Intersections of Law and Computational Intelligence in Health Governance

Komal Vig
Sharda School of Law, Sharda University, India

Christian Kaunert
Dublin City University, Ireland

Bhupinder Singh
Sharda School of Law, Sharda University, India

A volume in the Advances in Electronic Government, Digital Divide, and Regional Development (AEGDDRD) Book Series

IGI Global
Publishing Tomorrow's Research Today

Published in the United States of America by
IGI Global
Information Science Reference (an imprint of IGI Global)
701 E. Chocolate Avenue
Hershey PA, USA 17033
Tel: 717-533-8845
Fax: 717-533-8661
E-mail: cust@igi-global.com
Web site: http://www.igi-global.com

Library of Congress Cataloging-in-Publication Data

CIP DATA PENDING

ISBN13: 9798369359761
Isbn13Softcover: 9798369359778
EISBN13: 9798369359785

British Cataloguing in Publication Data
A Cataloguing in Publication record for this book is available from the British Library.

All work contributed to this book is new, previously-unpublished material.
The views expressed in this book are those of the authors, but not necessarily of the publisher.

For electronic access to this publication, please contact: eresources@igi-global.com.

Table of Contents

Preface xviii

Chapter 1
Intersections of Law and Computational Intelligence in Health Governance: Virtual Assistants in Health and Medicines 1
Nigar Kadar Mujawar, Womens College of Pharmacy, Peth Vadgaon, Kolhapur, India

Chapter 2
Role of Social Media and AI in Transforming Healthcare Communication 29
Divya Mishra, Sharda University, India

Chapter 3
Analyzing Human Genome and Embryo Editing: International Canons for Legal-Social Issues Concerning Women's Health and Reproductive Rights 52
Bhupinder Singh, Sharda University, India
Christian Kaunert, Dublin City University, Ireland
Kittisak Jermsittiparsert, Shinawatra University, Thailand
Bhumika Sharma, Sharda University, India
Anjali Raghav, Sharda University, India

Chapter 4
Issues and Challenges of Artificial Intelligence Implementation in Healthcare: A Review Study 81
Tarun Kumar Kaushik, Sharda University, India
Ravish, Meerut College, India
Anurag Singh, Meerut College, India
Anjali Raghav, Sharda University, India
Bhupinder Singh, Sharda University, India

Chapter 5
Impact of Artificial Intelligence in the Health Sector: Potential and Barriers... 100
Sahil Lal, School of Law, Sharda University, India
Anjali Raghav, Sharda University, India
Manmeet Kaur Arora, Sharda University, India
Sanskriti Mishra, Sharda University, India
Bhupinder Singh, Sharda University, India

Chapter 6
Intersection of Intellectual Property, Medicines, and Legal Concerns 117
Manvendra Singh, Sharda University, India
Vaishali Arora, Sharda University, India
Kushagra Kulshreshta, Raja Mahendra Pratap University, Aligarh, India

Chapter 7
A Socio-Legal Analysis of the Health and Well-Being of the Ageing Population 142
Urmila Yadav, Sharda School of Law, Sharda University, India
Bishwajeet Prakash, Sharda School of Law, Sharda University, India

Chapter 8
Balancing Innovation and Access: The Role of Patents and Traditional and Non-Traditional Trademarks in Healthcare.. 161
Karun Sanjaya, VIT School of Law, Vellore Institute of Technology, Chennai, India & Symbiosis Law School, Symbiosis International University (Deemed), Pune, India
P. R. L. Rajavenkatesan, VIT School of Law, Vellore Institute of Technology, Chennai, India

Chapter 9
Medical Tourism and Health Gateways in International Health Market Places: Stimulating Sustainability and Technological Advancements.............. 174
Bhupinder Singh, Sharda University, India
Christian Kaunert, Dublin City University, Ireland
Budi Agus Riswandi, Universitas Islam Indonesia, Indonesia
Manmeet Kaur Arora, Sharda University, India
Sahil Lal, Sharda University, India

Chapter 10
Safeguarding Data Privacy and Informed Consent: Ethical Imperatives in AI-Driven Mental Healthcare.. 197
Souvik Dhar, Brainware University, India
Utsa Sarkar, Calcutta High Court, India

Chapter 11
Cyber Terrorism in Health Information Systems: A Systematic Review and Bibliometric Analysis 220
Shashikant Rai, Indian Institute of Information Technology, Allahabad, India
Richa Sharma, Amity Global Business School, Amity University, India
Divya Mishra, Sharda University, India
Netranand Pathak, Indian Institute of Information Technology, Allahabad, India

Chapter 12
Exploring Menstrual Health and Hygiene in India: Understanding Usage Patterns of Menstrual Products Across Different Demographics 248
Amiya Abdul Khadar, Lovely Professional University, India
Pooja Kansra, Lovely Professional University, India
Kaushik Lodh, Health USA, USA

Chapter 13
Socio-Economic Factors of Maternal Healthcare in India: 15 Years of National Health Mission 271
Bishwajeet Prakash, Sharda University, India
Urmila Yadav, Sharda University, India
Indrajit Kumar, Parul University, India
Supriya Gautam, Amity University, India
Atul Arora, Sharda University, India
Mehak Arora, Delhi Technical Campus, India
Richa Sharma, Amity University, India

Chapter 14
Trips Plus Provisions: Implications for Access to Medicines 290
Raniyal Niyada P., National Law School of India University, Bengaluru, India
Karun Sanjaya, Symbiosis Law School, Symbiosis International University (Deemed), Pune, India

Chapter 15
Unconventional Trademarks in the Pharmaceutical Sector: Critical and Comparative Insights 306
Vaishnavi Yashasvi, Sharda University, India
Ruchir Singh, Bennett University, India

Chapter 16
Implications of Compulsory License Under WTO TRIPS Regime 325
Saurabh Chandra, Bennett University, India
Suparna Kundu, Amity University, Kolkata, India

Compilation of References 346

About the Contributors 412

Index 418

Detailed Table of Contents

Preface.. xviii

Chapter 1
Intersections of Law and Computational Intelligence in Health Governance: Virtual Assistants in Health and Medicines.. 1
Nigar Kadar Mujawar, Womens College of Pharmacy, Peth Vadgaon, Kolhapur, India

Virtual assistants in health and medicine utilize AI and NLP to revolutionize patient care and healthcare services. They engage patients with personalized interactions, improve access to healthcare, and support healthcare professionals. They assess symptoms, provide personalized health education, assist with medication management, and streamline appointment scheduling. Integration with telemedicine expands access to care, while wearable device integration monitors health metrics. Virtual assistants ensure secure access to medical records, adhere to regulations like HIPAA, and continuously improve through user feedback. Overall, they optimize patient engagement, improve accessibility, and enhance efficiency in healthcare delivery.

Chapter 2
Role of Social Media and AI in Transforming Healthcare Communication 29
Divya Mishra, Sharda University, India

This study explores the transformative impact of social media and AI on healthcare communication, emphasizing their transformative potential in information dissemination, patient engagement, and misinformation management. It highlights how social media platforms provide real-time updates and patient support, while AI technologies like machine learning and natural language processing revolutionize data analysis and personalized care. Despite these benefits, integrating these tools raises ethical concerns, such as privacy issues, data security risks, and informed consent complexities. It addresses challenges like data interoperability, infrastructure sufficiency, and system scalability, emphasizing the need for comprehensive provider training and unbiased AI algorithms. It also examines AI's role in curbing misinformation while balancing ethical considerations and free speech. The study advocates for a collaborative approach to ensure innovative and ethically sound healthcare communication, improve patient outcomes, and foster a more equitable and efficient healthcare system.

Chapter 3
Analyzing Human Genome and Embryo Editing: International Canons for Legal-Social Issues Concerning Women's Health and Reproductive Rights 52
Bhupinder Singh, Sharda University, India
Christian Kaunert, Dublin City University, Ireland
Kittisak Jermsittiparsert, Shinawatra University, Thailand
Bhumika Sharma, Sharda University, India
Anjali Raghav, Sharda University, India

The rapid progress in genetic research and technological advancements in recent years have revolutionized the field of reproductive medicine. Human genome and embryo editing, which involve the deliberate alteration of genetic material, hold immense potential for preventing genetic diseases, enhancing human traits, and even addressing infertility. However, these groundbreaking developments come with significant ethical, legal, and social implications that need to be carefully examined and addressed. The absence of a unified global regulatory framework for human genome and embryo editing has created a fragmented landscape. Various countries have adopted different approaches, ranging from strict regulations to more permissive policies. This chapter aims to provide a comprehensive analysis of the current state of affairs, highlighting the importance of establishing global standards to ensure responsible and equitable use of these technologies, while also prioritizing the protection of women's rights and ensuring reproductive justice.

Chapter 4
Issues and Challenges of Artificial Intelligence Implementation in Healthcare: A Review Study 81
Tarun Kumar Kaushik, Sharda University, India
Ravish, Meerut College, India
Anurag Singh, Meerut College, India
Anjali Raghav, Sharda University, India
Bhupinder Singh, Sharda University, India

In 1956, the United States of America was the birthplace of artificial intelligence (AI), which at the time consisted of an algorithm that was developed via the process of analyzing previously collected data and learning on its own. This chapter provides a discussion on the present applications of artificial intelligence in the medical field, as well as a summary of the existing challenges that are restricting the widespread acceptance of AI. Therefore, the implementation of technology and artificial intelligence in the healthcare industry may be beneficial to hospitals, particularly in situations where viruses such as COVID diminish the workforce. There is also a dependence on trustworthy sources, as well as worry over artificial intelligence and healthcare. To fulfill its objectives, however, the healthcare industry must contend with a great deal of difficulty.

Chapter 5
Impact of Artificial Intelligence in the Health Sector: Potential and Barriers... 100
Sahil Lal, School of Law, Sharda University, India
Anjali Raghav, Sharda University, India
Manmeet Kaur Arora, Sharda University, India
Sanskriti Mishra, Sharda University, India
Bhupinder Singh, Sharda University, India

In the contemporary era, artificial intelligence (AI) has made tremendous strides. The emergence of artificial intelligence had a significant impact on upgrading transformation in the medical field. However, there is enormous optimism that the application of artificial intelligence would significantly enhance pivotal aspects of health care. Furthermore, AI can also be useful for highly specific personal profiling, which plays a vital role in understanding and targeting behavioural patterns along with that it also has the potential to forecast healthcare. In addition, artificial intelligence systems are already increasing the precision and efficacy of diagnosis and treatment across a wide range of specialisations, especially when combined with the intense advancements in computer processing in the health sector. Nevertheless, there are many challenges with the application of artificial intelligence in medical practice which are often hindered by a series of problems, including problems of privacy, data security, lack of operational simplicity, the problem of medical ethics, and the risk of fraud in the health sector. However, recent developments in artificial intelligence and virtual health will be proven to have positive effects on the health sector. This chapter discusses the role of artificial intelligence in the medical field. It also discusses the potential and challenges of artificial intelligence applications in the health sector.

Chapter 6
Intersection of Intellectual Property, Medicines, and Legal Concerns 117
Manvendra Singh, Sharda University, India
Vaishali Arora, Sharda University, India
Kushagra Kulshreshta, Raja Mahendra Pratap University, Aligarh, India

Intellectual property is a group of property that contains intangible creations of the intellect of man. There are many types of intellectual property; the most renowned types are patents, copyrights, trademarks, and trade secrets. The intersection of intellectual property (IP), medicines, and legal concerns in India represents a dynamic landscape shaped by a complex interplay of domestic laws, international agreements, and socio-economic factors. This abstract provides a comprehensive overview of the multifaceted issues surrounding IP rights, access to medicines, and legal frameworks in the Indian context. India's pharmaceutical industry holds a prominent position globally, renowned for its production of affordable generic medicines. However, the introduction of product patents through amendments to the Patents Act in 2005 marked a significant shift in the IP landscape, posing challenges to the country's generic drug industry while aiming to align with international trade duty, specially under the Agreement on Trade-Related Aspects of Intellectual Property Rights (TRIPS). The implications of patents on access to medicines in India are profound. While patents promote innovation, they also have the potential to create monopolies, leading to high drug prices and limited accessibility, especially for marginalized populations. The debate surrounding the protection of intellectual property and public health imperatives has been aimed at issues such as compulsory licensing, parallel importation, and patent enforcement. India's proactive use of TRIPS flexibilities, including compulsory licensing, has been instrumental in addressing public health challenges. Compulsory licensing allows the government to license patented drugs to third-party manufacturers without the permission of the patent holder, thence facilitating the production of affordable generic versions of essential medicines. High-profile cases of compulsory licensing for drugs treating diseases like HIV/AIDS and cancer highlight India's commitment to ensuring access to life-saving treatments. Legal concerns surrounding IP rights and medicines extend beyond patents to encompass issues such as data exclusivity, regulatory barriers, and the associate between laws relating to intellectual property and competition law. On other hand, regulatory framework aims to balance innovation incentives with public health objectives, challenges persist in areas such as patent prosecution, enforcement, and the granting of ever greening patents. Recent developments in India's IP landscape, including judicial decisions, policy initiatives, and international trade negotiations, continue to shape the discourse on IP rights and medicines. The introduction of the National Intellectual Property Rights Policy in 2016 reflects India's commitment to fostering innovation while safeguarding public health interests. Additionally, initiatives such as the Drug Price Control Order aim to regulate drug pricing to ensure affordability and accessibility. The complex interplay between intellectual property, medicines, and legal concerns in India underscores the need for a holistic approach. Balancing the interests of innovators, generic manufacturers, and public health requires collaborative efforts, evidence-based policy interventions, and transparent regulatory mechanisms. Prioritizing access to affordable and quality medicines remains a fundamental imperative in achieving health equity and promoting socio-economic development.

Chapter 7
A Socio-Legal Analysis of the Health and Well-Being of the Ageing Population 142
Urmila Yadav, Sharda School of Law, Sharda University, India
Bishwajeet Prakash, Sharda School of Law, Sharda University, India

Approximately 10% of the global population, or 771 million people, are over 65 as of 2023. A further feature of ageing is the rise of multiple complex health states, collectively referred to as geriatric syndromes. Research indicated that this illness has been increasing daily and will reach 16% in 2050 and eventually 24% by 2100. Societal ageing can also have an impact on economic growth, retirement, and employment patterns, family dynamics, and the capacity of local governments and communities to provide sufficient resources for the elderly. This chapter's goals are to examine and evaluate the various aspects of wellbeing in an ageing population. This involved looking at things like statistical facts of aging populations, social dimensions and Support of ageing care, networks and ageing care and maintenance structure in India, as well as strategies for encouraging good ageing.

Chapter 8
Balancing Innovation and Access: The Role of Patents and Traditional and Non-Traditional Trademarks in Healthcare.. 161
Karun Sanjaya, VIT School of Law, Vellore Institute of Technology, Chennai, India & Symbiosis Law School, Symbiosis International University (Deemed), Pune, India
P. R. L. Rajavenkatesan, VIT School of Law, Vellore Institute of Technology, Chennai, India

The book chapter offers comprehensive coverage of the complex interplay between patents, trademarks, and health care. The chapter highlights the fine and tenuous line between stimulating innovation in the field and ensuring access to life-saving and essential medical technologies. The chapter investigates the positive and negative externalities produced by patents and trademarks in research and development and market contexts, as well as their effects on consumer behaviour in the healthcare sector. The authors have analysed the role played by both traditional and non-traditional trademarks in the healthcare sector. The chapter also addresses the ethical and accessibility dilemmas pertaining to the right to intellectual property and the potential policy reforms, which would alleviate the tension between creating incentives for innovation and protecting public health. By reviewing both the literature and specific case studies, the chapter enlightens the reader on the ways to tackle the dual challenge of promoting innovation and ensuring that health care is a right for all.

Chapter 9
Medical Tourism and Health Gateways in International Health Market Places: Stimulating Sustainability and Technological Advancements............... 174
Bhupinder Singh, Sharda University, India
Christian Kaunert, Dublin City University, Ireland
Budi Agus Riswandi, Universitas Islam Indonesia, Indonesia
Manmeet Kaur Arora, Sharda University, India
Sahil Lal, Sharda University, India

Medical tourism has the ability to reshape how patients move around in global healthcare, providing new opportunities for access to high standardised services and quality resources as industries progress through innovation and technological advancements. A critical factor for medical tourism is that this newfound option must be imbued with sustainability; it has to go hand in hand respecting equity and social responsibility. It is structured such that it provides insights for those interested in creating policies, practicing medicine, or dealing with diagnosis. This chapter investigates the contribution of medical tourism in supporting sustainability and technological transfer, at the global health market. It will look at what is driving the growth of medical tourism and why patients are seeking healthcare abroad, as well as some of the hurdles and benefits with this burgeoning space for both patient consumers and provider stakeholders.

Chapter 10
Safeguarding Data Privacy and Informed Consent: Ethical Imperatives in AI-Driven Mental Healthcare... 197
Souvik Dhar, Brainware University, India
Utsa Sarkar, Calcutta High Court, India

This chapter explores the ethical challenges surrounding data privacy and informed consent in artificial intelligence (AI)-driven mental healthcare in India. The integration of AI technologies in mental health services offers potential for enhanced patient outcomes, but also raises significant ethical issues. Emphasizing patient autonomy and the protection of personal information, the chapter examines the complexities of informed consent and data privacy. It highlights the importance of transparent communication and robust regulatory frameworks to safeguard patient rights. By analysing key principles and the Digital Personal Data Protection Act 2023, the chapter provides insights into balancing technological advancements with ethical imperatives. It advocates for comprehensive ethical guidelines and collaborative efforts among stakeholders to foster a responsible and patient-centred AI-driven mental healthcare system. The chapter emphasizes the need for education on AI's impact, potential biases, and the significance of maintaining trust and accountability in patient care.

Chapter 11
Cyber Terrorism in Health Information Systems: A Systematic Review and Bibliometric Analysis 220
Shashikant Rai, Indian Institute of Information Technology, Allahabad, India
Richa Sharma, Amity Global Business School, Amity University, India
Divya Mishra, Sharda University, India
Netranand Pathak, Indian Institute of Information Technology, Allahabad, India

This review examines the escalating threat of cyber terrorism in health information systems (HIS), highlighting the increasing frequency and sophistication of cyber-attacks targeting the healthcare sector. Healthcare institutions, holding critical data like electronic health records (EHR) and personally identifiable information (PII), are prime targets for cybercriminals. The study explores key security challenges, including ransomware, data breaches, denial of service attacks, and IoT vulnerabilities. Through a comprehensive literature review and bibliometric analysis, the study investigates encryption, blockchain technology, and training programs for healthcare providers. It also evaluates cybersecurity frameworks and emphasizes the need for continuous innovation in security measures. The findings underscore the urgent need for enhanced cybersecurity strategies to protect patient data and ensure the integrity of healthcare services. This review aims to initiate a dialogue on strengthening the cybersecurity resilience of healthcare systems.

Chapter 12
Exploring Menstrual Health and Hygiene in India: Understanding Usage Patterns of Menstrual Products Across Different Demographics 248
Amiya Abdul Khadar, Lovely Professional University, India
Pooja Kansra, Lovely Professional University, India
Kaushik Lodh, Health USA, USA

Menstrual health refers to a woman's overall physical and psychological well-being throughout their menstrual cycle. Having good menstrual health means that a person experiences a regular and predictable menstrual cycle, without significant pain or discomfort. It also involves having the availability of nontoxic and effective products for menstruation and adequate information about menstrual health. The absence of proper hygienic menstrual facilities and sanitation put women and girls at threat of several health issues, such as infections in the urinary and reproductive tract. Additionally, menstrual stigma often leads to communal separation and omission from daily activities like school and work. In the present study, an attempt has been made to explore the state of menstrual health and hygiene in India and also identify the most popular menstrual product types among women of different age groups, educational backgrounds, places of residence, and religions.

Chapter 13
Socio-Economic Factors of Maternal Healthcare in India: 15 Years of National Health Mission 271
Bishwajeet Prakash, Sharda University, India
Urmila Yadav, Sharda University, India
Indrajit Kumar, Parul University, India
Supriya Gautam, Amity University, India
Atul Arora, Sharda University, India
Mehak Arora, Delhi Technical Campus, India
Richa Sharma, Amity University, India

Pregnancy and childbirth should be times of joy. However, safe motherhood and childbirth depend on the care and attention provided to pregnant women and newborns. Maternal health remains major health problem in India, with large inter- and intra-state inequities in maternal health service use and maternal deaths. Maternal health care coverage includes maternal mortality; and antenatal care includes post- and pre-natal care. The post mortality in both women and child is increased in many countries throughout the world, especially in developing countries due to low level of socio-economic development. The present study examines the contribution of India's National Health Mission (NHM) to maternal health includes both pre- and post-natal care at health institution with inequalities in various determinates of major health outcomes, at least visit of six ANC. In furthermore, the study examines socio-demographic factors of maternal healthcare utilization among Indian women. The data has been collected from an Indian National Family health survey between 2005-06 and 2019-21. A multiple logistic regression model has been used to estimate ratios associated with various visited ANC. It has been observed from the data post implementation of National Health that the institutional delivery increased by 58 percent to 88 percent, which indicates persistent increase in both rural and urban areas. It further observed the proportion of ANC visit by pregnant women is increased dramatically, with a higher percent at 89.38 percent—indicating rich women are more times visited to ANC, compared to poorer women. In further, study has indicated that educational attainment among women and family is most significant predicators of maternal healthcare utilization. As a result, maternal mortality has removed the inter and intra state disparities and forces women to make their delivery in more institutional and ensuring the reduction of child and mother mortality rate in the country, which helps to meet the sustainable development goals.

Chapter 14
Trips Plus Provisions: Implications for Access to Medicines............................ 290
Raniyal Niyada P., National Law School of India University, Bengaluru, India
Karun Sanjaya, Symbiosis Law School, Symbiosis International University (Deemed), Pune, India

The primary goal of granting intellectual property rights was to encourage innovation, particularly in the healthcare industry. The Paris Convention provided for worldwide protection for ideas, and the global harmonization of intellectual property protection (TRIPs) broadened the scope of protection. The pharmaceutical sector, including Pfizer, played a key role in TRIPS lobbying. However, corporations were dissatisfied with TRIPS flexibilities used by developing nations. To combat this, they turned the forum towards bilateral and regional trade agreements, providing additional economic incentives. The United States is at the forefront of these efforts, which include clauses that restrict affordable access and generic entry. This research investigates the history, mechanisms, and techniques of forum shifting and outlines key areas of Free Trade Agreements that directly impact access to medicine.

Chapter 15
Unconventional Trademarks in the Pharmaceutical Sector: Critical and Comparative Insights 306
Vaishnavi Yashasvi, Sharda University, India
Ruchir Singh, Bennett University, India

In this chapter, an attempt has been made to understand the effects of non-traditional trademarks in the area of pharmaceutical products and issues of competition along with a normative case against the unconventional trademarks, further proceeding towards a discussion on inherently valuable freedom of expression and to assess why affording legal protection for non-traditional marks in this area may hamper access to medicine/health. In order to answer this question effectively, this chapter is divided into three parts: the first part explores the prevalence of non- traditional marks in the area of pharmaceuticals; the second part analyzes whether protection for non-traditional marks could pose impediments to access to medicine/health; and the last part ponders the issues of competition and freedom of expression with analytical approach.

Chapter 16
Implications of Compulsory License Under WTO TRIPS Regime 325
Saurabh Chandra, Bennett University, India
Suparna Kundu, Amity University, Kolkata, India

The beginning of humankind marks trade and exchange of goods and services across borders. In the earliest days, goods were exchanged for goods; this was termed as a barter system. With globalization and liberalisation of trade, goods and services travel across nations. In order to regulate these trading activities, a uniform set of rules and guidelines are required so as not to discriminate against nations and ensure peace and stability on a global level. The WTO which regulates these trading activities was formed so as to promote free and fair movement of trade, facilitate trade without discrimination, fair competition, etc. This chapter examines the utilization of compulsory licensing provisions within the TRIPS framework, focusing on India's experience and its implications for public health and intellectual property rights (IPR). Through a comprehensive analysis of legal frameworks, case studies, and policy implications, it elucidates India's approach to compulsory licensing, highlighting its role in enhancing access to essential medicines while balancing competing interests.

Compilation of References 346

About the Contributors 412

Index 418

Preface

Computational intelligence (CI) refers to computer capacities that correspond with the intelligence of humans. Artificial intelligence (AI) technologies are used in healthcare to improve services and solutions through the use of machine learning, cognitive computing, data analytics, wireless communication and mobile computing. Artificial intelligence (AI) provides efficient ways to gather, process and use the large amounts of knowledge required by contemporary healthcare through the use of methodologies like fuzzy models, artificial neural networks, evolutionary algorithms and probabilistic approaches.

Artificial intelligence (AI) technologies are being used in a variety of legal tasks, including contract analysis, legal research, and case outcome predicting. These technologies include computer vision, natural language processing, and machine learning algorithms. While using AI in law has the potential to increase productivity and reduce costs, there are concerns about privacy violations, biases and the requirement for explicit accountability protocols.

In the rapidly evolving landscape of technology and healthcare, computational intelligence (CI) plays a pivotal role in shaping innovative solutions. As the integration of artificial intelligence (AI) technologies becomes increasingly prevalent across various sectors, understanding their impact on healthcare and legal frameworks is essential. This book provides a comprehensive examination of the intersection between computational intelligence and healthcare, with a particular focus on the legal and ethical considerations that arise. The following chapter overview outlines the book's key themes and objectives, offering readers a roadmap for exploring the latest research developments and methodologies that are transforming the healthcare industry. By delving into diverse disciplines such as public health, law, computer science, and social sciences, the book aims to equip academicians and researchers with valuable insights into the challenges and opportunities presented by AI technologies in healthcare.

Chapter 1 explores how AI and natural language processing (NLP) revolutionize patient care and healthcare services through virtual assistants. These technologies engage patients with personalized interactions, improve access to healthcare, and support healthcare professionals by assessing symptoms, providing personalized health education, assisting with medication management, and streamlining appointment scheduling. Integration with telemedicine and wearable devices enhances healthcare delivery by expanding access to care and monitoring health metrics, all while ensuring secure access to medical records and adhering to regulations like HIPAA. Through continuous user feedback, virtual assistants optimize patient engagement, improve accessibility, and enhance efficiency in healthcare delivery.

Chapter 2 examines the transformative impact of social media and AI on healthcare communication. It emphasizes their role in information dissemination, patient engagement, and managing misinformation. Social media platforms provide real-time updates and patient support, while AI technologies like machine learning and NLP revolutionize data analysis and personalized care. Ethical concerns such as privacy, data security, and informed consent are addressed, alongside challenges like data interoperability, infrastructure sufficiency, and system scalability. The chapter advocates for a collaborative approach to ensure innovative and ethically sound healthcare communication, enhancing patient outcomes and fostering an equitable healthcare system.

Chapter 3 delves into the rapid progress in genetic research and technological advancements in reproductive medicine. Human genome and embryo editing offer immense potential for preventing genetic diseases, enhancing human traits, and addressing infertility. However, these developments raise significant ethical, legal, and social implications. The absence of a unified global regulatory framework creates a fragmented landscape, with various countries adopting different approaches. This chapter provides a comprehensive analysis of the current state, emphasizing the need for global standards to ensure responsible use of these technologies, prioritizing women's rights, and ensuring reproductive justice.

Chapter 4 discusses the evolution of artificial intelligence (AI) from its inception in 1956 to its current applications in the medical field. It highlights the benefits of AI in enhancing hospital efficiency, especially during workforce challenges like the COVID-19 pandemic. The chapter also addresses challenges restricting AI's widespread acceptance, emphasizing the need for reliable sources and addressing concerns about AI and healthcare. It concludes by discussing the significant difficulties the healthcare industry must overcome to effectively integrate AI technologies.

Chapter 5 highlights the impact of AI on healthcare transformation, emphasizing its potential to enhance key aspects of healthcare. AI contributes to personal profiling, understanding behavioral patterns, and forecasting healthcare needs. It also improves diagnosis and treatment precision across specializations. The chapter discusses

AI's potential and challenges in the health sector, exploring the synergy between AI advancements and computer processing improvements in medical applications.

Chapter 6 provides a comprehensive overview of the intersection of intellectual property (IP), medicines, and legal concerns in India. It explores the dynamic landscape shaped by domestic laws, international agreements, and socio-economic factors. The chapter examines the multifaceted issues surrounding IP rights, access to medicines, and legal frameworks, highlighting the challenges and opportunities in navigating this complex environment.

Chapter 7 examines the various aspects of wellbeing in an ageing population. It discusses the statistical facts of ageing populations, social dimensions of ageing care, networks, and maintenance structures in India. The chapter explores strategies for encouraging healthy ageing, addressing the impact of ageing on economic growth, retirement patterns, family dynamics, and the capacity of local governments and communities to provide adequate resources for the elderly.

Chapter 8 explores the complex interplay between patents, trademarks, and healthcare. It examines the fine line between stimulating innovation and ensuring access to essential medical technologies. The chapter investigates the externalities produced by patents and trademarks in research, development, and market contexts, analyzing their effects on consumer behavior. It addresses ethical and accessibility dilemmas related to IP rights and potential policy reforms to balance innovation incentives with public health protection.

Chapter 9 investigates the role of medical tourism in global healthcare, emphasizing its potential to reshape patient mobility and access to high-standard services. It explores the drivers of medical tourism growth, the benefits and challenges for patients and providers, and the importance of sustainability, equity, and social responsibility. The chapter provides insights for policymakers, medical practitioners, and stakeholders involved in this burgeoning industry.

Chapter 10 explores the ethical challenges of data privacy and informed consent in AI-driven mental healthcare in India. While AI technologies offer potential for improved patient outcomes, they raise ethical issues concerning patient autonomy and personal information protection. The chapter examines informed consent complexities, data privacy concerns, and the importance of transparent communication and robust regulatory frameworks. It advocates for comprehensive ethical guidelines and collaborative efforts to foster a responsible and patient-centered AI-driven mental healthcare system.

Chapter 11 examines the escalating threat of cyber terrorism in health information systems (HIS), highlighting the increasing frequency and sophistication of cyber-attacks targeting healthcare. It explores key security challenges, including ransomware, data breaches, denial of service attacks, and IoT vulnerabilities. The chapter investigates encryption, blockchain technology, and training programs for healthcare providers, emphasizing the need for enhanced cybersecurity strategies to protect patient data and ensure healthcare service integrity.

Chapter 12 explores the state of menstrual health and hygiene in India, emphasizing the importance of regular menstrual cycles, non-toxic menstrual products, and adequate information about menstrual health. It addresses health issues arising from inadequate menstrual facilities and sanitation and examines menstrual stigma's impact on women's social participation. The chapter analyzes menstrual product preferences among women of different age groups, educational backgrounds, places of residence, and religions.

Chapter 13 examines India's National Health Mission (NHM) and its contribution to maternal healthcare, including pre and postnatal care. It analyzes socio-demographic factors affecting maternal healthcare utilization and highlights the impact of NHM on institutional delivery rates in urban and rural areas. The chapter uses data from the Indian National Family Health Survey and a logistic regression model to assess health outcome determinants and healthcare access improvements.

Chapter 14 investigates the history, mechanisms, and techniques of forum shifting in intellectual property rights, focusing on access to medicines. It examines the global Harmonization of Intellectual Property Protection (TRIPs) and its impact on affordable access and generic entry. The chapter explores the role of corporations and trade agreements in shaping IP rights and discusses India's approach to balancing public health needs with IP protection through compulsory licensing provisions.

Chapter 15 explores the effects of non-traditional trademarks in the pharmaceutical industry, analyzing competition issues and the normative case against unconventional trademarks. It examines the impact of legal protection for non-traditional marks on access to medicine and health, addressing freedom of expression and competition challenges. The chapter is divided into three parts, focusing on non-traditional mark prevalence, access to medicine implications, and freedom of expression concerns.

Chapter 16 examines trade and globalization's impact on compulsory licensing within the TRIPS framework, focusing on India's experience and its implications for public health and intellectual property rights. It analyzes legal frameworks, case studies, and policy implications, highlighting India's approach to enhancing access to essential medicines while balancing competing interests. The chapter explores the role of the World Trade Organization (WTO) in promoting free and fair trade and ensuring global peace and stability.

This book systematically explores legal considerations within healthcare-related computational intelligence across various relevant disciplines, such as public health, law, nutrition, computer science, dentistry, psychology, engineering, medicine, nursing, pharmacy, social sciences and other healthcare professions. This book explains the fundamentals of computational intelligence and related approaches concerning healthcare and governance. It addresses issues with data analysis and storage inside healthcare facilities by covering state-of-the-art Computational intelligence (CI) methodologies and associated techniques used in healthcare systems. Its main goal is to provide academicians and researchers with the most recent research discoveries that are relevant to the healthcare industry. It does this by providing a thorough platform for cutting-edge developments, research techniques and implementation strategies. Its objectives include examining the extent to which these legal aspects are prioritized in different fields, analyzing the breadth and nature of research endeavors across disciplines, synthesizing and disseminating research outcomes to relevant stakeholders, and identifying research gaps within existing literature. These objectives form the cornerstone of a comprehensive review strategy aimed at advancing understanding and practice in this complex intersection.

Komal Vig
Sharda School of Law, Sharda University, India

Christian Kaunert
Dublin City University, Ireland

Bhupinder Singh
Sharda School of Law, Sharda University, India

Chapter 1

Intersections of Law and Computational Intelligence in Health Governance:

Virtual Assistants in Health and Medicines

Nigar Kadar Mujawar
https://orcid.org/0009-0001-7663-9279
Womens College of Pharmacy, Peth Vadgaon, Kolhapur, India

ABSTRACT

Virtual assistants in health and medicine utilize AI and NLP to revolutionize patient care and healthcare services. They engage patients with personalized interactions, improve access to healthcare, and support healthcare professionals. They assess symptoms, provide personalized health education, assist with medication management, and streamline appointment scheduling. Integration with telemedicine expands access to care, while wearable device integration monitors health metrics. Virtual assistants ensure secure access to medical records, adhere to regulations like HIPAA, and continuously improve through user feedback. Overall, they optimize patient engagement, improve accessibility, and enhance efficiency in healthcare delivery.

DOI: 10.4018/979-8-3693-5976-1.ch001

INTRODUCTION

Virtual assistants, often referred to as AI assistants or digital assistants, are sophisticated software applications that utilize AI and NLP algorithms to interact with users, understand natural language inputs, and provide real-time responses and assistance. In the realm of healthcare, these virtual assistants are designed to support patients, healthcare providers, and healthcare systems through various functionalities and services (Giachos et al. 2023).

The advent of virtual assistants within the medical and health fields signifies a profound paradigm change in the provision and utilization of healthcare services. Virtual assistants have become vital tools in contemporary healthcare systems, surpassing old boundaries with the introduction of cutting-edge AI and NLP technology (Soofastaei 2024).

The ability of virtual assistants to communicate with patients in a personalized way is at the forefront of this shift. These digital assistants can comprehend and react to patient questions, concerns, and demands in a way that feels human-like and customized to specific preferences by utilizing the power of AI and NLP. In addition to strengthening the bond between patients and their healthcare professionals, this individualized strategy gives people the confidence to adopt a more proactive approach to controlling their health.(Greene et al. 2017).

Additionally, virtual assistants have been essential in enhancing underprivileged and distant people's access to healthcare services. Virtual assistants facilitate remote monitoring and telemedicine support, allowing patients to contact with medical specialists from anywhere in the world. All people could benefit from timely and high-quality healthcare services thanks to this increased access to care. It also offers the ability to close healthcare disparities (Ali, & Noul).

Virtual assistants have not only improved accessibility and patient involvement, but they have also completely changed how healthcare professionals go about their everyday business. Virtual assistants help doctors focus more on providing patients with high-quality treatment by streamlining administrative tasks including prescription management, appointment scheduling, and symptom evaluation and triage. Virtual assistants help healthcare organizations operate more efficiently and productively by automating repetitive processes and offering real-time support (Verma et al. 2023).

Virtual assistants can also be used for clinical decision-making as well as patient care in addition to administrative help. Virtual assistants can help healthcare providers diagnose ailments, forecast patient outcomes, and provide individualized treatment strategies by using complex algorithms and data analytics. Better clinical workflows are the result of incorporating AI-driven insights, which also improve treatment outcomes and decision-making processes. All of these factors contribute to better patient care (Alowais et al. 2023).

Virtual assistants have a significant potential to influence healthcare delivery in the future as the need for individualized healthcare solutions grows. Virtual assistants will continue to change and adapt to suit the changing demands of patients, healthcare providers, and healthcare organizations as long as AI, NLP, as well as digital health technologies, continue to advance. Virtual assistants are leading the charge in changing the healthcare industry and achieving better results for patients all over the world, whether it is by promoting clinical innovation, increasing patient involvement, or bettering access to care (Senbekov et al. 2020).

Importance of AI and NLP Technologies in Healthcare

a) Enhanced Patient Care:

AI and NLP technologies play a crucial role in enhancing patient care by enabling virtual assistants to provide personalized support. These assistants can interact with patients, answer queries, provide medication reminders, and offer emotional support, improving patient engagement and satisfaction (Sarker 2023).

b) Efficient Diagnosis and Treatment:

AI and NLP empower virtual assistants to analyze symptoms described by patients, suggest potential diagnoses, recommend treatments, and assist healthcare professionals in making informed decisions swiftly. By processing vast amounts of medical literature and patient data, these technologies help identify patterns and insights that aid in diagnosis and treatment planning. (Chintala 2023).

c) Optimized Healthcare Operations:

AI-driven virtual assistants automate administrative tasks such as appointment scheduling, data entry, and medical record management. By streamlining these processes, healthcare providers can focus more on patient care, leading to increased efficiency and reduced workload (Alowais et al. 2023).

d) Continuous Learning and Improvement:

Virtual assistants powered by AI algorithms can continuously learn from their interactions with patients and healthcare professionals. This iterative learning process allows them to improve their accuracy, effectiveness, and understanding of natural language over time, leading to better performance in assisting users (Aslam 2023).

e) Data Analysis and Insights:

NLP enables virtual assistants to extract valuable insights from unstructured healthcare data, such as clinical notes, research papers, and patient records. These insights help in research, decision-making, resource allocation, and the development of evidence-based guidelines, ultimately contributing to improved healthcare outcomes. (Alowais et al. 2023).

Key Functionalities of Virtual Assistants

1) Symptom assessment and triage
2) Personalized health education and information
3) Medication management and adherence tracking
4) Appointment scheduling and management
5) Integration with telemedicine platforms
6) Monitoring health metrics through wearable devices
7) Secure access to medical records and adherence to regulations

In detail discussed below

Symptom Assessment and Triage

Virtual assistants in healthcare offer symptom assessment and triage functionalities, aiding in the initial evaluation of patient's health concerns. Here's an elaboration of this key functionality:

Symptom Assessment

Virtual assistants use natural language processing (NLP) to understand patients' descriptions of their symptoms. They ask relevant questions to gather additional information, such as the duration and severity of symptoms, medical history, and associated factors. By analysing this information, virtual assistants can generate a preliminary assessment of the potential health issue or condition (Zhou et al. 2022).

Triage

Based on the symptom assessment, virtual assistants categorize patients' conditions into urgency levels, such as emergent, urgent, and non-urgent. They provide appropriate recommendations, including seeking immediate medical attention, scheduling an appointment with a healthcare provider, or providing self-care advice.

Triage functionality helps prioritize patient care based on the severity of symptoms, ensuring timely intervention for critical cases while optimizing resource allocation and reducing unnecessary healthcare utilization. Virtual assistants streamline the initial patient interaction process, facilitating quicker access to healthcare services and enabling efficient utilization of healthcare resources (Božić)

Personalized Health Education and Information

Virtual assistants play a crucial role in delivering personalized health education and information to users. Here's a brief elaboration on this key functionality:

Personalized Content

Virtual assistants leverage AI algorithms and data analytics to provide tailored health education content based on users' demographics, medical history, preferences, and current health status. This personalized approach ensures that users receive information relevant to their specific needs and conditions (Tavakoli 2023).

Health Promotion

Virtual assistants actively promote healthy behaviors and lifestyles by offering tips, guidance, and reminders related to diet, exercise, medication adherence, and preventive healthcare measures. By delivering timely and relevant health education content, virtual assistants empower users to make informed decisions about their health and well-being (Sezgin et al. 2020).

Disease Management

For individuals managing chronic conditions or undergoing specific treatments, virtual assistants offer targeted education and support materials to assist with disease management. This includes information on symptom management, medication management, lifestyle modifications, and coping strategies, tailored to each user's unique situation (McGowan 2012).

Accessible Information

Virtual assistants serve as accessible sources of health information, available anytime and anywhere through digital devices. This accessibility promotes health literacy and empowers users to proactively engage in managing their health, ultimately leading to better health outcomes. By providing personalized health education and information, virtual assistants contribute to promoting health awareness, supporting disease management, and empowering individuals to take control of their health journey (Shorbaji, 2021).

Medication Management and Adherence Tracking

Virtual assistants in health and medicine leverage artificial intelligence (AI) and natural language processing (NLP) technologies to provide personalized support and assistance to patients and healthcare providers (Giachos et al.2023). One significant area where virtual assistants have made a considerable impact is in medication management and adherence tracking. These virtual assistants play a crucial role in ensuring patients adhere to their medication regimens, thereby improving treatment outcomes and reducing healthcare costs. By integrating AI and NLP, virtual assistants offer functionalities such as medication reminders, dosage tracking, refill notifications, interaction checks, and educational resources about prescribed medications (Raval et al. 2022). Key functionalities and benefits of virtual assistants in medication management and adherence tracking, highlighting their role in enhancing patient care and promoting better health outcomes discussed in brief as follows as

Medication Reminders

Virtual assistants help users stay on track with their medication schedule by sending timely reminders for doses. These reminders can be personalized based on the user's prescription, dosage frequency, and preferred timing (Dharmale, et al. 2023).

Dosage Tracking

Users can input their medication details into the virtual assistant, which then tracks their dosage history. This feature helps users keep an accurate record of the medications they've taken, reducing the risk of missed or double doses (Arun et al.2023).

Refill Notifications

Virtual assistants notify users when it's time to refill their prescriptions, ensuring continuity of medication supply. This feature prevents interruptions in treatment and helps users avoid running out of essential medications (Friedman et al. 1997).

Interaction Checks

Virtual assistants provide information about potential drug interactions by cross-referencing a user's medication list. This functionality alerts users and healthcare providers to potential risks associated with combining certain medications (Abigail et al.2021).

Educational Resources

Virtual assistants offer educational resources about prescribed medications, including information about dosage, side effects, and proper administration. Users can access this information to better understand their medications and make informed decisions about their healthcare (Scarborough & Smith 2018).

Integration With Healthcare Providers

Some virtual assistants integrate with healthcare providers' systems, allowing for seamless communication regarding medication management. This integration enables healthcare providers to monitor medication adherence remotely and intervene if necessary(Preum et al.2021), These functionalities contribute to improved medication adherence, better health outcomes, and enhanced patient-provider communication in healthcare settings.

Appointment Scheduling and Management

Virtual assistants play a crucial role in revolutionizing healthcare by streamlining various administrative tasks. Specifically, in appointment scheduling and management, they offer a range of key functionalities to enhance efficiency and patient experience. These functionalities include automated appointment scheduling, reminder notifications, calendar integration, customized patient communications, rescheduling and cancellation management, integration with electronic health records (EHR), multi-channel access, and patient education (Anastasiadou et al.2023). By leveraging these capabilities, virtual assistants optimize resource allocation, reduce administrative burden, improve patient engagement, and ultimately enhance the overall quality of healthcare delivery (Ali & Noul.) Key functionalities of appointment scheduling and management virtual assistants in health and medicine are discussed in brief as follows as

Automated Appointment Scheduling

Virtual assistants enable patients to schedule appointments conveniently without human intervention, reducing administrative burden and wait times (Sharmila et al.2024).

Reminder Notifications

They send timely reminders to patients about upcoming appointments, reducing no-show rates and improving healthcare provider efficiency. (Kizza 2023).

Calendar Integration

Virtual assistants sync with patients' calendars to avoid scheduling conflicts and ensure appointments fit seamlessly into their daily routines. (Sanchez et al.2023).

Customized Patient Communications

They facilitate personalized communication with patients, providing information about appointment details, preparation instructions, and any necessary documentation (Rathert et al.2017).

Rescheduling and Cancellation Management

Virtual assistants allow patients to reschedule or cancel appointments easily, optimizing healthcare resource allocation and improving patient satisfaction (Haleem et al. 2021).

Integration With Electronic Health Records (EHR)

They integrate with EHR systems to access patient information, update records, and streamline administrative processes for healthcare providers (Wager et al.(2021).

Multi-Channel Access

Patients can interact with virtual assistants through various channels, including voice commands, messaging platforms, and mobile applications, enhancing accessibility and convenience(Jesse 2019).

Patient Education

Virtual assistants provide educational resources to patients about healthcare services, procedures, and preventive measures, empowering them to make informed decisions about their health (Alpay et al. 2010). These functionalities streamline the appointment scheduling and management process, improve patient engagement, and optimize healthcare delivery in both traditional and telehealth settings.

Integration With Telemedicine Platforms

Incorporating telemedicine platforms, virtual assistants offer indispensable functionalities to optimize patient care delivery. These include seamless integration with telemedicine platforms for scheduling appointments, conducting virtual consultations, sharing medical records securely, facilitating medication management, providing remote monitoring support, and offering personalized health education. By bridging the gap between patients and healthcare providers, virtual assistants enhance the accessibility, convenience, and effectiveness of telemedicine services, ultimately improving healthcare outcomes and patient satisfaction (Chauhan et al.2024).Virtual assistants play a pivotal role in integrating with telemedicine platforms, facilitating streamlined healthcare delivery. Here's a detailed explanation of their key functionalities discuss in detail as follow as:

Appointment Scheduling

Virtual assistants enable patients to schedule, reschedule, or cancel appointments conveniently through telemedicine platforms, ensuring efficient time management for both patients and healthcare providers (Chandwani et al.2023).

Patient Consultation

They facilitate seamless virtual consultations by providing a user-friendly interface for patients to connect with healthcare professionals, discuss symptoms, receive diagnoses, and seek medical advice remotely (Wiedermann et al.2023).

Medical Records Management

Virtual assistants securely manage and update patients' medical records, ensuring accessibility to healthcare providers during telemedicine consultations for informed decision-making (Shorbaji 2021).

Medication Management

They assist in managing medication prescriptions, refills, and reminders, enhancing medication adherence, and reducing the risk of medication errors through telemedicine platforms (Karattuthodi et al. 2023).

Remote Monitoring

Virtual assistants enable remote monitoring of patient's health parameters, such as vital signs or chronic condition indicators, allowing healthcare providers to track patients' progress and intervene proactively when necessary (Comito et al.2020).

Health Education

They provide personalized health education resources and information tailored to patients' needs, empowering them to make informed decisions about their health and treatment plans during telemedicine interactions (Anshari et al.2021).

Administrative Support

Virtual assistants offer administrative support by handling tasks such as insurance verification, billing inquiries, and appointment confirmations, streamlining operational processes within telemedicine platforms (Haleem et al 2021).

Data Analytics

They analyze patient data collected during telemedicine interactions to generate insights for healthcare providers, supporting evidence-based decision-making and continuous improvement of telemedicine services. In summary, virtual assistants serve as invaluable tools for telemedicine integration in healthcare, enhancing accessibility, efficiency, and quality of care delivery for patients and providers alike (Amjad et al.2023).

Monitoring Health Metrics Through Wearable Devices

Virtual assistants are revolutionizing healthcare by leveraging wearable devices to monitor health metrics efficiently. Here's a concise introduction to their key functionalities: Virtual assistants enable seamless integration with wearable devices, allowing continuous monitoring of vital health metrics such as heart rate, blood pressure, sleep patterns, and physical activity. Through intuitive interfaces and real-time data analysis, they provide personalized insights and actionable recommendations to users, empowering them to proactively manage their health. By facilitating remote monitoring and early detection of health issues, virtual assistants enhance preventive care and contribute to better health outcomes. Here are the key functionalities of virtual assistants in monitoring health metrics through wearable devices, explained as below:

a) Data Integration: Virtual assistants seamlessly integrate with various wearable devices such as smartwatches, fitness trackers, and medical sensors. (Nahavandi et al.2022).
b) Real-Time Monitoring: They continuously collect data on vital health metrics like heart rate, blood pressure, sleep patterns, and physical activity (Valero et al.2021).
c) Data Analysis: Virtual assistants analyze the collected data in real time, identifying patterns, trends, and anomalies (Khatri 2023).
d) Personalized Insights: They provide personalized insights based on individual health data, offering tailored recommendations for improving health and wellness (Babatunde et al. 2024).
e) Alerts and Notifications: Virtual assistants send alerts and notifications for abnormal health readings or deviations from established patterns (Ghayvat et al.2019).
f) Goal Setting: Users can set health goals within the virtual assistant interface, with progress tracking and reminders to stay on track (Dingler et al. 2021).
g) Health Coaching: Some virtual assistants offer coaching features, guiding exercise routines, dietary habits, and lifestyle changes (Kulyk et al.2014).
h) Integration with Healthcare Providers: They can share health data with healthcare providers, enabling remote monitoring and timely interventions (Daniel & Stephen 2024).
i) Medication Reminders: Virtual assistants remind users to take medications at prescribed times, improving medication adherence (Janwaar & Singh 2021).
j) Long-Term Tracking: They maintain a history of health metrics over time, facilitating long-term tracking and trend analysis for better health management. These functionalities empower users to take control of their health by leveraging wearable devices and virtual assistant technology for continuous monitoring and personalized health insights (Trinh et al. 2018).

Secure Access to Medical Records and Adherence to Regulations

Virtual assistants in healthcare offer secure access to medical records while adhering to stringent regulations to safeguard patient privacy and confidentiality. Here's a detailed discussion of their key functionalities:

Authentication and Authorization

Virtual assistants implement robust authentication mechanisms to verify the identity of healthcare professionals before granting access to medical records. This includes password-based authentication, biometric authentication (e.g., fingerprint or facial recognition), or two-factor authentication for enhanced security (Shah & Kanhere 2019).

Encryption of Data

They employ encryption techniques such as SSL/TLS (Secure Sockets Layer/Transport Layer Security) to encrypt data during transmission between the virtual assistant and the healthcare provider's system. Additionally, data-at-rest encryption ensures that stored medical records remain protected from unauthorized access (Tyagi 2023).

Compliance With Regulations

Virtual assistants strictly adhere to healthcare regulations such as the Health Insurance Portability and Accountability Act (HIPAA) in the United States and the General Data Protection Regulation (GDPR) in the European Union. They maintain compliance by implementing necessary safeguards for handling and protecting sensitive patient information (Tzanou 2023).

Role-Based Access Control (RBAC)

RBAC allows virtual assistants to assign specific access permissions to different users based on their roles within the healthcare organization. This ensures that only authorized personnel can access certain types of medical records, minimizing the risk of data breaches (Park et al. 2021).

Audit Trails

They maintain detailed audit trails that record all interactions with medical records, including user access, modifications, and system activities. Audit trails provide transparency and accountability, allowing administrators to track and review access logs for security and compliance purposes (Fernández et al. 2013).

Data Integrity Checks

Virtual assistants employ checksums or hash functions to verify the integrity of medical records, ensuring that data remains unchanged and uncorrupted during storage or transmission. Any unauthorized modifications to records trigger alerts, enabling prompt investigation and remediation (Alenoghena et al.2022).

Regular Security Updates

To mitigate emerging threats and vulnerabilities, virtual assistants receive regular security updates and patches. These updates address known vulnerabilities and strengthen security measures to protect against evolving cybersecurity risks (Yaacoub et al. 2022).

User Training and Awareness

Healthcare organizations conduct regular training sessions to educate staff members about security best practices and regulatory requirements when using virtual assistants. This helps ensure that personnel are knowledgeable about safeguarding patient data and preventing security incidents. By integrating these functionalities, virtual assistants facilitate secure access to medical records while maintaining compliance with regulations, thus promoting trust and confidence in healthcare services (Baumgart 2005).

BENEFITS OF VIRTUAL ASSISTANTS

Enhanced Patient Engagement and Empowerment

Virtual assistants have revolutionized patient engagement and empowerment in healthcare. These digital tools offer personalized support, timely communication, access to information, self-management tools, continuous support, and encouragement, ultimately leading to improved health outcomes (BACHINA). Here's a detailed explanation of how virtual assistants enhance patient engagement and empowerment in health and medicine, discussed in detail as follows

Personalized Support

Virtual assistants offer personalized support tailored to individual patient needs, preferences, and medical conditions. Through advanced algorithms and natural language processing (NLP), they provide customized responses and recommendations, fostering a sense of personal connection.

Timely Communication

Virtual assistants facilitate timely communication by sending reminders for medication schedules, follow-up appointments, and health screenings. Patients receive notifications via various channels such as text, email, or mobile apps, ensuring they stay informed and engaged in their healthcare journey (Mo et al.2024).

Access to Information

Patients have access to a wealth of health information and educational resources through virtual assistants. They can ask questions, and receive explanations about medical terms, treatment options, and lifestyle modifications, empowering them to make informed decisions(Claessen et al.2017).

Self-Management Tools

Virtual assistants provide self-management tools like symptom trackers, medication reminders, and diet journals. Patients can actively monitor their health metrics, track progress, and adhere to treatment plans, fostering a sense of control over their well-being (Griffin et al.2021).

Continuous Support

Virtual assistants offer continuous support by being available 24/7, allowing patients to seek assistance at any time. This accessibility ensures patients receive prompt responses to queries, reducing anxiety and enhancing trust in the healthcare system (Robinson et al. 2024).

Encouragement and Motivation

Virtual assistants offer encouragement and motivation through positive reinforcement messages, goal-setting prompts, and progress tracking. Patients feel empowered to adopt healthier behaviors, adhere to treatment regimens, and achieve their health goals with ongoing support (BACHINA).

Improved Health Outcomes

By enhancing patient engagement and empowerment, virtual assistants contribute to improved health outcomes. Patients who actively participate in their care are more likely to experience better treatment adherence, disease management, and overall well-being. In summary, virtual assistants play a crucial role in enhancing patient engagement and empowerment by providing personalized support, timely communication, access to information, self-management tools, continuous support, encouragement, and motivation, and ultimately contributing to improved health outcomes (Maher et al. 2024).

Improved Healthcare Accessibility, Especially in Remote Areas

Virtual assistants play a pivotal role in enhancing healthcare accessibility, particularly in remote areas. By leveraging digital technologies, virtual assistants bridge geographical gaps, providing medical support and guidance to individuals who might otherwise face challenges in accessing healthcare services. Virtual assistants and improved healthcare accessibility, especially in remote areas discussed in detail as follows as

a) Telemedicine Support: Virtual assistants enable remote consultations, allowing patients in remote areas to connect with healthcare providers without the need for physical travel.
b) 24/7 Availability: With virtual assistants, individuals can access healthcare advice and information anytime, reducing the dependency on traditional healthcare facilities that may have limited operating hours (Robinson et al. 2024).
c) Health Monitoring: Virtual assistants can monitor health metrics remotely through wearable devices, providing real-time data to healthcare professionals for assessment and intervention.
d) Health Education: They offer educational resources and guidance on preventive measures, empowering individuals to manage their health proactively, which is particularly valuable in areas with limited access to healthcare professionals (Anshari et al. 2021).

e) Appointment Scheduling: Virtual assistants assist in scheduling appointments efficiently, ensuring timely access to healthcare services even in remote locations (Chandwani et al. 2023).
f) Medication Management: They facilitate medication reminders and adherence tracking, supporting patients in managing their treatment plans effectively, regardless of their geographical location (Karattuthodi et al. 2023).
g) Language Support: Virtual assistants can overcome language barriers, providing healthcare information and support in multiple languages, thus improving accessibility for diverse populations in remote areas (Giachos et al. 2023).
h) Remote Monitoring: They enable remote monitoring of chronic conditions, allowing healthcare providers to track patients' health status and intervene promptly, reducing the need for frequent in-person visits (Comito et al.2020).
i) Emergency Assistance: In emergencies, virtual assistants can provide immediate guidance and support until professional medical assistance arrives, potentially saving lives in remote areas with limited emergency services (Robinson et al. 2024).

Support for Healthcare Professionals in Daily Tasks

Virtual assistants offer crucial support to healthcare professionals in their daily tasks, enhancing efficiency and productivity across various healthcare settings.

a) Efficient Documentation: Virtual assistants help healthcare professionals in managing and documenting patient information, reducing the time spent on administrative tasks (Rathert et al. 2017).
b) Appointment Scheduling: They assist in scheduling appointments, managing calendars, and sending reminders, allowing healthcare providers to focus on patient care (Chandwani et al. 2023).
c) Clinical Decision Support: Virtual assistants provide real-time information and clinical decision support, aiding healthcare professionals in making informed decisions during patient consultations (Comito et al.2020).
d) Medication Management: They assist in medication reconciliation, tracking prescriptions, and providing medication reminders to ensure adherence and patient safety. (Karattuthodi et al. 2023).
e) Telehealth Support: Virtual assistants facilitate telehealth consultations by managing virtual waiting rooms, handling patient intake, and coordinating video calls between patients and healthcare providers (Poonsuph 2022).

f) Data Analysis: They can analyze healthcare data to identify trends, monitor patient outcomes, and support evidence-based decision-making for better patient care (Khatri 2023).
g) Patient Education: Virtual assistants offer educational resources and personalized health information to patients, empowering them to take control of their health and make informed decisions (Rathert et al. 2017).
h) Remote Monitoring: They enable remote patient monitoring by collecting and analyzing health metrics from wearable devices, providing early detection of health issues, and facilitating timely interventions (Comito et al. 2020).
i) Administrative Support: Virtual assistants handle administrative tasks such as billing, insurance verification, and processing referrals, streamlining workflows and reducing administrative burdens on healthcare professionals (Haleem, et al. 2021).
j) Language Interpretation: They offer language interpretation services, breaking down language barriers and ensuring effective communication between healthcare providers and patients with diverse linguistic backgrounds (Giachos et al. 2023).

Efficiency in Healthcare Delivery and Resource Utilization

Virtual assistants in health and medicine bring about a myriad of benefits, enhancing various aspects of healthcare delivery. One significant advantage is the efficiency they bring to healthcare delivery and resource utilization. By automating tasks and streamlining processes, virtual assistants optimize the allocation of resources and improve overall operational efficiency within healthcare systems. Here are detailed benefits of virtual assistants in enhancing efficiency in healthcare delivery and resource utilization as follow as.

a) Task Automation: Virtual assistants automate repetitive administrative tasks, such as appointment scheduling, data entry, and documentation, freeing up healthcare professionals' time (Preum et al. 2021).
b) Streamlined Workflow: They streamline workflow processes by organizing patient data, managing medical records, and facilitating communication between healthcare providers, leading to smoother operations (Kaledio et al. 2024).
c) 24/7 Availability: Virtual assistants are available round the clock, ensuring continuous support and accessibility for both patients and healthcare professionals (Robinson et al. 2024).

d) Resource Optimization: By efficiently managing appointments and resources, virtual assistants help in maximizing the utilization of healthcare facilities and staff, reducing idle time and improving productivity (Youn et al. 2022).
e) Data Analysis and Insights: They assist in data analysis, providing valuable insights into patient trends, population health management, and resource allocation, aiding in informed decision-making (Alowais et al.2023).
f) Cost Savings: Virtual assistants contribute to cost savings by optimizing resource allocation, reducing administrative overheads, and minimizing errors, ultimately leading to more efficient use of financial resources (Rane 2023).
g) Patient Satisfaction: Improved efficiency translates to shorter wait times, quicker responses, and smoother processes, enhancing patient satisfaction and overall experience (Chauhan et al. 2024).
h) Scalability: Virtual assistants can scale according to the demand, handling increased patient volumes without compromising the quality of care or efficiency of operations. These functionalities collectively contribute to making healthcare delivery more efficient and resource utilization more effective, thereby improving the overall quality of care provided to patients (Jaroodi et al. 2020).

Promotion of Preventive Care and Healthy Lifestyle Choices

Incorporating virtual assistants in healthcare offers numerous benefits, including the promotion of preventive care and healthy lifestyle choices. These assistants play a pivotal role in empowering individuals to take charge of their health proactively. By providing personalized guidance, education, and reminders, they encourage users to adopt healthy habits and preventive measures. Let's delve into the advantages of virtual assistants in promoting preventive care and fostering healthy lifestyle choices. How virtual assistants promote preventive care and healthy lifestyle choices is discussed in detail as follows:

Personalized Health Recommendations

Virtual assistants analyze user data and provide tailored recommendations based on individual health profiles. They offer personalized advice on nutrition, exercise routines, stress management, and sleep hygiene.

Health Monitoring and Tracking

These assistants help users track their health metrics such as physical activity, heart rate, sleep patterns, and calorie intake. By monitoring trends over time, they empower users to make informed decisions about their health behaviors (Comito et al. 2020 & Nahavandi et al.2022).

Medication and Appointment Reminders

Virtual assistants ensure adherence to medication schedules and remind users of upcoming medical appointments. Timely reminders enhance medication compliance and encourage regular health check-ups (Mo et al.2024).

Health Education and Information

They provide access to reliable health information and educational resources. Users can learn about preventive measures, early warning signs of diseases, and strategies for maintaining overall wellness (Anshari et al. 2021).

Behavioural Change Support

Virtual assistants employ behavior change techniques such as goal setting, feedback, and positive reinforcement. They motivate users to adopt healthier habits by celebrating achievements and offering encouragement (Sezgin et al. 2020).

Integration With Wearable Devices

These assistants seamlessly integrate with wearable health devices like fitness trackers and smartwatches. Data collected from wearables enhances the accuracy of health assessments and enables more personalized recommendations (Nahavandi et al. 2022).

24/7 Accessibility and Support

Users can access virtual assistants anytime, anywhere, fostering continuous engagement with their health. Immediate access to support encourages users to seek guidance and take proactive steps toward preventive care. By leveraging these functionalities, virtual assistants empower individuals to prioritize their health, prevent illnesses, and lead healthier lifestyles (Robinson et al. 2024).

Challenges and Considerations Virtual Assistants in Health and Medicine

Here's Table 1. outlining the challenges and considerations associated with virtual assistants in health and medicine:

Table 1. Challenges and considerations virtual assistants in health and medicine

Sr. No	Challenges & Considerations	Explanation
1	Accuracy and Reliability	Ensuring that virtual assistants provide accurate and reliable information and recommendations.
		Minimizing errors in diagnosis, treatment suggestions, and medication management (Maher et al. 2024).
2	Privacy and Security Concerns	Addressing concerns regarding the protection of patient data and compliance with privacy regulations.
		Safeguarding sensitive health information from unauthorized access or breaches (Chen & Esmaeilzadeh 2024).
3	Integration with Healthcare Systems	Ensuring seamless integration with existing electronic health records (EHR) and hospital systems.
		Compatibility with various healthcare software and interoperability standards (Janett & Yeracaris 2020).
4	Ethical Considerations in AI	Addressing ethical dilemmas surrounding AI decision-making in healthcare.
		Ensuring fairness, transparency, and accountability in algorithmic processes (Guan 2019).

FUTURE DIRECTIONS AND OPPORTUNITIES

In the future, virtual assistants in healthcare will undergo significant evolution, leveraging advanced technologies like AI, AR, and VR to offer personalized, context-aware support to both patients and healthcare professionals. These assistants will play an expanded role in chronic disease management, integrating genomics and precision medicine to provide tailored recommendations, while also facilitating remote patient monitoring, telehealth, and mental health support to address health-care disparities. Improved natural language understanding will enable intuitive interactions and seamless integration with EHR systems will ensure adherence to ethical and regulatory standards. Additionally, advancements in AI and NLP will lead to expanded capabilities and adoption in specialty areas, such as genomics and mental health, with virtual assistants collaborating synergistically with other emerging technologies like IoT and blockchain to foster a holistic and efficient healthcare ecosystem, ultimately revolutionizing patient care and improving outcomes (Preum et al. 2021 & Qadri et al. 2020).

CONCLUSION

In conclusion, the transformative impact of virtual assistants on healthcare delivery is undeniable, offering personalized, context-aware support, enhancing patient engagement, and improving outcomes across various aspects of healthcare. However, to fully realize the potential of virtual assistants and ensure their seamless integration into healthcare systems, continued research, development, and implementation efforts are essential. By investing in advancing technologies like AI, AR, and NLP, and fostering collaboration between healthcare professionals, technologists, and policymakers, we can further refine virtual assistants' capabilities, address ethical and regulatory challenges, and optimize their role in revolutionizing patient care. We must remain committed to driving innovation in this space to harness the immense promise virtual assistants hold in shaping the future of healthcare delivery.

REFERENCES

Abigail Swamidoss, S. K., Alghamdi, B., Hickman, R. L., Knighton, S., Pekarek, M., & Drummond, C. K. (2021, April). Medication Management System Design for Isolated Patient Care. In *Frontiers in Biomedical Devices* (*Vol. 84812*, p. V001T06A001). American Society of Mechanical Engineers. 10.1115/DMD2021-1036

Al-Jaroodi, J., Mohamed, N., & Abukhousa, E. (2020). Health 4.0: On the way to realizing the healthcare of the future. *IEEE Access : Practical Innovations, Open Solutions*, 8, 211189–211210. 10.1109/ACCESS.2020.303885834976565

Al-Shorbaji, N., & Al-Shorbaji, N. (2021). Improving healthcare access through digital health: the use of information and communication technologies. *Healthcare Access, 10.*

Alenoghena, C. O., Onumanyi, A. J., Ohize, H. O., Adejo, A. O., Oligbi, M., Ali, S. I., & Okoh, S. A. (2022). eHealth: A survey of architectures, developments in mHealth, security concerns, and solutions. *International Journal of Environmental Research and Public Health*, 19(20), 13071. 10.3390/ijerph19201307136293656

Alowais, S. A., Alghamdi, S. S., Alsuhebany, N., Alqahtani, T., Alshaya, A. I., Almohareb, S. N., Aldairem, A., Alrashed, M., Bin Saleh, K., Badreldin, H. A., Al Yami, M. S., Al Harbi, S., & Albekairy, A. M. (2023). Revolutionizing healthcare: The role of artificial intelligence in clinical practice. *BMC Medical Education*, 23(1), 689. 10.1186/s12909-023-04698-z37740191

Alpay, L. L., Henkemans, O. B., Otten, W., Rövekamp, T. A., & Dumay, A. C. (2010). E-health applications and services for patient empowerment: Directions for best practices in The Netherlands. *Telemedicine Journal and e-Health*, 16(7), 787–791. 10.1089/tmj.2009.015620815745

Amjad, A., Kordel, P., & Fernandes, G. (2023). A review on innovation in healthcare sector (telehealth) through artificial intelligence. *Sustainability (Basel)*, 15(8), 6655. 10.3390/su15086655

Anastasiadou, M. N., Isaia, P., Kolios, P., & Charalambous, C. (2023). Transitioning towards fit-for-purpose Public Health Surveillance Systems. arXiv preprint arXiv:2305.16821.

Anshari, M., Almunawar, M. N., Younis, M. Z., & Kisa, A. (2021). Modeling users' empowerment in e-health systems. *Sustainability (Basel)*, 13(23), 12993. 10.3390/su132312993

Arun, A. (2023). MedSync-App and Device to Promote Medication Adherence. [JIEEE]. *Journal of Informatics Electrical and Electronics Engineering*, 4(2), 1–8. 10.54060/jieee.2023.103

Aslam, F. (2023). The impact of artificial intelligence on chatbot technology: A study on the current advancements and leading innovations. *European Journal of Technology*, 7(3), 62–72. 10.47672/ejt.1561

Babatunde, S. O., Odejide, O. A., Edunjobi, T. E., & Ogundipe, D. O. (2024). The role of AI in marketing personalization: A theoretical exploration of consumer engagement strategies. *International Journal of Management & Entrepreneurship Research*, 6(3), 936–949. 10.51594/ijmer.v6i3.964

Baumgart, D. C. (2005). Personal digital assistants in health care: Experienced clinicians in the palm of your hand? *Lancet*, 366(9492), 1210–1222. 10.1016/S0140-6736(05)67484-316198770

Chandwani, A., Shrivastava, K., Sadashiv, S., Saha, I., & Mishra, P. (2023, April). Virtual Assistant for Appointment Booking. In *2023 IEEE 8th International Conference for Convergence in Technology (I2CT)* (pp. 1-5). IEEE. 10.1109/I2CT57861.2023.10126199

Chauhan, P., Bali, A., & Kaur, S. (2024). Breaking Barriers for Accessible Health Programs: The Role of Telemedicine in a Global Healthcare Transformation. In *Transformative Approaches to Patient Literacy and Healthcare Innovation* (pp. 283-307). IGI Global.

Chen, Y., & Esmaeilzadeh, P. (2024). Generative AI in medical practice: In-depth exploration of privacy and security challenges. *Journal of Medical Internet Research*, 26, e53008. 10.2196/5300838457208

Chintala, S. (2023). AI-Driven Personalised Treatment Plans: The Future of Precision Medicine. *Machine Intelligence Research*, 17(02), 9718–9728.

Claessen, V., Schmidt, A., & Heck, T. (2017). *Virtual Assistants*. Humboldt-Universität zu Berlin.

Comito, C., Falcone, D., & Forestiero, A. (2020, December). Current trends and practices in smart health monitoring and clinical decision support. In *2020 IEEE International Conference on Bioinformatics and Biomedicine (BIBM)* (pp. 2577-2584). IEEE. 10.1109/BIBM49941.2020.9313449

. Daniel, S., & Stephen, M. (2024). *Transforming Healthcare Delivery: The Role of AI in Telehealth Services*.

Dharmale, G., Shirsath, P., Shinde, A., Sawant, V., & Chougule, A. (2023, February). REMICARE—Medicine Intake Tracker and Healthcare Assistant. In *Proceedings of 3rd International Conference on Recent Trends in Machine Learning, IoT, Smart Cities and Applications: ICMISC 2022* (pp. 273-283). Singapore: Springer Nature Singapore.

Dingler, T., Kwasnicka, D., Wei, J., Gong, E., & Oldenburg, B. (2021). The use and promise of conversational agents in digital health. *Yearbook of Medical Informatics*, 30(01), 191–199. 10.1055/s-0041-172651034479391

Fernández-Alemán, J. L., Señor, I. C., Lozoya, P. Á. O., & Toval, A. (2013). Security and privacy in electronic health records: A systematic literature review. *Journal of Biomedical Informatics*, 46(3), 541–562. 10.1016/j.jbi.2012.12.00323305810

Friedman, R. H., Stollerman, J. E., Mahoney, D. M., & Rozenblyum, L. (1997). The virtual visit: Using telecommunications technology to take care of patients. *Journal of the American Medical Informatics Association : JAMIA*, 4(6), 413–425. 10.1136/jamia.1997.00404139391929

Ghayvat, H., Awais, M., Pandya, S., Ren, H., Akbarzadeh, S., Chandra Mukhopadhyay, S., Chen, C., Gope, P., Chouhan, A., & Chen, W. (2019). Smart aging system: Uncovering the hidden wellness parameter for well-being monitoring and anomaly detection. *Sensors (Basel)*, 19(4), 766. 10.3390/s1904076630781852

Giachos, I., Papakitsos, E. C., Savvidis, P., & Laskaris, N. (2023). Inquiring natural language processing capabilities on robotic systems through virtual assistants: A systemic approach. *Journal of Computer Science Research*, 5(2), 28–36. 10.30564/jcsr.v5i2.5537

Greene, S. M., Tuzzio, L., & Cherkin, D. (2012). A framework for making patient-centered care front and center. *The Permanente Journal*, 16(3), 49–53. 10.7812/TPP/12-02523012599

Griffin, A. C., Xing, Z., Mikles, S. P., Bailey, S., Khairat, S., Arguello, J., Wang, Y., & Chung, A. E. (2021). Information needs and perceptions of chatbots for hypertension medication self-management: A mixed methods study. *JAMIA Open*, 4(2), ooab021. 10.1093/jamiaopen/ooab02133898936

Guan, J. (2019). Artificial intelligence in healthcare and medicine: Promises, ethical challenges and governance. *Chinese Medical Sciences Journal*, 34(2), 76–83.31315747

Haleem, A., Javaid, M., Singh, R. P., & Suman, R. (2021). Telemedicine for healthcare: Capabilities, features, barriers, and applications. *Sensors International*, 2, 100117. 10.1016/j.sintl.2021.10011734806053

Janett, R. S., & Yeracaris, P. P. (2020). Electronic Medical Records in the American Health System: Challenges and lessons learned. *Ciencia & Saude Coletiva*, 25(4), 1293–1304. 10.1590/1413-81232020254.2892201932267432

Janwaar, A., & Singh, A. (2021, October). On the Design of Therapy Tracker: A Cross-platform Medication Management Application with Augmented Reality and Machine Learning. In *Proceedings of the Future Technologies Conference (FTC) 2021, (Vol. 358*, p. 29). Springer Nature.

Jesse, M. W. (2019). *Analysis of voice assistants in eHealth* [Doctoral dissertation, Master Thesis, Universität Klagenfurt].

.Kaledio, P., Doris, L., & Olaoye, F. (2024). *Optimizing Hospital Workflows with AI and Robotics.*

Karattuthodi, M. S., Krishnan, G., Aiswarya, A. V., Sarath Chandran, C., Nair, S. S., Thorakkatil, S. A., & Arain, S. (2023). A systematic review on pharmacist-led pharmaceutical care optimization through virtual platforms. *Journal of Pharmaceutical Health Services Research*, 14(1), 2–13. 10.1093/jphsr/rmac054

Khatri, M. R. (2023). Integration of natural language processing, self-service platforms, predictive maintenance, and prescriptive analytics for cost reduction, personalization, and real-time insights customer service and operational efficiency. *International Journal of Information and Cybersecurity*, 7(9), 1–30.

Kizza, P. (2023). *Implementation of Telemedicine to Reduce No-show Rates.*

Kulyk, O. (2014). Personalized virtual coaching for lifestyle support: Principles for design and evaluation. *International Journal on Advances in Life Sciences*, 6(3-4), 300–309.

Maher, C., Singh, B., Wylde, A., & Chastin, S. (2024). Virtual health assistants: A grand challenge in health communications and behavior change. *Frontiers in Digital Health*, 6, 1418695. 10.3389/fdgth.2024.141869538827384

McGowan, P. T. (2012). Self-management education and support in chronic disease management. *Primary Care*, 39(2), 307–325. 10.1016/j.pop.2012.03.00522608868

Mo, L., Zhang, L., Sun, X., & Zhou, Z. (2024). Unlock Happy Interactions: Voice Assistants Enable Autonomy and Timeliness. *Journal of Theoretical and Applied Electronic Commerce Research*, 19(2), 1013–1033. 10.3390/jtaer19020053

Nahavandi, D., Alizadehsani, R., Khosravi, A., & Acharya, U. R. (2022). Application of artificial intelligence in wearable devices: Opportunities and challenges. *Computer Methods and Programs in Biomedicine*, 213, 106541. 10.1016/j.cmpb.2021.10654134837860

Park, J., Sandhu, R., Gupta, M., & Bhatt, S. (2021). Activity control design principles: Next-generation access control for smart and collaborative systems. *IEEE Access : Practical Innovations, Open Solutions*, 9, 151004–151022. 10.1109/ACCESS.2021.3126201

Poonsuph, R. (2022). The design blueprint for a large-scale telehealth platform. *International Journal of Telemedicine and Applications*, 2022, 2022. 10.1155/2022/848650835035477

Preum, S. M., Munir, S., Ma, M., Yasar, M. S., Stone, D. J., Williams, R., & Stankovic, J. A. (2021). A review of cognitive assistants for healthcare: Trends, prospects, and future directions. *ACM Computing Surveys*, 53(6), 1–37. 10.1145/3419368

Qadri, Y. A., Nauman, A., Zikria, Y. B., Vasilakos, A. V., & Kim, S. W. (2020). The future of healthcare internet of things: A survey of emerging technologies. *IEEE Communications Surveys and Tutorials*, 22(2), 1121–1167. 10.1109/COMST.2020.2973314

Rathert, C., Mittler, J. N., Banerjee, S., & McDaniel, J. (2017). Patient-centered communication in the era of electronic health records: What does the evidence say? *Patient Education and Counseling*, 100(1), 50–64. 10.1016/j.pec.2016.07.03127477917

Raval, H. Y., Parikh, S. M., & Patel, H. R. (2022). Self-maintained health surveillance artificial intelligence assistant. In *Handbook of Research on Lifestyle Sustainability and Management Solutions Using AI, Big Data Analytics, and Visualization* (pp. 168-184). IGI Global. 10.4018/978-1-7998-8786-7.ch010

Robinson, C. L., D'Souza, R. S., Yazdi, C., Diejomaoh, E. M., Schatman, M. E., Emerick, T., & Orhurhu, V. (2024). Reviewing the Potential Role of Artificial Intelligence in Delivering Personalized and Interactive Pain Medicine Education for Chronic Pain Patients. *Journal of Pain Research*, 17, 923–929. 10.2147/JPR.S43945238464902

Sanchez-Segura, M. I., Dugarte-Peña, G. L., Medina-Dominguez, F., Amescua Seco, A., & Menchen Viso, R. (2023). Digital transformation in organizational health and safety to mitigate Burnout Syndrome. *Frontiers in Public Health*, 11, 1080620. 10.3389/fpubh.2023.108062037026125

Sarker, M. (2023). Assessing the Integration of AI Technologies in Enhancing Patient Care Delivery in US Hospitals. *Journal of Knowledge Learning and Science Technology, 2*(2), 338-351.

Scarborough, B. M., & Smith, C. B. (2018). Optimal pain management for patients with cancer in the modern era. *CA: a Cancer Journal for Clinicians*, 68(3), 182–196. 10.3322/caac.2145329603142

Senbekov, M., Saliev, T., Bukeyeva, Z., Almabayeva, A., Zhanaliyeva, M., Aitenova, N., Toishibekov, Y., & Fakhradiyev, I. (2020). The recent progress and applications of digital technologies in healthcare: A review. *International Journal of Telemedicine and Applications*, 2020, 2020. 10.1155/2020/883020033343657

Sezgin, E., Militello, L. K., Huang, Y., & Lin, S. (2020). A scoping review of patient-facing, behavioral health interventions with voice assistant technology targeting self-management and healthy lifestyle behaviors. *Translational Behavioral Medicine*, 10(3), 606–628. 10.1093/tbm/ibz14132766865

Shah, S. W., & Kanhere, S. S. (2019). Recent trends in user authentication–a survey. *IEEE Access : Practical Innovations, Open Solutions*, 7, 112505–112519. 10.1109/ACCESS.2019.2932400

Sharmila Nirojini, P., Kanaga, K., Devika, S., & Pradeep, P. (2024). Exploring the impact of artificial intelligence on patient care: A comprehensive review of healthcare advancements. *Sch Acad J Pharm*, 13(2), 67–81. 10.36347/sajp.2024.v13i02.003

Soofastaei, A. (Ed.). (2024). *Advanced Virtual Assistants-A Window to the Virtual Future*. BoD–Books on Demand.

Tavakoli, M. (2023). *Hybrid human-AI driven open personalized education.*

Trinh, H., Shamekhi, A., Kimani, E., & Bickmore, T. W. (2018, November). Predicting user engagement in longitudinal interventions with virtual agents. In *Proceedings of the 18th International Conference on Intelligent Virtual Agents* (pp. 9-16). ACM. 10.1145/3267851.3267909

Tyagi, A. K. (Ed.). (2023). *Privacy Preservation and Secured Data Storage in Cloud Computing*. IGI Global.

Tzanou, M. (2023). *Health Data Privacy Under the GDPR.* TAYLOR FRANCIS Limited.

Valero, M., Clemente, J., Li, F., & Song, W. (2021). Health and sleep nursing assistant for real-time, contactless, and non-invasive monitoring. *Pervasive and Mobile Computing*, 75, 101422. 10.1016/j.pmcj.2021.101422

Verma, A., Sharma, A., Singh, A., Malviya, R., & Fuloria, S. (2023). Digital Assistant in the Pharmaceutical Field for Advancing Healthcare Systems. In *Pharmaceutical industry 4.0: Future, Challenges & Application* (pp. 213-254). River Publishers. 10.1201/9781003442493-8

Wager, K. A., Lee, F. W., & Glaser, J. P. (2021). *Health care information systems: a practical approach for health care management*. John Wiley & Sons.

Wiedermann, C. J., Mahlknecht, A., Piccoliori, G., & Engl, A. (2023). Redesigning Primary Care: The Emergence of Artificial-Intelligence-Driven Symptom Diagnostic Tools. *Journal of Personalized Medicine*, 13(9), 1379. 10.3390/jpm1309137937763147

Yaacoub, J. P. A., Noura, H. N., Salman, O., & Chehab, A. (2022). Robotics cyber security: Vulnerabilities, attacks, countermeasures, and recommendations. *International Journal of Information Security*, 21(1), 115–158. 10.1007/s10207-021-00545-833776611

Youn, S., Geismar, H. N., & Pinedo, M. (2022). Planning and scheduling in healthcare for better care coordination: Current understanding, trending topics, and future opportunities. *Production and Operations Management*, 31(12), 4407–4423. 10.1111/poms.13867

Zhou, B., Yang, G., Shi, Z., & Ma, S. (2022). Natural language processing for smart healthcare. *IEEE Reviews in Biomedical Engineering*.36170385

Chapter 2
Role of Social Media and AI in Transforming Healthcare Communication

Divya Mishra
https://orcid.org/0000-0002-9375-8720
Sharda University, India

ABSTRACT

This study explores the transformative impact of social media and AI on healthcare communication, emphasizing their transformative potential in information dissemination, patient engagement, and misinformation management. It highlights how social media platforms provide real-time updates and patient support, while AI technologies like machine learning and natural language processing revolutionize data analysis and personalized care. Despite these benefits, integrating these tools raises ethical concerns, such as privacy issues, data security risks, and informed consent complexities. It addresses challenges like data interoperability, infrastructure sufficiency, and system scalability, emphasizing the need for comprehensive provider training and unbiased AI algorithms. It also examines AI's role in curbing misinformation while balancing ethical considerations and free speech. The study advocates for a collaborative approach to ensure innovative and ethically sound healthcare communication, improve patient outcomes, and foster a more equitable and efficient healthcare system.

DOI: 10.4018/979-8-3693-5976-1.ch002

INTRODUCTION

Communication in healthcare is changing rapidly due to the increased use of social media and Artificial Intelligence technology solutions. In general, communication in the context of healthcare has a very significant impact on the patient's outcomes, safety, and quality of care (Ratna, 2019). As noted by Teutsch (2003), communication should be effective both between providers and patients and within the teams of providers to ensure optimal patient care. In the past, healthcare communication used to be a one-way process where the physicians were expected to make the decisions while the patients passively received the information from the physicians (Will, 2011; Rees, 1993). Initially, based on the ethic of beneficence this model started changing towards patient's self-determination and voluntary consent in the middle of the twentieth century (Brock, 1991; Ballard-Reisch, 1990). This resulted in joint management making as well as multi-disciplinary cooperation and consultation (Siegler, 2021; Chung et al., 2011). Some research noted that this approach is beneficial, as patient-centered communication enhances patient satisfaction, adherence to treatment, and health outcomes (Haskard-Zolnierek & DiMatteo 2021; Mead & Bowers, 2000). Such measures as the teach-back technique that involves patients recounting what the provider has said to them also strengthen the communication channel between providers and patients.

Effective communication leads to better adherence to treatment plans, fewer medical errors, and enhanced overall patient health. For example, a study by Street et al. (2009) found that positive communication behaviors, such as active listening and empathy, significantly improve patient satisfaction and trust, resulting in better health outcomes. Additionally, programs like the University of Michigan Health System's communication and resolution program (CRP) encourage open communication with patients and families following adverse events, leading to a significant reduction in malpractice claims and improved patient-provider relationships (Kachalia et al., 2010).

However, in the traditional healthcare setting, effective communication remains a challenge as it does in any other practice. Traditional face-to-face communication process can be problematic due to large patient population, time constraints, and difficult medical information. Clinicians neglect the communication aspect due to short time they spend with patients hence provide less time in communication hence poor communication and patients' dissatisfaction (Lown et al.,2011). In addition, ineffectively managed hierarchical systems in many healthcare facilities can hinder free and appropriate disclosure of information between members of a team, which can negatively affect patient safety and care quality. According to the report by The Joint Commission, it was determined that close to 70 percent of sentinel events are caused by communication issues (Sentinel Event, n.d.). Tools such as the SBAR

(Situation, Background, Assessment, Recommendation) has been found to be useful in improving the organization and communication during handoffs and therefore reducing on the number of errors (*SBAR Tool: Situation-Background-Assessment-Recommendation*, n.d.).

SYNERGISTIC INTEGRATION OF SOCIAL MEDIA AND AI: REVOLUTIONIZING HEALTHCARE COMMUNICATION AND ENGAGEMENT

The use of social media platforms in conjunction with artificial intelligence is revolutionizing the healthcare conversation and interaction, opening up new possibilities and issues. Facebook, Twitter, and other social media applications are crucial tools used by healthcare providers in reaching out to patients and following trending topics in real time. AI augments these capabilities through analyzing, predicting, and automating communication in healthcare leading to efficient and effective interaction. This synergy is revolutionizing the healthcare sector as it allows physicians and patients to have closer and timely communication.

The intersection of social media platforms and artificial intelligence (AI) in the healthcare system has changed the overall concepts of communication and engagement. Facebook, Twitter, and Instagram are some of the most popular social media sites that have proven useful for the management of healthcare services and sharing of information on patient trends in real time. AI extends these capabilities by offering enhanced data analysis, forecasting algorithms, and self-service interactions, making healthcare communication more effective and efficient. These synergistic integrations are gradually redesigning the healthcare industry through timely and personalized interactions between providers and patients.

Social media has emerged as a powerful tool in healthcare, enabling providers to reach wider audiences and foster more interactive communication channels. It has significantly transformed the dissemination of medical information, patient interaction, and service delivery. Platforms such as Facebook, Twitter, and YouTube serve as critical tools for public health education, patient support, and community engagement. These platforms enable healthcare organizations to rapidly share essential health information, engage with patients, and receive real-time feedback on healthcare services. For instance, hospitals and health systems use YouTube to share patient education videos (Househ, 2013), significantly increasing patient engagement and leading to higher appointment rates. Many healthcare organizations create community pages where they post updates, share educational content, and interact with patients. For example, the Mayo Clinic and the Cleveland Clinic use Facebook to share patient stories, health tips, and live Q&A sessions with medical experts, fostering a sense of community and engagement (Ventola, 2014). Twitter is crucial for real-time updates and professional networking. During the COVID-19 pandemic, organizations like the CDC and WHO used Twitter to provide timely updates and control misinformation (Merchant & Lurie, 2020). Another successful example is the Know Your Lemons campaign, which used social media to educate women about the signs of breast cancer. The campaign's creative and visually engaging posts on platforms like Facebook and Instagram went viral, significantly increasing awareness and encouraging women to perform self-examinations. This campaign demonstrated the power of social media in spreading crucial health information quickly and effectively.

Social media is also very useful in crisis management and public health monitoring and surveillance. In cases of health emergencies, including diseases and natural disasters, social media has a role in quickly and accurately informing the public. During COVID-19, people used social media to promote awareness of precautionary measures, vaccines, and government guidelines (Neely et al., 2021). Social media platforms were used effectively to disseminate pertinent health information among the public hence ensuring strict compliance with the health guidelines. It was found that a large number of people got their updates and directives concerning COVID-19 from social media, thereby affirming its importance in the dissemination of Information during the pandemic (Olawunmi & Babatunde, 2022; Zang et al., 2022). Healthcare workers can also use SMM to gather insights about the general public's sentiments and information that is being spread around which is crucial when it comes to public health engagement (Bautista et al., 2021). Social media has the feature of giving real-time information on public opinions and actions hence is efficient in eradicating misinformation given to the public by healthcare providers. Therefore, interacting on social networks helps healthcare professionals dispel misconceptions and provide accurate guidance based on the principles of evidence-based medicine, which will positively affect public health and the overall trust in healthcare systems (Jeyaraman et al., 2023).

Another advantage of social media is that it may also create patient support groups by which, patients with similar diseases can get connected to each other, share their experiences, offer encouragement, and exchange information regarding different treatment and management techniques to enhance their power. For instance, research reveals that online support groups can enhance patients' quality of life and their compliance with medication through exchange of experiences among the patients (Hu et al., 2019). These virtual communities are important sources of information and support for patients of chronic diseases or rare diseases where there are fewer support groups available in the community.

In addition, social media brings the possibility of improving the sphere of healthcare marketing and patient relations: it allows healthcare providers to promote themselves as trustworthy and competent. Most health facilities post on social media platforms patient success stories and those who have undergone through a particular treatment, which has the tendency of creating a positive perception to anyone who is planning to undergo the same treatment. Integrating social media with healthcare big data can improve service delivery by providing insights into patient behaviors and preferences, enabling more targeted and effective interventions. As healthcare organizations continue to integrate social media into their strategies, they create more informed, engaged, and connected patient communities.

AI in healthcare communication has revolutionized the sector in recent years, mainly through ML and NLP. These technologies facilitate the processing, communication, and application of medical details, and hence, the improved delivery of health care. Machine learning algorithms function on pattern recognition and prediction from datasets without coding, enhancing the decision-making system and results (Esteva et al., 2019). NLP is a technique that allows computers to analyze, understand, and produce natural language and would be particularly useful in the analysis of large amounts of unstructured data such as clinical notes and patient records (Jiang et al., 2017).

Both, ML and NLP are becoming indispensable for the analysis of electronic health records (EHRs). In EHRs, the NLP algorithms are applied to identify relevant information from unstructured text to enhance data retrieval and patient records. This results in improved formation of clinical decisions and consequently, patient management and treatment (Wang et al., 2018). For example, in the case of Google's DeepMind, the AI models can diagnose over 50 eye diseases from retinal scans more accurately than expert ophthalmologists and with improved diagnostic accuracy (De Fauw et al., 2018). Also, it is applied in the prediction of the health status of the patients and the progression of the disease in order to prevent or counteract the occurrence of effects. Virtual health assistants and chatbots are also employed in managing patients' interactions, disseminating medical knowledge, and screening symptoms as well as scheduling appointments. These tools enable it to capture patient queries, answer the same to the highest likelihood, and minimize the amount of work for the healthcare provider. For instance, the Mayo Clinic has developed an AI chatbot that helps to identify possible COVID-19 symptoms and provide relevant recommendations. AI in research enhances the identification of relevant medical literature and clinical trial results to facilitate evidence-based practice by making the research findings more easily available (Jiang et al., 2017).

Telemedicine platforms have enhanced patient access due to the removal of travel requirements and the option for follow-up visits and chronic care management in the comfort of their homes especially in rural and other hard-to-reach areas. There has been an over 50% increase in the use of telemedicine during the COVID-19 pandemic and has been beneficial in decreasing missed appointments and enhancing patient compliance with recommended treatment plans (Quesada-Caballero et al., 2023). The integration of telemedicine during this pandemic also highlighted its effectiveness in ensuring the continuity of care of chronic patients and decreasing the load on healthcare facilities. For example, telemedicine has been applied successfully for follow-up in the family medicine clinic, which enhances the adherence level of chronic patients (AlAhmad et al., 2021). Further, telemedicine has been advantageous in managing patient consultations and follow-ups especially during rheumatology and neurology, to ensure that patients continue receiving care without risking exposure to COVID-19 (Bloem et al., 2020). Telemedicine has been an essential tool in the Indian context to address long-term illnesses and maintain constant care during the COVID-19 pandemic; it has facilitated epilepsy care in patients with video consults and in homeopathic research institutions, where patients reported high satisfaction during the second wave of the pandemic (Bhattacharjee et al., 2023). These examples show how the telemedicine approach can be used to address the gaps in the provision of healthcare and access to medical services in hard-to-reach areas in particular, in times of a pandemic.

mHealth applications and tools are effective in improving patients' involvement and adherence to prescribed treatments as well as in providing them with relevant medical data. Some examples include nutritional and workout applications such as MyFitnessPal and Glucose Buddy which assist patients in tracking their health status and getting a response (Peng et al., 2016). Some of the examples of mental health apps include Headspace and Calm, which help make users happy through meditation. However, some of the issues that may arise include data authenticity and protection, the privacy of users, and how to overcome digital inequality (Poduval et al., 2018). In general, it can be stated that by using AI technologies, including machine learning and natural language processing, communication in the sphere of healthcare is improved to a greater extent. These technologies enhance the accuracy and the rate and pave the way to personalized and patient-centered care.

Impact on Speed and Flexibility of Communication

Telemedicine platforms, mHealth apps, and EHRs have greatly improved the speed and convenience at which patients can communicate with their providers. Telemedicine includes virtual visits such as video calls, phone consultations, and messages, which help to provide quick medical advice and follow-up. For instance, institutions such as the Cleveland Clinic revealed that they witnessed a 1,700% surge in virtual visits during the COVID-19 outbreak (Keesara, Jonas, & Schulman, 2020). mHealth apps, such as MyChart, offer features such as health status monitoring, medication tracking, and secure messaging with the provider, who responds promptly (Free et al., 2013). Also, EHRs allow for the interoperability of information within the various providers' entities, which in turn ensures timely decision-making and minimizes errors (Wang et al., 2018).

These advancements have also helped in improving patient-physician communication since it has become easier for patients to interact with their physicians than they used to do in the past hence improving patient satisfaction and compliance with treatment regimes (Street et al., 2009). The social media that is employed by healthcare organizations in patient interaction as well as distribution of health information has enhanced these relationships (Ventola, 2014). These technological applications foster timely interaction and individualized attention, which are key components of patient-centered care, thereby enhancing the relationship between patients and providers and resulting in more efficient and satisfactory outcomes in healthcare.

BALANCING ETHICS AND TECHNOLOGY IN HEALTHCARE COMMUNICATION: PRIVACY, DATA SECURITY, AND INFORMED CONSENT

There are numerous advantages in the current digital healthcare communication but this also poses important ethical issues on privacy and security and more importantly on informed consent. Since most healthcare organizations have digitized patient data, they become a focal point for cyber criminals to steal personal health information that can be used for identity theft and the loss of consumer confidence. It is crucial to maintain the confidentiality of the patient details and this can only be achieved through the implementation of strong security measures and adherence to the data protection laws.

Patients' privacy is one of the essential components that determine the level of trust between the patient and the healthcare provider. It helps safeguard health information from other people who do not have a right to access this information and make patients comfortable to reveal crucial information required in the diagnosis and treatment of their diseases. The Health Insurance Portability and Accountability Act (HIPAA) in the United States is one of the leading regulations that safeguard the privacy of patients by putting into practice standard measures for the protection of health information across the country (U.S. Department of Health and Human Services, 2022). Though the availability of digital communication media and EHR has enhanced the healthcare sector's effectiveness, it has also raised the frequency and possibilities of privacy infringements. For instance, the health insurance company Anthem Inc. suffered a data breach in 2015 that put the identity details of over 78 million individuals at risk (Terhune, 2015). Likewise, in 2018, UnityPoint Health fell prey to a phishing attack that exposed the information of 1.4 million patients (*1.4 Million Patient Records Breached in UnityPoint Health Phishing*, 2018). Such incidents erode patient confidence and may have dire psychological and financial implications for the victims.

Cyber threats in healthcare manifest in several ways; hacking, phishing, and ransomware. The WannaCry ransomware cyberattack of 2017 impacted healthcare services and patient records in many organizations globally, proving that the outcomes can be massive (Ehrenfeld, 2017). Healthcare workers are the major victims of the phishing schemes as evidenced by the University of Washington Medicine breach which occurred in 2019 and affected over a million records (*PHI of Almost 1 Million UW Medicine Patients Exposed Online*, 2019). Another good example is the attack that took place in 2016 at Banner Health where the attackers were able to obtain data of 3. 7 million people via a targeted server (*Banner Health Nailed by Huge Cyberattack That Compromised Personal*, 2016). To address these security threats, there is a need for healthcare organizations to implement sound measures like applying enhanced forms of encryption, having regular security scans, and offering frequent training to employees on cybersecurity. Other measures that can prevent breaches include; adopting multi-factor authentication since it can minimize the probability of attacks and using up-to-date software systems. In addition, the successful implementation of incident response plans and conducting vulnerability assessments are essential strategies for improving healthcare cybersecurity (Kwon & Johnson, 2014).

Informed consent is one of the essential principles of medical ethics that refers to the patient's right to information regarding processes and consent to the procedures to be conducted on them. It entails informing the patient on the nature of a given procedure or treatment that is to be done and its implications for the patient. In the digital era, informed consent is not without challenges because of issues of intricacy in information, as well as the depersonalization of interactions through various forms of technology. For instance, the increase in the usage of telemedicine due to the COVID-19 pandemic to deliver consultations and medical advice brought to the forefront the issue of informed consent when patients consult the doctor virtually as opposed to physically and hence may not be fully attentive or even capable of fully understanding the information being imparted to them (Kruse et al., 2017). Also, most of the mobile health apps lack content standards in explaining the data utilization and privacy statement, which hinders the informed consent process. Such opacity often renders the user incapable of making rational decisions on how their personal information will be used hence not in adherence to the principle of informed consent. There are existing ways to enhance informed consent in the digital age, including the use of new technologies and tools for communication with patients, such as interactive informed consent forms and educational videos.

Several ethical dilemmas emerge when addressing diverse and unique healthcare practices such as the importance of the rapid response in the healthcare setting, especially during emergencies. This is why decision-making must be fast while at the same time not compromising the patients' right to autonomy and informed choices. Some of the relevant ethical issues concerning rapid response involve the need to provide patients with adequate information and their consent regardless of the time constraints. Due to the COVID-19 outbreak, healthcare workers experienced various ethical challenges, including the distribution of scarce resources like ventilators and Intensive Care Unit beds. For example, in Italy, physicians had to make fast decisions about which patients would be admitted to critical care based on their conditions, the prognosis of the health state, and survival chances, which raised the ethical dilemma of speed and accountability (Rosenbaum, 2020). Another example is the application of AI in sorting out patients during the pandemic, which, despite its effectiveness, questioned the rationality and equity of the algorithms implemented (Vorisek et al., 2023). Other scenarios observed during the Ebola outbreak also show that there is a dilemma between speedy response and ethical responses in the health system where the healthcare providers had to deal with the conflict between a faster response and a humane response (Venkat et al., 2015). These scenarios highlight the need to establish ethical standards and policies that help in coming up with quick decisions in the care of patients.

EVOLVING PATIENT EXPECTATIONS: ENHANCING ACCESS TO INFORMATION, AI-DRIVEN PERSONALIZATION, AND EXPECTATIONS MANAGEMENT

With the advancement of healthcare, the expectations of patients have also risen to the next level. The advances in the digital world have greatly improved the way patients are able to seek information about their health. Facebook, Instagram, and LinkedIn are also useful in spreading health information. Such organizations as the American Heart Association leverage these platforms to post updates, disseminate information on preventive measures, and carry out public engagements such as the "Life's Simple 7" (*Life's Simple 7*, n.d.). These platforms allow for an interactive discourse so patients have access to recent health information.

AI technologies are now helping patients transform the way they engage with their health care. For instance, chatbots used in the healthcare sector offer instant medical advice by considering the patient's reported symptoms and past medical history. For example, during the COVID-19 outbreak, AI chatbots assisted with answering patients' questions and minimising the load on doctors (Topol, 2020). IBM Watson Health, for instance, deploys artificial intelligence to study patients' characteristics and design individual treatment plans to improve the quality of patient care (Jiang et al., 2017). The recent studies indicate that AI has the capability to predict patient's deterioration much more effectively than conventional methods and its potential to enhance patient outcomes (Maan et al., 2021). However, there are several areas of ethical concern such as data privacy and bias in artificial intelligence (Cohen et al., 2020). Furthermore, the use of AI has been applied to increase patients' compliance with prescribed treatment plans and individual health management to result in better health outcomes (Kvedar et al., 2016).

Nevertheless, it is crucial to manage patient expectations as this is a key to providing quality patient care. These expectations should be managed through a proactive communication style. Engaging patients with their portals, explaining and discussing the reality during consultative sessions, and even carrying out educational campaigns can assist in the process of managing their expectations. For instance, Cleveland Clinic's patient portal provides detailed information about health, increasing the patients' involvement levels and their satisfaction (Davis et al., 2012). Moreover, it is crucial to mention the importance of combining technology with the more traditional face-to-face communication. While telemedicine is beneficial for establishing teleconsultations for routine follow-ups, actual face-to-face consults are crucial in handling complicated cases. For instance, the Mayo Clinic follows the hybrid model where it employs telemedicine for routine visits and face-to-face meetings for diagnosis and advanced treatment plans for additional patient care (*Telehealth: Technology Meets Health Care*, 2022). Studies conducted in the recent past point to the fact that telemedicine has had a high patient satisfaction rate and has helped to expand the reach of healthcare services, especially in the time of the COVID-19 pandemic (Gajarawala & Pelkowski, 2021). In addition, the use of secure messaging, video consultation, and other forms of communication technologies have delivered positive results in overall patient care, as a result, improving patient outcomes (Powell et al., 2017). Meeting these increased expectations proves challenging, and practicing healthcare providers must embrace technology while also maintaining personal connections with patients, so technological engagement stays a supplement to, rather than a replacement for, interpersonal contact. This process of a technology-mediated relationship between patients and clinicians is important to address rising expectations.

MISINFORMATION MANAGEMENT IN HEALTHCARE: ADDRESSING SPREAD, AI DETECTION, AND BALANCING CORRECTION WITH FREE SPEECH

Misinformation is a critical area of concern in the healthcare sector because the impacts of such information on the health of the public can be detrimental. Inaccurate information shared on social media leads to negative health practices that make the work of health care services challenging. AI is very significant in the prevention and management of false information because of the complicated structures applied in fact-checking and moderation. During crucial moments, such as the COVID-19 pandemic, the spread of fake news highlighted the need for proper identification and correction. Machine learning, NLP, and deep learning techniques have the potential to mitigate misinformation through AI-driven systems. For instance, models like the Bi-LSTM optimized by genetic algorithms have demonstrated high accuracy in detecting misinformation on social media platforms (Al Bataineh et al., 2023). Furthermore, the application of sentiment analysis and document similarity has proved helpful for fact-checking information in the field of healthcare (Barve & Saini, 2021).

The involvement of AI in the process of misinformation detection not only contributes to the speed of the task but also allows for solving the problems of transparency and interpretability, which is crucial in the sphere of healthcare. Other models like DETERRENT, which employs the use of knowledge graph and graph attention networks, were revealed to have enhanced healthcare misinformation detection by 21% when extra contextual information from medical knowledge bases was incorporated (Cui et al., 2020). These systems also provide rationales for their operations, which is important in the battle against false information since they help flag misleading content.

Nevertheless, addressing the issue of misinformation (Kaushal et al., 2023) is a delicate process that needs to be weighed against the rights of free speech, especially in the area of healthcare. AI interventions should be taken with ethical considerations that should include free speech so that there is both health integrity and democracy. Other legal systems such as the European Convention on Human Rights (ECHR) tries to achieve this balance by permitting the use of restrictions on free speech in order to protect public health provided that the restrictions are legal, necessary, and proportionate (Marecos et al., 2023). Therefore, other forms of solutions such as media literacy should be encouraged by the policymakers instead of focusing on speech regulation where it involves ethical and constitutional issues. It is important to stress that educational activities are necessary for creating an informed and reasoned society. Media literacy initiatives might improve cognition and show how misleading information works to help people make better decisions.

A diverse media diet and active information consumption from various sources can reduce the impact of biased or misleading information and encourage fair public debate. In conclusion, it is necessary to admit that the strategy of combating fake news and, at the same time, preserving freedom of speech is multifaceted and calls for further discussion. Through the establishment of sound laws, ethical moderation strategies, and educational initiatives, misinformation can be fought and freedom of speech preserved.

OVERCOMING TECHNOLOGICAL AND REGULATORY CHALLENGES IN INTEGRATING SOCIAL MEDIA AND AI IN HEALTHCARE COMMUNICATION

The combination of social media and artificial intelligence in healthcare communication poses several technological and legal challenges that need to be resolved to reap maximum benefits. Table 1 presents the challenges and solutions for integrating social media and AI in Healthcare Communication. This brings out the problem of data interoperability as one of the significant technological challenges. Health data interoperability can be defined as the effectiveness of conversion, sharing, and utilization of data between healthcare IT systems. It is imperative for patient care and allows healthcare practitioners to obtain a complete patient history that is crucial for treating the patient. Interoperability minimizes healthcare risks and increases the overall quality of the patient's care because all relevant practitioners receive the same information (Wang et al., 2018). One major challenge is the lack of standardized data formats across different healthcare systems, leading to difficulties in data exchange and integration. To overcome these problems, use of standards like the Health Level Seven International (HL7) and Fast Healthcare Interoperability Resources (FHIR) have been adopted to enhance data exchange in varied systems (Bender & Sartipi, 2013).

Another big issue is the sufficiency of infrastructure that is, the ability to provide the population with the necessary facilities and equipment. Most of the healthcare facilities are outdated having low budgets, which slows down the implementation of modern digital tools such as AI and social media platforms. To get the most out of these technologies, it is necessary to ensure the availability of powerful and modern infrastructure, including high-speed Internet, data security, and high-performance computing. The American Hospital Association identified that while the adoption of new technologies is challenging, the lack of sufficient training for healthcare staff exacerbates the issue (*Telehealth: A Path to Virtual Integrated Care | AHA*, n.d.). It is essential to stress educational initiatives that would prepare the staff of the healthcare sector and facilities to employ these tools and applications. For instance, in India, Apollo Hospitals has incorporated AI-based diagnostic and patient care systems throughout the network, enhancing the patient's well-being and process effectiveness (Nizam & Aslekar, 2021). AI applications in radiology include the analysis of images, risk assessment of patients' deterioration, and resource utilization planning. In addition, the Indian government has launched the National Digital Health Mission (NDHM) that aims at developing a digital health environment that includes a health ID for every citizen and interoperable EHRs.

Another problem is scalability since the volume of data in healthcare systems increases significantly when using AI technologies such as machine learning for diagnosis. Due to the increase in data size of electronic health records (EHRs), medical images, and wearable devices, these challenges are only getting worse (Jiang et al., 2017). The implementation of cloud computing solutions like Amazon Web Services (AWS) and Microsoft Azure can help in offering the right platform for the large-scale application of AI and big data storage. Moreover, through data compression and algorithm optimization, the amount of data and computations can be effectively controlled (Esteva et al., 2019).

Current regulatory frameworks in healthcare organizations deal with privacy rights, the security of patients' information, and proper technology utilization. Some of the key regulations include the Health Insurance Portability and Accountability Act (HIPAA) in the United States of America which establishes national-level standards for the protection of health information and the General Data Protection Regulation (GDPR) in the European Union which provides comprehensive guidelines on data protection and privacy. In India, the Digital Information Security in Healthcare Act (DISHA) is available to safeguard patient data and privacy in the digital health domain (Ganapathy, 2021). These frameworks need to be revised for the new challenges as technology progresses to improve the ethical use of AI and digital tools. Future regulatory changes should address improving data compatibility and sharing, increasing the AI algorithm decision process openness, and providing equal access to innovative solutions. Having standard sets of regulations and policies for the use of AI in healthcare across the world can go a long way in ensuring that the various applications of AI in the healthcare sector meet appropriate safety and efficacy standards (Pesapane et al., 2021; Li et al., 2023). Tackling the technological and regulatory issues in healthcare communication is crucial to enabling the use of social media and AI (Kaushal & Mishra, 2024) to the fullest. Potential opportunities for these technologies include advancing data exchange, refining infrastructure, expanding system capacity, and modernizing policies to provide better care to patients in need and deliver care that is more efficient, effective, and equitable.

Table 1. Challenges and solutions in integrating social media and AI in healthcare communication (table by author)

Challenges	Type	Description	Solutions	Impact
Data Interoperability	Technological	Lack of standardized data formats and protocols hinders seamless data exchange	Adoption of HL7 and FHIR standards	Improved data sharing and patient care
Infrastructure Sufficiency	Technological	Outdated technology and insufficient funding impede adoption of advanced digital tools	Investment in high-speed internet, secure data storage, and comprehensive training programs	Enhanced capability to leverage new technologies
Scalability	Technological	Managing large data volumes from EHRs, medical imaging, and wearable devices is challenging.	Use of cloud computing solutions (AWS, Microsoft Azure), data compression techniques, algorithm optimization	Efficient management of data and computational loads
Privacy Concerns	Ethical	Risk of unauthorized access to sensitive health information	Implementation of strong encryption, adherence to HIPAA and GDPR standards	Enhanced patient trust and data security
Data Breaches and Security Risks	Ethical	Vulnerability to cyberattacks like hacking, phishing, and ransomware	Regular security audits, multi-factor authentication, updated software systems	Reduced risk of data breaches
Informed Consent	Ethical	Complexity of obtaining informed consent in digital interactions	Use of interactive consent forms, educational videos, clear communication strategies	Improved patient understanding and consent processes
Balancing Promptness with Ethical Responsibility	Ethical/Regulatory	Need for rapid decision-making without compromising patient autonomy	Establishment of ethical frameworks and guidelines for rapid response scenarios	Better balance between speed and ethical responsibility in care provision

FUTURE DIRECTIONS AND RECOMMENDATIONS

While the current research indicates a promising shift in the area of healthcare communication through the use of social media and Artificial Intelligence, future research directions should aim at improving the technological infrastructure as well as addressing ethical issues in order to fully harness the potential of social media in the health care communication. The area that needs further development is the improvement of the interoperability standards. More resources should be aimed at increasing the adoption and utilization of such standards as HL7 and FHIR to promote compatible exchange of data between different healthcare systems. This can be supported by developing sound collaborative IT support and providing enhanced education to the practitioners. As a whole, the technology industry can only develop an integrated system through the cooperation of technology developers, healthcare providers, and policymakers that will help emphasize the efficient, secure, and quality medical care of the patients.

Moreover, there is also a need to bridge the digital divide that would make a lot of technologies in health care available to all. It should also include expanding funding for digital connectivity and focusing on extending broadband to areas that currently lack this vital resource so that patients of all demographics can make use of telemedicine and other digital health technologies. Such initiatives as the National Digital Health Mission (NDHM) in the context of India offer great examples of developing holistic digital health environments that will give every citizen their individual health identifier and use interoperable e-health records. Improving cybersecurity and introducing transparent AI algorithms and transparent and easily understandable AI algorithms will also be important. This means that the legal guidelines have to be updated periodically to remain relevant with the developments in technology, as well as protecting the patient's rights and their data. Global governance standards supporting the increasing application of AI in the medical sector could be beneficial in the alignment of the rules and guidelines for AI use, for example, in the domain of protecting patients' rights, and promoting ethical innovation.

The Integration of these recommendations will involve collective efforts from different stakeholders such as governments, health organizations, and technology firms. Overall, through integration, bridging the digital divide, and solidifying good regulatory policies, social media, and AI in the healthcare sector will revolutionize the way healthcare communication is managed, patients' well-being is enhanced, and the delivery of healthcare services becomes fair and efficient.

CONCLUSION

The implementation of digital solutions and technologies in healthcare communication is one of the significant developments in the field of healthcare concerning patients' care, access, and convenience. However, this also leads to several issues and ethical dilemmas that need to be addressed to guarantee equality and quality of health care. Both social media and artificial intelligence have affected the sharing of health information, patients and their interactions, and even the handling of misinformation in the health sector. Though helpful, these technologies have drawbacks in the areas of privacy, security, and the provision of fake information. To prevent these risks, there should be some positive practices like AI-supported fact-checking and reasonable content moderation policies.

Technology has impacted patients' expectations where they expect accurate and timely information, personal care, and effective communication channels. Achieving these expectations therefore requires continuous efforts in enhancing the education of these patients, ensuring that the health care professionals are equipped adequately with the digital technologies and making the AI algorithms more neutral.

However, it is equally important to note that the successful adoption of technologies within these settings features heavy infrastructural and regulatory barriers. Promoting the data standards, improving the healthcare system, and making it scalable should remain its key prerequisites when it comes to integrating new technologies. Specifically, the paper concludes that there is a need to adapt the regulatory stance for these technologies to reflect the possible ethical consequences of the advancement of these technologies in the medical field in order to protect the rights of the patient without hampering innovation. Moving forward, there is a need to enhance partnerships with key players such as healthcare providers, developers of technology, and policymakers to optimally manage these challenges. Regarding the key values associated with the patient's needs and ethical concepts, the healthcare area must benefit from the use of digital technologies and ensure that patients receive the best possible treatment for their conditions.

The study concludes that the use of new digital tools and technologies in healthcare communication is very promising but simultaneously it poses ethical, technological, and regulatory concerns. If these issues are tackled effectively, healthcare can continue improving its developments, becoming more available, and fair to patients across the globe.

REFERENCES

AlAhmad, Y., Haggeer, D., Alsayed, A., Haik, M., AbuAfifeh, L., Aljaber, M., Mohamed, A., Balideh, M., Almutawa, N., & Mahmoud, M. (2021). The effect of telemedicine on patients' compliance in family medicine follow-ups in Qatar. *Avicenna (Doha)*. 10.5339/avi.2022.3

Ballard-Reisch, D. S. (1990). A model of participative decision making for Physician-Patient interaction. *Health Communication*, 2(2), 91–104. 10.1207/s15327027hc0202_3

Barve, Y., & Saini, J. (2021). Healthcare misinformation detection and fact-checking: A novel approach. *International Journal of Advanced Computer Science and Applications*, 12(10), 407–414. 10.14569/IJACSA.2021.0121032

Bastiaan, R. (2020, August 01). Bloem, M., E.RayDorsey, M., & MichaelS.Okun, M. (2020). The Coronavirus Disease 2019 Crisis as Catalyst for Telemedicine for Chronic Neurological Disorders. *JAMA Neurology*, 77(8), 927. 10.1001/jamaneurol.2020.1452

Bataineh, A. A., Reyes, V., Olukanni, T., Khalaf, M., Vibho, A., & Pedyuk, R. (2023). Advanced misinformation detection: A Bi-LSTM model optimized by genetic algorithms. *Electronics (Basel)*, 12(15), 3250. 10.3390/electronics12153250

Bautista, J., Zhang, Y., & Gwizdka, J. (2021). Healthcare professionals' acts of correcting health misinformation on social media. *International Journal of Medical Informatics*, 148, 104375. 10.1016/j.ijmedinf.2021.10437533461008

Bender, D., & Sartipi, K. (2013). HL7 FHIR: An agile and RESTful approach to healthcare information exchange. In *Proceedings of the 26th IEEE International Symposium on Computer-Based Medical Systems* (pp. 326-331). IEEE. 10.1109/CBMS.2013.6627810

Bhattacharjee, B., Pal, P., Purkait, R., Chakraborty, P., & Choubey, G. (2023). Patient satisfaction survey for the telemedicine services during the second wave of the COVID-19 pandemic in the Homoeopathic Research Institutes of West Bengal. *Homoeopathic Links, 36*, 006-011. 10.1055/s-0043-1761429

Bloem, B. R., Dorsey, E. R., & Okun, M. S. (2020). The coronavirus disease 2019 crisis as catalyst for telemedicine for chronic neurological disorders. *JAMA Neurology*, 77(8), 927. 10.1001/jamaneurol.2020.145232329796

Brock, D. W. (1991). The ideal of shared decision making between physicians and patients. *Kennedy Institute of Ethics Journal*, 1(1), 28–47. 10.1353/ken.0.008410113819

Chung, G. S., Lawrence, R. E., Curlin, F. A., Arora, V., & Meltzer, D. O. (2011). Predictors of hospitalised patients' preferences for physician-directed medical decision-making. *Journal of Medical Ethics*, 38(2), 77–82. 10.1136/jme.2010.04061821697296

Cohen, I. G., Amarasingham, R., Shah, A., Xie, B., & Lo, B. (2020). The legal and ethical concerns that arise from using complex predictive analytics in health care. *Health Affairs*, 33(7), 1139–1147. 10.1377/hlthaff.2014.004825006139

Cui, L., Seo, H., Tabar, M., Ma, F., Wang, S., & Lee, D. (2020). DETERRENT: Knowledge guided graph attention network for detecting healthcare misinformation. In *Proceedings of the 26th ACM SIGKDD International Conference on Knowledge Discovery & Data Mining*. ACM. 10.1145/3394486.3403092

Davis, R. E., Sevdalis, N., & Vincent, C. A. (2012). Patient involvement in patient safety: The health-care professional's perspective. *Journal of Patient Safety*, 8(4), 182–188. 10.1097/PTS.0b013e318267c4aa23007240

De Fauw, J., Ledsam, J. R., Romera-Paredes, B., Nikolov, S., Tomasev, N., Blackwell, S., Askham, H., Glorot, X., O'Donoghue, B., Visentin, D., van den Driessche, G., Lakshminarayanan, B., Meyer, C., Mackinder, F., Bouton, S., Ayoub, K., Chopra, R., King, D., Karthikesalingam, A., & Ronneberger, O. (2018). Clinically applicable deep learning for diagnosis and referral in retinal disease. *Nature Medicine*, 24(9), 1342–1350. 10.1038/s41591-018-0107-630104768

Ehrenfeld, J. (2017). WannaCry, cybersecurity and health information technology: A time to act. *Journal of Medical Systems*, 41(1), 1. 10.1007/s10916-017-0752-128540616

Esteva, A., Robicquet, A., Ramsundar, B., Kuleshov, V., DePristo, M., Chou, K., Cui, C., Corrado, G., Thrun, S., & Dean, J. (2019). A guide to deep learning in healthcare. *Nature Medicine*, 25(1), 24–29. 10.1038/s41591-018-0316-z30617335

Free, C., Phillips, G., Galli, L., Watson, L., Felix, L., Edwards, P., Patel, V., & Haines, A. (2013). The effectiveness of mobile-health technology-based health behaviour change or disease management interventions for health care consumers: A systematic review. *PLoS Medicine*, 10(1), e1001362. 10.1371/journal.pmed.100136223349621

Gajarawala, S. N., & Pelkowski, J. N. (2021). Telehealth benefits and barriers. *The Journal for Nurse Practitioners*, 17(2), 218–221. 10.1016/j.nurpra.2020.09.01333106751

Ganapathy, K. (2021). Artificial intelligence and healthcare regulatory and legal concerns. *Telehealth and Medicine Today*, 6(2). 10.30953/tmt.v6.252

Haskard-Zolnierek, K., Snyder, M., Hernandez, R., & Thompson, T. L. (2021). *Patient-Provider communication and health outcomes*. Routledge eBooks. 10.4324/9781003043379-18

Househ, M. (2013). The use of social media in healthcare: Organizational, clinical, and patient perspectives. *Studies in Health Technology and Informatics*, 183, 244–248. 10.3233/978-1-61499-203-5-24423388291

Hu, G., Han, X., Zhou, H., & Liu, Y. (2019). Public perception on healthcare services: Evidence from social media platforms in China. *International Journal of Environmental Research and Public Health*, 16(7), 1273. 10.3390/ijerph1607127330974729

Jeyaraman, M., Ramasubramanian, S., Kumar, S., Jeyaraman, N., Selvaraj, P., Nallakumarasamy, A., Bondili, S., & Yadav, S. (2023). Multifaceted role of social media in healthcare: Opportunities, challenges, and the need for quality control. *Cureus*, 15. 10.7759/cureus.3911137332420

Jiang, F., Jiang, Y., Zhi, H., Dong, Y., Li, H., Ma, S., Wang, Y., Dong, Q., Shen, H., & Wang, Y. (2017). Artificial intelligence in healthcare: Past, present and future. *Stroke and Vascular Neurology*, 2(4), 230–243. 10.1136/svn-2017-00010129507784

Kachalia, A. (2010). Liability claims and costs before and after implementation of a medical error disclosure program. *Annals of Internal Medicine*, 153(4), 213. 10.7326/0003-4819-153-4-201008170-0000220713789

Kaushal, S., & Mishra, D. (2024). *Strategic implications of AI in contemporary business and society*. 2024 2nd International Conference on Disruptive Technologies (ICDT), Greater Noida, India. 10.1109/ICDT61202.2024.10489027

Kaushal, S., Nyoni, A. M., Sharma, A., & Saidi, J. A. K. (2023). Drawbacks of technology as an antecedent for knowledge sharing: Focus on curbing misinformation. *2023 9th International Conference on Advanced Computing and Communication Systems (ICACCS)*. IEEE. 10.1109/ICACCS57279.2023.10112895

Keesara, S., Jonas, A., & Schulman, K. (2020). Covid-19 and health care's digital revolution. *The New England Journal of Medicine*, 382(23), e82. 10.1056/NEJMp200583532240581

Kruse, C. S., Krowski, N., Rodriguez, B., Tran, L., Vela, J., & Brooks, M. (2017). Telehealth and patient satisfaction: A systematic review and narrative analysis. *BMJ Open*, 7(8), e016242. 10.1136/bmjopen-2017-01624228775188

Kvedar, J., Coye, M. J., & Everett, W. (2014). Connected health: A review of technologies and strategies to improve patient care with telemedicine and telehealth. *Health Affairs (Project Hope)*, 33(2), 194–199. 10.1377/hlthaff.2013.099224493760

Kwon, J., & Johnson, M. (2014). Proactive versus reactive security investments in the healthcare sector. *Management Information Systems Quarterly*, 38(2), 451–471. 10.25300/MISQ/2014/38.2.06

Li, P., Williams, R., Gilbert, S., & Anderson, S. (2023). Regulating AI/ML-enabled medical devices in the UK. *Proceedings of the First International Symposium on Trustworthy Autonomous Systems*. ACM. 10.1145/3597512.3599704

Lown, B. A., Rosen, J., & Marttila, J. (2011). An agenda for improving compassionate care: A survey shows about half of patients say such care is missing. *Health Affairs*, 30(9), 1772–1778. 10.1377/hlthaff.2011.053921900669

Mann, K. D., Good, N. M., Fatehi, F., Khanna, S., Campbell, V., Conway, R., Sullivan, C., Staib, A., Joyce, C., & Cook, D. (2021). Predicting patient deterioration: A review of tools in the digital hospital setting. *Journal of Medical Internet Research*, 23(9), e28209. 10.2196/2820934591017

Marecos, J., Shattock, E., Bartlett, O., Goiana-da-Silva, F., Maheswaran, H., Ashrafian, H., & Darzi, A. (2023). Health misinformation and freedom of expression: Considerations for policymakers. *Health Economics, Policy, and Law*, 18(2), 1–14. 10.1017/S174413312200026336718749

Martin, G., Martin, P., Hankin, C., Darzi, A., & Kinross, J. (2017). Cybersecurity and healthcare: How safe are we? *BMJ (Clinical Research Ed.)*, 358, j3179. 10.1136/bmj.j317928684400

Mead, N., & Bower, P. (2000). Patient-centredness: A conceptual framework and review of the empirical literature. *Social Science & Medicine*, 51(7), 1087–1110. 10.1016/S0277-9536(00)00098-811005395

Merchant, R. M., & Lurie, N. (2020). Social media and emergency preparedness in response to novel coronavirus. *Journal of the American Medical Association*, 323(20), 2011–2012. 10.1001/jama.2020.446932202611

Nair, P., Aghoram, R., Thomas, B., Bharadwaj, B., & Chinnakali, P. (2021). Video teleconsultation services for persons with epilepsy during COVID-19 pandemic: An exploratory study from public tertiary care hospital in Southern India on feasibility, satisfaction, and effectiveness. *Epilepsy & Behavior*, 117, 107863. 10.1016/j.yebeh.2021.10786333677363

Neely, S., Eldredge, C., & Sanders, R. (2021). Health information seeking behaviors on social media during the COVID-19 pandemic among American social networking site users: Survey study. *Journal of Medical Internet Research*, 23(6), e29802. 10.2196/2980234043526

Nizam, V., & Aslekar, A. (2021). Challenges of applying AI in healthcare in India. *Journal of Pharmaceutical Research International*, 203–209. 10.9734/jpri/2021/v33i36B31969

Olawunmi, B., & Babatunde, F. (2022). *Impact of mass media messaging on compliance with COVID-19 safety protocols among residents of Osogbo*. Caleb International Journal of Development Studies. 10.26772/cijds-2022-05-01-015

Peng, W., Yuan, S., & Holtz, B. (2016). Exploring the challenges and opportunities of health mobile apps for individuals with type 2 diabetes living in rural communities. *Telemedicine Journal and e-Health. Telemedicine Journal and e-Health*, 22(9), 733–738. 10.1089/tmj.2015.018026982017

Pesapane, F., Bracchi, D., Mulligan, J., Linnikov, A., Maslennikov, O., Lanzavecchia, M., Tantrige, P., Stasolla, A., Biondetti, P., Giuggioli, P., Cassano, E., & Carrafiello, G. (2021). Legal and regulatory framework for AI solutions in healthcare in EU, US, China, and Russia: New scenarios after a pandemic. *Radiation*, 1(4), 17–28. 10.3390/radiation1040022

Poduval, S., Ahmed, S., Marston, L., Hamilton, F., & Murray, E. (2018). Crossing the digital divide in online self-management support: Analysis of usage data from HeLP-Diabetes. *JMIR Diabetes*, 3(4), e10925. 10.2196/1092530522988

Powell, R. E., Henstenburg, J. M., Cooper, G., Hollander, J. E., & Rising, K. L. (2017). Patient perceptions of telehealth primary care video visits. *Annals of Family Medicine*, 15(3), 225–229. 10.1370/afm.209528483887

Quesada-Caballero, M., Carmona-García, A., Chami-Peña, S., Caballero-Mateos, A., Fernández-Martín, O., Fuente, G., & Romero-Béjar, J. (2023). Telemedicine in elderly hypertensive and patients with chronic diseases during the COVID-19 pandemic: A systematic review and meta-analysis. *Journal of Clinical Medicine*, 12(19), 6160. 10.3390/jcm1219616037834803

Ratna, H. (2019). The importance of effective communication in healthcare practice. *HPHR Journal*, 23(23). 10.54111/0001/W4

Rees, A. M. (1993). Communication in the physician-patient relationship. *Bulletin of the Medical Library Association*, 81(1), 1–10.8428183

Rosenbaum, L. (2020). Facing Covid-19 in Italy - Ethics, logistics, and therapeutics on the epidemic's front line. *The New England Journal of Medicine*, 382(20), 1873–1875. 10.1056/NEJMp200549232187459

Schairer, C. E., Rubanovich, C. K., & Bloss, C. S. (2018). How could commercial terms of use and privacy policies undermine informed consent in the age of mobile health? *AMA Journal of Ethics*, 20(9), E864–E872. 10.1001/amajethics.2018.86430242818

Siegler, M. (2021). Clinical medical ethics and the historical background of shared decision making. In *Oxford University Press eBooks* (pp. 27–36). 10.1093/med/9780197598573.003.0003

Street, R. L.Jr, Makoul, G., Arora, N. K., & Epstein, R. M. (2009). How does communication heal? Pathways linking clinician–patient communication to health outcomes. *Patient Education and Counseling*, 74(3), 295–301. 10.1016/j.pec.2008.11.01519150199

Sunyaev, A., Dehling, T., Taylor, P. L., & Mandl, K. D. (2014). Availability and quality of mobile health app privacy policies. *Journal of the American Medical Informatics Association : JAMIA*, 22(e1), e28–e33. 10.1136/amiajnl-2013-00260525147247

Telehealth: A Path to Virtual Integrated Care | AHA. (n.d.-b). American Hospital Association. https://www.aha.org/center/emerging-issues/market-insights/telehealth/path-virtual-integrated-care

Telehealth: Technology meets health care. (2022, June 18). Mayo Clinic. https://www.mayoclinic.org/healthy-lifestyle/consumer-health/in-depth/telehealth/art-20044878

Terhune, C. (2015, February 5). Anthem hack exposes data on 80 million; experts warn of identity theft - Los Angeles Times. *Los Angeles Times*. https://www.latimes.com/business/la-fi-anthem-hacked-20150204-story.html

Teutsch, C. (2003). Patient–doctor communication. *The Medical Clinics of North America*, 87(5), 1115–1145. 10.1016/S0025-7125(03)00066-X14621334

Topol, E. (2020). High-performance medicine: The convergence of human and artificial intelligence. *Nature Medicine*, 25(1), 44–56. 10.1038/s41591-018-0300-730617339

U.S. Department of Health and Human Services. (2022, October 19). *Summary of the HIPAA Security Rule*. HHS.gov. https://www.hhs.gov/hipaa/for-professionals/security/laws-regulations/index.html

Venkat, A., Asher, S. L., Wolf, L., Geiderman, J. M., Marco, C. A., McGreevy, J., Derse, A. R., Otten, E. J., Jesus, J. E., Kreitzer, N. P., Escalante, M., & Levine, A. C. (2015). Ethical issues in the response to Ebola virus disease in United States Emergency Departments: A position paper of the American College of Emergency Physicians, the Emergency Nurses Association, and the Society for Academic Emergency Medicine. *Academic Emergency Medicine*, 22(5), 605–615. 10.1111/acem.1264225903144

Ventola, C. L. (2014). Social media and health care professionals: Benefits, risks, and best practices. *P&T*, 39(7), 491–520.25083128

Vorisek, C., Stellmach, C., Mayer, P., Klopfenstein, S., Bures, D., Diehl, A., Henningsen, M., Ritter, K., & Thun, S. (2023). Artificial intelligence bias in health care: Web-based survey. *Journal of Medical Internet Research*, 25, e41089. 10.2196/4108937347528

Wang, Y., Kung, L., & Byrd, T. A. (2018). Big data analytics: Understanding its capabilities and potential benefits for healthcare organizations. *Technological Forecasting and Social Change*, 126, 3–13. 10.1016/j.techfore.2015.12.019

Will, J. F. (2011). A brief historical and theoretical perspective on patient autonomy and medical decision making. *Chest*, 139(3), 669–673. 10.1378/chest.10-253221362653

Yen, P. H., & Leasure, A. R. (2019). Use and effectiveness of the Teach-Back method in patient education and health outcomes. *Federal Practitioner*, 36(6), 284–289.31258322

Zang, S., Zhang, X., Xing, Y., Chen, J., Lin, L., & Hou, Z. (2022). Applications of social media and digital technologies in COVID-19 vaccination: Scoping review. *Journal of Medical Internet Research*, 25, e40057. 10.2196/4005736649235

Chapter 3
Analyzing Human Genome and Embryo Editing:
International Canons for Legal–Social Issues Concerning Women's Health and Reproductive Rights

Bhupinder Singh
https://orcid.org/0009-0006-4779-2553
Sharda University, India

Christian Kaunert
https://orcid.org/0000-0002-4493-2235
Dublin City University, Ireland

Kittisak Jermsittiparsert
https://orcid.org/0000-0003-3245-8705
Shinawatra University, Thailand

Bhumika Sharma
https://orcid.org/0000-0002-3963-6036
Sharda University, India

Anjali Raghav
https://orcid.org/0009-0004-0248-7956
Sharda University, India

DOI: 10.4018/979-8-3693-5976-1.ch003

ABSTRACT

The rapid progress in genetic research and technological advancements in recent years have revolutionized the field of reproductive medicine. Human genome and embryo editing, which involve the deliberate alteration of genetic material, hold immense potential for preventing genetic diseases, enhancing human traits, and even addressing infertility. However, these groundbreaking developments come with significant ethical, legal, and social implications that need to be carefully examined and addressed. The absence of a unified global regulatory framework for human genome and embryo editing has created a fragmented landscape. Various countries have adopted different approaches, ranging from strict regulations to more permissive policies. This chapter aims to provide a comprehensive analysis of the current state of affairs, highlighting the importance of establishing global standards to ensure responsible and equitable use of these technologies, while also prioritizing the protection of women's rights and ensuring reproductive justice.

INTRODUCTION

Reproductive medicine has undergone a radical transformation because to recent fast advances in genetic science and technology. The intentional modification of genetic material via human genome and embryo editing has enormous promise for curing genetic illnesses, improving human characteristics, and even treating infertility. These revolutionary advancements do, however, have important moral, legal, and societal ramifications that should be thoroughly considered and handled (Alsubai et al., 2023). The lack of a single, worldwide regulatory framework for modifying human genomes and embryos has led to a fragmented environment. Various measures have been taken by various nations, ranging from stringent laws to more lax rules. This lack of consistency creates worries about the possibility of abuse and uneven access to these technologies in addition to impeding international cooperation (Chen et al., 2023). For the human genome and embryo editing technologies to be used responsibly and equitably, global governance guidelines must be established. This study examines the complicated world of human genome editing and embryo editing, examining the need for international governance norms and the moral, legal, and societal concerns related to reproductive justice. The development of genetic technology has created new opportunities and brought up difficult issues with relation to the editing of human genomes and the morality of embryonic stem cell research. In addition to emphasizing the need for international norms to guarantee the ethical and responsible use of these technologies, this presentation will provide a thorough analysis of the existing situation, with a special emphasis on the defense of women's rights and the maintenance of reproductive justice (Krishnamoorthy et al., 2023).

A new age in reproductive medicine has emerged with the development of human genome and embryo editing tools, bringing with it both unparalleled potential and moral conundrums. As gene-editing techniques—most especially, CRISPR-Cas9 become more sophisticated, the international community must work quickly to develop comprehensive guidelines governing the moral, legal, and societal implications of these revolutionary technologies. This study explores the complex interactions between the human genome, embryo editing, and the larger context of reproductive justice (Kuranga et al., 2023). The idea of reproductive justice, which includes the freedom to have or not bear children as well as the opportunity to raise children in secure and nurturing homes, offers a prism through which to assess how genome editing may affect various communities (Khan et al., 2023). In light of the international character of scientific research and medical therapies, investigating global standards is essential. This introduction lays the groundwork for a thorough examination by highlighting the need of strong governance to negotiate the tricky waters of genome and embryo editing and make sure that scientific discoveries are consistent with moral standards and preserve social values (Simões-Marques et al., 2023).

The capacity to alter genetic material at the molecular level is at the heart of the human genome and embryo editing concepts, which have significant ramifications for both human existence and medicine in the future (Annoni et al., 2023). With the use of precise modifications to the DNA sequence within the cells, human genome editing makes it possible to improve certain features or fix genetic abnormalities. This capacity also applies to embryos, allowing for interventions during the most formative phases of development (Singh & Kaunert,2024). The groundbreaking gene-editing instrument CRISPR-Cas9 has become a major force in this area. The prospect of curing genetic disorders and developing therapeutic approaches coexists with concerns about unexpected effects and ethical issues surrounding designer babies. While scientists work through the complexities of science, society must negotiate the moral, legal, and social ramifications of using this technology responsibly. The review of the human genome and embryo editing highlights the potential for significant medical advancements but also poses important ethical and social problems about the manipulation of life itself (De Giovanni, 2023).

Objectives of the Chapter

The purpose of this study is to further the scholarly conversation, provide policymakers with information, and direct future genome editing research with an emphasis on moral, legal, and social issues in the framework of reproductive justice (Obiuto et al., 2023).

- **Analyze Existing Technologies:** Give a summary of the human genome and embryo editing techniques that are already in use, with an emphasis on techniques like CRISPR-Cas9 and the implications they have for genetic manipulation.
- **Examine Global Governance Frameworks:** Look at the current national and international legal frameworks that control the altering of the human genome and embryos. Examine these frameworks' advantages and disadvantages in handling moral, legal, and social challenges.
- **Examine the Ethical Implications:** Go over the ethical issues surrounding the altering of the human genome and embryos, such as worries about designer babies, unforeseen outcomes, and possible social effects.
- **Assess Legal state:** Taking into account current court decisions and disputes, assess the legal state of genome and embryo editing in different nations. Talk about the potential and difficulties of developing unified international legal norms.
- **Examine Social and Cultural Aspects:** Investigate how genome and embryo editing may affect society, with a particular emphasis on problems like inequality, prejudice, and healthcare access. Examine how the public's views, beliefs, and cultural influences have shaped the conversation around these technologies (Singh et al., 2024).
- **Define Reproductive Justice:** Explain what reproductive justice is, including how it relates to the modification of the human genome and embryos. Examine the ways in which genome editing technology might help or hurt reproductive justice.
- **Identify Future Directions and Challenges**: Determine the gaps and difficulties in the existing global governance framework pertaining to genome and embryo editing. Talk about possible areas for development and the need of changing standards.

Figure 1. Displays the objectives of this chapter

(Source- Original)

TECHNOLOGIES FOR EDITING EMBRYOS AND THE HUMAN GENOME

The field of genetic engineering has made significant strides with the development of the human genome and embryo editing technologies, which have the potential to drastically alter human health and the basic structure of life. Leading the charge in these technologies is the groundbreaking CRISPR-Cas9 system. Bacteria naturally possess a defensive mechanism called CRISPR, which stands for Clustered Regularly Interspaced Short Palindromic Repeats. This technique has been used by scientists to accurately target and edit certain DNA sequences in animals, allowing for the molecular alteration or correction of genes. The required genetic alterations are then either introduced or the current sequence is disrupted by subsequent cellular repair processes (Esposito et al., 2023). With this degree of accuracy, genetic modification might possibly eradicate inherited disorders or improve desirable features in creatures, among other far-reaching effects. These technologies may be used in the earliest phases of development when it comes to embryo editing (Singh et al., 2024). Because scientists may alter an embryo's genetic coding, the possibility of producing genetically altered people raises serious ethical concerns. Although there is a great deal of promise for prenatal genetic disease prevention, strong arguments have been triggered by worries about unexpected effects and the ethical limits of changing the human germline (Skapetze et al.,2023)

In addition to fueling scientific excitement, the rapid development of these technologies has spurred a demand for careful consideration of their social ramifications. The idea of "designer babies," in which certain features may be chosen or improved, raises moral questions about eugenics and the monetization of human existence. The human genome and embryo editing technologies represent a turning point in the history of biotechnology, requiring careful thought and ethical governance at the nexus of science, ethics, and social values (Qadir & Fatah, 2023).

Biomedical and Gene-Editing Fields: Significant Scientific Progress

A slew of significant scientific discoveries in the biomedical and gene-editing fields has led to the field's foray into new territory and its revolutionary possibilities for healthcare and beyond. The ground-breaking CRISPR-Cas9 gene-editing technique, which has emerged as a key component of the genomic toolkit, is at the vanguard of these advances.

CRISPR-Cas9 Precision: A naturally occurring defensive system in bacteria, CRISPR stands for Clustered Regularly Interspaced Short Palindromic Repeats. Editing certain DNA sequences with unmatched accuracy is made possible by the use of CRISPR-Cas9. The "Cas9 enzyme" is guided by the guide RNA, which is intended to match the target DNA, to precisely cut the desired regions of the DNA, allowing for the insertion, removal, or change of genetic information. The ability to precisely target medicines for a variety of illnesses and rectify genetic abnormalities has created previously unheard-of therapeutic opportunities (Skapetze et al.,2023).

Healthcare Applications of Genome Mapping and Editing: Thanks to developments in genome mapping technology, including high-throughput sequencing, scientists can now quickly and cheaply sequence the human genome. Personalized medicine has been made possible by the abundance of genetic data that has helped to understand the hereditary causes of many illnesses. CRISPR and other gene-editing technologies have been used to investigate possible therapies for hereditary illnesses. This involves repairing cellular abnormalities that cause illness, providing hope for ailments that were previously thought to be incurable (Doherty, 2023)

Stem Cell Therapies: The regenerative potential of stem cells has been greatly advanced by biomedical research. Through the exact manipulation of stem cells made possible by CRISPR technology, tailored cell treatments for a range of medical problems may one day be developed. This has the potential to transform the area of regenerative medicine by restoring damaged tissues and organs (Sharifi et al.,2023).

Human Germline Editing: The prospect of editing human germlines, as shown by CRISPR, has raised both ethical questions and enthusiasm. Modifying the genetic composition of next generations has significant ethical ramifications, even if it may help avoid genetic illnesses and birth abnormalities (Singh & Kaunert, 2024). The scientific community is in constant communication to develop moral standards for the appropriate use of germline editing technology (Morrison & Buhalis, 2023).

New Gene-Editing Technologies and CRISPR variations: Researchers are investigating and creating novel CRISPR variations in addition to CRISPR-Cas9. Systems such as prime editing and base editing are designed to increase the accuracy and range of genetic alterations. These new technologies have the potential to alleviate some of the drawbacks and difficulties related to CRISPR-Cas9(Modarress et al.,2023).

Figure 2. Conveys significant scientific discoveries in the biomedical and gene-editing fields

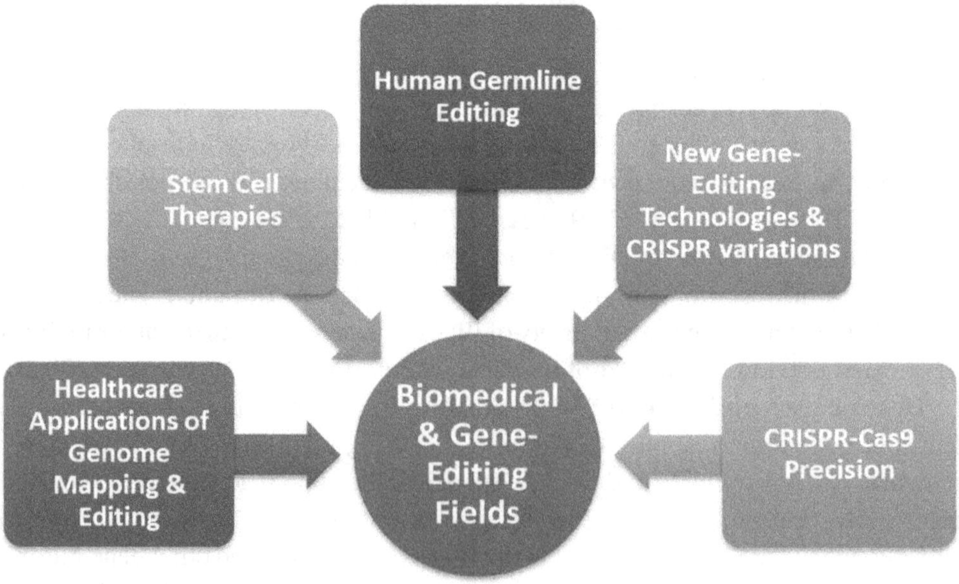

(Source- Original)

The rapid breakthroughs in the fields of biomedicine and gene editing highlight how revolutionary these technologies are, guaranteeing that scientific discoveries are in line with society ideals and improve health and welfare worldwide.

Understanding Concepts Regarding Genome Editing and Transgenic Technology

While both genome editing and transgenic technologies are effective tools in genetic engineering, their workings and applications are different. With the use of genome editing technology, an organism's DNA may be precisely altered by adding, removing, or replacing certain DNA sequences. For genome editing, tools like CRISPR-Cas9 are often used. It directly modifies the sequences of the organism's preexisting DNA. For instance, CRISPR-Cas9 targets certain DNA sequences using a guide RNA and then cuts the DNA using the Cas9 enzyme to introduce modifications via natural repair processes(Hemachandran & Rodriguez, 2023).

The process of transgenic technology entails introducing foreign genes into the genome of an organism. As a consequence, the foreign genes' encoded proteins or characteristics are expressed by the organism. It entails the introduction of alien genes into the genetic code. This is often accomplished by introducing the foreign DNA into the cells of the host organism via vectors, such as viruses or plasmids (Kitada et al.,2023).

With the use of genome editing technology, precise modifications to certain genes or DNA sequences are possible. It has excellent precision when aiming at and altering certain areas. It is mostly used in functional genomics research, disease modeling, and targeted gene alterations for medicinal reasons. It is also used in agriculture to enhance crop yields.

Transgenic technology: Usually causes foreign genes to be randomly integrated into the host genome. When it comes to genome editing, gene insertion precision is higher. Transgenic technology is often utilized to give an organism certain characteristics. Transgenic crops in agriculture may be modified to withstand pests, tolerate herbicides, or have higher nutritional value (Singh, 2024). While transgenic technology includes inserting foreign genes into an organism's genome to give certain features, genome editing technology entails directly and very precisely altering an organism's existing DNA. While there are many uses for both technologies in research, medicine, agriculture, and other domains, their methods and the kind of genetic alterations they cause are different (Skapetze et al., 2023).

Editing the Human Germline and Heritable Genome

Heritable genome editing and human germline editing are two novel yet hotly debated genetic research topics. The exact alteration of genetic material in reproductive cells, such as eggs and sperm, or during the embryonic stage is known as human germline editing. The special quality of germline editing is that any modifications are inherited and will be passed on to the next generation. With the use of this technology, hereditary illnesses and disorders may be completely eradicated and their transmission stopped. However, there are significant ethical ramifications as well, including issues with "designer babies," accidentally introducing genetic effects, and the larger matter of interfering with human development (Khizar et al.,2023).

This idea is expanded upon by heritable genome editing, which highlights the goal of creating genetic alterations meant to become a permanent component of the human gene pool. Even while there are exciting scientific prospects, these techniques present more ethical challenges. The changes are inheritable and permanent, which emphasizes the need of strong moral standards and social agreement. In the conversation around new technologies, issues of permission, equality, and the possibility of unforeseen social effects are brought to the fore (Kopplin et al.,2023).

Globally, there are many different ethical and legal frameworks pertaining to heritable genome editing and human germline modification. Numerous nations have imposed stringent laws or complete prohibitions on these kinds of activities. A rising number of people are calling for international collaboration to create precise, widely-accepted rules and norms because of the global character of genetic research and the far-reaching effects of these technologies (Singh & Kaunert,2024). The ethical issues and social ramifications of human germline and heritable genome editing remain crucial to the proper development of this innovative discipline as scientists continue to push the frontiers of genetic technology (Zawish et al.,2024).

IMPLICATIONS OF HUMAN GENOME AND EMBRYO EDITING FOR WOMEN'S REPRODUCTIVE JUSTICE

The emergence of human genome editing and embryo editing has significant ramifications for reproductive justice, presenting a challenging landscape where ethical issues and technology progress collide (Periyasamy et al.,2023). On the one hand, family planning and reproductive autonomy may be improved by the prospect of eliminating genetic illnesses before birth. The moral quandaries are complex, however. Concerns about building a society where certain genetic qualities are valued arise from the potential to selectively modify genes, raising issues with equality and social expectations. Uncertainties that might disproportionately affect disadvantaged populations are introduced by the possibility of unanticipated genetic risks and unintended effects. It is also critical to address concerns of cost and fair distribution of these cutting-edge reproductive alternatives since the availability of genome editing technology has the potential to worsen already-existing imbalances. To guarantee that the application of genome editing technologies is in line with the values of reproductive justice, protecting individual choices, fostering inclusivity, and responsibly and fairly addressing societal concerns, a careful balance between scientific advancement and ethical considerations must be struck (/Singh,2024).

Women's agency in reproductive decision-making is one of the ethical issues raised by modifying the human germline or editing embryos. The capacity to make knowledgeable decisions on genetic interventions raises questions regarding the possibility of excessive pressure, coercion, or restricted autonomy in women's reproductive choices, particularly in the germline or in the early stages of embryogenesis. Consent difficulties and the long-term effects of genetic changes on women's health and the health of future generations are challenges that legal systems must address. It is important to establish clear guidelines for acceptable genetic modifications and make sure that laws are consistent with moral values in order to protect women's reproductive rights (Bohan & Dumbrell,2023).

Social conceptions of women's responsibilities in reproduction may be affected by genome and embryo editing. The idea of "designer babies" and the possibility of cultural expectations or preferences for certain genetic features might serve to further entrench stereotypes and existing gender norms (Eriksson & Regoczi,2023). This calls into doubt the viability of discrimination based on genetic traits and contradicts the goals of reproductive justice, which aim to guarantee that everyone has the freedom to make their own choices about reproduction without facing prejudice. The equitable distribution of access to these therapies is also influenced by the cost and accessibility of genome editing technology (Singh & Kaunert,2024). Maintaining the ideals of reproductive justice and avoiding the escalation of current disparities depend on making reproductive technology accessible to all women, regardless of financial background(Grassini & Ratcliffe, 2024).

A thorough and inclusive strategy is necessary to navigate the relationship between reproductive justice for women and the human genome and embryo editing. This entails taking into account a variety of viewpoints, placing an emphasis on informed consent, resolving any power disparities, and creating moral and legal frameworks that defend women's autonomy and rights when it comes to reproductive technology (Suratiningsih, 2023). In light of fast developing genetic technology, the continuing discussion around these concerns should take into account the larger implications for women's reproductive rights, health, and justice (Ishida et al., 2023).

GLOBAL GOVERNANCE FRAMEWORK: MONITORING EMBRYO EDITING AND HUMAN GENOME

The development of technology for modifying the human genome and embryos has highlighted the need for a strong global governance structure to regulate their use. Since new technologies cut beyond national boundaries, it is essential to address the ethical, legal, and social ramifications via a cogent and all-encompassing international strategy (Kumar et al., 2023). It is essential to establish protocols and benchmarks that maintain the values of openness, responsibility, and diversity in order to effectively traverse the intricate terrain of genetic engineering (Singh, 2023). International organizations like the World Health Organization (WHO) are essential in helping countries work together to create a common position on the moral use of these technologies (Tonelli & Morandi, 2023). It need an open conversation that takes into account many cultural, ethical, and religious viewpoints to strike a balance between advancing scientific discoveries and protecting against their abuse. Establishing a global governance framework promotes international cooperation, prevents ethical transgressions, and guarantees equitable access to the advantages of these innovative technologies by guaranteeing that the responsible application of human genome and embryo editing remains at the forefront (Dobrauz-Saldapenna & Huras, 2023).

The lack of a single, worldwide regulatory framework for modifying human genomes and embryos has led to a fragmented environment. various measures have been taken by various nations, ranging from stringent laws to more lax rules (Derval,2023). This lack of consistency creates worries about the possibility of abuse and uneven access to these technologies in addition to impeding international cooperation. For the human genome and embryo editing technologies to be used responsibly and equitably, global governance guidelines must be established (Skapetze et al.,2024).

International Organizations and Frameworks Controlling Embryo Editing and Genome Editing

A wide range of institutions and organizations are involved in attempts to control and manage genome and embryo editing on a global basis, which reflects the intricate ethical, legal, and scientific issues these technologies entail. Leading worldwide health organization, the World Health Organization (WHO), holds talks to create guidelines for the appropriate use of genome editing on a global scale. It is essential to organizing efforts to address issues of public health and ethical concern about genetic therapies (Sharifi et al.,2024).

By offering rules and ethical standards for stem cell research, including applications requiring genome editing, the “International Society for Stem Cell Research (ISSCR)” makes a substantial contribution to the regulatory environment. These recommendations emphasize responsible behavior and ethical issues in the use of developing genetic technologies, making them an invaluable resource for researchers worldwide (Grassini & Ratcliffe, 2024).

Scientists, ethicists, and politicians get together as the Hinxton Group to discuss the moral and legal implications of genome editing technology. In order to guarantee that ethical issues continue to be at the forefront of both the research and use of genetic therapies, this worldwide consortium encourages communication and cooperation (Singh et al.,2024). The establishment of the International Commission on the Clinical Use of Human Germline Genome Editing in response to high-profile human germline editing incidents highlights the necessity for specialized organizations tasked with examining the technological, medical, and ethical ramifications of these advances. In order to address the complicated ethical situation surrounding germline editing, this committee brings together specialists from across the world (Min et al.,2024).

The United Nations Educational, Scientific, and Cultural Organization (UNESCO) participates in global dialogues on bioethics, including genetic technology-related issues. The International Bioethics Committee of UNESCO emphasizes the significance of universal ethical standards in scientific breakthroughs by offering a forum for international discussion on the ethical implications of genome and embryo editing. Even though these global frameworks and organizations provide insightful analysis and helpful suggestions, the environment is ever-changing and vulnerable to new innovations. The ongoing evolution of issues around genome and embryo editing underscores the need of international cooperation and governance systems in guiding the ethical and responsible deployment of these innovative technologies on a global scale (Matebese et al.,2024).

Conventions, Treaties, and Accords Pertaining to These Technologies

Human Rights and Bioethics: A Universal Declaration (UNESCO)

Adopted in 2005, the Universal Declaration on Bioethics and Human Rights by UNESCO establishes guidelines for the moral conduct of research and medical endeavors, including genetic technology-related ones. Its tenets—human dignity, consent, and solidarity—offer a fundamental framework for ethical concerns in biomedicine even if they do not directly address genome editing (Molavi et al.,2024).

Oviedo Convention is a Human Rights and Biomedical Convention

The Oviedo Convention of the Council of Europe deals with the defense of human rights in the biomedical industry. While not specifically addressing genome editing, it does highlight the need of nondiscrimination, informed consent, and respect for human dignity—all of which are pertinent to the moral issues raised by genetic technology.

CBD or Convention on Biological Diversity

The primary goal of the United Nations-sponsored international convention known as the CBD is to conserve biological variety. Although genome editing is not formally regulated, debates in the CBD have touched on issues of the possible effects that genetically modified organisms (GMOs), particularly those produced using genetic editing technology, may have on the environment.

UNESCO-Published International Declaration on Human Genetic Data

The gathering, handling, and preservation of genetic data are covered under the 2003 International Declaration on Human Genetic Data by UNESCO. It highlights permission, privacy, and genetic information protection principles, all of which are pertinent to conversations about genetic technology even if they are not specifically related to genome editing.

World Health Organization (WHO) Frameworks for Governance

Global governance frameworks for genome editing have been the subject of ongoing deliberations by the World Health Organization. The WHO's engagement shows a commitment to creating standards and guidelines for the appropriate use of these technologies, even if it is not a treaty. For the most current advances in the regulation of genome and embryo editing, it is important to consult the most recent information and updates from relevant international organizations and legal agencies.

Figure 3. Conventions, treaties, and accords pertaining to these technologies

(Source- Original)

Evaluating the Current Governance Mechanisms' Effectiveness

The usefulness of the present governance frameworks for modifying the human genome and embryos is still being examined and discussed. Although several international organizations and ethical frameworks provide useful ideals, there are obstacles in the way of their actual application and enforcement. There are sometimes supervision gaps because of how quickly technology is developing at the expense of regulatory framework development. Furthermore, there is a lack of consistency in regulatory methods due to the differences in cultural, ethical, and legal settings across nations. Differences in national regulations might result in differences in ethical norms and practices since there isn't a single international convention that addresses genome editing. Furthermore, enforcing rules mostly depends on each country's desire to do so, which makes establishing a reliable and consistent global governance system difficult. In order to properly address the ethical, legal, and social aspects of human genome and embryo editing, there is a growing agreement on the necessity for more international collaboration, openness, and accountability as talks continue and scientific capabilities advance. Sustaining these governance structures calls for constant communication, cooperation, and a dedication to respecting moral principles worldwide.

HUMAN GENOME AND EMBRYO EDITING: ETHICAL CONSIDERATIONS

In the discussion of the human genome and embryo editing, ethics are crucial. The capacity to alter a person's genetic composition presents concerns of consent, autonomy, and the possibility of unforeseen outcomes. Ethical problems are also raised by the idea of "designer babies" and the potential for genetic differences to be created between people.

The essence of life, human involvement, and the possible ramifications for future generations are among the many complicated and nuanced ethical considerations raised by the human genome and embryo editing controversy. The idea of "designer babies" and the capacity to change genes selectively to improve certain features are two main ethical issues. Because of the potential for access to these technologies to create gaps between those who can purchase genetic alterations and those who cannot, this raises concerns about equality. Furthermore, since changes made today will affect countless people in the future without their express agreement, the permanence and inheritability of germline modifications generated by embryo editing create ethical challenges that span generations (Tong et al.,2024).

Another crucial ethical factor is informed permission, especially when modifying the genomes of germline cells or embryos. It is difficult to predict every possible outcome of genetic alterations, and it is yet unknown how they will affect people's health and well-being in the long run. Since those impacted by genome editing would not have the autonomy to agree or object, this calls into question established medical ethics. Editing the human germline raises questions about unknown genetic risks and unintended repercussions. Concerns about acting as "genetic gatekeepers" and possible social pressure to adhere to certain genetic standards are also raised in the ethical discussion. This raises the possibility of discrimination based on genetic traits, undercutting the values of inclusion, variety, and personal freedom. Beyond personal decisions, ethical issues have wider social ramifications, therefore careful consideration of cultural, religious, and philosophical viewpoints is required. In the rapidly developing field of genetic technologies, striking a balance between the advancement of scientific knowledge and the upholding of ethical standards in the areas of human genome and embryo editing is a constant challenge that calls for constant communication, international cooperation, and a dedication to upholding the principles of beneficence, non-maleficence, autonomy, and justice (Ahmed et al.,2024)

LEGAL ENVIRONMENT FOR WOMEN'S REPRODUCTIVE JUSTICE: EXAMINING EMBRYO EDITING AND GENOME

The legal environment pertaining to modifying human genomes and embryos is complicated and differs across nations. While some countries have passed laws governing these technologies, others still lack complete frameworks. It is difficult to guarantee the proper use of new technologies, defend individual rights, and stop any abuses when there are inconsistent legal requirements. To guarantee a unified approach to human genome and embryo editing, these gaps may be filled with the adoption of international legal rules (Singh et al.,2024).

The development of genome and embryo editing technology has created new obstacles and difficulties in the legal environment for women's reproductive justice. These cutting-edge biotechnologies bring up complex legal issues pertaining to women's autonomy, rights, and the laws that control assisted reproductive technologies. The ability of women to make knowledgeable decisions concerning genetic treatments in the context of reproduction is at the core of the issue. Legal systems have to work out what constitutes consent and make sure that women are given the knowledge they need to make choices regarding genome and embryo editing, which may have a significant impact on future generations' genetic make-up as well as their own health. The crucial element pertains to the oversight of therapeutic procedures concerning genome editing in reproductive settings. The licensing, accreditation, and supervision of reproductive clinics and genetic labs that perform these operations must be covered by legal frameworks. Legal responses to genome and embryo editing must be based on ensuring that practitioners follow ethical guidelines, provide women and couples thorough information, and get legitimate permission) (Al-Dahidi et al.,2024).

Access and equality concerns must be taken into account in the legal system. These technologies' accessibility and cost may lead to inequality, preventing certain groups of women from using them. Legal frameworks should protect the ideals of reproductive justice, which stress the freedom to make reproductive choices without experiencing obstacles or inequities, by working to avoid discrimination in access to genome and embryo editing based on socioeconomic reasons. The worldwide consequences of genome editing technologies need international cooperation and the formation of generally acknowledged norms in order to navigate the legal terrain for women's reproductive rights. International treaties, conventions, and agreements may help to ensure that moral and legal principles are respected uniformly around the world and help to shape a unified global response.

However, legislative solutions must safeguard women's access to advantageous genetic therapies that help fend off inherited illnesses and promote healthier pregnancies in addition to focusing on limitations. It is a challenging issue for legal systems across the world to strike a balance between the need of monitoring and the desire to protect women's autonomy. Instead of impeding scientific advancement, the legal system should support the values of reproductive justice for women everywhere by offering a strong and moral foundation that permits responsible genome and embryo editing. The way that these legal frameworks continue to develop will probably have a significant impact on how justly and ethically genome and embryo editing technologies are used in the field of women's reproductive health (Singh & Kaunert, 2024).

SOCIAL IMPLICATIONS: GENOME AND EMBRYO EDITING AND WOMEN'S REPRODUCTIVE JUSTICE

Beyond personal decisions, the societal ramifications of human genome editing and embryo editing affect society as a whole. Fairness and social justice are called into question by the possibility of generating hereditary inequities and escalating preexisting injustices. In addition, the price and accessibility of these technologies need to be taken into account in order to guarantee reproductive justice for every person, irrespective of their geographic location or socioeconomic standing. Ensuring fair access to these technologies and addressing societal problems may be facilitated by global norms for governance.

The social ramifications of genome and embryo editing technologies have a profound influence on women's reproductive justice, bringing with them a range of issues that go beyond personal preferences to have an impact on society as a whole. The most important thing to consider is how society's expectations and conventions around women's reproductive duties can change. The concept of choosing or altering certain genetic characteristics in embryos raises concerns about cultural values and preferences, as it may serve to reinforce gender stereotypes and establish new ones about the responsibilities that women should play in reproduction (Singh,2024).

The notion of "designer babies," where certain qualities may be selected or increased, is introduced by the development of genome and embryo editing. This creates questions regarding how women may be unduly pressured to adhere to desired genetic norms, perpetuating beauty standards, intellect, or other socially valued attributes. By restricting women's autonomy in choosing decisions that are consistent with their beliefs and preferences, such cultural expectations have the potential to undermine the fundamentals of reproductive justice.

The possibility of discrimination based on genetic traits is another aspect of the social ramifications. People who defy these genetic norms may be stigmatized or subjected to discrimination if certain qualities are seen to be more desirable. Reproductive justice concepts, which seek to guarantee that people may make reproductive decisions without facing discrimination, are called into question by this. Social inequality are exacerbated by genome editing technologies' price and accessibility. If wealthy people or communities are the only ones with access to these technologies, it may worsen already-existing social and economic disparities and restrict equitable access to reproductive options. This brings up important issues of justice, equality, and the ability of all women to profit from genetic technology breakthroughs, irrespective of their financial situation (Singh & Kaunert,2024).

A comprehensive strategy that takes into account varied cultural viewpoints, encourages public discussion, and includes the voices of women from diverse backgrounds is required to address these societal ramifications. In order to enable women to make decisions that are in line with their beliefs and to increase public understanding of the societal ramifications of genome and embryo editing, educational initiatives must be developed. In the end, negotiating these technologies' social ramifications in the framework of women's reproductive justice necessitates an intelligent and inclusive public conversation to guarantee that the advantages of genetic advancements are distributed fairly and that women's autonomy and rights continue to be fundamental to the developing field of reproductive technologies (Agaton et al.,2024)

Social Issues' Intersectionality With Women's Reproductive Health

Figure 4. Intersection of social issues with women's reproductive health

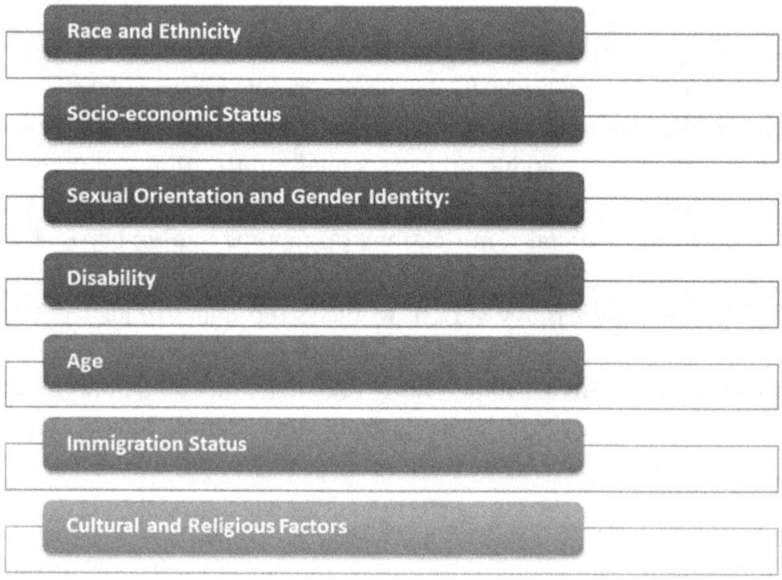

(Source- Original)

The intricate interaction of several social elements that shape the experiences of distinct groups of women is acknowledged by the intersectionality of social concerns in women's reproductive health (Singh,2023). This intersectionality approach recognizes that factors such as race, class, ethnicity, sexual orientation, ability, and gender influence women's reproductive health in addition to other aspects of identity. Reproductive justice requires an understanding of how these interlocking issues affect women's autonomy over reproductive decisions, access to healthcare, and general well-being(Rahimieh & Nosrati, 2024).

Race and Ethnicity: There are often differences in the reproductive health outcomes for women from various racial and ethnic origins. Disparities in reproductive rights, increased rates of maternal mortality, and uneven access to high-quality healthcare are all consequences of structural racism. For example, women who identify as Indigenous, Black, or Hispanic may have greater rates of maternal mortality and encounter obstacles while trying to get reproductive healthcare services.

Socioeconomic Status: Women's reproductive health is significantly impacted by socioeconomic variables. It may be difficult for women from lower socioeconomic backgrounds to get fertility therapies, prenatal care, and contraception. Economic inequality may affect mother and child health outcomes as well as family planning choices.

Sexual Orientation and Gender Identity: People who identify as LGBTQ+ may encounter particular difficulties while seeking reproductive healthcare, such as prejudice, a lack of cultural sensitivity on the part of medical professionals, and restricted access to family-building alternatives that are inclusive. Reproductive justice demands attending to the unique needs and rights of people who identify as LGBTQ+.

Disability: Stigmatization, inaccessibility, and insufficient support during pregnancy and delivery are some of the obstacles faced by women with disabilities while trying to receive reproductive healthcare services. Policies and services that are inclusive and take into account the various needs of women with disabilities are necessary for reproductive justice.

Age: Women of different ages may have different reproductive health issues. Older women may have age-related reproductive problems, while younger women may face obstacles to complete sex education and access to contraception. Support for customized reproductive healthcare is needed for both populations.

Immigration Status: Women who are immigrants may face particular difficulties, such as restricted access to healthcare because of linguistic or legal constraints. There are dangers to the health of mothers and children when women are deterred from obtaining essential reproductive healthcare due to fear of deportation.

Cultural and Religious Factors: Perceptions about abortion, family planning, and reproductive health may be influenced by religious doctrine and cultural norms. Providing reproductive healthcare treatments that are culturally competent requires an understanding of and respect for various cultural viewpoints.

Thus, tackling the interconnectedness of social concerns with women's reproductive health necessitates an all-encompassing strategy. Policies and interventions should take into account the varied needs and experiences of women, recognizing the manner in which many social variables interact to influence the course of reproduction. By aiming to eliminate structural injustices, a reproductive justice framework makes sure that all women, regardless of how their identities intersect, have the autonomy, information, and support they need to make choices about having children.

FUTURE DIRECTIONS

The rapid progress in human genome and embryo editing technology demands the creation of international guidelines for governance that tackle the moral, legal, and societal concerns related to reproductive justice. A coordinated strategy will guarantee ethical behavior, defend individual liberties, and advance fair access to these technology. We can manage the intricacies of human genome and embryo editing while respecting the values of ethics, fairness, and equality by encouraging worldwide cooperation and discourse. The landscape at the junction of social concerns and women's reproductive health is intricate and multidimensional, influenced by the interactions of age, immigrant status, gender, race, socioeconomic position, sexual orientation, disability, and cultural influences.

Figure 5. Rapid advances in human genome and embryo editing technologies

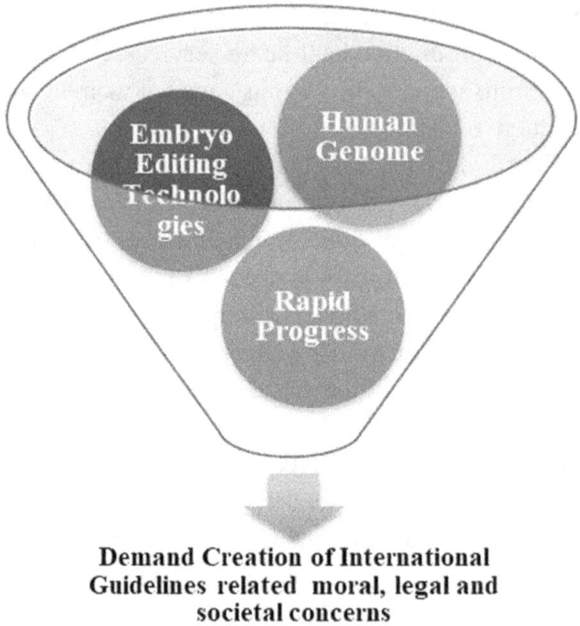

(Original)

The achieving of reproductive justice a framework that defends the rights to have children, not to have children, and to parent in secure and supportive environments requires acknowledging and addressing these interlocking elements. The conversation around reproductive justice now emphasizes the need of accessible healthcare, inclusive legislation, and tearing down structural obstacles that disproportionately impact underprivileged communities. The creation of treatments that take into account the varied needs and experiences of women, as well as educational programs and cultural competency training for healthcare professionals, are all essential components of strategies (Singh & Kaunert,2024).

CONCLUSION AND FUTURE SCOPE

The sufficient research, activism and policy development are crucial in addressing the dynamic state of women's reproductive health. Technology integration creates new levels of complexity and raises ethical questions, as shown by developments in genome and embryo editing. Future efforts should strive to achieve a balance between ethical protections and scientific advancement, making sure that technology advancements support reproductive justice rather than undermine it. Advocating for reproductive justice must become a worldwide movement in the future, taking into account regional differences in healthcare results and access. Fair and equitable reproductive health practices will need international cooperation and the creation of global standards. In order to ensure that policies and initiatives are informed by the stories of women from varied backgrounds and experiences, attention should also be placed on elevating the voices of these women. The core tenet of reproductive justice is empowering women to actively participate in choices about their reproductive health. The future of women's reproductive justice and health thus rests on a comprehensive, inclusive, and rights-based strategy. It entails continuing discussion, investigation, and policy formulation that take into account the complex interplay between social variables, technological developments, and the varied experiences that women have on a global scale. We can work toward a future in which every woman, regardless of her intersecting identities, has access to the full range of reproductive rights and health by promoting an all-encompassing and inclusive vision of reproductive justice.

REFERENCES

Agaton, C. B., & Guila, P. M. C. (2024). Success Factors and Challenges: Implications of Real Options Valuation of Constructed Wetlands as Nature-Based Solutions for Wastewater Treatment. *Resources*, 13(1), 11. 10.3390/resources1301001138187013

Ahmed, S. F., Islam, N., Tasannum, N., Mehjabin, A., Momtahin, A., Chowdhury, A. A., Almomani, F., & Mofijur, M. (2024). Microplastic removal and management strategies for wastewater treatment plants. *Chemosphere*, 347, 140648. 10.1016/j.chemosphere.2023.14064837952815

Al-Dahidi, S., Alrbai, M., Al-Ghussain, L., Alahmer, A., & Hayajneh, H. S. (2024). Data-driven analysis and prediction of wastewater treatment plant performance: Insights and forecasting for sustainable operations. *Bioresource Technology*, 391, 129937. 10.1016/j.biortech.2023.129937

Alsubai, S., Dutta, A. K., Alkhayyat, A. H., Jaber, M. M., Abbas, A. H., & Kumar, A. (2023). Hybrid deep learning with improved Salp swarm optimization based multi-class grape disease classification model. *Computers & Electrical Engineering*, 108, 108733. 10.1016/j.compeleceng.2023.108733

Annoni, A., Nativi, S., Çöltekin, A., Desha, C., Eremchenko, E., Gevaert, C. M., Giuliani, G., Chen, M., Perez-Mora, L., Strobl, J., & Tumampos, S. (2023). Digital earth: Yesterday, today, and tomorrow. *International Journal of Digital Earth*, 16(1), 1022–1072. 10.1080/17538947.2023.2187467

Bohan, D., & Dumbrell, A. (Eds.). (2023). *Advances in Ecological Research: Roadmaps Part B*. Elsevier.

Chen, L., Wu, T., Wang, Z., Lin, X., & Cai, Y. (2023). A novel hybrid BPNN model based on adaptive evolutionary Artificial Bee Colony Algorithm for water quality index prediction. *Ecological Indicators*, 146, 109882. 10.1016/j.ecolind.2023.109882

De Giovanni, P. (2023). Sustainability of the Metaverse: A transition to Industry 5.0. *Sustainability (Basel)*, 15(7), 6079. 10.3390/su15076079

Derval, D. (2023). *Frontiers in Product Innovation Strategy: Predicting Market Outcomes and Creating Winning Products for a People and Planet-friendly Future.*

Dobrauz-Saldapenna, G., & Huras, N. (Eds.). (2023). *Circular Economy: New solutions for a better tomorrow*. Stämpfli Verlag.

Doherty, P. (2023). *Smart Cities: Reimagining the Urban Experience*. Quality Press.

Eriksson, R. O., & Regoczi, B. (2023). *Diving into venture creation: An exploratory study of how external enabler combinations facilitate sustainable venture creation in the marine sector.*

Esposito, M., Halkias, D., Tse, T., & Harkiolakis, T. (2023). Environmental and Climate Impacts of the Metaverse. *Available atSSRN* 4616695. 10.2139/ssrn.4616695

Grassini, S., & Ratcliffe, E. (2024). The Virtual Wild: Exploring the Intersection of Virtual Reality and Natural Environments. *Managing Protected Areas*, 327.

Grassini, S., & Ratcliffe, E. (2024). The Virtual Wild: Exploring the Intersection of Virtual Reality and Natural Environments. *Managing Protected Areas*, 327.

Hemachandran, K., & Rodriguez, R. V. (Eds.). (2023). *The Business of the Metaverse: How to Maintain the Human Element Within this New Business Reality*. CRC Press.

Ishida, S., Matsui, T., Haga, C., Hori, K., Hashimoto, S., & Saito, O. (2023). Twitter Mining for Detecting Interest Trends on Biodiversity: Messages from Seven Language Communities. *Sustainability (Basel)*, 15(17), 12893. 10.3390/su151712893

Khan, A., Pin, K., Aziz, A., Han, J. W., & Nam, Y. (2023). Optical coherence tomography image classification using hybrid deep learning and ant colony optimization. *Sensors (Basel)*, 23(15), 6706. 10.3390/s2315670637571490

Khizar, H. M. U., Younas, A., Kumar, S., Akbar, A., & Poulova, P. (2023). The progression of sustainable development goals in tourism: A systematic literature review of past achievements and future promises. *Journal of Innovation & Knowledge*, 8(4), 100442. 10.1016/j.jik.2023.100442

Kitada, M., Johannesen, E., Ojwala, R. A., Buckingham, S., Sun, Z., Rodríguez-Chaves, M., & Schofield, C. (2023). Barriers to the Collection of Gender-Disaggregated Data in Ocean Science. *Human Factors in Management and Leadership*, 71

Kopplin, C. S. (2023). Sports fashion and sustainability: A perfect match? *International Journal of Sports Marketing & Sponsorship*, 24(5), 891–912. 10.1108/IJSMS-04-2023-0078

Krishnamoorthy, G. D., Balasubramanian, K., Govindaraj, S., Ayyavu, P. G., & Geetha, D. A. D. (2023, June). Energy management system using binary particle swarm optimization technique. In *AIP Conference Proceedings* (*Vol. 2766*, No. 1). AIP Publishing. 10.1063/5.0139459

Kumar, R., Gupta, S. K., Wang, H. C., Kumari, C. S., & Korlam, S. S. V. P. (2023). From Efficiency to Sustainability: Exploring the Potential of 6G for a Greener Future. *Sustainability (Basel)*, 15(23), 16387. 10.3390/su152316387

Kuranga, C., Muwani, T. S., & Ranganai, N. (2023). A multi-population particle swarm optimization-based time series predictive technique. *Expert Systems with Applications*, 233, 120935. 10.1016/j.eswa.2023.120935

Matebese, F., Mosai, A. K., Tutu, H., & Tshentu, Z. R. (2024). Mining wastewater treatment technologies and resource recovery techniques: A review. *Heliyon*, 10(3), e24730. 10.1016/j.heliyon.2024.e2473038317979

Min, X. Z., Zhang, Z. F., Lu, X. M., Chen, J. C., Ma, W. L., Liu, L. Y., & Kallenborn, R. (2024). Occurrence and fate of pharmaceuticals and personal care products in a wastewater treatment plant with Bacillus bio-reactor treatment. *The Science of the Total Environment*, 924, 171589. 10.1016/j.scitotenv.2024.17158938461988

Modarress-Fathi, B., Ansari, A., & Ansari, A. (2023). Examining Sustainability Alignment of Supplier Selection Criteria during Industrial Revolutions. *Sustainability (Basel)*, 15(22), 15930. 10.3390/su152215930

Molavi, H., Mirzaei, K., Jafarpour, E., Mohammadi, A., Salimi, M. S., Rezakazemi, M., Nadagouda, M. M., & Aminabhavi, T. M. (2024). Wastewater treatment using nanodiamond and related materials. *Journal of Environmental Management*, 349, 119349. 10.1016/j.jenvman.2023.119349

Morrison, A. M., & Buhalis, D. (Eds.). (2023). *Routledge Handbook of Trends and Issues in Global Tourism Supply and Demand*. Taylor & Francis. 10.4324/9781003260790

Obiuto, N. C., Ugwuanyi, E. D., Ninduwezuor-Ehiobu, N., Ani, E. C., & Olu-lawal, K. A. (2024). Advancing wastewater treatment technologies: The role of chemical engineering simulations in environmental sustainability. *World Journal of Advanced Research and Reviews, 21*(3), 019-031.

Periyasamy, A. P., & Periyasami, S. (2023). Critical Review on Sustainability in Denim: A Step toward Sustainable Production and Consumption of Denim. *ACS Omega*, 8(5), 4472–4490. 10.1021/acsomega.2c0637436777581

Qadir, A. M. A., & Fatah, A. O. (2023). Platformization and the metaverse: Opportunities and challenges for urban sustainability and economic development. *EAI Endorsed Transactions on Energy Web, 10*(1).

Rahimieh, A., & Nosrati, M. (2024). A Review on Biochemistry, Microbiology and Thermodynamic Aspects of Propionate: The Key Intermediate in the Anaerobic Digestion and Wastewater Treatment. *Desalination and Water Treatment*, 317, 100191. 10.1016/j.dwt.2024.100191

Sharifi, A., Allam, Z., Bibri, S. E., & Khavarian-Garmsir, A. R. (2024). Smart cities and sustainable development goals (SDGs): A systematic literature review of co-benefits and trade-offs. *Cities (London, England)*, 146, 104659. 10.1016/j.cities.2023.104659

Sharifi, A., Allam, Z., Bibri, S. E., & Khavarian-Garmsir, A. R. (2024). Smart cities and sustainable development goals (SDGs): A systematic literature review of co-benefits and trade-offs. *Cities (London, England)*, 146, 104659. 10.1016/j.cities.2023.104659

Simões-Marques, M., Água, P., Frias, A., & Correia, A. (2023). Metaverse and Digital Twins: Contributions, Opportunities and Challenges to a Sustainable Use of the Ocean. *Human Factors and Systems Interaction, 84*(84).

Singh, B. (2023). Blockchain Technology in Renovating Healthcare: Legal and Future Perspectives. In Kaushik, K., Dahiya, S., Aggarwal, S., & Dwivedi, A. (Eds.), *Revolutionizing Healthcare Through Artificial Intelligence and Internet of Things Applications* (pp. 177–186). IGI Global. 10.4018/978-1-6684-5422-0.ch012

Singh, B. (2024). Lensing Legal Dynamics for Examining Responsibility and Deliberation of Generative AI-Tethered Technological Privacy Concerns: Infringements and Use of Personal Data by Nefarious Actors. In Ara, A., & Ara, A. (Eds.), *Exploring the Ethical Implications of Generative AI* (pp. 146–167). IGI Global. 10.4018/979-8-3693-1565-1.ch009

Singh, B. (2024). Evolutionary Global Neuroscience for Cognition and Brain Health: Strengthening Innovation in Brain Science. In Prabhakar, P. (Ed.), *Biomedical Research Developments for Improved Healthcare* (pp. 246–272). IGI Global. 10.4018/979-8-3693-1922-2.ch012

Singh, B. (2024). Social Cognition of Incarcerated Women and Children: Addressing Exposure to Infectious Diseases and Legal Outcomes. In Reddy, K. (Ed.), *Principles and Clinical Interventions in Social Cognition* (pp. 236–251). IGI Global. 10.4018/979-8-3693-1265-0.ch014

Singh, B., Dutta, P. K., & Kaunert, C. (2024). Replenish Artificial Intelligence in Renewable Energy for Sustainable Development: Lensing SDG 7 Affordable and Clean Energy and SDG 13 Climate Actions With Legal-Financial Advisory. In Derbali, A. (Ed.), *Social and Ethical Implications of AI in Finance for Sustainability* (pp. 198–227). IGI Global. 10.4018/979-8-3693-2881-1.ch009

Singh, B., Jain, V., Kaunert, C., Dutta, P. K., & Singh, G. (2024). Privacy Matters: Espousing Blockchain and Artificial Intelligence (AI) for Consumer Data Protection on E-Commerce Platforms in Ethical Marketing. In Saluja, S., Nayyar, V., Rojhe, K., & Sharma, S. (Eds.), *Ethical Marketing Through Data Governance Standards and Effective Technology* (pp. 167–184). IGI Global. 10.4018/979-8-3693-2215-4.ch015

Singh, B., & Kaunert, C. (2024). Computational Thinking for Innovative Solutions and Problem-Solving Techniques: Transforming Conventional Education to Futuristic Interdisciplinary Higher Education. In Fonkam, M., & Vajjhala, N. (Eds.), *Revolutionizing Curricula Through Computational Thinking, Logic, and Problem Solving* (pp. 60–82). IGI Global. 10.4018/979-8-3693-1974-1.ch004

Singh, B., & Kaunert, C. (2024). Augmented Reality and Virtual Reality Modules for Mindfulness: Boosting Emotional Intelligence and Mental Wellness. In Hiran, K., Doshi, R., & Patel, M. (Eds.), *Applications of Virtual and Augmented Reality for Health and Wellbeing* (pp. 111–128). IGI Global. 10.4018/979-8-3693-1123-3.ch007

Singh, B., & Kaunert, C. (2024). Harnessing Sustainable Agriculture Through Climate-Smart Technologies: Artificial Intelligence for Climate Preservation and Futuristic Trends. In Kannan, H., Rodriguez, R., Paprika, Z., & Ade-Ibijola, A. (Eds.), *Exploring Ethical Dimensions of Environmental Sustainability and Use of AI* (pp. 214–239). IGI Global. 10.4018/979-8-3693-0892-9.ch011

Singh, B., & Kaunert, C. (2024). Salvaging Responsible Consumption and Production of Food in the Hospitality Industry: Harnessing Machine Learning and Deep Learning for Zero Food Waste. In Singh, A., Tyagi, P., & Garg, A. (Eds.), *Sustainable Disposal Methods of Food Wastes in Hospitality Operations* (pp. 176–192). IGI Global. 10.4018/979-8-3693-2181-2.ch012

Singh, B., & Kaunert, C. (2024). Revealing Green Finance Mobilization: Harnessing FinTech and Blockchain Innovations to Surmount Barriers and Foster New Investment Avenues. In Jafar, S., Rodriguez, R., Kannan, H., Akhtar, S., & Plugmann, P. (Eds.), *Harnessing Blockchain-Digital Twin Fusion for Sustainable Investments* (pp. 265–286). IGI Global. 10.4018/979-8-3693-1878-2.ch011

Singh, B., & Kaunert, C. (2024). Wind and Solar Energy as Renewable Energy for Sustainable Global Future: Projecting Future Multi-Sector Sustainable Policies and Innovation. In Ara, A., & Thakore, R. (Eds.), *Promoting Multi-Sector Sustainability With Policy and Innovation* (pp. 210–245). IGI Global. 10.4018/979-8-3693-2113-3.ch009

Singh, B., & Kaunert, C. (2024). Aroma of Highly Smart Internet of Medical Things (IoMT) and Lightweight EdgeTrust Expansion Medical Care Facilities for Electronic Healthcare Systems: Fortified-Chain Architecture for Remote Patient Monitoring and Privacy Protection Beyond Imagination. In Hassan, A., Bhattacharya, P., Tikadar, S., Dutta, P., & Sagayam, M. (Eds.), *Lightweight Digital Trust Architectures in the Internet of Medical Things (IoMT)* (pp. 196–212). IGI Global. 10.4018/979-8-3693-2109-6.ch011

Singh, B., & Kaunert, C. Reinventing Artificial Intelligence and Blockchain for Preserving Medical Data. In *Ethical Artificial Intelligence in Power Electronics* (pp. 77–91). CRC Press. 10.1201/9781032648323-6

Singh, B., Vig, K., Dutta, P. K., & Kaunert, C. (2024). Unraveling Agile Transformation for Customer Satisfaction in Changing Market Conditions: Roadmap for Industry Embracing Change in Project Management. In Misra, S., Jadeja, R., & Mittal, M. (Eds.), *Practical Approaches to Agile Project Management* (pp. 305–321). IGI Global. 10.4018/979-8-3693-3318-1.ch017

Skapetze, L., Zha, C., Yin, X., von Brueck, D., & Önkü, E. (2023). Promoting Pro-Environmental Behavior based on the Psychology of Perception. *Briefe zur Interdisziplinarität*, (31).

Skapetze, L., Zhao, C., Yin, X., von Brueck, D., & Önkü, E. (2023). 6 Promoting pro-environmental behaviour based on the. *Balanced Sustainability In A Changing World, 10*, 111.

Skapetze, L., Zhao, C., Yin, X., von Brueck, D., & Önkü, E. (2024). Promoting pro-environmental behaviour based on the psychology of perception—Can the metaverse be a potential solution? In *Balanced Sustainability in a Changing World* (pp. 111-136).

Skapetze, L., Zhao, C., Yin, X., von Brueck, D., & Önkü, E. (2024). Promoting pro-environmental behaviour based on the psychology of perception—Can the metaverse be a potential solution? In *Balanced Sustainability in a Changing World* (pp. 111-136).

Suratiningsih, D. (2023). Strategy for Establishing the World Mangrove Center as a Climate Change Mitigation Effort. *Journal of Namibian Studies: History Politics Culture*, 34, 2474–2494.

Tonelli, C., & Morandi, A. (2023). *The impact of 3D technology on sustainability in fashion luxury product design: evidences from an exploratory analysis.*

Tong, Y., Liao, X., He, Y., Cui, X., Wishart, M., Zhao, F., & Chen, G. (2024). Mitigating greenhouse gas emissions from municipal wastewater treatment in China. *Environmental Science and Ecotechnology*, 20, 100341. 10.1016/j.ese.2023.10034138094258

Zawish, M., Dharejo, F. A., Khowaja, S. A., Raza, S., Davy, S., Dev, K., & Bellavista, P. (2024). AI and 6G into the metaverse: Fundamentals, challenges and future research trends. *IEEE Open Journal of the Communications Society*, 5, 730–778. 10.1109/OJCOMS.2024.3349465

Zhan, J., Xu, S., Zhu, Y., Han, Y., Li, L., Liu, J., & Guo, X. (2024). Potential pathogenic microorganisms in rural wastewater treatment process: Succession characteristics, concentration variation, source exploration, and risk assessment. *Water Research*, 254, 121359. 10.1016/j.watres.2024.12135938428237

Chapter 4
Issues and Challenges of Artificial Intelligence Implementation in Healthcare:
A Review Study

Tarun Kumar Kaushik
https://orcid.org/0000-0002-3279-8307
Sharda University, India

Ravish
Meerut College, India

Anurag Singh
Meerut College, India

Anjali Raghav
https://orcid.org/0009-0004-0248-7956
Sharda University, India

Bhupinder Singh
https://orcid.org/0009-0006-4779-2553
Sharda University, India

ABSTRACT

In 1956, the United States of America was the birthplace of artificial intelligence (AI), which at the time consisted of an algorithm that was developed via the process of analyzing previously collected data and learning on its own. This chapter provides

DOI: 10.4018/979-8-3693-5976-1.ch004

a discussion on the present applications of artificial intelligence in the medical field, as well as a summary of the existing challenges that are restricting the widespread acceptance of AI. Therefore, the implementation of technology and artificial intelligence in the healthcare industry may be beneficial to hospitals, particularly in situations where viruses such as COVID diminish the workforce. There is also a dependence on trustworthy sources, as well as worry over artificial intelligence and healthcare. To fulfill its objectives, however, the healthcare industry must contend with a great deal of difficulty.

INTRODUCTION

Researchers and healthcare professionals are focusing on artificial intelligence (AI) in the healthcare sector in the era of data science and robots. Even the word "artificial intelligence" conjures up images of robots, code, and the internet for most people. Any digital programme that can perform jobs typically performed by humans is considered artificial intelligence, in our opinion. AI is therefore defined as a computer programme with intelligent decision-making capabilities. This comprises data-driven models and computer programmes that operate according to preset rules. Artificial Intelligence (AI) encompasses a wide range of sophisticated technological forms and combinations, including machine learning, deep learning, neural networks, robotics, robotics, and computational statistics. AI was therefore designed to finish repeated tasks, but that is no longer the case. Following several decades of research and development, artificial intelligence has progressively been incorporated into routine medical practice. Additionally, significant advancements have been achieved in the fields of medical image processing, medical process optimisation, medical education, and other applications. The fast growth of artificial intelligence technology has, however, been accompanied by the emergence of a number of challenges; hence, it has not yet been significantly used in clinical practice or public health. A search was conducted in the PubMed database to locate publications that were published during the past five years on the subject of artificial intelligence medical applications, legislation, and ethics (Lei et. al, 2020).

Although people are gaining a deeper comprehension of the circumstances surrounding healthcare and are being pushed to extend their perspectives on the possibilities presented by computerised technology, people continue to be apprehensive about the impact that artificial intelligence will have in the field of medicine. In addition to this, we investigate and talk about various approaches to problem-solving. Patients' varied perspectives on the use of artificial intelligence (AI) in healthcare are a significant factor in determining how people feel about AI applications in this fast-paced, automated digital environment (Hao & Zheng, 2022). The four primary objectives of healthcare are to enhance the health of the population, to improve the experience of patients and careers, to reduce the growing cost of care, and to improve the overall quality of treatment. Therefore, if artificial intelligence is successfully implemented, we might observe a rapid change in the hospital experience, a reduction in the amount of work that is required in the hospital, protection of healthcare professionals from viruses or infections that could potentially be fatal, and diagnosis that is efficient, effective, quick, and accurate (Singh, 2023).

The need for more people in the medical field is growing along with the population. AI can help with this. These days, AI is far more capable than doctors at doing the same duties. Because the AI database is infinite, significantly more individualised treatment is possible. Computers are frequently observed operating far more rapidly, effectively, and efficiently than humans (Zhu et. al.,2023). A small number of earlier studies in the fields of accounting, management and business, decision sciences, and healthcare sciences have looked at this topic. AI has the ability to save healthcare expenses while simultaneously greatly improving patient care. As the population increases, getting healthcare would become more difficult. Solutions to healthcare problems that are both extremely useful and successful include computational technologies and data-centric methods (Ramalingamm& Chinnaiyan, 2023).

Furthermore, AI is becoming more potent and frequently capable of doing human duties more successfully. Although these new technologies are highly anticipated, few comprehensive analyses of their potential for moral use in clinical practice have been conducted (Ramalingamm& Chinnaiyan, 2023). Additionally, there hasn't been much engagement with those impacted by AI's usage in healthcare. Artificial intelligence (AI) is a helpful technology that can be used to improve several healthcare fields' primary objectives. AI has several applications that can enhance the patient experience (Holzinge et. al.,2023). One such is an IBM Watson-created app that allows patients to share their fears with the doctor ahead of time. By understanding what patients are frightened of, physicians can better plan to treat them. It can assist them in creating a strategy that makes patients feel at ease without having direct contact with them(Ahmed & Kadhem,2021).

The analysis of patterns in vast volumes of data is another use for AI. In order to forecast new cancer medication targets, scientific research is combined with genetic and clinical patient data from the Institute of Cancer Researchers' SAR database. This can expedite the process of receiving the medication, expediting the diagnosis and treatments. Artificial Intelligence is also utilised in surgical assistive technology, such as robotic arms, and can analyse many scans to forecast various illnesses (Xiong & Wang, 2017). AI also has the ability to monitor water and other sources in order to identify disease outbreaks early. Because AI can be applied to a wide range of issues, we can thus see how it will enhance many aspects of healthcare just from these examples alone. Sections comprise the remainder of the paper's structure. The methods for using AI in healthcare are shown in the next section (Li et. al,2017). The progress and perspectives on AI for healthcare are reviewed and explained in brief in the part that follows. Thereafter, several perspectives on AI in healthcare are explored and condensed. This work is concluded in the last section. In the penultimate portion, we address many research difficulties of AI implementation and possible future paths (Sharma & Singh., 2022).

Approaches for AI in Healthcare

Artificial Intelligence often concentrates on automation, which may be utilised to do repetitive tasks. However, this does not imply intellect. In this instance, we wish to create a computer process that uses one or more machine learning-based models to algorithmically make judgments based on a variety of factors. A technology known as machine/deep learning uses data patterns found in the input to build a prediction model. Next, the model forecasts using fresh data. Furthermore, there is a wide range in the public's perception of non-medical applications of AI, with factors such as media coverage significantly influencing public opinion. Given how popular the internet is in the twenty-first century, it is difficult for someone to be unaware of non-medical AI uses (Zhu et. al,2020). If you share our enthusiasm for technology and its uses, you've probably heard about the Japanese hotel receptionist who is a robotic dinosaur. This is but a small portion of artificial intelligence's potential. AI is completely superior to humans in terms of computational abilities. Can AI, however, use those abilities in real-world situations? When people hear that AI will replace humans, they often raise this important question. Because they are sentient beings, people can take the appropriate safety measures in different situations than do digital machine (Ye et. al.,2023).

In the medical field, however, people are expected to report any annoyance they may be experiencing as well as any other health-related issues they may be having to their doctor. AI can link words to any data in its database by using voice recognition. Emotional robots are not a thing of the future. For instance, an Indian youngster from Chennai was able to build an emotional robot that could sense when it was being reprimanded. AI is also capable of faster, more accurate, and reliable illness detection (Sujatha et. al,2021). AI is capable of making quite accurate predictions by comparing data from earlier diagnoses. In addition, we employed many machine learning algorithms (Naïve Byes, SVM, Decision Tree, Regression, etc.). Convolutional neural network (CNN), recurrent neural network (RNN), and XG-Boost are a few deep learning algorithms that may be used to predict and identify melanoma early on, which is the most serious and common type of skin cancer in the world.

To ensure that these developments are integrated into healthcare in a way that upholds society's confidence, new elements highlight the importance of patient engagement. Artificial intelligence (AI) apps give human professionals more data for decision-making and are becoming a vital part of the medical team. In order to ensure that these advancements in AI are not only well-received but also created and used in a morally acceptable manner that improves patient care, it is imperative to more thoroughly characterise patients' needs, beliefs, and preferences, since they are frequently the intended targets of these developments. Currently, there is a dearth of research describing patients' and other partners' perspectives on the application of AI in healthcare (Wang et. al,2022).

Advancement and Opinion of AI for Healthcare

There were 87 participants in 15 focus groups conducted by NPJ Digital Medicine between November 2019 and February 2020. Focus groups consisted of three to seven participants and lasted ninety minutes each. The mean age of the participants was 53.5 years, and 49.4% of the participants were female. The majority of participants (93.1%) and non-Hispanic/Latinos (94.3%) were White. Eighty-three percent of participants have completed more schooling than just high school. These focus groups' primary objective was to learn about various people's perspectives on artificial intelligence in healthcare (Singh,2022).

These conversations reveal a range of patient concerns and excitement around the use of AI to medicine. Most patients are excited about the prospect of using AI to improve their care. However, our study indicates that they are also concerned about the administration and security of AI in the healthcare industry. In our earlier investigation of early and accurate melanoma skin cancer diagnosis and prevention with melanoma skin cancer, we started by gathering five separate datasets. Next, we trained a CNN with the VGG16 network architecture to recognise visual patterns using the biggest one. The model was tested on four different datasets after it had been trained on one to evaluate how well it would function with other datasets (Guo et. al,2019). In order to avoid training the model pointlessly when the metrics stopped rising, we included early stopping in addition to 13 convolutional layers, five pooling layers, and epochs. Another callback that we added reduced the model's learning rate as the number of epochs rose. The pace at which the weights change over time is influenced by the learning rate. We made the distinctions between each period smaller and smaller as we went along. These together created our model and provided our findings. Nevertheless, our test did not significantly improve the models' performance metrics to the point where we could suggest using it on any fresh dataset (Gupta et. al,2021).

The datasets were tested, and the findings showed a wide range of improvements, some good and many negative. The test results showed 89% accuracy and 0.19 F1 Score for dataset 1. These were average results. Since the F1 Score metric would save the greatest lives, we concentrated more on it (Wu et. al,2023). The reason for this is that the F1 Score is the mean of two numbers. First, divide the total number of malignant photos accurately identified by the total number of malignant images. This is the number of cancer-related lives it will help spare. The precision, or degree of accuracy, is the second parameter. The mode produces fewer false diagnoses the better this parameter is. More lives are lost or more money is squandered on false positives the lower this number is (Singh,2022).

Thus, Dataset saw the largest improvement. The F1 Score increased to 75% despite the accuracy dropping to 78%. This represents a decent balance between money lost and lives saved. The fact that we are not taking into consideration the variations in data is now one of the main problems with our system. While the photos may vary greatly because they come from various sources, all the data is preprocessed using the same methods as the other datasets. The severely unbalanced dataset is another problem (Khan et. al, 2021). This complicates the model's ability to identify cancerous pictures since so many of them are benign. A dataset with fewer imbalances during training could aid the model's ability to identify patterns. Dataset is an excellent choice to test this idea because it performs well even when it isn't utilised as training data. In a trial, the Cloud Medx AI performed a medical checkup and outperformed human doctors in terms of results. The medical exam included of questions that described the patient's condition and required the test taker to make decisions based on intricate medical processes (MacLean,2021).

The AI completed the analysis in five minutes, compared to the seventy-three minutes that the human doctors required on average. This indicates that AI is far more adept at analysis than humans. The AI answered 85% of the questions correctly, while humans scored as high as 81%. The aforementioned case study demonstrates AI's superiority in data analysis. AI will be able to analyse a vast number of scenarios in a matter of minutes in the healthcare industry of the future. However, when humans and AI collaborated, they received a 91% score. Even if AI is far more analytical than humans, humans are still required for tasks requiring common sense (Xia & Qi 2023).

Opinion on AI in Healthcare

People were generally enthusiastic about artificial intelligence's potential to improve healthcare. They thought that the goal of medicine, which is to cure as many people as possible, might be accomplished by using AI in healthcare. In addition, they conveyed that healthcare AI faults should be prevented by experts acting as a safety net for patients. Furthermore, it's been proposed that even when AI is used, clinicians still have accountability for their patients. Furthermore, respondents admitted that their level of satisfaction with AI in healthcare was affected by the preservation of choice. They desired to have the option of using AI or not in their process. Four areas exist for the use of AI in biomedicine to diagnose and forecast illnesses, as well as to solve healthcare problems. The applications of AI in biomedical research include efficiently completing the difficult task of summarising the literature on a particular topic, living assistance for the elderly and disabled, biomedical information processing for quick and accurate answers to user-formulated questions, and diagnostics and prediction for health professionals to provide earlier and more accurate diagnose (Lv et al.,2021).

Additionally, there was worry expressed that the use of AI technology would increase healthcare costs, which might then be passed on to patients. The public was against paying for these AI instruments. Concerns about technological systems that may become overly dependent on emerging AI technologies are also present, as is the fear that some problems may worsen if they were to become extensively employed in medical. One of these concerns was how a therapeutic system that heavily depends on AI skills will be affected in the event of a system failure or broad technical issue.

AI may result in improved viral protection. AI and technology may be utilised to track down viral origins and assist in the identification of disease outbreaks. For a number of reasons, however, many are excited about the application of AI in the medical profession. Radiologists discovered in 2017 that deep learning could classify TB lesions with 96% accuracy. If we train these machine learning algorithms more, we can get greater accuracy rates. Additionally, Oxitone is a startup that makes smart home appliances that work with AI to deliver individualised treatment. When taken as a whole, these elements lower transit expenses and time complexity. Similar to this, AI has very high beginning prices but also has a number of potential price-reducing variables. Neoteric claims that the initial cost of integrating AI into medical systems might range from $20,000 to USD 1,000,000. Value varies according to what you provide to the ecosystem (Binder et.al,2022).

Limitations of AI: Implementation and its Future

Our literature review revealed that various people's perspectives on AI applications and approaches varied widely. Some contend that developing AI like IBM Watson and others is the best way to integrate it into our healthcare systems. Some contended that developing artificial intelligence to help surgeons during procedures was essential. I have to admit that after reading these viewpoints, each is accurate in its own particular manner. Future expenses and the scarcity of workers in the medical field would drastically decrease if we apply such technologies.

Moral Dilemmas (Data Morality)

AI is built on data ethics, which has five main pillars: ownership, impartiality, informed consent, privacy and data protection, and openness. Can we quantify our own health data in monetary terms? Regretfully, these kinds of data exchanges are not unusual; Deep Mind's collaboration with the Royal Free London Foundation Trust is one such instance. Who is the owner of so much private health information? Canada's regulations acknowledge that consumers own their private health data and those healthcare providers are the "information custodians" of such data. The fact that there are legitimate interests in patient medical records that are legally protected is reflected in this "guardianship." Patients therefore have a right to know how and to what extent their personal health data are stored and used because they are the data owners (Kumar et. al.,2022).

Fairness

Bias in data sources leading to unfairness is the most prevalent ethical problem. There will always be some bias in every data set, whether it comes from sociological, environmental, economic, racial, or sexual orientation considerations. AI systems are created using the data that already exists in order to learn and draw relevant conclusions. Healthcare disparities are also reflected in historical data, and machine learning models that are trained on this data may reinforce these disparities. For instance, an American research revealed that physicians may have disregarded the better outcomes for African Americans because they believed the model's positive predictive value for this population was poor. False-positive findings were more common, and the low positive rate was really a result of the tiny number of African Americans who took part in the first investigation (Wang,2022). Injustices may also occur throughout the model's development, application, and assessment phases. When delivering medical care, medical professionals never continue treating individuals who exhibit specific symptoms (such severe brain damage or premature delivery). AI will pick up on these disparities in human inclinations, which will cause grave ethical issues that might endanger patients' lives. When allocating resources, the approach will leave out inhabitants of underprivileged communities who have to stay in hospitals for extended periods of time because of their poverty or distance. Resources for case management may be disproportionately given to patients from affluent, predominately white neighbourhoods by the paradigm. Deviations from automation will also make it more difficult to use AI in real-world applications.

AI choices that are based on minute details that are invisible to humans aggravate this dilemma. Because there is no local expert to challenge these conclusions, the danger of automation bias may be increased in areas with little resources (Rana &Bhushan, 2023).).

It could be challenging for us to predict ahead of time if an AI system or enhancement plan would be detrimental to or beneficial to a certain population.

Ethics of Clinical Practice

The use of AI in healthcare presents new difficulties for physicians. When making difficult clinical practice judgements, an ethical person is more trustworthy than a strictly rule-oriented robot, despite the latter's first seeming superiority. Regardless of the precise clinical interactions, AI has a tendency to magnify biassed findings. In a real-world example, AI incorrectly categorised patients with asthma and pneumonia as low-risk even though co-occurring asthma exacerbates pneumonia. Patients with pneumonia alone were correctly identified as high-risk.

Some academics have argued that participants in an algorithm cannot take moral responsibility if they are unable to anticipate the machine's future actions. This will make the conflict between physicians and patient's worse, which is unworkable in the healthcare industry. Physicians took on the persona of the "guardian of the machine" in collaborative AI ethical declarations from North America, Europe, and Canada. They operated as active operators as opposed to passive users. Consequently, whether or not the patient's diagnostic plan benefited entirely from the AI system, clinicians were still in charge of how the plan turned out. Furthermore, the difficulty in explaining AI-generated models and the fact that many physicians are ignorant of the inner workings of algorithms provide significant ethical difficulties for medical professionals (Liu & Lang, 2019).

Legal Issues Arising in AI

Before being hired, healthcare professionals must pass stringent exams, and they should follow a number of norms of behaviour on a daily basis. As of right now, there are no internationally harmonised rules or regulations governing the use of AI in medicine to standardise the conduct of practitioners. Criminals may employ AI to commit AI-crime, a novel and damaging kind of criminal activity. Thus, it is imperative that comprehensive and precise AI legislation be developed. Nonetheless, there are a few things to think about. First, creating such laws will not be the sole responsibility of legal professionals. Stakeholders engaged in the creation or building of AI-based medical solutions must be involved. Secondly, in the event of an AI-related violation, we ought to ascertain who is at fault—the AI's creator, user, or maintainer. Where does each stakeholder's obligation end? Rather than putting all the risk of AI medical treatment on doctors, what share of accountability should be shared when a complex situation emerges? Lastly, we need to keep improving the laws that have already been created. Research have revealed that health-related data has far surpassed what the original privacy protection rules (such the US Congress's 1996 HIPAA Act) were intended to safeguard. Thankfully, a slew of new rules governing AI data protection, accountability, and oversight have been implemented (Singh,2022).

There is presently no clear AI regulatory body or accountability pathway to more effectively control AI, even in the event that a legal foundation is formed. For instance, the Medicines and Healthcare Products Regulatory Agency classified the NHS 111 powered by Babylon, a kids' intelligent inquiry app, as a medical device even though there was insufficient evidence and no thorough clinical verification.

Security

When it comes to applying AI to the medical field, security is the most crucial concern and also needs the most thorough examination.

Hardware Security

Currently, in order for any AI product to work, a number of electrical devices, including computers, smartphones, and wristbands, are needed. It is important to recognise three major concerns about the security of such devices. First, external variables like cost, temperature fluctuations, and electromagnetic interference will impair the performance of even the greatest physically unclonable operations. Second, physicians and engineers find it challenging to employ AI that combines different technologies due to the complexity and professionalism of medical knowledge and information technology. On the one hand, the medical workflow may be disrupted and data leakage may occur if engineers are retrained in accessing and processing medical system data. Conversely, physicians could not fully comprehend the tenets and practical applications of AI technologies, which might lead to issues like decreased productivity and a rise in mistakes. Third, we need to talk about the security of AI networks. If important nodes in the intricate network transmission process are compromised or fail, a worldwide cascade effect can happen (Gazzotti et. al,2022).

Software Security

Algorithm programmes, even with robust capabilities, are quite vulnerable to design attacks. The AI system does not always perform well in a targeted design confrontation, even though it did well in the initial design assessment. All stages of the AI algorithm creation process will really be targeted, supposing that the attacker is aware of every aspect related to the trained neural network model, such as the number of layers, activation function, training data, and model architecture (Gazzotti et. al,2022). A false-positive attack that generates a negative sample or a false-negative assault that generates a positive sample might confuse the system categorization. It is possible for unknown attacks to target not just the target model but also its parameters and structure inside the training data set. The system is also prone to error in the absence of outside intervention. The original algorithm will ultimately deviate from the intended course as a result of errors in autonomous updates, missing data, and shifting patterns of sickness (Cui et al.,2022).

Human Factors

Software codes enable AI of today. Errors are inevitable when engineers work with thousands of codes. Patches and upgrades over time might enhance an AI system. However, these mistakes might directly jeopardise patients' health in AI systems utilised in the medical industry. The efficacy of the AI system is frequently the final goal that engineers focus on, not security. Medical professionals are fallible as well, and when the often dependable AI system confirms a patient's diagnosis, time-pressed physicians stop thinking about other options (Long et al.,2020).

Protection of Human Genetic Resources

To finish mapping the human genome, all of the chromosomes' DNA sequences have been mapped, and a common information system has been set up. The link between function and genes, particularly the association between genes and illnesses, is the main emphasis of this information system (Jinlei et al.,2022). Over the last three decades, scientists have mapped the whole human genome, which has made it possible to do far more in-depth genetic and cellular research on clinical disorders. Human genetic resources can be extremely helpful in diagnosing and treating medical conditions, but if used unlawfully, they might have disastrous effects on all people (Singh,2020). A biologic weapon known as a "gene weapon"—a term used by the People's Republic of China Ministry of National Defense—consists of bacteria, insects, or other microorganisms that have been genetically modified to carry disease-causing genes. These weapons may be extremely lethal in combat (Avci et al.,2021). The study of genetic traits may be used to engineer genetic variations unique to particular ethnic groups; for this reason, safeguarding the human genome resources is essential. In addition, more patients are getting genetic testing to help with diagnosis and treatment as a consequence of the growth of the Internet and gene testing technologies, and hospitals and testing organisations are keeping track of the test findings. Inappropriate staff may be exposed to confidential information as a result, and discrimination in insurance or employment may result. Therefore, it is necessary to strengthen the legislative safeguards safeguarding patients' privacy during DNA collection, transmission, and storage (kou et al.,2022).

Societal Acceptance

Patients are generally inclined to accept an AI-based diagnosis, but when the AI-based diagnosis is different from the physicians' diagnosis, they are more likely to trust the doctors. According to one poll, medical students and resident physicians wanted to learn about artificial intelligence (AI), but few of them got the chance to take individual data science or machine learning courses. Furthermore, medical professionals in developing nations are quite concerned about whether AI may eventually replace them (Xia et. al.,2021).

Ethical Adoption of AI in Medicine

Ethicists must be involved in the oversight of the whole AI development process in order to address ethical concerns with data, resource allocation, and application. We must first guarantee the ethics committee's independence. The “land” policy, which asserts that patients own medical data in the same way that landowners do, may then be discussed in relation to the data ethics issue. However, it is possible to argue that other parties, such the government or healthcare providers, have a right to access the data in order to improve healthcare. The fairness of distribution in certain clinical and organisational settings, as well as marginalised communities, must be carefully taken into account in order to guarantee justice. The “three fairs”—equal allocation, performance, and outcomes—must be upheld. To guarantee that the development of AI in medical care does not contradict ethics, we think that ethics committees must create consistent guidelines, standards, and codes of behaviour that must be decided upon and updated on a regular basis (Pan et al.,2021).

Establishment and Perfection of the Legal System

A comprehensive legal framework has to be created. Strict and cautious regulations are developed for each stage of AI, from laboratory research to clinical use, based on the "no harm" philosophy. The legal framework ought to be adaptable; that is, it shouldn't impede AI research and development. Regulations that have already been put in place must instead direct the development of AI. Laws cannot be fixed in stone; they must evolve with the times. As technology advances, laws and regulations based on AI technology from earlier stages will inevitably fall short of the requirements for monitoring. As a result, we must review the existing rules, swiftly resolve any new legal ambiguities or deficiencies, and enhance the legal terminology.

Improvement in Feasibility of AI in the Real World

It is necessary to give more robust AI solutions with a user-friendly interface, dependable outcomes, and steady operation to both individuals and communities. Then, production may be enhanced in accordance with the flaws that the users have pointed up. Therefore, there should be more ways to expose people to AI, such using live broadcast platforms, offline experiential shops in tandem with social media, and other strategies.

Above all, in terms of lowering costs, saving time, and minimising errors and disputes, AI solutions may really help patients and medical personnel. We think that after some time and effort, more people will come around to accepting AI solutions in the medical field.AI is also required in health services, particularly in the management of health services, to make medical judgements, particularly in the area of predictive analytics, which is used in patient diagnosis and treatment. Safety, effectiveness, privacy, information and consent, the ability to make one's own decisions, expenses, and access are a few ethical issues that AI clinical applications must address (Jin et al., 2021).

The virtual branch also addresses the core of artificial intelligence, encompassing the investigation of comprehensive knowledge processing for electronic health records, health management systems, and the active monitoring of physicians in the making of medical choices. A significant amount of health or other data must be entered into the AI model during training. When insufficient or incomplete data is utilised to train AI models, as well as when the training data does not accurately represent the target population, such bias may arise. Another issue is that boosting user trust does not always lead to the greatest choices. The user takes the AI's recommendations at face value when their level of trust is at its highest.

Even while AI is capable of making better decisions than humans, its limits imply that placing too much faith in the technology might have disastrous results. It can be difficult to build a strong trusting connection with AI because of its unpredictable behaviour as it develops. The model should have three characteristics in order to get the most trust: robustness, transparency, and fairness.

Furthermore, there are a lot of concerns about whether AI may exercise physicians' rights and duties regarding privacy, and the relevant legal framework is not quite ready for this development. Additionally, if AI is used to gather location data from cellphones, it may be utilised for clandestine monitoring. Since AI may also be used for cyberattacks, many are calling experts to become ready for AI to be utilised maliciously (Singh,2019).

CONCLUSION

Our research indicates that in order to apply AI to the healthcare industry, medical judgements must be made, especially when it comes to managing healthcare services and using predictive analytics for patient diagnosis and treatment. A few ethical concerns that AI clinical applications must address are safety, efficacy, privacy, information and consent, and costs. Positive or negative, every cause has its own viewpoints. Even if technology, AI in particular, might be unpredictable, a lot of things can go wrong. For this reason, much thought and testing must go into the implementation. As a consequence, these study findings address our concerns regarding the financial and welfare implications of AI in healthcare.) Only a small portion of all healthcare employment consists of menial and repetitive tasks. Although AI has a high upfront cost, the benefits over time more than offset this expense. I did see, nevertheless, that AI in healthcare only marginally improves efficiency. Certain medical services could also be too expensive initially. We could encounter these and other problems if we look at the advantages of AI in healthcare and how to apply it in the medical field. We will discuss potential government financing options, AI emotion development, and other potential methods to evaluate these issues.

REFERENCES

Ahmed, S. T., & Kadhem, S. M. (2021). Using Machine Learning via Deep Learning Algorithms to Diagnose the Lung Disease Based on Chest Imaging: A Survey. *International Journal of Interactive Mobile Technologies*, 15(16).

Avci, O., Abdeljaber, O., Kiranyaz, S., Hussein, M., Gabbouj, M., & Inman, D. J. (2021). A review of vibration-based damage detection in civil structures: From traditional methods to Machine Learning and Deep Learning applications. *Mechanical Systems and Signal Processing*, 147, 107077. 10.1016/j.ymssp.2020.107077

Binder, J., Ursu, O., Bologa, C., Jiang, S., Maphis, N., Dadras, S., Chisholm, D., Weick, J., Myers, O., Kumar, P., Yang, J. J., Bhaskar, K., & Oprea, T. I. (2022). Machine learning prediction and tau-based screening identifies potential Alzheimer's disease genes relevant to immunity. *Communications Biology*, 5(1), 125. 10.1038/s42003-022-03068-735149761

Che, M., Yao, K., Che, C., Cao, Z., & Kong, F. (2021). Knowledge-graph-based drug repositioning against COVID-19 by graph convolutional network with attention mechanism. *Future Internet*, 13(1), 13. 10.3390/fi13010013

Cui, Z., Yuan, Z., Wu, Y., Sun, X., & Yu, K. (2023). Intelligent Recommendation for Departments Based on Medical Knowledge Graph. *IEEE Access : Practical Innovations, Open Solutions*, 11, 25372–25385. 10.1109/ACCESS.2023.3254303

Gazzotti, R., Faron, C., Gandon, F., Lacroix-Hugues, V., & Darmon, D. (2022). Extending electronic medical records vector models with knowledge graphs to improve hospitalization prediction. *Journal of Biomedical Semantics*, 13(1), 1–20. 10.1186/s13326-022-00261-935193692

Gazzotti, R., Faron, C., Gandon, F., Lacroix-Hugues, V., & Darmon, D. (2022). Extending electronic medical records vector models with knowledge graphs to improve hospitalization prediction. *Journal of Biomedical Semantics*, 13(1), 1–20. 10.1186/s13326-022-00261-935193692

Guo, Y., Ren, X., Chen, Y. X., & Wang, T. J. (2019). Artificial intelligence meets Chinese medicine. *Chinese Journal of Integrative Medicine*, 25(9), 648–653. 10.1007/s11655-019-3169-531650485

Gupta, R., Srivastava, D., Sahu, M., Tiwari, S., Ambasta, R. K., & Kumar, P. (2021). Artificial intelligence to deep learning: Machine intelligence approach for drug discovery. *Molecular Diversity*, 25(3), 1315–1360. 10.1007/s11030-021-10217-333844136

Hao, F., & Zheng, K. (2022). Online disease identification and diagnosis and treatment based on machine learning technology. *Journal of Healthcare Engineering*, 2022, 2022. 10.1155/2022/673624935449857

Holzinger, A., Saranti, A., Hauschild, A. C., Beinecke, J., Heider, D., Roettger, R., & Pfeifer, B. (2023, August). Human-in-the-Loop Integration with Domain-Knowledge Graphs for Explainable Federated Deep Learning. In *International Cross-Domain Conference for Machine Learning and Knowledge Extraction* (pp. 45-64). Cham: Springer Nature Switzerland. 10.1007/978-3-031-40837-3_4

Jin, S., Zeng, X., Xia, F., Huang, W., & Liu, X. (2021). Application of deep learning methods in biological networks. *Briefings in Bioinformatics*, 22(2), 1902–1917. 10.1093/bib/bbaa04332363401

Jinlei, L., Wenchao, D., Nuo, C., Wenjing, L., Peirong, Q., Hui, Z., & Jie, W. (2022, July). Knowledge Graph of Artificial Intelligence in Medicine: A Scientometric Analysis. In *2022 7th IEEE International Conference on Data Science in Cyberspace (DSC)* (pp. 142-153). IEEE. 10.1109/DSC55868.2022.00026

Khan, P., Kader, M. F., Islam, S. R., Rahman, A. B., Kamal, M. S., Toha, M. U., & Kwak, K. S. (2021). Machine learning and deep learning approaches for brain disease diagnosis: Principles and recent advances. *IEEE Access : Practical Innovations, Open Solutions*, 9, 37622–37655. 10.1109/ACCESS.2021.3062484

Kou, Z., Shang, L., Zhang, Y., & Wang, D. (2022). Hc-covid: A hierarchical crowdsource knowledge graph approach to explainable covid-19 misinformation detection. *Proceedings of the ACM on Human-Computer Interaction, 6*(GROUP), (pp. 1-25). ACM. 10.1145/3492855

Kumar, A., Khan, S. F., Sodhi, R. S., Khan, I. R., Kumar, S., & Tamrakar, A. K. (2022, February). Deep learning Based Patient-Friendly Clinical Expert Recommendation Framework. In *2022 2nd International Conference on Innovative Practices in Technology and Management (ICIPTM)* (*Vol. 2*, pp. 736-741). IEEE. 10.1109/ICIPTM54933.2022.9754157

Lei, Z., Sun, Y., Nanehkaran, Y. A., Yang, S., Islam, M. S., Lei, H., & Zhang, D. (2020). A novel data-driven robust framework based on machine learning and knowledge graph for disease classification. *Future Generation Computer Systems*, 102, 534–548. 10.1016/j.future.2019.08.030

Li, Z. Q., Fu, Z. X., Li, W. J., Fan, H., Li, S. N., Wang, X. M., & Zhou, P. (2023). Prediction of Diabetic Macular Edema Using Knowledge Graph. *Diagnostics (Basel)*, 13(11), 1858. 10.3390/diagnostics1311185837296709

. Liu, H., & Lang, B. (2019). Machine learning and deep learning methods for intrusion detection systems: A survey. *Applied Sciences, 9*(20), 4396.

Long, J., Chen, Z., He, W., Wu, T., & Ren, J. (2020). An integrated framework of deep learning and knowledge graph for prediction of stock price trend: An application in Chinese stock exchange market. *Applied Soft Computing*, 91, 106205. 10.1016/j.asoc.2020.106205

Lv, H., Shi, L., Berkenpas, J. W., Dao, F. Y., Zulfiqar, H., Ding, H., Zhang, Y., Yang, L., & Cao, R. (2021). Application of artificial intelligence and machine learning for COVID-19 drug discovery and vaccine design. *Briefings in Bioinformatics*, 22(6), bbab320. 10.1093/bib/bbab32034410360

MacLean, F. (2021). Knowledge graphs and their applications in drug discovery. *Expert Opinion on Drug Discovery*, 16(9), 1057–1069. 10.1080/17460441.2021.191067333843398

Pan, X., Lin, X., Cao, D., Zeng, X., Yu, P. S., He, L., Nussinov, R., & Cheng, F. (2022). Deep learning for drug repurposing: Methods, databases, and applications. *Wiley Interdisciplinary Reviews. Computational Molecular Science*, 12(4), e1597. 10.1002/wcms.1597

Ramalingam, R., & Chinnaiyan, V. (2023). A comparative analysis of chronic obstructive pulmonary disease using machine learning, and deep learning. *Iranian Journal of Electrical and Computer Engineering*, 13(1), 389. 10.11591/ijece.v13i1.pp389-399

Ramalingam, R., & Chinnaiyan, V. (2023). A comparative analysis of chronic obstructive pulmonary disease using machine learning, and deep learning. *Iranian Journal of Electrical and Computer Engineering*, 13(1), 389. 10.11591/ijece.v13i1.pp389-399

Rana, M., & Bhushan, M. (2023). Machine learning and deep learning approach for medical image analysis: Diagnosis to detection. *Multimedia Tools and Applications*, 82(17), 26731–26769. 10.1007/s11042-022-14305-w36588765

Sharma, A., & Singh, B. (2022). Measuring Impact of E-commerce on Small Scale Business: A Systematic Review. *Journal of Corporate Governance and International Business Law*, 5(1).

Singh, B. (2019). Profiling Public Healthcare: A Comparative Analysis Based on the Multidimensional Healthcare Management and Legal Approach. *Indian Journal of Health and Medical Law*, 2(2), 1–5.

Singh, B. (2020). GLOBAL SCIENCE AND JURISPRUDENTIAL APPROACH CONCERNING HEALTHCARE AND ILLNESS. *Indian Journal of Health and Medical Law*, 3(1), 7–13.

Singh, B. (2022). Understanding Legal Frameworks Concerning Transgender Healthcare in the Age of Dynamism. *ELECTRONIC JOURNAL OF SOCIAL AND STRATEGIC STUDIES*, 3(1), 56–65. 10.47362/EJSSS.2022.3104

Singh, B. (2022). Relevance of Agriculture-Nutrition Linkage for Human Healthcare: A Conceptual Legal Framework of Implication and Pathways. *Justice and Law Bulletin*, 1(1), 44–49.

Singh, B. (2022). COVID-19 Pandemic and Public Healthcare: Endless Downward Spiral or Solution via Rapid Legal and Health Services Implementation with Patient Monitoring Program. *Justice and Law Bulletin*, 1(1), 1–7.

Singh, B. (2023). Blockchain Technology in Renovating Healthcare: Legal and Future Perspectives. In *Revolutionizing Healthcare Through Artificial Intelligence and Internet of Things Applications* (pp. 177-186). IGI Global.

Sujatha, R., Chatterjee, J. M., Jhanjhi, N. Z., & Brohi, S. N. (2021). Performance of deep learning vs machine learning in plant leaf disease detection. *Microprocessors and Microsystems*, 80, 103615. 10.1016/j.micpro.2020.103615

Wang, S., Lin, M., Ghosal, T., Ding, Y., & Peng, Y. (2022). Knowledge Graph Applications in Medical Imaging Analysis: A Scoping Review. *Health Data Science*, 2022, 9841548. 10.34133/2022/984154835800847

Wang, S., Xu, F., Li, Y., Wang, J., Zhang, K., Liu, Y., Wu, M., & Zheng, J. (2021). KG4SL: Knowledge graph neural network for synthetic lethality prediction in human cancers. *Bioinformatics (Oxford, England)*, 37(Supplement_1), i418–i425. 10.1093/bioinformatics/btab27134252965

Wu, X., Duan, J., Pan, Y., & Li, M. (2023). Medical knowledge graph: Data sources, construction, reasoning, and applications. *Big Data Mining and Analytics*, 6(2), 201–217. 10.26599/BDMA.2022.9020021

Xia, F., Sun, K., Yu, S., Aziz, A., Wan, L., Pan, S., & Liu, H. (2021). Graph learning: A survey. *IEEE Transactions on Artificial Intelligence*, 2(2), 109–127. 10.1109/TAI.2021.3076021

Xiong, W., Hoang, T., & Wang, W. Y. (2017). Deeppath: A reinforcement learning method for knowledge graph reasoning. *arXiv preprint arXiv:1707.06690*. 10.18653/v1/D17-1060

Ye, Q., Xu, R., Li, D., Kang, Y., Deng, Y., Zhu, F., Chen, J., He, S., Hsieh, C.-Y., & Hou, T. (2023). Integrating multi-modal deep learning on knowledge graph for the discovery of synergistic drug combinations against infectious diseases. *Cell Reports. Physical Science*, 4(8), 101520. 10.1016/j.xcrp.2023.101520

Zhu, D., Xie, L., Chen, B., Tan, J., Deng, R., Zheng, Y., & Andrew, W. H. (2023). Knowledge graph and deep learning based pest detection and identification system for fruit quality. *Internet of Things : Engineering Cyber Physical Human Systems*, 21, 100649. 10.1016/j.iot.2022.100649

Zhu, Y., Che, C., Jin, B., Zhang, N., Su, C., & Wang, F. (2020). Knowledge-driven drug repurposing using a comprehensive drug knowledge graph. *Health Informatics Journal*, 26(4), 2737–2750. 10.1177/146045822093710132674665

Chapter 5
Impact of Artificial Intelligence in the Health Sector:
Potential and Barriers

Sahil Lal
https://orcid.org/0000-0001-9827-3717
School of Law, Sharda University, India

Anjali Raghav
https://orcid.org/0009-0004-0248-7956
Sharda University, India

Manmeet Kaur Arora
Sharda University, India

Sanskriti Mishra
https://orcid.org/0009-0008-4225-1648
Sharda University, India

Bhupinder Singh
https://orcid.org/0009-0006-4779-2553
Sharda University, India

ABSTRACT

In the contemporary era, artificial intelligence (AI) has made tremendous strides. The emergence of artificial intelligence had a significant impact on upgrading transformation in the medical field. However, there is enormous optimism that the application of artificial intelligence would significantly enhance pivotal aspects of

DOI: 10.4018/979-8-3693-5976-1.ch005

health care. Furthermore, AI can also be useful for highly specific personal profiling, which plays a vital role in understanding and targeting behavioural patterns along with that it also has the potential to forecast healthcare. In addition, artificial intelligence systems are already increasing the precision and efficacy of diagnosis and treatment across a wide range of specialisations, especially when combined with the intense advancements in computer processing in the health sector. Nevertheless, there are many challenges with the application of artificial intelligence in medical practice which are often hindered by a series of problems, including problems of privacy, data security, lack of operational simplicity, the problem of medical ethics, and the risk of fraud in the health sector. However, recent developments in artificial intelligence and virtual health will be proven to have positive effects on the health sector. This chapter discusses the role of artificial intelligence in the medical field. It also discusses the potential and challenges of artificial intelligence applications in the health sector.

INTRODUCTION

Artificial intelligence is an important aspect of the research and development of new technologies (Abomhara et al., 2015). Besides this, it undoubtedly plays a major role in rapidly expanding healthcare and medicine (Raghavi et al.,2021). Artificial intelligence is being incorporated into acute care to bring a new intellectual perspective to the Health Sector. The potential for AI technologies and human intellect now together deliver healthcare (Lynn, 2019).

In recent years, artificial intelligence has become increasingly important in the Healthcare sector. The healthcare sector has benefited immensely from the use of Artificial Intelligence technology. The use of Artificial Intelligence in technology can also be referred to as the study of "intelligent agents," which are any agents or machines that can observe and comprehend their environment and take appropriate action to increase their chances of success (Guoguang et al. 2020). Moreover, a branch of computing science concerned with the development of intelligent computer systems is known as artificial intelligence (AI). This intelligent system can be compared to the behavioral intelligence of humans. AI can be used to create computers with reasoning skills like humans (Jimma & Bahiru,2003).

Besides this, AI plays a crucial part in advancing technologies for impressive advancement in the health sector. Moreover, the use of artificial intelligence in healthcare enhances disease diagnosis, classification, and prediction, which is advantageous to both patients and healthcare professionals. a rise in interest in Artificial Intelligence, partly due to significant advances in computing power and even more rapid growth in data generation (Muzeeb & Ashutosh,2021). The benefits of

AI have received a lot of attention in the medicinal literature. AI may use complex algorithms to 'learn' information from vast volumes of patient data and then use the findings to enhance medical care.

Additionally, based on the data, it might be able to learn and self-correct to increase accuracy. Specialists may receive assistance from AI frameworks that provide outstanding clinical data from journals, textbooks, and medical techniques in communicating sufficient patient attention. In human medical care, diagnostic and therapeutic errors are inevitable, but an AI system can minimize them. Additionally, an AI device collects crucial information from a large patient population to continuously conclude health risk warnings and predictions (Muzeeb & Ashutosh,2021).

Artificial Intelligence and the Health Sector: Significance

In today's era, advanced digital devices and technologies are extensively utilised nowadays but throughout the Fourth Industrial Revolution, the primary focus was on innovation and creating value across industries (Lee & Lim,2018). Additionally, this is also true concerning the healthcare industry. Besides this, digital technologies like artificial intelligence (AI), machine learning, smart sensors and robots, big data analytics, and the Internet of Things are being swiftly adopted by hospitals and care providers around the world, particularly in developed economies, to improve operational efficiency and care quality (Lee & Donhee,2018). Hence, Artificial Intelligence emerged as one of the pivotal pillars of advanced technology in all sectors. However, applications of AI-supported technologies have been widely used recently in healthcare facilities to increase the effectiveness of medical resources and the quality of treatment (Seong & Donhee,2019).

Moreover, due to its potential for revolutionary advancements in the treatment of human illnesses and public health, AI has sparked the interest of academics, clinicians, technology and program developers, and consumers in a broad spectrum of disciplines (Huiying et al., 2019). In Addition, AI-supported techniques have an enormous impact on enhancing clinicians' decisions for diagnosis and treatment since they acquire knowledge and diagnosis from medical research and patient treatment data (Filippo et al.,2013).

Although, there are some prime concerns about privacy, cybersecurity, data integrity, data ownership, the issue of data sharing by different organisational barriers, medical ethics concerns, responsibility for medical errors, and failure of systems risks are a few of the notable difficulties associated with the widespread use of AI and digital devices in Health Care System (Abomhara & Køien, 2015).

Additionally, Bertalan Mesko (Mesko, 2016) also emphasised the potential impact of AI-enabled gadgets, for example, personal assistants, on observing patients and care during times when healthcare providers are not accessible. Smart robots with AI help may also execute procedures and assist doctors' work with certain diagnoses, and treatment options, reducing costs and time, and improving reaction times to patient requirements (lee, 2018).

Artificial Intelligence for the Health Sector: Implementations

AI has made an innovative penetration into the healthcare industry (Panch et al.,2018). AI has aided doctors and other medical workers in medical imaging, epidemic, syndromic surveillance, geocoding health data, health information systems, and predictive modeling and decision support (Jiang F, 2017).

Diagnoses and Treatments: Innovative technologies are becoming progressively more crucial in enhancing medical professionals in practically every field, as highlighted in everyday life scenarios involving AI applications in the healthcare medical treatment of patients. To enhance the quality-of-care services provided using imaging techniques, AI has been shown to be especially efficient when confronted with a high number of radiological data (Pesapane et al.,2018). Patients as well as the work of healthcare providers will benefit immensely, if AI-based technologies increase the precision of patient treatments. Perhaps many intriguing applications of AI in healthcare are the promise of improved diagnosis and treatment accuracy. Healthcare providers may be able to identify problems faster with their assistance. AI can increase diagnostic accuracy by emulating human doctors' capacity to predict outcomes through rapidly analysing electronic medical records of patients on both a horizontal and vertical plane (Jimma & Bahiru,2003).

Application of Management: Machine learning, which enables probabilistic database matching, is another AI technology that is relevant to the claims and payment administration process. Insurance companies have a responsibility to confirm that the millions of claims are accurate.

Health insurers, governments, and health providers save time, money, and effort by accurately recognising, assessing, and correcting coding problems and false claims. between data matching and claim audits, inaccuracies in claims that fall between the cracks represent considerable income potential waiting to be realized. Once considered the ultimate hurdle between ineffective and beneficial health outcomes, patient engagement and adherence constitute the “last miles” issue in healthcare. Utilisation, financial results, and member satisfaction all improve as a result of patients adopting an active part in their health and care. Artificial intelligence and big data are being used more and more to address these issues.

Advantages and Assistance of AI in Healthcare Sector

In the recent decade, the introduction of AI in various fields has transformed the Conventional route and practices, especially in the field of medical diagnostics. With the help of AI diagnostic accuracy has enhanced efficiently as it can rapidly process vast amounts of data and Patterns for recognition. the traditional diagnostic procedures rely upon the healthcare professional expertise and experience, which often results in discrepancies in diagnoses. The introduction of AI technologies, for instance, machine learning algorithms and deep neural networks, has changed the scope of the healthcare sector by augmenting human insights with computational power and data-driven capabilities. With the help of AI-enabled diagnostic tools professionals can diagnose more precisely and faster medical images including X-rays, MRI, CT- Scans, etc. Laboratory results, and patient data for advanced identification of patterns, anomalies, and potential diagnoses (Meskó, B., & Görög, M. 2020).

The advantages of AI assistance in diagnostics in comparison to the conventional methods (Khanna, N et al 2022).

- It helps in the early detection of disease and conditions, which further leads to timely intervention and improved prognosis.
- AI algorithms can easily reduce the risk of misinterpretation enhance diagnostic accuracy and help healthcare professionals in interpreting complex medical images.
- AI technologies can efficiently analyse through vast databases like health records and genomic data, which will further identify subtle correlations and risk factors that might have been eluded by human observation (Date et al., 2023).

The high adoption of AI assistance in diagnostic procedures has many caveats to its potential usage, loopholes, challenges, and considerations. This includes issues regarding Patient data privacy and security, lack of regulatory controls, computation and algorithm transparency, and interpretability. This integration requires robust training and validation of AI Tools and AI models and vice versa with continuous monitoring and refinement to achieve optimal performance and safety (Khanna et al., 2022).

Adoption of AI in Genomic Medicine

Genomic medicine is a revolutionary healthcare strategy that provides genetically tailored medical care according to Individual genetic makeup, with advanced treatment strategies and insights into disease risk management. AI and genomic integration emerged as powerful tools for managing the complexities of the human genome and converting it into genomic data into actionable insights for clinical practice.

AI technologies brought revolutionary changes with the help of machine learning, deep learning, and natural language

- The Genomic Data Analysis: - With the help of AI Algorithms in genomic datasets, identification of patterns, and mutations associated with the disease vulnerability, prognosis, and treatment response can be analysed effectively (Bangash & Kullo, 2020).
- Variant Interpretations: - AI technologies advance in interpreting genetic variants by predicting their functional impact, working on variants that have a significant impact on clinical studies, and recommending suitable follow-up procedures.
- Risk prediction of Disease: - AI prototypes work with genomic and clinical data to predict an individual's capacity to develop certain diseases, which further chances of early interventions and prevention.
- Personalizes treatment regimens and Drug Discovery: - AI transformed personalized treatment regimens by predicting drug efficacy and toxicity based on an Individual's genomic profile.
- Clinical Decision support system: - Healthcare providers benefit from AI-powered decision support systems that incorporate genomic information into clinical decision-making, treatment guidance support, and management strategies (Bhatt, 2022).

AI- Assistance in Population Health Management

The comprehensive approach to improve the health outcomes of entire populations can be achieved efficiently and proactively with the help of Population health management (PHM) and Artificial Intelligence. It offers advanced analytics, predictive models and Decision support competencies to healthcare and policymakers.

Adoption of AI in Population Health Management (PHM)

Targeted Healthcare With AI: Predicting and Preventing Risks

AI algorithms act as powerful tools in healthcare, analyzing vast amounts of data like medical records, insurance claims, social factors, and even environmental influences. This analysis helps categorize individuals based on their risk of developing chronic illnesses or facing health complications. By identifying high-risk groups, AI empowers healthcare systems to implement targeted interventions and allocate resources more effectively, potentially preventing future health issues (Shaban-Nejad et al., 2018).

Tracking Diseases in Real-Time: AI for Outbreak Detection and Prevention

Imagine AI systems acting as vigilant sentinels, continuously monitoring the health of entire populations. By analyzing diverse data sources like social media, online searches, and even sensor data, these AI "watchers" can detect disease outbreaks and emerging threats faster than ever before. This allows for early warnings and rapid response efforts, potentially containing outbreaks before they spread widely (Al Kuwaiti et al., 2023).

Predicting the Future: AI Optimizes Healthcare Resources

Imagine healthcare providers equipped with a crystal ball, accurately predicting future needs for services, staffing, and budget allocation. This is the promise of AI-powered predictive analytics. By analyzing vast amounts of data, AI models can forecast future healthcare utilization, demand for specific services, and overall healthcare expenditures at a population level (Zeng et al., 2021). This empowers healthcare organizations to:

Optimize Resource Allocation: Resources can be strategically directed towards areas with anticipated high demand, ensuring efficient use of personnel, equipment, and facilities. Plan Capacity Effectively: Knowing future needs allows for proactive capacity planning, preventing bottlenecks and ensuring timely access to services for everyone.

Budget Wisely: Accurate predictions enable informed budgeting decisions, ensuring efficient use of financial resources and equitable distribution of services across the population. Ultimately, AI-powered predictive analytics helps healthcare organizations deliver efficient and equitable services, ensuring everyone receives the care they need when they need it (MacIntyre et al., 2023).

Bridging the Gaps: AI Streamlines Healthcare Coordination

A healthcare ecosystem where information flows effortlessly between doctors, social workers, and community organizations is the potential of AI-driven care coordination platforms. These platforms act as intelligent hubs, enabling: Early

Identification of High-Risk Patients: AI analyses data to identify individuals at increased risk of complications, allowing for proactive intervention and prevention.

Seamless Care Transitions: As patients move between different healthcare settings, AI platforms ensure smooth handovers and continuity of care, minimizing disruptions and potential complications.

Targeted Referrals: AI-powered systems match patients with the most appropriate specialists and services based on their specific needs, ensuring timely access to the right care. By facilitating communication and collaboration, AI platforms enhance care coordination, leading to better patient outcomes and a more efficient healthcare system.

Understanding Patients, Tailoring Interventions: AI for Healthier Communities

AI can delve into the complex world of health behaviors, uncovering the hidden influences that shape individual and community well-being by analysing vast amounts of data, AI algorithms can:

- Identify Key Factors: Uncover the individual and societal factors, like social determinants of health or environmental influences, that impact health outcomes.
- Tailor Interventions: Develop personalized behaviour change strategies, educational campaigns, and community programs based on specific needs and challenges.
- Promote Healthier Habits: Encourage healthy behaviours, disease prevention, and overall well-being through targeted interventions.

This deep understanding empowers healthcare professionals and communities to create effective solutions that address the root causes of health issues, leading to a healthier and more resilient population.

Legal Implications of AI in the Healthcare Sector

The healthcare sector is currently undergoing a major transition due to the amalgamation of Artificial Intelligence in its fundamental process by serving assistance in the treatment, diagnosis & care of patients. Further, it provides numerous benefits such as minimizing human error, affording accuracy in clinical decision-making, and many more. One of the major added advantages AI comes along with it with regards healthcare industry is that it can access and reach the remote parts of the society making it easier for all sections of society to avail medical facilities.

However, the integration of Artificial Intelligence in the healthcare industry presents various ethical & critical issues as well such as the privacy & security of data, ethical issues concerning the consent of the patients, and a very pertinent issue regarding the liability of artificial intelligence for the error committed by it. Further, the rapid emergence of AI has also posed a direct threat to individuals by giving rise to loss of employment. Hence, the following part of this paper will discuss the advantages, challenges, and legal implications of AI's integration into the healthcare industry.

Transforming Healthcare: Benefits of AI

The advent of new-age technology such as Artificial Intelligence is transformative in nature and with its rapid growth it has changed the dynamics of the healthcare industry. According to the World Economic Forum (WEF) report, by the year 2025, India's expected AI expenditure is to reach \$11.78 billion and it is further expected to add \$ 1 trillion by 2035 to India's economy. Furthermore, the integration of AI in the healthcare sector is predicted to rise in 2023 from \$14.6 to \$102.7 billion by 2028. (J, 2023)

Utilising the ability of AI, the healthcare industry is poised for a revolution. No longer restricted to the realm of science fiction, AI tools act as a keen-eyed diagnostician, swiftly and precisely identifying and detecting diseases & medical conditions. The intricate medical images from X-rays to MRIs and CT scans, once the sole domain of human experts are now analyzed by AI with precision and accuracy. This newfound ability empowers healthcare professionals to detect diseases and medical conditions at their earliest stages, potentially paving the way for earlier interventions and improved patient outcomes. It is a testament to the ingenuity of human innovation, harnessing the power of AI to guide in a new era of medical care. With the integration of AI, repetitive administrative tasks can be automated by AI tools, which would reduce the burden on the medical professional and allow them to invest more time and focus on their patients. Further, AI would ensure minimizing human error and provide precision and accuracy.

Due to the scarcity of doctors and medical/healthcare professionals in many rural, urban, and remote areas, it becomes stringent for people to avail healthcare services they require; therefore, AI becomes a valuable tool in such situations. AI systems can provide basic healthcare services and help diagnose illness, making healthcare more accessible to everyone. However, it is pertinent to note that such AI assistance must be acquired and used responsibly in the healthcare industry. This means addressing the concerns about data privacy, ethics, and regulations to ensure that patient's well-being and safety are the utmost priority.

Challenges In Integrating AI In the Healthcare Sector

While advancements in AI hold great promise for the healthcare sector, concerns remain regarding its ethical and responsible implementation. The World Health Organisation (WHO) in its 1st global report on AI in Health entitled, "Ethics and Governance of Artificial Intelligence for Health" (WHO, *Ethics and Governance of Artificial Intelligence for Health* 2021) highlighted the potential risks associated with Artificial Intelligence. The reports provide caution against over-emphasizing the benefits of AI and urge caution regarding:

- Data Privacy & Security: the report raises concerns about the collection and use of sensitive health data in AI systems. It emphasizes the need for robust data security measures to protect patient privacy.
- Patient Safety: the report emphasizes the importance of ensuring patient safety when integrating AI into the healthcare sector. It stresses the need for thorough testing and evaluation to ensure the accuracy and reliability of AI algorithms.
- Algorithmic Bias: the report acknowledges the risk of bias being encoded into AI algorithms, which could lead to unfair and discriminatory outcomes for certain patient groups. It underscores the need for diverse datasets and transparent development processes to mitigate the risk.

Dr Tedros Adhanom Ghebreyesus (*Director General of WHO*), emphasized the negative aspects of AI as well when he stated, "Like all new technology, artificial intelligence holds enormous potential for improving the health of millions of people around the world, but like all technology, it can also be misused and cause harm." (Srivastav, 2023)

Many advanced AI systems rely on complex deep learning models that achieve highly accurate results but cannot often explain how they reached those conclusions. In the healthcare sector, where decisions directly impact human lives, transparency is crucial for both doctors and patients to understand the reasoning behind AI-driven recommendations. Therefore, implement consequences that must be tackled before widespread adoption.

Data Privacy and Security

The deployment of AI in healthcare raises critical concerns regarding data privacy and security, given the sensitive and personal nature of medical information. These concerns carry significant potential consequences and require diligent management.

- Firstly, the rise in cybercrime poses a serious threat to sensitive patient data accessed by AI systems, which often require comprehensive medical histories. Maintaining the confidentiality of this information is paramount to protecting patient privacy. Addressing unauthorized access, data breaches, and cyberattacks becomes crucial before AI deployment.
- Secondly, collaborations with third-party AI vendors necessitate vigilance. Healthcare organizations must ensure these vendors adhere to stringent data privacy and security standards. A thorough review of vendor practices and data protection protocols is essential before entrusting patient information.

By proactively addressing these data privacy and security concerns, the healthcare sector can leverage the potential of AI while safeguarding patient trust and well-being.

Ethical Considerations in AI Driven Healthcare

Integrating AI into healthcare presents crucial ethical considerations due to the inherent trust healthcare providers hold for their patient's well-being. Several key factors require careful consideration:

i. ***Patient Preference and Consent*:** Recognizing that some patients may express a strong preference for human interaction and distrust AI-driven decisions, particularly in critical situations, is vital. Obtaining informed consent throughout the process is paramount, ensuring patients understand the AI's role and purpose in their care.
ii. ***Transparency and Trust:*** Maintaining transparency in AI algorithms and decision-making processes is essential. Both patients and healthcare providers deserve to understand the reasoning behind AI-generated recommendations, fostering trust and informed decision-making.
iii. ***Mitigating Bias:*** Addressing potential biases in AI systems is critical. Improper training and testing can lead to disparities in care, perpetuating existing inequalities. Therefore, understanding and mitigating potential biases must be addressed before implementation.

iv. ***Patient Autonomy:*** Emphasizing patient autonomy remains paramount. The decision to incorporate AI in their care ultimately rests with the patient. If a patient expresses discomfort or declines AI involvement, their wishes must be respected and alternative pathways explored.

By proactively addressing these ethical considerations, the healthcare sector can ensure responsible AI integration that upholds patient autonomy, trust, and equitable care.

Liability and Accountability

Integrating AI into healthcare raises critical questions regarding accountability and liability, areas where current practices around the world remain unprepared. Unlike traditional diagnostic tools, AI cannot be held directly accountable for its decisions. This necessitates a clear framework assigning responsibility throughout the entire development and deployment process. Determining who bears the weight of errors made by AI in healthcare presents a complex ethical dilemma. Patients deserve clear avenues for recourse in the event of AI-related errors. Legal frameworks need to evolve to address liability concerns, particularly when AI systems influence clinical decisions and treatments. Developers and vendors of these AI systems might share liability when their solutions impact clinical decisions or patient care. They carry the responsibility of ensuring their systems are safe, effective, and compliant with regulations. Consequently, establishing clear mechanisms for assigning liability and accountability in case of errors becomes crucial before widespread AI adoption in healthcare.

Loss of Employment

The potential impact of AI on healthcare employment has sparked concerns about widespread job losses. While automation may streamline routine tasks, it is important to remember that AI systems themselves require human oversight and operation. While AI can undoubtedly expedite and simplify tasks formerly performed by humans, it's unlikely to completely replace them. In specific circumstances, where tasks lack complexity and require minimal human intervention, some healthcare providers might see their roles shift or be replaced by AI. It is important to emphasize that this likely affects a very small number of positions. Furthermore, the adoption of AI may present opportunities for certain doctors. For instance, well-versed physicians utilizing AI could potentially take over roles currently held by those less comfortable with advanced technology. However, it's crucial to acknowledge that no technology can replicate the irreplaceable human touch, empathy, and emotional support that healthcare providers offer patients. The unique level of emotional connection established by humans simply cannot be replicated by AI. Therefore, while AI undoubtedly holds transformative potential for healthcare, its impact on employment is anticipated to be nuanced and unlikely to result in mass job losses. Instead, it may necessitate shifts in existing roles and create new opportunities within the healthcare landscape.

Unlike humans, AI systems may struggle to adapt to unforeseen circumstances or rapidly evolving patient conditions, situations not explicitly accounted for in their training data. Furthermore, healthcare decisions often involve nuanced ethical and legal considerations that necessitate human judgment and empathy. While AI can play a valuable role in assisting with such decision-making, entrusting patient lives solely to its calculations would be unwise. Therefore, it's crucial to view AI as a tool within the healthcare ecosystem, designed to enhance and refine care, not replace human involvement entirely. Its core function should be to streamline tasks, improve efficiency, and provide valuable insights, not eradicate human presence from the sector.

Regulating AI in Healthcare: Legal Considerations and Challenges

The rapid rise of AI has sparked discussions about its potential within healthcare, but this potential necessitates a robust regulatory framework. Regulations are crucial to ensure safe and ethical practices in this sensitive domain. Healthcare inherently involves complex issues like data privacy, security, ethical considerations, and liability in case of errors. Establishing clear regulations for AI application in healthcare becomes even more critical to address these challenges and ensure patient well-being remains paramount.

Indian Council of Medical Research (ICMR) in its report entitled, '*Ethical Guidelines for Application of Artificial Intelligence in Biomedical Research and Healthcare*' emphasized, "AI-assisted platforms available for the benefit of the largest section of common people with safety and highest precision possible." (*ICMR,* 2023)

Acknowledging the nascent stage of AI regulation in healthcare, even in developed nations, the document emphasizes the need for regular internal and external audits to guarantee optimal AI system performance. These audits, ideally made public, aim for seamless human-technology integration. Patient consent remains paramount under the ICMR regulations, which further prioritize privacy and data protection throughout AI development and deployment. Additionally, the document addresses potential misuse, exploitation, and safety concerns associated with AI in the healthcare sector.

India has taken proactive steps to integrate AI technologies into its healthcare sector through several key policies and initiatives. Notably, the National Health Policy (2017) establishes a framework for promoting innovation and accessibility in healthcare (Welfare, 2017), while the National Digital Health Blueprint (NDHB 2019) outlines a roadmap for digitizing the healthcare system. Additionally, the proposed Digital Information Security in Healthcare Act (2018) focuses on ensuring data privacy and security within the healthcare domain. Together, these initiatives pave the way for the establishment of the National Data Health Authority, which will facilitate secure Health information exchange and ultimately contribute to a more streamlined and efficient healthcare system.

CONCLUSION

AI holds great promise in healthcare. It can analyze medical images, manage complex data, aid in drug development, and even assist in diagnosing illnesses. By providing valuable insights, AI can help healthcare workers make better decisions. However, it's important to remember that AI is a powerful tool, not a replacement for human expertise. The best approach is to view AI and healthcare professionals as partners, working together for improved patient care. As AI technology continues to develop, doctors, policymakers, technology experts, and legal professionals must collaborate. Together, they can create guidelines and laws to ensure AI is used safely, transparently, and effectively within the healthcare system.

REFERENCES

Abomhara, M., & Køien, G. (2015). Cyber Security and the Internet of Things: Vulnerabilities, Threats, Intruders and Attacks. *Journal of Cybersecurity*, 65–88.

Al Kuwaiti, A., Nazer, K., Al-Reedy, A., Al-Shehri, S., Al-Muhanna, A., Subbarayalu, A. V., Al Muhanna, D., & Al-Muhanna, F. A. (2023). A Review of the Role of Artificial Intelligence in Healthcare. *Journal of Personalized Medicine*, 13(6), 951. 10.3390/jpm1306095137373940

Bangash, H., & Kullo, I. J. (2020, December 29). Implementation Science to Increase Adoption of Genomic Medicine: An Urgent Need. *Journal of Personalized Medicine*, 11(1), 19. 10.3390/jpm1101001933383675

Bhatt, P. (2022, March 15). AI adoption in the hiring process – important criteria and extent of AI adoption. *Foresight*, 25(1), 144–163. 10.1108/FS-07-2021-0144

Date, P., Pimprale, V., & Mandke, S. (2023, December 26). Explorative study on potential of machine learning and artificial intelligence for improved healthcare diagnosis and treatment. *Journal of Autonomous Intelligence*, 7(3). Advance online publication. 10.32629/jai.v7i3.1084

Filippo Amato, A. L.-M. (2013). Artificial neural networks in medical diagnosis. *Journal of Applied Biomedicine*, 11(2), 47–58. 10.2478/v10136-012-0031-x

Guoguang Rong, A. M. (2020). Artificial Intelligence in Healthcare: Review and Prediction Case Studies. *Engineering (Beijing)*, 6(3), 291–301. 10.1016/j.eng.2019.08.015

Huiying Liang, B. Y. (2019). Evaluation and accurate diagnoses of pediatric diseases using artificial intelligence. *Nature Medicine*, 25(3), 433–438. 10.1038/s41591-018-0335-930742121

Indian Council of Medical Research (ICMR), Ethical Guidelines for Application of Artificial Intelligence in Biomedical Research and Healthcare. (2023). Retrieved January 12, 2024, from https://main.icmr.nic.in/sites/default/files/upload_documents/Ethical_Guidelines_AI_Healthcare_2023.pdf

J, J. (2023a, June 30). Rapid transformation. artificial intelligence in indian healthcare: a promising future with challenges. *The Hindu*. https://www.thehindubusinessline.com/news/science/artificial-intelligence-in-indian-healthcare-a-promising-future-with challenges/article67015361.ece#:~:text=AI%20expenditure%20in%20India%20is,to%20%24102.7%20Billion%20by%202028.

Jiang, F. J. Y., Jiang, Y., Zhi, H., Dong, Y., Li, H., Ma, S., Wang, Y., Dong, Q., Shen, H., & Wang, Y. (2017). Artificial intelligence in healthcare: Past, Present and Future. *Stroke and Vascular Neurology*, 2(4), 230–243. 10.1136/svn-2017-00010129507784

. Jimma, B. L. (March 2003). Artifical Intelligence in the Health Care: A Bibliometic Analysis. *Telematics and Informatics Reports, 4.*

Khanna, N. N., Maindarkar, M. A., Viswanathan, V., Fernandes, J. F. E., Paul, S., Bhagawati, M., Ahluwalia, P., Ruzsa, Z., Sharma, A., Kolluri, R., Singh, I. M., Laird, J. R., Fatemi, M., Alizad, A., Saba, L., Agarwal, V., Sharma, A., Teji, J. S., Al-Maini, M., & Suri, J. S. (2022). Economics of Artificial Intelligence in Healthcare: Diagnosis vs. Treatment. *Healthcare (Basel)*, 10(12), 2493. 10.3390/healthcare1012249336554017

Lavigne, M., Mussa, F., Creatore, M. I., Hoffman, S. J., & Buckeridge, D. L. (2019). A population health perspective on artificial intelligence. *Healthcare Management Forum*, 32(4), 173–177. 10.1177/084047041984842831106580

Lee, D. (2019). Effects of Key Value Co-creation Elements in the Healthcare System: Focusing on Technology Applications. *Service Business*, 13(2), 389–417. 10.1007/s11628-018-00388-9

Lee, S. (2018). *Living Innovation: From Value Creation to the Greater Good*. Emerald Publishing Limited. 10.1108/9781787567139

Lee, D. (2018). Strategies for technology-driven service encounters for patient experience satisfaction in hospitals. *International Journal Technological Forecasting and Social Change*, 118-127.

Lynn, L. A. (2019). Artificial intelligence systems for complex decision-making in acute Care Medicine: A Review. *Patient Safety in Surgery*, 13(1), 6. 10.1186/s13037-019-0188-230733829

MacIntyre, C. R., Chen, X., Kunasekaran, M., Quigley, A., Lim, S., Stone, H., Paik, H. Y., Yao, L., Heslop, D., Wei, W., Sarmiento, I., & Gurdasani, D. (2023, March). Artificial intelligence in public health: The potential of epidemic early warning systems. *The Journal of International Medical Research*, 51(3), 030006052311593. 10.1177/0300060523115933536967669

Mesko, B. (2016). Artificial Intelligence Will Redesign Healthcare. *Brain.*

Meskó, B., & Görög, M. (2020). A short guide for medical professionals in the era of artificial intelligence. *NPJ Digital Medicine*, 3(1), 126. 10.1038/s41746-020-00333-z33043150

Muzeeb Ur Rehman, A. P. (2021). Review on Artificial Intelligence in Healthcare. *Innovations*, •••, 66.

Panch, T. S. P., Szolovits, P., & Atun, R. (2018). Artifcial intelligence, machine learning and Health System. *Journal of Global Health*, 8(2), 020303. 10.7189/jogh.08.02030330405904

Pesapane, F., Codari, M., & Sardanelli, F. (2018). *Artificial Intelligence in Medical Imaging: Threat or Opportunity? Radiologists again at tEuprohe Forefront of Innovation in Medicine*. European Radiology Exprimental.

Ragavi, V. S., Santha Sheela, A. C., & Narayanan Kannaiyan, G. (2021). Impact of Artificial Intelligence in the field of Health. *Journal of Physics: Conference Series*, 1831(1), 012006. 10.1088/1742-6596/1831/1/012006

Secinaro, S., Calandra, D., Secinaro, A., Muthurangu, V., & Biancone, P. (2021). The role of artificial intelligence in healthcare: A structured literature review. *BMC Medical Informatics and Decision Making*, 21(1), 125. 10.1186/s12911-021-01488-933836752

Seong No Yoon, D. L. (2019). Artificial Intelligence and Robots in Healthcare: What are the Success Factors for Technology-based Service Encounters? *International Journal of Healthcare Management*, 12(3), 218–225. 10.1080/20479700.2018.1498220

Srivastav, S. (2023, June 19). AI in healthcare: the regulations conundrum. *Financial Express*. https://www.financialexpress.com/healthcare/healthtech/ai-in-healthcare-the-regulations-conundrum/3131045/

World Health Organization (WHO). (n.d.). (rep.). *Ethics and Governance of Artificial Intelligence for Health*. WHO. https://www.ncdirindia.org/Downloads/WHO_AI_Ethics.pdf

Zeng, D., Cao, Z., & Neill, D. B. (2021). Artificial intelligence–enabled public health surveillance—From local detection to global epidemic monitoring and control. *Artificial Intelligence in Medicine*, 437–453. 10.1016/B978-0-12-821259-2.00022-3

Chapter 6
Intersection of Intellectual Property, Medicines, and Legal Concerns

Manvendra Singh
https://orcid.org/0000-0001-8750-5877
Sharda University, India

Vaishali Arora
Sharda University, India

Kushagra Kulshreshta
https://orcid.org/0009-0002-9445-120X
Raja Mahendra Pratap University, Aligarh, India

ABSTRACT

Intellectual property is a group of property that contains intangible creations of the intellect of man. There are many types of intellectual property; the most renowned types are patents, copyrights, trademarks, and trade secrets. The intersection of intellectual property (IP), medicines, and legal concerns in India represents a dynamic landscape shaped by a complex interplay of domestic laws, international agreements, and socio-economic factors. This abstract provides a comprehensive overview of the multifaceted issues surrounding IP rights, access to medicines, and legal frameworks in the Indian context. India's pharmaceutical industry holds a prominent position globally, renowned for its production of affordable generic medicines. However, the introduction of product patents through amendments to the Patents Act in 2005 marked a significant shift in the IP landscape, posing

DOI: 10.4018/979-8-3693-5976-1.ch006

challenges to the country's generic drug industry while aiming to align with international trade duty, specially under the Agreement on Trade-Related Aspects of Intellectual Property Rights (TRIPS). The implications of patents on access to medicines in India are profound. While patents promote innovation, they also have the potential to create monopolies, leading to high drug prices and limited accessibility, especially for marginalized populations. The debate surrounding the protection of intellectual property and public health imperatives has been aimed at issues such as compulsory licensing, parallel importation, and patent enforcement. India's proactive use of TRIPS flexibilities, including compulsory licensing, has been instrumental in addressing public health challenges. Compulsory licensing allows the government to license patented drugs to third-party manufacturers without the permission of the patent holder, thence facilitating the production of affordable generic versions of essential medicines. High-profile cases of compulsory licensing for drugs treating diseases like HIV/AIDS and cancer highlight India's commitment to ensuring access to life-saving treatments. Legal concerns surrounding IP rights and medicines extend beyond patents to encompass issues such as data exclusivity, regulatory barriers, and the associate between laws relating to intellectual property and competition law. On other hand, regulatory framework aims to balance innovation incentives with public health objectives, challenges persist in areas such as patent prosecution, enforcement, and the granting of ever greening patents. Recent developments in India's IP landscape, including judicial decisions, policy initiatives, and international trade negotiations, continue to shape the discourse on IP rights and medicines. The introduction of the National Intellectual Property Rights Policy in 2016 reflects India's commitment to fostering innovation while safeguarding public health interests. Additionally, initiatives such as the Drug Price Control Order aim to regulate drug pricing to ensure affordability and accessibility. The complex interplay between intellectual property, medicines, and legal concerns in India underscores the need for a holistic approach. Balancing the interests of innovators, generic manufacturers, and public health requires collaborative efforts, evidence-based policy interventions, and transparent regulatory mechanisms. Prioritizing access to affordable and quality medicines remains a fundamental imperative in achieving health equity and promoting socio-economic development.

INTRODUCTION

In today's rapidly evolving global marketplace, the value of ideas often surpasses that of physical assets. Intellectual property (IP) has emerged as a cornerstone of modern business strategy, providing individuals and organizations with the means to protect their creative works, innovations, and intangible assets. From groundbreaking inventions to artistic masterpieces, intellectual property encompasses a wide array of creations that drive innovation, fuel economic growth, and shape our cultural landscape. Intellectual property rights are necessary for enhancing innovation, skills, creativity, and economic growth (Rauf & Tamang, 2023). By providing innovators, a legal option to protect their intellectual assets, IP rights incentivize investment in research and development, spur technological advancement, and drive entrepreneurship and job creation. Furthermore, intellectual property rights promote the dissemination of knowledge and technology by enabling creators to license their innovations and creative works to others for commercial use. This licensing framework encourages collaboration, fosters the exchange of ideas, and facilitates the development of new products, services, and industries.

Despite its numerous benefits, the safeguard of intellectual property faces various challenges in the online era. Piracy, counterfeiting, infringement, and other forms of unauthorized exploitation pose significant threats to the cost of intellectual property and the interests of creators and innovators (Tenni et al., 2022). Additionally, the global nature of intellectual property presents complexities in terms of enforcement, harmonization of laws, and cross-border protection. To address these challenges concerted efforts are required from governments, businessmen, and international organizations to strengthen intellectual property rights, enhance enforcement mechanisms, and promote awareness and respect for intellectual property rights (Teremetskyi, 2021). By providing creators and innovators with the legal protections to safeguard their ideas, creations, and innovations, intellectual property rights attract investors towards research and development, spur technological advancement, and drive entrepreneurship among large number of people. As we navigate the complexities of the digital age, it is essential to recognize the value of intellectual property and the importance of protecting and promoting intellectual property rights (Kianzad & Wested, 2021). By fostering a supportive environment for innovation and creativity, we can unlock the full potential of intellectual property to drive sustainable economic growth, foster cultural expression, and improve the quality of life for people around the world.

Important Definitions of "Intellectual Property"

Intellectual property rights (IPR) are territorial rights by which owner can sell, buy or license his Intellectual Property (IP) similar to physical property.

World Intellectual Property Organization (WIPO)

"Intellectual property (IP) refers to creations of the mind, such as inventions; literary and artistic works; designs; and symbols, names, and images used in commerce."

United States Patent and Trademark Office (USPTO)

"Intellectual property (IP) refers to creations of the intellect for which a monopoly is assigned to designated owners by law. Intellectual property rights (IPRs) are the protections granted to the creators of IP, and include patents, copyrights, trademarks, and trade secrets. "

European Union Intellectual Property Office (EUIPO)

"Intellectual property (IP) refers to creations of the mind, such as inventions, literary and artistic works, designs, and symbols, names, and images used in commerce. IP rights protect the interests of creators by giving them exclusive rights over their creations for a certain period."

Cornell Law School Legal Information Institute

"Intellectual property (IP) refers to creations of the mind: inventions; literary and artistic works; and symbols, names, images, and designs used in commerce.".

The World Trade Organization (WTO)

"Intellectual property (IP) refers to creations of the mind, such as inventions; literary and artistic works; designs; and symbols, names, and images used in commerce. IP rights protect these creations by giving the creators exclusive rights over their use for a certain period."

United Nations Conference on Trade and Development (UNCTAD)

"Intellectual property (IP) refers to creations of the mind, such as inventions, literary and artistic works, and symbols, names, and images used in commerce. IP rights protect these creations by granting creators exclusive rights over their use for a certain period."

These definitions provide a comprehensive overview of intellectual property, highlighting its broad scope and significance in fostering innovation, creativity, and economic development worldwide.

Types of Intellectual Property

The development of any society directly depends on IPR and its policy frame work. At its core, intellectual property refers to the legal rights given to the innovators for their creations. These rights help creators to safeguard their works from unauthorized use or exploitation, thereby incentivizing innovation and creativity.

Intellectual property can be said to be of following types:

Patents: Patents are long understood to involve a trade-off or balance. A patent is a document issued by government to the inventor granting permission to exclusively make, use and sell on disclosure of the invention for a definite period of time. Unlike patents, monopoly existed where inventions were not disclosed and exclusively sold. Patents provide exclusive rights to the inventor for a limited period of time, granting them the ability to prevent others from using, or selling the patented invention without the permission of patent holder (Lee et al., 2021). Patents have a wide range of inventions, including new processes, products, machines, and compositions of matter. Securing a patent involves a rigorous application process, including a thorough examination by patent offices to ensure that the invention meets the criteria of novelty, non-obviousness, and utility. Once granted, patents serve as a valuable asset for businesses, attracting investment, and facilitating technology transfer through licensing agreements. However, obtaining a patent is sometimes a complex and costly endeavor, requiring extensive research, documentation, and legal expertise. Furthermore, patents are subject to public disclosure, meaning that inventors must weigh the benefits of exclusivity against the risk of disclosing sensitive information to competitors.

Copyrights: Copyright is a branch of Intellectual Property Rights and an exclusive legal right given by the judiciary to the creator on his creation. Copyrights protect original works of authorship from unauthorized copying, distribution, performance, and display. These works encompass a broad spectrum of creative expressions, including literary works, musical compositions, films, softwares, architectural designs and artistic creations. Unlike patents, copyrights automatically apply upon creation, providing creators with immediate protection for their works. Copyrights are used to allow creators to reproduce, distribute, and display their works, and allowing them to control how their creations are used and monetized. Copyright infringement has now a days become a grave concern, as the ease of copying and distributing digital work has made it easier for individuals to infringe upon the rights of creators (Stim, 2024). As such, effective copyright enforcement strategies, including digital rights management (DRM) technologies and legal recourse against infringers, are essential for protecting the value of creative works and ensuring fair compensation for creators.

Trademarks: A trademark is an easily recognizable symbol, phrase, or word that denotes a specific product. Trademarks are used to safeguard brands, logos, slogans, and other identifiers that distinguish goods and services in the marketplace. By securing exclusive rights to their trademarks, businesses can build brand recognition, establish consumer trust, and prevent competitors from misleading consumers or diluting their brand value. Trademarks serve as the bedrock of brand identity and consumer trust in the marketplace. They encompass logos, brands, tag lines, and other identifiers that distinguish goods and services from competitors. By securing exclusive rights to their trademarks, businesses can build brand recognition, establish consumer loyalty, and protect their reputation from unauthorized use or infringement. Trademark protection enables businesses to prevent competitors from using confusingly similar marks that may deceive consumers or dilute the distinctiveness of their brand. Through trademark registration, businesses gain enhanced legal remedies and enforcement mechanisms, including the ability to pursue legal action against infringers and counterfeiters. Maintaining and enforcing trademark rights requires ongoing vigilance, including monitoring the marketplace for unauthorized use, taking swift action against infringers, and defending against challenges to the validity of the trademark.

Trade Secrets: "The secret of the business is to know something that nobody knows." - Aristotle Onassis. Trade secrets cover confidential information that provide businesses with a competitive advantage. Formulas, recipes, algorithms, customer lists, and manufacturing processes are covered in trade secrets. Unlike patents, which require disclosure to the public, trade secrets rely on confidentiality to maintain their value. Protecting trade secrets requires security measures like restricted access, non-disclosure agreements (NDAs), and employee training programs. The most essential part of the trade secrets is that their secrecy as opposed to the novelty. By safeguarding their trade secrets, business owners can preserve their competitive edge and prevent competitors from unauthorized access to proprietary information. In the event of a misappropriation or unauthorized disclosure of trade secrets, businesses can pursue legal remedies, including injunctions, damages, and trade secret theft prosecutions (Upadhyay & Rathee, 2020). However, proving trade secret misappropriation can be challenging, requiring evidence of unauthorized access, use, or disclosure of the protected information.

However, the protection of intellectual property is not without its challenges. Effective intellectual property management requires a comprehensive approach that encompasses legal protection, enforcement, licensing, and strategic planning. By leveraging intellectual property rights strategically, individuals and organizations can monetize their innovations, attract investment, foster collaboration, and drive sustainable growth in the knowledge-based economy. Intellectual property serves as a stimulus to innovation, creativity, and development, empowering creators and innovators to unleash their potential and create value for society (Chidede, 2022). As we navigate the complexities of the digital age, protecting and promoting intellectual property rights will remain essential for building a prosperous and vibrant future built on innovation, ingenuity, and imagination.

Issues surrounding intellectual property rights:

a) ***Balancing Innovation and Access to Knowledge:*** Intellectual property rights are designed to motivate innovation by providing creators and inventors exclusive rights over their creations for a limited period. Excessive protection can however cause hinderance to easy access to essential knowledge and technologies (Mamanazarov, 2023). Striking a balance between rewarding innovators and ensuring access to knowledge such as healthcare, education for societal benefit is a big challenge that requires focused consideration of competing interests and values.
b) ***Digital Technologies and Copyright Enforcement:*** The advent of digital technologies has transformed the path of production, distribution and consumption. While digital platforms offer unprecedented opportunities for creativity and expression, they also pose significant challenges in terms of copyright enforcement (Hanafi et al., 2023). The ease of copying and sharing online content has led to inevitable piracy, undermining the livelihoods of creators and the viability of creative industries. Effective enforcement measures must navigate legal, technological, and ethical considerations to protect the rights of copyright holders while preserving the principles of freedom of expression and access to information.
c) ***Socio-Economic Implications:*** Intellectual property rights intersect with broader socio-economic issues, including access to essential medicines, cultural diversity, and indigenous knowledge. The debate over patents on life-saving drugs hovers between rising pharmaceutical innovation and making affordable medicines. Addressing these socio-economic implications requires policymakers and stakeholders to consider the broader social and ethical implications of intellectual property rights and to develop policies that promote equitable access to knowledge and resources.
d) ***Globalization and International Trade:*** Globalization has intensified the need for harmonized intellectual property standards and enforcement mechanisms to facilitate international trade and investment. Several International agreements set minimum standards of enforcement and protection for intellectual property rights, aiming to create a standard field for global businesses. However, disparities in economic development, legal systems, and cultural norms present challenges in implementing and enforcing these standards across countries.

e) ***Emerging Technologies and Ethical Considerations:*** The rapid pace of technological innovation, including advancements in artificial intelligence, biotechnology, and blockchain, raises new ethical considerations in the realm of intellectual property rights. Issues such as the ownership of AI-generated inventions, the patentability of genetic sequences, and the protection of data and algorithms present complex challenges that require careful consideration of legal and societal factors (Jorstad, 2020). Addressing these challenges requires interdisciplinary collaboration and ongoing dialogue among policymakers, technologists, ethicists, and other stakeholders.

The multifaceted issues surrounding intellectual property rights demand a nuanced and holistic approach that considers the interplay of legal, ethical, economic, and social indicators. Access to Medicines explored several critical barriers to drug accessibility and affordability (Gerke et al.,2020). Stakeholders can work together to address these challenges and create a more sustainable intellectual property system that promotes innovation, protects rights, and is in the interest of public.

Legal Framework of Intellectual Property in Indian Context

In the Indian context, intellectual property rights (IPR) are governed by a comprehensive legal framework that encompasses various statutes and regulations aimed at protecting and promoting innovation, creativity, and economic development. In India, the legal framework for intellectual property is designed to align with international standards while addressing the country's unique socio-economic challenges and cultural diversity.

The primary legislation governing intellectual property rights in India includes:

1) ***The Patents Act, 1970:*** India's principal regulation for patents is The Patents Act, 1970, which exclusively gives inventors rights in respect of their discoveries within a given span, usually twenty years after registration. Specially, it is purposed at encouraging development through creativity, technological development and this is done by granting industrial property rights in form of patents for new things which constitute an improvement over-existing ones. Additionally, the Act outlines the procedures for filing patent applications, examination, and grant of patents, as well as provisions for compulsory licensing, revocation, and infringement proceedings.
2) ***The Copyright Act, 1957:*** The Copyright Act of 1957 protects the original literary, artistic, musical, and dramatic works among others like cinematographic films and sound recordings and it gives creators of such works exclusive rights to reproduce, distribute, perform and display their works as well as remedies for

dealing with cases of copyright infringement such as injunctions, damages, and account of profits. The Act contains copyright registration provisions, copyright duration, as well as provisions for copyright exceptions and limitations like fair use and education purposes.

3) ***The Trade Marks Act, 1999:*** The Trade Marks Act, 1999 is the law that regulates the registration and safeguarding of trademarks in India. It was designed to prohibit the unlawful utilization of trademarks that would result in consumers' misunderstandings and weaken the distinctiveness of protected labels. As far as their items and services are concerned, companies are allowed by this statute only to use their trademarks exclusively and enables them to take legal action against infringers, including seeking injunctions, damages, and seizure of infringing goods.
4) ***Patent Act 2005:*** The Patent Act of 2005 marked a significant shift in India's intellectual property landscape, aligning the country's patent regime with international standards while introducing new challenges for the generic drug industry. The Act, which came into effect on January 1, 2005, replaced the Patents Act of 1970 and introduced product patents for pharmaceuticals, chemicals, and food products, ending India's long-standing practice of granting only process patents for drugs. While the Act aimed to promote innovation and investment in research and development (R&D), it also presented formidable obstacles for India's thriving generic drug industry.

Intellectual Property Rights (IPRs) and Healthcare

Intellectual property rights (IPRs) have a strong effect on access to medicines, especially in the field of health and pharmaceuticals. They have the purpose of stimulating innovation by giving inventors exclusive privileges, yet at the same time they can restrict access, especially in essential medication and treatment (Nomani, 2020). Balancing innovation promotion against ensuring patients get affordable treatment is a difficult and disputable matter which demands due regard be given to ethics, legal matters and socio- economic aspects. Strong intellectual property protections are an essential factor for encouraging investment in research and development (RD) and driving innovation in the pharmaceutical industry. In order to come up with new drugs and treatments, drug manufacturers usually invest much money and often stand a chance to go wrong thus losing a great deal of money. They apply too patents as a copyright thereby enabling themselves earn exclusively for some time intervals generally lasting a short time so that they can get back the capital spent in addition generating receipts for their drugs in order to sponsor further research and development on the same area. Expensive patented drugs can be a real problem for low- and middle-income countries where many people cannot afford them where healthcare budgets are limited and millions of people lack access to essential medicines (Pley et al., 2020). Patented drugs are often priced beyond the reach of many patients, Thus, contributing to the gap in the availability of essential medicines and increasing the disparities in public health at an international level. What is more, such a maneuver as evergreening used by pharmaceutical manufacturers who tend to modify slightly existing products for the sake of prolonging patents hampers free competition and, consequently, results in the preservation of expensive medications at unnecessarily high prices.

Attempts made in dealing with the access to medicines challenge have sparked arguments as well as strategies for establishing a middle ground that allows for a culture of innovation while at the same time ensuring that the drugs are within reach of the ordinary citizen. Strategies such as compulsory licensing, which allows governments to license generic versions of patented drugs to increase competition and lower prices, have been employed to improve access to essential medicines in resource-constrained settings. The Medicines Patent Pool and other similar initiatives aim to promote voluntary licensing deals between those who own patents and those who make stuff that are not real so that they can sell things like HIV/AIDS medicine, tuberculosis medicine, as well as medicines meant for treating different diseases. The issue of access to medicines highlights the complex interplay between intellectual property rights, public health, and social justice. While strong intellectual property protections are essential for incentivizing innovation, efforts to ensure affordable access to life-saving medicines must be prioritized to address global health challenges and promote equitable access to healthcare for all. Finding sustainable solutions that balance the interests of innovators with the needs of patients globally requires collaborative efforts by governments, pharmaceutical companies, civil society organizations, and international agencies (Sharma & Thakkalapelli, 2023).

Generic Drug Industry and its Challenges

Judicial decisions in some countries have not only mandated that individuals be provided with specific medications; they have also commanded governments to make particular medications available to all citizens.

a) ***Patent Hurdles:*** Transitioning from process patents to product patents meant that generic drug manufacturers could no longer rely on reverse engineering to create cheaper versions of patented drugs. Before the Patent Act of 2005, generic manufacturers could tweak the manufacturing process of a drug to avoid infringing on the patent. However, with product patents, they had to develop entirely new methods of making the drug or obtain licenses from the patent holders (Abbott & Reichman, 2020). This significantly increased the cost and complexity of manufacturing generic drugs, making it more challenging for generic manufacturers to compete in the market.

b) ***Legal Battles:*** The introduction of product patents led to a surge in patent litigation between multinational pharmaceutical companies and Indian generic drug manufacturers. Patent holders aggressively pursued legal action to protect their intellectual property rights, often filing legal action which involves patenting something in which is copyrightable. These legal battles were protracted and costly, draining resources and time from both sides. As a result, generic drug manufacturers faced significant challenges in defending their right to produce cheaper versions of essential medicines, which undermined their competitiveness in the industry.

c) ***Market Access:*** The stringent patent regime introduced by the Patent Act of 2005 delayed the entry of generic versions of essential medicines into the market. It is a problem because it prevents many people in India and other developing countries from getting cheap medicines which are often their main form of healthcare and it affects millions of patients. High drug prices resulting from patent monopolies exacerbated healthcare inequalities, as many patients could not afford the brand-name alternatives. Additionally, the strain on government healthcare budgets increased as they had to allocate more funds to procure expensive patented medicines, further limiting access to healthcare services for vulnerable populations.

d) ***Innovation vs. Access:*** The core of the policy discourse regarding the Patent Act, 2005, is the controversy surrounding advocating novelty and maintaining access to primary medicines. While strong patent protection incentivizes pharmaceutical innovation by rewarding companies for their investments in R&D, concerns arise about the potential negative impact on public health, particularly for life-saving drugs. Stricter patent protection might limit the availability of necessary drugs to the world's worst-off sufferers of diseases such as HIV/AIDS, tuberculosis, or cancer where the price of drugs is a very important factor. It remains vital to find an appropriate balance between encouraging inventions and facilitating the citizens' access to drugs generally if health sector problems must be dealt with in the society where discrepancies in healthcare provision persists.

Trade Related Aspects of Intellectual Property Rights (TRIPS)

The agreement on Trade-Related Aspects of Intellectual Property Rights (TRIPS), which is under the supervision of the World Trade Organization (WTO), serves as a cornerstone of global intellectual property (IP) regulation. Enforced since 1995, TRIPS aims to harmonize and standardize IP laws across WTO member countries, facilitating international trade while safeguarding the rights of creators, innovators, and patent holders. The major challenges ahead involve the development of new drugs and vaccines, and putting into place mechanisms to allow their wide-scale distribution, including to those with limited financial resources (Chattu, 2021). This is a multidimensional set of tasks. A number of the moving parts bear only a tangential relationship to intellectual property (IP) protection. This research explores the key provisions and implications of TRIPS, as well as its impact on innovation, access to medicines, and socio-economic development.

Key Provisions of TRIPS

The TRIPS agreement establishes the minimum levels of protection and enforcement of IP rights which are to be followed by all the member countries, and includes patents, copyrights, trademarks and service marks, geographical indications and trade secrets. the agreement further mandates that member states should grant patents for any inventions, whether products or processes, in all fields of technology without discrimination and the rights conferred by such patents must be available for a specified period of time. TRIPS also requires us to look after the copyrights for literary, artistic and musical works as well as ensure that unauthorized use of trademarks does not take place.

i. ***Patents:*** The TRIPS agreement directs member countries to give patents for new gadgets or methods in all fields of tech without any differences, thus ensuring that any person who holds a patent has complete monopoly control over it for a fixed time frame, commonly around 20 years.
ii. ***Copyrights:*** The agreement requires member countries to grant creators exclusive rights to copy, distribute, and display their works through copyright protection of literary, artistic, and musical works.
iii. ***Trademarks:*** That the owners of marks have the sole right in relation to products and services, mandates protecting the trademarks from being used by other parties illegally or without permission regulated focuses on guarding the trademarks to prevent others from misusing or violating, hence allowing trademark owners have the only say over the use of their marks in association with goods and services.

iv. ***Geographical Indications:*** An analysis regarding the protection of geographical indications (GI) which attribute products to a particulate geographical area and have characteristics, reputation or qualities that are as a result of that area and so on and so forth is made in the agreement.
v. ***Enforcement:*** The Agreement has regulations to enforce intellectual rights, like civil and criminal measures against piracy fake products at national borders, and coordination among rights owners and agents at entry and exits.

Implications for Innovation and Access to Medicines

While TRIPS aims to promote innovation and investment in R&D by providing strong IP protections, concerned that this will make it harder for folks who need medicines badly across poor nations to take them. They say the rules on intellectual property rights for drugs have been attacked since they make sure that cheaper versions don't hit the shelves which can increase prices and hence prevent some sick persons from benefiting from them. Various measures to curb these fears constitute exceptions like mandatory licensing and the Doha Declaration on TRIPS and Public Health, which acknowledge the World Trade Organization (WTO) participants' ability to protect public health and guarantee everyone acquire drugs.

Innovation: TRIPS aims to provide to a dioxide platform its high property rights amplify that would make hold them invest any form in into new inventions and discoveries. By granting patent holders exclusive rights to their inventions, TRIPS encourages innovation by ensuring that creators and innovators can profit from their discoveries and investments. This creates a motive for companies to put money into Research & Development, because they are confident of what they can gain back from the money put into it by having patents (Drexl, 2021). Additionally, TRIPS aides in technological progress through establishing a regime for protecting copyrights, trademarks as well as other types of intellectual property resulting in increased creativity and innovation throughout different sectors. Overall, TRIPS serves as a catalyst for innovation-driven economic growth, driving advancements in technology, science, and industry while promoting competitiveness and entrepreneurship on a global scale.

Access to Medicines: Despite its aim to promote innovation, TRIPS expresses worries over the entry to crucial drugs especially for developing countries. In particular, the deal's clauses related to IP rights in pharmaceutical products have met with criticisms for delaying the availability of generic versions of essential medicines, driving up drug prices, and limiting access for patients in need. Many persons in developing nations depend on affordable generic drugs to treat killer diseases which makes it of profound consequence to public health too. Efforts to address this issue have included flexibilities such as compulsory licensing and this is since these populations cannot afford expensive patented drugs The Doha Declaration on TRIPS and Public Health affirmed the right of WTO Members to provide public health protection measures by making sure that all individuals had access to drugs especially during times of emergency or health crisis situations.

A lot more than simply the adding of value through high technology and the provision of affordable drugs is involved in the Trade-Related Aspects of Intellectual Property Rights (TRIPS) agreement. TRIPS influences various aspects of trade, investment, technology transfer, and cultural diversity, shaping the socio-economic landscape of member countries. TRIPS provisions impact trade by facilitating the exchange of IP-protected goods and services across borders, promoting international commerce and economic integration. The agreement encourages technology transfer through licensing agreements, joint ventures, and collaborations between domestic and foreign companies (Abbott, 2020). This facilitates the dissemination of knowledge and expertise, supporting the development of local industries and enhancing technological capabilities. Furthermore, TRIPS intersects with cultural diversity by safeguarding traditional knowledge and expressions of indigenous communities. The agreement acknowledges the significance of defending Geographical Indications (GIs) and Traditional Cultural Expressions, in addition to the preservation of cultural heritage and enhancement of cultural diversity in the global market.

The Trade Related Aspects of Intellectual Property Rights (TRIPS)agreement has a central role in the orientation of the worldwide IP situation as well as in generating an impact on the domain of creativity, pharmaceutical facility and the overall economic status. On the other hand, merely establishes minimum thresholds for protection and enforcement of intellectual property, its implementation raises complex challenges and trade-offs for policymakers, particularly in balancing the rights of IP holders with the imperative of ensuring public health and socio-economic development. By fostering dialogue, cooperation, and capacity-building, stakeholders can work towards harnessing the potential of TRIPS to promote innovation, foster economic growth, and advance public health objectives on a global scale.

Striking a Balance: Intellectual Property Protection and Public Health Imperatives

The intersection of IP protection and public health imperatives poses a complex challenge for policymakers, stakeholders, and society at large. Protection of intellectual property encourages progress and investment in research and development (R&D), which would not be possible without the latter access to essential medicines and healthcare services, particularly in developing countries. This research explores the delicate balance between IP protection and public health imperatives, examining the impact of IP regimes on access to medicines, healthcare innovation, and global health outcomes.

IP Protection and Access to Medicines: Strong IP protections, such as patents, copyrights, and trademarks, play a crucial role in promoting innovation by rewarding creators and innovators for their contributions. But strict IP regimes might prevent individuals from accessing important drugs since licensing rights are as a matter of fact often equated to control and monopoly over life-saving pharmaceuticals, consequently the prices go beyond the reach of people (Ragavan, 2021). Since the majority of people cannot afford good quality healthcare services in low and middle-income countries, then these patients' lives are put at stake due to lack of access to care (Velásquez, 2022). Several strategies have been proposed to mitigate this problem including issuing compulsory licenses for production of essential medications to balance IP protection with the imperative of ensuring access to medicines for all.

Healthcare Innovation and IP: While IP protection incentivizes innovation by providing a framework for creators and innovators to protect their intellectual assets, it can also stifle competition and hinder the diffusion of knowledge and technology. This can impede progress in healthcare innovation, as companies may prioritize profits over public health needs, leading to a lack of investment in research and development for neglected diseases and underserved populations. Balancing IP protection with public health imperatives requires promoting innovation while ensuring that new technologies and for the people in need, solutions as well as treatments are within reach and cost-effective.

Global Health Outcomes: The balance between IP protection and public health imperatives has significant implications for global health outcomes. Access to essential medicines and healthcare services is essential for achieving health equity and reducing health disparities worldwide. Strengthening health systems, promoting technology transfer, and fostering international cooperation are essential for addressing global health challenges and ensuring that IP regimes contribute to improving health outcomes for all.

For several decades, India has witnessed various health crisis, the situation became worst due to the unavailability of medicines and inadequate health infrastructure (Sekalala et al., 2021chatt). Based on such scenarios, it becomes essential that the patented medicine shall be provided at a reasonable rate by pharmaceutical companies. Policymakers, by giving attention to public health needs and at the same time appreciating intellectual property rights would be able to construct a healthcare system that is much equitable, lasting and benefits all people in irrespective of where they come from or their economic status.

Compulsory Licensing: A Critical Tool for Access to Medicines

Theoretically, the term compulsory licensing means, "When the government permits other interested parties or itself to make use of patented invention for manufacture and sell without the consent of the patent holder. It is a statutorily created license that allows certain people to pay a royalty and use an invention without patentee's permission" (Dratler, 2023). This tool is essential for promoting access to medicines, particularly in situations where patented drugs are priced prohibitively high, limiting access for patients in need. The main reason for compulsory licensing is to reconcile the concerns of patent owners and the interests of the general public in obtaining vital medicines (Gomulkiewicz et al., 2023). By authorizing generic manufacturers to produce patented drugs at a lower cost, compulsory licensing enables governments to address public health crises and ensure that regardless of a person's financial status, everyone can be able to access lifesaving cures. But some people question it because it might infringe on patent rights and affect production incentives.

Compulsory licensing of pharmaceuticals is a vital mechanism for broadening the consumption of drugs and addressing the uneven distribution of healthcare, underscoring the interrelationship and conflicts existing between intellectual property and health matters in the drug making industry.

Compulsory Licensing: Case Studies of HIV/AIDS and Cancer Drug Access

Compulsory licensing is now considered crucial in dealing with public health issues of access to medical treatment for life threatening illness such as AIDS, cancer among others. This part deals case studies where compulsory licensing has been utilized to facilitate access to essential drugs for these diseases, highlighting the impact of this mechanism on public health outcomes and the pharmaceutical industry.

Case Studies of Compulsory Licensing for HIV/AIDS Drugs

The HIV/AIDS epidemic has presented an important health issue which most affects the developing countries whose populations can hardly afford antiretroviral therapy due to exorbitant cost of drugs. In response, nations like Brazil, Thailand, & India have utilized compulsory licensing to facilitate access to generic versions of patented HIV/AIDS drugs. For instance, in 2007, Brazil issued a compulsory license for efavirenz, a key component of ART, allowing generic manufacturers to produce and distribute the drug at a lower cost. This move significantly reduced the financial burden on Brazil's healthcare system and increased access to treatment for HIV/AIDS positive people.

Similarly, Thailand approved the use of compulsory licensing for different HIV/AIDS drugs, including efavirenz and lopinavir/ritonavir, enabling the government to negotiate lower prices with generic manufacturers and expand access to treatment across the country. In India, the landmark case of compulsory licensing for the HIV/AIDS drug, Sorafenib Tosylate, highlighted a balance between protecting IP while also considering public health concerns. Natco Pharma was given a compulsory license by Indian Patent Office in 2012 for a drug produced by an American company enabling it to produce generic version of the drug at mere fraction of cost rendering it more affordable to Indian cancer patients.

Brazil: Brazil stands out as a pioneer in using compulsory licensing to expand access to HIV/AIDS treatment. In 2007, the Brazilian government issued a compulsory license for efavirenz, a crucial component of ART, amidst concerns about the exorbitant prices charged by patent-holding pharmaceutical companies. This move enabled generic manufacturers to produce affordable versions of efavirenz, significantly reducing treatment costs and increasing accessibility for HIV/AIDS positive people across the country. The implementation of compulsory licensing in Brazil served as a groundbreaking example of how governments can prioritize public health imperatives over intellectual property rights to ensure equitable access to essential medicines.

Thailand: Thailand has also employed compulsory licensing to enhance access to HIV/AIDS treatment. In 2006, the Thai government issued a compulsory license for efavirenz and later for lopinavir/ritonavir, two critical drugs used in ART regimens. By doing so, Thailand aimed to overcome barriers posed by high drug prices and expand access to treatment for its population. The issuance of compulsory licenses empowered the government to negotiate lower prices with generic manufacturers, resulting in significant cost savings and broader availability of HIV/AIDS medications across the country.

India: India is also known as the pharmacy of the developing world and has been very instrumental in producing generic drugs that are affordable especially those used for HIV (Human Immunodeficiency Virus) and AIDS (Acquired Immune Deficiency Syndrome). The local patent authority awarded a compulsory licence on Sorafenib Tosylate, an anticancer drug used in treating specific cancers such as kidney cancer as of 2012 (Khachigian, 2020). The aforementioned license permitted Natco Pharma (a generic manufacturer) to develop cheaper generic editions of the medicine which were far much cheaper than the original one hence being available to patients at just a small fraction of the cost it would have entailed otherwise. It was such decisions that showed how deeply ingrained in policy-making were both protection of intellectual property rights and considerations over health among other things affecting general public)

Case Studies of Compulsory Licensing for Cancer Drugs

Cancer is another disease area where access to medicines remains a pressing issue, particularly in developing countries where high drug prices pose a significant barrier to treatment. Compulsory licensing has been utilized to address access to cancer drugs in countries such as Colombia, Malaysia, and Ecuador. For example, in 2012, the Colombian government issued a decree declaring the public interest in accessing generic versions of the cancer drug imatinib due to its high price and the urgent need for treatment (Cousins et al., 2021). This paved the way for the issuance of a compulsory license, enabling generic manufacturers to produce and distribute the drug at a lower cost, expanding access to treatment for cancer patients in Colombia.

Similarly, in Malaysia, the government invoked compulsory licensing for the cancer drug, sorafenib, in 2016, citing the need to ensure access to affordable treatment for patients with liver and kidney cancer. This move allowed generic manufacturers to produce and distribute the drug at a significantly lower cost, reducing the financial burden on patients and the healthcare system. In Ecuador, the government issued a decree in 2017 declaring the public interest in accessing generic versions of the cancer drug, letrozole, under compulsory licensing provisions. This initiative aimed to increase access to treatment for breast cancer patients and alleviate the financial strain on the healthcare system.

Colombia: In 2012, the Colombian government issued a decree declaring the public interest in accessing generic versions of the cancer drug imatinib due to its exorbitant price. The decree paved the way for the issuance of a compulsory license, enabling local generic manufacturers to produce and distribute the drug at significantly lower costs. This initiative aimed to alleviate the financial burden on cancer patients and improve access to life-saving treatment across Colombia.

Malaysia: Malaysia invoked compulsory licensing for the cancer drug sorafenib in 2016 to ensure access to affordable treatment for patients with liver and kidney cancer. The government's decision to issue a compulsory license enabled generic manufacturers to produce and distribute the drug at a fraction of the price, expanding access to treatment options for cancer patients in Malaysia.

Ecuador: In 2017, the Ecuadorian government issued a decree declaring the public interest in accessing generic versions of the cancer drug letrozole under compulsory licensing provisions. This initiative aimed to increase access to treatment for breast cancer patients and reduce the financial burden on the healthcare system. In its efforts to guarantee a balance in accessibility of necessary cancer medication to the public, Ecuador invoked obligatory licensing.

The case studies of compulsory licensing for HIV/AIDS and cancer drugs underscore the critical role of this mechanism in promoting access to essential medicines and addressing health inequities. By leveraging compulsory licensing, governments can negotiate lower prices for patented drugs, expand access to treatment, and improve health outcomes for patients with life-threatening diseases. The trade-off between intellectual property rights and incentives for innovation in the pharmaceutical industry still causes heated debate, but there is a need to find middle ground concerning compulsory licensing. One way forward is striking a balance between IP protection as well as public health needs so that drugs can be accessed fairly by every person.

Drug Price Control Order (DPCO)

The Drug Price Control Order (DPCO) is a regulatory framework established by the Government of India to ensure the affordability and accessibility of essential medicines for the general public. The DPCO is a law enacted under the Essential Commodities Act that allows the government to control the price of particular drugs and medical devices so as to prevent unreasonable price hikes as well as promote public health. In India, due to a lack of population-level financial risk protection mechanisms, the expenditure on healthcare is primarily out-of-pocket in nature. Through Drug Price Control Orders (DPCOs), the Indian Government attempts to keep medicine prices under check. Its objectives include ensuring affordable access to essential medicines, preventing monopolistic practices by pharmaceutical companies, promoting rational use of medicines, addressing healthcare disparities, and fostering competition in the pharmaceutical market (Krikorian, 2021). This is achieved through price adjustment exercises that are done from time to time; by doing so DPCO tries to make sure that it maintains a middle ground between what pharmaceuticals want (business interests) and what patients need urgently as regards healthcare: availability at inexpensive cost throughout every stratum of populace (social justice).

Key Objectives of the Drug Price Control Order

Ensuring Affordable Access to Essential Medicines: The DPCO aims to ensure that essential medicines, which are critical for treating prevalent diseases and maintaining public health, remain affordable and accessible to all segments of society.

Preventing Unjustified Price Escalation: Unjustified price escalation refers to the arbitrary increase in drug prices by pharmaceutical companies without any valid justification, such as increased production costs or significant improvements in drug efficacy (Sharma & Dube, 2021). Such price hikes can severely burden patients, healthcare providers, and the healthcare system as a whole.

Promoting Rational Use of Medicines: The promotion of the Rational Use of Medicines is achieved when medicines are prescribed and used by people in a way that ensures they work the best for them medically; this also puts into consideration the fact that such use carries less danger compared to using other drugs which may make someone spend more money without getting better results.

Addressing Disparities in Healthcare Access: Disparities in healthcare access refer to inequalities in the availability and affordability of healthcare services, including essential medicines, across different regions and socio-economic groups.

Promoting Competition in the Pharmaceutical Market: Healthy competition in the pharmaceutical market is essential for driving innovation, ensuring quality, and keeping drug prices affordable.

Balancing the Interest of Innovators and Generic Drug Manufacturers

It is important to strike a balance between the research and development (R&D) investments of the innovators who invest substantial amounts in order to introduce new medicines into the pharmaceutical market and those of the generic drug producers who start producing affordable copies once the relevant patents come to an end (Smith, 2009). While innovators seek to protect their intellectual property rights to recoup investments and foster further innovation, generic drug manufacturers aim to provide low-cost alternatives to ensure broader access to essential medicines (Gurgula, 2020). Achieving this balance requires implementing intellectual property regulations that incentivize innovation while also facilitating timely entry of generic drugs to the market. It involves striking a delicate equilibrium where innovators are rewarded for their contributions to medical progress, while generic manufacturers can compete fairly to drive down drug prices and improve accessibility for patients.

Collaborative Efforts of Public Health: Public health efforts play a pivotal role in ensuring access to essential medicines, disease prevention, and promoting overall well-being within communities. Collaborative initiatives involving government agencies, healthcare providers, non-governmental organizations (NGOs), and other stakeholders are essential for addressing public health challenges effectively. These efforts encompass a wide range of activities, including disease surveillance, vaccination campaigns, health education, and policy advocacy. Stakeholders can join hands to contribute resources, skills and information towards coming up with inclusive public health strategies that cater for various population needs. Collaboration also fosters innovation and knowledge sharing, leading to the development of evidence-based interventions that yield positive health outcomes. Furthermore, collaborative efforts enhance coordination between different sectors, ensuring a holistic approach to public health that considers social, economic, and environmental determinants of health.

Evidence-Based Policy Interventions: Evidence-based policy interventions are crucial for informing decision-making and guiding effective strategies to address public health challenges. Using data, research findings and scientific evidence, policymakers can create specific interventions to meet community and population needs. Evidence-based approaches help identify priority areas, assess the impact of interventions, and allocate resources efficiently (Zeilinger, 2021). They also enable policymakers to assess the competence of the current systems to be modified in line with emerging information or changing times. By adopting evidence-based practices, policymakers can maximize the impact of their interventions and achieve better health outcomes for populations.

Transparent Regulatory Mechanism: A transparent regulatory mechanism is essential for ensuring accountability, fairness, and public trust in the healthcare system. Regulatory bodies responsible for overseeing pharmaceuticals, medical devices, and healthcare services must operate with transparency and openness to uphold the highest standards of safety, efficacy, and quality (Garagancea, 2021). Transparent regulatory processes involve clear guidelines, procedures, and decision-making criteria that are accessible to stakeholders. They also include mechanisms for soliciting feedback, engaging with the public, and addressing concerns or complaints. Transparency in regulatory decision-making promotes confidence in the regulatory system, fosters industry compliance, and facilitates timely access to safe and effective healthcare products. It also enhances accountability by holding regulatory authorities accountable for their actions and decisions. Ultimately, a transparent regulatory mechanism contributes to a well-functioning healthcare system that prioritizes patient safety, public health, and regulatory compliance.

CONCLUSION

In today's knowledge-driven global landscape, intellectual property rights (IPRs) serve as foundational pillars that bolster innovation, foster creativity, and drive economic progress (Napoleon, 2020). India's legal framework for intellectual property not only conforms to international standards but also customizes solutions to address the nation's distinctive socio-economic makeup and cultural diversity. This dual approach ensures that India maintains global standards while also accommodating the nuances of its own context.

However, the intersection of intellectual property protection and public health objectives presents a multifaceted challenge for policymakers, stakeholders, and society at large (Bently et al., 2022). Strong IP rights are central to fostering innovation and attracting investments in R&D, they simultaneously create barriers to accessing essential medicines and healthcare services, especially in developing nations where affordability remains a pressing concern.

This research delves into the intricate balance between IP protection and public health imperatives, shedding light on the nuanced interplay between these two domains. By scrutinizing the impact of IP regimes on medication accessibility, healthcare innovation, and global health outcomes, it navigates the complex terrain where legal, ethical, and humanitarian considerations converge. This deeper understanding empowers policymakers and stakeholders to make well-informed decisions that prioritize both innovation and public health.

Striking a tradeoff between encouraging creativity and keeping health care even-handedly emerges as a paramount challenge on the global stage. Addressing this challenge necessitates the development of innovative policy frameworks, the cultivation of collaborative partnerships, and a person and community first approach, especially for those who are poor. Only through concerted efforts can policymakers reconcile these seemingly conflicting objectives and advance inclusive growth and sustainable development.

As we navigate the evolving landscape of intellectual property and public health, it becomes increasingly evident that a holistic approach is imperative. By fostering dialogue, nurturing collaboration, and harnessing technology and innovation, we can chart a course toward a future where intellectual property serves as a catalyst for inclusive growth, sustainable development, and improved health outcomes for all members of society, irrespective of their socio-economic background or geographic location.

To sum up, nuanced policy development and collaborative action are required due to the fine line that exists between safeguarding intellectual property rights and serving public health interests. Innovating first while making sure healthcare is available to everyone is how we will prepare a brighter and healthier destiny for all.

REFERENCES

Abbott, F. M. (2020). The TRIPs agreement article 73 security exceptions and the COVID-19 pandemic. *Research Paper, 116*, 20-16.

Abbott, F. M., & Reichman, J. H. (2020). Facilitating access to Cross-border supplies of patented pharmaceuticals: The case of the COVID-19 pandemic. *Journal of International Economic Law*, 23(3), 535–561. 10.1093/jiel/jgaa022

Bently, L., Sherman, B., Gangjee, D., & Johnson, P. (2022). *Intellectual property law*. Oxford university press. 10.1093/he/9780198869917.001.0001

Chattu, V. K., Singh, B., Kaur, J., & Jakovljevic, M. (2021). COVID-19 vaccine, TRIPS, and global health diplomacy: India's role at the WTO platform. *BioMed Research International*, 2021, 2021. 10.1155/2021/665807034485525

Chidede, T. (2022). The role of intellectual property rights' protection in advancing development in South Africa. *Law, Democracy & Development, 26*(1).

Cousins, T., Pentecost, M., Alvergne, A., Chandler, C., Chigudu, S., Herrick, C., Kelly, A., Leonelli, S., Lezaun, J., Lorimer, J., Reubi, D., & Sekalala, S. (2021). The changing climates of global health. *BMJ Global Health*, 6(3), e005442. 10.1136/bmjgh-2021-00544233758015

. Dratler J. Licensing of intellectual property. Law Journal Press; 2023 Dec 28.

Drexl, J., Hilty, R., Desaunettes-Barbero, L., Globocnik, J., Otero, B. G., Hoffmann, J., & Kim, D. (2021). *Artificial intelligence and intellectual property law-Position statement of the max planck institute for innovation and competition of 9 april 2021 on the current debate*. Max Planck Institute for Innovation & Competition.

Garagancea, L. (2021). Access to Medicines: The Interplay between Parallel Imports, Compulsory Licensing, and Voluntary Licensing. *EPLR*, 5(1), 37–56. 10.21552/eplr/2021/1/6

Gerke, S., Minssen, T., & Cohen, G. (2020). *"Ethical and legal challenges of artificial intelligence-driven healthcare." Artificial intelligence in healthcare*. Academic Press.

Gomulkiewicz, R., Nguyen, X. T., & Conway, D. M. (2023). *Licensing intellectual property: law and application*. Aspen Publishing.

Gurgula, O. (2020). Strategic patenting by pharmaceutical companies–should competition law intervene? *IIC; International Review of Industrial Property and Copyright Law*, 51(9), 1062–1085. 10.1007/s40319-020-00985-033132411

Hanafi, I., & Lubis, A. F. (2023). Protection of Privacy and Intellectual Property Rights in Digital Data Management in Indonesia. *The Easta Journal Law and Human Rights*, 2(01), 33–40. 10.58812/eslhr.v2i01.151

Jorstad, K. T. (2020). Intersection of artificial intelligence and medicine: Tort liability in the technological age. *Journal of Medical Artificial Intelligence*, 3, 3. 10.21037/jmai-20-57

Khachigian, L. M. (2020). Pharmaceutical patents: Reconciling the human right to health with the incentive to invent. *Drug Discovery Today*, 25(7), 1135–1141. 10.1016/j.drudis.2020.04.00932325020

Kianzad, B., & Wested, J. (2021). 'No-One Is Safe until Everyone Is Safe'-Patent Waiver, Compulsory Licensing and COVID-19. *EPLR*, 5(2), 71–91. 10.21552/eplr/2021/2/4

Krikorian, G., & Torreele, E. (2021). We cannot win the access to medicines struggle using the same thinking that causes the chronic access crisis. *Health and Human Rights*, 23(1), 119.34194206

Lee, J. A., Hilty, R., & Liu, K. C. (Eds.). (2021 Feb 25). *Artificial intelligence and intellectual property*. Oxford University Press. 10.1093/oso/9780198870944.001.0001

Mamanazarov, S. (2023). Intellectual Property Theories as Applied to Big Data. *International Journal of Law and Policy.*, 1(7). 10.59022/ijlp.164

Napoleon, E. A. (2020). Patent Eligibility: Exploring the Intersection Between Patent Law and Biomedical Data. *Pitt. J. Tech. L. & Pol'y*, 21, 117.

Nomani, M. Z. M., & Alaa, K. K. (2020). Alhalboosi, and Mohammad Rauf. "Legal & intellectual property dimension of health & access to medicines in India.". *Indian Journal of Forensic Medicine Toxicology*, 14(1), 118–122.

Pley, C., van Der Heijden, M. R., & Tulinius, C. (2020). A health professional's guide to the intersection of public health with intellectual property rights in trade and investment: The case of tobacco plain packaging. *Journal of Public Health Policy*, 41(1), 52–62. 10.1057/s41271-019-00195-031685934

Ragavan, S., & Vanni, A. (Eds.). (2021). *Intellectual property law and access to medicines: TRIPS agreement, health, and pharmaceuticals*. Taylor & Francis. 10.4324/9781003176602

Rauf, M., & Tamang, R. (2023). Access to Medicines and Intellectual Property Law: Balancing Innovation and Public Health. *Interdisciplinary Studies in Society, Law, and Politics*, 2(3), 37–43. 10.61838/kman.isslp.2.3.5

Sekalala, S., Forman, L., Hodgson, T., Mulumba, M., Namyalo-Ganafa, H., & Meier, B. M. (2021). Decolonising human rights: How intellectual property laws result in unequal access to the COVID-19 vaccine. *BMJ Global Health*, 6(7), e006169. 10.1136/bmjgh-2021-00616934253631

Sharma, A. K., & Dube, D. (2021). The relevance of criminal law in intellectual property law research. *Handbook of intellectual property research: Lenses, methods, and perspectives.* Oxford University Press. 10.1093/oso/9780198826743.001

Sharma, S., & Thakkalapelli, D. (2023). Corporate patenting AI and ML in healthcare: Regulatory and ethical considerations. *International Journal of New Media Studies: International Peer Reviewed Scholarly Indexed Journal*, 10(1), 232–235.

Stim, R. (2024). *Patent, copyright & trademark: an intellectual property desk reference*. Nolo.

Tenni, B., Moir, H. V., Townsend, B., Kilic, B., Farrell, A. M., Keegel, T., & Gleeson, D. (2022). What is the impact of intellectual property rules on access to medicines? A systematic review. *Globalization and Health*, 18(1), 40. 10.1186/s12992-022-00826-435428250

Teremetskyi, V., Duliba, Y., Drozdova, O., Zhukovska, L., Sivash, O., & Dziuba, I. (2021). Access to Justice and Legal Aid for Vulnerable Groups: New Challenges Caused by the Covid-19 Pandemic. *J. Legal Ethical & Regul. Isses*, 24, 1.

Upadhyay, N. K., & Rathee, M. 2020, June. Impact of Artificial Intelligence on Intellectual Property Rights. In *Proceedings of International Young Scholars Workshop* (Vol. 9). 10.47344/iysw.v9i0.192

Velásquez, G., & Velásquez, G. (2022). *Medicines and intellectual property: 10 years of the WHO global strategy*. Springer International Publishing.

Yu, P. K. (2022). Intellectual property paradoxes in pandemic times. *GRUR International*, 71(4), 293–294. 10.1093/grurint/ikac014

Chapter 7
A Socio-Legal Analysis of the Health and Well-Being of the Ageing Population

Urmila Yadav
https://orcid.org/0000-0002-3716-9059
Sharda School of Law, Sharda University, India

Bishwajeet Prakash
Sharda School of Law, Sharda University, India

ABSTRACT

Approximately 10% of the global population, or 771 million people, are over 65 as of 2023. A further feature of ageing is the rise of multiple complex health states, collectively referred to as geriatric syndromes. Research indicated that this illness has been increasing daily and will reach 16% in 2050 and eventually 24% by 2100. Societal ageing can also have an impact on economic growth, retirement, and employment patterns, family dynamics, and the capacity of local governments and communities to provide sufficient resources for the elderly. This chapter's goals are to examine and evaluate the various aspects of wellbeing in an ageing population. This involved looking at things like statistical facts of aging populations, social dimensions and Support of ageing care, networks and ageing care and maintenance structure in India, as well as strategies for encouraging good ageing.

DOI: 10.4018/979-8-3693-5976-1.ch007

INTRODUCTION

"One who always serves and respects the elderly is blessed with four things: long life, wisdom, fame, and power". Manusmriti, 121.

"A society for all ages is one that does not caricature older persons as patients and pensioners. Instead, it sees them as both agents and beneficiaries of development. It honours traditional elders in their leadership and consultative roles in communities throughout the world." -Kofi Annan, United Nations Secretary-General 1 October 1998. The popular saying, "old is gold' which implies the gravity of age on earth. All the things get older. The things around us, both animate and inanimate, go through this ageing process. The old people are not treated well, and they need special care and policies for their autumn days. The increasing number of elderly people, due to advancements in medical sciences, health care, etc., is a problem in both developed as well as developing countries. Policy makers and social scientists focus their attention on abating the seriousness of the problems, they pose to countries, particularly third world countries. To understand the issue of the elderly, there is a need to understand basic concepts like ageing.

Concept of Aging

The medicinal sciences use the term elderly to describe individuals who are attaining the later stage of their lives after living more than 60 years of life. An individual, due to the process of ageing, starts experiencing a decline in effective motor activities, a lack of ability to carry out various physiological functions, the immune system will get affected and the digestive system will get disturbed, as a result of the increased in risk of being affected by various illnesses and infections. All these physiological changes make them feel unable to perform day -to-day activities as adults do. Psychological functions will also be affected due to the impact of ageing the risk of age-related psychological illnesses like Alzheimer's, dementia, and many more will increase. The medicinal sciences focus on studies and the development of appropriate strategies to address the healthcare needs of the elderly.

The social sciences focus on understanding the social, psychological, and physical changes that occur as individuals age, and how these changes can impact their quality of life. This includes examining the impact of social structures, social policies, and cultural norms on the well-being and social integration of older adults. Social scientists also study issues related to caregiving, intergenerational relationships, and the social networks and support systems that are important for the elderly population. The study of the elderly population is interdisciplinary, drawing on theories and methods from sociology, psychology, anthropology, economics, social work, and other fields. Handler defined "ageing is the deterioration of nature's organisms resulting from the dependent, essentially irreversible changes intrinsic to all members of a species such that, with the passage of time, they become increasingly unable to cope with the stresses of the environment, thereby increasing the probability of death." Beckar defined ageing in the broader sense as "changes coursing in an individual as the result of the passage of time." He added, "aging consists of two simultaneous components: anabolic building up and catabolic breaking down." Comfort regards it as "the total effect of all changes which occur in a living being with increasing chronological age and which render it more vulnerable or less viable." Birren and Renner define "ageing as the regular changes that occur in mature genetically representative organisms living under representative environmental conditions as they advance in chronological age." According to Hurlock, old age is the closing period in the life span. It is a period when people move away from previous, more desirable periods or times of usefulness. Stieglitz has rightly observed that "aging is a part of living." Ageing begins with conception and terminates with death. It cannot be arrested unless we arrest life. We may retire aging or accelerate it, but we cannot arrest it while life goes on because it is essentially an element in living."

STATISTICAL FACTS OF AGING

Global statistics: The latest projections by the United Nations suggest that the global population could grow to around 8.5 billion in 2030, 9.7 billion in 2050, and 10.4 billion in 2100. Many of the 46 least-developed countries are projected to double in population between 2022 and 2050, posing challenges to the achievement of the Sustainable Development Goals. Similarly, the World Health Organisation (WHO) reported that between 2015 and 2050, the proportion of the world's population over 60 years old will nearly double from 12% to 22%. By 2030, 1 in 6 people in the world will be aged 60 years or older. At this time, the share of the population aged 60 years and over will increase from 1 billion in 2020 to 1.4 billion. By 2050, the world's population of people aged 60 years and older will double (2.1 billion). The number of people aged 80 years or older is expected to triple between 2020 and 2050 to reach 426 million. (WHO, 2022). Here's what that's projected to look like, for every country and territory.

Figure 1. A graph showing the growth of world's ageing population

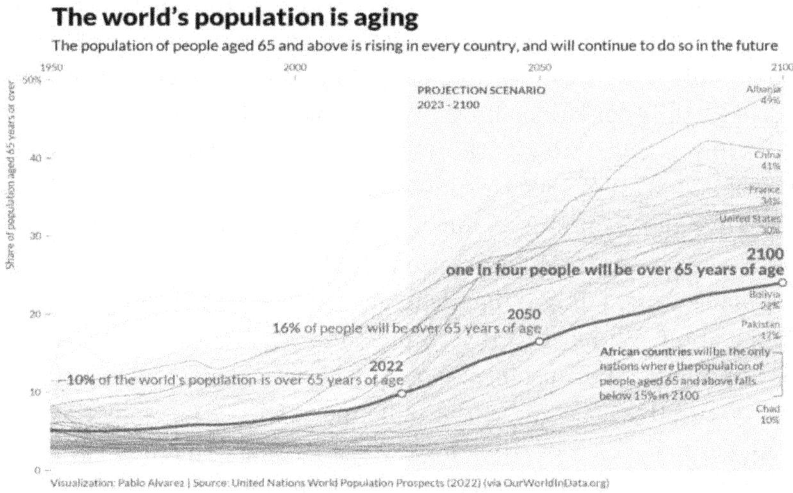

Indian Statistics, Facts of Ageing

Figure 2. Projected share of the elderly population, India and states, 2021 versus 2036

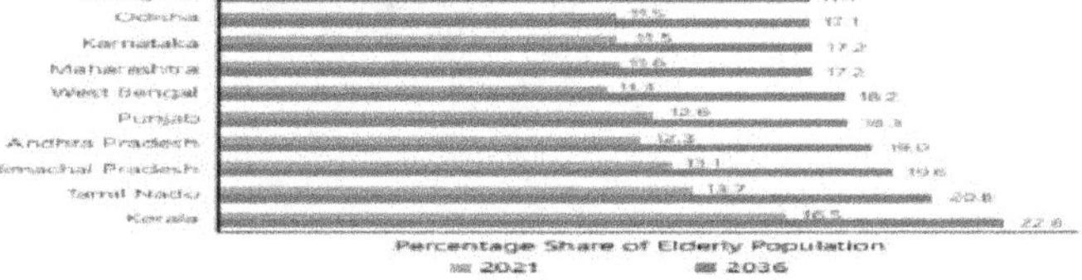

India is not an exception to this phenomenon. According to the Census of India, the elderly population aged 60 years or older in India was 103 million in 2011, which was 8.6% of the total population (Registrar General & Census Commissioner India,

2011).There will be 149 million persons aged 60 years and older in 2022 (as of July-1), comprising around 10.5 percent of the country's population. By 2050, the share of older people will double to 20.8 percent, with the absolute number at 347 million. A good part of the world's population is growing older, and India mirrors this trend as well. The reality is that, according to the United Nations Population Fund (UNFPA) the population above 60 years old will double from 10.5%, or 14.9 crore (as of July 1, 2022), to 20.8%, or 34.7 crore, by 2050. (UNFPA 2023).

In Kerala and West Bengal, for instance, there is a growing population of the elderly who live alone as children migrate for better opportunities. With life expectancy increasing, thanks to better ways to fight disease, and decreasing fertility rates in many countries, including India, there are challenges in nurturing an expanding elderly population. Within this macro phenomenon, there are myriad other data points of importance. For instance, women elderly citizens outnumber their male counterparts. At 60 years, a person in India may expect to live another 18.3 years, which is higher in the case of women at 19 years compared to men at 17.5 years. If women in India, where labour force participation is low at 24%, do not have economic and social security, they will become more vulnerable in old age. There are also significant inter-state variations. Most states in the south reported a higher share of the elderly population than the national average in 2021, a gap that is expected to widen by 2036. While States with higher fertility rates, such as Bihar and Uttar Pradesh, expect to see an increase in the share of the elderly population by 2036, the level will remain lower than the Indian average. Overall, more than two-fifths of the elderly are in the poorest wealth quintile, ranging from 5% in Punjab to 47% in Chhattisgarh; also, 18.7% of the elderly do not have any income. A high proportion of the rural population is among the elderly and often economically deprived.

DIMENSIONS OF ELDERLY CARE

Figure 3. Shows the dimensions of elderly care

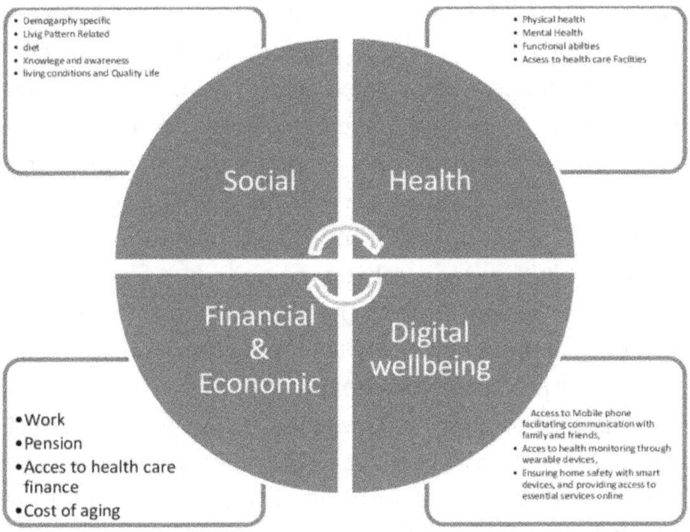

In India, the challenges associated with population ageing are further exacerbated by the lack of affordable healthcare services, shifting disease burden, evolving nuclear family structures, and altered consumption patterns. India will have 319 million older adults by 2050, accounting for 20% of the total population, putting additional strain on India's already overburdened healthcare system. Nearly one-half (45%) of India's disease burden is projected to be borne by older adults in 2030, when the population age groups with high levels of chronic conditions will represent a much greater share of the total population. Further, neuro-degenerative diseases like dementia mostly affect older adults, though they are not part of normal ageing. According to the WHO, there are approximately 50 million people worldwide who are living with dementia, and this number is expected to triple by 2050. In India, an estimated 4 million people are living with dementia, and this number is projected to increase to 13.4 million by 2050. The burden of dementia on healthcare systems is substantial, with global costs estimated at US$1 trillion annually. In addition, there is a need to address mental health concerns such as depression and anxiety as well as issues related to mobility and independence, such as fall prevention, assistive technology, and accessible transportation. Moreover, many seniors, especially women and those residing in rural areas, face challenges in accessing healthcare due to the limited availability of geriatric specialists and services, high out-of-pocket costs, and a lack of awareness about age-related health issues. So, healthcare systems will face numerous challenges in providing affordable and accessible healthcare services to older adults because of their diverse physical and mental needs, along with their social and financial challenges. Apart from the health issues, hygiene related issues also affect the quality of life among the elderly negatively. Maintaining good hygiene is essential for the health and wellbeing of elderly individuals, but certain age-related changes can make it difficult for them to maintain proper hygiene. Though open defecation was a major concern earlier, the steps taken by the government have curtailed the issue to a large extent, but disabled-friendly sanitation facilities are still lacking in most public spaces. The ageing population also has significant implications for India's social and welfare systems. Many older adults in India rely on their children for financial support and care in their later years. However, with the shift towards smaller nuclear families and increased migration due to work, education, and marriage; the elderly are left behind with a scarce or practically no support system. Further, there are numerous negative stereotypes and stigmas associated with ageing in India. Traditionally, ageing was seen as a natural part of life, and the elderly were respected and valued for their wisdom and life experience. However, in recent years, there has been a shift towards a more westernized view of ageing, where ageing is often associated with decline and loss. The elderly are often viewed as a burden and are marginalised in society. This shift may be due to the influence of media and globalisation, which have created a culture that values youth and beauty. These negative stereotypes about ageing can have a detrimental effect on the health and well-being of older adults, leading to social isolation, depression, and other health problems. The economic impact of an ageing population is also a significant concern for India. As the proportion of older adults in the population increases, their contribution to the labour force decreases. Also, the social benefits extended by the elderly population through their unpaid work, which includes care tasks, volunteer activities, etc., are neither recognised nor quantified. Additionally, the shift in consumption patterns as people age can significantly impact the demand for goods and services, including housing, healthcare, and social protection. The country's pension system leaves many older adults without a reliable sources of income in their retirement, so it needs to be strengthened and funded with additional resources. Digital technology has become an essential part of our daily lives, and it has transformed the way we live, work, and interact with others. However, there is still a significant digital divide between different age groups, particularly when it comes to senior citizens. Seniors may face challenges in using digital devices and accessing online services due to physical, cognitive, or socio-economic reasons. According to a survey conducted by the National Sample Survey Organisation (NSSO), only 13% of people aged 60 years or older have ever used the internet. This is significantly lower than the overall internet penetration rate in India, which is around 50%. The reasons for this low rate of internet use among seniors in India include limited access to digital devices, a lack of digital literacy, and limited awareness of online services. Thus, there is a growing need to bridge the digital divide for seniors.

MAJOR TRENDS IN THE SOCIAL DOMAIN

The world's population is living longer and growing older. Embracing and planning for this massive demographic transition is one of the greatest social challenges of the 21st century. It is high time to make people aware of it because it is having an impact on our society. Societal ageing can affect economic growth, patterns of work and retirement, family's function, the ability of governments and communities to provide adequate resources for older adults, and the prevalence of chronic disease and disability. The following Social assertions are supported by findings from the examination of Indian Statistics.

The number of elderly Indians is increasing: India has the highest number of young people and ageing is rapidly progressing. The current elderly population of 153 million (aged 60 and above) is expected to reach a staggering 347 million by 2050. **Increasing dependency ratios:** India's population is relatively young at present, however, a substantial decline in fertility rates and death rates indicates an increase in the elderly population in the coming decades. Rising life expectancy rates make it important for the government to convert these years into healthy years. A high dependency ratio means a higher burden on the economically active population to support and provide for the economically dependent older population. **Rural-Urban Divide:** Increased proportion of the elderly residing in rural areas. Out of the total population of the elderly in India, a very high proportion of them reside in rural India. Rural India still lacks medical infrastructure and other basic facilities such as electricity, communication, etc. Further, rural seniors reflect low healthcare utilisation, along with poor financial cover.

There are also significant inter-state variations in the elderly population. States with higher fertility rates, such as Bihar and Uttar Pradesh, expect to see an increase in the share of the elderly population by 2036; the level will remain lower than the Indian average.

Migration and socio-cultural shift: Globalisation and migration of the younger working people are leading to an increase in the number of elderly population living alone, particularly in urban areas. Moreover, there are more elderly women than men who live alone. In Kerala and West Bengal, for instance, there is a growing population of the elderly who live alone as children migrate for better opportunities.

Loss of family and social support for seniors: The disintegration of traditional family structure and shift to nuclear families have reduced the amount of family support, home-based care, and day-to-day psychosocial support for the elderly.

Need for senior living communities: 19% of the elderly are divorced, separated, deserted, or live alone. The COVID-19 pandemic exposed the vulnerability of seniors living alone and requiring housing support. Moreover, the traditional housing system is unable to cater to the specific needs of seniors, such as fall-resistant flooring, no sharp edges, and required medical facilities closer to the living place.

Increased probability of abuse and ill-treatment in the elderly population: According to a report by HelpAge India, a charity platform that works for the cause of the disadvantaged elderly people. The survey stated that 35% of elders suffered abuse at the hands of their sons, and 21% reported abuse by their daughters-in-law. About 2% of elders were abused by their house help, who is not a family member. The abuse reported ranged from 'disrespect' and 'verbal abuse' to 'neglect' and 'physical violence'. The elderly population is more likely to suffer abuse and ill-treatment because of a decline in their financial status and functional capabilities. Abuse and mistreatment are more common among elderly women and those living in rural areas. Carer are found to be the primary abusers, making the elderly even more helpless and reluctant to report such incidents

Societal transformation of unparalleled magnitude with far-reaching implications: This demographic shift is not merely a statistic, it's a societal transformation of unparalleled magnitude with far-reaching implications. "As India experiences demographic ageing, it is crucial to ensure that our elderly population has access to the care and support required for them to lead healthy, dignified, and fulfilling lives," remarked Saurabh Garg, Secretary, the Ministry of Social Justice and Empowerment (Government of India).

Ageing is a complex and intricate issue: The United Nations Decade of Healthy Ageing (2021-2030) recognises the far-reaching impact of ageing to encompass not just health systems but labour and financial markets, social protection, and education, among other facets.

Indian elderly are poor: In India, a significant portion of the elderly—roughly half—have no income at all, and 40% of them are in the lowest wealth quintile. The vulnerability of older people is multiplied by social-cultural mindsets and conventions that view them as a "burden," senior maltreatment, and a lack of complete safety nets. It is crucial to emphasise that the senior population is further burdened by the distinct phenomena of feminization and ruralisation.

Ageing & Gender: Women who are elderly citizens outnumber their male counterparts. As per the ***LASI India Report, 2020*-1065/1000 is the senior sex ratio (females vs. males**), and only 10% (rural) and 11% (urban) of senior females are financially independent. The sex ratio of the elderly population is on the higher side for females as compared to their male counterparts. Further, the average life expectancy has increased; however, it has not risen equally for males and females. This gap means that India's older female population is growing faster. 2.8 million and 0.8 million senior women live alone in rural and urban areas, respectively 54% of women are widows and are at higher risk of social exclusion due to a lack of social and financial security. Poor physical health and the stigma around widowhood further increase their vulnerability.

Women elderly do not have economic and social security; they will become more vulnerable in old age. If women in India, where labour force participation is low at 24%, do not have economic and social security, they will become more vulnerable in old age.

Low Access to Social Security measures: As per the India Ageing Report 2023, there is low awareness and utilisation of social security schemes among the elderly. Only 28% of the elderly aware of any concessions for senior citizens. 24% experienced problems in providing documents. A little more than 50% of the elderly are aware of IGNOAPS (Indira Gandhi National Old Age Pension Scheme) and 44% of IGNWPS (Indira Gandhi Widow Pension Scheme). Awareness of the Annapurna scheme is very limited (12%). Further, only 12% of the elderly are aware of the Maintenance and Welfare of Parents and Senior Citizens Act 2007. Further, due to many reasons, awareness of social security schemes does not necessarily lead to their utilization. More than a third (35%) of elderly people could not utilize these schemes because the process of getting benefits is cumbersome.

EFFORTS FOR ELDERLY CARE BY THE INDIAN GOVERNMENT

The Indian government has been very active in addressing the demographic shift driven by the ageing of the population by implementing various initiatives, policies, programmes, and action plans for the welfare of the elderly population. (MoSJE) The Ministry of Social Justice and Empowerment is the nodal ministry responsible for the welfare of senior people in India. It has been leading the overall policy and programme development for senior people in close collaboration with other line ministries such as Finance, Health and family welfare, state governments, NGOs, civil society, and the private sector. MoSJE has led the way in framing India's National Policy on Older Persons and is also implementing the Atal Vayo Abhyudaya Yojana (AVYAY). Under the MOSJE, the National Institute of Social Defence has been the nodal institute tasked with training and research focusing on social defence issues, including the welfare of senior citizens, for over a decade. Further, the maintenance and welfare of parents and senior citizens act, 2007 is landmark legislation that was initiated by MOSJE. In order to provide the elderly with long-term, comprehensive, and dedicated care services that are accessible, affordable, and of high quality, the Ministry of health and family welfare launched the National Programme for the Health Care of the Elderly (NPHCE) in 2010–2011. This initiative helped to create a new “architecture” for ageing and an environment that was conducive to the creation of “a society for all ages.” This programme aligned with various national and international commitments like the UN Convention on the Rights of Persons with Disabilities (UNCRPD), the National Policy on Older Persons (NPOP) adopted by the Government of India in 1999, and Section 20 of “The Maintenance and Welfare of Parents and Senior Citizens Act, 2007” dealing with provisions for medical care of people aged 60 and above. It provides dedicated healthcare facilities to senior citizens at various levels of primary, secondary, and tertiary health care.

Additionally, the Ministry of Rural Development has been administering the National Social Assistance Programme (NSAP), which provides social assistance benefits to vulnerable groups, including seniors, widows, disabled persons, and transgender people. Presently, NSAP, through the Indira Gandhi National Old Age Pension Scheme (IGNOAPS), provides social protection to the elderly through pensions. The central contribution of pension under IGNOAPS is `200 per month per beneficiary up to 79 years and 500 per month per beneficiary from 80 years onwards, and the state governments may contribute over and above this amount. According to the Ministry of Rural Development, more than 2.85 crore senior citizens were receiving social pensions under the NSAP as of December 2020. Besides this, India’s policy response to population ageing encompasses multiple programmes, schemes, and laws that include social protection, financial security, and healthcare service provisions for senior people, especially those belonging to socio-economically vulnerable groups.

Figure 4. Elderly care maintenance structure in India

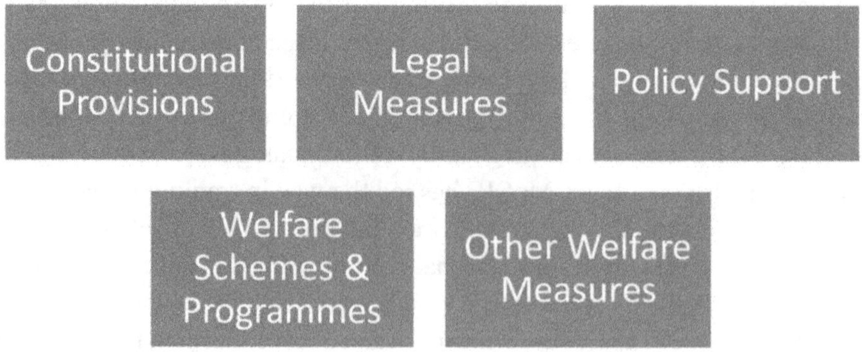

CONSTITUTIONAL PROVISIONS

The provisions of Article 41: The State shall, to the extent of its economic development and capability, provide effective measures to ensure the right to work, education, and public assistance in situations involving old age, illness, or disability, unemployment, as well as in other instances of unreasonable desperation.

The provisions of Article 46: Advancement of the educational and economic interests of Scheduled Tribes, Scheduled Castes, and other marginalised groups include the elderly, the disabled, and others.

7th Schedule of the Indian Constitution: The Seventh Schedule of the Indian Constitution covers economic and social planning, social security and insurance, and old- age pensions. These subjects are particularly covered by items No. 9 of the State List and items 20, 23, and 24 of the Concurrent List. The Concurrent List's entry number 24 is titled "Welfare of Labour, including conditions of work, provident funds, liability for workmen's compensation, invalidity and old age pension, and maternity benefits."

LEGAL MEASURES

Under the Hindu Adoption and Maintenance Act, 1956, Section 20, it is mandatory to make provisions for an ageing parent.

The Criminal Procedure Code's Section 125 allows elderly parents to sue their children for maintenance payments.

Under the Income Tax Act, seniors can claim a tax discount under sections 88-B, 88-D, and 88-DDB.

The 2007 Act Concerning the Maintenance and Well-Being of Senior Citizens and Their Parents.

The NALSA Scheme (2016 provided legal services to senior citizens).

POLICY SUPPORT

National policy for older persons (NPOP): The National Policy on Older Persons (NPOP), which was adopted in 1999, calls for state assistance to guarantee older people's access to resources for bettering their quality of life, as well as their financial and food security, health care, housing, and other needs. It also calls for an equitable share of development and protection from exploitation and abuse. In addition, topics like social security, intergenerational relationships, the role of non-governmental organisations, the family as the primary carer, workforce training, research, and training are covered by the policy.

Welfare Schemes and Programmes

NSAP (National Social Assistance Programme): It is a centrally sponsored scheme that offers financial support ranging from around $200 to $500 per month to the elderly, widowed, and disabled people who meet the BPL qualifying requirements outlined in the NSAP standards. Additionally, the grieving family receives lump sum aid in the event of the breadwinner's death, up to ~20,000/-. States and UTs are responsible for putting the plan into action, and state governments and UT administrations give a top-up on top of the central aid. The following is a description of the NSAP programmes for Disabled people (divyangs) and the elderly:

The scheme for Indira Gandhi Old Age Pension (IGNOAPS): Older people 60–79 years old who fall under the BPL category receive a monthly stipend of 200/-. When an individual reaches the age of 80, their pension is increased to 500 per month. There are 221 lakh beneficiaries in total under the plan.

The IGNDPS, or Indira Gandhi National Disability Pension Scheme,: BPL individuals with severe and numerous disabilities (80% disability level) aged 18-79 years are granted a monthly stipend of 300/-. After turning 80 years old, the pension rises to 500 per month. There are 10.58 lakh beneficiaries in total under the plan.

AVYAY (Atal Vayo Abhyudaya Yojana): The National Action Plan for Senior Citizens (NAPSrc), which preceded the AVYAY, was redesigned and renamed the Atal Vayo Abhyuday Yojana in April 2021. It is a centrally sponsored scheme designed to give Indian seniors more power. The four essential requirements of older adults that AVYAY aims to address are food, health care, human connection, and a life of dignity. Seniors who are impoverished are given free access to basic amenities, including food, shelter, entertainment, and other necessities. It also addresses issues of societal sensitization and awareness-raising, as well as the safety and protection of seniors. Since its launch on April 1, 2021, AVYAY has served as an umbrella programme for the following schemes:

-Integrated Program for Senior Citizens (IPSrC)

- State Action Plan for Senior Citizens (SAPSrC).
- Rashtriya Vayoshree Yojana' (RVY)

-National Helpline (Elderline)

- Senior care Ageing Growth Engine (SAGE)- Promoting Silver Economy*
- Livelihood and Skilling Initiatives for Senior Citizens
- Channeling CSR funds for elderly care

National Programme for Health Care of the Elderly (NPHCE): NPHCE is a state-oriented programme that was introduced in 2010–2011. Its primary goal is to offer senior citizens over 60 comprehensive and specialised health care services at different levels of primary, secondary, and tertiary health care. an all-encompassing programme that was established on April 1, 2021, and which consists of the following programmes:

Pradhan Mantri Vaya Vandana Yojana: The programme was available for enrolment from May 4, 2017, to May 3, 2018, or a full year. Under the policy, a family might purchase a property for as little as 1.5 lakh, with a minimum pension of 1,000 per month, and as much as 7.5 lakh, with a maximum pension of 5,000 per month. The programme's objectives are to safeguard senior citizens (60 years of age and older) against potential interest income declines brought on by erratic market conditions and to offer social security in old life. The Indian Life Insurance Corporation (LIC) is in charge of carrying it out. For ten years, it offers a guaranteed return of 8% annually, payable on a monthly basis. After the first three policy years are up, a financing facility becomes accessible. Each year, the Government of India will subsidise the differential return, which is the difference between the return produced by LIC and the 8% annual guaranteed return. **Varishtha Pension Bima Yojana:** Members of this scheme receive a guaranteed annual pension (payable on a monthly basis) upon payment of a lump sum amount. The Government of India makes up any difference between the guaranteed return and the return that the LIC generates on the fund by paying subsidies under the scheme. After fifteen years after purchasing the policy, the annuitant is permitted to withdraw the amount of deposits made under the scheme. By means of the Life Insurance Corporation of India, the programme is administered.

Atal Pension Yojana: In order to establish a universal social security system for all Indians, particularly the impoverished, the disadvantaged, and those employed in the unorganised sector, the programme was introduced on May 9, 2015. All Indian nationals between the ages of 18 and 40 who have a bank account at a bank or post office are eligible. The scheme offers five pension plan slabs, which are guaranteed by the Government of India to the subscriber at the age of sixty: 1000 Rs., 2000 Rs., 3000 Rs., 4000 Rs., and 5000 Rs.

Ayushman Bharat, (PMJAY): In order to assist over 10 crore impoverished and vulnerable families (about 50 crore beneficiaries), the Government of India introduced ABPMJAY. This programme covers up to ~ 5 lakhs per family year for secondary and tertiary hospitalisation. Since the PMJAY's debut, SCHIS and RSBY have been incorporated into it. Benefits under PMJAY are available to all SCHIS and RSBY enrolled beneficiary families.

(VayoMitra) Ayush Geriatric Healthcare Services under Ayush Public Health Programmes (National Ayush Mission): The National Ayush Mission provides funding for Ayush public health programmes. Vayo Mitra, one of the most recently approved programmes under its purview, is tasked with offering specialised and comprehensive Ayush Geriatric Health Care Services to raise community awareness of various aspects of ageing and ways to lower morbidity in old age. It also aims to promote the importance of maintaining the quality of life and the value of healthy elderly people in the community.

Ayurswasthya Yojana: Ayush and Public Health (PHI), a sub-component of this scheme, is required to provide Ayush interventions on common public health issues related to mental health, non-communicable diseases, MCH, geriatric care, and infectious diseases, among other things. It also has to promote the importance of maintaining quality of life and the value of healthy elderly people to the community.

Annapurna Scheme: The Department of Food and Public Distribution distributes food in accordance with the Ministry of Rural Development's projections under the Annapurna Scheme, which provides 10 kg of free food grains per person per month to impoverished senior citizens who do not receive a pension under the IGNOAPS.

Antyodaya Anna Yojana: Under this programme, households headed by widows, terminally sick individuals, disabled people, or senior citizens receive significantly subsidised rice and wheat, but there is no guarantee of maintenance or social support.

National Council of Senior Citizens (NCSrC): The National Council for Older Persons (NCOP) was established in 1999 in accordance with the National Policy for Older Persons (NPOP) to supervise the Policy's implementation and provide guidance to the Government in the development and execution of policies and programmes for the elderly. In 2012, it was reorganised and given a new name, the National Council of Senior Citizens (NCSrC), with the aim of advising the federal and state governments on a wide range of matters pertaining to senior citizen welfare and improving their standard of living.

Rashtriya Vayoshri Yojana (RVY): The Citizens' Welfare "Senior Fund" provides 100% of the funding for the scheme, which is entirely supported by the Central Government. The amount of free assistance provided in the form of "Physical Aids and Assisted-Living Devices" varies according to the degree of disability or infirmity that the older citizens who qualify for them exhibit. When a person has more than one illness or disability, assistive gadgets will be provided according to each one that shows up in that person. The aids and assisted living gadgets that they supply will receive free maintenance from the Implementing Agency for a period of one year. The maximum cost of the equipment for each recipient citizen and the improvement of their quality of life will not be more than $7,000.

Senior Care Ageing Growth Engine (SAGE): To inspire young people to consider issues facing the elderly and develop creative solutions for their care, then support these ideas as they launch their own businesses by offering equity. On behalf of the Ministry, Industrial Finance Corporation of India (IFCI) Venture Capital Ltd. shall keep the equity support (not to exceed 49%) granted to the creative startup initiatives. A maximum of one crore is given as an equity share to each selected startup.

Senior Able Citizens for Re-Employment in Dignity (SACRED): An IT platform called Senior Able Citizens for Re-Employment in Dignity (SACRED) connects senior citizens looking for work with employers. On October 1, 2021, the Ministry of Social Justice & Empowerment's Department of Social Justice and Empowerment launched the platform.

Action Groups Aimed at Social Reconstruction (AGRASR Self-Help Groups): Action Groups Targeted at Social Reconstruction (AGRASR Groups): Senior citizens are invited to form self-help groups (SHGs) to give them a forum for spending time together in a positive manner.

ADDITIONAL WELFARE PROVISIONS

National Helpline for Senior Citizens, i.e., Elder Line, With Toll-Free Number 14567

For all senior citizens in the nation, the National Helpline for Senior Citizens' toll-free number is 14567. It was established on October 1st, 2021, with the goal of enhancing the quality of life for older adults by offering free advice, information, emotional support, and field action in cases of abuse and rescue. Elderline is open seven days a week; from eight in the morning until eight at night. The Elderline Central Nodal Agency nominee is the National Institute of Social Defence (NISD).

Senior Citizens' Welfare Fund: This welfare fund was established in accordance with the Budget Announcement 2015–16 and will be used to further the welfare of older residents. The Department of Financial Services, the Ministry of Health and Family Welfare, the Ministry of Rural Development, the Ministry of Housing & Urban Affairs, and the Ministry of Labour and Employment make up the Inter-Ministerial Committee that oversees the fund's administration. The Ministry of Social Justice and Empowerment serves as the committee's nodal ministry.

Vayoshreshtha Samman: Since October 1, 2005, the Ministry of Social Justice and Empowerment has observed the International Day of Older Persons (IDOP) to honour the contributions made by notable senior citizens and institutions that have provided outstanding services for the benefit of the aged. Thirteen categories are used to present the awards. To commemorate the International Day of Older Persons (IDOP) on October 1, 2013, the National Awards were first given out.

Accessible India Campaign (Sugamya Bharat Abhiyaan): As a national initiative to achieve universal accessibility for people with disabilities (PwDs), the campaign was started in 2015. In order to develop age-friendly communities, this involves making public restrooms, bus stops, buildings, airports, and other public areas barrier-free and elder-friendly.

E-Anudaan Portal: Through the Ministry of Social Justice and Empowerment's e-Anudaan initiative, non-governmental organisations (NGOs) can register online and log in to apply for grants-in-aid to support the implementation of several ministry programmes. Seats are reserved for buses, railways, and metro trains.

Overall, the government has taken foundational affirmative steps for the welfare of senior citizens, but its presence across the various domains of senior care remains limited. Further, the senior care segment is currently fragmented across a range of other providers, such as voluntary and philanthropic organisations, NGOs, private providers, and industry associations.

SUGGESTION RELATED TO ELDERLY WELL-BEING

- When addressing the health and well-being of the ageing population, a comprehensive strategy that takes into account social, mental, physical, and environmental issues is required. Social services and neighbourhood associations are critical in encouraging older people to live healthy lives and maximising their well-being.
- In order to overcome loneliness and promote emotional resilience, social support might be quite important. Intergenerational activities and community programmes can improve social interaction and lessen loneliness. For older folks, frequent physical activity and mental and physical health examinations are also crucial.
- An important factor in elderly individuals' well-being is their family. It is our responsibility to look after our senior citizens; family should observe their activities and give them advice on what to do and what not to do. Additionally, we must see whether they are receiving enough nourishment.
- Promoting age-friendly surroundings, increasing healthcare service accessibility, and funding projects that target the social determinants of health, affordable housing, access to transportation, and social support networks should be the main objectives of policy initiatives.

- To provide high-quality, reasonably priced care options for senior citizens, long-term care regulations must be changed. This includes providing carer support programmes, ageing-in-place assistance, and increased payment for geriatric services.
- To provide older persons with complete care, multidisciplinary teamwork among healthcare professionals including geriatricians, nurses, social workers, and physical therapists—should be prioritised.
- Community-based organisations actively engage in digital empowerment through computer and internet usage sessions.
- Ministerial committees are dedicated to shaping policies for welfare of the elderly. The enhancement of geriatric care to cater to the unique healthcare needs of seniors must be done.

CONCLUSION

There are several schemes to take care of the elderly, but to ensure that senior citizens live with dignity, public and private policies must provide a more supportive environment. To meet the challenges, physical and mental health, the basic needs of food and shelter, income security, and social care, a 'whole-of-society' approach is required. Geriatric care must be fine-tuned to their unique health-care needs. India needs to realign, reorganise, and re-orient its existing policy landscape to map out an effective and efficient senior care ecosystem. Which contains various programmes and policies that address the specific needs of the ageing population, such as increasing access to affordable healthcare services, strengthening the social welfare system, and promoting economic opportunities to safeguard seniors against economic hardships, in line with the concept of ageing and senior care. Additionally, there is a need for increased public awareness and education about the issues facing older adults and the importance of including them in policy decisions.

REFERENCES

Arti & Mittal J.K. (2020). Indian *Journal of Public Health Research & Development*, *2*(11). _https://doi.org/10.37506/ijphrd.v11i1

Department of Economic and Social Affairs. (2022). *Population Division, World Population Prospects 2022, Online Edition*. UN. https://population. un.org/wpp/)

Goswami, A., Reddaiah, V. P., Kapoor, S. K., Singh, B., Dwivedi, S. N., & Kumar, G. (2005). *Tobacco and alcohol use in rural elderly Indian population*. Ind Joul of Psy. 10.4103/0019-5545.43050

The Hindu. (2023). India must attune its policies to ensure the elderly live a life of dignity. *The Hindu.*

Ministry of social Justice & Empowerment. (2023). *Critical Insights Into Elderly Care In India.* Press information Bureau government of India. https://pib.gov.in/ pressReleasePage.aspx?PRID=1961168)

Vats, S. (2022). 35% senior citizens in India suffer abuse by sons, 21% by daughters-in-law, finds survey. *The Print.* (https://theprint.in/india/35-senior-citizens-in-india -suffer-abuse-by-sons-21-by-daughters-in-law-finds-survey/997283/)

Chapter 8
Balancing Innovation and Access:
The Role of Patents and Traditional and Non-Traditional Trademarks in Healthcare

Karun Sanjaya
VIT School of Law, Vellore Institute of Technology, Chennai, India & Symbiosis Law School, Symbiosis International University (Deemed), Pune, India

P. R. L. Rajavenkatesan
VIT School of Law, Vellore Institute of Technology, Chennai, India

ABSTRACT

The book chapter offers comprehensive coverage of the complex interplay between patents, trademarks, and health care. The chapter highlights the fine and tenuous line between stimulating innovation in the field and ensuring access to life-saving and essential medical technologies. The chapter investigates the positive and negative externalities produced by patents and trademarks in research and development and market contexts, as well as their effects on consumer behaviour in the healthcare sector. The authors have analysed the role played by both traditional and non-traditional trademarks in the healthcare sector. The chapter also addresses the ethical and accessibility dilemmas pertaining to the right to intellectual property and the potential policy reforms, which would alleviate the tension between creating incentives for innovation and protecting public health. By reviewing both the literature and specific case studies, the chapter enlightens the reader on the ways to tackle the dual challenge of promoting innovation and ensuring that health care is a right for all.

DOI: 10.4018/979-8-3693-5976-1.ch008

INTRODUCTION

A patent is a legal document that grants an inventor exclusive rights to develop, use, or sell the invention for a limited time, usually 20 years from the filing date (World Intellectual Property Organization, 2019a). A trademark is a sign or symbol that is distinctively used by an organization to identify and differentiate its goods from those produced by others (World Intellectual Property Organization, 2019b). In the healthcare sector, patents protect innovative drugs, medical equipment, and biotechnology, while trademarks enable companies to develop their brand identity and market trust in products (European Union, 2022). The two aspects play a crucial role in the healthcare sector. A patent encourages innovative thinking by offering inventors and developers the exclusive right to monetize their innovations, which motivates investment in research (Williams, 2017). It also enables those that risk fortunes in research to secure their invention and help cover the investment costs, especially in drug development (Williams, 2017). Trademarks help organizations develop a brand that consumers can trust and get attached to while providing organizations with an asset to base their market operations (Abou Naja Intellectual Property, 2024). They are thus a valuable asset for these companies and have a notable influence on the market culture and consumers.

In this chapter, the authors will shed light on more diverse roles of patents and trademarks in healthcare that include shaping the context for innovation, driving market forces, and facilitating consumer choices. The chapter will further identify ethical and access implications of such intellectual property rights in healthcare and suggest a balanced approach toward innovation promotion over public health. Finally, the chapter offers suggestions that help advance access to healthcare without undermining the innovation in the field.

PATENTS IN HEALTHCARE

A patent is a legal instrument that gives an inventor exclusive rights to their invention, making it possible to benefit financially from their innovative idea and prevent others from using the invention without their approval (Sanjaya, 2020). In the field of healthcare, patents help secure new pharmaceuticals, unique medical appliances, and at times novel biotechnologies by making potential financial backers and developers confident that the inventor has a time frame when they can benefit exclusively from the innovation (European Union, 2022). The significance of patents in stimulating innovation cannot be overestimated. Patents give inventors the reassurance that they will eventually recoup their massive investment in R&D because they would be able to charge the monopoly price of their products for a limited period of time granted by the patent (Grabowski, 2002). This monetary reward encourages businesses to pursue high-risk research projects because they realize that they may generate money for a certain period of time by selling those foods and not having to worry about the competition copying their goods (Guellec, 2007). If companies were unable to patent their inventions, many would be unable to afford the cost of developing new healthcare technologies and would never see the light of day.

Patents are fundamental to the company's efforts to recoup the cost of research and development. Patents confer monopolistic property rights on inventors, allowing them to charge higher prices that consumers may not be able to afford. Patents are used to incentivize companies to engage in long-term research and development projects that are tough to license. Patents enable inventors to safeguard their intellectual property rights by allowing them to publish preferred technological know-how anchored on that information (Cameron & Hajhashem, 2015). However, broad patents especially in sectors like genetic testing and personalized medicine have generated a lot of speculation about access to critical tools and the defeat of the competitive operation (Chandrasekharan & Cook-Deegan, 2009).

Several instances serve as proof of the essential contribution of patents to healthcare innovation. For instance, "two long patented treatments, the invention of insulin (1923) and the Polymerase Chain Reaction (PCR) technique for DNA amplification ", were originally developed with the help of the financial support from investors who were encouraged by the opportunity to rely on a legal patent and intellectual property protection regime (McDowell, 2006). As these examples prove, patents have become a pivotal tool to encourage the necessary investment in R&D and the possibility of progress in the healthcare domain.

TRADEMARKS IN HEALTHCARE

A trademark is an identifying symbol, sign, or logo that is used to distinguish one product or service from those of other companies. For instance, in the field of healthcare, pharmaceuticals, medical devices, and service providers are branded using unique trademarks that help consumers to quickly determine a product or service's source (Chouhan, 2020).

Importance of Trademarks in the Healthcare Sector

Trademarks have the following significant implications in a healthcare setting: first and foremost, strong trademarks are vehicles for rigorous branding and product differentiation. A strong and established trademark signifies stability, quality, and dependability with a user and providers' consumer confidence. It leads to brand loyalty, with users and providers depending on a specific name, coupled with availability in relying on a specific product or service (De Penning & De Penning, 2024). Contemporarily, trademarks have become eponymous, with some being synonymous with the products they represent. Pfizer's Viagra and Johnson & Johnson's Band-Aid are some of the established trademarks that have become self-describing (Chow, 2012). Secondly, the presence of trademarks influences the choice of an operator and the level of competition. Established names, logos, symbols, and signs have a superior advantage gained though reputational systems from established clientele making it hard for new operators to thrive. Due to the existence of trademarks, a single company with similar products can have different products on the market thereby enhancing market competition and transparency (Maniatis, 1998).

There are instances that show the impact trademarks have on healthcare products. For example, trademarks have contributed to the commercial success of certain drugs by creating impressions of market authorities in their respective therapeutic classifications (Nimje, 2022). "Crestor", a pharmaceutical remedy for high cholesterol and a product of rosuvastatin, and "Advair", a prescription medicine that combines fluticasone and salmeterol, are two examples (Anwar et al., 2015). Similarly, trademarks are used to identify medical devices, such as "MRI-compatible" implants, which have been promoted on the factor that they can be used with magnetic resonance imaging (Rapacke, 2018). These situations underscore the significance of trademarks in achieving market dynamics and influencing consumer attitudes about healthcare goods.

Role of Non-Traditional Trademarks in the Healthcare Sector

Non-traditional trademarks are identifiers that expand beyond primary logos and brand names. Thus, in the sector of pharmaceuticals, they may be colours, shapes, sounds, or scents that can even be product packaging. Their primary role is to enable the industry to distinguish its products from those of competitors and ensure that consumers recognize the brand. Pharmaceutical companies have discovered alternative methods to safeguard their products through unconventional trademarks. One of the most well-known examples is Nexium, developed by AstraZeneca plc. Known as the 'purple pill', Nexium® is a medication prescribed for chronic heartburn. Its unique purple and gold colour combination has been trademarked (Wasserman, 2015). In addition, the mark has already been utilised to block Dr Reddy's Laboratories Ltd, an Indian generic manufacturer, from introducing its purple-colored heartburn pills into the US market (Dandekar, 2015). After making some adjustments, Dr Reddy's successfully launched its drug, which now features blue pills (Dandekar, 2015).

Viagra serves as an illustration of another distinctive trademark for a pharmaceutical drug that deviates from the norm. More precisely, the unique blue colour and diamond-shaped tablet have been officially recognised as a trademark for pharmaceuticals intended to address sexual dysfunction (Gallant, 2009). However, there are challenges when it comes to acquiring unconventional marks for pharmaceuticals. At times, the functional purpose of colour has been discovered, just like when Pepto-Bismol® made efforts to safeguard its renowned pink hue (McVean, 2023).

Non-traditional trademarks play a significant role in the pharmaceutical sector, with companies using unique shapes and colours to distinguish their products (Calboli, 2019). An outstanding example of a non-traditional trademark in the pharma industry is Viagra's pill's unique shape that has become a distinguishing feature of the drug (Daly & Emery, 2019). Pharmaceutical companies like Gilead Sciences, Pfizer, and AstraZeneca have utilized non-traditional marks such as unique shapes and colours for products like Viread, Viagra, and Nexium, respectively (Scaria & Mammen, 2018). Other examples include AstraZeneca's heartburn medicine Nexium, known for its distinctive purple and gold colour combination, and Gilead Sciences' Truvada, Ranexa, Letairis, and Stribild, each having unique visual characteristics (Scaria & Mammen, 2018). These non-traditional trademarks add uniqueness to products and help in brand recognition and product differentiation in the competitive pharmaceutical market (Scaria & Mammen, 2018).

AstraZeneca's successful branding strategy with Prilosec and Nexium showcased the power of branding in retaining customer loyalty even after generic competitors entered the market (Fritch, 2006). However, there are concerns regarding branded drugs being granted monopoly rights over the physical attributes which enforce the notion of low-quality generics, affecting consumer perceptions and adherence (Aivalli et al., 2018). Other works argue the importance of physical attributes in pharmaceuticals for patient adherence, placebo effects, and public health considerations (Miller et al., 2009). For instance, the consumers may associate colour, shape, and size of medications with quality and increase adherence and placebo effects (Alessandrini et al., 2023). This reiterates the need for similar physical appearances of the branded and generic drugs. Furthermore, the courts of law have acknowledged physical attributes of pharmaceuticals as functional with regard to patient populations, thus, impacting the decisions on trademark protection (Halabi, 2021).

However, it should be remembered that the protection of non-traditional marks in the pharmaceutical sphere can result in barriers to access to medicine for the population, the increase in transaction costs, and limitations on the generics entry to the market (Scaria & Mammen, 2018). Policymakers should take the implications for public health into account when considering the protection of non-traditional marks to pharmaceuticals. Trademark protection should not be employed to extend the manufacturers' branded drug monopolies perpetually with protection, and functionality should be taken into consideration to avoid the abovementioned barriers to the access to medicine-affordability (Nimje, 2022). It has been seen that the international and national health policies often overlook the public health implications of extending protection to non-traditional marks in the pharmaceutical sector (Scaria & Mammen, 2018).

ETHICAL AND ACCESS CONCERNS

Patents and trademarks in the healthcare sector are fraught with significant ethical issues. Specifically, patent protections confer inventors with exclusive rights to control the production, distribution, and pricing of their inventions. Therefore, it incentivized the development of the innovation but became a monopoly practice to acquire substantial profit and restricted access to vital drugs. Similarly, trademarks grant brand recognition, but they may be unethical as they may lead to deceptive advertising and promotion of healthcare inventions. Therefore, the pursuit of inventors' interests should combine and balance healthcare access and affordability of the community.

Patents and trademarks protection may act as major barriers to access to healthcare services and products, especially in an environment with resource constraints (Sellin, 2015). The exorbitant costs of medications due to exclusive patents could make life-saving treatments financially out of reach for individuals, resulting in unequal availability and compromised health. In a similar vein, trademarks may aim at restricting competition even among generic manufacturers, thus leading to issues with access to affordable alternatives (Sellin, 2015). Such disparities move across generations and socio-cultural backgrounds, and, as such, dealing with those is an ethical matter.

On a global level, disparities in healthcare access are also fuelled by intellectual property rights, consisting of patents and trademarks (Salazar, 1998). In developed countries, these systems act effectively such by creating incentives to innovate and protect product quality, and it is not rare that denials of access to medication are created by such branded healthcare products (Khachigian, 2020). However, developing countries face challenges in affording costly patented medication and branded healthcare products due to limited resources. In addition, unfair intellectual property laws can hinder the transfer of technology and the local manufacturing of essential healthcare products, resulting in low-income countries being reliant on multinational pharmaceutical companies (Diependaele et al., 2016). In this context, it is crucial to create a balance taking into consideration the rights of individuals, the availability of public health services, the affordability and access to the same. There are several examples that portray the ethical and access concerns in the healthcare sector caused due to patents and trademarks. For instance, the exorbitant price of patented drugs for the treatment of cancer and HIV has been criticised for being unaffordable and hence inaccessible (Bognar et al., 2016). Besides, trademark disputes between patented and generic drugs pertaining to the renaming of generic drugs also acts as entry barriers for the generic drugs after the expiry of the patent thereby extending their monopoly and delaying the entry of generics into the market. (Sarpatwari & Kesselheim, 2016). These instances highlight the importance of considering reflectivity and policymaker interventions to mitigate the adverse effects of intellectual property on access and equity.

STRATEGIES FOR BALANCING INNOVATION AND ACCESS

Addressing the Dual Role of Patents and Trademarks

The ultimate goal for the policy- and decision-makers is to strike a balance between promoting innovation through patents and trademarks and ensuring that life-saving health technologies are affordable for all citizens. The challenge arises in determining the extent to which innovation must be protected through patents and trademarks, on the one hand, and the need to ensure broad access, on the other. The former is necessary to stimulate investments and innovations, but they must not compromise access to products they enable by any means. Protecting property rights is critical as it can lead to potential abuse under conditions of private control. It can be addressed by introducing price controls and compulsory licencing that would facilitate wider access to patented medicines (Urias & Ramani, 2020). Policymaking can also stimulate transparency and accountability in the area of patents and trademarks to establish a conducive environment for fair play and further innovations (West, 2008).

Therefore, to consider the complex nature of the governance response to the healthcare challenges, the thoughtful and holistic approach should be used. It must consider both incentives for innovation and public health needs. Although patents and trademarks are essential tools to drive innovation and maintain high quality levels, their management must be centered on patient needs (World Health Organisation, World Intellectual Property Organisation & World Trade Organisation, 2013). Policymakers in the area of intellectual property rights must assess the potential consequences of their decisions. They must make decisions that would avoid limiting access to the medicine and drive costs up. Monopolistic practices and unfair pricing can prove to have more adverse effects than advantageous (Bhattacharya &

Saha, 2011). Hence, evidence-based policy-making and stakeholder collaboration would help the government introduce policies that would maximize incentives for intelligence and minimize fragmentation for access.

Addressing the Ethical and Access Concerns

While addressing ethical and access concerns related to healthcare, it is also necessary to consider potential reforms or alternatives to the existing patent and trademark systems. First, this can be achieved through the use of differential pricing mechanisms that would make patented medicines affordable for residents of relatively low-income countries and remain profitable in relatively high-income markets (Danzon & Towse, 2003). Secondly, it is worthwhile to pay more attention to open innovation models, such as patent pools and technology sharing agreements, in cases where patent protection works against access to innovations. Such an approach would create conditions for researchers who could consolidate their resources on specific projects and deliver high-quality products to as many consumers as possible (Lee et al., 2010). Finally, additional ways to protect intellectual property, such as data exclusivity and regulatory exclusivity, can complement patents and trademarks, promoting innovation, and maintaining competition in the health care industry.

Moreover, based on the analysis of case studies, some evidence-based conclusions regarding the most appropriate ways of creating a regulatory environment that can satisfy innovation needs without sacrificing patients' access to medicine. Thus, one of such unique initiatives is a medicines patent pool that has enabled a series of voluntary licensing agreements among prominent pharmaceutical companies to increase access to affordable drugs for the treatment of HIV/AIDS in low-income countries (Gore et al., 2023). Moreover, the US experience demonstrates the effect of the regulatory framework for the creation and promotion of the production of generic drugs, as well as faster launch (Kovács et al., 2021). Therefore, these examples prove that it is possible to resolve this issue through special measures and the participation of interested parties.

CONCLUSION AND SUGGESTIONS

Patents and trademarks are continuing to steer the legal front of the healthcare sector. On the one hand, this is based on technological advances that have led to the de-fragmentation of health services across borders and patients, each with unique needs. Some of the changes in the legal front are instigated by globalization, for example, individual property rights in biotechnological, digital health innovation, and personalized medicine. Bhattacharya and Saha (2011) indicate that there have been recent changes and novel avenues such as personalized medicine in the new innovation value chain. Policymakers have faced increased legal complexity linked to the new forms of intellectual property, such as the right granted through data exclusivity and trade secrets (Diependaele et al., 2016). The laws have primed on international agreements and partnerships such as TRIPS agreement under the World Trade Organization (World Trade Organization, 2019). This approach influences the availability of health care essential medicine and technologies globally.

Given that the existing legal policies have failed to promote innovation and increase access to healthcare technologies, there is a need for researchers and policymakers to work in varied areas to address these dynamic problems. Meanwhile, based on the study conducted by Yamabhai & Smith (2012), it has been found that the existing policies didn't ensure access to healthcare services and protection of innovation. Furthermore, there is a need for a new approach to managing intellectual property (Lee et al., 2010). The new approach should improve transparency, accountability, and equity in the system to reduce inequalities in the healthcare sector hence improving long-term innovation. The utilization of non-traditional trademarks by the pharma industry is also a recent threat that may affect the generic industry to a great extent. To sum up, the patents, trademarks and the healthcare trio gives rise to a number of problems and opportunities as far as innovation and access are concerned. The focus should be to overcome the challenges and make the best use of the opportunities without compromising access.

REFERENCES

Abou Naja Intellectual Property. (2024). *7 Reasons Why Trademarks are Important for Startups*. Abounaja.com. https://abounaja.com/blogs/7-reasons-why-trademarks-are-important#:~:text=Trademarks%20also%20provide%20legal%20protection

Aivalli, P. K., Elias, M. A., Pati, M. K., Bhanuprakash, S., Munegowda, C., Shroff, Z. C., & Srinivas, P. N. (2018). Perceptions of the quality of generic medicines: Implications for trust in public services within the local health system in Tumkur, India. *BMJ Global Health*, 2(Suppl 3), e000644. 10.1136/bmjgh-2017-00064429531844

Alessandrini, E., Gonakova, M., Batchelor, H., Gizurarson, S., Iurian, S., Klein, S., Schaufelberger, D., Turner, R., Walsh, J., & Tuleu, C. (2023). Colour of Medicines and Children's Acceptability? A Systematic Literature Review of Children's Perceptions about Colours of Oral Dosage Forms. *Pharmaceutics*, 15(7), 1992. 10.3390/pharmaceutics1507199237514178

Anwar, M. M., El-Haggar, R. S., & Zaghary, W. A. (2015). Salmeterol Xinafoate. *Profiles of Drug Substances, Excipients, and Related Methodology*, 40, 321–369. 10.1016/bs.podrm.2015.02.00226051688

Bhattacharya, S., & Saha, C. N. (2011). Intellectual property rights: An overview and implications in pharmaceutical industry. *Journal of Advanced Pharmaceutical Technology & Research, 2*(2), 88. 10.4103/2231-4040.82952

Bognar, C. L. F. B., Bychkovsky, B. L., & Lopes, G. de L.Jr. (2016). Compulsory Licenses for Cancer Drugs: Does Circumventing Patent Rights Improve Access to Oncology Medications? *Journal of Global Oncology*, 2(5), 292–301. 10.1200/JGO.2016.00536328717715

Calboli, I. (2019). Beyond Patents: The Problems of Non-Traditional Trademark Protection for Medicines and Health Technologies. *IIC - International Review of Intellectual Property and Competition Law, 51*. 10.1007/s40319-019-00893-y

Cameron, H., & Hajhashem, M. (2015). *THE INTERSECTION OF INTELLECTUAL PROPERTY RIGHTS AND INNOVATION POLICY MAKING -A LITERATURE REVIEW*. WIPO. https://www.wipo.int/edocs/pubdocs/en/wipo_report_ip_inn.pdf

Chandrasekharan, S., & Cook-Deegan, R. (2009). Gene patents and personalized medicine - what lies ahead? *Genome Medicine*, 1(9), 92. 10.1186/gm9219804612

Chouhan, N. (2020, April 30). *Introduction to Pharmaceutical Trademarks*. Sagacious IP. https://sagaciousresearch.com/blog/introduction-pharmaceutical-trademarks/

Chow, D. (2012). Lessons from Pfizer's Disputes Over its Viagra Trademark in China. *Maryland Journal of International Law, 27*(1), 82. https://digitalcommons.law.umaryland.edu/mjil/vol27/iss1/9

Danzon, P. M., & Towse, A. (2003). Differential Pricing for Pharmaceuticals: Reconciling Access, R&D and Patents. *International Journal of Health Care Finance and Economics*, 3(3), 183–205. https://www.jstor.org/stable/3528839. 10.1023/A:1025384819575146259999

De Penning & De Penning. (2024, March 4). *Decoding Consumer Perception: How Trademarks Shape Your Choices*. De Penning & de Penning. https://depenning.com/blog/trademarks-on-consumer-perception/

Diependaele, L., Cockbain, J., & Sterckx, S. (2016). Raising the Barriers to Access to Medicines in the Developing World - The Relentless Push for Data Exclusivity. *Developing World Bioethics*, 17(1), 11–21. 10.1111/dewb.1210526818105

European Union. (2022). *Intellectual Property and the Pharma & Healthcare Sectors in India*. EU. https://www.cde.ual.es/wp-content/uploads/2022/06/EA0722284ENN.en-1.pdf

Fritch, D. (2006). SHOULD "THE PURPLE PILL" BY ANY OTHER DRUG COMPANY STILL BE AS PURPLE? THE CHANGING FACE OF TRADE DRESS PROTECTION FOR PHARMACEUTICAL MANUFACTURERS. *IDEA - the Intellectual Property Law Review, 47*(2). https://ipmall.law.unh.edu/sites/default/files/hosted_resources/IDEA/idea-vol47-no2-fritch.pdf

Gore, C., Morin, S., Røttingen, J.-A., & Kieny, M. P. (2023). Negotiating public-health intellectual property licensing agreements to increase access to health technologies: An insider's story. *B. Journal of Global Health*, 8(9), e012964. 10.1136/bmjgh-2023-01296437669799

Grabowski, H. (2002). Patents, Innovation and Access to New Pharmaceuticals. *Journal of International Economic Law*, 5(4), 849–860. https://ideas.repec.org/a/oup/jieclw/v5y2002i4p849-860.html. 10.1093/jiel/5.4.849

Guellec, D. (2007). Patents as an Incentive to Innovate. In D. Guellec & B. van P. Potterie (Eds.), *The Economics of the European Patent System: IP Policy for Innovation and Competition*. Oxford University Press.

Halabi, S. F. (2021). Trademarks, Trade Dress, and the Patient Costs of Pharmaceutical Branding. *New York University Journal of Intellectual Property & Entertainment Law, 11*(2). https://jipel.law.nyu.edu/wp-content/uploads/2022/03/JIPEL-Halabi-Fall-2021.pdf

Khachigian, L. M. (2020). Pharmaceutical patents: Reconciling the human right to health with the incentive to invent. *Drug Discovery Today*, 25(7), 1135–1141. Advance online publication. 10.1016/j.drudis.2020.04.00932325020

Kovács, B., Darida, M., & Simon, J. (2021). Drugs Becoming Generics—The Impact of Genericization on the Market Performance of Antihypertensive Active Pharmaceutical Ingredients. *International Journal of Environmental Research and Public Health*, 18(18), 9429. 10.3390/ijerph18189429345 74353

Lee, N., Nystén-Haarala, S., & Huhtilainen, L. (2010). *Interfacing Intellectual property rights and Open innovation*. WIPO. https://www.wipo.int/edocs/mdocs/mdocs/en/wipo_ipr_ge_11/wipo_ipr_ge_11_topic6.pdf

Maniatis, S. M. (1998). *The communicative aspects of trade marks: a legal, functional and economic analysis* [Thesis]. https://core.ac.uk/download/pdf/30695616.pdf

McDowell, D. (2006). The polymerase chain reaction patents: Going, going, still going. *Journal of the Royal Society of Medicine*, 99(2), 62–64. 10.1258/jrsm.99.2.6216449778

Miller, F. G., Colloca, L., & Kaptchuk, T. J. (2009). The Placebo Effect: Illness and Interpersonal Healing. *Perspectives in Biology and Medicine*, 52(4), 518–539. 10.1353/pbm.0.011519855122

Nimje, P. (2022, May 10). *The Need for Trademark in Pharmaceutical Industry*. Sagacious IP. https://sagaciousresearch.com/blog/the-need-for-trademark-in-pharmaceutical-industry/

OECD. (2004). *Patents And Innovation: Trends And Policy Challenges Organisation For Economic Co-Operation And Development*. OECD. https://www.oecd.org/science/inno/24508541.pdf

Rapacke, A. (2018, September 18). *The Role Trademarks Play in Medical Device Technologies - The Rapacke Law Group*. Arapackelaw.com. https://arapackelaw.com/trademarks/role-trademarks-medical-devices/

Salazar, S. (1998). *INTELLECTUAL PROPERTY AND THE RIGHT TO HEALTH*. WIPO. https://www.wipo.int/edocs/mdocs/tk/en/wipo_unhchr_ip_pnl_98/wipo_unhchr_ip_pnl_98_3.pdf

Sanjaya, K. (2020). Competition Law and IPRs: Friends or Foes? *International Journal of Law Management & Humanities*, 3(6). 10.1732/IJLMH.25187

Sarpatwari, A., & Kesselheim, A. S. (2016). The Case for Reforming Drug Naming: Should Brand Name Trademark Protections Expire upon Generic Entry? *PLoS Medicine*, 13(2), e1001955. 10.1371/journal.pmed.100195526859662

Scaria, A. G., & Mammen, K. S. (2018). Non-Traditional Trademarks in the Pharmaceutical Sector. In Calboli, I., & Senftleben, M. (Eds.), *The Protection of Non-Traditional Trademarks: Critical Perspectives* (pp. 271–286). Oxford University Press. 10.1093/oso/9780198826576.003.0015

Sellin, J. A. (2015). Does One Size Fit All? Patents, the Right to Health and Access to Medicines. *Netherlands International Law Review*, 62(3), 445–473. 10.1007/s40802-015-0047-5

Urias, E., & Ramani, S. V. (2020). Access to medicines after TRIPS: Is compulsory licensing an effective mechanism to lower drug prices? A review of the existing evidence. *Journal of International Business Policy*, 3(4), 367–384. Advance online publication. 10.1057/s42214-020-00068-4

West, J. K. (2008). Competition, Patents and Innovation. In SSRN *Electronic Journal*. 10.2139/ssrn.1081332

Williams, H. L. (2017). How Do Patents Affect Research Investments? *Annual Review of Economics*, 9(1), 441–469. 10.1146/annurev-economics-110216-10095929104716

World Health Organization, World Intellectual Property Organization and World Trade Organization. (2013). *Promoting Access to Medical Technologies and Innovation Intersections between public health, intellectual property and trade*. WHO. https://www.wto.org/english/res_e/booksp_e/pamtiwhowipowtoweb13_e.pdf

World Intellectual Property Organization. (2019a). *Patents*. WIPO. https://www.wipo.int/patents/en/

World Intellectual Property Organization. (2019b). *Trademarks*. WIPO. https://www.wipo.int/trademarks/en/

World Trade Organization. (2019). *WTO | intellectual property - overview of TRIPS Agreement*. WTO. https://www.wto.org/english/tratop_e/trips_e/intel2_e.htm

Yamabhai, I., & Smith, R. D. (2012). A review of the health and economic implications of patent protection, with a specific focus on Thailand. *Health Research Policy and Systems*, 10(1), 24. 10.1186/1478-4505-10-2422849392

Chapter 9
Medical Tourism and Health Gateways in International Health Market Places:
Stimulating Sustainability and Technological Advancements

Bhupinder Singh
https://orcid.org/0009-0006-4779-2553
Sharda University, India

Christian Kaunert
https://orcid.org/0000-0002-4493-2235
Dublin City University, Ireland

Budi Agus Riswandi
Universitas Islam Indonesia, Indonesia

Manmeet Kaur Arora
https://orcid.org/0009-0002-5071-117X
Sharda University, India

Sahil Lal
https://orcid.org/0000-0001-9827-3717
Sharda University, India

ABSTRACT

Medical tourism has the ability to reshape how patients move around in global

DOI: 10.4018/979-8-3693-5976-1.ch009

healthcare, providing new opportunities for access to high standardised services and quality resources as industries progress through innovation and technological advancements. A critical factor for medical tourism is that this newfound option must be imbued with sustainability; it has to go hand in hand respecting equity and social responsibility. It is structured such that it provides insights for those interested in creating policies, practicing medicine, or dealing with diagnosis. This chapter investigates the contribution of medical tourism in supporting sustainability and technological transfer, at the global health market. It will look at what is driving the growth of medical tourism and why patients are seeking healthcare abroad, as well as some of the hurdles and benefits with this burgeoning space for both patient consumers and provider stakeholders.

INTRODUCTION

The Movement of persons across national borders to seek medical treatment is rapidly becoming a worldwide, multibillion-dollar industry known as Medical Tourism. A variety of reasons has led to this trend, the main ones being expensive healthcare in developed countries satellite by long waitlist for certain procedures and affordable high-end technology available in emerging economies. As a result, the medical tourism industry has flourished in recent years and it is believed that by 2012 this business could become from $60 to nearly US$100 billion yearly. Purpose: This research paper explores the role played by medical tourism in sustainability and advancement of technology for global healthcare marketplace. This chapter explore the primary drivers of medical tourism and reasons for its growth, an examination of benefits and risks associated with this type services faced by patient as well as healthcare providers (HCPs) (Ansari et al., 2024).

Figure 1. Dimensions of introduction section

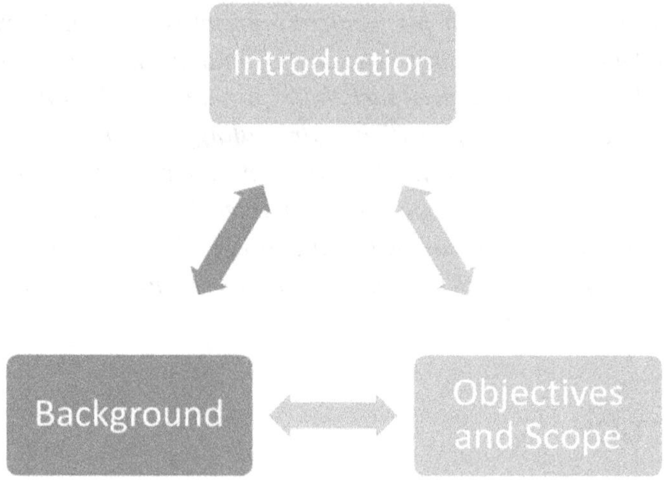

(Source- Original)

The most notable contributor to medical tourism is the large potential savings that patients have when they resort to foreign healthcare providers. Cardiac surgery at Apollo Hospital in New Delhi, India costs $4.000 whereas the same cost around 30K$ in USA. Likewise, an American could get a knee replacement for as little $12,000 in India compared to costs of well over US$30. Those cost savings is what has made medical tourism an appealing solution for uninsured, underinsured or those who have to wait long periods of time domestically due to the need. The availability of stem cell therapies at a lower cost has been one major reason medical tourism has proliferated, and the proliferation will continue with the advance healthcare technologies across developing countries.

In countries such as India, Thailand and Singapore there are numerous hospitals that have spent big on world-class facilities and equipment - including hiring physicians/technicians trained to international standards. This has helped them provide top-notch medical services at an affordable prize range, thus bringing in patients from all over the world. Meanwhile, the rise of medical tourism has entailed a variety of potential sustainability and inequality impacts on healthcare systems that worry public health scholars especially in developing countries. However, there is a danger the arrival of medical tourists will come at the expense of resources and attention to local population which could create two-tier system in which high-quality care was available only for affluent people while hundreds are denied base health services. Finally, and importantly, the environmental impact of medical tourism including the carbon footprint associated with travelling internationally must be taken into consideration. This research paper reviews how these concerns may be addressed by promoting sustainable and equitable medical tourism practices. For instance, it could be investing in local healthcare infrastructure, training and keeping health human resources or carrying out environment sustainability actions. The possible positive impacts of technology to stimulate improved efficiency, accessibility and quality health care delivery. For example telemedicine or data analytics in medical tourism service provisions will also be discussed.

Medical tourism has the ability to reshape how patients move around in global healthcare providing new opportunities for access to high standardised services and quality resources as industries progress through innovation and technological advancements. But, the critical factor for medical tourism is that this new found option must be imbued with sustainability; it has to go hand in hand respecting equity and social responsibility. It is structured such that it provides insights for those interested in creating policies, practicing medicine, or dealing with diagnosis.

Background of the Chapter

Over the last couple of years, one industry that has begun to back its head in a big way is Medical Tourism as it grows exponentially on global front. Medical tourism involves individuals from one country who seek medical treatment in another, often at a lower cost and with shorter waiting times or to receive specialized care. The trend has been buoyed by the expensive healthcare of developed countries, prolonged waiting times for some treatments and advanced medical technology available in developing nations.

The growth potential for the medical tourism industry has been cited as a $100 billion revenue opportunity by 2012. With 2006 the industry was making in excess of $60 billion dollars a year world-wide. Medical tourism has also benefited from a global pattern in which patients of affluent nations including Americans traveling to former "third world" locales for inexpensive medical procedures executed by top-notch doctors (Poornima & Subramanian, 2024). But medical tourism involves equally serious concerns including the sustainability and equity of healthcare systems, especially in developing economies. The availability of advanced healthcare service could be diverted or may have to accomodate too many medical tourists and the local populace would need contrastingly different quality care under limited resources leading into a two tier system. Moreover, the environmental toll of medical tourism such as international travel related carbon footprint needs to be complemented.

Objectives and Scope of the Chapter

This chapter investigates the contribution of medical tourism in supporting sustainability and technological transfer, at the global health market. It will look at what is driving the growth of medical tourism and why patients are seeking healthcare abroad, as well as some of the hurdles and benefits with this burgeoning space for both patient consumers and provider stakeholders. This will be done against the backdrop of our experience and knowledge we have as to some approaches that may potentially reverse or mitigate current forms of unsustainable medical tourism, which includes investing in local infrastructure for healthcare services, training and retaining health workers, adding sustainability markers. Also, it will delve into the part of technology in increasing medical tourism performance (telemedicine & data analytics). This chapter seeks to add the sources of evidence and enable a more informed discussion of what policymakers, healthcare providers and patients could learn from medical tourism as part its future -or unconstrained growth-especially in light potential impact on global health systems. These results are of special interest to countries worldwide, particularly developing nations endeavouring to compete with developed ones by occupying a unique niche in the growing health tourism industry as well as for those facing increasing healthcare prices and low levels access.

GLOBAL MEDICAL TOURISM INDUSTRY

Medical tourism, known as health tourism or medical travel, is when individuals cross international borders to obtain medical treatment. The main reasons for becoming a medical tourist are preferable costs, availability of technology, or opportunity to see the specialist quickly after arriving in the country where medical services are of the best possible quality . The rise of medical tourism is largely due to the high cost of healthcare in developed countries and the long waiting times for operations or their total unavailability. Currently, emerging markets are trying to attract medical tourists by offering new technologies that have lower costs in order to obtain profit from the industry (Dar & Kashyap, 2023).

Figure 2. Emerging and motivating factors of global medical tourism industry

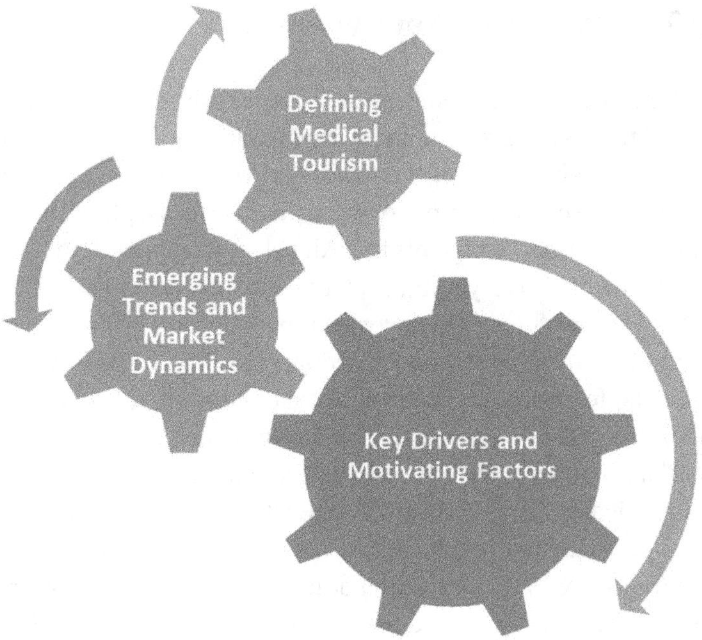

(Source- Original)

Medical Tourism

Medical Tourism association states that the purpose of the industry is "to promote high standards and best practices in all aspects of the patient experience, for treatment and care provision to ambience and amenities, to meet the patients' expectations of standards and to create a positive experience for the patients". According to The UNWTO and ETC, medical tourism may be defined as a subspecies of health tourism, which, in turn, refers to wellness and medical tourism. The last specifically includes evidence-based medical healing resources and services, including practices which are more invasive than not. Wellness tourism, on the other hand, refers to all types of treatment activities geared toward prevention and a healthy lifestyle: fitness training, beauty treatments, healthy eating, relaxation, etc. The difference is blurry: many wellness activities are correlated with purchasing goods and services on the medical tourism market, such as beauty therapy or retreat centers, while medical tourists most likely use wellness activities along with medical procedures and therapies. However, in the current research, I will focus on medical tourism as one of the major parts of the global health tourism branch (Xu et al., 2023).

Emerging Trends and Market Dynamics

It reports that in 2007 the business could be worth up to $100 billion a year, becoming one of the fastest growing industries worldwide. As of 2006, the industry was already grossing about $60 billion annually worldwide and has been growing ever since (Shabankareh, 2023). A major trend that boosts the global medical tourism market is the rising number of patients from developed countries, including US who are looking for cost-effective yet high-quality medical treatment in novel nations (Sardar, 2024). The trend has been driven in part by the cost of care at home, as well prolonged wait times for certain procedures (Khurana, 2024). One of the more recent trends is the formation of medical tourism hubs and clusters, or geographic areas in which countries or regions cooperate to form a network that attracts patients (Li, 2021). Singapore, for instance, has targeted a million foreign patients by 2012; India's medical tourism industry is expected to be worth $2. There are now professional, specialized intermediaries, to act as an intermediary between patients and providers (Sejdic & Falk, 2018). In addition, the services act like travel agents investigating healthcare providers to insure quality as well as screening customers for physical fitness for traveling. They usually employ medical personnel to help patients choose the right procedures and providers (Luo et al., 2016).

Key Drivers and Motivating Factors

All these factors can help sign up the large players in the travel insurance market and incentivize them to add medical tourism coverage as a rider on their existing product offerings (Mohammadi et al., 2018).

Affordability: One of the most decisive factors contributing to medical tourism is that patients can screen international treatments at a cheaper price (Scarpato et al., 2017). For instance, cardiac surgery at Apollo Hospital New Delhi costs about $4,000 in India as against 30 grand to have the similar process with no insurance within United States (Dash et al., 2019). A knee replacement that would cost $30,000 in the U.S. can be done for as little as $12,000 in India (Singh, 2024).

Shorter wait times- patients in nations with national health insurance, akin to Canada and the UK, will usually come across a long delay before they could go into treatment within their own government healthcare systems if they choose to ration care themselves (Singh & Kaunert, 2024).

The main drivers of high levels or reliance on non-EU patients are Access to specialized care: some countries/regions offer world leading procedures e.g. re-implantation and attract global expertise (Al-Jarrah et al., 2015). Patient flows driven by individual healthcare providers have created markets for services which cross national borders. Barrier in patient flow is the hurdle across EU3 tariffs is another unnecessary barrier (Zhou et al., 2021).

Coordinated service between provider - potential ethical/legal issues i.e. Costs follow on post operatively back through, transplant i.e. policy/service coordination implications (Muthu et al., 2020). For instance, India serves as a destination for wholesale high-quality cardiac care but is outcompeted on cosmetics and reconstructive surgeries by the Thais (Miller & Brown, 2018).

Higher Quality of Care: As newer technology intrudes the independence; patients are not hesitant to travel distance beyond borders for an exchange in improved quality of care and more skilled professionals which prevails as contemporary challenges (Bhattacharyya et al., 2023). Such driving factors have contributed to the industry of medical tourism at a pace that has led it from being non-existent towards globalized, where healthcare providers and policymakers are encouraged with new opportunities for desiring patients (Malik & Tyagi, 2022).

TECHNOLOGICAL ADVANCEMENTS IN MEDICAL TOURISM

Role of Digital Health Technologies

Digital health tools have also enabled better coordination and communication along the medical tourism journey (Singh, 2023). They are now able to interact with healthcare providers, share their medical data, and ask for individual consultation and support right from the early stages of considering their health trip (Rodrigues, 2021). That has gone a long way in terms of integration and transparency, which contributes to the trust factor that is so important for this still nascent industry called medical tourism (Pramanik, 2022).

Telemedicine and Remote Patient Monitoring

One such technology that has made a significant impact in the medical tourism industry is telemedicine, allowing patients to avail healthcare services without having to be physically present at the facility where their provider of choice practices (Zhou, et al., 2017). Telemedicine has helped make health care more efficient and cost-effective by providing video consultations, virtual appointments and remote monitoring that have bridged the gap between patients & providers (Bahri, 2018).

For Medical Tourists, There Are Several Benefits with Telemedicine (Kashyap, 2015). It provides an opportunity to interview specialists from their destination country prior to traveling so they can address any concerns or questions that arise (Elbadawi, 2021). This might help to reduce anxiety before medical procedure and having patients being fully prepped. In addition, telemedicine affords a streamlined experience in the healing journey with follow-up visits and remote monitoring which reduce prolonged stays, as well as additional travel (Cabello, 2020).

Telemedicine in medical tourism is made a lot easier through wearable and IoMT sensors (with remote patient monitoring technologies), that adds to the spectrum of telehealth (Chen et al., 2014). These sensors allow healthcare providers to monitor the vital signs, medication compliance and other health metrics of patients even after they have returned home (Stephens et al., 2015). Benefits include more informed treatment planning, real-time information to rapidly manage care and quickly identify issues as they arise-resulting in improved patient outcomes (Tiwari et al., 2022).

Artificial Intelligence and Data Analytics

The integration of AI and data analytics is transforming medical tourism, bringing a number of chances for personalized care as well as improved decision-making along with increased operational effectiveness (Singh, 2023). Artificial intelligence algorithms can crunch massive data sets of patient records, treatment success rates or population-wide health trends to uncover patterns that influence the types of individualized recommendations a medical tourist receives. This enables them to find the most suitable healthcare providers, treatments and locations according to their specific requirements (Sukeshini et al.,2021). In addition, AI and data analytics could help healthcare providers in medical tourism destinations to efficient resource allocation and administrative work as well as allow them to analyses patterns (Jordan et al., 2015). For instance, hospitals and clinics can rely on predictive analytics to forecast patient demand which will enable them to have the right staffs (Singh, 2024).Technologies along with equipments in place (and adequate rooms) needed for a smooth flow of care delivery towards medical tourists (Singh & Kaunert, 2024).

The deployment of such state-of-the-art technologies could also increase the sustainability of medical tourism (Reddy, 2023). Using data-driven intelligence, industry stakeholders can take advantage of the informed strategic decisions related to infrastructure investments for all parties and minimizing environmental impact as well developing healthcare systems which are both good locally and also serve medical tourists (Keikhosrokiani, 2022).

PROMOTING SUSTAINABLE MEDICAL TOURISM

The imbibing of digital health technologies has a lot to do with the spurt and metamorphosis in medical tourism (Viceconti et al., 2015). These technologies have been extremely useful in changing the scope of things especially for patients who are looking to avail treatments overseas (Ahmed et al., 2013). In medical tourism, digital health technologies plays a major role in terms of making the patient experience better (Panesar, 2019). Medical tourists can now and then get a lot of data about medicinal services suppliers, treatment alternatives and goal contributions by means of tolerant entries, portable applications or online platforms. This is a way for the patient to learn more so that they can spend their dollars in an informed manner about what type of medical intervention makes best sense for them, and there by leading to higher levels of consumer satisfaction with better health outcomes (Sengan, 2020).

Figure 3. Highlights sustainable considerations to promote medical tourism industry

(Source- Original)

Environmental Sustainability Considerations

The environmental cost of this billion dollar industry is substantial when considering the growth trajectory of medical tourism (Kashyap et al., 2016). Although international travel is increasing the carbon footprint, resource consumption and emissions related with healthcare facilities cannot be ruled out when considering long-term sustainability (Manyika, 2011). Reducing greenhouse gas emissions from air travel is a significant aspect of environmental sustainability for medical tourism. Healthcare recipients and their entourage, as well the healthcare workforce have to travel from other countries extensively for meeting medical services (Hilbert, 2016). Encouraging the use of greener transportation methods, like high-speed rail or carbon-neutral aviation can help to offset some of their environmental effects (Jain, 2023).

Similarly, medical destinations have to run their operations in a manner that is sustainable on the clinical front (Ariffin et al., 2021). This involves utilization of energy, water and other resources in an efficient manner & the correct disposal / recycling of medical waste. Green building standards, renewable energy sources and closed-loop waste management systems have the potential to make medical tourism environmentally sustainable (Bao et al., 2019).

Social and Cultural Sustainability

Second, the expansion of medical tourism poses a concern for social and cultural sustainability (Zhou et al., 2021). the local population (Padmaja et al., 2022). Another is to make it certain that the local people derive some benefit from increasing number of medical tourists (Shah et al., 2017). This will be accomplished primarily by the establishment of local jobs, investment in community health care infrastructure and ensuring ethical labor treatment within medical tourism industry. The cultural ramifications of medical tourism must also be monitored closely (Singh & Kaunert, 2024). The promotion of medical tourism can, for one thing, result in the commodification of local health practices and further erode traditional healing (Marjan et al., 2017). Balancing the needs of international patients and respecting cultural heritage & identity of host community When the stakeholders are local such as healthcare providers, community leaders and cultural organizations they will be inclined to ensure that medical tourism develops in accordance with their social values which is important (Singh, 2024).

Economic Sustainability and Local Development

While there are financial advantages to medical tourism, these must be evenly distributed and used in a way that aids the overall development of the host community (Chen & Zhang, 2014) further important dimension of economic sustainability concerns the need to reinvest medical tourism earnings within local healthcare provision and infrastructure (Thapa & Camtepe, 2021). Once the aforementioned is addressed then they can focus on improving local access to healthcare services by increasing funding for: developing medical facilities, training and retaining health care workers (Behura et al., 2021). In addition, medical tourism development should be harmonized with wider economic diversification strategies that include industrial clusters initiatives to stimulate local industries as well as the broader creation of job potential (Olshannikova et al., 2015). The aim of such an initiative would be to help ensure that the financial wealth generated from medical tourism is not only revered in a capitalistic economy, but prospers through all echelons of local economic value within any host community (Rudin, 2019). The medical tourism industry can become a vehicle of sustainable development, serving the interests not only to international patients but also local communities by addressing environmental, social and economic sustainability considerations (Wu et al., 2013).

REGULATORY FRAMEWORKS AND POLICY INITIATIVES

Examining the emergence of medical tourism, which has grown in importance being driven by shortfalls or limitations with existing systems and regulatory mechanisms (Saadat & Shuaib, 2020). There is a pressing need to garner international consensus around robust regulation as well as guidelines incorporating patient safety, quality care processes and ethical considerations. The medical tourism sector has seen initiatives from several organizations taken the lead in establishing accreditation standards and best practices (Kitchin, 2013). One of the largest and most well-known health care provider accreditors in medical tourism is an international organization, The Joint Commission International (JCI), which has set guidelines for medical facilities targeting healthcare tourists (Shahid, 2021). The standards include those that relate to patient safety, quality of care, and patient rights. For medical tourism providers seeking to attract international patients, JCI accreditation is a powerful seal of quality and its importance cannot be underestimated (Monteiro et al., 2021).

International Guidelines and Accreditation Standards

Another example is the Global Healthcare Accreditation (GHA) program, which was created in 2016 to address medical travel providers uniquely (Qureshi et al., 2023). In this way, these facilities make use of GHA standards and guidelines to improve patient experience, care coordination or cultural competency for medical tourists ensuring that their healthcare journey is a smooth one from pre-travel preparation until post-op follow-ups (Leung. 2021) These international accreditation standards are pivotal and central in promoting transparency as well as quality assurance across the whole medical tourism sector throughout (Faaique. 2024). Adherence to these standards allows healthcare providers a way of holding themselves accountable for patient safety and ethical behavior, which translates into increased trust and confidence on the part of medical tourists (Pradhan et al., 2024).

National Policies and Strategies

In addition to the international guidelines, various national governments have also embraced policies and strategies in support of health tourism regardless of allowing or restricting medical facilitation/brokering services within their respective borders (Singh, & Kaunert 2024). One such example could be the government of India that identified medical tourism as a priority sector and implemented various initiatives to support its growth (Singh et al.,2024). These include the creation of dedicated medical tourism zones, granting taxation privileges to support providers and easing visa regulations for overseas patients (Kong et al., 2024). Similarly, the Thailand Medical Hub initiative is created by the government in order to make a country where excellent healthcare and affordability coincide. This includes the creation of medical tourism clusters, quality standards and promoting Thailand as a global leader in medical travel (Aghabiglou et al., 2024).

Malaysia: In Malaysia, the government has established a dedicated agency as "the Malaysia Healthcare Travel Council" (MHTC) which work for development and promotion of medical tourism in this country (Wang et al., 2024). MHTC collaborates closely with healthcare providers, tourism agencies and other medical tourism partners to offer a comprehensive approach towards building an ideal environment for medical tourists (Dalkıran. 2023) Further emphasizing the weight that governments place on medical tourism, these are national level initiatives with their respective countries working towards crafting a pro-patient safe regulatory environment for economic equity and global competitiveness (Wright & Zascerinska 2023).

Addressing Ethical Concerns

The exponential development has also led to various ethical questions in the medical tourism industry that need emphasis by regulatory frameworks and policy making. Medical tourism is a source of concern because it can potential impede existing healthcare inequalities in the host countries (Akhavan et al., 2023). According to Prof Jayashri Kulkarni, director of the Monash Alfred Psychiatry research centre in Melbourne and founder of a women's mental health program at St Vincent's for disadvantaged and marginalised communities "It will be those that can afford it coming here first versus limited supplies available to manage migrants". In order to guard against this risk, policymakers should ensure that the development of medical tourism are paired with investments in domestic health infrastructure and increased accessibility for population (Baran & Karaca 2023).

This could include implementing policies that obligate medical tourism providers to divert at least a portion of their revenue towards public health or setting up mechanisms where the economic gains from medical tourism are fairly shared. Further ethical issues arise from a concern associated with the vulnerability of medical tourists (Gajić., 2023). Policymakers should work to make sure that medical tourists receive accurate information about the risks and quality of care they can expect, are not subject to unethical practices (e.g., receiving substandard care or consent for experimental treatments is obtained properly (Sahar. 2024)

CONCLUSION AND FUTURE SCOPE

While there were many other such technologies like digital health, telemedicine and artificial intelligence which changed the whole game of travel medical tourism. By combining medical tourism and technological innovations, significant strides can be made to convert the global healthcare environment into a more sustainable one that is not only accessible but also equitable. The research paper discussed the various dimensions shaping the landscape of this maturing industry, including key drivers and emerging trends through regulatory frameworks and policy initiatives. Over the past few years, medical tourism has enjoyed a considerable growth in popularity due to various factors including cost benefits, reduced waiting times and some special care. The growth of this sector with the principle of sustainability is necessary, seen that so we can guarantee a more balanced partitioning and also not to increase significantly on negative environmental impacts.

This has made it possible to improve care coordination, facilitate a better patient experience and even promote more personalized decisions based on data. The advent of next-generation technologies in this industry must be accompanied with the right strategy, one that is designed for innovation and better patient care as well as sustainable healthcare. This is not leaving out the significant impact of strong and supportive encumbrances as well expedite on a top scheme for health tourism. International guidelines, accreditation standards and national-level strategies have been developed in order to ensure the safety of patients, quality outcomes, and ethical practice. Nevertheless, continued work is required to tackle new issues like increasing inequalities in healthcare and the ethical considerations regarding medical tourism. Partnering with policymakers, healthcare professionals and industry to promote sustainable medical tourism. In this way, addressing environmental and social determinants of health with medical tourism can help to create a more livable world where meaningful access is equally accessible; perhaps even moving away from only people leaving their local region for better care.

So, incorporating medical tourism with technological advancements paired up together creates an exclusive space which will help change the face of healthcare on a global scale. Through embracing this transformation, and tackling the challenges it presents with new innovative models of care delivery, we can harness what medical tourism has to offer, towards a vision for sustainable healthcare services that are available for global patients who chose our city as their next healing destination. This research paper has a done an extensive research on understanding what this fluid industry contains which in turn will allow further developments and innovative solutions be made to the change that is inevitable for global healthcare.

REFERENCES

Aghabiglou, A., Chu, C. S., Dabbech, A., & Wiaux, Y. (2024). The R2D2 deep neural network series paradigm for fast precision imaging in radio astronomy. *arXiv preprint arXiv:2403.05452*.

Ahmed, Y. A. E., Yue, B., Gu, Z., & Yang, J. (2023). An overview: Big data analysis by deep learning and image processing. *International Journal of Quantum Information*, 21(7), 2340009. 10.1142/S0219749923400099

Akhavan, P., Azizi, N., Akhtari, S., Haass, O., Jan, T., & Sajeev, S. (2023). Understanding critical success factors for implementing medical tourism in a multi-case analysis. *Knowledge Management & E-Learning*, 15(1), 43.

Al-Jarrah, O. Y., Yoo, P. D., Muhaidat, S., Karagiannidis, G. K., & Taha, K. (2015). Efficient machine learning for big data: A review. *Big Data Research*, 2(3), 87–93. 10.1016/j.bdr.2015.04.001

. Ansari, A. I., & Singh, A. (2024). Growth and Opportunity of Medical Tourism in the Indian Healthcare Sector: A Critical Review. *Impact of AI and Robotics on the Medical Tourism Industry*, 290-301.

Ariffin, N. A., Yunus, A. M., & Kadir, I. K. (2021). The role of big data in the healthcare industry. *Journal of Islamic*, 6(36), 235–245.

Bahri, S., Zoghlami, N., Abed, M., & Tavares, J. M. R. (2018). Big data for healthcare: A survey. *IEEE Access : Practical Innovations, Open Solutions*, 7, 7397–7408. 10.1109/ACCESS.2018.2889180

Bao, Y., Tang, Z., Li, H., & Zhang, Y. (2019). Computer vision and deep learning–based data anomaly detection method for structural health monitoring. *Structural Health Monitoring*, 18(2), 401–421. 10.1177/1475921718757405

Baran, Z., & Karaca, Ş. (2023). Next-Generation Technologies in Health Tourism. In *Global perspectives on the opportunities and future directions of health tourism* (pp. 138–164). IGI Global. 10.4018/978-1-6684-6692-6.ch006

Behura, A., Sahu, S., & Kabat, M. R. (2021). Advancement of Machine Learning and Cloud Computing in the Field of Smart Health Care. *Machine Learning Approach for Cloud Data Analytics in IoT*, 273-306.

Bhattacharyya, D., Stephen Neal Joshua, E., & Thirupathi Rao, N. (2023). Medical Image Analysis of Lung Cancer CT Scans Using Deep Learning with Swarm Optimization Techniques. *Machine Intelligence, Big Data Analytics, and IoT in Image Processing: Practical Applications*, 23-50.

Cabello, J. C., Karimipour, H., Jahromi, A. N., Dehghantanha, A., & Parizi, R. M. (2020). Big-data and cyber-physical systems in healthcare: Challenges and opportunities. *Handbook of Big Data Privacy*, 255-283.

. Chen, C. P., & Zhang, C. Y. (2014). Data-intensive applications, challenges, techniques and technologies: A survey on Big Data. *Information sciences, 275*, 314-347. Mayer-Schönberger, V., & Cukier, K. (2013). *Big data: A revolution that will transform how we live, work, and think*. Houghton Mifflin Harcourt.

Chen, M., Mao, S., Zhang, Y., & Leung, V. C. (2014). *Big data: related technologies, challenges and future prospects* (Vol. 100). Springer. 10.1007/978-3-319-06245-7

Dalkıran, G. B. (2023). Health Tourism Components and Intermediary Institutions as Supplier Businesses in the Context of Health 4.0. In *Health 4.0 and Medical Supply Chain* (pp. 147–162). Springer Nature Singapore. 10.1007/978-981-99-1818-8_12

Dar, H., & Kashyap, K. (2023). Smart healthcare system (SHS): Medical tourism delivering, consumption, and elevating tool in the ages of smart technologies. *Tourism Planning & Development*, 20(3), 397–415. 10.1080/21568316.2022.2109206

Dash, S., Shakyawar, S. K., Sharma, M., & Kaushik, S. (2019). Big data in healthcare: Management, analysis and future prospects. *Journal of Big Data*, 6(1), 1–25. 10.1186/s40537-019-0217-0

Devika, G., & Karegowda, A. G. (2021). Deep Learning in IoT: Introduction, Applications, and Perspective in the Big Data Era. In *Deep Learning Applications and Intelligent Decision Making in Engineering* (pp. 1-54). IGI Global.

Elbadawi, M., Gaisford, S., & Basit, A. W. (2021). Advanced machine-learning techniques in drug discovery. *Drug Discovery Today*, 26(3), 769–777. 10.1016/j.drudis.2020.12.00333290820

Faaique, M. (2024). Overview of Big Data Analytics in Modern Astronomy. *International Journal of Mathematics, Statistics, and Computer Science*, 2, 96–113. 10.59543/ijmscs.v2i.8561

Gajić, T., Minasyan, L. A., Petrović, M. D., Bakhtin, V. A., Kaneeva, A. V., & Wiegel, N. L. (2023). Travelers'(in) Resilience to environmental risks emphasized in the media and their redirecting to medical destinations: Enhancing sustainability. *Sustainability (Basel)*, 15(21), 15297. 10.3390/su152115297

Hilbert, M. (2016). Big data for development: A review of promises and challenges. *Development Policy Review*, 34(1), 135–174. 10.1111/dpr.12142

Jain, L. (2023). *Artificial Intelligence and Machine Learning for Healthcare.*

Jordan, M. I., & Mitchell, T. M. (2015). Machine learning: Trends, perspectives, and prospects. *Science*, 349(6245), 255–260. 10.1126/science.aaa841526185243

Kashyap, H., Ahmed, H. A., Hoque, N., Roy, S., & Bhattacharyya, D. K. (2015). Big data analytics in bioinformatics: A machine learning perspective. *arXiv preprint arXiv:1506.05101.*

Kashyap, H., Ahmed, H. A., Hoque, N., Roy, S., & Bhattacharyya, D. K. (2016). Big data analytics in bioinformatics: Architectures, techniques, tools and issues. *Network Modeling and Analysis in Health Informatics and Bioinformatics*, 5(1), 1–28. 10.1007/s13721-016-0135-4

Keikhosrokiani, P. (Ed.). (2022). *Big data analytics for healthcare: datasets, techniques, life cycles, management, and applications*. Academic Press.

Khurana, V. (2024). Accelerating Pace of Scientific Discovery and Innovation through Big Data Enabled Artificial Intelligence and Deep Learning. *Emerging Trends in Machine Intelligence and Big Data*, 16(1), 38–53.

Kitchin, R. (2013). Big data and human geography: Opportunities, challenges and risks. *Dialogues in Human Geography*, 3(3), 262–267. 10.1177/2043820613513388

Kong, W., You, Z., Lyu, S., & Lv, X. (2024). Multi-dimensional stereo face reconstruction for psychological assistant diagnosis in medical meta-universe. *Information Sciences*, 654, 119831. 10.1016/j.ins.2023.119831

Leung, P. H., Chui, K. T., Lo, K., & de Pablos, P. O. (2021). A support vector machine–based voice disorders detection using human voice signal. In *Artificial Intelligence and Big Data Analytics for Smart Healthcare* (pp. 197–208). Academic Press. 10.1016/B978-0-12-822060-3.00014-0

Li, W., Chai, Y., Khan, F., Jan, S. R. U., Verma, S., Menon, V. G., & Li, X. (2021). A comprehensive survey on machine learning-based big data analytics for IoT-enabled smart healthcare system. *Mobile Networks and Applications*, 26(1), 234–252. 10.1007/s11036-020-01700-6

. Luo, J., Wu, M., Gopukumar, D., & Zhao, Y. (2016). Big data application in biomedical research and health care: a literature review. *Biomedical informatics insights, 8*, BII-S31559.

Malik, S., & Tyagi, A. K. (Eds.). (2022). *Intelligent Interactive Multimedia Systems for E-Healthcare Applications*. CRC Press. 10.1201/9781003282112

Manyika, J., Chui, M., Brown, B., Bughin, J., Dobbs, R., Roxburgh, C., & Hung Byers, A. (2011). *Big data: The next frontier for innovation, competition, and productivity*.

. Marjani, M., Nasaruddin, F., Gani, A., Karim, A., Hashem, I. A. T., Siddiqa, A., & Yaqoob, I. (2017). Big IoT data analytics: architecture, opportunities, and open research challenges. *ieee access, 5*, 5247-5261.

Miller, D. D., & Brown, E. W. (2018). Artificial intelligence in medical practice: The question to the answer? *The American Journal of Medicine*, 131(2), 129–133. 10.1016/j.amjmed.2017.10.03529126825

Mohammadi, M., Al-Fuqaha, A., Sorour, S., & Guizani, M. (2018). Deep learning for IoT big data and streaming analytics: A survey. *IEEE Communications Surveys and Tutorials*, 20(4), 2923–2960. 10.1109/COMST.2018.2844341

Monteiro, A. C. B., França, R. P., Arthur, R., & Iano, Y. (2021). An overview of medical Internet of Things, artificial intelligence, and cloud computing employed in health care from a modern panorama. *The Fusion of Internet of Things, Artificial Intelligence, and Cloud Computing in Health Care*, 3-23.

Sahar, S. N., & Dar, H. (2024). Artificial Intelligence-Enhanced Global Healthcare: The Future of Medical Tourism. In *Impact of AI and Robotics on the Medical Tourism Industry* (pp. 194-216). IGI Global.

Muthu, B., Sivaparthipan, C. B., Manogaran, G., Sundarasekar, R., Kadry, S., Shanthini, A., & Dasel, A. (2020). IOT based wearable sensor for diseases prediction and symptom analysis in healthcare sector. *Peer-to-Peer Networking and Applications*, 13(6), 2123–2134. 10.1007/s12083-019-00823-2

Olshannikova, E., Ometov, A., Koucheryavy, Y., & Olsson, T. (2015). Visualizing Big Data with augmented and virtual reality: Challenges and research agenda. *Journal of Big Data*, 2(1), 1–27. 10.1186/s40537-015-0031-2

Padmaja, M., Shitharth, S., Prasuna, K., Chaturvedi, A., Kshirsagar, P. R., & Vani, A. (2022). Grow of artificial intelligence to challenge security in IoT application. *Wireless Personal Communications*, 127(3), 1829–1845. 10.1007/s11277-021-08725-4

Panesar, A. (2019). *Machine learning and AI for healthcare*. Apress. 10.1007/978-1-4842-3799-1

Poornima, A. S., & Subramanian, S. (2024, May). Fostering Global Wellness: Harnessing Social Media to Enhance Cross-Cultural Trust to propel Medical Tourism Ensuring Economic Growth. In *European Conference on Social Media* (Vol. 11, No. 1, pp. 216-224). 10.34190/ecsm.11.1.2408

Pradhan, T., Nimkar, P., & Jhajharia, K. (2024). Machine Learning and Deep Learning for Big Data Analysis. In *Big Data Analytics Techniques for Market Intelligence* (pp. 209–240). IGI Global. 10.4018/979-8-3693-0413-6.ch008

Pramanik, P. K. D., Pal, S., & Mukhopadhyay, M. (2022). Healthcare big data: A comprehensive overview. *Research anthology on big data analytics, architectures, and applications*, 119-147.

Qureshi, R., Irfan, M., Ali, H., Khan, A., Nittala, A. S., Ali, S., & Alam, T. (2023). Artificial Intelligence and Biosensors in Healthcare and its Clinical Relevance: A Review. *IEEE Access : Practical Innovations, Open Solutions*, 11, 61600–61620. 10.1109/ACCESS.2023.3285596

. Reddy, B. M. (2023). Amalgamation of Internet of Things and Machine Learning for Smart Healthcare Applications–A Review. *Int. J Comp. Eng. Sci. Res, 5*, 08-36.

Rodrigues, J. F.Jr, Florea, L., de Oliveira, M. C., Diamond, D., & Oliveira, O. N.Jr. (2021). Big data and machine learning for materials science. *Discover Materials*, 1(1), 1–27. 10.1007/s43939-021-00012-033899049

Rudin, C. (2019). Stop explaining black box machine learning models for high stakes decisions and use interpretable models instead. *Nature Machine Intelligence*, 1(5), 206–215. 10.1038/s42256-019-0048-x35603010

Saadat, M. N., & Shuaib, M. (2020). Advancements in deep learning theory and applications: Perspective in 2020 and beyond. *Advances and Applications in Deep Learning, 3*.

Sardar, T. H., Khatun, A., Sengupta, S., Alam, Y., & Ara, T. (2024). Machine Learning in the Healthcare Sector and the Biomedical Big Data: Techniques, Applications, and Challenges. *Big Data Computing*, 336-352.

Scarpato, N., Pieroni, A., Di Nunzio, L., & Fallucchi, F. (2017). E-health-IoT universe: A review. *management, 21*(44), 46.

Sejdic, E., & Falk, T. H. (Eds.). (2018). *Signal processing and machine learning for biomedical big data*. CRC press. 10.1201/9781351061223

Sengan, S., Kamalam, G. K., Vellingiri, J., Gopal, J., Velayutham, P., & Subramaniyaswamy, V. (2020). Medical information retrieval systems for e-Health care records using fuzzy based machine learning model. *Microprocessors and Microsystems*, 103344.

Shabankareh, M., Nazarian, A., Golestaneh, M. H., & Dalouchi, F. (2023). Health tourism and government supports. *International Journal of Emerging Markets*.

Shah, F., Li, J., Shah, Y., & Shah, F. (2017, November). Broad big data domain via medical big data. In *2017 4th International Conference on Systems and Informatics (ICSAI)* (pp. 732-737). IEEE.

Shahid, Z. (2021). *Distributed Machine Learning for Anomalous Human Activity Recognition using IoT Systems.*

Singh, B. (2023). Blockchain Technology in Renovating Healthcare: Legal and Future Perspectives. In *Revolutionizing Healthcare Through Artificial Intelligence and Internet of Things Applications* (pp. 177-186). IGI Global.

Singh, B. (2023). Unleashing Alternative Dispute Resolution (ADR) in Resolving Complex Legal-Technical Issues Arising in Cyberspace Lensing E-Commerce and Intellectual Property: Proliferation of E-Commerce Digital Economy. *Revista Brasileira de Alternative Dispute Resolution-Brazilian Journal of Alternative Dispute Resolution-RBADR*, 5(10), 81–105. 10.52028/rbadr.v5i10.ART04.Ind

Singh, B. (2024). Lensing Legal Dynamics for Examining Responsibility and Deliberation of Generative AI-Tethered Technological Privacy Concerns: Infringements and Use of Personal Data by Nefarious Actors. In Ara, A., & Ara, A. (Eds.), *Exploring the Ethical Implications of Generative AI* (pp. 146–167). IGI Global. 10.4018/979-8-3693-1565-1.ch009

Singh, B. (2024). Social Cognition of Incarcerated Women and Children: Addressing Exposure to Infectious Diseases and Legal Outcomes. In Reddy, K. (Ed.), *Principles and Clinical Interventions in Social Cognition* (pp. 236–251). IGI Global. 10.4018/979-8-3693-1265-0.ch014

Singh, B. (2024). Evolutionary Global Neuroscience for Cognition and Brain Health: Strengthening Innovation in Brain Science. In *Biomedical Research Developments for Improved Healthcare* (pp. 246-272). IGI Global.

Singh, B., & Kaunert, C. (2024). Salvaging Responsible Consumption and Production of Food in the Hospitality Industry: Harnessing Machine Learning and Deep Learning for Zero Food Waste. In Singh, A., Tyagi, P., & Garg, A. (Eds.), *Sustainable Disposal Methods of Food Wastes in Hospitality Operations* (pp. 176–192). IGI Global. 10.4018/979-8-3693-2181-2.ch012

Singh, B., & Kaunert, C. (2024). Harnessing Sustainable Agriculture Through Climate-Smart Technologies: Artificial Intelligence for Climate Preservation and Futuristic Trends. In *Exploring Ethical Dimensions of Environmental Sustainability and Use of AI* (pp. 214-239). IGI Global.

Singh, B., & Kaunert, C. (2024). Salvaging Responsible Consumption and Production of Food in the Hospitality Industry: Harnessing Machine Learning and Deep Learning for Zero Food Waste. In *Sustainable Disposal Methods of Food Wastes in Hospitality Operations* (pp. 176-192). IGI Global.

. Singh, B., & Kaunert, C. (2024). Future of Digital Marketing: Hyper-Personalized Customer Dynamic Experience with AI-Based Predictive Models. *Revolutionizing the AI-Digital Landscape: A Guide to Sustainable Emerging Technologies for Marketing Professionals*, 189.

Singh, B., Kaunert, C., & Vig, K. (2024). Reinventing Influence of Artificial Intelligence (AI) on Digital Consumer Lensing Transforming Consumer Recommendation Model: Exploring Stimulus Artificial Intelligence on Consumer Shopping Decisions. In Musiolik, T., Rodriguez, R., & Kannan, H. (Eds.), *AI Impacts in Digital Consumer Behavior* (pp. 141–169). IGI Global. 10.4018/979-8-3693-1918-5.ch006

Stephens, Z. D., Lee, S. Y., Faghri, F., Campbell, R. H., Zhai, C., Efron, M. J., & Robinson, G. E. (2015). Big data: Astronomical or genomical? *PLoS Biology*, 13(7), e1002195. 10.1371/journal.pbio.100219526151137

Sukeshini, S., P., Ved, M., Chintalapti, J., & Pal, S. N. (2021). Big data analytics and machine learning technologies for HPC applications. In *Evolving Technologies for Computing, Communication and Smart World:Proceedings of ETCCS 2020* (pp. 411-424). Springer Singapore.

Thapa, C., & Camtepe, S. (2021). Precision health data: Requirements, challenges and existing techniques for data security and privacy. *Computers in Biology and Medicine*, 129, 104130. 10.1016/j.compbiomed.2020.10413033271399

Tiwari, S. K., Kaur, J., Singla, P., & Hrisheekesha, P. N. (2022, September). A Comprehensive Review of Big Data Analysis Techniques in Health-Care. In *International Conference on Emergent Converging Technologies and Biomedical Systems* (pp. 401-420). Singapore: Springer Nature Singapore.

Viceconti, M., Hunter, P., & Hose, R. (2015). Big data, big knowledge: Big data for personalized healthcare. *IEEE Journal of Biomedical and Health Informatics*, 19(4), 1209–1215. 10.1109/JBHI.2015.240688326218867

Wang, M. H., Xing, L., Pan, Y., Gu, F., Fang, J., Yu, X., Pang, C. P., Chong, K. K.-L., Cheung, C. Y.-L., Liao, X., Fang, X., Yang, J., Zhou, R., Zhou, X., Wang, F., & Liu, W. (2024). AI-based Advanced approaches and dry eye disease detection based on multi-source evidence: Cases, applications, issues, and future directions. *Big Data Mining and Analytics*, 7(2), 445–484. 10.26599/BDMA.2023.9020024

Wright, D. W. M., & Zascerinska, S. (2023). Becoming immortal: Future wellness and medical tourism markets. *Journal of Tourism Futures*, 9(2), 168–195. 10.1108/JTF-05-2021-0119

Wu, X., Zhu, X., Wu, G. Q., & Ding, W. (2013). Data mining with big data. *IEEE Transactions on Knowledge and Data Engineering*, 26(1), 97–107.

Xu, A., Johari, S. A., Khademolomoom, A. H., Khabaz, M. T., Umurzoqovich, R. S., Hosseini, S., & Semiromi, D. T. (2023). Investigation of management of international education considering sustainable medical tourism and entrepreneurship. *Heliyon*, 9(1), e12691. 10.1016/j.heliyon.2022.e1269136685466

Zhou, L., Pan, S., Wang, J., & Vasilakos, A. V. (2017). Machine learning on big data: Opportunities and challenges. *Neurocomputing*, 237, 350–361. 10.1016/j.neucom.2017.01.026

Zhou, S., Zhang, R., Chen, D., & Zhu, X. (2021). A novel framework for bringing smart big data to proactive decision making in healthcare. *Health Informatics Journal*, 27(2), 14604582211024698. 10.1177/14604582211024698341598 34

Zhou, S. K., Greenspan, H., Davatzikos, C., Duncan, J. S., Van Ginneken, B., Madabhushi, A., Prince, J. L., Rueckert, D., & Summers, R. M. (2021). A review of deep learning in medical imaging: Imaging traits, technology trends, case studies with progress highlights, and future promises. *Proceedings of the IEEE*, 109(5), 820–838. 10.1109/JPROC.2021.305439037786449

Chapter 10
Safeguarding Data Privacy and Informed Consent:
Ethical Imperatives in AI-Driven Mental Healthcare

Souvik Dhar
https://orcid.org/0000-0002-5472-9193
Brainware University, India

Utsa Sarkar
https://orcid.org/0009-0001-1997-3086
Calcutta High Court, India

ABSTRACT

This chapter explores the ethical challenges surrounding data privacy and informed consent in artificial intelligence (AI)-driven mental healthcare in India. The integration of AI technologies in mental health services offers potential for enhanced patient outcomes, but also raises significant ethical issues. Emphasizing patient autonomy and the protection of personal information, the chapter examines the complexities of informed consent and data privacy. It highlights the importance of transparent communication and robust regulatory frameworks to safeguard patient rights. By analysing key principles and the Digital Personal Data Protection Act 2023, the chapter provides insights into balancing technological advancements with ethical imperatives. It advocates for comprehensive ethical guidelines and collaborative efforts among stakeholders to foster a responsible and patient-centred AI-driven mental healthcare system. The chapter emphasizes the need for education on AI's impact, potential biases, and the significance of maintaining trust and accountability

DOI: 10.4018/979-8-3693-5976-1.ch010

in patient care.

INTRODUCTION

Data privacy and informed consent are emerging as critical ethical problems in the burgeoning field of AI-driven mental healthcare. The increasing use of technology in India's mental health services has made it imperative to protect patient information and uphold their right to make their own decisions. This study examines the complex relationship between informed consent and data privacy, emphasising the hurdles and constraints involved in navigating this ethically challenging sector. For instance, psychoanalysis is a comprehensive approach to understanding human behaviour, emotions, and thought processes through the lens of unconscious dynamics and motivations (Tarzian, Ndrio and Fakoya, 2023). Psychoanalysis, which was developed by Sigmund Freud and later developed by other theories and practitioners, holds that memories, unconscious conflicts, and early childhood experiences are the driving forces behind many aspects of human activity (Tarzian, Ndrio and Fakoya, 2023). Artificial intelligence (AI) is currently being used to enhance cognition of the onset of illness, facilitate the early detection of diseases, optimise therapy and drug dosages, and find novel cures. The chapter focuses at the ethical implications of using AI in mental healthcare in an effort to promote ethical frameworks that put patients' rights and dignity first in the context of AI-driven mental healthcare and to promote a better understanding of the intricacies involved. Through an analysis of key principles and regulatory frameworks, this chapter aims to provide insights into how stakeholders in AI-driven mental healthcare can effectively balance ethical imperatives while leveraging technological advancements for improved patient care and well-being.

RESEARCH OBJECTIVE

This chapter aims to emphasise the critical importance of both data privacy and informed consent within the domain of AI-driven mental healthcare. The intention is to increase awareness and spark discussion on the need for a balanced integration of AI technologies while respecting patient rights and dignity by shedding light on the ethical issues raised by these imperatives. This discourse's main objective is to aid in the creation of a technologically sophisticated, morally sound, and patient-centred healthcare environment. The goal is to emphasise how important it is to incorporate moral values into the creation, use, and supervision of AI-powered mental health care programmes. In order to take full advantage of their right to informed consent, patients should be encouraged to deny AI treatments if they have reservations or treatment preferences. In order to preserve patient data privacy and stop unauthorised access or exploitation for financial gain, the author advocates for the establishment of strict protections and encryption procedures.

The two main research objectives are as follows:

- To advocate for policies and practices that prioritize patient empowerment and involvement in their own care, as exemplified by informed consent.
- To provide comprehensive strategies and frameworks that safeguard patient data privacy in AI-driven mental healthcare settings.

By fostering collaboration among stakeholders, including healthcare providers, patients, policymakers, and technologists, our mission is to promote ethical decision-making and ensure the protection of patient rights in the face of technological advancements.

CONCERNS

Data privacy and informed consent become interwoven ethical imperatives in the context of AI-driven mental healthcare, requiring careful thought and well-balanced integration. Unprecedented prospects for individualised and effective treatment delivery are presented by the widespread use of AI technology in mental health services. But these developments also bring with them serious ethical problems, especially when it comes to preserving patient autonomy and privacy. The ethical foundation of healthcare that guarantees information security and confidentiality is data privacy. Significant risks include unauthorised access, data leakage, and commercial exploitation when it comes to AI-based mental healthcare. AI techniques could undermine the connection between patients and physicians in the lack of strong security and encryption measures, rendering this instrument less useful than necessary and eroding public confidence in mental healthcare system.

Informed consent is still a core ethical issue that preserves patients' autonomy and an opportunity to decide on their attitude towards their medical treatment (Jeyaraman et al. 2023). Transparent communication through shared-decision-making is essential since it is the only way to brief patients in a clear and an understandable manner about the potential risks and benefits of AI interventions, and motivate or allow them to give or refuse their informed consent (Naik et al., 2022). Informed consent and data protection in AI-driven mental health treatment must coexist in harmony, which calls for a multifaceted strategy (Jeyaraman et al. 2023). This calls for the creation of thorough ethical and legal structures that put the interests and wellbeing of patients first. Furthermore, in order to promote a culture of accountability, transparency, and ethical responsibility, stakeholders must work together (Jeyaraman et al. 2023).

METHOD

This chapter employs a multidisciplinary approach to explore the critical ethical issues of data privacy and informed consent in AI-driven mental healthcare in India. The methodology encompasses the following key components:

- Conduct a comprehensive review of existing literature on data privacy, informed consent, and AI applications in mental healthcare.
- Examine relevant regulatory frameworks, including the Digital Personal Data Protection Act 2023 (DPDPA) and its implications for data privacy in healthcare.
- Assess the compliance requirements and ethical standards mandated by Indian healthcare laws and international guidelines.
- Explore the ethical principles underlying informed consent and data privacy, particularly in AI-driven mental healthcare.
- Identify potential ethical dilemmas and conflicts that arise from the use of AI technologies in patient care.
- Investigate real-world cases where AI has been implemented in mental healthcare settings.
- Analyze the outcomes, challenges, and ethical issues encountered in these cases to draw practical insights.
- Gather perspectives on the ethical, legal, and practical aspects of informed consent and data privacy in AI-driven mental healthcare.
- Propose strategies for integrating these frameworks into the development, deployment, and oversight of AI technologies in mental healthcare.
- Examine the legal implications of non-compliance with data privacy regulations and informed consent requirements.

SAFEGUARDING PATIENT DATA PRIVACY

In the realm of AI-driven mental healthcare, safeguarding patient data privacy is a paramount concern. These systems are designed to process and analyze vast amounts of sensitive personal data to provide accurate diagnoses and personalized treatment plans. However, the complexity and scale of data involved introduce significant vulnerabilities. Understanding these vulnerabilities, along with the regulatory frameworks that address data privacy and the delicate balance between data utility and patient confidentiality, is crucial for ethical AI implementation in mental health research and practice. Clinical Decision Support Systems (also known as CDSS) are vital instruments in modern healthcare that improve patient outcomes and physician decision-making (Elhaddad et al., 2024). Currently, the incorporation of artificial intelligence (AI) is further revolutionising CDSS (Elhaddad et al., 2024).

The Vulnerabilities in AI-Driven Mental Healthcare Systems

AI-driven mental healthcare systems are particularly susceptible to a range of vulnerabilities that can compromise patient data privacy (Frank and Olaoye 2024). One primary vulnerability is the risk of data breaches. These systems often collect and store extensive amounts of sensitive information, including personal identifiers, medical histories, and treatment records (Frank and Olaoye 2024). If these data repositories are not adequately protected, they become attractive targets for cyberattacks. Hackers can exploit security weaknesses to access, steal, or manipulate sensitive patient information, leading to severe privacy violations (Frank and Olaoye 2024).

Another vulnerability lies in the potential for algorithmic bias and misuse of data (Mensah 2023). AI systems are trained on large datasets that may contain inherent biases, reflecting social prejudices or inaccuracies present in the data (Mensah 2023). This can result in biased outcomes, where certain groups may receive inadequate or inappropriate mental health care based on flawed algorithmic predictions (Mensah 2023). Additionally, the misuse of data for purposes other than those originally intended, such as for marketing or profiling without patient consent, raises significant ethical and legal concerns (Mensah 2023).

Moreover, the complexity of AI algorithms often makes them "black boxes," meaning their decision-making processes are not easily interpretable by humans (Hassija et al. 2024). This opacity can prevent healthcare providers and patients from understanding how decisions are made, making it difficult to identify and correct errors or biases (Hassija et al. 2024). The lack of transparency undermines trust and accountability in AI-driven mental healthcare systems, further exacerbating privacy and ethical issues.

Regulatory Frameworks and Compliance in India's Healthcare Landscape

In response to these vulnerabilities, regulatory frameworks have been established to address data privacy concerns in AI-driven mental healthcare. In India, the Digital Personal Data Protection Act 2023 (DPDPA) is a landmark legislation that provides a comprehensive framework for data protection (Sarkar and Shukla 2024). The DPDPA grants individuals rights to access, rectify, delete, limit, and carry their personal data, as well as the right to object to data processing (Sarkar and Shukla 2024). These provisions ensure that patients have control over their data and can make informed decisions about its use.

The DPDPA also establishes the Data Protection Authority (DPA), an autonomous body responsible for enforcing the Act (Sarkar and Shukla 2024). The DPA monitors compliance, investigates breaches, and imposes penalties on organizations that fail to adhere to data protection standards (Sarkar and Shukla 2024). This regulatory oversight is crucial in ensuring that AI-driven mental healthcare systems operate transparently and ethically, protecting patient data from misuse and breaches (Sarkar and Shukla 2024).

Compliance with the DPDPA requires healthcare organizations to implement robust data protection measures. This includes employing advanced encryption techniques to secure data during transmission and storage, conducting regular security audits to identify and mitigate vulnerabilities, and training staff on data privacy principles and practices (Sarkar and Shukla 2024). Organizations must also develop clear data governance frameworks that outline how data is collected, processed, and stored, ensuring that these practices align with the DPDPA's requirements.

Balancing Data Utility With Patient Confidentiality

While regulatory frameworks are essential for safeguarding patient data privacy, striking a balance between data utility and patient confidentiality is equally important in AI-driven mental health research (Jeyaraman et al. 2023). Data utility refers to the ability to use data effectively to achieve desired outcomes, such as improving mental health diagnoses and treatments. However, maximizing data utility often involves extensive data collection and analysis, which can conflict with the need to protect patient confidentiality (Jeyaraman et al. 2023).

One approach to balancing data utility with patient confidentiality is the adoption of privacy-preserving techniques in data processing. Techniques such as data anonymization and pseudonymization can protect patient identities while allowing data to be used for research and analysis (Stalla-Bourdillon and Knight 2016). Anonymization involves removing personally identifiable information from data sets, whereas pseudonymization replaces identifiable information with pseudonyms (Stalla-Bourdillon and Knight 2016). These techniques can reduce the risk of re-identification and ensure that patient data remains confidential (Stalla-Bourdillon and Knight 2016).

Another important aspect is the concept of data minimization (Senarath and Arachchilage 2019). Data minimization involves collecting only the data that is strictly necessary for a specific purpose, thereby reducing the exposure of sensitive information (Senarath and Arachchilage 2019). In AI-driven mental healthcare, this means designing systems to require the minimal amount of personal data needed to achieve their objectives (Senarath and Arachchilage 2019). By limiting data collection, organizations can reduce the risk of privacy breaches and misuse.

Furthermore, obtaining informed consent from patients is crucial in maintaining the ethical balance between data utility and confidentiality (Jeyaraman et al. 2023). Patients should be fully informed about how their data will be used, the potential risks involved, and their rights under data protection laws. This empowers patients to make informed decisions about their participation in AI-driven mental health research and treatment. Ongoing communication with patients about any changes in data use or technology is essential to maintaining their trust and ensuring ethical practices (Jeyaraman et al. 2023).

Ethical considerations also extend to the transparency of AI algorithms (Jeyaraman et al. 2023). Ensuring that AI systems are interpretable and their decision-making processes are transparent helps build trust and accountability. When patients and healthcare providers understand how AI systems make decisions, they are better positioned to identify and address any biases or errors, ensuring that patient data is used ethically and effectively (Jeyaraman et al. 2023).

Thus, safeguarding patient data privacy in AI-driven mental healthcare involves addressing significant vulnerabilities, adhering to regulatory frameworks, and balancing data utility with patient confidentiality. The DPDPA provides a robust legal foundation for protecting patient data, but effective implementation requires healthcare organizations to adopt comprehensive data protection measures (Sarkar and Shukla 2024). By employing privacy-preserving techniques, practicing data minimization, and ensuring informed consent, organizations can navigate the ethical challenges of AI in mental health research and practice. Transparency and interpretability of AI algorithms further enhance trust and accountability, ensuring that patient data is used responsibly and ethically. As AI technologies continue to evolve, maintaining this delicate balance will be crucial in advancing mental healthcare while protecting patient privacy.

INFORMED CONSENT: UPHOLDING PATIENT AUTONOMY IN AI INTERVENTIONS

Health AI applications, such as imaging, diagnostics, and surgery, are poised to revolutionize the patient-clinician relationship (Gerke, Minssen and Cohen, 2020). These technologies promise to enhance the accuracy of diagnoses, streamline surgical procedures, and provide personalized treatment plans (Gerke, Minssen and Cohen, 2020). However, the integration of AI in patient care raises significant ethical concerns regarding informed consent, an issue that has not been sufficiently addressed in ethical debates (Cohen, Amarasingham, Shah, Xie and Lo, 2014). Informed consent will be one of the most immediate challenges as AI becomes more prevalent in clinical practice (Gerke, Minssen and Cohen, 2020).

Informed consent is a cornerstone of medical ethics, ensuring that patients are fully aware of the nature, benefits, risks, and alternatives of a proposed intervention (Gerke, Minssen and Cohen, 2020). Traditionally, informed consent involves direct communication between the patient and clinician, where the latter explains the procedures, answers questions, and addresses concerns (Farhud and Zokaei 2019). The introduction of AI into this dynamic complicates the process significantly (Farhud and Zokaei 2019). AI systems in healthcare often function as black boxes, meaning their decision-making processes are not transparent even to the developers (Gerke, Minssen and Cohen, 2020). Machine learning (ML) algorithms can process vast amounts of data and identify patterns that might be imperceptible to human clinicians (Gerke, Minssen and Cohen, 2020). However, these algorithms can also perpetuate existing biases in the data, leading to skewed or unfair outcomes (Farhud and Zokaei 2019). For instance, if an AI diagnostic tool is trained primarily on data from a specific demographic, it might perform less accurately for patients from other demographics (Farhud and Zokaei 2019).

Understanding Informed Consent in Healthcare Ethics

A patient must willingly accept to a suggested medical treatment or intervention through the process of informed consent, which is based on a complete understanding of the procedure, its possible risks, benefits, and alternatives (Kadam 2017). Because of the complexity and unpredictability of AI technologies, informed consent is even more important in the case of AI-driven mental healthcare. The conventional approach to informed consent calls for open lines of communication between the patient and the healthcare professional, during which the professional describes the nature of the intervention in terms the patient can comprehend. This procedure has to cover the data collection, processing, and storage methods, as well as how AI algorithms will be used to their care (Kadam 2017). Given the sophistication of AI technologies, it is imperative that patients are fully aware of the scope and limitations of AI systems, the potential biases in AI decision-making, and the possibility of data breaches.

Ensuring informed consent in AI-driven mental healthcare requires overcoming significant challenges. Healthcare providers must possess a deep understanding of the AI tools they are using to effectively communicate their complexities to patients. Moreover, the dynamic nature of AI systems, which can evolve and learn over time, necessitates ongoing consent processes where patients are regularly updated about changes in the technology and its implications for their treatment. This continuous dialogue helps maintain transparency and trust between patients and providers, reinforcing the ethical foundation of informed consent.

Transparency in AI Algorithms

Transparency in AI algorithms is a critical ethical requirement in AI-driven mental healthcare. Transparency refers to the extent to which the inner workings of AI systems are open and understandable to users, stakeholders, and regulatory bodies (Singhal 2024). In mental healthcare, where decisions made by AI can significantly impact patient outcomes, transparency ensures that these systems are accountable and that their decisions can be scrutinized and understood by human operators (Singhal 2024).

Achieving transparency in AI involves several layers. Firstly, there must be clarity about how AI models are developed, including the data sources used for training and the methodologies applied. This includes disclosing potential biases in the data that could affect the AI's performance and outcomes. Secondly, the decision-making processes of AI algorithms should be interpretable, meaning that clinicians and patients can understand how specific inputs lead to particular outputs or recommendations. This interpretability is crucial for clinicians to validate and trust AI-driven insights and for patients to feel confident in their treatment.

One of the primary challenges in achieving transparency is the inherent complexity of many AI models, particularly deep learning systems that operate as "black boxes" with intricate layers of computation that are not easily interpretable (Hassija et al. 2024). To address this, researchers and developers are working on techniques for explainable AI (XAI), which aim to make AI decisions more transparent (Hassija et al. 2024). XAI techniques provide insights into the model's behavior and decision-making processes, helping to demystify how AI arrives at its conclusions (Hassija et al. 2024).

Transparency also involves ethical disclosure practices (Singhal 2024). AI developers and healthcare providers must be forthcoming about the limitations and uncertainties of AI systems (Singhal 2024). This includes being honest about the potential for errors and the steps taken to mitigate these risks. By fostering an environment of openness and honesty, transparency not only enhances the reliability and acceptance of AI tools but also upholds the ethical principles of trust and accountability in mental healthcare.

Ethical Dilemmas Involving Negotiation of the Right to Decline AI Interventions in Mental Healthcare Settings

The integration of AI in mental healthcare introduces unique ethical dilemmas, particularly regarding patients' rights to decline AI interventions (Singhal 2024). While AI has the potential to revolutionize mental health services by providing accurate diagnoses, personalized treatments, and continuous monitoring, it is crucial to respect patients' autonomy and their right to make informed decisions about their care, including the choice to refuse AI-based interventions (Singhal 2024).

One ethical dilemma arises from the tension between the potential benefits of AI and the patient's right to decline its use (Farhud and Zokaei 2019). AI systems can offer significant advantages, such as early detection of mental health issues and customized therapeutic approaches. However, patients may have valid reasons for declining AI interventions, such as concerns about privacy, the accuracy of AI diagnoses, or a lack of trust in technology. It is essential for healthcare providers to respect these concerns and support patients' decisions without coercion.

Negotiating the right to decline AI interventions involves balancing respect for patient autonomy with the ethical duty of beneficence, which is the commitment to act in the patient's best interests. (Farhud and Zokaei 2019). Healthcare providers must engage in meaningful conversations with patients, thoroughly explaining the potential benefits and risks of AI interventions and addressing any misconceptions or fears. This dialogue should be patient-centered, prioritizing the individual's values and preferences and ensuring that their decision is respected.

Another ethical challenge is the potential for implicit pressure on patients to accept AI interventions due to the authority of medical professionals and the perceived infallibility of technology (Farhud and Zokaei 2019). Patients might feel compelled to agree to AI-based treatments out of deference to their healthcare providers or because they believe that refusing might negatively impact their care. To mitigate this, providers must create a supportive environment where patients feel empowered to voice their preferences and concerns without fear of judgment or repercussions (Farhud and Zokaei 2019).

Moreover, the decision to decline AI interventions should not compromise the quality of care a patient receives. Healthcare systems must be designed to offer equivalent non-AI alternatives that meet the same standards of care (Farhud and Zokaei

2019). This ensures that patients who opt out of AI interventions still have access to high-quality treatment options, reinforcing the principle of justice in healthcare.

NAVIGATING THE INTERSECTION: ETHICAL CONSIDERATIONS AND POLICY IMPLICATIONS

Artificial intelligence (AI) has the potential to completely transform patient care once it is included into mental health procedures (Graham et al. 2019). AI-driven solutions provide considerable improvements in a variety of areas, including personalised treatment regimens and improved diagnostic accuracy (Graham et al. 2019). Nevertheless, in order to protect patient welfare and preserve ethical norms, these developments raise important ethical questions and policy consequences that need to be carefully considered (Graham et al. 2019). The work examines the necessity of strong patient rights through open communication and consent processes, the necessity of thorough ethical frameworks for AI-driven mental health services, and the critical role that regulatory organisations play in upholding moral norms.

The Promise of AI in Mental Health

AI technologies have shown promise in various aspects of mental health care (D'Alfonso 2020). Machine learning algorithms can analyze vast amounts of data to detect patterns and predict mental health conditions with greater accuracy than traditional methods (D'Alfonso 2020). AI-driven chatbots and virtual therapists can provide immediate support and bridge gaps in mental health services, particularly in underserved areas (D'Alfonso 2020). Personalized treatment plans generated by AI can enhance therapeutic outcomes by tailoring interventions to individual needs.

Ethical Challenges

Despite these benefits, the use of AI in mental health care raises several ethical challenges (Gerke, Minssen and Cohen, 2020). These include concerns about privacy, data security, bias, and the potential for AI to make decisions that could adversely affect patients. Without robust ethical guidelines, the risk of harm increases, potentially undermining the trust between patients and healthcare providers.

Developing Comprehensive Ethical Frameworks

To address these challenges, there is a pressing need for comprehensive ethical frameworks that guide the development and deployment of AI in mental health care (Gerke, Minssen and Cohen, 2020). These frameworks should encompass the following principles:

- Beneficence and Non-Maleficence: AI systems should aim to do good and avoid causing harm. This involves rigorous testing to ensure that AI tools are safe and effective before they are used in clinical settings.
- Justice and Fairness: AI should be designed to promote equity in mental health care. This includes ensuring that AI systems do not perpetuate existing biases in mental health diagnosis and treatment. Special attention should be given to populations that have historically been marginalized or underserved.
- Autonomy: Patients should have control over their data and the use of AI in their treatment. This requires clear communication about how AI tools work and the implications for patient care.
- Transparency and Accountability: The decision-making processes of AI systems should be transparent. This involves making the algorithms and data sources used by AI systems accessible for review by independent experts. Additionally, there should be mechanisms for accountability if AI systems fail or cause harm.
- Privacy and Confidentiality: Given the sensitive nature of mental health data, robust measures must be in place to protect patient privacy. This includes secure data storage, strict access controls, and anonymization techniques to prevent unauthorized access to patient information.

Strengthening Patient Rights Through Transparent Communication and Consent Procedures

- The Importance of Informed Consent

Informed consent is a cornerstone of ethical medical practice. In the context of AI-driven mental health care, obtaining informed consent becomes even more critical. Patients must understand how AI tools will be used in their care, what data will be collected, how it will be used, and the potential risks and benefits (Gerke, Minssen and Cohen, 2020).

- Challenges in Achieving Informed Consent

One of the primary challenges in achieving informed consent for AI-driven mental health care is the complexity of the technology. Many patients may not have the technical background to fully understand how AI works. This can lead to confusion and mistrust, particularly if patients feel that they are not being adequately informed (Gerke, Minssen and Cohen, 2020).

Strategies for Transparent Communication

To overcome these challenges, healthcare providers should adopt strategies that enhance transparent communication:

- Simplified Explanations: Use plain language to explain how AI tools work and how they will be used in patient care. Avoid technical jargon that may confuse patients.
- Visual Aids and Demonstrations: Use visual aids and demonstrations to illustrate how AI tools function. This can help patients better understand the technology and its implications.
- Interactive Consent Processes: Implement interactive consent processes that allow patients to ask questions and receive real-time answers. This can help ensure that patients fully understand what they are consenting to.
- Continuous Communication: Keep patients informed about any updates or changes to the AI tools being used in their care. This includes communicating any new risks or benefits that may arise.

Strengthening patient rights also involves enhancing patient autonomy. This can be achieved by:

- Providing Choices: Give patients the option to opt-out of AI-driven care if they are uncomfortable with the technology. Provide alternative treatment options that do not rely on AI.
- Empowering Patients: Educate patients about their rights and how they can take control of their mental health care. This includes providing resources and support for patients to make informed decisions about their treatment.

ROLE OF REGULATORY BODIES IN ENFORCING ETHICAL STANDARDS AND SAFEGUARDING PATIENT WELFARE IN AI-DRIVEN HEALTHCARE: NEED FOR REGULATION

Given the ethical challenges associated with AI-driven mental health care, regulatory bodies play a crucial role in safeguarding patient welfare. Effective regulation ensures that AI tools are safe, effective, and used in ways that protect patient rights. Regulatory bodies should establish standards for the development and deployment of AI in mental health care. These standards should cover (Gerke, Minssen and Cohen, 2020):

- Safety and Efficacy: AI tools should undergo rigorous testing to demonstrate their safety and efficacy. This includes clinical trials and independent reviews to validate the performance of AI systems (Gerke, Minssen and Cohen, 2020).
- Bias and Fairness: Regulatory standards should require that AI tools are tested for bias and designed to promote fairness (Gerke, Minssen and Cohen, 2020). This includes guidelines for data collection and algorithm development to ensure that AI systems do not perpetuate existing inequities.
- Transparency and Accountability: Standards should mandate transparency in the development and use of AI tools. This includes requiring developers to disclose their algorithms and data sources, as well as implementing mechanisms for accountability if AI systems cause harm (Gerke, Minssen and Cohen, 2020).
- Privacy and Data Protection: Regulatory bodies should enforce strict data protection standards to safeguard patient privacy. This includes requirements for secure data storage, anonymization techniques, and strict access controls (Gerke, Minssen and Cohen, 2020).

Monitoring and Enforcement

Regulatory bodies should also be responsible for monitoring the use of AI in mental health care and enforcing compliance with established standards. This can be achieved through:

- Regular Audits: Conducting regular audits of AI tools and their use in clinical settings to ensure compliance with ethical and regulatory standards.
- Reporting Mechanisms: Implementing mechanisms for patients and healthcare providers to report concerns or adverse events related to AI-driven care. This includes establishing clear procedures for investigating and addressing these reports.

- Sanctions and Penalties: Enforcing sanctions and penalties for non-compliance with regulatory standards. This includes penalties for developers and healthcare providers who fail to adhere to ethical guidelines and regulatory requirements.

Promoting Collaboration and Innovation

Regulatory bodies should also promote collaboration and innovation in the development of AI-driven mental health care. This includes:

- Supporting Research and Development: Providing funding and support for research and development of ethical AI tools. This includes encouraging collaborations between researchers, healthcare providers, and technology developers.
- Fostering Public-Private Partnerships: Promoting public-private partnerships to drive innovation while ensuring that ethical standards are maintained. This includes facilitating dialogue between stakeholders to address ethical and regulatory challenges.
- Encouraging Best Practices: Sharing best practices and guidelines for the ethical use of AI in mental health care. This includes creating platforms for knowledge exchange and collaboration among stakeholders.

DIGITAL PERSONAL DATA PROTECTION ACT 2023 (DPDPA) AND DATA PRIVACY IN HEALTHCARE: AN INSIGHT

The Digital Personal Data Protection Act 2023, (DPDPA), serves as an example of a lighthouse that enables people to retain their fundamental rights to privacy through an era when such rights are constantly endangered (Sarkar and Shukla 2024). The DPDPA grants the right to access, rectify, delete, limit, and carry personal data as well as the right to object to data processing (Sarkar and Shukla 2024). The autonomy of the DPA to enforce the DPDPA, an independent authority tasked with ensuring compliance and responsibility from organizations processing personal data (Sarkar and Shukla 2024). Therefore, this legislation represents a major milestone in data governance, sending a clear signal to the AI-driven mental healthcare community about the significance of ethical conduct. The balance of privacy rights and technological advancements is done by allowing individuals the freedom to choose what information they want to share about themselves while imposing strict rules on how data processors operate. By not being compliant with the DPDPA, organizations in AI-driven mental healthcare have to face the legal consequences and moral considerations to meet its provisions actively (Sarkar and Shukla 2024). The DPDPA basically serves as a pragmatic tool toward fostering a responsible and accountable environment of data management where transparency, fairness, and security are one of its key specifications (Sarkar and Shukla 2024).

The DPDPA provides individuals with several critical rights concerning their personal data. The right to access allows individuals to obtain their personal data held by organizations, ensuring transparency in how their data is being used (Sarkar and Shukla 2024). The right to rectify enables individuals to correct inaccuracies in their data, ensuring that the information held about them is accurate and up-to-date. The right to delete permits individuals to request the deletion of their data, particularly if it is no longer needed for the purpose it was collected or if they withdraw their consent (Sarkar and Shukla 2024). The right to limit allows individuals to restrict the processing of their data, especially in scenarios where they contest the accuracy of the data or object to its processing. The right to data portability enables individuals to transfer their data between service providers, promoting interoperability and giving them greater control over their data (Sarkar and Shukla 2024). Lastly, the right to object allows individuals to oppose the processing of their data, particularly in cases where the data is being used for direct marketing or profiling purposes.

The DPDPA establishes the DPA as an autonomous authority responsible for enforcing the Act (Sarkar and Shukla 2024). The DPA's role includes ensuring compliance by monitoring and ensuring that organizations adhere to the provisions of the DPDPA (Sarkar and Shukla 2024). It also involves enforcement, which includes investigating breaches and imposing penalties on organizations that fail to comply with the Act. Additionally, the DPA provides guidance and support to organizations on best practices for data protection. Another critical function of the DPA is public awareness, which involves educating the public about their data protection rights and the importance of privacy (Sarkar and Shukla 2024).

The DPDPA's emphasis on privacy and data protection has profound implications for AI-driven mental healthcare (Sarkar and Shukla 2024). This sector, which relies heavily on sensitive personal data, must navigate the balance between leveraging technological advancements and safeguarding patient rights. AI-driven mental healthcare systems process vast amounts of sensitive data to diagnose, treat, and support patients (Sarkar and Shukla 2024). The DPDPA mandates that these systems operate transparently and ethically by adhering to principles such as data minimization, which involves collecting only the data that is strictly necessary for the intended purpose, thereby reducing the risk of misuse (Sarkar and Shukla 2024). Purpose limitation ensures that data is used only for the purposes for which it was collected, preventing unauthorized use (Sarkar and Shukla 2024). Data security entails implementing robust security measures to protect data from breaches and unauthorized access.

The rights granted under the DPDPA empower patients to take control of their personal data (Sarkar and Shukla 2024). In the context of AI-driven mental healthcare, this means that patients must be fully informed about how their data will be used and must consent to its processing, known as informed consent (Sarkar and Shukla 2024). Transparency ensures that patients have the right to know what data is being collected, how it is being used, and who it is being shared with. Choice and control allow patients to limit the use of their data or withdraw their consent, ensuring that they are not subjected to unwanted data processing.

For organizations in AI-driven mental healthcare, complying with the DPDPA presents several challenges (Sarkar and Shukla 2024). Implementing systems that comply with the DPDPA's requirements can be technically complex and resource-intensive (Sarkar and Shukla 2024). Establishing robust data governance frameworks is essential to ensure ongoing compliance with the Act (Sarkar and Shukla 2024). Ensuring that staff are trained on data protection principles and understand their responsibilities under the DPDPA is also critical. Despite these challenges, the DPDPA presents significant opportunities. By complying with the DPDPA, organizations can build trust with patients, who will feel more confident in sharing their data. Organizations that prioritize data protection and ethical conduct can differentiate themselves in the market, gaining a competitive advantage. Enhanced data governance can lead to better data quality, improving the effectiveness of AI-driven mental health tools.

Non-compliance with the DPDPA can result in severe legal consequences (Sarkar and Shukla 2024). Organizations that fail to comply with the Act can face substantial fines and penalties (Sarkar and Shukla 2024). Data breaches or misuse can result in significant reputational damage, impacting an organization's credibility and patient trust. Patients whose data rights are violated may take legal action against the organization, leading to costly litigation. Beyond legal compliance, organizations have a moral responsibility to protect patient data. This includes ensuring that data processing is conducted ethically, respecting patient rights and dignity. Prioritizing patient welfare ensures that AI-driven tools do not harm patients or compromise their privacy (Sarkar and Shukla 2024). Being accountable for data protection practices and taking responsibility for any breaches or misuse is essential (Sarkar and Shukla 2024).

The Digital Personal Data Protection Act 2023 serves as a landmark in data governance, providing a robust framework for protecting privacy rights in an increasingly digital world (Sarkar and Shukla 2024). For the AI-driven mental healthcare sector, the DPDPA offers a roadmap for ethical conduct, emphasizing transparency, fairness, and security (Sarkar and Shukla 2024). By empowering patients and imposing stringent regulations on data processors, the DPDPA ensures that technological advancements do not come at the expense of fundamental privacy rights.

As organizations navigate the complexities of compliance, they must embrace the opportunities for innovation and trust-building that the DPDPA presents. Ultimately, the Act fosters a responsible and accountable environment where patient welfare is paramount, setting a high standard for ethical data management in AI-driven mental healthcare (Sarkar and Shukla 2024).

INFORMED CONSENT: LEGAL CONSIDERATION IN INDIA

It is already discussed above, informed consent, from the point of view of balancing ethical imperatives in informed consent in ai-driven mental healthcare, is of paramount importance (Prakash et al. 2023). Consent, here, stands as a legal requirement for medical practice and not as a procedural formality (Prakash et al. 2023). Getting consent by mere signing has no consent but assumes a lot of rights and liberties, especially where a competent patient is concerned. Oftentimes, medical professionals either ignore or are ignorant of the requirements of a valid consent and its legal implications. In this medical ethics context, valid consent is premised upon the patient's competence and informed decision-making capacity (Prakash et al. 2023). In other words, valid consent lies upon the presumption that an adult can understand the risk, benefit, and alleged advantages of the proposed treatment (Prakash et al. 2023). The legal frame is usually predicated upon the assumption that on reaching adulthood, there will be an operational presumption of capacity. However, this presumption of competence is not absolute; where there is doubt regarding a patient's understanding, then, medical practitioners need to assess whether the individual is capable of providing informed consent. In the cases where the patient is incapable of providing consent, it will be obtained from the surrogate decision-maker (Prakash et al. 2023).

Moreover, the professional opinion of medical practitioners in ensuring informed consent as part of their professional obligations is laid out in the legal framework (Banerjee 2023). The principle of autonomy, encapsulated in Article 21 of the Indian Constitution, states that the rights of an individual to make decisions regarding his or her own health (Banerjee 2023). However, the common law principles of consent are merely mentioned in the Indian legal landscape, lacking a full-fledged consent practices framework. The doctrine of informed consent, an American judicial concept, lays down the obligation of the medical practitioners, alongside the patient's right to knowledge about the proposed interventions, implications, and choices available. Informed consent involves more than just a mere signature on the consent form. It further lays down the ethical duty of medical practitioners to ensure that adequate information is passed on to patients regarding the nature, risks, benefits, and alternatives of the proposed interventions. In particular, ensuring informed consent becomes more critical in the context of AI-driven mental health where technological interventions could sometimes be complex and opaque to patients. Patients should be able to grasp the effects of AI algorithms and the possible consequences, including treatment options and privacy.

CONCLUSION AND SUGGESTIONS

As technological evolution redefines the limits of mental health care in India, data privacy and informed consent are important focal points for ethical concerns. This is a delicate balance whereby one tries to use technological advancements for better patient outcomes and at the same time keep privacy and rights. What is of great importance is the responsibility of stakeholders such as clinicians, policymakers, technologists, and lawyers to design ethical frameworks that encourage patient autonomy and dignity. It should be realized that with the regulatory landscape surrounding stakeholders of AI-driven mental healthcare, they are obliged to uphold the ethical imperatives by embracing the principles of the DPDPA, ensuring that patient privacy and autonomy are respected and protected. Balancing the ethical imperatives of data privacy and informed consent requires transparency, patient education, and the provision of information that makes sense to patients on AI-driven interventions. There is responsibility of healthcare providers towards empowering patients to make autonomous decisions on their mental health journey while safeguarding their privacy rights in the digital age. As AI continues to evolve, stakeholders need to prioritize ethical concerns, especially those of patient autonomy and data privacy. Given the complexities and potential biases associated with AI, clinicians have a heightened responsibility to educate patients about these technologies. This education should encompass:

- **Types of ML Algorithms Used:** Patients should be informed about the specific types of AI being employed in their care. For example, they should understand whether a decision is being made by a supervised learning algorithm, which relies on labeled training data, or an unsupervised one, which identifies patterns without predefined labels.
- **Nature of Data Inputs:** Patients should know what kind of data the AI system uses to make decisions. This includes demographic information, medical history, genetic data, and real-time health metrics. Transparency about data sources helps patients understand the breadth and depth of the information influencing their care.
- **Potential Biases and Shortcomings:** Clinicians must disclose any known limitations or biases in the AI system. For example, if an AI tool is known to

perform better on certain populations or under specific conditions, patients should be made aware of these limitations. This transparency is crucial in maintaining trust and enabling informed decision-making.

- **When to Inform Patients About AI Use:** Determining the circumstances under which clinicians must notify patients about the use of AI is complex.
- **Significance of AI's Role:** If AI plays a critical role in diagnosis or treatment decisions, full disclosure is essential. For example, if an AI system is used to diagnose cancer from imaging scans, patients should be informed about its use and the degree to which the diagnosis relies on AI versus human judgment.
- **Impact on Treatment Options:** When AI influences the choice of treatment options, patients should be informed. They need to understand how AI recommendations are generated and how much weight clinicians place on these recommendations in their decision-making process.
- **Patient Autonomy and Preference:** Patients' rights to autonomy must be respected. Some patients may prefer not to have AI involved in their care, while others might welcome it. Clinicians should gauge patient preferences and respect their choices, ensuring that they feel comfortable and informed about their care.
- **Trust and Reliability:** Trust in AI systems is crucial for their acceptance. Clinicians should not only educate patients about AI but also provide reassurance about the reliability and safety of these systems. Highlighting the benefits of AI, such as improved diagnostic accuracy or personalized treatment plans, can help build trust.
- **Ethical Imperatives:** Addressing potential biases in AI systems is an ethical imperative. Clinicians should advocate for AI tools that have been rigorously tested for fairness and equity. They should also be vigilant about detecting and mitigating any biases that could affect patient care.
- **Changes in Legal and Regulatory Frameworks:** The legal and regulatory environment for AI in healthcare is still evolving. Clinicians must stay informed about current regulations and ensure that their use of AI complies with legal standards. This includes adhering to guidelines on informed consent and data privacy.

REFERENCES

Banerjee, D. (2023). *Ethical Dilemmas and Legal Questions Involved in Use of AI in Surgeries: Discrepancies in Indian Medical Jurisprudence*.

Carr, S. (2020). 'AI gone mental': Engagement and ethics in data-driven technology for mental health. *Journal of Mental Health (Abingdon, England)*, 29(2), 125–130. 10.1080/09638237.2020.171401132000544

Cohen, I. G., Amarasingham, R., Shah, A., Xie, B., & Lo, B. (2014). The legal and ethical concerns that arise from using complex predictive analytics in health care. *Health Affairs (Project Hope)*, 7(7), 1139–1147. 10.1377/hlthaff.2014.004825006139

D'Alfonso, S. (2020). AI in mental health. *Current Opinion in Psychology*, 36, 112–117. 10.1016/j.copsyc.2020.04.00532604065

Elhaddad, M., & Hamam, S. (2024). AI-Driven Clinical Decision Support Systems: An Ongoing Pursuit of Potential. *Cureus*, 16(4). 10.7759/cureus.5772838711724

Farhud, D. D., & Zokaei, S. (2021). Ethical issues of artificial intelligence in medicine and healthcare. *Iranian Journal of Public Health*, 50(11), i–v. 10.18502/ijph.v50i11.760035223619

Frank, E., & Olaoye, G. (2024). *Privacy and data protection in AI-enabled healthcare systems*. Research Gate. https://www.researchgate.net/publication/378287462_Privacy_and_data_protection_in_AI-enabled_healthcare_systems

. Gerke S, Minssen T & Cohen G (2020). Ethical and legal challenges of artificial intelligence-driven healthcare. *Artificial Intelligence in Healthcare*. Academic Press. .10.1016/B978-0-12-818438-7.00012-5

Graham, S., Depp, C., Lee, E. E., Nebeker, C., Tu, X., Kim, H. C., & Jeste, D. V. (2019). Artificial Intelligence for Mental Health and Mental Illnesses: An Overview. *Current Psychiatry Reports*, 21(11), 116. 10.1007/s11920-019-1094-031701320

Hassija, V., Chamola, V., Mahapatra, A., Singal, A., Goel, D., Huang, K., Scardapane, S., Spinelli, I., Mahmud, M., & Hussain, A. (2024). Interpreting Black-Box Models: A Review on Explainable Artificial Intelligence. *Cognitive Computation*, 16(1), 45–74. 10.1007/s12559-023-10179-8

Jeyaraman, M., Balaji, S., Jeyaraman, N., & Yadav, S. (2023). Unraveling the ethical enigma: Artificial intelligence in healthcare. *Cureus*, 15(8). 10.7759/cureus.4326237692617

Kadam, R. A. (2017). Informed consent process: A step further towards making it meaningful! *Perspectives in Clinical Research*, 8(3), 107–112. 10.4103/picr.PICR_147_1628828304

Mensah, G. B. (2023). *Artificial Intelligence and Ethics: A Comprehensive Review of Bias Mitigation*. Transparency, and Accountability in AI Systems.

Mohammad Amini, M., Jesus, M., Fanaei Sheikholeslami, D., Alves, P., Hassanzadeh Benam, A., & Hariri, F. (2023). Artificial Intelligence Ethics and Challenges in Healthcare Applications: A Comprehensive Review in the Context of the European GDPR Mandate. *Machine Learning and Knowledge Extraction*, 5(3), 1023–1035. 10.3390/make5030053

Murdoch, B. (2021). Privacy and artificial intelligence: Challenges for protecting health information in a new era. *BMC Medical Ethics*, 22(1), 122. 10.1186/s12910-021-00687-334525993

Naik, N., Hameed, B. M. Z., Shetty, D. K., Swain, D., Shah, M., Paul, R., Aggarwal, K., Ibrahim, S., Patil, V., Smriti, K., Shetty, S., Rai, B. P., Chlosta, P., & Somani, B. K. (2022). Legal and ethical consideration in artificial intelligence in healthcare: Who takes responsibility? *Frontiers in Surgery*, 9, 266. 10.3389/fsurg.2022.86232235360424

Prakash, S., Balaji, J. N., Joshi, A., & Surapaneni, K. M. (2022). Ethical Conundrums in the application of artificial intelligence (AI) in healthcare—A scoping review of reviews. *Journal of Personalized Medicine*, 12(11), 1914. 10.3390/jpm1211191436422090

Rubeis, G. (2022). iHealth: The ethics of artificial intelligence and big data in mental healthcare. *Internet Interventions : the Application of Information Technology in Mental and Behavioural Health*, 28, 100518. 10.1016/j.invent.2022.10051835257003

Sarkar, G., & Shukla, S. K. (2024). Reconceptualizing online offenses: A framework for distinguishing cybercrime, cyberattacks, and cyberterrorism in the Indian legal context. *Journal of Economic Criminology*, 4, 100063. 10.1016/j.jeconc.2024.100063

Senarath, A., & Arachchilage, N. A. G. (2019). A data minimization model for embedding privacy into software systems. *Computers & Security*, 87, 101605. 10.1016/j.cose.2019.101605

Singhal, A., Neveditsin, N., Tanveer, H., & Mago, V. (2024). Toward Fairness, Accountability, Transparency, and Ethics in AI for Social Media and Health Care: Scoping Review. *JMIR Medical Informatics*, 12, e50048. 10.2196/5004838568737

Stalla-Bourdillon, S., & Knight, A. (2016). Anonymous data v. personal data-false debate: An EU perspective on anonymization, pseudonymization and personal data. *Wis. Int'l LJ*, 34, 284.

Tarzian, M., Ndrio, M., & Fakoya, A. O. (2023). An Introduction and Brief Overview of Psychoanalysis. *Cureus*, 15(9), e45171. 10.7759/cureus.4517137842377

Chapter 11
Cyber Terrorism in Health Information Systems:
A Systematic Review and Bibliometric Analysis

Shashikant Rai
https://orcid.org/0000-0002-1781-9181
Indian Institute of Information Technology, Allahabad, India

Richa Sharma
Amity Global Business School, Amity University, India

Divya Mishra
https://orcid.org/0000-0002-9375-8720
Sharda University, India

Netranand Pathak
https://orcid.org/0009-0008-9001-6482
Indian Institute of Information Technology, Allahabad, India

ABSTRACT

This review examines the escalating threat of cyber terrorism in health information systems (HIS), highlighting the increasing frequency and sophistication of cyber-attacks targeting the healthcare sector. Healthcare institutions, holding critical data like electronic health records (EHR) and personally identifiable information (PII), are prime targets for cybercriminals. The study explores key security challenges, including ransomware, data breaches, denial of service attacks, and IoT vulnerabilities. Through a comprehensive literature review and bibliometric analysis, the study investigates encryption, blockchain technology, and training programs for healthcare providers. It also evaluates cybersecurity frameworks and emphasizes

DOI: 10.4018/979-8-3693-5976-1.ch011

the need for continuous innovation in security measures. The findings underscore the urgent need for enhanced cybersecurity strategies to protect patient data and ensure the integrity of healthcare services. This review aims to initiate a dialogue on strengthening the cybersecurity resilience of healthcare systems.

INTRODUCTION

Health Information System has much to offer regarding controlling healthcare expenditures and enhancing the standard of care (Chaudhry et al., 2006).However, data stored in HIS that can be used for personal or business purposes is of interest to cybercriminals. In most information technology sectors, there are present controls in place to thwart the activities of these cybercriminals, but in some, innovation is required to address a security gap (Kraemer-Mbula et al., 2013).

To accomplish the Joint Commission's National Patient Safety Goal (NPSG) number 13, healthcare professionals can use health information systems to let patients access test results, refill medicines, securely interact with their clinicians, and possibly participate in medical decisions (Ryals et al., 2011). HIS provides strategic decision-making for the healthcare executive and suggests areas for investment or emphasis. HIS offers compiled data to the researcher for evaluation. For the government, HIS supports data-driven public policy and assists public health in identifying health trends throughout a nation or region (Kwon & Johnson, 2013). Access to health information is essential for providing adequate medical care. Even in the face of denial-of-service assaults, system outages, and natural disasters, health informatics systems must continue functioning. Within the last ten years, cybercrime in the healthcare sector has grown significantly and become a significant danger; an example is Anthem Health and the 80 million patient data breach (Wilner et al., 2021). The healthcare sector is seriously threatened by cybercrime, and data breaches remain a significant source of worry. Many governments are working towards safeguarding the health information system in their country. In this context, HIPPA was introduced. The Clinton Administration created the Health Insurance Portability and Accountability Act (HIPAA) of 1996 as a set of rules to safeguard patients' privacy rights (Kulynych & Korn, 2003). These regulations specifically call for the hiring of a full-time privacy officer, the documentation of any access to patient medical information, the hiring of doctors, hospitals, insurance providers, and pharmacies, and the provision of patient access to their data and the ability to make corrections (Agaku et al., 2014). HINTS is one of several other groups battling for the security of patient data. The Health Information Technology for Economic and Clinical Health (HITECH) Act was created to safeguard patient confidentiality and privacy. The act requires compliance and breach reporting from healthcare companies and professionals (Seh et al., 2020).

METHODOLOGY

This study aims to review previous research to prevent cybercrime in healthcare. A literature review (LR) and bibliometric analysis have been conducted to do the analysis. Four research questions were developed to guide this analysis:

RQ1- What attacking strategy is most favored and used in healthcare devices?

RQ2- From a privacy protection perspective, what are the current requirements and recommended security platforms for medical equipment?

RQ3- What part does training and awareness serve in raising healthcare providers' awareness of cyber threats, and how can the effectiveness of training and awareness initiatives implemented inside an organization be measured?

RQ4- Which cyber defense techniques have national and international organizations implemented to increase cyber resilience?

Various search engines and academic databases were utilized to gather relevant content. The digital research tools frequently referenced for obtaining related scientific studies are specified. The keywords used to encompass nearly all relevant sources include:

Keywords: Security challenges, Security requirements, Security Solutions, Security Threats, Information Security, Internet of Things (IoT), Privacy, U-Healthcare Monitoring, Smart Hospital, Personal Health Information, Service-Technology-Organization-Finance model (STOF), Healthcare, Cyber Terrorism, Cybercrime, Cyber-attack, Cyberthreats, Cybersecurity, Health, ransomware, Medical and Healthcare.

The study examined relevant literature (Table 4 & Table 5) on health, ransomware, and medical and healthcare security, filtering articles from January 2012 to August 2024. Four research questions (RQ1-RQ4) guided the analysis, with the number of articles reducing significantly after duplicate removal, abstract review, and full-text scanning. Data was sourced from Google Scholar, Scopus, Springer, IEEE, Web of Science, ResearchGate, and through Google Search.

Table 1. Filtering procedure: A list of all relevant articles published between January 2012 and August 2024

Study Questions	Number Reference Retrieved	After Removing the Duplicates	After Abstract	After Full-text Scanning
RQ1	78	35	28	18
RQ2	56	24	16	10
RQ3	43	30	21	16
RQ4	72	54	36	14

Table 2. A list of search engines and databases

Sources	Name of the Source
Databases	Google Scholar, Scopus, Springer, IEEE, Web of Science, ResearchGate
Search Engines	Google Search

LITERATURE REVIEW

Because of the importance of the healthcare business, the rapid advancement of cybersecurity in this field, and the severe consequences of cyberattacks, many research articles examine the architecture of healthcare organizations, identifying weaknesses in systems and looking into possible assaults (Acar & Acar, 2012). These studies also highlight strategies for lowering the likelihood of breaches and dealing with their fallout productively (Alharam & Elmedany, 2017).

Analyzing the numerous information security technologies used in the healthcare sector will identify the key factors that place it at the top of the list of industries attacked the most (Kjaerland, 2006). Furthermore, it will investigate the recommended approaches to enhancing industrial security, specifically to protect and defend healthcare applications based on the Internet of Things (IoT) (Kouicem et al., 2018). This article analyses encryption-based solutions for the Advanced Encryption Standard (AES) applications and suggests a hybrid approach to protect commercial and Electronic Healthcare Record (EHR) applications against cyber-attacks (Chenthara et al., 2019).

Data breaches, Events involving cybersecurity throughout the past ten years (2012-22), the healthcare sector, its effects, and its current amount of data breaches that primarily have personal effects on the data (Angst et al., 2017). The research emphasizes the several distinct groups of breaches across several industrial organizations employing the straightforward moving average and straightforward soothing average techniques for analyzing and evaluating modern data security attacks targeting health care. The research aims to thoroughly investigate security concerns and provide data that can be used to recommend changes and solutions centered on safeguarding patient information's privacy. The article stated that there are two typical assaults conducted in most data breaches, i.e., IT incidents and internal revelation, that were not authorized.

These days, identity theft and fraud are among the most common. Identity fraud and identity theft are distinct concepts. The only activity involved in identity theft is information extraction. Identity fraud refers to the illicit use of personal information for malicious purposes. The primary motivations for initiating a cyber-attack are often driven by financial gain and disgruntled personnel. During a cyberterrorism symposium at the University of California Davis, it was revealed that hackers begin their assaults by sending "phishing" emails to inject malware packages into a hospital network (Kierkegaard, 2012).

These packages launched waves of strikes separated by days. Infected patient records and modified medicine orders would result from the initial attack. The second attack would obstruct portable equipment used by healthcare professionals to record patient data. Monitors in intensive care units would be the target of the third attack, which would trigger alarms and change displays. Infected software would control medicine infusion pumps and other similar medical devices in the fourth and final strike (Bansal et al., 2010).

According to a survey published by CloudSEK, an artificial intelligence startup that deals with cyber risks, India stands second among all nations regarding cyber assaults on healthcare systems in 2021. 7.7% of all cyberattacks on healthcare systems last year originated in India (Shenoy & Appel, 2017). A model is being developed to enhance data transmission safety between users, mobile devices, and cloud servers in the healthcare system. The rising utilization of mobile technologies in the healthcare industry encouraged the author to conduct the study because of the massive security risk in mobile devices. Information stored on handheld devices is also very prone to losing its integrity and confidentiality (Win et al., 2006).

The proposal recommends using a Wireless Body Area Network (WBAN) to create a cloud-based platform for secure healthcare equipment (Khan et al., 2014). They previously employed a combination of multi-biometric critical generation methodology to enhance the security of the cross-functional and cross-connection. Additionally, they were used to protect the EHR that was centrally kept in the healthcare sector's cloud to guarantee patient data privacy. They tested their system in an experimental setting, and the findings showed that it generated a secure cloud-based architecture that protected the security and privacy of patient data and communication methods (Kahn & Sheshadri, 2008).

Any system that must be HIPAA compliant must take crucial legal considerations into account. Recently, there has been pressure to gain Food and Drug Administration (FDA) approval for a few telemedicine applications. Not all mobile health applications need FDA approval. Patient monitoring is the foundation of many different sorts of healthcare applications. However, a clearly defined law for FDA approval, or SOI(k), must still exist for mobile healthcare applications. One of its distinguishing features is that a mobile health application is employed as a diagnostic tool (Win et al., 2006).

BIBLIOMETRIC ANALYSIS

The process of investigating cyber-related hazards in the medical and health information domains encompasses several intricate stages. Firstly, a specific search word is established to capture pertinent research while excluding similar-sounding but unrelated subjects. The selected search phrases are “Cyber Crime” OR “Cyber Security” OR “Cyber Terrorism” AND “Medical” OR “Health Information.” In the subsequent stage, it is necessary to choose a suitable academic database, and Scopus is selected due to its extensive coverage of the relevant literature. Table 3 presents the methodological steps of bibliometric analysis

The search is enhanced by using particular criteria to guarantee the pertinence and controllability of the outcomes. The specified requirements include publications from 2010 to 2024, document categories such as articles, review articles, book chapters, and conference papers, and the limitation to the English language. Data analysis and visualization include the use of many software packages. R Biblioshiny is used specifically for constructing word clouds, tables, and bar graphs. On the other hand, VOSViewer is applied for bibliometric network analysis and mapping.

The analysis is divided into two primary components. Performance Analysis primarily examines many metrics to comprehend publishing and citation patterns, contributions from different nations and affiliations, identification of leading journals, often referenced publications, and the most famous disciplines within the field. Science Mapping entails the use of co-keyword analysis to uncover shared themes and patterns in research, co-author analysis to investigate cooperation among scholars, and co-country analysis to comprehend international partnerships. This comprehensive approach seeks to provide a detailed examination of the convergence of cyber risks and medical and health information, emphasizing significant patterns, contributions, and partnerships within the academic community.

Table 3. Methodological steps bibliometric analysis

Step	Description	Details
Step1: Determining the Search Term	The initial step involves defining a precise search term to capture research on social cohesion while avoiding irrelevant concepts that might have similar-sounding terms.	Term: "Cyber Crime" OR "Cyber Security" OR "Cyber Terrorism" AND "Medical" OR "Health Information"
Step 2: Selection of Database	The next step is to select an appropriate academic database that provides comprehensive coverage of the relevant literature.	Database: Scopus
Step 3: Selection Criteria for Search	The search is refined using specific criteria to ensure the relevance and manageability of the results.	Years: 2010–2024 Document Types: Articles, review articles, book chapters, and proceedings papers Language: English
Step 4: Selection of Software	Different software tools are employed for data analysis and visualization.	R Biblioshiny: word cloud, Table, Bar graph VOSViewer: Bibliometric network analysis and mapping
Step 5: Analysis and Results	The analysis is divided into two main parts:	Performance Analysis: Publication and citation trends, Contribution by country, Contribution by affiliation, Top journals, frequently cited documents, Top disciplines, Science Mapping: Co-keyword analysis, Co-author analysis, Co-country analysis

Table 4. Completeness of bibliographic metadata - 642 documents from Scopus

Completeness of bibliographic metadata - **642** documents from **Scopus**

Metadata	Description	Missing Counts	Missing %	Status
AB	Abstract	0	0.00	Excellent
DT	Document Type	0	0.00	Excellent
SO	Journal	0	0.00	Excellent
LA	Language	0	0.00	Excellent
PY	Publication Year	0	0.00	Excellent
TI	Title	0	0.00	Excellent
TC	Total Citation	0	0.00	Excellent
AU	Author	1	0.16	Good
C1	Affiliation	7	1.09	Good
CR	Cited References	25	3.89	Good
DI	DOI	57	8.88	Good
DE	Keywords	63	9.81	Good
ID	Keywords Plus	71	11.06	Acceptable
RP	Corresponding Author	257	40.03	Poor
WC	Science Categories	642	100.00	Completely missing

Table 4 provides an overview of the several types of information, including Abstract (AB), Document Type (DT), Journal (SO), Language (LA), Publication Year (PY), Title (TI), and Total Citation (TC), and it analyses the completeness of the bibliographic metadata for 642 documents that were derived from Scopus. These categories have a perfect status with 0% missing as there are no missing data. The missing count for the Author (AU) category is 1, or 0.16%, which is regarded as excellent. Similar to this, the missing counts for Affiliation (C1) and Cited References (CR) are 7 and 25, respectively. These amounts equal 1.09% and 3.89%, both of which are considered satisfactory. The missing numbers for the DOI (DI) and Keywords (DE) categories are higher—57 (8.88%) and 63 (9.81%), respectively—but they are still within the acceptable range. The missing count for Keywords Plus (ID) is 71, or 11.06%, which is considered acceptable. With 257 items missing (40.03%), the Corresponding Author (RP) field is classed as having considerable missing data, meaning it needs improvement. Interestingly, the Science Categories (WC) have a 100% missing rate and are entirely absent from all papers. As a whole, the research shows that most metadata fields are excellent to good complete, with the exception of Keywords Plus, Corresponding Author, and Science Categories, which all have substantial or whole data missing.

FINDINGS

Figure 1. Corresponding author's countries

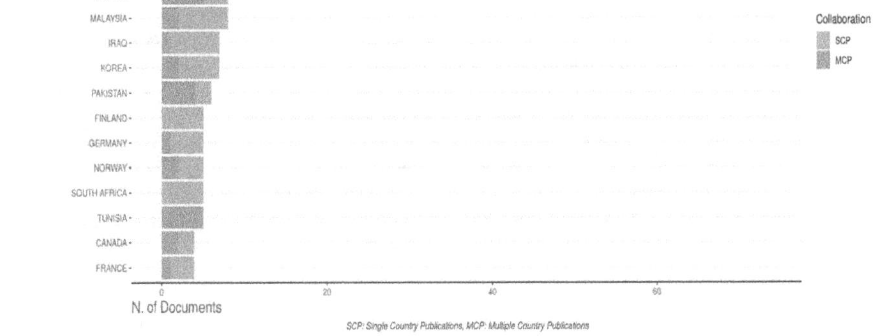

Categorized by Single Country Publications (SCP) and Multiple Country Publications (MCP), the bar chart (Figure 1: Corresponding Author's Countries) displays the distribution of papers ascribed to associated authors from different nations. India has the top spot with the most papers, mostly SCP. The USA, which contributes the second most, has a balanced combination of SCP and MCP. China and the United Kingdom also stand out as major donors, exhibiting a noteworthy combination of both kinds of cooperation. Australia and Saudi Arabia own a large quantity of papers, mostly SCP. India is the country that observes SCP the most, while the United States, the United Kingdom, China, Saudi Arabia, and Australia all make significant contributions as well. In terms of MCP, the United States of America and a number of European nations, such as Ireland, Italy, Germany, Norway, and Finland, demonstrate significant figures, highlighting global cooperation. Furthermore, MCP contributions are noteworthy in nations like France, Canada, and South Africa that value teamwork.

Notable nations such as Iraq, Korea, Pakistan, Malaysia, Italy, Ireland, and Malaysia exhibit a combination of SCP and MCP, with SCP being more common. Finland, Germany, Norway, South Africa, Tunisia, Canada, and France are among the nations that make modest contributions; Tunisia and France are more inclined toward MCP. In conclusion, India leads the world in overall document submissions, mostly via SCP. China, the United States, and the United Kingdom all make significant contributions with a balanced mix of SCP and MCP. Higher MCP tendencies are seen in European nations and other regions, suggesting a strong preference for international cooperation. Overall, MCP is still important in areas recognized for their cooperative research endeavors, even if SCP is more common in many other nations. The distribution of research contributions and patterns of cooperation among various nations is adequately shown in the chart.

Figure 2. Trending topics

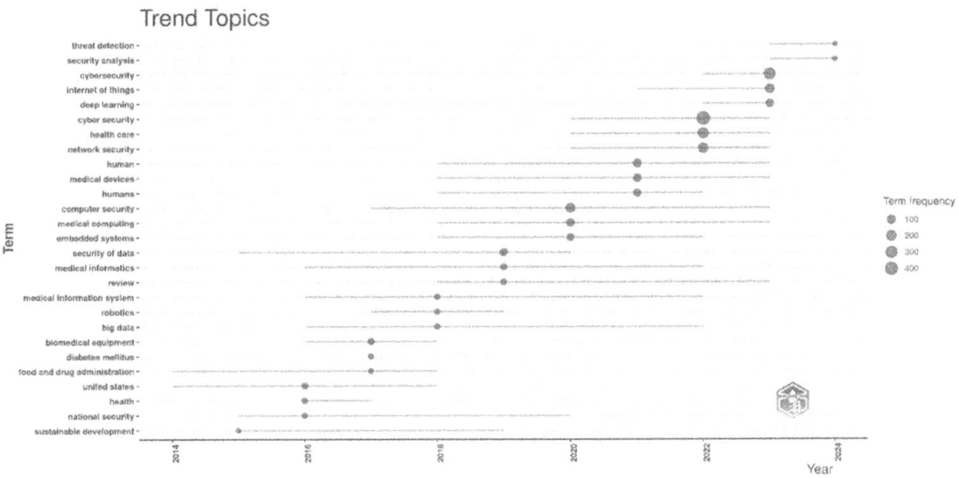

Figure 2 provides a comprehensive examination of popular subjects over a period of time, where the size of the circles represents the frequency of the terms. The themes are listed on the vertical axis, while the years from 2014 to 2024 are shown on the horizontal axis. Greater circles represent greater word frequency. Cybersecurity and network security have seen a noteworthy increase in occurrence, particularly starting from 2018, in conjunction with healthcare and medical equipment. The Internet of Things and deep learning are prominent topics that have been steadily growing in popularity over the years. Terms like threat detection, security analysis, and cyber security have gained prominence in the years 2023-2024. The fields of medical informatics and medical computing began to attract significant interest about 2017 and have since maintained their relevance. Enduring long-term patterns include embedded systems, computer security, and data security, while big data and biomedical equipment saw significant increases between 2018 and 2020. Terms such as sustainable development, national security, and food and drug administration have remained present, but with lower frequency. In addition, there have been intermittent rises in interest or relevance seen for keywords such as health, United States, and review, suggesting periodic surges. This graphic clearly demonstrates the tendencies of many themes over the previous decade, highlighting both long-lasting trends and new issues in technology, security, and healthcare.

Figure 3. Words' frequency over time

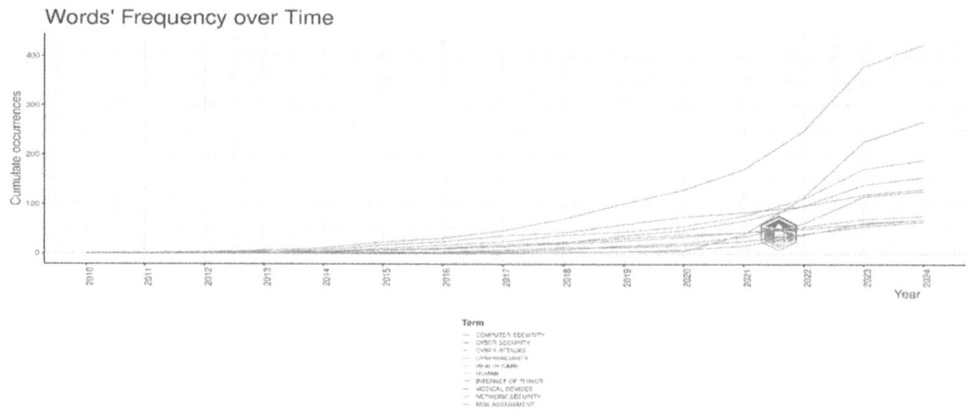

The chart (Figure 3: Words' Frequency over Time) displays the total number of instances of different phrases from 2010 to 2024. The vertical axis represents the cumulative occurrences, while the horizontal axis represents the years. Each line refers to a distinct phrase, as shown by the legend. The word "Cyber Security" (shown by the orange line) exhibits the most notable surge among the high-frequency terms, particularly starting from around 2016. It is projected to reach 400 total occurrences by 2024. The "Health Care" category, shown by the green line, has significant growth, notably starting from 2018, indicating a rise in interest and importance. Within the moderate to high-frequency range, the subjects of "Cybersecurity" (shown by the purple line) and "Computer Security" (represented by the yellow line) demonstrate consistent expansion, particularly throughout the period from 2017 to 2024. The "Internet of Things" (shown by the blue line) experiences a notable rise beginning in 2016 and continues to steadily grow.

Terms exhibiting constant and continuous growth include "Network Security" (shown by the pink line) and "Medical Devices" (represented by the light blue line), both demonstrating sustained rising trends after 2017. The term "Cyber-Attacks" (shown by the red line) began to acquire popularity in 2015, indicating a consistent rising trend that implies an increasing awareness or occurrence of such attacks. Among the less common but noteworthy phrases, the term "Human" (shown by the light green line) has a slower but constant development pattern, suggesting a continuous but less pronounced rise. The "Risk Assessment" (shown by the dark green line) similarly shows a progressive increase, indicating a modest and consistent level of interest over time.

The significant rise in words such as "Cyber Security" and "Health Care" beyond 2020 may be attributed to worldwide occurrences like the COVID-19 pandemic and an upsurge in cyber attacks, underscoring the increasing significance of these domains. The general patterns indicate an increasing emphasis on cybersecurity and health-related subjects, which align with wider socioeconomic and technical advancements. This figure highlights the growing importance of cybersecurity and healthcare in the last ten years, as seen by the significant increase in their use and debate. Additionally, the consistent growth in technology and security phrases indicates the continuous progress and difficulties faced in these areas.

Figure 4. Bibliometric network visualization

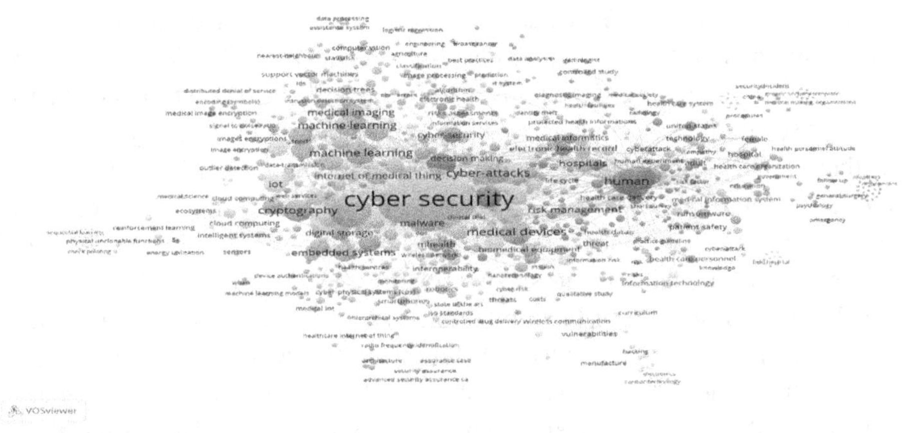

The figure 4 is a bibliometric network visualization generated using VOSviewer. It illustrates the connections between various terms by analysing their co-occurrence in academic literature. The main findings from this visualization demonstrate that "cyber security" is the most prominent keyword, indicating its central importance in the literature. Other noteworthy keywords, such as "human" and "medical devices," underscore a strong emphasis on human factors and the intersection of cyber security with medical devices. The network is partitioned into many clusters, each depicted by distinct colours, indicating sets of interconnected keywords. The green cluster specializes in medical devices and medical informatics; the red cluster focuses on human factors and healthcare systems; the blue cluster centres on machine learning and medical imaging; the yellow cluster encompasses IoT and cryptography; and the purple cluster is dedicated to cyber-attacks and malware.

Figure 5. Word cloud

This word cloud (Figure 5)visualizes key topics in cybersecurity and health information systems, with word size indicating frequency in academic literature. The most prominent terms are "Cyber Security," highlighting its central importance, followed by "Health Care," emphasizing the critical intersection of cybersecurity and healthcare. Other significant terms include "Network Security," "Computer Security," and "Internet of Things (IoT)," reflecting the growing relevance of securing networks and IoT devices in healthcare. Additionally, "Medical Devices" and "Cyber-Attacks" underscore the security challenges and threat landscape, while "Human" highlights the role of human factors. The presence of terms like "Deep Learning," "Machine Learning," "Risk Assessment," "Cryptography," and "Security of Data" shows the application of advanced technologies and methodologies in understanding and mitigating cybersecurity risks in healthcare. This visualization underscores the multidisciplinary nature of research focused on protecting sensitive health data and integrating innovative technologies.

Figure 6. Bibliometric analysis summary

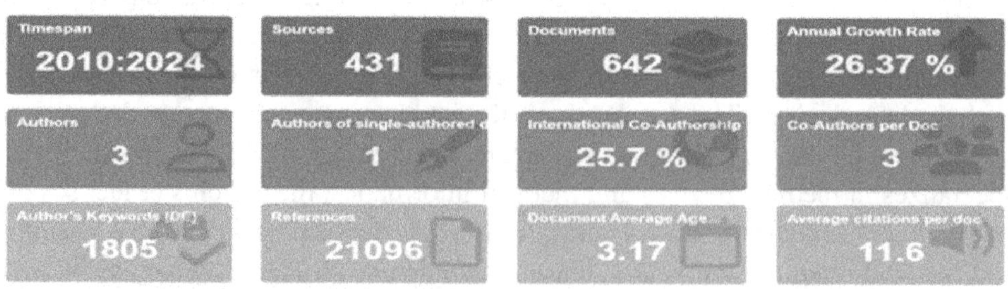

(Prepared by R Biblioshiny)

The dataset (Figure 6: Bibliometric Analysis Summary (Prepared by R Biblioshiny) spans publications from 2010 to 2024, comprising 642 documents from 431 journals, books, and other outlets. With an impressive annual growth rate of 26.37%, the collection has a relatively young average document age of 3.17 years. Each document garners an average of 11.6 citations, collectively citing 21,096 references. The richly detailed content features 3,771 Keywords Plus (ID) and 1,805 Author's Keywords (DE). Authorship data indicates contributions from three authors, including one single-authored document, reflecting a collaborative nature with an average of three co-authors per document and 25.7% involving international co-authorship. Document types are diverse: 224 articles, 6 books, 28 book chapters, 348 conference papers, smaller numbers of errata, letters, retractions, reviews, and short surveys. This dataset highlights a robust and growing body of research with significant international collaboration and a wide range of publication formats.

Figure 7. Author collaboration network

The VOSviewer representation of the author network (Figure 7) reveals a complex web of collaborative connections among academics in a particular topic. Clusters, represented by varying hues, indicate frequent cooperation. The yellow cluster comprises writers Gupta, Sumeet; Bhalla, Heena; and Joshi, Kapil, while the green cluster consists of Pant, Bhasker; Petikam, Sailaja; and De Castro Dantas Sales, Felipe. The blue cluster includes Saxena, Divya; Reddy Dornadula Venkata Harsh; and Kumar, Sentosh, whereas the purple cluster comprises Gautam, Siddharth; Sharma, Nikhil; and Bhardwaj, Jatin. Furthermore, there is another grouping of yellow entities on the right side, consisting of Alazab, Mamoun; Bhattacharya, Sweta; and Jhaveri, Rutvij H. Key individuals such as Pant, Bhasker, and Bhushan play a central role in connecting different groups, enabling collaborations across different disciplines. On the other hand, peripheral writers like Gupta, Sumeet; Bhalla, Heena; and Joshi, Kapil mostly engage in collaborations inside their own cluster. The temporal trends exhibit a color gradient ranging from blue to yellow, which represents the progression of partnerships from about 2021 to the present years, extending up to 2023. The yellow cluster located on the right side signifies the continuing research endeavors. The thickness of the lines connecting writers represents the intensity of their collaboration links, emphasizing the interrelated and ever-changing character of the study area, propelled by influential connectors such as Pant, Bhasker, and Bhushan, Bharat.

Figure 8. Country collaboration network

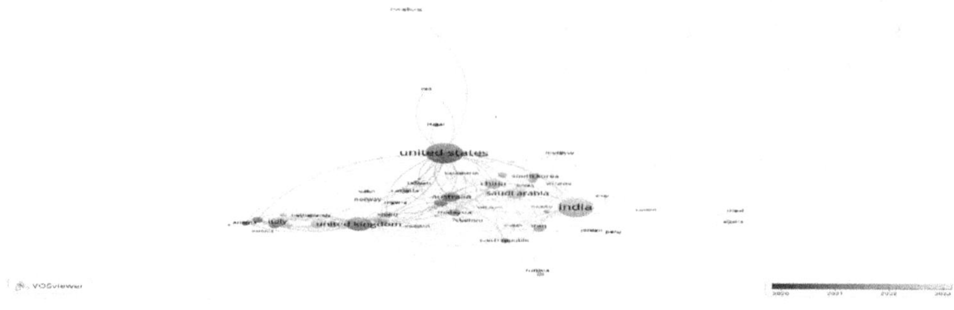

The depiction of the country collaboration network (Figure 8) depicts the complex interconnections between nations, which presumably include commerce, research, or other forms of cooperation. The United States, India, and Saudi Arabia are prominent central nodes, highlighting their substantial contributions to global cooperation. The United States, with extensive diplomatic ties to nations such as Israel, Canada, and the United Kingdom, assumes a crucial role. India has robust diplomatic relations with Saudi Arabia, China, and South Korea, while Saudi Arabia's prominent geographical location highlights its vast global engagements. The network unveils many clusters, including those centered on the United Kingdom and Italy, indicating strong intra-European collaborations. The thickness of the lines connecting the nodes indicates the intensity or frequency of these interactions, with thicker lines indicating stronger relationships. The history of these relationships from 2020 to 2023 is shown by color coding, spanning from blue to yellow, with newer connections emphasized in yellow. Peripheral nodes such as Hong Kong, Nepal, and Algeria have a lower number of connections, suggesting a lesser degree of engagement compared to major nodes. In summary, these graphic highlights the significant contributions of the United States, India, and Saudi Arabia to global cooperation, the formation of regional collaboration clusters, and the changing dynamics of international connections over time.

Figure 9. Co-authorship or citation network

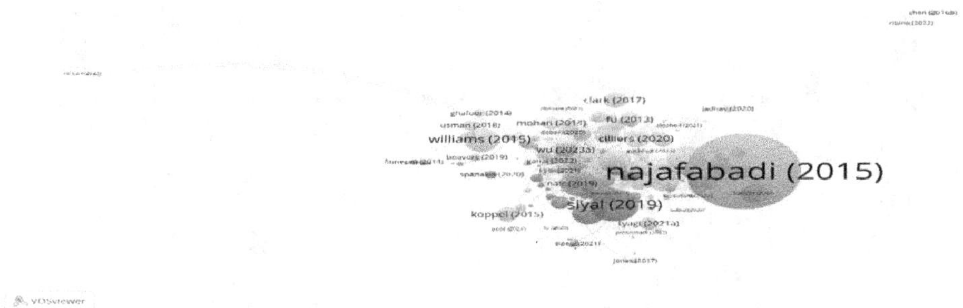

The depiction of the co-authorship or citation network (Figure 9) depicts the connections and partnerships between researchers, emphasizing important individuals and their affiliations. The network is mostly controlled by central nodes such as Najafabadi (2015), Siyal (2019), and Williams (2015), suggesting their substantial impact and wide connections with other authors or works. Najafabadi (2015) is the most prominent node, indicating that it is a very important work or author with a significant number of citations or co-authorships. Siyal (2019) and Williams (2015) are prominent figures in the academic community, known for their significant influence. The network consists of many clusters of highly interconnected nodes, which indicate groups of scholars that interact regularly or articles that are frequently referenced together. Notable scholars that have significant collaboration relationships include Clark (2017), Mohan (2014), and Cilliers (2020). The connections, shown as lines connecting nodes, vary in width to indicate the intensity or frequency of interactions, with wider lines suggesting stronger relationships. The history of contacts from 2013 to 2023 is represented by a color-coding system that ranges from blue to yellow. Blue indicates earlier connections, while yellow indicates more current connections. Peripheral nodes such as Ranjan (2023) and Chen (2016b) have lower connectivity, suggesting a lower level of engagement in comparison to center nodes. In summary, this visualization offers a thorough perspective on academic partnerships or citations, highlighting prominent scholars or articles and the development of their connections over time. Notably, Najafabadi (2015) stands out as a significant figure in the network.

Figure 10. Tree map

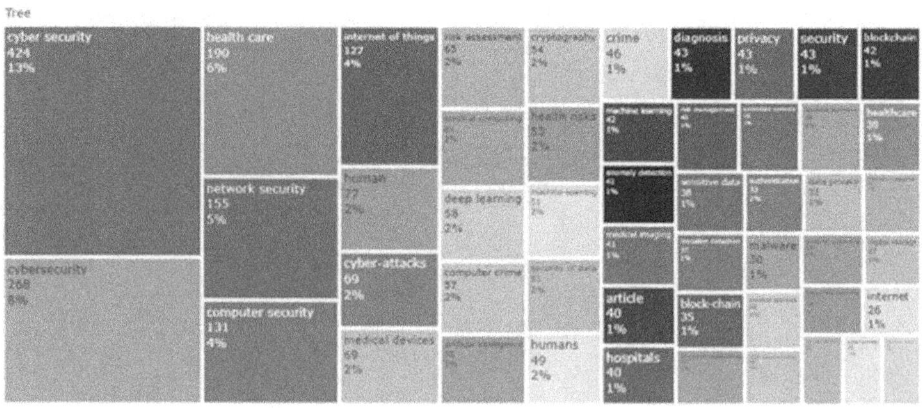

The tree map visualization (Figure 10) classifies different study subjects based on their frequency of recurrence, providing several significant insights. Cyber Security is the dominant subject, with 13% of the occurrences (424 instances). Cybersecurity is another important area, accounting for 8% (268 instances). The area of Health Care is significant, accounting for 6% of occurrences (190 instances). Network Security accounts for 5% of the occurrences, which is equivalent to 155 instances. On the other hand, Computer Security represents 4% of the occurrences, which is equivalent to 131 instances. The Internet of Things (IoT) is a significant domain, accounting for 4% (127 instances). Additional subjects, such as risk assessment, cryptography, crime, diagnostics, privacy, and blockchain, have a lower occurrence rate, making up just 1-2% of the overall occurrences. This distribution highlights a main emphasis on cybersecurity-related matters, with significant focus also given to health care and associated technology fields.

IoT has limitations. In recent years, there have been numerous large-scale cyber-attacks on connected devices; if there is anything to be learned from these cyber-attacks, the Internet of Things (IoT) has countless flaws that can be exploited (Kimani et al., 2019). Amid the rapid development of the IoT, many small devices are connected to the internet for controlling and tracking purposes (Kadhim et al., 2020).

RQ1- What attacking strategy is most favored and used in healthcare devices?(Mazhar et al., 2023).

Many substantial cyberattack are initiated daily, targeting and attacking the healthcare industry (Muthuppalaniappan & Stevenson, 2021). Based on our analysis, the healthcare business is most often targeted by the following cyberattacks (Figure 11):

Figure 11. Categories of cyber crime threats

Incidents involving Internal and External Data Breach

Internal attacks pose a more significant threat to the infrastructure since the attacker has direct access to the IT assets and resources, resulting in more substantial damage (Stellios et al., **2018)**.Either internal or external actors inside the firm may carry out data breaches (Hu et al., 2007).

Ransomware

Ransomware is often used to target the healthcare business, particularly hospitals and other healthcare industries. It is a kind of malicious software. Ransomware specifically targets the servers of a hospital or healthcare institution by encrypting the data and blocking access to the systems. It then demands a ransom. The assailants provide the encryption keys necessary to decipher the data and get access once the victim fulfils the ransom payment. During the first six months of 2020, there was a substantial rise in ransomware attacks. Statistics indicate that January saw the highest number of ransomware assaults, with 19.20% of all reported complaints, compared to 12.82% during the same period in 2019 (Minnaar & Herbig, 2021).

Disruptive Service Attack (DoS)

This attack inundates the server with fabricated or unauthenticated requests to hinder the provision of services to genuine users. Following the attack, a server or the healthcare system may completely cease functioning, leading to financial losses incurred in recovering from the catastrophe. Another prominent kind of this attack is a distributed denial of service (DDoS) attack, which utilizes a botnet to disperse and reduce the attack's duration (Zargar et al., 2013).

Active attacks

During these assaults, a non-authorized user can modify data or introduce malicious material into the Electronic Health Record (EHR). This may be achieved by modifying data that has been sent or stored or by introducing new data streams into the healthcare equipment (Kaddoura & Grati, 2021). There are seven distinct subcategories of current assaults. Examples of attacks that impersonate genuine users include "Masquerade Attacks," "Replay Attacks," "Message Modification Attacks," "Denial-of-Service Attacks," "Interception Attacks," "Session-Stealing Attacks," and "Malicious Codes."

Cybersquatting

Cybersquatting is a prevalent threat in health information systems. It refers to the act of a third party registering a well-known trademark as an Internet domain name to profit from it. This can be done by demanding a ransom from the trademark owner for the domain name or by redirecting customers away from the trademark owner towards the domain name's owner (Luna et al., 2016).

RQ2- From a privacy protection perspective, what are the current requirements and recommended security platforms for medical equipment?

Security guidelines include a collection of physical, specialized, and procedural tasks to ensure the integrity, safety, and accessibility of the health Information. Popular PHR architectures Wearable technology, particularly mobile health, may deliver sophisticated monitoring to any location at any time without mandating that the patient attend the facilities (Safavi & Shukur, 2014).

- Medical information about a patient is often documented using two main methods: Electronic Health Records (EHR) and Personal Health Records (PHR). A PHR is generated and maintained by the patient, while an EHR is created and maintained by medical facilities such as clinics or hospitals (Chomutare et al., 2011).
- Right now, Google Healthcare Service and Microsoft are the two leading Personal Health Record (PHR) service providers. Both businesses provide products that let users control their Personal Health Information (PHI) via the Internet and Internet of Things (IoT) devices. This method enables the collection of varied data from several sources and its storage in a single database (Jian et al., 2011).
- The user can modify the data in the existing record and distribute it to family members or healthcare providers (Azaria et al., 2016).

Blockchain technology can alter the healthcare ecosystem, which encompasses a wide variety of technologies utilized by the healthcare system to allow a learning health system to exchange information easily (Pilkington, 2016).

- Since blockchain relies on preserving all data on immutable, transparent blocks, it may be the most excellent option to log data safely(Putz et al., 2019).
- The blockchain's potential to substitute for a personal health record (PHR) by providing readily accessible patient data to all individuals and compatible third-party platforms is one of the critical benefits of this technology regarding healthcare interoperability (Houtan et al., 2020).
- Data archiving, identity management, and innovative contract software that makes use of a common data infrastructure are all included in a blockchain system (Paik et al., 2019).
- It would be necessary to switch to new techniques to link the data onto the blockchain utilizing the data from a traditional database to manage data access via blockchain (Azaria et al., 2016). For instance, existing databases should preserve data such that the blockchain provides users with the best way to "decrypt" the material, enabling patients to take ownership of their personal information (Dagher et al., 2018).
- The security and stability of the underlying blockchain technology are primarily attributed to the requirement for any malicious actor attempting to alter the chain (known as a 51% attack) to control a substantial portion of the computational power associated with the blockchain (Shrestha & Nam, 2019).

RQ3- What part does training and awareness serve in raising healthcare providers' awareness of cyber threats, and how can the effectiveness of training and awareness initiatives implemented inside an organization be measured?

RQ4- Which cyber defense techniques have national and international organizations implemented to increase cyber resilience?

According to a study by (Kahn & Sheshadri, 2008), HIPAA implemented a comprehensive framework of guidelines and mandates for healthcare providers. These guidelines include the obligation to inform patients about their privacy rights, restricting the usage of protected health information to only necessary purposes such as treatment, payment, or operations, and ensuring that all staff members in covered entities (which are businesses that handle or utilize personal health records in the course of providing services) receive training on privacy matters (Winker et al., 2000).

According to (Kwon & Johnson, 2014), every healthcare company has a crucial duty to secure protected health information. The study aimed to analyze the level of patient data security in healthcare institutions in the United States. The product distribution was conducted by interviewing 250 randomly selected US hospital managers responsible for privacy and security (Aiken et al., 2012). Each organization was limited to submitting just one responder for this poll. The researchers examined information security protocols and identified behaviour patterns associated with improved regulatory compliance (Bulgurcu et al., 2010). The data included in this study was obtained from a telephone survey of 250 healthcare organizations in the United States done by Kroll and the Healthcare Information and Management Systems Society (HIMSS) (van Deursen Hazelhoff Roelfze, 2014). While high levels of practice adoption were generally associated with high levels of perceived compliance, the study discovered distinct patterns in security practices and their relationship to compliance (Chan et al., 2005). Hospitals with the highest levels of compliance were found to place significant emphasis on monitoring third-party breaches and providing training. On the other hand, audit practices were essential for hospitals that scored in the middle range of compliance (Hysong et al., 2006). The study's results suggest that managers must gain awareness of their behaviours and the necessary steps to achieve compliance, resulting in low perceived compliance levels. The findings indicate that hospitals made efforts to evenly distribute the adoption of security measures across four key areas: safeguarding, auditing, HR management, and third-party security management. We analyzed the implementation of security measures to determine typical setups and their correlation with regulatory compliance. A total of 204 hospitals were categorized into three groups according to survey findings that detailed the implementation of security standards (Narayana Samy et al., 2010). Groupings were established according to similarities in practice and corresponding degrees of compliance. Although hospitals in all three groups extensively use technological tools, we observed substantial variation in non-technical practices.

According to a study by Khansa et al., 2012, HIPAA's advantages include facilitating the systematic adoption of EHRs, expediting insurance claims, enhancing information accuracy, reducing administrative costs in the long run, and centralizing medical care to advance contemporary medicine. Patient EHRs Although HIPAA has a negative economic impact in the short term, possibly because of its financial burden on healthcare companies, the longer-term impact is likely favorable. HIPAA was created to reduce healthcare providers' long-term expenses by permitting standardization and simplification. Future research on the advantages of practical HIPAA implementations should be done to confirm the anticipated long-term benefits and to determine when the benefits start to be felt by regulated organizations (Yaraghi & Gopal, 2018).

As was already mentioned, several studies that did not include the issue of phishing addressed the need for cybersecurity training among healthcare personnel. The authors suggested providing user training and simulations to increase knowledge and training on cybersecurity-related IT systems. Based on the target audience, the writers also distinguished between awareness-raising and training efforts. On the one hand, persons who can recognize possible security concerns and take necessary action are the target audience for awareness-raising programs. On the other hand, formal training programs aim to increase understanding and proficiency in cybersecurity measures (Mäses et al., 2018).

HIS has much to offer regarding controlling healthcare expenditures and enhancing the standard of care. However, data stored in HIS that can be used for personal or business purposes is of interest to cybercriminals. In most information technology sectors, there are presently controls in place to thwart the activities of these cybercriminals, but in some, innovation is required to address a security gap (Berg, 2001).This manuscript aims to delineate the inherent benefits offered by the presence and proper utilization of Health Information Systems (HIS), the potential risks to HIS, easily accessible safeguards, and areas necessitating further investigation and advancement to ensure security for patients and organizations effectively (Argaw et al., 2020).

CONCLUSION

The escalating rate of successful cyber breaches(Farrokhi et al., 2020) in the healthcare sector, increasing by approximately 27% annually, underscores the pressing need for robust cybersecurity measures. This review highlights the growing complexity, frequency, and impact of cyberattacks on health information systems (HIS). Healthcare institutions, due to their extensive repositories of sensitive data such as electronic health records (EHR) and personally identifiable information (PII), are prime targets for cybercriminals. The analysis identifies key security challenges including ransomware, data breaches, denial of service (DoS) attacks, and the exploitation of IoT vulnerabilities. By examining various cybersecurity technologies and frameworks, the study emphasizes the critical role of encryption, blockchain technology, and comprehensive training programs for healthcare providers. National and international regulatory frameworks like HIPAA and HITECH are evaluated for their effectiveness in mitigating cyber threats. The findings stress the importance of continuous innovation and adaptive strategies to safeguard patient data and maintain the integrity of healthcare services. This comprehensive review aims to foster a deeper understanding of the vulnerabilities in healthcare cybersecurity and initiate proactive measures to enhance resilience against cyber threats.

REFERENCES

Acar, A. Z., & Acar, P. (2012). The Effects of Organizational Culture and Innovativeness on Business Performance in Healthcare Industry. *Procedia: Social and Behavioral Sciences*, 58, 683–692. 10.1016/j.sbspro.2012.09.1046

Agaku, I. T., Adisa, A. O., Ayo-Yusuf, O. A., & Connolly, G. N. (2014). Concern about security and privacy, and perceived control over collection and use of health information are related to withholding of health information from healthcare providers. *Journal of the American Medical Informatics Association : JAMIA*, 21(2), 374–378. 10.1136/amiajnl-2013-00207923975624

Aiken, L. H., Sermeus, W., den Heede, K. V., Sloane, D. M., Busse, R., McKee, M., Bruyneel, L., Rafferty, A. M., Griffiths, P., Moreno-Casbas, M. T., Tishelman, C., Scott, A., Brzostek, T., Kinnunen, J., Schwendimann, R., Heinen, M., Zikos, D., Sjetne, I. S., Smith, H. L., & Kutney-Lee, A. (2012). Patient safety, satisfaction, and quality of hospital care: Cross sectional surveys of nurses and patients in 12 countries in Europe and the United States. *BMJ (Clinical Research Ed.)*, 344(mar20 2), e1717. 10.1136/bmj.e171722434089

Alharam, A. K., & Elmedany, W. (2017). The Effects of Cyber-Security on Healthcare Industry. *2017 9th IEEE-GCC Conference and Exhibition (GCCCE)*, (pp. 1–9). IEEE. 10.1109/IEEEGCC.2017.8448206

Angst, C. M., Block, E. S., D'Arcy, J., & Kelley, K. (2017). When Do IT Security Investments Matter? Accounting for the Influence of Institutional Factors in the Context of Healthcare Data Breaches. *Management Information Systems Quarterly*, 41(3), 893–916. 10.25300/MISQ/2017/41.3.10

Argaw, S. T., Troncoso-Pastoriza, J. R., Lacey, D., Florin, M.-V., Calcavecchia, F., Anderson, D., Burleson, W., Vogel, J.-M., O'Leary, C., Eshaya-Chauvin, B., & Flahault, A. (2020). Cybersecurity of Hospitals: Discussing the challenges and working towards mitigating the risks. *BMC Medical Informatics and Decision Making*, 20(1), 146. 10.1186/s12911-020-01161-732620167

Azaria, A., Ekblaw, A., Vieira, T., & Lippman, A. (2016). MedRec: Using Blockchain for Medical Data Access and Permission Management. *2016 2nd International Conference on Open and Big Data (OBD)*, (pp. 25–30). IEEE. 10.1109/OBD.2016.11

Bansal, G., Zahedi, F., & Gefen, D. (2010). The impact of personal dispositions on information sensitivity, privacy concern and trust in disclosing health information online. *Decision Support Systems*, 49(2), 138–150. 10.1016/j.dss.2010.01.010

Berg, M. (2001). Implementing information systems in health care organizations: Myths and challenges. *International Journal of Medical Informatics*, 64(2), 143–156. 10.1016/S1386-5056(01)00200-311734382

Bulgurcu, B., Cavusoglu, H., & Benbasat, I. (2010). Information Security Policy Compliance: An Empirical Study of Rationality-Based Beliefs and Information Security Awareness. *Management Information Systems Quarterly*, 34(3), 523–548. 10.2307/25750690

Chan, M., Woon, I., & Kankanhalli, A. (2005). Perceptions of Information Security in the Workplace: Linking Information Security Climate to Compliant Behavior. *Journal of Information Privacy and Security*, 1(3), 18–41. 10.1080/15536548.2005.10855772

Chaudhry, B., Wang, J., Wu, S., Maglione, M., Mojica, W., Roth, E., Morton, S. C., & Shekelle, P. G. (2006). Systematic Review: Impact of Health Information Technology on Quality, Efficiency, and Costs of Medical Care. *Annals of Internal Medicine*, 144(10), 742–752. 10.7326/0003-4819-144-10-200605160-0012516702590

Chenthara, S., Ahmed, K., Wang, H., & Whittaker, F. (2019). Security and Privacy-Preserving Challenges of e-Health Solutions in Cloud Computing. *IEEE Access : Practical Innovations, Open Solutions*, 7, 74361–74382. 10.1109/ACCESS.2019.2919982

Chomutare, T., Fernandez-Luque, L., Årsand, E., & Hartvigsen, G. (2011). Features of Mobile Diabetes Applications: Review of the Literature and Analysis of Current Applications Compared Against Evidence-Based Guidelines. *Journal of Medical Internet Research*, 13(3), e65. 10.2196/jmir.187421979293

Dagher, G. G., Mohler, J., Milojkovic, M., & Marella, P. B. (2018). Ancile: Privacy-preserving framework for access control and interoperability of electronic health records using blockchain technology. *Sustainable Cities and Society*, 39, 283–297. 10.1016/j.scs.2018.02.014

Houtan, B., Hafid, A. S., & Makrakis, D. (2020). A Survey on Blockchain-Based Self-Sovereign Patient Identity in Healthcare. *IEEE Access : Practical Innovations, Open Solutions*, 8, 90478–90494. 10.1109/ACCESS.2020.2994090

Hu, Q., Hart, P., & Cooke, D. (2007). The role of external and internal influences on information systems security – a neo-institutional perspective. *The Journal of Strategic Information Systems*, 16(2), 153–172. 10.1016/j.jsis.2007.05.004

Hysong, S. J., Best, R. G., & Pugh, J. A. (2006). Audit and feedback and clinical practice guideline adherence: Making feedback actionable. *Implementation Science : IS*, 1(1), 9. 10.1186/1748-5908-1-916722539

Jian, W.-S., Wen, H.-C., Scholl, J., Shabbir, S. A., Lee, P., Hsu, C.-Y., & Li, Y.-C. (2011). The Taiwanese method for providing patients data from multiple hospital EHR systems. *Journal of Biomedical Informatics*, 44(2), 326–332. 10.1016/j.jbi.2010.11.00421118726

Kaddoura, S., & Grati, R. (2021). Blockchain for Healthcare and Medical Systems. In *Enabling Blockchain Technology for Secure Networking and Communications* (pp. 249–270). IGI Global. 10.4018/978-1-7998-5839-3.ch011

Kadhim, K. T., Alsahlany, A. M., Wadi, S. M., & Kadhum, H. T. (2020). An Overview of Patient's Health Status Monitoring System Based on Internet of Things (IoT). *Wireless Personal Communications*, 114(3), 2235–2262. 10.1007/s11277-020-07474-0

Kahn, S., & Sheshadri, V. (2008). Medical Record Privacy and Security in a Digital Environment. *IT Professional*, 10(2), 46–52. 10.1109/MITP.2008.34

Khan, F. A., Ali, A., Abbas, H., & Haldar, N. A. H. (2014). A Cloud-based Healthcare Framework for Security and Patients' Data Privacy Using Wireless Body Area Networks. *Procedia Computer Science*, 34, 511–517. 10.1016/j.procs.2014.07.058

Khansa, L., Cook, D. F., James, T., & Bruyaka, O. (2012). Impact of HIPAA provisions on the stock market value of healthcare institutions, and information security and other information technology firms. *Computers & Security*, 31(6), 750–770. 10.1016/j.cose.2012.06.007

Kierkegaard, P. (2012). Medical data breaches: Notification delayed is notification denied. *Computer Law & Security Report*, 28(2), 163–183. 10.1016/j.clsr.2012.01.003

Kimani, K., Oduol, V., & Langat, K. (2019). Cyber security challenges for IoT-based smart grid networks. *International Journal of Critical Infrastructure Protection*, 25, 36–49. 10.1016/j.ijcip.2019.01.001

Kjaerland, M. (2006). A taxonomy and comparison of computer security incidents from the commercial and government sectors. *Computers & Security*, 25(7), 522–538. 10.1016/j.cose.2006.08.004

Kouicem, D. E., Bouabdallah, A., & Lakhlef, H. (2018). Internet of things security: A top-down survey. *Computer Networks*, 141, 199–221. 10.1016/j.comnet.2018.03.012

Kraemer-Mbula, E., Tang, P., & Rush, H. (2013). The cybercrime ecosystem: Online innovation in the shadows? *Technological Forecasting and Social Change*, 80(3), 541–555. 10.1016/j.techfore.2012.07.002

Kulynych, J., & Korn, D. (2003). The New HIPAA (Health Insurance Portability and Accountability Act of 1996) Medical Privacy Rule: Help or Hindrance for Clinical Research? *Circulation*, 108(8), 912–914. 10.1161/01.CIR.0000080642.35380.5012939240

Kwon, J., & Johnson, M. E. (2013). Security practices and regulatory compliance in the healthcare industry. *Journal of the American Medical Informatics Association : JAMIA*, 20(1), 44–51. 10.1136/amiajnl-2012-00090622955497

Kwon, J., & Johnson, M. E. (2014). Proactive Versus Reactive Security Investments in the Healthcare Sector. *Management Information Systems Quarterly*, 38(2), 451–471. 10.25300/MISQ/2014/38.2.06

Luna, R., Rhine, E., Myhra, M., Sullivan, R., & Kruse, C. S. (2016). Cyber threats to health information systems: A systematic review. *Technology and Health Care*, 24(1), 1–9. 10.3233/THC-15110226578272

Mäses, S., Randmann, L., Maennel, O., & Lorenz, B. (2018). Stenmap: Framework for Evaluating Cybersecurity-Related Skills Based on Computer Simulations. In Zaphiris, P., & Ioannou, A. (Eds.), *Learning and Collaboration Technologies. Learning and Teaching* (pp. 492–504). Springer International Publishing. 10.1007/978-3-319-91152-6_38

Mazhar, T., Talpur, D. B., Shloul, T. A., Ghadi, Y. Y., Haq, I., Ullah, I., Ouahada, K., & Hamam, H. (2023). Analysis of IoT Security Challenges and Its Solutions Using Artificial Intelligence. *Brain Sciences*, 13(4), 683. 10.3390/brainsci1304068337190648

Minnaar, A., & Herbig, F. J. (2021). Cyberattacks and the Cybercrime Threat of Ransomware to Hospitals and Healthcare Services During the COVID-19 Pandemic. *Acta Criminologica : African Journal of Criminology & Victimology*, 34(3), 155–185. 10.10520/ejc-crim_v34_n3_a10

Muthuppalaniappan, M., & Stevenson, K. (2021). Healthcare cyber-attacks and the COVID-19 pandemic: An urgent threat to global health. *International Journal for Quality in Health Care : Journal of the International Society for Quality in Health Care*, 33(1), mzaa117. 10.1093/intqhc/mzaa11733351134

Narayana Samy, G., Ahmad, R., & Ismail, Z. (2010). Security threats categories in healthcare information systems. *Health Informatics Journal*, 16(3), 201–209. 10.1177/146045821037746820889850

Paik, H.-Y., Xu, X., Bandara, H. M. N. D., Lee, S. U., & Lo, S. K. (2019). Analysis of Data Management in Blockchain-Based Systems: From Architecture to Governance. *IEEE Access : Practical Innovations, Open Solutions*, 7, 186091–186107. 10.1109/ACCESS.2019.2961404

Pilkington, M. (2016). Blockchain technology: Principles and applications. In Olleros, F. X., & Zhegu, M. (Eds.), *Research Handbook on Digital Transformations*. Edward Elgar Publishing. 10.4337/9781784717766.00019

Putz, B., Menges, F., & Pernul, G. (2019). A secure and auditable logging infrastructure based on a permissioned blockchain. *Computers & Security*, 87, 101602. 10.1016/j.cose.2019.101602

Ryals, C. A., Pierce, K. L., & Baker, J. W. (2011). INR Goal Attainment and Oral Anticoagulation Knowledge of Patients Enrolled in an Anticoagulation Clinic in a Veterans Affairs Medical Center. *Journal of Managed Care Pharmacy : JMCP*, 17(2), 133–142. 10.18553/jmcp.2011.17.2.13321348546

Safavi, S., & Shukur, Z. (2014). Conceptual Privacy Framework for Health Information on Wearable Device. *PLoS One*, 9(12), e114306. 10.1371/journal.pone.011430625478915

Seh, A. H., Zarour, M., Alenezi, M., Sarkar, A. K., Agrawal, A., Kumar, R., & Ahmad Khan, R. (2020). Healthcare Data Breaches: Insights and Implications. *Health Care*, 8(2), 133. 10.3390/healthcare802013332414183

Shenoy, A., & Appel, J. M. (2017). Safeguarding Confidentiality in Electronic Health Records. *Cambridge Quarterly of Healthcare Ethics*, 26(2), 337–341. 10.1017/S096318011600093128361730

Shrestha, R., & Nam, S. Y. (2019). Regional Blockchain for Vehicular Networks to Prevent 51% Attacks. *IEEE Access : Practical Innovations, Open Solutions*, 7, 95033–95045. 10.1109/ACCESS.2019.2928753

Stellios, I., Kotzanikolaou, P., Psarakis, M., Alcaraz, C., & Lopez, J. (2018). A Survey of IoT-Enabled Cyberattacks: Assessing Attack Paths to Critical Infrastructures and Services. *IEEE Communications Surveys and Tutorials*, 20(4), 3453–3495. 10.1109/COMST.2018.2855563

Van Deursen Hazelhoff Roelfze, N. (2014). *HI-Risk: A socio-technical method for the identification and monitoring of healthcare information security risks in the information society*. Naiper Repository. https://napier-repository.worktribe.com/output/181044

Wilner, A. S., Luce, H., Ouellet, E., Williams, O., & Costa, N. (2021). From public health to cyber hygiene: Cybersecurity and Canada's healthcare sector. *International Journal (Toronto, Ont.)*, 76(4), 522–543. 10.1177/00207020211067946

Win, K. T., Susilo, W., & Mu, Y. (2006). Personal Health Record Systems and Their Security Protection. *Journal of Medical Systems*, 30(4), 309–315. 10.1007/s10916-006-9019-y16978011

Winker, M. A., Flanagin, A., Chi-Lum, B., White, J., Andrews, K., Kennett, R. L., DeAngelis, C. D., & Musacchio, R. A. (2000). Guidelines for Medical and Health Information Sites on the Internet: Principles Governing AMA Web Sites. *Journal of the American Medical Association*, 283(12), 1600. 10.1001/jama.283.12.160010735398

Yaraghi, N., & Gopal, R. D. (2018). The Role of HIPAA Omnibus Rules in Reducing the Frequency of Medical Data Breaches: Insights From an Empirical Study. *The Milbank Quarterly*, 96(1), 144–166. 10.1111/1468-0009.1231429504206

Zargar, S. T., Joshi, J., & Tipper, D. (2013). A Survey of Defense Mechanisms Against Distributed Denial of Service (DDoS) Flooding Attacks. *IEEE Communications Surveys and Tutorials*, 15(4), 2046–2069. 10.1109/SURV.2013.031413.00127

Chapter 12
Exploring Menstrual Health and Hygiene in India:
Understanding Usage Patterns of Menstrual Products Across Different Demographics

Amiya Abdul Khadar
https://orcid.org/0009-0002-0861-8115
Lovely Professional University, India

Pooja Kansra
https://orcid.org/0000-0003-2229-0662
Lovely Professional University, India

Kaushik Lodh
Health USA, USA

ABSTRACT

Menstrual health refers to a woman's overall physical and psychological well-being throughout their menstrual cycle. Having good menstrual health means that a person experiences a regular and predictable menstrual cycle, without significant pain or discomfort. It also involves having the availability of nontoxic and effective products for menstruation and adequate information about menstrual health. The absence of proper hygienic menstrual facilities and sanitation put women and girls at threat of several health issues, such as infections in the urinary and reproductive tract. Additionally, menstrual stigma often leads to communal separation and omission from daily activities like school and work. In the present study, an attempt has been

DOI: 10.4018/979-8-3693-5976-1.ch012

made to explore the state of menstrual health and hygiene in India and also identify the most popular menstrual product types among women of different age groups, educational backgrounds, places of residence, and religions.

INTRODUCTION

Menstrual Health refers to the overall physical and psychological well-being of a woman throughout their menstrual cycle (Gupta et al., 1992; Torondel et al., 2018; Belayneh & Mekuriaw, 2018; Anbesu & Asgedom, 2023). The menstrual cycle is the monthly process where a woman's body prepares for conception. If conception doesn't occur, the body sheds the lining of the uterus, resulting in bleeding from the vagina (Baisley et al., 2009, Borg et al., 2023). Having good menstrual health means that a person experiences a regular and predictable menstrual cycle, without significant pain or discomfort (Gupta et al., 1992; Pednekar et al., 2022; Khatoon et al., 2023). It also involves having the availability of nontoxic and effective products for menstruation and adequate information about menstrual health (Torondel et al., 2018).

Menstrual health can be impacted by a diversity of factors, including genetics, hormonal imbalances, stress, diet, and exercise (Kamath et al., 2013; Muralidharan et al., 2015). Certain health conditions, such as polycystic ovary syndrome (PCOS) and endometriosis can also affect menstrual health (Aniebue et al., 2010; Sharma et al., 2022). It is essential to prioritize menstrual health by practising good menstrual hygiene, using safe and effective menstrual products, and seeking medical attention if there are any concerns or irregularities with the menstrual cycle. Additionally, education and de-stigmatization around menstruation can help improve overall menstrual health and well-being (Nair et al., 2012; Hennegan et al., 2019).

Joint Monitoring Programs by WHO and UNICEF highlight the significance of handling menstruation in a sanitized and respectable manner (WHO-UNICEF, 2012; Sharma et al., 2022). To achieve this, women and girls need hygienic menstrual products, privacy, clean water for washing, and proper facilities for disposal that can be availed as frequently as necessary. Additionally, they need knowledge about menstrual well-being and hygiene. Effective menstrual well-being and sanitization are essential for women and girls to live a healthy, fruitful and respectful life (Anand et al., 2015; Sharma et al., 2022).

The way people manage their menstrual hygiene can be different depending on their social and cultural background, level of education, and financial situation (UNICEF 2019). There is also an important distinction concerning the management of menstrual hygiene practices among countries and even within countries (Standing et al., 2018; Singh et al., 2022). Guaranteeing women a safe and respectable experience during menstruation is essential for achieving several sustainable development goals (SDGs) (Fakhri et al., 2012). These goals include SDG No.3 which focuses on promoting healthy lives and well-being for all, SDG No.4, which aims to provide a complete and rightful education, and SDG No. 5 which emphasizes gender equality (Guterres, 2020).

Menstrual health is a significant issue in India, where there is a cultural silence and stigma surrounding menstruation and menstrual hygiene (Garg et al., 2012; Gurunget al.,2023). Many women in India don't have adequate hygienic menstrual protection methods and often resort to using unhygienic and potentially harmful methods like cloth, paper and husk for their periods (Upashe et al., 2015; Hennegan et al., 2019). The absence of proper hygienic menstrual facilities and sanitation also put women and girls at threat of several health issues such as infections in the urinary and reproductive tract. Additionally, menstrual stigma often leads to communal separation and omission from daily activities like school and work (Krishnan & Twigg, 2016; Malik et al., 2023). This study will explore the current state of menstrual health and hygiene in India and identify the preferred menstrual products among Indian women.

Specifically, in the present study, an attempt has been made to explore the state of menstrual health and hygiene in India. An attempt was also made to identify the most popular menstrual product types among women of different age groups, educational backgrounds, places of residence and religions.

REVIEW OF LITERATURE

A systematic Literature review was conducted to identify the research gap for the present study. Previously published studies that talked about menstrual health and hygiene management were used for the study. The search was conducted on 5th March 2023, and three main online databases were used for finding previously published papers: Scopus database, PubMed and Google Scholar the search was without any time restriction, to include a broad range of research. Keywords for finding papers included: *"Menstrual Health"*, *Menstrual Well-being*", *Menstrual Hygiene Management*" and "*Social effect on Menstrual health in India*". The article that was analyzed for the review included three types of study designs: qualitative, quantitative and mixed methods. The review did not include training manuals, organizational reports and policy statements.

A total of 70 were identified through a database search, but after removing 30 duplicates and screening titles and abstracts a total of 15 papers were selected for the study.

Figure 1. Search strategy with PRISMA flow diagram

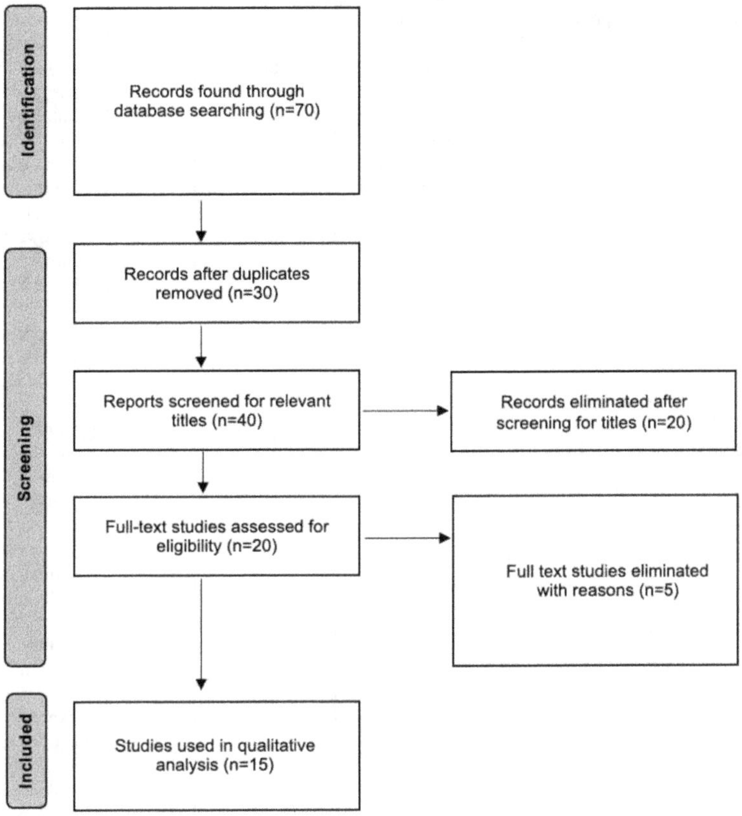

(Moher et al., 2009)

Key features of the 15 studies included in this review are the type of research design, methods used, publication year, and primary outcomes measured. The studies were published between 2011 and 2022, with a majority being published in 2021 and 2022. Most studies focused on menstrual health and hygiene, while others examined the potential risk factors related to menstrual products.

Table 1. Study description

S.No	Author	Journal	Purpose	Study design	Sample	Results
1,	Rupe et al., 2022.	Reproductive Health	To examine the reproductive health during the monthly cycle among individuals in the age group of adolescents and young adults.	Cross sectional study	200	The study involved 200 participants, and the median age was 20 years with an interquartile range of 17-22. Of the participants, 50 per cent were attending school at least three days a week, and 96 per cent were not married. Based on the MPNS-36 questionnaire, 67 per cent of the participants had unmet mental health needs. Additionally, 77 per cent of the participants reused some of their menstrual products at some point in their last menstruation, and 44 per cent reported often or always skipping school during menstruation, while 30 per cent sometimes skipped. The participants also expressed concerns about their safety while removing menstrual products at home and school.
2,	Babbar et al., 2022.	The Lancet Public Health	To analyse the Impact of menstrual health on societal well-being and human rights issues	Prospective Study	-	People who identify as women and experience menstruation are frequently overlooked, even in emergency situations, which has a direct impact on their basic human rights. It is important to acknowledge menstrual well-being as a fundamental right in the right to health.

continued on following page

Table 1. Continued

S.No	Author	Journal	Purpose	Study design	Sample	Results
3,	Sharma et al., 2022	Reproductive Health	To examine the menstrual well-being and sanitation in Nepal	Descriptive Study	129	The study's main objectives were to examine concerns related to reproductive health and menstrual hygiene practices. The research found that Nepali women face various difficulties in managing menstruation due to factors such as no knowledge regarding menstrual well-being, inadequate WASH (Water, Sanitation, and Hygiene) facilities, absence of sex education and superstitious beliefs
4,	Holst et al., 2022	Reproductive Health	To explore experiences of menstrual well-being and inequity among women in Barcelona and surrounding areas (Spain).	Qualitative Study	250	The cost and availability of menstrual products frequently influenced people's choices, with some participants experiencing menstrual poverty. Many reported a lack of formal education about menstruation, often relying on personal experience, self-teaching, or information from family and friends. Menstruation significantly impacted their daily lives.
5,	Singh et al., 2022	BMC Public Health	To examine the factors that impacted women's use of menstrual products in rural India.	Quantitative study	95,551	In rural areas of India, only 42 per cent of young girls used a clean methods for menstruation protection. There were significant differences in the usage of such methods across different states and districts, with Tamil Nadu having the highest usage at 85 per cent and Uttar Pradesh having the lowest at 23 per cent.

continued on following page

Table 1. Continued

S.No	Author	Journal	Purpose	Study design	Sample	Results
6,	Hennegan et al., 2021	Sexual and Reproductive Health Matters	To define menstrual health policies, practices and research	Qualitative study	-	In order to make progress in the field of menstrual health, it is crucial to establish a precise definition that serves several purposes. Firstly, it should study the significance of menstrual well-being in areas such as global health, development, national policies, and funding frameworks. Secondly, it should clarify the various concerns associated with menstrual health, even though different sectors may prioritize different aspects. Lastly, it should encourage collaboration and information exchange among stakeholders from diverse fields.
7,	Hennegan et al., 2019	PLoS Medicine	To explore experiences of women during menstruation in developing and underdeveloped countries	Exploratory Study	150	Study found that most of the studies they reviewed focused on the experiences of young girls. The study noticed a gap in research on menstrual health experiences of adult women and women from certain geographic regions. This lack of representation reflects the overall focus of menstrual health research worldwide.

continued on following page

Table 1. Continued

S.No	Author	Journal	Purpose	Study design	Sample	Results
8,	Torondel et al., 2018	BMC Infectious Diseases	To explore connection between improper practices for managing menstrual sanitation.	Cross Sectional Study	558	The study found that women who had bacterial vaginosis (BV) tended to wash themselves less often and were more likely to change their absorbent materials outside of a bathroom facility. Women who changed their menstrual products more frequently were less likely to have infections .
9,	Verma et al., 2017.	Reproductive Health	To examine the reproductive risk during menstruation	Descriptive study	6431	According to the study, only 20 percent of men possess an accurate understanding of the subject matter. Additionally, the findings indicate that factors such as education level, societal beliefs, caste, and communication with their spouse regarding reproductive matters significantly impact men's understanding about the risks of conception during the menstruation.

continued on following page

Table 1. Continued

S.No	Author	Journal	Purpose	Study design	Sample	Results
10,	Chandra-Mouli & Patel, 2017	Reproductive Health	Mapping the knowledge and understanding of menarche, menstrual hygiene and menstrual health among adolescent girls in low- and middle-income countries	Qualitative study	89	Girls in underdeveloped and developing countries often lack adequate knowledge and preparation for their first menstruation, and typically rely on female family members for information. However, these sources may not have the necessary knowledge to address gaps in girls' understanding, which can lead to misunderstandings and unhygienic practices during menstruation. Girls may avoid seeking medical help and instead skip school, medicate without seeing a doctor, and withdraw from social activities
11,	Van Eijk et al., 2016	BMJ Open	To analyse the situation of menstrual hygiene management amongst young girls in India.	Qualitative Study	138	It was found that half of the respondents knew about menstruation before their 1st period. Urban girls were more likely to use commercial pads than rural girls and this increased over time. Improper disposal of menstrual products was common. Girls faced many restrictions during their periods, especially for religious activities.

continued on following page

Table 1. Continued

S.No	Author	Journal	Purpose	Study design	Sample	Results
12,	Das et al., 2015	PLoS ONE	To assess the menstrual practices, availability of water and sanitation and risk of infection among women in Odisha.	Case Study	485	In comparison to women using disposable pads, those who opted for reusable pads for their menstrual hygiene were more prone to developing urogenital infections or being diagnosed with at least one such infection. Women with greater financial resources and access to personal hygiene facilities at home were found to be less vulnerable to bacterial vaginosis (BV). Additionally, lower educational attainment was found to be the sole factor associated with urinary tract infection (UTI), even after controlling for all other factors.
13,	Muralidharan et al., 2015	Waterlines	To examine the policy management for menstrual hygiene and health in India	Qualitative Study	50	The research discovered that when it comes to addressing menstrual hygiene management (MHM), most policy initiatives concentrate on adolescent girls, emphasizing the hardware (such as infrastructure and sanitary napkins) or software (such as health education) aspects. Programs are usually carried out in schools, but the guidelines for implementation are not always clear. Programs encourage coordination with other government initiatives, but there is a shortage of effective mechanisms to put this into action.

continued on following page

Table 1. Continued

S.No	Author	Journal	Purpose	Study design	Sample	Results
14,	Shah et al., 2013	Reproductive Health Matters	To analyse the menstrual health and hygiene practices among young girls in rural Gujarat.	Mixed Method	164	Out of all the teenage girls surveyed, 67 per cent preferred using falalin cloths, whereas 31 per cent preferred sanitary pads, and none of the respondents preferred old clothes. The use of falalin cloths had a notable positive effect on the girls' quality of life, while the effect of sanitary pads was relatively minor. Falalin cloth was used majorly because of how easily it was available locally and it was also much cheaper than sanitary napkins.
15,	Fakhri et al., 2012	BMC Public Health	To investigated project promoting menstrual hygiene and health for women in Iran	Quasi Experimental Study	698	One of the key findings was that educational sessions had a significant effect on women's bathing and genital hygiene during menstruation. In the group that received the education, 61 per cent of women practiced usual bathing, compared to 49.2 per cent in the control group. Additionally, a woman's individual health status was found to have a significant correlation with her menstrual health, and her attitude towards menstruation also had a significant impact.

After several literature reviews, it was observed that menstrual health is still an ignored part of the healthcare system (Table 1). The social stigma and lack of awareness are major contributors to it.

RESEARCH METHODOLOGY

To identify the most popular menstrual product types among women of different age groups, educational backgrounds, places of residence and religions the secondary data published by the National Family Health Survey (NFHS-5) (International Institute for Population Sciences, 2020) by the Ministry of Health and Family Welfare (MoHFW), Government of India was used. The NFHS-5 was designed to provide comprehensive insight into health and social indicators at multiple levels. It's a valuable tool for understanding not just national trends but also regional variations, which can be crucial for targeted interventions and policy planning. The data concerning menstrual health and hygiene practices were used for analysis for the present study. The NFHS-5 used a stratified two-stage sample and followed the 2011 census as a sampling framework. The districts were divided into urban and rural stratum and each rural and urban stratum was subdivided into smaller regions based on the population density. NFHS-5 survey women aged 15-24 were inquired about their most preferred menstrual product usage. The respondents' Demographic variables and preferred menstrual hygiene practices were analysed in the present study.

ANALYSIS AND INTERPRETATION

Menstrual Product Preferences With Respect to Different Demographics

Table 2. Menstrual product preferences among women aged 15 -24

Age	Cloth	Locally Prepared Napkins	Sanitary Napkins	Tampons	Menstrual Cup	Others	Nothing	Number of Women	%
15-19 years	49.3	15.2	64.5	1.7	0.3	0.2	0.2	1,21,803	78
20-24 years	50	14.7	64.2	1.6	0.3	0.2	0.2	1,19,309	77.2

Source: National Family Health Survey (NFHS-5), 2020.

Table 2 showed that out of 1,21,803 women aged 15-19, 49.3 per cent, women used cloth as a protection method for menstruation, 15.2 preferred locally prepared napkins, 64.5 preferred sanitary napkins and only 1.7 per cent used tampons, 0.3 used a menstrual cup,0.2 used other methods of protection and 0.2 used nothing (Figure 2). Out of 1,19,309 women aged 20-24, 50 per cent used cloth, 14.7 used locally prepared napkins, 64.2 used sanitary napkins, 1.6 used tampons, 0.3 used a menstrual cup and 0.2 responded to other methods and 0.2 said nothing.

Sanitary napkins were the protection method used by most women followed by cloths. The study also showed that 78 per cent aged 15-19 used hygienic methods for menstruation and 77.2 per cent aged 20-24 used hygienic methods as protection.

Figure 2. Menstrual product preferences among women aged 15 -24

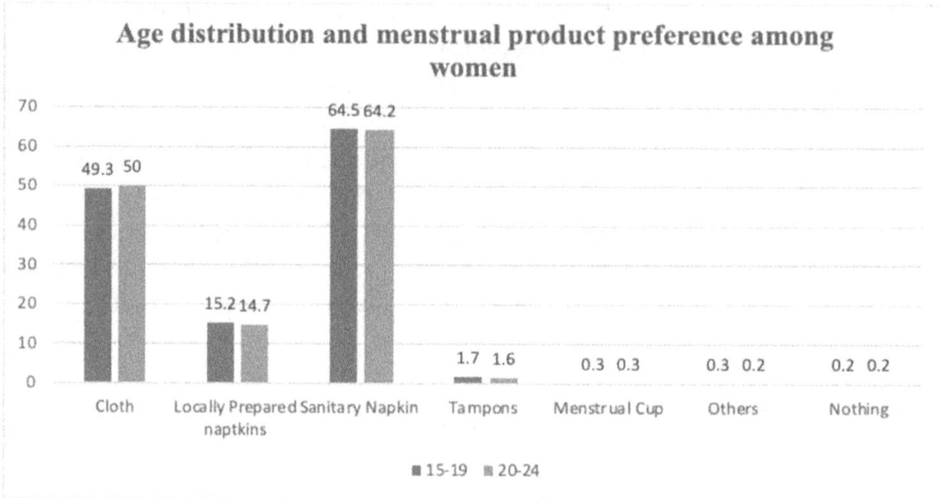

Source: National Family Health Survey (NFHS-5), 2020.

Table 3. Menstrual preference among women with respect to place of residence

Residence	Cloth	Locally Prepared Napkins	Sanitary Napkins	Tampons	Menstrual Cup	Others	Nothing	Number of Women	%
Urban	31.5	14.1	77.5	1.8	0.5	0.2	0.1	70,941	89.6
Rural	57.2	15.3	58.9	1.6	0.2	0.2	0.3	1,70,171	72.6

Source: National Family Health Survey (NFHS-5), 2020.

Regarding the place of residence, 77.5 per cent of women living in urban areas preferred using sanitary napkins, 31.5 preferred using cloths, and 14.1 per cent preferred locally prepared napkins. Very few from urban regions preferred tampons, menstrual cups and other products (Figure 3). The same trend was seen in rural areas, 58.9 per cent of respondents preferred using sanitary napkins, 57.2 preferred cloths and 15.3 preferred using locally prepared napkins. Cloth and sanitary napkins were the most commonly used products in both rural and urban regions (Table 3).

Figure 3. Place of residence and menstrual product preference

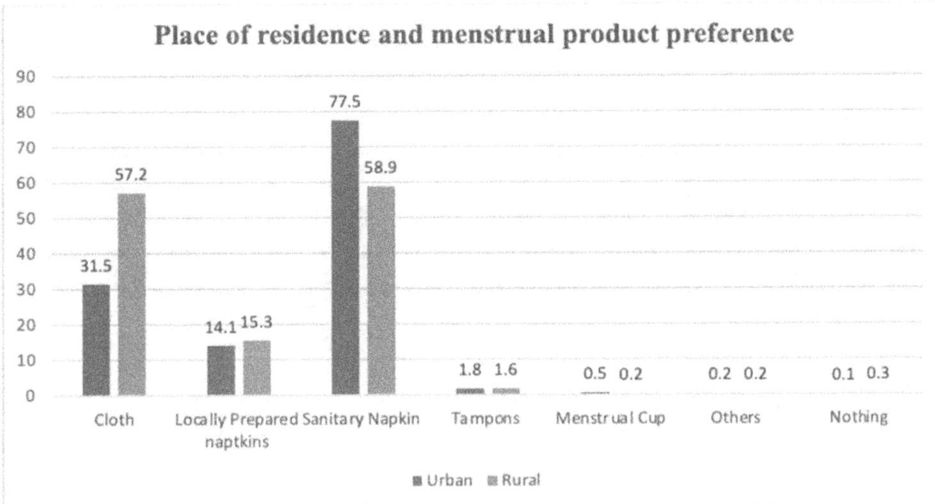

Source: National Family Health Survey (NFHS-5), 2020.

Table 4. Menstrual preference among women concerning level of schooling

Education	Cloth	Locally Prepared Napkins	Sanitary Napkins	Tampons	Menstrual Cup	Others	Nothing	Number of Women	%
No Schooling	80	11	32.6	1.1	0.1	0.2	1.2	15,833	43.5
<5 years Complete	73.7	11.6	40.3	1.1	0.3	0.2	0.6	5,501	51.3
8-9 years Complete	57.8	14.4	58.7	1.7	0.3	0.2	0.2	59,189	71.9
10-11 years Complete	43.3	16.3	70.7	1.7	0.4	0.2	0.1	55,504	84.7
12 or more years	53.2	15.9	76.8	1.9	0.4	0.2	0.1	82,265	90.3

Source: National Family Health Survey (NFHS-5), 2020.

Figure 4. Menstrual preference among women concerning level of schooling

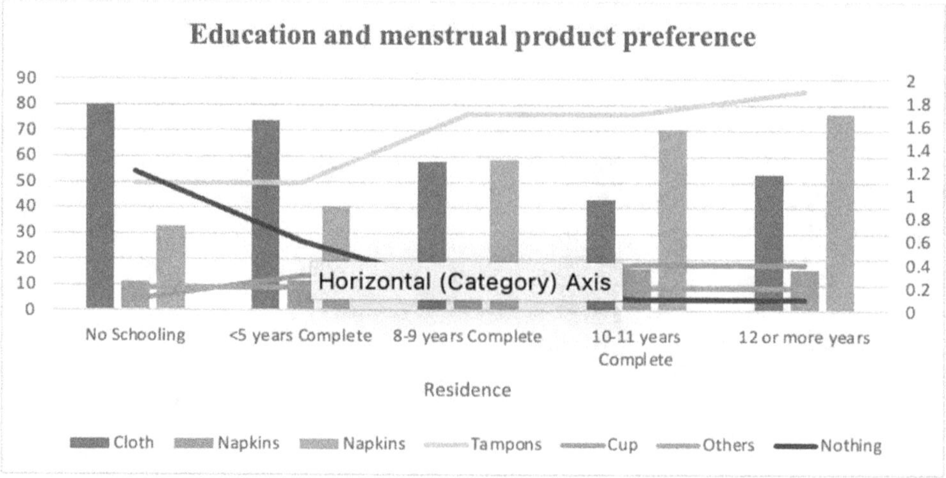

Source: National Family Health Survey (NFHS-5), 2020.

Schooling of the respondents showed that 80 per cent of respondents who had no schooling preferred using clothes, 32.6 per cent preferred using sanitary napkins, and 11.0 preferred using locally prepared napkins (Figure 4). 73.7 per cent of the respondents who had less than 5 years of schooling used cloths, 40.3 per cent used sanitary napkins, 11.6 per cent used locally prepared napkins and only 1.1 per cent used tampons. Among respondents who had 5-7 years of schooling 69 per cent preferred using cloths, 46.8 per cent used sanitary napkins and 13.5 per cent used locally prepared napkins. 58.7 per cent of respondents who had completed 8-9 years of schooling preferred using sanitary napkins, 57.8 per cent still preferred clothes and 14.4 per cent used locally prepared napkins. 70.7 per cent of respondents who had completed 10-11 years of schooling preferred sanitary napkins and 43.3 per cent used cloths, 16.3 used locally prepared napkins. 76.8 per cent of respondents who had completed 12 or more years of schooling used sanitary napkins, 35.2 used clothes and 15.9 used locally prepared napkins. Hardly more than 1 per cent respectively used tampons, menstrual cups and other methods as was the same among all levels of schooling (Table 4).

Table 5. Menstrual preference among women concerning religion

Religion	Cloth	Locally Prepared Napkins	Sanitary Napkins	Tampons	Menstrual Cup	Others	Nothing	Number of Women	%
Hindu	49.2	15.3	64.2	1.6	0.3	0.2	0.2	1,93,622	77.6
Muslim	56.2	13.4	61	2	0.3	0.2	0.2	36,757	74.7
Christian	36.1	11	77	1.1	0.5	0.8	0.1	4,955	85.7
Sikh	28.4	25.5	72.8	0.9	0.5	0	0	3,174	93.6
Buddhist	21.7	11.4	78.9	0.8	0.3	1.8	0.3	1,272	86.6
Jain	21	6.1	88.7	0.8	0	0	0	422	94.7
Other	59.5	15	57.7	1	0.1	0.2	0.3	910	71.5

Source: National Family Health Survey (NFHS-5), 2020.

Figure 5. Menstrual preference among women concerning religion

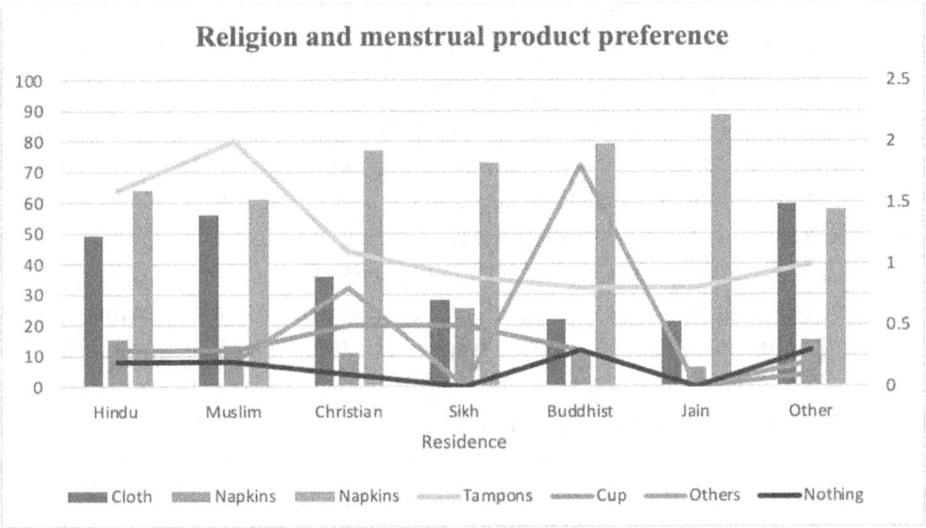

Source: National Family Health Survey (NFHS-5), 2020.

The data showed that 64.2 per cent of respondents who belonged to the Hindu community preferred using sanitary napkins, 49.2 preferred cloths, and 15.3 preferred locally prepared napkins. 62 per cent of respondents belonging to the Muslim Community preferred sanitary napkins, 56.2 preferred clothes and 13.4 per cent used locally produced napkins. 77 per cent of respondents belonging to the Christian community used sanitary napkins, 36.1 per cent used cloths and 11 per cent used locally produced napkins. 72.8 per cent of respondents belonging to the Sikh community preferred sanitary napkins, 28.4 per cent preferred clothes and 25.5 per cent used local napkins. 78.9 per cent of respondents from the Buddhist community used sanitary napkins as a protection method, 21.7 used cloths and 11.4 used local napkins. 88.7 of respondents belonging to the Jian community preferred sanitary napkins, 21 per cent used clothes and only 6 per cent used locally produced brands. 57.7 respondents who belonged to other communities preferred sanitary napkins, 59.5 per cent used clothes and 15 per cent used locally produced napkins (Figure 5). Very few respondents used other methods of menstrual protection like tampons, cups and other alternatives. The sanitary napkin was the most used menstrual product followed by clothes among the respondents (Table 5).

DISCUSSION

Menstrual hygiene and menstrual health, an important aspect towards the overall well-being of women's health, it is a complex and multifaceted issue that impacts a woman's socioeconomic as well as cultural factors (Dasgupta & Sarkar, 2008). The current study sheds light on the usage preferences of menstrual products for women aged between 15 to 24 years. The study found that most of the women in India still lacked significant awareness regarding the different types of menstrual products that are available in the market. Tampons and Menstrual cups which are prevalently used in developed countries are still a new concept among Indian women (Singh et al., 2022). The data published by NHFS-5 depicts the usage disparity. Sanitary napkins were found to be the most preferred menstrual products by women (Garg et al., 2012; Muralidharan et al., 2015; Ram et al., 2020; Singh et al., 2022). Cloth was the second most favoured product among Indian women (Garg et al., 2012; Shah et al., 2013; Torondel et al., 2018).

Demographic factors such as age, socio-economic status and geographical location were observed to be factors that significantly impact the usage patterns among women in India (Ram et al., 2020; Rossouw & Ross, 2021; Tembo et al., 2022). Improving menstrual health and hygiene in India will require a diverse approach which involves awareness regarding proper hygiene practices, knowledge regarding menstruation, accessibility towards better menstrual products and improved sanitation facilities with proper availability of clean water and disposal options and destigmatize the society regarding menstruation (Majeed et al., 2022). It can be achieved by challenging taboos and misconceptions surrounding menstruation to promote open discussion, education and acceptance (Thakre et al., 2011; Garg et al., 2012; Kansal et al., 2016; Kaur et al., 2018; Sharma et al., 2022). It is also important to provide proper healthcare services for any kind of menstrual-related disorders and infections.

CONCLUSION AND POLICY IMPLICATIONS

Menstruation is a natural process affecting a large portion of the population for a significant portion of their lives. Despite this fact, there remains a stigma surrounding the topic in many societies. This taboo can lead to a lack of awareness, education, and access to menstrual products and healthcare. The shame associated with menstruation can have serious consequences for those who menstruate. In some cultures, it is viewed as something dirty or embarrassing, and those who are menstruating may be excluded from certain activities or social gatherings. This can create feelings of isolation and lead to poor mental health. Furthermore, the lack of access to menstrual products and healthcare can also impact menstrual health. Those who cannot afford these products may resort to using unhygienic materials like rags or leaves, which can lead to infections and other health problems. Additionally, the lack of education about menstruation can prevent individuals from understanding the normalcy of menstrual cycles and recognizing signs of potential health issues.

To promote menstrual health and gender equality, we need to break down the taboo surrounding menstruation. This involves creating safe spaces where people can openly discuss the topic, ensuring access to menstrual products and healthcare, and promoting comprehensive sex education that includes information about menstrual health. By doing so, we can ensure that everyone has the right to a healthy and dignified menstrual experience. In conclusion, menstrual health is a crucial aspect of women's health that has long been stigmatized and overlooked. The lack of knowledge and education about menstruation among women can lead to negative consequences, such as shame, stigma, and harmful beliefs and practices. It is important to prioritize comprehensive sexual education, destigmatizing conversations around menstruation, and providing access to menstrual products and resources to empower women and improve their menstrual health. By addressing the issue of menstrual health, we can help women feel more comfortable, confident, and healthy during their menstrual cycles, and promote gender equality and social justice.

REFERENCES

Anand, E., Singh, J., & Unisa, S. (2015). Menstrual hygiene practices and its association with reproductive tract infections and abnormal vaginal discharge among women in India. *Sexual & Reproductive Healthcare : Official Journal of the Swedish Association of Midwives*, 6(4), 249–254. 10.1016/j.srhc.2015.06.00126614609

Anbesu, E. W., & Asgedom, D. K. (2023). Menstrual hygiene practice and associated factors among adolescent girls in sub-Saharan Africa: A systematic review and meta-analysis. *BMC Public Health*, 23(1), 33. 10.1186/s12889-022-14942-836604734

Aniebue, U., Aniebue, P., & Nwankwo, T. (2010). The impact of pre-menarcheal training on menstrual practices and hygiene of Nigerian school girls. *The Pan African Medical Journal*, 2(1), 1–9. 10.4314/pamj.v2i1.5170821532905

Babbar, K., Martin, J., Ruiz, J., Parray, A. A., & Sommer, M. (2022). Menstrual health is a public health and human rights issue. *The Lancet. Public Health*, 7(1), e10–e11. 10.1016/S2468-2667(21)00212-734717798

Baisley, K., Changalucha, J., Weiss, H. A., Mugeye, K., Everett, D., Hambleton, I., Hay, P., Ross, D., Tanton, C., Chirwa, T., Hayes, R., & Watson-Jones, D. (2009). Bacterial vaginosis in female facility workers in north-western Tanzania: Prevalence and risk factors. *Sexually Transmitted Infections*, 85(5), 370–375. 10.1136/sti.2008.03554319473997

Belayneh, Z., & Mekuriaw, B. (2019). Knowledge and menstrual hygiene practice among adolescent school girls in southern Ethiopia: A cross-sectional study. *BMC Public Health*, 19(1), 1–8. 10.1186/s12889-019-7973-931783741

Borg, S. A., Bukenya, J. N., Kibira, S. P., Nakamya, P., Makumbi, F. E., Exum, N. G., Schwab, K. J., & Hennegan, J. (2023). The association between menstrual hygiene, workplace sanitation practices and self-reported urogenital symptoms in a cross-sectional survey of women working in Mukono District, Uganda. *PLoS One*, 18(7), e0288942. 10.1371/journal.pone.028894237471386

Chandra-Mouli, V., & Patel, S. V. (2017). Mapping the knowledge and understanding of menarche, menstrual hygiene and menstrual health among adolescent girls in low- and middle-income countries. *Reproductive Health*, 14(1), 1–16. 10.1186/s12978-017-0293-628249610

Das, P., Baker, K. K., Dutta, A., Swain, T., Sahoo, S., Das, B. S., Panda, B., Nayak, A., Bara, M., Bilung, B., Mishra, P. R., Panigrahi, P., Cairncross, S., & Torondel, B. (2015). Menstrual hygiene practices, WASH access and the risk of urogenital infection in women from Odisha, India. *PLoS One*, 10(6), 1–16. 10.1371/journal.pone.013077726125184

Dasgupta, A., & Sarkar, M. (2008). Menstrual hygiene: How hygienic is the adolescent girl? *Indian Journal of Community Medicine*, 33(2), 77–80. 10.4103/0970-0218.4087219967028

Fakhri, M., Hamzehgardeshi, Z., Hajikhani Golchin, N. A., & Komili, A. (2012). Promoting menstrual health among persian adolescent girls from low socioeconomic backgrounds: A quasi-experimental study. *BMC Public Health*, 12(1), 2–6. 10.1186/1471-2458-12-19322420743

Garg, R., Goyal, S., & Gupta, S. (2012). India moves towards menstrual hygiene: Subsidized sanitary napkins for rural adolescent girls - Issues and challenges. *Maternal and Child Health Journal*, 16(4), 767–774. 10.1007/s10995-011-0798-521505773

Gupta, N., Pal, P., Bhargava, M., & Daga, M. (1992). Health of Women and Children in Rajasthan. *Economic and Political Weekly*, 27(42), 2323–2330.

Gurung, P., Rajbanshi, R., Bastien, S., & Luitel, B. C. (2023). Menstrual Hygiene Management: A Case Study Through Participatory Action Research in Rural Nepal. In *Implementing Transformative Education With Participatory Action Research* (pp. 14-29). IGI Global. 10.4018/979-8-3693-0607-9.ch002

Hennegan, J., Shannon, A. K., Rubli, J., Schwab, K. J., & Melendez-Torres, G. J. (2019). Women's and girls' experiences of menstruation in low-and middle-income countries: A systematic review and qualitative metasynthesis. In *PLoS Medicine, 16*(5). 10.1371/journal.pmed.1002803

Hennegan, J., Winkler, I. T., Bobel, C., Keiser, D., Hampton, J., Larsson, G., Chandra-Mouli, V., Plesons, M., & Mahon, T. (2021). Menstrual health: A definition for policy, practice, and research. *Sexual and Reproductive Health Matters*, 29(1), 31–38. 10.1080/26410397.2021.191161833910492

Holst, A. S., Jacques-Aviñó, C., Berenguera, A., Pinzón-Sanabria, D., Valls-Llobet, C., Munrós-Feliu, J., Martínez-Bueno, C., López-Jiménez, T., Vicente-Hernández, M., & Medina-Perucha, L. (2022). Experiences of menstrual inequity and menstrual health among women and people who menstruate in the Barcelona area (Spain): A qualitative study. *Reproductive Health*, 19(1), 1–16. 10.1186/s12978-022-01354-535183195

International Institute for Population Sciences. (2020). National Family Health Survey(NFHS-5) India 2019-21. *Ministry of Health and Family Welfare National*, 361, 2.

Kamath, R., Ghosh, D., Lena, A., & Chandrasekaran, V. (2013). A study on knowledge and practices regarding menstrual hygiene among rural and urban adolescent girls in Udupi Taluk, Manipal, India. *Global journal of medicine and public health, 2*(4), 1-9.

Kansal, S., Singh, S., & Kumar, A. (2016). Menstrual hygiene practices in context of schooling: A community study among rural adolescent girls in Varanasi. *Indian Journal of Community Medicine*, 41(1), 39–44. 10.4103/0970-0218.17096426917872

Kaur, R., Kaur, K., & Kaur, R. (2018). Menstrual hygiene, management, and waste disposal: Practices and challenges faced by girls/women of developing countries. *Journal of Environmental and Public Health*, 2018, 2018. 10.1155/2018/173096429675047

Khatoon, R., Ansari, S., Asghar, S. A., Sachan, B., Zaidi, Z. H., & Ahmad, S. (2023). Knowledge, attitude, and practices of adolescent school girls regarding menstrual hygiene in Lucknow district. *Asian Journal of Medical Sciences*, 14(2), 90–95. 10.3126/ajms.v14i2.49421

Krishnan, S., & Twigg, J. (2016). Menstrual hygiene: A "silent" need during disaster recovery. *Waterlines*, 35(3), 265–276. 10.3362/1756-3488.2016.020

Majeed, J., Sharma, P., Ajmera, P., & Dalal, K. (2022). Menstrual hygiene practices and associated factors among Indian adolescent girls: A meta-analysis. *Reproductive Health*, 19(1), 148. 10.1186/s12978-022-01453-335739585

Malik, V. S., Behmani, S., Singh, V., Behmani, R. K., Kumar, S., & Kumar, K. (2023). The effects of a menstrual distress coping education program for adolescents and young adult females. In *Perspectives on coping strategies for menstrual and premenstrual distress* (pp. 156–174). IGI Global. 10.4018/978-1-6684-5088-8.ch009

Moher, D., Liberati, A., Tetzlaff, J., & Altman, D. G. (2009). Preferred reporting items for systematic reviews and meta-analyses: The PRISMA statement. *BMJ (Clinical Research Ed.)*, 339(7716), 332–336. 10.1136/bmj.b253519622551

Muralidharan, A., Patil, H., & Patnaik, S. (2015). Unpacking the policy landscape for menstrual hygiene management: Implications for school WASH programmes in India. *Waterlines*, 34(1), 79–91. 10.3362/1756-3488.2015.008

Nair, M. K. C., Chacko, D. S., Ranjith Darwin, M., Padma, K., George, B., & Ps, R. (2012). Menstrual disorders and menstrual hygiene practices in higher secondary school girls. *Indian Journal of Pediatrics*, 79(S1), 74–78. 10.1007/s12098-011-0431-z21625846

Pednekar, S., Some, S., Rivankar, K., & Thakore, R. (2022). Enabling factors for sustainable menstrual hygiene management practices: A rapid review. *Discover Sustainability*, 3(1), 28. 10.1007/s43621-022-00097-4

Ram, U., Pradhan, M. R., Patel, S., & Ram, F. (2020). Factors associated with disposable menstrual absorbent use among young women in India. *International Perspectives on Sexual and Reproductive Health*, 46, 223–234. 10.1363/46e032033108760

Rossouw, L., & Ross, H. (2021). Understanding period poverty: Socio-economic inequalities in menstrual hygiene management in eight low-and middle-income countries. *International Journal of Environmental Research and Public Health*, 18(5), 1–15. 10.3390/ijerph1805257133806590

Rupe, E. R., Rodean, J., Hurley, E. A., Miller, M. K., Boncoeur, M. D., & Masonbrink, A. R. (2022). Menstrual health among adolescents and young adults in rural Haiti. *Reproductive Health*, 19(1), 1–10. 10.1186/s12978-022-01533-436539795

Shah, S. P., Nair, R., Shah, P. P., Modi, D. K., Desai, S. A., & Desai, L. (2013). Improving quality of life with new menstrual hygiene practices among adolescent tribal girls in rural Gujarat, India. *Reproductive Health Matters*, 21(41), 205–213. 10.1016/S0968-8080(13)41691-923684203

Sharma, A., McCall-Hosenfeld, J. S., & Cuffee, Y. (2022). Systematic review of menstrual health and hygiene in Nepal employing a social ecological model. *Reproductive Health*, 19(1), 1–21. 10.1186/s12978-022-01456-035773696

Singh, A., Chakrabarty, M., Singh, S., Chandra, R., Chowdhury, S., & Singh, A. (2022). Menstrual hygiene practices among adolescent women in rural India: A cross-sectional study. *BMC Public Health*, 22(1), 1–18. 10.1186/s12889-022-14622-736401238

Standing, K., & Parker, S. L. (2018). Girls' and Women's Rights to Menstrual Health in Nepal. In *Handbook of research on women's issues and rights in the developing world* (pp. 156-168). IGI Global.

Tembo, M., Renju, J., Weiss, H. A., Dauya, E., Gweshe, N., Ndlovu, P., Nzombe, P., Chikwari, C. D., Mavodza, C. V., Mackworth-Young, C. R. S., & Ferrand, A., R., & Francis, S. C. (. (2022). Integration of a menstrual health intervention in a community-based sexual and reproductive health service for young people in Zimbabwe: A qualitative acceptability study. *BMC Health Services Research*, 22(1), 1–12. 10.1186/s12913-022-07818-535354445

Thakre, S. B., Thakre, S. S., Reddy, M., Rathi, N., Pathak, K., & Ughade, S. (2011). Menstrual hygiene: Knowledge and practice among adolescent school girls of Saoner, Nagpur district. *Journal of Clinical and Diagnostic Research : JCDR*, 5(5), 1027–1033.

Torondel, B., Sinha, S., Mohanty, J. R., Swain, T., Sahoo, P., Panda, B., Nayak, A., Bara, M., Bilung, B., Cumming, O., Panigrahi, P., & Das, P. (2018). Association between unhygienic menstrual management practices and prevalence. *BMC Infectious Diseases*, 18(1), 473. https://bmcinfectdis.biomedcentral.com/articles/10.1186/s12879-018-3384-2. 10.1186/s12879-018-3384-230241498

UNICEF. (2019). Guidance on menstrual health and hygiene. *New York: UNICEF*.

Upashe, S. P., Tekelab, T., & Mekonnen, J. (2015). Assessment of knowledge and practice of menstrual hygiene among high school girls in Western Ethiopia. *BMC Women's Health*, 15(1), 1–8. 10.1186/s12905-015-0245-726466992

Van Eijk, A. M., Sivakami, M., Thakkar, M. B., Bauman, A., Laserson, K. F., Coates, S., & Phillips-Howard, P. A. (2016). Menstrual hygiene management among adolescent girls in India: A Systematic review and meta-analysis. *BMJ Open*, 6(3), e010290. Advance online publication. 10.1136/bmjopen-2015-01029026936906

Verma, P., Singh, K. K., & Singh, A. (2017). Pregnancy risk during menstrual cycle: Misconceptions among urban men in India. *Reproductive Health*, 14(1), 1–8. 10.1186/s12978-017-0332-328606153

WHO-UNICEF. (2012). *Consultation on Draft Long List of Goal, Target and Indicator Options for Future Global Monitoring of Water, Sanitation and Hygiene*. World Health Organization. https://www.wssinfo.org/fileadmin/user_upload/resources/Consultation_JMP_post2015_August2012.pdf

Chapter 13
Socio-Economic Factors of Maternal Healthcare in India:
15 Years of National Health Mission

Bishwajeet Prakash
Sharda University, India

Urmila Yadav
Sharda University, India

Indrajit Kumar
https://orcid.org/0000-0002-6976-6376
Parul University, India

Supriya Gautam
https://orcid.org/0009-0001-9269-1990
Amity University, India

Atul Arora
Sharda University, India

Mehak Arora
Delhi Technical Campus, India

Richa Sharma
Amity University, India

ABSTRACT

Pregnancy and childbirth should be times of joy. However, safe motherhood and childbirth depend on the care and attention provided to pregnant women and newborns. Maternal health remains major health problem in India, with large inter- and intra-state inequities in maternal health service use and maternal deaths. Maternal health care coverage includes maternal mortality; and antenatal care includes post- and pre-natal care. The post mortality in both women and child is increased in many countries throughout the world, especially in developing countries due to low level of socio-economic development. The present study examines the contribution of

DOI: 10.4018/979-8-3693-5976-1.ch013

India's National Health Mission (NHM) to maternal health includes both pre- and post-natal care at health institution with inequalities in various determinates of major health outcomes, at least visit of six ANC. In furthermore, the study examines socio-demographic factors of maternal healthcare utilization among Indian women. The data has been collected from an Indian National Family health survey between 2005-06 and 2019-21. A multiple logistic regression model has been used to estimate ratios associated with various visited ANC. It has been observed from the data post implementation of National Health that the institutional delivery increased by 58 percent to 88 percent, which indicates persistent increase in both rural and urban areas. It further observed the proportion of ANC visit by pregnant women is increased dramatically, with a higher percent at 89.38 percent—indicating rich women are more times visited to ANC, compared to poorer women. In further, study has indicated that educational attainment among women and family is most significant predicators of maternal healthcare utilization. As a result, maternal mortality has removed the inter and intra state disparities and forces women to make their delivery in more institutional and ensuring the reduction of child and mother mortality rate in the country, which helps to meet the sustainable development goals.

INTRODUCTION

Child birth and pregnancy should became joyfull event for the parents, however safe motherhood and child birth mainly depends upon the attention and care facilities provided to pregnant women and newborn babies (UNICHEF, 2008). According to United Nation inter agency It has been estimated that global maternal mortality ratio (MMR) decline from 339 death per 100000 live birth in 2000 to 223 deaths in 2020, indicate 34% decline in MMR during 20 years of period(Shahabuddin, 2016). It translate annual decline rate of MMR is around 2.1 per cent, however to achieve sustainable development goals (SDGs) it should be decline at the rate of 6.4 percent annual till 2030. Notable, India showed an ever greater decline rate in MMR in integer age group from 384 in 2000 to 103 in 2020, which is higher than world MMR decline rate 6.03 per cent annual. Regrettable despite of higher decline rate, India still account 12 percent of global maternal morality and rank second after south African countries in absolute number of maternal death (WHO,2015). Nearly half of the all maternal death in developing countries occurs during the labour, delivery of babies or immediate postpartum period are major key factors influencing major programs and aim to reduce death during pregnancy of women in delivery and places of delivery (Ghosh & Ghosh,2020). To ascertain the well being of both pregnant women and child, it is most important there should be at least four antenatal care (ANC) visits, to supervision of child and women to reduce more MMR. Antenatal care is comprehensive planned healthy examination, observation and guidance of pregnant women until postnatal period. The primary objective of ANC to regular monitoring fetal growth, detecting threat of mother and unborn baby fostering and preventing maternal complication including the guidance of nutrition and guidance towards family planning after the birth of babies (Arokiasamy & Jalandhar, 2013) The child and mother mortality rate are reduced due to institutional delivery, availability of life equipment and hygienic condition. It has been found that higher mother mortality on first week of the birth of child (Carine & Wendy, 2006), the maternal healthcare coverage depend upon efficiency uses of medical equipment and availability of resources, the four visit of antenatal improves the care of delivery and post natal care. Best utilization of healthcare services is crucial for improvement of health services and well being of mother as well child. In India, Maternal and Child health care was given an importance in 1997, with the launching of the Reproductive and Child health-I (RCHI) initiative. The objective of this initiative to empowering health organization, intensify the quality, coverage and productiveness of current well being, accessible, affordable, more accountable and effective reliable healthcare services especially for vulnerable section society. In order to achieve more effective health services to rural population the national rural health mission (NRHM) was launched in April, 2005. The major motive of this policy was to improving the availability and access of quality of health care facilities in rural areas especially poor women and children (Garg & Laskar, 2010). In further, to improving the maternal, neonatal, child, adolescent health central government created National Health Mission (NHM) in 2013, which summed up of two previous policies likely NRHM and National Urban Health Mission (NUHM). Under the NHM, Central government introduced Janani Suraksha Yojna and Janani Shishu Sudhar Karyakaram was introduced to focus more on pregnant women, neonatal care. JSY program is largest cash transfer program in worldwide, to provide additional cash benefits to women to child delivery at public health centers (Balhasan et.al, 2020). The present paper is examine the role and impact of NHM, since 2005 to improving the maternal health care in India, which comparing the rate of Institutional and use of ANC services. In addition this study investigates inequalities in the determinants of the major maternal health at least four ANC visits during (2010-2020).

Methods

The study mainly used data from the National Family Health Survey (NFHS). India's first National Health Survey (NFHS1) was conducted by the Ministry of Health and Family Welfare, Govenment of India, in 199293, with the aim of obtaining national data on fertility status, family planning, ANC practice, child nutrition and health, diseases.,Prevention and maternal and child health. The goal is to assist policymakers, administrators, and researchers in evaluating population and family programs. The survey covers 24 states and the national capital Delhi, which covers 99 percent of India's population. This is a household survey with a total sample size of 89,777 married women aged 13 to 49 years. The second survey (NFHS-2) was conducted in 1998 99 and covered over99% of India's population across all 26 states, including a sample size of over 90,000 women aged 15 to 49 years. The Third National Health Survey (NFHS3) was conducted in June 2005 and provides information on important factors such as fertility, mortality, family planning, HIV awareness, nutrition, health and treatment. NFHS3 collects data from a nationally respective sample of 109,041 households, 124,385 women ages 15-49 and 74,369 men ages 15-54. The NFHS 3 model covers 99% of the population in 29 states of India. The Fourth National Health Survey (NFHS-4), conducted in 2015 16, provides demographic, health and nutrition data across India as well as states and union territories. In NFHS-4, a two stage model has been applied to rural and urban areas across regions in India to provide regional estimates. NFHS4 interviewed 601,509 households, 699,686 women aged 15-49 and 112,122 men aged 15 54 in 28,586 sample units (PSUs) consisting of villages and census tracts, including 6 epizootic zones (CEB) districts, India. NFHS 5 was conducted in 2019-21 provides district level estimates of various indicators of health, population, and nutrition for India. NFHS 5 was conducted in two phase June 2019- January 2020 and phase two from February 2020 to April 2021. NFHS interviewed 636,699 household, includes 724,115 women 101,839 men consisting various age group at villages level, panchayat level, district level and includes all six zones of India

Outcome Variables

The present study includes two domains of maternal health care coverage extracted from NFHS. Firstly the number of ANC visit during pregnancy obtained with 4 or fewer than 4. It indicates ANC visit means skilled pregnancy care received by women. Secondly the place of delivery (home vs Health care), uses binary system if delivery at healthcare center mark as 1 otherwise 0.

Explanatory Variables

The facility at delivery center and utilization of ANC visits is highly depended upon socio-demographic and economic structure of the areas. On the basis of previous literature factors to maternal healthcare services has been used and dependent and independent variables are decided. The variable includes age group(three categorized 15-19,20-34 & 34-49 years), type of resident (rural and urban),educational qualification no schooling,<5 years, 5–7 years, 8–9 years, 10–11 years, and 12 or more years), birth order (1 to 6), Religion, wealth index of household (poorest, poor, middle, richer, richest), health insurance (insured and uninsured). The wealth score has been decided or obtained by Principal Component Analysis (PCA), based on list of household specified under Demographic and Health Surveys (DHS), which include household building structure sanitation, water facilities, roof structure, household components (ratio, television, refrigerators, motorcycles) on that based household weighted score has been classified in to poorest, poorer, middle, richer and richest)

Statistical Analysis

The analysis of the data includes descriptive analysis (includes mean, standard Deviation, charts, tables and others), its describe maternal characteristics, ANC visit, place of delivery.

Multivariate logistic regression models were used to examine factors associated with at least four ANC visits. . All analyses were conducted using STATA 16 or measures the probability that the dependent variable explains the effect after adjusting for the effect of other explanatory factors.

Independent variables in this regression model included mother's age and education, birth rate, place of residence, family wealth, and gender of the household head.

Results

Table 1 indicates the distribution of maternal healthcare by uses of ANC service (at least 1) and institutional delivery during the period of 1992-1993 and 2019-21. The period during 1992-93 to 2005-06 was the performance before the introduction of NRHM, while post 2005-06 indicate the impact of NRHM/NHM on the institutional delivery. The proportion of pregnant women in India aged 15-49 who has at least one ANC visit and maximum 5 years preceding services, the result of the NRHM indicate with positive increase 17.5 percent point over pre- NRHM. Further the rate of growth of institutional delivery during the same period it has significantly increase 15.1 percent during the both time period of NRHM/NHM. The figure 1 depicts the mother mortality rate during 20 years of pre NRHM era (1999-2006) decline from 330 to 254 per 100000 live birth and post NRHM it declined from 254 (2004-06) to 130 (2014-16) and further it declined to 73 (2018-20) (Rode, 2018) The infant mortality rate during 20 years pre NRHM (1992-2006) decline from 80 to 57 per 1000 births and 57 to 34 (2006-2014-15) post NRHM with annual decline rate 2.4 percent, Now according to World Health organization date 2021 the IMR decline from 34 to 25 (2.33% annually). The annual MMR decline rate during 1999-01 to 2004-06 was 4.93 percent in later part post NRHM the MMR decline rate (2004-06 to 2019-21) was 7.05 per cent. The decline rate in MMR indicate the performance of

NRHM was remarkable and various policies related of facilitates health services are working together and more effort to achieve the Sustainable development Goal 70 per 100,000 live birth (Gedefaw G, et al, 2016). An institutional environment capable of providing effective obstetric and neonatal care could help to reduce maternal deaths, still births. Table 1 also reveals that institutional delivery also increased 12.6 (pre NRHM period) but intervention of NRHM in 2006 institutional delivery has been increased more than 42.53 percent during the period of 2005-06 to 2019-20. In further, Its also indicate all the religion, caste and educated women mostly refer to adopt ANC services regurly and more depend on institutional deliveries.

Table 1. Distribution of maternal characteristics at least one antenatal care (ANC) visit and institutional delivery (1992–2020)

	ANC Visit (atleast 1)							Institutional Delivery		
	92–93	**98–9**	**2005–06**	**2015–16**	**2019-20**	**92–93**	**98–9**	**2005–06**	**2015–16**	**2019-20**
India	62.7	65.4	77.1	83.5	91	26.1	34	38.7	78.9	88.6
Mother's age at birth										
<20 years	64.3	67.8	80.5	85.8	87.9	24.0	31.8	38.0	81.5	87.0
20–34 years	62.1	65.7	78.0	84.1	87.8	27.0	35.0	39.8	79.2	88.6
35–49 years	41.7	44.0	54.9	68.2	82.9	12.5	19.9	21.7	61.8	87.2
Birth order										
1	72.8	77.6	88.4	90.2	90.6	38.2	50.6	57.0	88.2	88.7
2–3	65.8	69.5	82.4	84.4	87.8	26.9	33.8	39.4	77.7	88.7
4–5	53.5	51.2	64.2	69.2	80.1	14.5	17.5	19.6	60.6	86.1
Residence										
Urban	81.1	85.8	90.7	90.8	89.4	57.6	65.1	67.5	88.7	90.0
Rural	56.7	59.6	72.3	80.5	86.9	16.0	24.6	28.9	75.1	87.9
Education										
No schooling	50.2	51.6	62.1	67.8	78.7	11.8	17.4	18.4	61.6	86.0
<5 years complete	78.1	79.5	82.4	82.1	84.7	33.3	34.1	36.3	70.0	86.4
5–7 years complete	81.3	81.2	87.0	86.6	86.7	38.7	44.0	47.9	80.1	88.2
8–9 years complete	89.4	86.4	91.4	88.2	89.1	53.1	54.4	57.7	85.3	88.9
10–11 years complete	94.6	91.8	95.1	91.6	90.2	65.6	66.5	72.2	91.5	89.5
12 or more years complete	94.3	96.6	98.3	93.9	92.4	78.7	83.6	86.4	94.7	89.5
Religion										
Hindu	NA	NA	58.7	65.2	88.0	NA	NA	12.7	59.6	88.6
Muslim	NA	NA	69.2	81.9	85.0	NA	NA	23.5	75.1	87.3
Christian	NA	NA	80.1	88.7	91.3	NA	NA	39.2	85.0	89.1
Sikh	NA	NA	90	92.2	89.7	NA	NA	57.9	90.5	91.6

continued on following page

Table 1. Continued

	ANC Visit (atleast 1)					Institutional Delivery				
	92–93	**98–9**	**2005–06**	**2015–16**	**2019-20**	**92–93**	**98–9**	**2005–06**	**2015–16**	**2019-20**
Buddhist/Neo-Buddhist/ others	NA	NA	97.3	95.0	90.3	NA	NA	83.7	95.3	88.1
Caste/tribe	NA	NA	NA	NA		NA	NA	NA	NA	
Scheduled caste	NA	NA	NA	NA	87.2	NA	NA	NA	NA	88.6
Scheduled tribe	NA	NA	NA	NA	88.3	NA	NA	NA	NA	90.1
Other backward class	NA	NA	NA	NA	87.1	NA	NA	NA	NA	88.7
Other	NA	NA	NA	NA	88.8	NA	NA	NA	NA	87.1

NA: Not Available.
Data source: NFHS Survey report 1, report 2, report 3 Report 4, Report 5

Figure 1. Maternal mortality ratio (Graph)

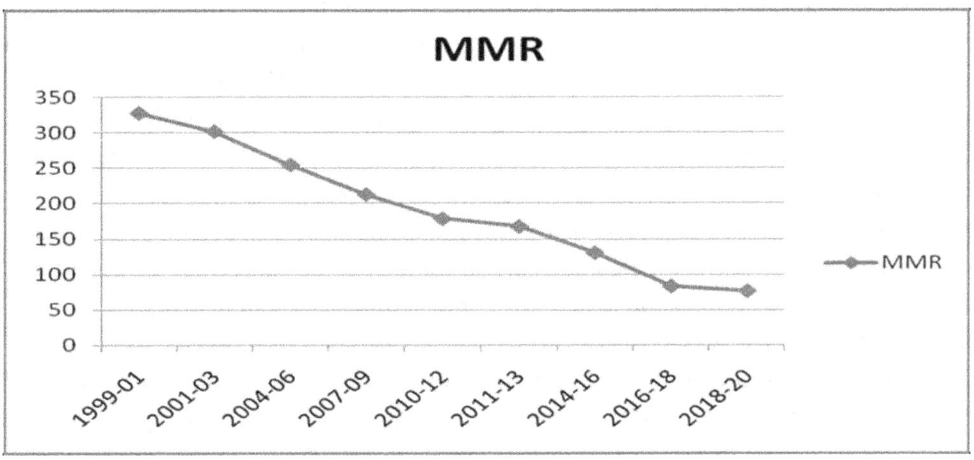

Institutional Delivery in India

Table 2 shows the present scenario of institutional delivery in Indian states in 2019-21. It has found that significant increase in institutional deliveries and women utilizing more institutional services but still shows the disparities among various states (9). It has been depicted that highest institutional delivery in western states with top position in small state like Goa (99.8%), followed by Kerala (99.75%), Tamil Nadu (99.1%) and Karnataka (97.5). It has indicated the southern states /west zone states have majorly adopted institutional delivery rather than other zones. On the other hand, it is lowest in Nagaland with 51.9%, followed by Meghalaya (68.5%)

and Bihar (71.1%). The institutional delivery in rural areas is 85% against 93.10% in urban areas. It indicates a wider gap between rural and urban areas to adopt institutional services. It also indicates the highest rural urban gap in northeastern states and lowest in southern regions. The highest rural urban gap was in Meghalaya (28.4%), followed by Mizoram (26.3%) and Nagaland (26.2%). It has been indicated that with the highest disparities among northeastern hilly states, the effectiveness of NRHM policies can need more focus. Rural-urban disparities lowest in Kerala (0.1%), Goa (-0.4%), Punjab (-3.5%) indicates these states rural area women are more adopting the institutional delivery services rather than urban area.

Figure 2 depicts a comparative study of two period NFHS 4 and NFHS 5. The chart indicates the percentage of institutional delivery in topmost institutional delivery is remain almost same, however Goa registration a spike, the rate of institutional delivery almost higher from 96% (NFHS4) to 99.5% (NFHS 5) during 5 year of period. Among the northeastern states Sikkim performed best with 94.7 percent institutional delivery, but Nagaland was still on the bottom side in proportion of institutional births. However, it has seen a positive outlook in comparison to both periods. To evaluate the gap between urban and rural in northeastern states, except Sikkim all states were far below than western states institutional delivery in rural areas. On average it has been observed that most of the state's urban area were performing well as compared to rural area however, Punjab, Kerala, Goa were marginally higher rural institutional delivery as compared to urban areas. In further, observed in north-eastern states have wider gaps in urban and rural area delivery. Southern states/western zone states performed remarkably well in terms of institutional delivery as well terms of difference in rural and urban institutional birth. It has been observed from fig 2 that many states performed remarkably between in terms of percentage of institutional birth more than 90 percent.

Table 2. Institutional delivery in Indian states (2019-21)

Region	State	Total (%)	Urban (%)	Rural (%)	Urban – Rural Difference (%)
Central	Chhattisgarh	88.5	93.1	83.9	9.2
	Madhya Pradesh	92.5	95.8	89.2	6.6
	Uttar Pradesh	84.2	85.5	82.9	2.6
	Central Region	88.4	91.46	85.35	6.13

continued on following page

Table 2. Continued

Region	State	Total (%)	Urban (%)	Rural (%)	Urban – Rural Difference (%)
East	Bihar	73.5	80	67	13
	Jharkhand	81.1	89.1	73.1	16
	Odisha	94.4	97.5	91.3	6.2
	West Bengal	91.95	92.3	91.6	0.7
	Eastern Region	85.23	89.72	80.75	8.97
Northern Region	Haryana	95.25	96.1	94.4	1.7
	Himachal Pradesh	90.35	93.1	87.6	5.5
	Jammu & Kashmir	94.55	98.6	90.5	8.1
	Punjab	93.75	92	95.5	-3.5
	Rajasthan	95.85	97.5	94.2	3.3
	Uttarakhand	84.9	89.4	80.4	9
	Northern Region	92.44	94.45	90.43	4.016
North-East	Arunachal Pradesh	83.95	90.6	77.3	13.3
	Assam	88.2	93.5	82.9	10.6
	Manipur	83.2	92.5	73.9	18.6
	Meghalaya	68.5	82.7	54.3	28.4
	Mizoram	85.65	98.8	72.5	26.3
	Nagaland	51.9	65	38.8	26.2
	Sikkim	93.2	92	94.4	-2.4
	Tripura	91.15	94.8	87.5	7.3
	North-East	80.71	88.73	72.7	16.03
South Region	Andhra Pradesh	97.15	98.6	95.7	2.9
	Karnataka	97.25	98.3	96.2	2.1
	Kerala	99.75	99.7	99.8	-0.1
	Tamil Nadu	99.1	99.8	98.4	1.4
	Telangana	97.15	97.7	96.6	1.1
	South Region	98.08	98.53	97.63	1.15
West Region	Goa	99.8	99.6	100	-0.4
	Gujarat	95	97.8	92.2	5.6
	Maharashtra	94.9	96.7	93.1	3.6
	West Region	97.3111111	98.4222	96.2	2.22

Source: NFHS5 2019-21

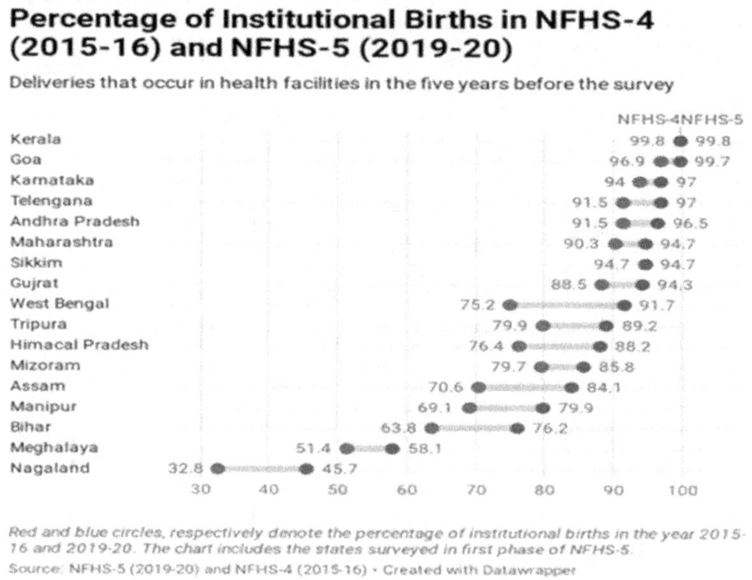

Source: NFHS 5 (2019-20)

Table 3. Antenatal cares by state and union territory

ANC from Skilled Provider				**ANC from Semi -Skilled Provider**			
State/union territory	**Doctor**	**ANM/ nurse/ midwife**	**Percentage**	**Dai/ TBA**	**Anganwadi/ ICDS worker**	**Community/ village Other No ANC**	**Percentage**
Chandigarh	63.1	31.8	94.9	1.8	0.7	2.6	5.1
Delhi	74.1	12.6	86.7	3.6	0.2	9.5	13.3
Haryana	62.8	24.4	87.2	0.3	6.2	6.3	12.8
Himachal Pradesh	69.6	15.6	85.2	1.6	0.9	12.3	14.8
Jammu & Kashmir	86.1	8.1	94.2	0.1	0.2	5.5	5.8
Ladakh	78.3	13.3	91.6	0.5	0.5	7.4	8.4
Punjab	52.2	33.6	85.8	0.5	2	11.7	14.2
Rajasthan	61.7	27.4	89.1	0.4	3.5	7	10.9
Uttarakhand	66.7	20.5	87.2	0.5	2.6	9.7	12.8
Chhattisgarh	40.7	44.8	85.5	0.7	7.3	6.5	14.5
Madhya Pradesh	36.3	44.1	80.4	0.4	11.1	8.1	19.6
Uttar Pradesh	47.8	33.7	81.5	0.7	5.3	12.5	18.5

continued on following page

Table 3. Continued

ANC from Skilled Provider				ANC from Semi -Skilled Provider			
State/union territory	**Doctor**	**ANM/ nurse/ midwife**	**Percentage**	**Dai/ TBA**	**Anganwadi/ ICDS worker**	**Community/ village Other No ANC**	**Percentage**
Bihar	38.7	29	67.7	0.5	9.2	22.6	32.3
Jharkhand	42.9	36.4	79.3	0.6	10.2	9.9	20.7
Odisha	82.1	8.1	90.2	0	5.7	4.1	9.8
West Bengal	70.7	13.4	84.1	0.2	1.1	14.6	15.9
Arunachal Pradesh	59.4	16.7	76.1	0.4	0.2	23.3	23.9
Assam	59.4	25.4	84.8	0.5	0.9	13.8	15.2
Manipur	91	1.2	92.2	0.1	0	7.7	7.8
Meghalaya	61.9	21.8	83.7	0.6	0.5	15.2	16.3
Mizoram	69.4	17.1	86.5	0.2	1.4	11.9	13.5
Nagaland	49.8	20.6	70.4	0.2	0.5	28.9	29.6
Sikkim	67	14.4	81.4	0	3.2	15.4	18.6
Tripura	82.1	1.5	83.6	0.1	0.2	16.1	16.4
Dadra & Nagar Haveli and Daman & Diu	75.3	21.6	96.9	0.4	0.5	2.2	3.1
Goa	97.7	0.9	98.6	0	0.4	1	1.4
Gujarat	75.2	11.1	86.3	0.2	5	8.5	13.7
Maharashtra	80.9	11.8	92.7	0.2	1.4	5.7	7.3
Andaman Islands	45.7	46.9	92.6	0	0.1	7.3	7.4
Andhra Pradesh	90.2	5.1	95.3	0	1.7	3	4.7
Karnataka	84.2	12.6	96.8	0	0.7	2.5	3.2
Kerala	97.9	0.1	98	0	0.1	1.9	2
Lakshadweep	100	0	100	0	0	0	0
Pondicherry	86.4	8.7	95.1	0	0.3	4.6	4.9
Tamil Nadu	86.8	8.5	95.3	0	0.5	4.2	4.7
Telangana	93.5	3.5	97	0	1.5	1.5	3
Average	**70.21**	**17.95**	**88.16**	**0.425**	**2.38**	**9.02**	**11.83**

Source: NFHS 2019-21

** Percent distribution of women age 15-49 who had a live birth in the 5 years preceding

Table 3 shows the skilled assistance service provided during pregnancy, skilled includes doctors, ANM nurse and midwifes and semi-skilled ANC provider includes Skilled Dai, Aganwadi Workers and others (Community/ village health worker ASHA Other No ANC).

Eighty-five percent of women aged 15-49 who had a live birth in the five years before the survey received antenatal care from a skilled provider at least once for their last birth. It is found that the majority of women received antenatal care from doctors (70%), followed by ANM/Nurse Midwives (17%), and other women received antenatal care from different semi trained sources (including Dai, community village center, and others). Table indicate that Lakshadweep (100%) women received antenatal care from doctors, followed by Goa (98.6%), Karnata (96.8%), on the other side skilled provider ANC is low in Bihar (67.7%), followed by Nagaland (70.4%) and Arunachal Pradesh (76.1%). The ANC services are basically based on background characteristics of women in both areas rural and urban. It has been found that ANC services are increasing with rising in education as well health services in particular states.

Trends of Maternal Care India

The table shows the trends in utilization of maternal health care service with comparative understanding of NFHS 4 (2015-16) and NFHS 5 (2019-21). (15-17) The participants are taken in the study group were women aged 15-49 including rural and urban. The Table indicate that upward trends in percentage of women who receive antenatal care services in NFHS 4 (85.55%) to NFHS (94.4%), annual growth with 2.13% per annual indicate the various government schemes was highly impacted to women to regular visit the center for their healthy delivery. In further, it was indicated that four antenatal care visits are higher 55% to 61.5% in both periods. Even though women percentage of delivery with health facilities with skilled assistance move towards positive trends with also 2.14% annual upwards.

Table 4. Trends in maternal care indicators—Maternal care indicators for births to women age 15-49 during the 5 years preceding the survey by residence, NFHS-5 and NFHS-4, India

Indicator	NFHS-4 (2015-2016			NFHS-5 (2019-2021)		
	URBAN	RURAL	Total	URBAN	RURAL	Total
Percentage antenatal care	90.7	80.4	85.55	95.7	93.1	94.4
Percentage at least four antenatal care visits	66.4	44.8	55.6	68.5	54.5	61.5
Percentage antenatal care within the first trimester of pregnancy	69.1	54.2	61.65	75.4	67.9	71.65
Percentage of births delivered with health facility	88.7	75.1	81.9	93.8	86.7	90.25
Percentage of deliveries assisted by a skilled provider	90.0	78.0	84	94.0	87.8	90.9

Source: NFHS 5 2019-21 & Author Computation

Table 5. Multiple logistic regression of factors associated with underutilization of 4 ANC visits in India, NFHS-5

Variable		**COR**	**95% Confidence Level**	**P value**
Residence				
	Urban [ref]	1		
	Rural	1.86	1.82–1.90	.005
Region	North	2.24	2.09–2.39	.005
	Central	4.07	3.81–4.34	.005
	East	3.64	3.41–3.89	.005
	Northeast	3.24	3.00–3.51	.005
	West	1.19	1.08–1.31	.005
	South [ref]	1		
Age	15–19 [ref	1		
	20–29	1.06	1.05–1.18	.005
	25–29	1.05	0.99–1.11	0.075
	30–34	1.01	0.95–1.07	0.743
	35–39	1.18	1.10–1.26	.005
	40–44	1.35	1.23–1.48	.005
	45–49	2.19	1.86–2.58	.005
Religion	Hindu	1.44	1.34–1.55	.005
	Muslim	1.51	1.40–1.63	.005
	Christian [ref	1		
	Sikh	1.31	1.17–1.46	.005
	Neo-Buddhist	1.01	0.86–1.18	0.917
	Others	1.37	1.19–1.59	.005
Caste	Scheduled Caste	1.51	1.47–1.56	.005
	Scheduled Tribe	1.37	1.32–1.42	.005
	Other Backward Class	1.40	1.37–1.44	.005
	Other (ref)	1		.005
Education	No education	3.85	3.73–3.98	.005
	Primary	2.23	2.15–2.31	.005
	Secondary	1.49	1.45–1.54	.005
	Higher [ref]	1		.005

continued on following page

Table 5. Continued

Variable		COR	95% Confidence Level	P value
Household wealth index	Poorest	3.6	3.55–3.79	.005
	Poorer	2.28	2.20–2.35	.005
	Middle	1.56	1.51–1.61	.005
	Richer	1.24	1.20–1.28	.005
	Richest [ref]	1		.005
Health insurance coverage	Covered [ref]	1		.005
	Not covered	1.35	1.32–1.38	.005

Source: Authors computation

Table 5 presents the multivariate logistic regression results for the determinants of having at least four ANC visits in India. The cumulative odds ratios (CORs) in table 1.5 indicate the impact of explanatory/ dependent variables after adjusting the other various parameters/variables in this model. Age of mother, type of residence, education level of mother, regional area of women, household wealth, insurance coverage all variables are played important roles in having at least four ANC visits. Women aged group 30-49 years were more likely to visit ANC (average COR: 1.43; 95% confidence interval with range 0.95-1.63 respectively) to have at least higher ANC visit as compared to 15-30 years age group of women. There was a significance of difference in region wise structure, west region indicate they have more ANC visit as compared to North region, its significantly indicate higher number of COR (4.07). Women who had only primary education (1-4 years of schooling) or completed 5-7 years schooling were minimum 73% more likely to have at least four ANC visits (COR: 2.23; CI: 2.15–2.31 and COR 1.49; CI; 1.45–1.54 respectively) than women without schooling/no schooling. The study is not much significantly differentiate based on education of women and antenatal care center visit. The pregnant women from Sikh community have least co-relationship (COR: 1.31; CI: 1.17–1.46) as compared to the other communities. The women of Schedule tribes and scheduled caste, other backwards caste have negatively influenced with four antenatal care center visit prospects. Women belongs to higher income group based on wealth indexing parameters were highly likely (COR 1.24; CI 1.20–1.28) to have four ANC visits than those are belongs to poorer category. Women residing in rural area if their household head was female and highest ANC visit with highest level of economic stratum.

DISCUSSION/CONCLUSION

In India to reduce the Mother maternal death and effective universal access to sexual reproductive health of global level is highly progressive agenda to achieve Sustainable Development of Goal (SDGs) by 2030(Mezgebu et.al,2019) Globally found that 47 percent of all neonatal death during the first five year period, and two region accounted almost 95 percent of all maternal death occurred in low and middle income countries in 2021 with 87 percent (253000) contribution of Sub-Saharan African and southern Asian countries. The sub-Saharan African countries contribute 70 percent (202,000) maternal death, while southern Asian countries contribute 16 percent (47,000). On the other hand, Western Europe and Southern Asia achieved higher reduction in MMR during the of 2000-2020. In India, and Pakistan alone contribute about one third of maternal death in 2020. The present empirical evidence present maternal care facilities in India have been improved over last two decades but reduction ratio has been slow and uneven condition in Country, during first one decade 1992-2006. For Instance, during 1992-2006 the percentage of women in India who receive at least three ANC during their last pregnancies and medical assistance has been increased from 44 percent to 51 percent. (Trujillo et.al, 2014). The study reveals that introduction of NRHM/NHM brough significant reduction in MMR and IMR and increase ANC visit by the pregnant women. It is also found that institutional delivery during post NRHM 1992-2006 increased 40.2 percent while rate of institutional delivery in pre NRHM was very low around 1.6 percent. It has been observed that inequality in institutional delivery in various states declined considerably. Although still exists disparities with various Indian states in terms of institutional delivery and rural- urban disparities. However, it is found that few states i.e. Goa, Puducherry, Tamilnadan, Kerala has almost 100 percent institutional delivery and least gap between rural and urban outfit, where as Nagaland has lowest institutional delivery but highest gap between rural and urban (26.2%). Furthermore, leading risk factors for death in neonatal includes premature birth, birth complication, infection from tetanus, sepsis and pneumonia (Kuhnt & Vollmer,2017; Barbosa et.al,20115). These risk factors can be reduced or prevented through maximum visits of ANC centers by pregnant women (Hong & Beltran, 2007; UNICEF, 2019; Hogan, 2010). It is recommended by World Health Organisation (WHO) to atleast Four ANC visit effective for pregnant women in low-income countries. According to WHO recommendation, the first two ANC visits are required in the first two trimesters, and last two visit in last trimester. It must be ensured by health center to provide ANC service package including screening for complications, health education, two tetanus injection, iron, calcium and folic acid tablets (Mohanty, 2012; NFHS, 3, 2007; NFHS5, 2022; Singh et.al, 2014). Reproductive health will benefit substantially through health sector transforms since the flaws that plague the financing and delivery of reproductive health services are closely related to those that plague health services generally and are typically systemic in nature (Malachi et.al, 2017). If there is any reform in the health sector, it should make basic infrastructure facilities and preventive healthcare facilities including reproductive health services (Sabrina, Hussain & Chen Lincoln, 2013). The health sector reforms in various countries like Bangladesh, Egypt aiming to deliver universal access with pluralistic health system with numerous stakeholders including government and non-government agency; it also accesses of basic packages of healthcare service to the population. The motive of wide spread of health care program to equity-oriented work and development of children as well as reduction in malnutrition among the pregnant women to meet the target of SDG goals and decline 75% infant mortality rate (Nair et.al, 2017). In India, Janani Suraksha Yojana (JSY) is a cash incentive scheme has promoted population to more adopt institutional delivery, specially rural vulnerable section (Saggurti N, et al, 2018). It seems difficult to make significant changes in household wealth indices through income redistribution because factors like head of household, birth order, and level of education involve decisions and situations that are out of one's control in the short term. To enhance overall performance in maternity healthcare, the NHM, however, focuses primarily on low-income mothers. For example, low-income mothers who use maternal care services receive financial transfers. In spite of the remarkable advancements in institutional delivery rates in India through NRHM/NHM interventions, extra attention is still needed to maintain the proportion of women who receive at least four ANC visits. There are significant differences between and within states, and the national rate of having at least four ANC visits is still only 51.2%. A gap in receiving at least four ANC visits is shown in this study, that is caused by sociodemographic and economic characteristics such as the mother's age and educational attainment, birth order, type of dwelling, household wealth, and gender of the head of the household. To achieve the anticipated targets for the IMR and MMR, attempts must be undertaken to remove the obstacles to receiving at least four ANC visits. The Ananya program, which the Bill and Melinda Gates Foundation implemented in eight districts of Bihar in 2011, combines supply-side and demand-side interventions to improve reproductive, maternal, newborn, and child health services and outcomes. This initiative aims to address inter-regional variations in reproductive health service and utilization [Garg S, Laskar AR, 2012]. Similar initiatives should be taken to address the challenges faced by states like Nagaland in the Northeast, where institutional delivery and ANC visits have been historically low.

REFERENCES

Abebe, E., Seid, A., Gedefaw, G., Haile, Z. T., & Ice, G. (2019). Association between antenatal care follow-up and institutional delivery service utilization: Analysis of 2016 Ethiopia demographic and health survey. *BMC Public Health*, 19(1), 1472. 10.1186/s12889-019-7854-231699062

Arokiasamy P. & Pradhan J. (2014). Maternal health care in India: access and demand determinants. Prim Health Care Maternal Survival steering group. Maternal Mortality: Who, When, Where, and Why? *Maternal Survival. Lancet Mater Surv Series.*

Balhasan, A., Dhillon, P., & Mohanty Sanjay, K. (2020). Inequalities in the utilization of maternal health care in the pre- and post-National Health Mission periods in India. *Journal of Biosocial Science*, 52(2), 198–216. 10.1017/S002193201900038531232249

Barbosa, I., Roberta, C., Silva, W. B. M., Cerqueira, G. S. G., Novo, N. F., Almeida, F. A., & Novo, J. L. V. G. (2015). Maternal and fetal outcome in women with hypertensive disorders of pregnancy: The impact of prenatal care. *Therapeutic Advances in Cardiovascular Disease*, 9(4), 140–175. 10.1177/175394471559762226220808

Fekadu, A., Yitayal, M., & Alemayehu, G. (2019). Frequent Antenatal Care Visits Increase Institutional Delivery at Dabat Health and Demographic Surveillance System Site, Northwest Ethiopia. *J Pregn.*

Garg, S., & Laskar, A. R. (2012). Community Based Monitoring; Key to success of National Health Programs, Department of community Medicine, MAMC, New Delhi, India. *Indian Journal of Community Medicine*, 35(2), 214–226.20922094

Ghosh. A. & Ghosh, R. (2020) Maternal health care in India: A reflection of 10 years of National Health Mission on the Indian maternal health scenario. *Sexual Reproductive health care, 25*, 1-8.

Gogia, S., & Sachdev, H. S. (2010). Home Visits by Community Health Workers to Prevent Neonatal Deaths in Developing Countries: A Systematic Review. *Bulletin of the World Health Organization*, 88(9), 658–666. 10.2471/BLT.09.06936920865070

Gupta, S. K. (2012). Impact of Janani Suraksha Yojana on Institutional Delivery Rate and Maternal Morbidity and Mortality: An Observational Study in India. *Journal of Health, Population and Nutrition*, 30(4), 464–471.23304913

Hogan, M. C., Foreman, K. J., Naghavi, M., Ahn, S. Y., Wang, M., Makela, S. M., Lopez, A. D., Lozano, R., & Murray, C. J. L. (2010). Maternal mortality for 181 countries, 1980–2008: A systematic analysis of progress towards Millennium Development Goal 5. *Lancet*, 375(3), 1609–1623. 10.1016/S0140-6736(10)60518-120382417

Hong, R., & Ruiz-Beltran, M. (2007). Impact of prenatal care on infant survival in Bangladesh. *Maternal and Child Health Journal*, 11(1), 199–206. 10.1007/s10995-006-0147-217136460

IIPS and Macro International. (2007). *National Family Health Survey (NFHS 3), 2005–06; India* (Vol. I). IIPS.

Kuhnt, J., & Vollmer, S. (2017). Antenatal care services and its implications for vital and health outcomes of children: Evidence from 193 surveys in 69 low-income and middle income countries. *BMJ Open*, 7(11), e017122. 10.1136/bmjopen-2017-01712229146636

Malachi, A., Anders, E., & Asamoah, B. O. (2017). Effectiveness of antenatal care services in reducing neonatal mortality in Kenya: Analysis of national survey data. *Global Health Action*. 10.1080/16549716.2017.127222328621201

Mohanty, S. K. (2012). Multiple Deprivations and Maternal Care in India. *International Perspectives on Sexual and Reproductive Health*, 38(1), 6–14. 10.1363/380061222481144

Nair, N. S., Darak, S., Parsekar, S. S., Parchure, R., Darak, T., Nelson, H., Vijayamma, R., & Menon, S. (2017). *Effectiveness of Behaviour Change Communication interventions in improving the delivery of health messages for ante-natal care in limited literacy settings: An evidence summary*. London: EPPI-Centre, Social Science Research Unit, UCL Institute of Education, University College London.

Rode, S. J. (2018). Effect of Complete Antenatal Care on Birth Weight of Children in India: Evidence from National Family Health Survey (NFHS) Data. *Journal of Women's Health Care*, 7(1), 412. 10.4172/2167-0420.1000412

Sabrina, H. Z., & Chen, L. C. (2013). The Bangladesh Paradox: Exceptional Health Achievement despite Economic Poverty. *Lancet*, 382(9906), 1734–1745. 10.1016/S0140-6736(13)62148-024268002

Saggurti, N., Atmavilas, Y., Porwal, A., Schooley, J., Das, R., Kande, N., Irani, L., & Hay, K. (2018). Effect of health intervention integration within women's self-help groups on collectivization and healthy practices around reproductive, maternal neonatal and child health in rural India. *PLoS One*, 13(8), 2010–2020. 10.1371/journal.pone.020256230138397

Shahabuddin, A. S. M., De Brouwere, V., & Adhikari, R. (2017). *Determinants of institutional delivery among young married women in Nepal: Evidence from the Nepal Demographic and Health Survey*. BMJ. bmj.com/content/bmjopen/7/4/e012446.full.pdfhttps://doi.org/10.1136/bmjopen-2016-012446

Singh, A., Pallikadavath, S., Ram, F., & Alagarajan, M. (2014). Do antenatal care interventions improve neonatal survival in India? *Health Policy and Planning*, 29(7), 842–848. 10.1093/heapol/czt06624038077

Trujillo, J. C., Carrillo, B., & Iglesias, W. J. (2014). Relationship between professional antenatal care and facility delivery: An assessment of Colombia. *Health Policy and Planning*, 29(4), 443–449. 10.1093/heapol/czt03323735737

United Nations Children's Fund. (2008) *The State Of The World's Children Maternal And Newborn Health*. UNICEF. https://www.unicef.org/sowc09/docs/SOWC09-FullReport-EN.pdf

World Health Organization. (2015). *Trends in estimates of maternal mortality ratio 1990–2015*. WHO.

Chapter 14
Trips Plus Provisions:
Implications for Access to Medicines

Raniyal Niyada P.
National Law School of India University, Bengaluru, India

Karun Sanjaya
Symbiosis Law School, Symbiosis International University (Deemed), Pune, India

ABSTRACT

The primary goal of granting intellectual property rights was to encourage innovation, particularly in the healthcare industry. The Paris Convention provided for worldwide protection for ideas, and the global harmonization of intellectual property protection (TRIPs) broadened the scope of protection. The pharmaceutical sector, including Pfizer, played a key role in TRIPS lobbying. However, corporations were dissatisfied with TRIPS flexibilities used by developing nations. To combat this, they turned the forum towards bilateral and regional trade agreements, providing additional economic incentives. The United States is at the forefront of these efforts, which include clauses that restrict affordable access and generic entry. This research investigates the history, mechanisms, and techniques of forum shifting and outlines key areas of Free Trade Agreements that directly impact access to medicine.

INTRODUCTION

Access to life-saving medicines is hampered by the recent boom of intellectual property rights. (Sell, 2007) The high cost of essential medicines was exacerbated by intellectual property protections. The primary manifestation of the intellectual property rights' concern for health is the increasing levels of protection afforded to

DOI: 10.4018/979-8-3693-5976-1.ch014

pharmaceutical businesses. This culminated in a delay in the introduction of generic drugs to the market, resulting in increased prices for governments and restricted access to essential medications.

The relevance of patents in the pharmaceutical business arises from the fact that medicines are not ordinary commodities and are vital owing to their curative and therapeutic capabilities, which are required for the effective functioning of health systems. In addition, they contribute to the enhancement of life quality and the decrease of illness and death rates through enhancing various forms of healthcare services. In addition, questions of life, death, and social justice pertaining to medications cannot be handled merely by the "rules" of market supply and demand. (Jung and Kwon, 2015)

However, pharmaceutical patent protection is a comparatively recent development in the history of intellectual property. The majority of countries, including India, have not issued patents for medicinal products. In addition, pharmaceutical items were not patentable in West Germany, France, Italy, or Spain until 1967, 1979, or 1992, respectively. Canada did not authorise product patents until 1993. (Chang, 2001). In the 1990s, the emergence of WTO and TRIPS prompted states to extend product patents to all sectors. ("Agreement on the Trade Related Aspects of Intellectual Property Rights" (TRIPS), 1994)

In addition to the multilateral constraints they face as World Trade Organization members, developing countries are also subject to bilateral efforts from rich nations, headed by the United States, to impose even greater levels of intellectual property protection (TRIPS-Plus). This was the case despite the fact that TRIPS offers a rather high degree of protection for intellectual property rights. "Some of the fields of protection extended to data exclusivity, banning of parallel importing, linkage of the marketing approval process and the patent status of a drug, increase in the scope for patentability, and extension of the patent protection period". (Sell, 2003)

The issue that has developed due to the monopoly granted on pharmaceutical products is that the production, importation, and availability of cheaper generic medicines are delayed. The protection of pharmaceutical patents in developing and developed countries has made the problem worse. As a consequence, the average price of medications has risen, and middle and low-income strata of society cannot afford or access them, resulting in a severe scarcity of pharmaceutical supplies and limited access to medicines. (Sell, 2007) In addition, mounting evidence suggests that the increased protection of intellectual property rights for pharmaceuticals has had a detrimental influence on the pricing of medications and the capacity of poor nations to develop and manufacture medicines. (Duggan and Goyal, 2012)

Adding oil to an already soaring fire, increasing medicine prices, pharmaceutical R& D disparities are expected to grow. The existing IPR system does not provide pharmaceutical firms with an incentive to invest in the making of medications for the treatment of neglected diseases in poor countries. (Pecoul, 1999) According to Me´decins Sans Frontie`res estimates, "90% of the world's health research and development expenditure is devoted to conditions that affect just 10% of the world's population, with priority conditional upon ability to pay". (Miller, 2003)

Research and development of medical technology advancements are expensive and fraught with failure in the pharmaceutical sector. On the other hand, manufacturing costs are usually on the lower side, especially for small chemical molecules. In the lack of intellectual property protection, competitors may enter the market with cheaper generic copies of new products soon after the registration of the original versions. (The High-Level Panel on Access to Health Technology, 2016) This would make medicines more accessible and affordable to individuals in need.

TRIPS PLUS PROVISIONS: IMPLICATIONS FOR ACCESS TO MEDICINES

TRIPS and Access to Medicine

"A patent is an exclusive right that allows the patent holder to exclude competing suppliers for the duration of the patent. In return, the patent holder divulges their innovation to the general public, allowing for its unrestricted usage once the patent expires". (World Trade Organization, World Health Organization, World Intellectual Property Organization, 2020) Despite this utopian condition, intellectual property regulations have contributed to the high cost of essential medications, rendering them unavailable to the impoverished of the globe. (Sell, 2007)

Since 1883, intellectual property has been a part of worldwide multilateral forums. "The Paris Convention for the Protection of Industrial Property" was the first international agreement pertaining to the protection of intellectual property. (Bravo, 2001) Later, on April 12-15, 1994, GATT Ministers gathered in Marrakesh to complete the "Uruguay Round of Multilateral Trade Negotiations". "The WTO Signatories (the WTO Members) also became parties to the Agreement on Trade-Related Aspects of Intellectual Property Rights (TRIPS), which is annexed to the WTO Agreement, along with thirteen Multilateral Agreements on Trade in Goods, a General Agreement on Trade in Services, and a number of other measures, such as an Understanding on the Settlement of Disputes". (Matthews, 2002)

TRIPS mainly represents the interests of intellectual property right holders. The patent rights were extended by twenty years. In addition, "it mandates that developing nations provide pharmaceutical patent protection, severely restricts the conditions for issuing compulsory licences, and reduces the autonomy of states in formulating domestic intellectual property policies suited to their varying degrees of innovation and economic development". (Sell, 2007) This was made possible by the lobbying activities of international firms, such as Pfizer. After securing the backing of the United States government, they obtained the support of Europe and Japan. They were mainly successful in harnessing the WTO process and tailoring international law to their own requirements. (Braithwaite and Drahos, 2004) (Matthews, 2002) (Sell, 2003)

However, the TRIPS agreement itself was drafted by the corporates and is largely pro-industry. The vast majority of restrictions, including the term of protection, restrict access. The twenty-year term period acts as a hurdle wherein the generics cannot produce the medicine within the periods, especially where protection is given to the product. The limited scope of issuance of compulsory licence further restricted access. In addition, the demand for product patents in the pharmaceutical business has hindered worldwide accessibility. In 2001, The Doha Declaration and subsequent agreements in 2002, 2003, and 2005 confirmed the authority of WTO members to exercise inherent flexibilities to safeguard public health. (World Health Organisation, 2002)

Forum Shifting

The pharma industry continues to want more protection notwithstanding the protection envisaged in the TRIPS agreement. The TRIPS agreement set a minimum level of intellectual property protection. However, as a result of the interpretation of the rules throughout time, several inherent and associated flexibilities have been established. This includes mechanisms for compulsory licences, parallel imports, limits on patent rights, etc., that member nations may use to ensure that their people have access to these essential medicines. (Mittal, 2017)

This led to a continuing controversy about TRIPS-plus measures. On one side of the TRIPS is the need for enhanced protection of intellectual property, and on the other is access to medications. Their arguments centred on the premise that TRIPS is inadequate. They highlight the enormous expenses of producing new medicines, the necessity for robust property rights as innovation incentives, and the need for considerable recompense for supplying lifesaving drugs. (Grabowski, 2002) The arguments are mostly presented by brand corporations, the United States, and the USTR. Global pharma emphasises the possible health risks of extensive generic manufacture to boost their claims and prevent the flow of medications into the markets of high-income industrialised nations, which would further erode their market. They drew attention to the problem of piracy in the pharmaceutical sector and the usage of medicines without supervision, dosage instructions, and regulatory protocols covering the goods of global pharma. (Gervais, 2002) The underlying problem is poverty, not patents, is one of the most prevalent arguments made by advocates of global pharma. (Sell, 2007) The Pharmaceutical Research and Manufacturing Association (PhRMA), a U.S.-based corporate lobbying body, lobbies academics to support this position. They typically cite a Harvard research that demonstrates that patents do not hinder Africa's access to antiretroviral drugs. (Attaran, 2001) PhRMA supporters oppose the public health exemption on the grounds that it undermines intellectual property protection. In addition, they opposed mandatory licencing and parallel imports as policy tools to cut the price of essential medicines. To solve the problem of access to essential medicines, they suggest increasing foreign assistance and pharmaceutical contributions from businesses (Gervais, 2002).

In contrast, a coalition of poor nation governments and non-governmental organisations had initiated a push for access to essential medications. "They argue that patent protection is a barrier to access and that public health exceptions to patent regulations are essential to avoid needless deaths. They favoured mandatory licencing, generic competition, parallel imports, and predetermined rates of remuneration for pharmaceutical companies. James Love of Ralph Nader's Consumer Project on Technology (CPTech) and Ellen 't Hoen of Me'decinsSans Fronti'res (MSF) are notable advocates for this perspective. She contends that patent protection leads to high costs and limited access". (Ellen 't Hoen, 2002)

In response to these disputes, India, Brazil, and the African Group of Countries created the Access to Medicine Campaign. The campaign promotes the right of poor countries to issue compulsory licence pharmaceuticals, to make, export, and import generic medications, and to use parallel importation to locate the most cost-effective medications. (Sell, 2007) In November 2001, the Doha Declaration recognised the rights of WTO Member States to apply TRIPS in a way that safeguards public health and promotes universal access to medicines.

To prevent poor countries from building coalitions and using them in talks, proponents of TRIPS-plus shifted the global platform from multilateral to bilateral and regional trade agreements. Industry lobbyists were quick to emphasise that TRIPS does not restrict governments from implementing greater levels of protection. The United States and its businesses have committed to this framework and collaborated progressively for the implementation of TRIPS-plus in a number of venues. (Sell, 2007) Since 2001, the United States has signed 11 bilateral and regional free trade agreements with 23 nations. (Correa, 2006)

A new wave of bilateral international agreements arose as developed and developing nations sought to leverage the flexibilities and address the problem of access to medication by enacting measures to control the projected rise in the cost of medicines. (Correa, 2006) They are negotiated outside the WTO's framework. They need a greater degree of protection than TRIPS, such as the US-Jordan Free Trade Agreement. The wave began with U.S. attempts to convince other countries to embrace willingly a large extension of IPRs. The programme began in Jordan in 2000. Even since then, TRIPS provisions have been minimal compared to the current US IP blueprint, which surpasses TRIPS by a wide margin. Consequently, the protection of intellectual property has drastically and astoundingly grown in recent years. This is made feasible not just by WTO TRIPS, but also bilateral and regional free trade agreements (FTAs). (Sell, 2007)

Since bilateral and regional agreements were easier to arrange, multilateral agreements eventually gave way to bilateral ones. The United States government used bilateral FTAs to influence regional and multinational TRIPS-plus discussions. The United States and the European Union have pushed actively measures to elevate TRIPS requirements. (Drahos, 2005) (Dutfield, 2005) The purpose is to eradicate all so-called "TRIPS loopholes" and "TRIPS flexibilities." A thorough reading of the TRIPS-plus clauses in the leaked RCEP plans of Japan and South Korea, US Free Trade Agreements with Vietnam, Jordan, Singapore, Chile, Morocco, Australia, Bahrain, etc., and the Trans-Pacific Partnership (hereinafter "TPP") Agreement suggest that industry lobbyists were successful in establishing a higher TRIPS-plus standard, which would have a catastrophic effect on access to pharmaceuticals. (Townsend, Gleeson and Lopert, 2016) Peter Drahos claims that the United States and its IP activist businesses have engaged in a "one-way ratchet" for intellectual property, continuously procuring enhanced levels of protection. (Drahos, 2004) These bilateral agreements offered a greater degree of protection than that envisaged under TRIPS. (Correa, 2006) The stronger and longer protection contemplated by the TRIPS Plus clauses substantially restricts access to pharmaceuticals in low and middle-income countries. (Correa, 2006)

Major FTA's

The United States and Jordan inked their first free trade agreement in 2000. Over time, the United States and other countries signed several other free trade agreements with Vietnam, Singapore, Chile, Morocco, Australia, and Bahrain. Through clauses like patent term extension and data exclusivity, FTAs have established a TRIPS-plus norm.

Various regional agreements are also being negotiated. The TPP and the Regional Comprehensive Economic Partnership (hereinafter "RCEP") are significant discussions. In addition, the India EU–India negotiations were ongoing. (Wouters et al., 2014) Due to Brexit, however, present discussions are stalled.

On October 5, 2015, after seven years of discussions, the TPP Agreement was signed. It comprises twelve Pacific Rim countries, including the United States (US). The TPP is a free trade agreement (FTA) of the next generation that creates new-generation commitments between the parties by building on previous accords. Certain TPP clauses imitate TRIPS Plus provisions. (Vilchez, 2018)

The RCEP is an initiative to maintain ASEAN's centrality in the region. However, the most striking aspect of the RCEP is the United States' absence and the inclusion of India and China, who are not members of the TPP. The leaked plans of Japan and South Korea suggest that these countries sought to ratchet up intellectual property norms inside RCEP to levels akin to the TPP (Townsend, Gleeson, and Lopert, 2016). It is anticipated that RCEP would include all five ASEAN+1 FTAs into a regional economic framework (Das, 2014).

STANDARDS WITH IMPLICATIONS FOR ACCESS TO MEDICINES

Various factors play a crucial role in prolonging or even curtailing access to medicines. The pharmaceutical industry in the United States considered that TRIPS fell short of its original objective. Due to the inclusion of flexibilities, it failed to lessen the delay in the establishment of patent protection in countries that are key suppliers of generic medications, such as India. Therefore, the proliferation of bilateral and regional free trade agreements (FTAs) post-TRIPS is characterised by an escalation of intellectual property (IP) protection for medicines. It has features intended to extend monopolies, promote high pricing, prevent the market entrance of generic drugs, and delay access to affordable medicines. (Sell, 2007)

Even while TRIPS created worldwide identical patent requirements, it did so only at a basic level. The language itself provided great space for interpretation and freedom. It just offered guidance. However, TRIPS itself included a number of exceptions and restrictions on patentability exclusions (for example, for diagnostic, therapeutic, and surgical methods). This resulted in a degree of flexibility in the application of patentability requirements, yet protections like as pre-grant opposition and parallel importation were maintained. (Smith S., 2008)

The flexibilities are a must for affordable access to medicines. It is a trade-off that generics imitators boost societal value by offering affordable alternatives to brand name drugs, hence expanding access for the disadvantaged. However, the continued trend of free trade, bilateral, and regional agreements restricts these flexibilities. The bulk of U.S. free trade agreements featured provisions for longer data exclusivity, patent linkages, and an expansion to the scope of subject matter, patent period extension, restriction of parallel import, harsher border procedures, and stricter issuing of compulsory licences.

Subject Matter

Subject Matter determines the scope of applicability of the protection. As a result of the present trend in free trade agreements, more innovations and even discoveries are protected by intellectual property laws. For instance, inventions generated from plants are given patent protection in the draft language of the TPP Agreement. (Gervais, 2002) Article 18.37.4 of the Plant Protection Convention is both TRIPS-plus and UPOV 1991-plus, since it requires nations to offer plant varieties patent protection in addition to the sui generis protection afforded by UPOV 1991. (Vilchez, 2018) Chapter 15.9(2) of the US–Morocco Free Trade Agreement requires Morocco to forego its authority under TRIPs 27.3(b) to exclude plants and animals from patentability, essentially enlarging the scope of subject matter eligible for patent protection. (United States-Morocco Free Trade Agreement, 2004) This clause clearly exceeds the TRIPS standards. "Article 27.3(a) of the TRIPS Agreement, 1994 allows parties to preserve plant varieties through patents, an effective sui generis system, or any combination of the two". This flexibility is expressly taken away by the patentability requirement for plant derivatives.

Another tendency evident in the current wave of agreements is the patentability of new uses of a known product, new ways of employing a known product, and new processes of using a known product. This would enable the patents to be perpetually renewed. The cumulative impact of this clause is to expand the span of protection, thereby delaying the entry of generics and increasing the cost of access. These regulations are in direct contradiction with the Indian Patent Act of 1970, should they ever be enacted in India.

Patent Extension

Another trait shared by TRIPS-plus agreements is the extension of the duration of protection beyond the twenty-year term stipulated under TRIPs. Although there is no specific term extension, governments are compelled to prolong the protection period to compensate for delays in patent clearance. Surprisingly, none of the provisions of the agreements include a maximum extension duration. Some contracts include provisions for automatic extensions in the event that patent review and marketing authorisation are delayed. The industry's argument in favour of the term extension is that the approval delay decreases the effective period of patent protection and the prospect of collecting R&D spending. Nonetheless, the sole consequence of the period extension is the prolongation of monopoly rights. (Correa, 2006)

As per Art. 17.9.8 [a] and [b] of the Australian-US FTA, "patent term adjustments are needed to compensate for unreasonable delays in the issuing of patents and for unreasonable shortening of the effective patent term induced by delays in marketing approval". (ustr.gov, 2016) The TPP agreements' Articles 18.46.3 and 18.46.4 have similar text. (Lopert and Gleeson, 2013)

The term extension is often provided to compensate for unreasonable delays in the processes for marketing clearance of medicines and/or the evaluation of patent applications that exceed a specific duration. Nonetheless, it is unclear whether the extension must apply simply to delays in the nation where it is sought or if delays in the country where the original clearance was received should also be taken into account. However, subsequently in the instance of the Bahrain-US FTA, Article 14.8.6(b)(ii) emphasises that the foreign country's delays must also be included when determining the delay.

In practice, the undefined period extension provision is not just a TRIPS Plus provision, but also a US Plus provision, since the term extension for market clearance delays is restricted to five years in the United States. However, owing to a significant shortage of human resources, this would be catastrophic for emerging and poor countries. In these nations, permission delays are unavoidable.

Data Exclusivity

The introduction of new rights in the form of data protection is a danger in every FTA. These regulations allow for the maximisation of profits by delaying the market introduction of generics that are unable to furnish the needed data for approval, hence stifling competition. Article 39.3 of TRIPS provides solely the protection of non-disclosed pharmaceutical test data against unfair competition. Nonetheless, the FTA provisions go farther than this.

FTA regulations include a clause giving at least five years of data exclusivity from the day the product was authorised, regardless of whether the product is patentable or not or whether the data has been revealed. It also includes chemical entities that are not new. According to Art XX.G.3 of the leaked proposal of Japan in the RCEP, it applies to applicants seeking marketing authorisation for new pharmaceutical products. It is unlawful for applicants to rely on or make reference to tests or other information provided by the originator. It stipulates a minimum of six years from the approval date. (Townsend, Gleeson and Lopert, 2016)

Moreover, this requirement requires governments to guarantee that no permits are issued based on the data. Article 18.47.1 reads, "...parties must not authorise the marketing of such information without the authorization of the individual who originally supplied it." (ustr.gov, 2016) It results in the shift of the burden of a private right to a public right. In the United States, the Hatch-Waxman Act merely requires the ANDA applicant to inform the patent holder. (Sell, 2007)

A clause of this kind is an effective barrier to generic medicine competition since it makes it practically difficult to apply compulsory licencing as authorised by TRIPS, as approval would be expensive and time-consuming even then. Whether or not the new pharmaceutical product is covered by a patent, the goal of this rule is to prohibit the entry of identical or similar products into the market before the patent expires.

Patent Linkage

Patent Linkage refers to the relationship between drug registration and patent protection. Before approving a medicine in these cases, the drug's patent protection must be considered. The law mandates the national health authority to refuse marketing approval to a generic drug if a patent on the drug is in force unless the patent owner consents to such approval. Moreover, authorities are required to inform patent holders of requests. (Correa, 2006)

In line with South Korea-US Free Trade Agreement Article 18.9.5, "the authorities are obligated to inform patent holders of generic marketing applications asking marketing authorisation within the period of patent on a product or authorised use." The TPP's patent linkage section mandates that regulatory agencies should keenly look for existing patents.

Such ties simply serve to prolong the introduction of generics. By restricting the marketing of third-party medications throughout the period of patents, the language of the clause shows that it was designed to reduce the efficacy of compulsory licencing. (Abbott, 2011)

Required License

Not surprisingly, the FTAs restrain WTO Members' freedom, confirmed by the Doha Declaration, to determine the grounds for compulsory licences. Article 16.7 (6) (b) of the United States-Australia-Jordan-Singapore Free Trade Agreement states that "the provisions on grounds for issuance of compulsory licence are limited to cases of anticompetitive practises, public non-commercial use, national emergency, or other situations of extreme urgency."

Chapter 15 of the US–Morocco Free Trade Agreement limits the use of TRIPs flexibilities to certain illnesses (HIV/AIDS, malaria, TB, and other epidemics) and instances of "great urgency" or "national emergency."

Interestingly, TRIPs retained far more flexibility to issue compulsory licenses than bilateral and regional agreements. A reading of the provisions of various FTAs sheds light on how each of them had limited the scope of grounds to grand a Compulsory License. This has a chilling and considerable impact on the accessibility of the drug. The primary aim of the provisions was to curtail the flexibilities recognised by Doha declaration.

Parallel Importing

Parallel importation is the act of importing a patented product that has been lawfully sold in a foreign nation without the patent owner's permission. This is conceivable owing to the notion of exhaustion. The theory argues that after a patented product has been sold for the first time, the patent holder loses ownership of it and it becomes a commodity. The nation's method of depletion either facilitates or impedes parallel import.

US free trade agreements have led to national exhaustion. The TRIPS agreement permits flexibility, and the parties are allowed to choose the form of exhaustion to follow. By enforcing national exhaustion, however, the United States has moved to further limit parallel imports and access to emerging poor countries.

Article 17.9.4 of the Australia–United States Free Trade Agreement forbids parallel imports without patent holder approval. (Office of the United States Trade Representative, 2005) By imposing national exhaustion regimes, then, FTAs implement TRIPS plus. Thus, the requirements attempt to limit access to cheaper patented pharmaceuticals, which would otherwise be a TRIPS-compliant opportunity for access.

Border Controls

Recent disputes between intellectual property and international commerce have ignited a heated debate. The nations that export intellectual property have passionately asserted that the increased traffic in counterfeits and fake items has decimated the market for the originals and tricked customers into buying possibly harmful counterfeits. (Grosse Ruse -Khan, 2011) On the other hand, the emerging nations were concerned that it would operate as an effective trade barrier due to their increasing competency.

While TRIPS merely mandates border procedures against the importation of counterfeit trademark or copyright products, the current wave of FTAs has raised the standard and breadth of border measures. According to Article X.G.5 of the leaked RCEP papers, the following is South Korea's proposal in this regard: "Rights holders may request the suspension or detention of allegedly infringing imported, exported, or transhipment products." (Townsend, Gleeson and Lopert, 2016).

Article 18.76.2 of the TPP requires just a prima facie breach for the enforcement of the Border measure. Subparagraph 5 extends the application of this rule to goods in transit. Such a regulation has the effect of restricting the opportunity for parallel imports to developing countries.

CONCLUSION

Despite mounting worries about the detrimental impacts of free trade agreements and TRIPS-plus agreements, a number of developing nations have consented to/ are in the process of negotiating and entering into FTAs. This is often done to get tax reductions and trade connections, perceived business benefits that these nations so profoundly want. Concerns must be expressed, however, about the effects of expanding patent protection rules, notably in the pharmaceutical business. These higher protection standards might result in an unacceptable delay and/or impede generic competition, thereby curtailing affordable and easy access to medicines.

However, the concerns presented by these agreements, which are TRIPS-plus, are antithetical to the word and spirit of the agreement itself and would consequently violate and conflict with TRIPS. The bulk of these agreements are in opposition to both the language and the spirit of the Doha declaration and would restrict the capacity of nations to realise the human right to health. These bilateral and regional agreements threaten to undercut any multilateral advantages negotiated or achieved by poor nations. Statistics indicate that the introduction of data exclusivity in Jordan as a prerequisite of the Jordan-United States free trade agreement caused substantial delays in the introduction of generic versions of 79 percent of the tested drugs. Immediate evaluation of the free trade agreements and comprehension of the negative consequences they offer for these trade discussions is the need of the hour.

REFERENCES

Abbott, F. M. (2011). *The Doha Declaration on the TRIPS Agreement and Public Health and the Contradictory Trend in Bilateral and Regional Free Trade Agreements*. SSRN. https://papers.ssrn.com/sol3/papers.cfm?abstract_id=1977300

Agreement on the Trade Related Aspects of Intellectual Property Rights, 1994, Art. 27.

Attaran, A. (2001). Do Patents for Antiretroviral Drugs Constrain Access to AIDS Treatment in Africa? *Journal of the American Medical Association*, 286(15), 1886. 10.1001/jama.286.15.188611597292

Braithwaite, J., & Drahos, P. (2004). *Global business regulation*. Cambridge University Press.

Bravo, G. (2001). From Paris Convention to TRIPS: A Brief History. *Journal of Contemporary Legal Issues*, 12, 445.

Chang, H.-J. (2001). Intellectual Property Rights and Economic Development: Historical lessons and emerging issues. *Journal of Human Development*, 2(2), 287–309. 10.1080/14649880120067293

Correa, C. M. (2006). Implications of bilateral free trade agreements on access to medicines. *Bulletin of the World Health Organization*, *84*(5), 399–404. https://www.ncbi.nlm.nih.gov/pmc/articles/PMC2627342/10.2471/BLT.05.023432

Das, S. B. (2014). *Understanding the regional comprehensive economic partnership and the trans- pacific partnership: An ASEAN perspective*. Brookings. https://www.brookings.edu/wp-content/uploads/2014/01/11-asia-pacific-economic-integration-presentation-basu-das.pdf

Drahos, P. (2004). Securing the Future of Intellectual Property: Intellectual Property Owners and Their Nodally Coordinated Enforcement Pyramid Recommended Citation. *Case Western Reserve Journal of International Law*, *36*(1), 55–61. https://scholarlycommons.law.case.edu/cgi/viewcontent.cgi?article=1385&context=jil.

Drahos, P. (2005). Bits and Bips. *The Journal of World Intellectual Property*, 4(6), 791–808. 10.1111/j.1747-1796.2001.tb00138.x

Duggan, M., & Goyal, A. (2012). Pharmaceutical patents and prices: a preliminary empirical assessment using data from India. *Policy Research Working Paper Series*. https://ideas.repec.org/p/wbk/wbrwps/6063.html

Dutfield, G. (2005). Sharing the Benefits of Biodiversity. *The Journal of World Intellectual Property*, 5(6), 899–931. 10.1111/j.1747-1796.2002.tb00186.x

Gervais, D. (2002). The Internationalization of Intellectual Property: New Challenges The Internationalization of Intellectual Property: New Challenges from the Very Old and the Very New from the Very Old and the Very New. *Fordham Intellectual Property, Media and Entertainment Law Fordham Intellectual Property, Media and Entertainment Law Journal Journal, 12*(4). https://ir.lawnet.fordham.edu/cgi/viewcontent.cgi?article=1232&context=iplj

Grabowski, H. (2002). Patents, Innovation and Access to New Pharmaceuticals. *Journal of International Economic Law*, 5(4), 849–860. 10.1093/jiel/5.4.849

Grosse Ruse -Khan. H. (2011). *A Trade Agreement Creating Barriers to International Trade?: ACTA Border Measures and Goods in Transit.* Digital Commons. https://digitalcommons.wcl.american.edu/cgi/viewcontent.cgi?article=1711&context=auilr [Accessed 17 Nov. 2022].

High-Level Panel on Access to Health Technologies. (2016). *Report of the UNITED NATIONS SECRETARY-GENERAL'S HIGH-LEVEL PANEL ON ACCESS TO MEDICINES Promoting innovation and access to health technologies.* https://static1.squarespace.com/static/562094dee4b0d00c1a3ef761/t/57d9c6ebf5e231b2f02cd3d4/1473890031320/UNSG+HLP+Report+FINAL+12+Sept+2016.pdf

Jung, Y., & Kwon, S. (2015). The Effects of Intellectual Property Rights on Access to Medicines and Catastrophic Expenditure. *International Journal of Health Services*, 45(3), 507–529. 10.1177/0020731415584560 26077858

Lopert, R., & Gleeson, D. (2013). The High Price of 'Free' Trade: U.S. Trade Agreements and Access to Medicines. *The Journal of Law, Medicine & Ethics*, 41(1), 199–223. 10.1111/jlme.1201423581666

Matthews, D. (2002). *Globalising intellectual property rights: the TRIPs Agreement.* Routledge.

Miller, E. (2003). *Introduction A Progress Report on TRIPS and Access to Medicines Médecins Sans Frontières Briefing for the 5th WTO Ministerial Conference, Cancún 2003 See back cover for recommendations.* https://www.msfaccess.org/sites/default/files/MSF_assets/Access/Docs/ACCESS_report_DohaDerailed_ENG_2003.pdf

Mittal, S. (2017). *Effects of TRIPSPlus Provisions in International Trade Agreements Upon Access to Medicines in Developing Countries.* 10.2139/ssrn.2975649

Office of the United States Trade Representative. (2005). *Australia-United States Free Trade Agreement.* USTR. ustr.gov.in. https://ustr.gov/sites/default/files/uploads/agreements/fta/australia/asset_upload_file469_5141.pdf

Paris Convention for the Protection of Industrial Property, 1883.

Pécoul, B. (1999). Access to Essential Drugs in Poor CountriesA Lost Battle? *Journal of the American Medical Association*, 281(4), 361. 10.1001/jama.281.4.3619929090

Sell, S. K. (2003). *Private power, public law: the globalization of intellectual property rights*. Cambridge University Press. 10.1017/CBO9780511491665

Sell, S. K. (2007). TRIPS-Plus Free Trade Agreements and Access to Medicines. *The Liverpool Law Review*, 28(1), 41–75. 10.1007/s10991-007-9011-8

Smith, S. R. (2008). Introduction to Intellectual Property, Trade and Access to Medicines. In: *Our Health, Our Right: The Roles And Experiences Of PLHIV Networks in Securing Access to Generic ARV Medicines in Asia*. Asia Pacific Network of People Living with HIV/AIDS. https://rest.neptune-prod.its.unimelb.edu.au/server/api/core/bitstreams/cbf59c92-a665-5808-817b-e7d878d3dfc5/content

't Hoen, E. (2002). Number 1 Article 6 4-1-2002 From Seattle to Doha. *Chicago Journal of International Law Chicago Journal of International Law*, *3*(1), 27-29. https://chicagounbound.uchicago.edu/cgi/viewcontent.cgi?article=1171&context=cjil

Townsend, B., Gleeson, D., & Lopert, R. (2016). The Regional Comprehensive Economic Partnership, Intellectual Property Protection, and Access to Medicines. *Asia-Pacific Journal of Public Health*, 28(8), 682–693. 10.1177/101053951667633827920239

United States -Morocco Free Trade Agreement. (2004). TCC. https://tcc.export.gov/static/final_text_Morocco_FTA.pdf

ustr.gov. (2016). *TPP Full Text*. United States Trade Representative. https://ustr.gov/trade-agreements/free-trade-agreements/trans-pacific-partnership/tpp-full-text

Vilchez, G. C. (2018). *Legal and Policy Implications of the Trans-Pacific Partnership Agreement: Focus on Intellectual Property*. PidsWebs. pidswebs.pids.gov.phhttps://pidswebs.pids.gov.ph/CDN/PUBLICATIONS/pidspjd2016-2_intellectual_property.pdf [Accessed 16 Nov. 2022].

World Health Organisation, World Trade Organisation and World Intellectual Property Organisation. (2020). *Intersections between public health, intellectual property and trade Promoting Access to Medical Technologies and Innovation*. WHO. https://www.wto.org/english/res_e/booksp_e/who-wipo-wto_2020_e.pdf

World Health Organization. (2002). *Implications of the Doha Declaration on the TRIPS agreement and public health*. WHO.

Wouters, J., Goddeeris, I., Natens, B., & Ciortuz, F. (2014). Some Critical Issues in the EU-India Free Trade Agreement Negotiations. *European Law Journal*, 20(6), 848–869. 10.1111/eulj.12109

Chapter 15
Unconventional Trademarks in the Pharmaceutical Sector: Critical and Comparative Insights

Vaishnavi Yashasvi
Sharda University, India

Ruchir Singh
Bennett University, India

ABSTRACT

In this chapter, an attempt has been made to understand the effects of non-traditional trademarks in the area of pharmaceutical products and issues of competition along with a normative case against the unconventional trademarks, further proceeding towards a discussion on inherently valuable freedom of expression and to assess why affording legal protection for non-traditional marks in this area may hamper access to medicine/health. In order to answer this question effectively, this chapter is divided into three parts: the first part explores the prevalence of non- traditional marks in the area of pharmaceuticals; the second part analyzes whether protection for non-traditional marks could pose impediments to access to medicine/health; and the last part ponders the issues of competition and freedom of expression with analytical approach.

DOI: 10.4018/979-8-3693-5976-1.ch015

INTRODUCTION

This chapter aims to examine the impact of non-traditional trademarks on pharmaceutical products and competition issues, while also presenting a case against unconventional trademarks. The discussion will also delve into the potential limitations on access to medicine/health due to legal protection for non-traditional marks in this sector. The chapter is divided into three parts: the first part looks at the prevalence of non-traditional marks in pharmaceuticals, the second part considers the potential barriers to access to medicine/health posed by protection for non-traditional marks, and the final part explores competition and freedom of expression from an analytical perspective.

To explore ways of addressing this challenge posed by competing international human rights, trade, intellectual property rights, and public health imperatives, the United Nations Secretary General formed a High-Level Panel on Access to Health Technologies in November 2015. In this regard, a report published by the Panel in September 2016 considers the ways countries can use the flexibilities within the TRIPS Agreement to achieve innovative and production on health technologies.

Not surprisingly, the report primarily emphasized the significance of patent law. In the Report's Annexes, it was pointed out that trademarks and copyright, in addition to patents, can have monopolistic effects in the market, and their impact can be comparable or even greater due to their longer duration and broader scope of protection. It was observed that greater emphasis should be placed on these rights in order to address their collective impact on the affordability, availability, and distribution of medications and health technologies.''

This topic hit home recently with the ruling of a court in the UK. Lord Justice Arnold dismissed GlaxoSmithKline (GSK), the makers of a purple inhaler, passing off claims against generic manufacturer Sandoz. Although Sandoz did use the colour purple, its inhaler was of a different shape and intended use than GSK's. Meanwhile, in a trial better known for its deceptive advertising charges relating to the color red, an allegedly unauthorized usage of the color in passing off claims was also being tried since the European Union Trademark (EUTM) for the same color had been summarily judged invalid. According to Justice Arnold Misrepresentation as to the origin of the products because the inhaler had been prescribed by doctors based on their ingredients, and not because of their color He also denied allegations that he had misled healthcare professionals and the public by saying the products were equivalent, citing lack of evidence. While GSK failed to enforce its passing-off claim in the UK and lost the mark in the EU, the US trademark over the same color of the inhaler continues into effect. Complicating this, however, is the fact that trademark rights are territorial: refusal or cancellation in one country does not by itself guarantee refusals (or cancellations) elsewhere. Many of the licensing agreements typically have a "worldwide license" clause baked into them, which seemingly obliges to the terms of the agreement in multiple geographies based on the strength of a mark as a trademark in one country, even though the same mark may have been cancelled or never registered in another (*Glaxo Wellcome UK Limited and Anor v. Sandoz Limited & Ors,* 2019)

Non-traditional trademarks therefore can provide a complementary avenue to secure exclusive rights over medicines and health technologies to that granted by patent protection in terms of both scope and duration. This might trigger invasive, non-patient centric legal battles which might dissuade generics companies and impede effective patient access to healthcare. This should worries us not so much for the intellectual property rights itself, even if that does not refer to the main ingredients of the medicines or the technology of the devices. Trademarks might not cover the substance of the treatment itself — but they still stand in the way of access to medicines, health and care devices. If generics are already discouraged from entering a market because of the extended patent protection from secondary patents and similar strategies then, we should not add other hurdles for them to clear through non-traditional trademarks. Although manufacturers can use such features solely during the patent term, the shapes, colours and more generally, the other characteristics of medicines and medical equipment might well be considered as unique, they all tend to be functional aspects, supporting its correct use in delivering the treatment.

This form of functionality may not align with traditional utilitarian purposes, but it is rooted in therapeutic benefits as patients have come to rely on these indicators as an essential aspect of their treatment. Additionally, even if these indicators serve primarily as visual enhancements to products that are otherwise recommended by healthcare professionals based on their ingredients and technical attributes, they enhance the appeal of the products and therefore have aesthetic functionality. Because of these considerations, some argue that these indicators should not be eligible for trademark protection.

Unconventional Trademarks in Pharmaceutical Sector

A brief overview of some categories of non-traditional trademarks actually being used at the present time and specific questions attached to their registration in some of the most frequently mentioned geographies was covered in the preceding part of this piece. This post will analyze the use of non-traditional marks in the pharmaceutical industry. Researchers conducted two surveys to address this question. The American study had reviewed the nine top products from the nine top pharmaceutical companies and found that the majority of marks were meaningless and did not indicate the pharmaceutical effects of the products. The second survey consisted of the analysis of different case laws from other jurisdictions. This technique was adopted to under the extent of new entry of nontraditional marks in the pharmaceutical industry.

An examination of pharmaceutical company practices suggests that most tend to choose unusual symbols to differentiate their products. Interesting examples we found in this regard include Viread (Gilead Sciences), Viagra (Pfizer), Aubagio (Sanofi), Xarelto [20mg] (Johnson& Johnson), and Senisipar (Amgen), which were of a unique shape and colour.

The work is not in a position to establish whether any of the marks referred to above currently enjoy protection in various jurisdictions as to their shape, colour, or a combination thereof. However, obviously some of them are protected in its shape and colour per trademark law. Details of Pfizer's trademark registration for the diamond shape of Viagra tablets appear in the EUIPO database and the purple and gold colours of Nexium (commonly known as the "purple pill") are registered to AstraZeneca (USPTO database) (George, 2015). The survey of case-laws reveals that companies such as AstraZeneca and Pfizer have also brought suits against competitors which have attempted to produce infringing equivalents of those tablets.

An example includes the purple and gold colour combination (being seen as the unique colours) of the Nexium brand (the heart-burn medication of AstraZeneca), used by Dr Reddy's Laboratories in Indian for its own generic version of Nexium, launched in 2015. AstraZeneca quickly sued Dr Reddy's Laboratories. To grant an injunction, the court must find at least a likelihood that the plaintiffs will be successful in their trademark infringement claim. Examining the factors relevant to a likelihood of confusion determination, the court found the plaintiff had demonstrated it was likely to prevail on the merits of its case and would be irreparably harmed absent an injunction. Therefore, the Delaware District Court issued a temporary restraining order in favour of AstraZeneca and prevented Dr Reddy's from selling its generic version of Nexium. After this order, Dr Reddy's has reportedly gone ahead and changed the colour of its generic tablets from purple to blue (Stanton, 2016).

In the case of Viagra, the special case of male erectile dysfunction tablets, which are blue in color proposed in the diamond shape and must be manufactured by Pfizer, many generic businesses were faced with claims from Pfizer and litigations initiated by the Tribunal of Delhi High Court. The generic makers were naming their products Penegra, Kamagra or Edagra, and they had also been using a blue colour which is a bad play on Viagra's blue tablet and packaging. Order of the Court Pfizer had initiated a passing off action for injunction and damages. Moreover, the basic contention of Pfizer that the consumers might buy generic products such that of Penegra in the market thinking it as the some sort of equivalent of the Viagra being manufactured by Pfizer in India, basically remained unassuaged with the IPAB. The court, in view of the fact that Pfizer did not have a trademark registration in

India for the word Viagra and that it was not marketing the product in India at the relevant time, held that a consumer would, therefore, perceive the term Vega as only an Indian equivalent of Viagra, and hence, there was no likelihood of confusion. The bench also observed that there was no misrepresentation on part of a chemist, who had described the medicine as the "desi version of Viagra", as what was sold was not Viagra but an Indian product of the same substance." The court consequently refused the application for interim injunction filed by Pfizer, holding that the balance of convenience was in the favour of the defendant. But it is also noteworthy that the court maintained that the defendants cannot use the blue color that Pfizer uses.

The trend of non-traditional marks as prime players in many litigations particularly in the pharmaceutical sector, with special reference to the United States, has also been well established from the case-law survey. Let us now discuss some of the cases where protection was somewhere granted and somewhere denied.

The respondents were making valentine's heart shaped Benzedrine and Dexedrine tablets in pinkish brown and orange colors respectively. With the patents on those products coming to an end, dozens of knockoffs have ensued, all bearing different brand names. A generic Dexedrine tablet of the same size, colour and shape as the respondent's Dexedrine tablet, manufactured by Ross Whitney Corp. was additionally labelled "Heart brand Dexedrine". SKF on the other hand brought an action against the respondents seeking two remedies, namely an injunction and damages, for infringement of their registered trade mark and for passing off. The court explained that in these circumstances, it is likely that consumers, regardless of the appellant's labeling, will confuse the two products .The appellants were, therefore, injuncted from manufacturing a tablet of any colour or shape or a tablet of any combination of colour and shape that resembled the tablet of the respondents. The Court of Appeal decided that dexedrine was a valid trade-mark and added that SKF had established that the unique dexedrine tablet shape and color had become distinctive of SKF due to secondary meaning (Ross Whitney Corp. v. SKF, 1953).

SK&F was manufacturing patented oral diuretic – Dyazide- in a maroon and white hard gelatin capsule. The same drug was sold in Europe under the trade name Irenor (Merck, Sharpe and Dohme) as an orange-colored tableted drug, purportedly for the treatment of menstrual disorders. Premo, another pharmaceutical company that produced generic versions, used similar maroon and white hard gelatin capsules for the same drug. In late 1987, SK&F filed a complaint alleging, among other things, unfair competition and trademark infringement and seeking a preliminary injunction. In that case, one of the central issues was the concern that the introduction of generically equivalent products would lead to "unscrupulous pharmacists dispensing cheaper generic preparations instead of Dyazide (produced by SK&F) while keeping the cost savings for themselves. In this case, the court held that the use of the maroon and white colors, which were used by SK&F, were non-functional.

The court found that SK&F's trade dress was "arbitrary, having nothing to do with the purpose or performance of the drug or with its processing". The court observed that there was no industry practice of identifying diuretic by colours or the capsule form and that the same identical diuretic preparation was launched in a orange tablet form which was a success. Finally, the court upheld the District Courts decision to issue a preliminary injunction that trade dress must be as dissimilar to the trade dress of the proprietary brand as possible (SK&F v. Premo, 1980).

We saw numerous cases above where courts had rejected protection for non-traditional features. The most famous example of this is the case of Where Eli Lilly was making chocolate flavoured and colored liquid quinine and called it Coco Quinine. When the petitioner started manufacturing the same preparation at a cheaper price with chocolate color and flavour under the name Quin-Coco, Eli Lilly filed a suit against the petition. Eli Lilly asserted that the petitioner was transgressing upon their agreed exclusive right to manufacture, market and sell the chocolate flavoured paste. The court said to the Petitioners, there is no objection to you making and selling the chocolate flavoured quinine mixture because chocolate was functional. Functional in that the use of chocolate lent the medicine a palatability that was challenging to replace (William R. Warner & Co. v. Eli Lilly & Co. 1924.)

In the company had sought trademark registration for orange flavour of its quick dissolving anti-depressant tablets. The Appellate Board rejected this application on three grounds. Firstly, since this was a pill that dissolved on a patient's tongue, there was a "practical need for the medicine to have a good taste" (which was stressed by applicant in its advertisements) and hence orange flavour was functional. Further, orange was a popular flavour and granting monopoly over the flavour would leave few popular alternatives for other anti-depressant medications. Secondly, the Appellate Board expressed doubts as to whether orange flavour could act as a mark, since most consumers would perceive orange flavour as a common product feature to hide any unpleasant taste of medicine. Finally, the Appellate Board raised the question of how trademarks could practically function as a trademark given that consumers had no way of perceiving it prior to purchase. Similarly, in the EU, Eli Lilly's application for taste mark for the artificial flavour of strawberries for a drug was rejected on grounds similar to those seen in N.V.Organon case ***(N V Organon*, 2000).**

All the data discussed in this section indicate that the pharmaceutical sector has not shied away from seeking protection for non-traditional features/ marks.

Protection for Unconventional Trademarks and Access to Medicine

The previous section illustrates the prevalence of non-traditional marks in the pharmaceutical sector. In that context, it would be pertinent to analyze some of the important consequences of affording protection to non-traditional trademarks, on access to medicine. I would like to highlight three of them.

Firstly, there would be an increase in transaction costs due to protection afforded to non-traditional marks. Empirical studies have shown that patients might be reluctant to take bioequivalent drugs, if the physical attributes of the branded drug and generic drug are different (Aaron S. Kesselheim et.al, 2012). Studies show that some patients may even discontinue their prescribed drug regimen, due to doubts over the efficacy of the drug. In this context, studies have suggested that doctors and pharmacists need to educate and reassure patients, while providing a different looking generic bioequivalent. As one can imagine, this would require substantial investments in terms of time. Some studies even point out that pharmacies may need to adapt existing information technology systems in order to provide updates to the consumers when such changes occur. With rising protection for non-traditional marks in the pharmaceutical sector, these transaction costs are bound to increase, thereby adversely affecting the budgets for access to medicine.

One can see the court making some interesting observations in this regard. This case was a passing off action relating to the black and green chlordiazepoxizide capsules (brand name Librium) manufactured by Hoffmann-La Roche. One of the arguments used by DDSA was that the consumers who were accustomed to the black and green capsules would have resisted the drug if the same drug had appeared subsequently in different colours. The court ultimately ruled against the defendant (Hoffmann-La Roche & Co. A.G. v. DDSA Pharmaceuticals Ltd., 1972).

This challenge of increased transaction costs was also highlighted in a recent interview conducted by us with a pharmacist in a leading hospital in India. According to the pharmacist, many hours are still being spent in offering explanations to convince patients to switch from a familiar tablet identifiable in a particular colour/ shape to a generic equivalent in a different colour/ shape. In this context, it needs to be asked whether the increased transaction costs by virtue of monopoly rights over colour/ shape are justifiable, particularly when viewed in the context of limited social benefits accrued by way of grant of monopoly rights over colour/ shape.

Secondly, it is important to note that protection of non-traditional marks may create additional barriers for entry of generic drugs. There are two important aspects to be considered in this regard. First, non-traditional marks may perpetuate the monopoly position enjoyed by the branded drugs. Second, non-traditional marks may further reinforce the myth that generics are of low quality.

Branded drugs often enjoy a monopoly position due to patent protection and they also undertake extensive advertising campaigns to market and promote the uniqueness of the drug during the patent term. Sometimes such campaigns can be so successful in capturing the imagination of the customer that it becomes difficult for generic companies to break into that market even after the expiry of the patent term, with a cheaper version of the drug. In such instances, the trademark is slowly metamorphosing into a "brand" (Bentley et al., 2010). While there is no general definition for the term 'brand', it's usually understood "to have a value which transcends the product (Brennan, 2015).

AstraZeneca's 'Nexium' is a classic example which can illustrate how a branded drug can maintain its hold over the market through the use of trade dress in spite of the presence of cheaper generics in the market. AstraZeneca had a patent over a new class of acid reflux medications which were known as proton-pump-inhibitors (PPIs). The particular drug omeprazole was sold under the brand name Prilosec in purple and gold trade dress and was heavily advertised with the popular sobriquet "the purple pill". This campaign ensured that the patients remembered the colour, even if they forgot the name of the drug (Fritch, 2007). Prilosec was a commercial success and when the patent on that drug was set to expire, AstraZeneca came out with a slightly modified version of omeprazole, known as esomeprazole, which was duly patented and marketed as Nexium. Though it had more or less the same effect as Prilosec, it was marketed as the "new purple pill" by giving it the same physical appearance as Prilosec. The fact that Nexium was able to hold on to its customer base even after the entry of generic manufacturers into the market at much lower prices illustrates the power of branding in this sector.

It is evident that if other branded pharmaceutical companies were to adopt similar practices, it could portend considerable difficulties to the generic manufacturers trying to break into the market. As pointed out by a commentator, such factors which inhibit the generic market come at a great cost to consumers and affect the efficient functioning of the healthcare market. Hence it is important that generic companies are allowed to copy the physical appearances such as colour, shape and size of the drug.

An additional point of concern is the fact that monopoly rights over physical attributes of branded drugs may perpetuate the myth of "low quality" generics". There are regulatory mechanisms in most jurisdictions to ensure that generic drugs are manufactured under safe conditions. Further, no studies have conclusively established that generics manufacture products of low quality. However, there is a perception among many patients that generics are not as effective as branded drugs. In order to understand the underlying reasons behind this, a survey was undertaken by a team of researchers in the US who used a random sample of commercially insured beneficiaries (Shrank et al., 2009). The survey found that over 70% broadly agreed that "generic drugs are a better value than branded drugs" and 56% agreed with the statement that "Americans should use more generic drugs". However only 37.6% agreed that they would take generics over branded drugs. More interesting was that over 42% disagreed with the statement that "Generics are safer than branded drugs". It was suggested that this may be due to the perceptions associated with the term "generic" itself, which connoted low quality, or the belief that more expensive products are more effective. A more serious aspect was that such perceptions about generics even led to non-adherence among those who could not afford branded drugs. When one views non-traditional marks in the pharmaceutical sector in the light of this evidence regarding the "low quality" generic myth, it becomes important that generics be allowed to adopt the external attributes of branded drugs.

If these aspects are not given due consideration, the barriers to entry for generics may only be perpetuated with harmful repercussions for public health.

Thirdly, it is important to note that many of these non-traditional marks may also be serving different functions. For example, a significant group to which a combination of colour and shape is compelling is children. Interviews with medical practitioners confirm that certain shapes/ colours/ flavours make medicines more palatable for children. In such cases, a finding of functionality would be necessary to prevent monopolization of those physical attributes by the manufacturers of branded drugs.

Further, there are also public health considerations which necessitate a finding of functionality. As briefly discussed earlier, empirical studies have indicated that changes in colour, size or shape can have negative results such as drug regimen non-adherence, patient confusion and prescription errors.

One of those studies, which focused on adults who were on anti-epileptic drugs, found that though "colour and shape discordances occurred infrequently, it was more common preceding cases of anti-epileptic drug non-persistence". This assumes significance when read in the light of previous research which has shown that non-adherence to treatment in epilepsy patients leads to "increased risk of seizure-related emergency and even mortality". Another study which focused on patients, who had been discharged after myocardial infarction, also came to similar conclusions with regard to non-persistence. As mentioned earlier, apart from drug non-adherence, it was also observed that changes in the appearances of medication can also cause patients to doubt the efficacy of their medication or lead to confusion that could contribute to prescription errors. This is a serious issue, particularly among groups such as the elderly and those with limited health literacy.

In this regard, it becomes necessary to also look at the link between physical attributes of a pharmaceutical drug and placebo effects. placebo effects are *"nonspecific psychological, or psycho physiological therapeutic effect produced by a placebo, or the effect of spontaneous improvement attributed to the placebo"*. Experiments conducted over time have indicated that there exists a relationship between the physical appearance of a branded tablet and the placebo effect to be garnered from it by patients. In particular, it showcases how the placebo effect from a tablet varies with the size, shape and colour of the tablet (Arthur Shapiro and Elaine Shapiro, 1999).

Patients react best when colour corresponds with the intended results of the medication.

Given the correlation between pill appearance and non-persistence in otherwise bioequivalent drugs, studies have recommended similarity in appearance between branded drugs and generic drugs. One study even proposed that FDA should require generic drug manufacturers to retain the physical attributes of branded drugs.

Courts have also recognized this important aspect in some of the cases. For example, in the, Shire, a branded manufacturer of Adderall (a prescription drug for the treatment of Attention Deficit Hyperactivity Disorder (ADHD)) had brought an action against Barr Laboratories, a generic producer, for copying the colours and shapes used by Shire to indicate dosage. In this case, the court noted that, Shire had failed to show that its product configuration was non-functional. Interestingly enough, one of the arguments raised by the generic companies with the help of an expert witness was that there was "clinical functionality" when a generic drug is physically similar to the branded drugs. The court, while accepting this argument, also recognized that such similarity "materially benefitted the patient population" and denied injunction to Shire (Shire v. Barr, 2003).

All the three aspects highlighted above demonstrate how protection afforded to non-traditional marks can pose non-traditional barriers to access to medicine/ health. Policymakers would need to take into account these public health aspects while framing recommendations with regard to non-traditional marks. Unfortunately, most of the international and national health policies have not yet given due consideration to these aspects.

CONCLUSION

I did not agree with a prior critical comment that countries ought to refuse to register and protect trademark rights in non-traditional marks whose own message was internal before being exploited as a trademark. Modification of non-conventional trademark laws will immunise freedom of expression non-IP claims, while also ensure that potential product & marketing segments continue to be unmappable by any established businesses to their detriment and future disruptors benefits. For brands not predisposed to such potentially expansive reforms to non-traditional trademark laws, it is important to remember that in our global, digital, and growing economy, brands must continue to be able to evolve through new means of expressing themselves and compete effectively from the advertising and sales of new goods or services that consumers want. The shape of their products or packaging, the colors in their stores or advertising may be adjusted by the companies. Perhaps they will decide they want to send a message or compel us using another sense than vision such as the scent, sound, taste or texture of their products or marketing. Our trademark laws should empower them to make this statement. Since companies can separate their products through words, logos and other "traditional" marks, presumably such will not reduce the quality of their products or that consumers will be unable to find the products they specific want if unable to register or protect these non-traditional trademarks as a trademark.

Seemingly unrelatedly, the conversations in this chapter clarify the fact that any policy or judicial decision on traditional mark should be not limited in trademark law, but indeed pay heed of global public health policy highlighted. We must avoid the temptation to expand the monopoly of a patented drug by never-ending trademark protection. As mentioned earlier, allowing the protection of non-traditional marks in the pharmaceutical industry could pose significant challenges to the availability of medicine as high transaction costs and generic competition hindrances. Also run through the packaging of pharmaceutical products a difficult task, since the product is usually functional due to its physical properties that determines the advance of a trademark: the degree of rotation of the area involved leads to one conclusion, the material strength of the damaged packaging to another! We have to rely heavily on traditional legal principles such as the rule of functionality in order to avoid erecting new barriers in front of patients trying to get to medicine. This chapter is analytical in nature and aims to address the criticism regarding why these marks should not be given trademark protection but it does not completely reject non-traditional trademarks.

REFERENCES

R120/2001-2, Eli Lilly & Company, Appeal Relating to Community Trade mark application no: 1452853. (2004).

Aaker, D. (2004). *Brand portfolio strategy* (1st ed.). Simon & Schuster.

Ahuja, V. K. (2010). Non-traditional trade marks: New dimension of trade marks law. *European Intellectual Property Review*, 32.

Ahuja, V. K. (2013). *Law relating to intellectual property rights* (2nd ed.). Lexis Nexis Butterworths.

AIPPI. (2014). *Report Q181*. AIPPI.

AstraZeneca v. DRL Civ No.15-988 SLR. p.13-14.

Bentley, L., & Davis, J., (Eds.). (2008). *Trademarks and brands: An interdisciplinary critique* (2nd ed.). Cambridge University Press. 10.1017/CBO9780511495212

Bently, L., & Sherman, B. (2009). *Intellectual property law* (3rd ed.). Oxford University Press.

Bereskin, D. R. (1993). A comparison of the trademark provisions of NAFTA and TRIPS. *Trademark Reporter, 1*.

Bereskin, D. R., & Sawchuk, A. (2003). Crocker revisited: The protection of trademarks of foreign nationals in the United States. *Trademark Reporter, 93*.

Bravo, G. (2001–2002). From Paris Convention to TRIPS: A brief history. *Journal of Contemporary Legal Issues, 12*.

Brennan, H. (2015). The cost of confusion: The paradox of trademarked pharmaceuticals. *SSRN*, 22(1), 14. 10.2139/ssrn.2690889

Brown, G. (1948). Advertising and the public interest: The legal protection of trade symbols. *The Yale Law Journal*, 57(7), 57. 10.2307/793310

Carter, S. (1990). The trouble with trademark. *The Yale Law Journal*, •••, 99.

Classen, C., Howes, D., & Synnott, A. (1994). *Aroma: The cultural history of smell* (1st ed.). Routledge.

Cornish, W., & Llewelyn, D. (2007). *Intellectual property: Patents, copyright, trade marks and allied rights* (6th ed.). Sweet & Maxwell.

Cornish, W., & Llewelyn, D. (2010). *Intellectual property: Patents, copyright, trademarks and allied rights* (7th ed.). Sweet & Maxwell Limited.

Cornish, W., Llewelyn, D., & Aplin, T. (2010). *Intellectual property, patents, copyrights, trademarks and allied rights* (7th ed.). Sweet & Maxwell.

Correa, C. M., & Yusuf, A. A. (Eds.). (2008). *Intellectual property and international trade: The TRIPS Agreement* (1st ed.). Kluwer Law International.

Cutter, B. (1990). The rational basics of trademark protection; Control of quality and dilution - estranged bedfellows? *Journal Marshall Law Review, 24.*

D. I. (2004). Smell, sound, colour and shape trade marks: An unhappy flirtation. *Journal of Business Laws, 12.*

Davis, J. (2008). *Intellectual Property Law* (3rd ed.). Oxford University Press.

Davis, J. (2010). Between a sign and a brand: Mapping the boundaries of a registered trademark in European Union trademark law. In Bentley, L., (Eds.), *Trademarks and Brands* (pp. 65–81).

Dinwoodie, G. B. (1999). The death of ontology: A teleological approach to trademark law. *Iowa Law Review*, 84.

Dinwoodie, G. B., & Dreyfuss, R. C. (2009–2010). Designing a global intellectual property system responsive to change: The WTO, WIPO and beyond. *Houston Law Review*, 46.

Drawnbaugh, K. (2001). *Brands in the balance: Meeting the challenges to commercial identity* (1st ed.). Reuters.

. Drescher, T. D. (1992). The transformation and evolution of trademarks: From signals to symbols to myth. *The Trademark Reporter, 301.*

Dutfield, G., & Suthersanes, U. (2008). *Global intellectual property law* (1st ed.). Edward Elgar Publishing Ltd.

. Elias, B. (1992). Do scents signify source? An argument against trademark protection for fragrances. *Trademark Reporter, 82.*

. Ellwood, L. A. (1956). The Industrial Property Convention and the "Telle Quelle" clause. *Trademark Reporter, 46.*

Epstein, M. E. (2008). *Intellectual property.* Wolters Kluwer Law & Business.

F.-K., & Reimer, A. (1955). Preparatory study for the establishment of a uniform international trademark definition. *Trademark Reporter, 5.*

Fritch, D. M. (2006-2007). Should the purple pill by any other drug company still be as purple? The changing face of trade dress protection for pharmaceutical manufacturers. *IDEA*, 47, 171–188.

Gallagher, T. A. (2015). Non traditional trademarks: Taste/Flavour. *Trademark Reporter*, 105, 806.

Gallagher, T. A. (2015). Non-traditional trademarks: Taste/flavour. *Trademark Reporter, 105.*

George. (2015, December 22). AstraZeneca v. Dr Reddy's - Colour as a pharmaceutical trade dress. *SPICY IP BLOG.*https://spicyip.com/2015/12/astrazeneca-v-dr-reddys-colour-as-a-pharmaceutical-trade-dress.html

Gilson, J., & LaLonde, A. G. (2005). Cinnamon buns, marching ducks and cherry-scented racecar exhaust: Protecting nontraditional trademarks. *Trademark Review, 95*(4).

Glaxo Wellcome UK Ltd & Anor v. Sandoz Ltd & Ors [2019] EWHC 2545 (Ch) (04 October 2019).

Gonzale, M. (2014). So let the paint be spread, we're painting the soles red. *Wake Forest Journal of Business and Intellectual Property Law, 52.*

Greene, J. A., & Kesselheim, A. S. (2011). Why do the same drugs look different? Pills, trade dress and public health. *The New England Journal of Medicine*, 365(1), 83–89. 10.1056/NEJMhle110172221732842

Grimes, C. W., & Battersby, G. J. (1979). The protection of merchandising properties. *Trademark Reporter, 69.*

Hoffmann-La Roche' & Co. A.G. v. DDSA Pharmaceuticals Ltd., [1972] RPC 1, 20.

Inwood Labs Inc. v. Ives Labs Inc., 456 U.S. 844 (1982).

Kerly. (2007). *Law of trademarks and trade names* (South Asian ed.). Sweet and Maxwell.

Kesselheim, A. S. (2012). Variations in pill appearance of antiepileptic drugs and the risk of nonadherence. *Archives of Internal Medicine*, 173(3), 1.23277164

Kesselheim, A. S., Bykov, K., Avorn, J., Tong, A., Doherty, M., & Choudhry, N. K. (2014). Burden of changes in pill appearance for patients receiving generic cardiovascular medications after myocardial infarction. *Annals of Internal Medicine*, 161(2), 96. 10.7326/M13-238125023248

Kitchin, D., & Llewelyn, D., (Eds.). (2005). *Kerly's law of trademarks and trade-names* (44th ed.). Sweet & Maxwell.

. Ladas, S. P. (1948). Trademark and foreign trade. *Trademark Reporter, 38.*

. Landes, W. M., & Posner, R. A. (1986). The economics of trademark law. *Trade-mark Reporter, 78.*

Lemley, M. A., & Volokh, E. (1998). Freedom of speech and injunctions in intellectual property cases. *Duke Law Journal*, 48.

Lindstrom, M. (2005). *Brand sense: Build powerful brands through touch, taste, smell, sight and sound* (1st ed.). Free Press.

Lukose, L. P. (2013). Consumer protection vis-a-vis trademark law. *Journal on Consumer Law and Practice*, 1(1).

MacQueen, H., Waelde, C., & Laurie, G. (2008). *Contemporary intellectual property, law and policy* (1st ed.). Oxford University Press.

Maniatis, S. (2006). *Trade marks in Europe: A practical jurisprudence* (1st ed.). Sweet & Maxwell.

Marsoof, A. (2012). TRIPS compatibility of Sri Lankan trademark law. *The Journal of World Intellectual Property*, 15(1), 15. 10.1111/j.1747-1796.2011.00430.x

McCarthy, J. T. (1998). *McCarthy on trademarks and unfair competition* (3rd ed.). Legal Solutions, Thomas Reuters.

Norwich Pharmacal co: v. Sterling Drug, Inc., 271 F.2d 569 (1959)

O'Reilly, V. (2004). The Community Trademark System: A brief introduction and overview. *Marquette Intellectual Property Law Journal, 8.*

Office of the Controller General of Patents, Designs and Trade Marks (India). (2007-2008). *Annual report.*

Pauwelyn, J. (2010). The dog that barked but didn't bite: 15 years of intellectual property disputes at the WTO. *Journal of International Dispute Settlement*, 1.

Pfizer. (n.d.). EUIPO Registration No: 001909472.

Pfizer Products Inc. v. B.L. and Company, [Case citation]. Indian Kanoon. (2002). https://indiankanoon.org/doc/145093/

Pires de Carvalho, N. (2006). *The TRIPS regime of trademarks and designs* (5th ed.). Kluwer Law International.

Praniskas, J. (1968). Trade name creation: Processes and patterns. *Journal of Economics*, 101.

Ramsey, L. P. (2010). Free speech and international obligations to protect trademarks. *The Yale Journal of International Law*, 35.

Ricketson, S. (2015). *The Paris Convention for the Protection of Industrial Property: A commentary* (1st ed.). Oxford University Press.

Ross Whitney Corp v. SKF, 207 F.2d 190 (9th Cir. 1953).

Schechter, F. (1927). The rational basis of trademark protection. *Harvard Law Review*, •••, 40.

Schecter, F. I. (1927). The rational basis of trademark protection. *Harvard Law Review*, •••, 40.

Seligsohn, E. (1973). Recent developments in the law of trademarks and unfair competition in Israel. *Trademark Reporter, 63.*

Shire v. Barr, 329 F.3d 348.

Shrank, W. H. (2009). Patients' perceptions of generic medicines. Health Affairs, 28 • Shapiro, A. K., & Shapiro, E. (1999). The placebo: Is it much ado about nothing? In Harrington, A. (Ed.), *The placebo effect* (pp. 12–30).

Singh, B. (2023). Blockchain technology in renovating healthcare: Legal and future perspectives. In Kaushik, K., Dahiya, S., Aggarwal, S., & Dwivedi, A. (Eds.), *Revolutionizing healthcare through artificial intelligence and internet of things applications* (pp. 177–186). IGI Global. 10.4018/978-1-6684-5422-0.ch012

Singh, B. (2024). Lensing legal dynamics for examining responsibility and deliberation of generative AI-tethered technological privacy concerns: Infringements and use of personal data by nefarious actors. In A. Ara & A. Ara (Eds.), *Exploring the ethical implications of generative AI* (pp. 146-167). IGI Global. 10.4018/979-8-3693-1565-1.ch009

Singh, B. (2024). Social cognition of incarcerated women and children: Addressing exposure to infectious diseases and legal outcomes. In Reddy, K. (Ed.), *Principles and clinical interventions in social cognition* (pp. 236–251). IGI Global. 10.4018/979-8-3693-1265-0.ch014

Singh, B. (2024). Evolutionary global neuroscience for cognition and brain health: Strengthening innovation in brain science. In Prabhakar, P. (Ed.), *Biomedical research developments for improved healthcare* (pp. 246–272). IGI Global. 10.4018/979-8-3693-1922-2.ch012

Singh, B., Dutta, P. K., & Kaunert, C. (2024). Replenish artificial intelligence in renewable energy for sustainable development: Lensing SDG 7 affordable and clean energy and SDG 13 climate actions with legal-financial advisory. In Derbali, A. (Ed.), *Social and ethical implications of AI in finance for sustainability* (pp. 198–227). IGI Global. 10.4018/979-8-3693-2881-1.ch009

Singh, B., Jain, V., Kaunert, C., Dutta, P. K., & Singh, G. (2024). Privacy matters: Espousing blockchain and artificial intelligence (AI) for consumer data protection on e-commerce platforms in ethical marketing. In Saluja, S., Nayyar, V., Rojhe, K., & Sharma, S. (Eds.), *Ethical marketing through data governance standards and effective technology* (pp. 167–184). IGI Global. 10.4018/979-8-3693-2215-4.ch015

Singh, B., & Kaunert, C. (2024). Computational thinking for innovative solutions and problem-solving techniques: Transforming conventional education to futuristic interdisciplinary higher education. In Fonkam, M., & Vajjhala, N. (Eds.), *Revolutionizing curricula through computational thinking, logic, and problem solving* (pp. 60–82). IGI Global. 10.4018/979-8-3693-1974-1.ch004

Singh, B., & Kaunert, C. (2024). Wind and solar energy as renewable energy for sustainable global future: Projecting future multi-sector sustainable policies and innovation. In Ara, A., & Thakore, R. (Eds.), *Promoting multi-sector sustainability with policy and innovation* (pp. 210–245). IGI Global. 10.4018/979-8-3693-2113-3.ch009

Singh, B., & Kaunert, C. (2024). Aroma of highly smart Internet of Medical Things (IoMT) and lightweight EdgeTrust expansion medical care facilities for electronic healthcare systems: Fortified-chain architecture for remote patient monitoring and privacy protection beyond imagination. In Hassan, A., Bhattacharya, P., Tikadar, S., Dutta, P., & Sagayam, M. (Eds.), *Lightweight digital trust architectures in the Internet of Medical Things (IoMT)* (pp. 196–212). IGI Global. 10.4018/979-8-3693-2109-6.ch011

Singh, B., & Kaunert, C. (2024). Augmented reality and virtual reality modules for mindfulness: Boosting emotional intelligence and mental wellness. In Hiran, K., Doshi, R., & Patel, M. (Eds.), *Applications of virtual and augmented reality for health and wellbeing* (pp. 111–128). IGI Global. 10.4018/979-8-3693-1123-3.ch007

Singh, B., & Kaunert, C. (2024). Salvaging responsible consumption and production of food in the hospitality industry: Harnessing machine learning and deep learning for zero food waste. In Singh, A., Tyagi, P., & Garg, A. (Eds.), *Sustainable disposal methods of food wastes in hospitality operations* (pp. 176–192). IGI Global. 10.4018/979-8-3693-2181-2.ch012

Singh, B., & Kaunert, C. (2024). Revealing green finance mobilization: Harnessing FinTech and blockchain innovations to surmount barriers and foster new investment avenues. In Jafar, S., Rodriguez, R., Kannan, H., Akhtar, S., & Plugmann, P. (Eds.), *Harnessing blockchain-digital twin fusion for sustainable investments* (pp. 265–286). IGI Global. 10.4018/979-8-3693-1878-2.ch011

Singh, B., & Kaunert, C. (2024). Harnessing sustainable agriculture through climate-smart technologies: Artificial intelligence for climate preservation and futuristic trends. In Kannan, H., Rodriguez, R., Paprika, Z., & Ade-Ibijola, A. (Eds.), *Exploring ethical dimensions of environmental sustainability and use of AI* (pp. 214–239). IGI Global. 10.4018/979-8-3693-0892-9.ch011

Singh, B., & Kaunert, C. (Eds.). (2024). *Reinventing artificial intelligence and blockchain for preserving medical data*. CRC Press. 10.1201/9781032648323-6

Singh, B., Vig, K., Dutta, P. K., & Kaunert, C. (2024). Unraveling agile transformation for customer satisfaction in changing market conditions: Roadmap for industry embracing change in project management. In Misra, S., Jadeja, R., & Mittal, M. (Eds.), *Practical approaches to agile project management* (pp. 305–321). IGI Global., 10.4018/979-8-3693-3318-1.ch017

SK&F v. Premo Pharm. Labs., Inc., 625 F.2d 1055 (3rd Cir. 1980).

Soldrzano, R. (1952). Registrations of foreign trade-marks in Mexico. *Trademark Review, 42*.

Stanton, D. (2016, January 6). AstraZeneca's purple Reign? Dr Reddy's relaunches Nexium generic in blue. *IN-PHARMA TECHNOLOGIST BLOG*.http://www.in-pharmatechnologist.com/Processing/AZ-retains-purple-reign-Dr-Reddy-s-relaunches-Nexium-generic-in-blue

Swann, J. B. (1986). The design of restaurant interiors – A new approach to aesthetic functionality. *Trademark Reporter, 76*.

Szalewski, J. (1998). The international protection of trademarks after the TRIPS Agreement. *Duke Journal of Comparative & International Law, 9*.

Torremans, P. (2008). *Holyoak & Torremans, Intellectual Property Law* (5th ed.). Oxford University Press.

U.N. Secretary-General's High-Level Panel on Access to Medicines. (2016). *Promoting innovation and access to health technologies*. Annex by Professor Ruth Okediji. High-Level Panel.

Vaver, D. (2005). Recent trends in European trademark law: Of shapes, senses and sensation. *The Trademark Reporter, 95*.

William R Warner & Co. v. Eli lilly & Co., 265 US 526 (1924).

Zelnick, A. (1977). Shake the lemon tree: Use and Paris Union Treaty. *Trademark Reporter, 67*.

Chapter 16
Implications of Compulsory License Under WTO TRIPS Regime

Saurabh Chandra
https://orcid.org/0000-0003-4172-9968
Bennett University, India

Suparna Kundu
https://orcid.org/0009-0000-5142-8945
Amity University, Kolkata, India

ABSTRACT

The beginning of humankind marks trade and exchange of goods and services across borders. In the earliest days, goods were exchanged for goods; this was termed as a barter system. With globalization and liberalisation of trade, goods and services travel across nations. In order to regulate these trading activities, a uniform set of rules and guidelines are required so as not to discriminate against nations and ensure peace and stability on a global level. The WTO which regulates these trading activities was formed so as to promote free and fair movement of trade, facilitate trade without discrimination, fair competition, etc. This chapter examines the utilization of compulsory licensing provisions within the TRIPS framework, focusing on India's experience and its implications for public health and intellectual property rights (IPR). Through a comprehensive analysis of legal frameworks, case studies, and policy implications, it elucidates India's approach to compulsory licensing, highlighting its role in enhancing access to essential medicines while balancing competing interests.

DOI: 10.4018/979-8-3693-5976-1.ch016

LITERATURE REVIEW

The WTO's amendment to the TRIPS agreement in 2005 allowed member states to use compulsory licensing to produce lower-cost generic pharmaceutical products for export to countries in need (Herget, 2006). However, the effectiveness of this mechanism has been questioned (Herget, 2006). The procedural requirements for issuing compulsory licenses under TRIPS are explored by Desai (2016), who emphasizes that they should be a rare event and not an instrument of industrial policy. Jain (2008) provides a comprehensive analysis of the provisions and standards for granting compulsory licenses under TRIPS, with a focus on the Indian intellectual property laws. Lidgard (2006) discusses the use of compulsory licensing in the developing world, particularly in response to the AIDS crisis, and the suppression of parallel trade in pharmaceuticals.

The TRIPS Agreement, a key component of the WTO, has significantly impacted India's patent regime, particularly in the pharmaceutical industry. Raju (2004) and Chaudhuri (2005) both highlight the challenges and implications of these changes, with Raju (2004) suggesting that the Indian patent regime is inadequate to meet TRIPS obligations. Nair (2008) further explores the impact of TRIPS on the pharmaceutical industry, emphasizing the need for amendments to the Patents Act. Lee (2008) discusses the legal implications of these changes, particularly in the context of a legal challenge by Novartis. These studies collectively underscore the complex and evolving nature of India's patent regime in response to TRIPS.

A range of studies have explored the concept and application of compulsory licensing in India. Chaudhry (2016) and Basheer (2005) both provide comprehensive overviews of the legal framework and historical context of compulsory licensing in the country. They highlight the balance it strikes between innovators' rights and public interest. Rathod (2017) and Kumutha (2023) focus on specific cases and the criteria for obtaining compulsory licenses, with Rathod noting the rejection of subsequent applications after the Natco/Sorafenib case. These studies collectively underscore the significance of compulsory licensing in India's patent system and its potential impact on public access to essential products.

Kumutha (2023) and Lamping (2023) provide a broader context, discussing the background criteria for compulsory licensing of patents in India and the European Union, respectively. These studies underscore the need for a balanced approach to compulsory licensing, which the Indian judiciary will likely play a crucial role in shaping.

The TRIPS agreement has had a significant impact on the Indian patent regime, particularly in the pharmaceutical industry. Malhotra (2010) notes the evolution of India's patent laws, while Chadha (2009) finds that the stricter patent regime has led to increased patenting activity in the pharmaceutical sector. However, Raju (2004) argues that the Indian patent system is still inadequate in meeting the challenges posed by TRIPS, and suggests improvements. Basheer (2009) highlights the controversy surrounding the 2005 amendment to the patent regime, particularly in relation to pharmaceutical product patents and parallel imports.

The implementation of TRIPS and the Indian Patent Act has been a contentious issue, particularly in the pharmaceutical sector. Unni (2019) highlights the increase in patent-related disputes, while Sampat (2015) argues that the timing of India's adoption of pharmaceutical patents is a more significant factor than Section 3(d) in understanding the current patenting landscape. These studies collectively underscore the complex and evolving nature of patent regulation in India, and the need for ongoing analysis and adaptation.

The introduction of the TRIPS Agreement and the subsequent amendments to the Indian Patent Act have had a significant impact on the pharmaceutical industry in India. Nair (2008) and Sato (2012) both note that the industry has continued to grow, despite concerns about the potential negative effects of the new patent regime. This growth is further supported by Chadha (2009), who found that the patenting activity of Indian pharmaceutical firms increased after the implementation of TRIPS. However, the industry has had to adapt to the new challenges, as highlighted by Rai (2008), with firms adopting a mix of competitive and collaborative strategies to maintain their competitiveness and profitability.

The Indian Patent Act has undergone significant changes in the last two decades to comply with TRIPS, leading to a surge in patent-related disputes, particularly in the pharmaceutical sector (Unni, 2019). The 1999 Patent Amendment Act introduced the "mailbox" facility and Exclusive Marketing Rights, which provided temporary protection for patents (Ganguli, 1999). However, the Act has been criticized for not effectively promoting R&D and controlling potential misuse of patent rights (Damodaran, 2008). The Indian pharmaceutical industry has responded to these changes by adopting competitive and collaborative strategies (Rai, 2008).

The Indian patent act has seen significant developments after 2020, with a focus on innovative activities and intellectual property rights. Yurchyshyn (2023) highlights the importance of research and development expenditures in driving patent activity, while Kumar (2023) emphasizes the need for increased awareness and use of intellectual property rights in India. Jumde (2020) discusses the evolution of the patent law regime in response to global influences, particularly in the context of access to medicines. These studies collectively underscore the dynamic nature of the Indian patent act and the ongoing efforts to align it with the country's socio-economic needs and global standards.

The Indian Patent Regime has seen significant developments from 2020 onwards, particularly in the pharmaceutical and medical research and development sectors (Mucke 2020). These changes are in line with the global trend of rapid evolution in intellectual property law, driven by technological advancements (Menell 2020). Notably, China has also made amendments to its Patent Law, indicating a broader trend of strengthening patent protection (Long 2021). In the context of India, these changes are crucial for balancing patent rights with access to medicine, a challenge that has been addressed through judicial decisions and the National IPR Policy (Nomani 2020).

The 20th anniversary of TRIPS has sparked a range of reflections and studies. Duffy (2021) and Davis-Berman (2012) both explore the impact of time on various aspects of life, with Duffy focusing on the evolution of tourist studies and Davis-Berman on the long-term effects of a wilderness therapy trip. Rodríguez (2012) delves into the motivations and behaviors of tourists visiting heritage cities, while Thill (2010) provides a critical review of the literature on multiple-trip journeys, emphasizing the need for a more comprehensive theoretical framework.

INTRODUCTION

In the recent years, there has been a norm for the policymakers to appreciate the "emerging global economy", however there always existed a global economy. With advancement of the technology and exchange of thoughts, ideas and expressions, the world is moving towards globalisation. The branch of commerce and trade is no exception in this regard. In earlier times, it was confined to the exchange of goods. However, with the changing times even services are traded, for instance, telecommunications, computer and information services; transport services; intellectual properties etc.

In order to govern and regulate trade between nations, a uniform set of rules and regulations were required. International Trade Law as a branch of law fills in that void by providing certain remedies to the nations of the world at large.

Since the establishment of the World Trading Organization (WTO) in the year 1995, it is the only organization which regulates global trade among the nations. In order to ensure this, the WTO has time and again formulated a number of agreements, which has been negotiated, signed and ratified by a bulk of nations. The aim of the WTO is to ensure the free flow of trade across nations. Further, the WTO also has a Dispute Resolution Body (DSB) which addresses and resolves the disputes of the trading nations. (Bunting, G. A. 1995)

Along with the regulation of exchange of goods and services internationally, the WTO also regulates and protects the Intellectual Properties through the WTO-TRIPS Agreement.

During 1980s, the newly industrialising nations in Asia and Latin America increased competitiveness for manufactured exports with some of the most economically developed industrialised countries, notably the USA and several EU members. Due to this increased competitiveness, attention has been drawn to these countries' internal policies that could unjustly or negatively impact American or European commercial interests. As evidenced by the extensive intellectual property provisions in both the Uruguay Round Final Act and the North American FTA, as well as the extremely comprehensive TRIPs Plus provision in more recent Preferential Trade Agreements, the issue of IP rights has thus become a prominent item on the trade agenda.(Trebilcock, M. J., 2005).

In the present times, the protection of these intellectual properties has emerged as a significant issue globally. Countries have taken a number of steps to address these issues and TRIPS Agreement attempted to establish a global structure for IP rights that would standardise the laws for all WTO members.

Even after the development of a standard set of agreement between the nations, the past few years have been a roller coaster ride, especially for the pharmaceutical sector. Pharmaceutical monopoly rights have often been shown to obstruct timely and appropriate access to life-saving medications, vaccines, and other medical technologies. These obstacles still make it difficult for medical professionals to address health issues including HIV/AIDS, TB, hepatitis C, and even the COVID-19 pandemic. It has been consistently debated that by using the flexibilities provided under the WTO-TRIPS Agreement, such as 'compulsory licensing', 'government use licenses' etc, these issues can be resolved. Especially during the peak of the COVID-19 disease, nations around the world urged that the WTO and its members should undertake further steps in order to put a halt on the applications and enforcements pertaining to relevant intellectual property so as to manufacturing and distribution of crucial COVID-19 medical technology. In this paper the researcher aims to discuss and elaborate the concept of Compulsory Licenses under the WTO TRIPS regime and its implications especially during the COVID times.

COMPULSORY LICENSE: CONCEPT AND OVERVIEW

A permit which is granted by the government allowing the importation and manufacturing of generic varieties of medical products which are patented, without the right holder's consent and approval is referred to as a 'Compulsory License'. This agreement authorises Compulsory License as part of its broader endeavour to achieve a balance between promoting research and development of novel drugs and improving access to currently available ones. The term Compulsory License is not mentioned under the TRIPS Agreement; rather the title only mentions about the right to use without the permission of the patent holder. Compulsory licensing is governed by Article 31 of the TRIPS Agreement, which outlines the conditions and procedures under which such licenses can be granted. According to Article 31, compulsory licenses can be issued for reasons of public interest, such as addressing anti-competitive practices, ensuring access to essential medicines, or addressing national emergencies. However, certain procedural safeguards must be adhered to, including attempts to negotiate with the patent holder in good faith and providing adequate remuneration.

The ***Doha Declaration*** reiterated that the member countries are free to undertake measures so as to protect the health of the community at large, while providing accessible & affordable medicines for all. The member states have the authority to enact measures like Compulsory Licensing and are allowed to choose the criteria for granting such licences. It further confirmed that the members are also permitted to avail the flexibilities that are listed under the Agreement. McGill, A. M. (2009).

Under the Agreement the countries can implement the measures in cases of "national emergencies, other circumstances of extreme urgency or in cases of public non-commercial use". However, it is noteworthy that the Agreement does not clarify as to what all situations or circumstances will be considered under these categories. Health problems including HIV/AIDS, TB, malaria, and other epidemics might be characterised as emergency situation of national importance and conditions of extreme urgency, according to the Doha Declaration. Before the Government organizations issue a Compulsory License, discussions for a voluntary license on fair circumstances may be attempted in some cases. However, for national crises, other situations of exceptional urgency, or non-commercial uses, no prior conversations or agreements with the patent owners are required.

The use of compulsory licensing can have significant economic implications for both patent holders and recipient countries. On the one hand, patent holders may experience reduced revenues and diminished incentives for innovation if their patents are subject to compulsory licensing. This could potentially deter investment in research and development, particularly in sectors where intellectual property protection is crucial for recouping investments.

On the other hand, compulsory licensing can promote competition and lower prices, particularly in sectors such as pharmaceuticals, where access to affordable medicines is a pressing concern. By allowing generic manufacturers to produce patented drugs at lower costs, compulsory licensing can enhance access to essential medicines, particularly in developing countries where affordability is a barrier to healthcare.

Compulsory licensing has profound implications for public health, particularly in the context of access to medicines. In countries facing health crises such as HIV/AIDS, tuberculosis, or COVID-19, compulsory licensing can be a vital tool for ensuring access to life-saving treatments at affordable prices. By circumventing patent barriers, compulsory licensing enables the production and distribution of generic versions of essential medicines, thereby saving lives and mitigating the burden of disease.

However, the use of compulsory licensing has also sparked controversies, particularly in the pharmaceutical industry. Patent holders often argue that compulsory licensing undermines the incentives for innovation by eroding intellectual property rights. Furthermore, concerns have been raised about the potential for abuse or misuse of compulsory licensing provisions, particularly in cases where commercial interests clash with public health imperatives.

Beyond its immediate economic and public health implications, compulsory licensing under the TRIPS regime has broader implications for global governance, development, and access to knowledge. The use of compulsory licensing reflects tensions between intellectual property rights and public policy objectives, highlighting the need to strike a balance between promoting innovation and ensuring access to essential goods and services, particularly in sectors critical to human welfare.

The concerns pertaining to the issuance of Compulsory Licenses has remained highly debatable over the years, especially during the COVID-19 years to enable the production of generic medicines and its supply.

COVID-19: IMPLICATIONS OF COMPLUSORY LICENSING

During the pandemic, there was a shortage of certain permitted medicines that were effective in treating COVID-19. There is no doubt that the Covid-19 pandemic was a national emergency as well as a matter of extreme urgency for the world at large. There have been certain instances wherein the Governments have issued Compulsory licenses in order to ensure the affordability and accessibility of medicines for the countries.

One such instance occurred in the latter half of 2020, when the Government of Hungary had issued a Compulsory License for remdesivir, quoting a recently passed law and thereby the Government asked the Hungarian business Richter to manufacture the medicines domestically and thus encourage local manufacturing.

The HIV medication lopinavir, which was being evaluated and repurposed for the treatment of COVID-19 at the time, was given a mandatory licence by Israel in March 2020. At that time, AbbVie was not able to supply enough lopinavir/ritonavir, following which the patents on lopinavir/ritonavir for all uses, including HIV and Covid-19, were deemed to be unenforceable worldwide (Kamin-Friedman, S., & Peled Raz, M. 2021).

In another instance, civil society groups requested the Russian government to grant a remdesivir compulsory licence in August 2020. Pharmasyntez, a Russian producer who had created a generic version of the medication, was denied a voluntary licence by the patent holder, Gilead Sciences. In conformity with the current bilateral voluntary licence agreements with 9 generic producers, Gilead prevented Russia from receiving remdesivir in a generic form. Finally, Pharmasyntez received what amounts to a compulsory licence in December 2020, allowing it to manufacture and distribute generic remdesivir to the people of the Russian Federation without Gilead's consent (Flynn, M. B., & Silva, E. O. 2021).

The aforementioned compulsory licences are still in place even though lopinavir/ritonavir and remdesivir were later determined by the WHO to be ineffective for COVID-19 (Bonadio, E., & Baldini, A. 2020).

LIMITATIONS OF COMPULSORY LICENSE

Countries have often adopted the issuance of Compulsory Licenses as a crucial public health precaution and safeguard. However, in order to overcome and tackle these Intellectual Property hurdles and barriers, particularly during a pandemic, nations also require a short-term waiver of the IP. The TRIPS Agreement's present regulations pertaining to the issuance of compulsory licensing were not framed to address several important issues brought on by a pandemic or a general emergency. Utilization of Compulsory Licenses to gain access to medications have been wrongly politicised and the fear of trade retaliation has discouraged countries from such usage.

As a result of pressure from pharmaceutical companies and business partners, the developing nations have always been discouraged from using Compulsory Licenses for accessing pharmaceuticals. This has also been a trend especially during the Covid-19 Pandemic. One example of this is the conflict of interest between Gilead and the Russian Government for issuing Compulsory Licenses. The fear of trade retaliations has time and again prevented Governments from using Compulsory Licenses. On one such instance, the Indian Government contended before the Apex Court that the use of Compulsory Licenses would have severe and significant negative impacts globally.

The procedural and substantive conditions for the usage of Compulsory Licenses can pose many limitations. The Agreement mandates a case and product based approach for the usage of Compulsory Licenses. Due to tedious pre-requisites including the usage of voluntary license on commercially reasonable terms in the first attempt (except in cases of emergency or urgent situations) results in time delays. Effective establishment of patent-free supply chains for products which have several components, such as the vaccines, might create a coordination crisis as it could be necessary to start and win compulsory licensing cases in multiple jurisdictions.

Compulsory Licenses only provide a remedy for the already existing patent barriers on certain medical items and not on the emerging and evolving patents. Due to the pandemic's changing needs, the Intellectual Property landscapes were constantly changing, making the usage of Compulsory Licenses worthless.

Further, Art. 31 of the TRIPS Agreement read as under:

"(f) ...authorized predominantly for the supply of the domestic market of the Member authorizing such use"

It can be inferred from the abovementioned provision that Compulsory Licenses can be used for the supply of national market predominantly and a justification is necessary regarding the quantity for export if the countries wish to export generic products under such license. In April 2021, Gilead filed a law suit before the Supreme Court of Russia contesting the Compulsory Licenses issued on remdesivir. As a part of humanitarian assistance, the Russian Government had issued Compulsory Licenses to aid and support India which faced a shortage of the drug during the peak of the COVID-19 cases. However, this could not be given effect to as under the national law of Russia, in compliance with Agreement, production of generic products under these licenses are predominantly meant for national use, limiting exports even for humanitarian aid (Erfani, P. 2021).

ANALYSIS OF THE TRIPS WAIVER: 12th MINISTERIAL CONFERENCE

In order to avoid applying and/or enforcing patents, protection of undisclosed information, & copyrights relating to medications, vaccines, diagnostics, and other COVID-19 related health technologies, nations like India and South Africa proposed for a TRIPS waiver during the COVID-19 pandemic. Under this, nations would not have been subjected to legal action for failing to properly implement the TRIPS Agreement in the event of the pandemic before the WTO dispute settlement body. Further, at the national level, it might have lessened the restrictions imposed by the present laws requiring compulsory permits and provide a rapid method for importing and exporting items made by generic companies. However, it would be desirable if such waiver does not go beyond its objective of eradicating the pandemic. On the other hand, even if the compulsory licensing permits the Governments to import and manufacture products of a generic version without the consent and approval right holder, the process of issuance of these licenses is time consuming (Peter, K. Y. 2024).

The 12th Ministerial Conference which took place this year, and the decision arrived at by the countries might have different consequences for the developing and developed countries, wherein the countries adopted a partial waiver of the provisions pertaining to Compulsory Licenses. The proposed complete waiver by countries like India and South Africa was not accepted completely; rather the countries adopted a partial waiver of Compulsory Licenses in the Conference. The decision arrived at by the member nations clarified that 'law' under Art. 31 shall include orders of the executive, emergency decrees, judicial or administrative orders and shall not only be limited to the legal provisions of compulsory licensing (Rutschman, A. S. (2023).

Also agreed upon was the fact that the developing nation Members did not have to demand that the intended user in their countries make an effort to procure, within the time period prescribed by Article 31 (b), a voluntary licence on reasonable commercial conditions. It was further agreed by the member nations that countries can waive the requirement of Art 31 which only authorised the use of Compulsory Licenses for the predominant use and supply for the domestic market. Further it also permitted the member nations to export any portion of the goods produced through global or regional joint programmes designed to guarantee qualified Members' equitable access to the COVID-19 vaccine. However, it also restricted the same by implementing a limitation that the countries shall prohibit 're-exportation' of the goods that have been produced and imported into their nations according to the permission set out in the 12th Ministerial Conference's Decision. On the other hand, Art. 31 *bis*, was intended to help African nations wherein they are not required to inform the WTO of usage if it was a part of an Regional Trade Agreement with the majority of its members being Least Developed Countries (LDCs).

Furthermore, the countries also agreed that the humanitarian and non-profit goals of particular programmes for distributing vaccinations to ensure that everyone has access to COVID-19 vaccines be taken into consideration when determining adequate remuneration under Article 31(h), which are carried out to support producers in eligible member countries to develop and provide these vaccinations for eligible members at affordable costs. It also advised countries to adopt the current best practises in situations of national catastrophes, pandemics, or comparable conditions when determining the appropriate compensation in these scenarios. On the other hand, under Art.31*bis* remunerations are required to be based on the authorization's economic worth to the importing member. Furthermore, the decision also prescribes a time limit of 5 years from the date of adoption with respect to its applicability, which may possibly be extended by the General Council after considering the "exceptional circumstances" of COVID-19. On the other hand, no such time period has been prescribed under the TRIPS Articles. It is noteworthy that with the exception of paragraph 3(b), which outlines the new waiver, paragraph 9 of the Decision specifically indicates that it does not affect any current flexibility under the TRIPS Agreement. This shows that neither Article 31(f), which continues to permit the non-predominant portion of goods manufactured under a compulsory licence to be exported, nor Article 31*bis*, which includes the initial exemptions issued under Article 31(f), are replaced by this Ministerial Conference. However, it is still unclear as to why countries adopted a third option through this decision of waiver instead of simplifying Art. 31*bis*.

TRIPS AND COMPULSORY LICENSES: THE INDIAN PERSPECTIVE

The principle of utilitarianism, which stands for the welfare of everyone, serves as the justification for the idea of compulsory licensing. The innovator and user, however, are put in a conflict of interest by this "benefit of all approach" theory. Numerous international commissions have focused on the inherent conflict between intellectual property protection and healthcare access. The UN Secretary-General's High-Level Panel on Access to Medicines, which was formed in 2016–18, recommended that developing and underdeveloped nations should enact and implement laws on compulsory licenses. The recommendations of the panel were:

"Governments should adopt and implement legislation that facilitates the issuance of compulsory licenses. Such legislation must be designed to effectuate quick, fair, predictable and implementable compulsory licenses for legitimate public health needs, and particularly with regards to essential medicines. The use of compulsory licensing must be based on the provisions found in the Doha Declaration and the grounds for the issuance of compulsory licenses left to the discretion of member governments."

The nations implemented procedures through local law to implement the concept of compulsory licensing based on these proposals. In this regard, India's Indian Patent Act, 1970, incorporated the idea of compulsory licensing. The Indian Patent Act of 1970 has provisions pertaining to compulsory licenses in Sections 82 to 94. The purpose of the legislation is to give monopolies to patent holders and, when required, to make inventions accessible to the general public. To ensure that new ideas are promoted and used as soon as feasible for commercial purposes in India, the main objective is to provide broad guidelines for how patents function.

The Controller of Patents is given discretionary power if an invention fails to meet a "reasonable requirement of the public," "is not available and reasonably affordable to the public," or "is not worked within territory of India," taking into account all other factors mentioned under Section 83 of the Indian Patent Act. If someone applies and expresses interest, the Controller may issue a compulsory licence; however, the licence will expire three years from the date of patent issuance. The existence of a monopoly that the legislature clearly intended to award for the first three years in order to recover the costs of research and development demonstrates the well-thought-out balance between the patentee's rights and the state's duty to provide access to affordable healthcare The statute does, however, allow the Central government to grant a compulsory licence by notice in cases when the three-year mandate does not need to be followed. Moreover, the Indian legislation expressly states that, under certain conditions, pharmaceutical items must have a mandatory licence. This encompasses pharmaceutical goods, which are defined as the "product", the "process," "diagnostic kits," and the "ingredients" required for their production. The objectives behind these provisions are in line with international norms and standards, which include safeguarding public health and human life while also encouraging innovation and advancements. Despite the existence of legal frameworks in theory, it is important to note that there are very few examples in which mandatory licenses have been given for the purpose of protecting public health. In the *Natco Pharma Ltd. vs. Bayer Corporation* case, the Controller General of Patents gave *Natco Pharma* an obligatory licence to market the anti-cancer medication in India (Raju, K. D. 2016).. The prices of this drug were too high and beyond the affordability of the Indian population. It was retireated by the Court that *"We must bear in mind that these proceedings are in public interest; they are neither against the inventor, nor in favour of the compulsory licensee."*

In many other instances compulsory licenses have been rejected by the Indian authorities which reflects a number of challenges for protection of public health and human lives (Ramanujam, P., & Goyal, Y. 2014).

CHALLENGES IN PUBLIC HEALTH AND IPR: INDIAN PERSPECTIVE

It is believed that compulsory licensing is one of the best instruments for balancing public health and innovation. It is one of the ways that countries, including India, have chosen to guarantee that ideas and technology are both safeguarded and used for the benefit of society at large. In order to control and regulate the national patent protection system, the Indian legislature passed the Compulsory Licensing provisions of the Indian Patent Act, 1970. It is notable, therefore, that these rules have been the subject of discussions and arguments and have a restricted reach. These frequently provide difficulties for the application of these rules, which leads to uncertainty in the governance and regulation.

a. It's frequently seen as a rejection of the patent holders' ownership rights. In accordance with the requirements, the Indian legislature has said nothing about what should happen when a patent is no longer justified for use. There remains an ambiguity in regard.
b. It is crucial to ascertain and assess whether the granting of compulsory licensing results in the denial of the patentee's constitutionally mandated fundamental rights. However, in the context of the Constitutional requirements, the granting of a compulsory licence should be seen as a lawful and acceptable limitation, resulting in a harmonious construction between the rights and the constraints.
c. Any interested party may submit an application for compulsory licensing, according to the Indian legal framework controlling the conditions of the programme. Nevertheless, the statute is unclear as to the "interests" of the applicant. This may cause the patent holder to experience emotional anguish and persecution, which would discourage new ideas and advancements.
d. Furthermore, the Indian laws do not provide any guidelines or provisions for the negotiation of the prices of compulsory licensing. It is left at the discretion of the Government to decide as to such matters and there is a lack of involvement of the patent holder in such decisions. This might further lead to discouragement of innovations and techniques. An innovation for the development and well being of others in any field requires a lot of time, effort, and capital. However, an absence of provisions relating to negotiation of prices may act as a demotivation for the inventors.

On the other hand, stringent laws for the sole protection of the inventors rights might also lead to challenges for the countries in accessing essential technologies and medications in the healthcare sector, thereby compromising public health at the cost of the inventors interests. The following are some of the challenges which are faced in instances of stringent IPR laws.

CHALLENGES TO ACCESS: IMPLICATIONS OF STRONG INTELLECTUAL PROPERTY PROTECTION

The strong protection of intellectual property rights (IPRs) often lead to certain issues and challenges, thereby creating barriers to access the essential innovations and developments in healthcare. These barriers are of various natures, some of them are listed below:

a. **Exorbitant Drug pricing:** The capacity of pharmaceutical corporations to establish exorbitant pricing for patented pharmaceuticals is one of the most obvious effects of robust intellectual property protection. Patients frequently cannot pay these costs, especially in low- and middle-income nations where healthcare resources are constrained. The unreasonably high cost of patented medications may force patients to experience financial hardship or even to forgo critical medical care.
b. **Monopolies and Market Exclusivity:** Patents provide inventors the only right to use their creations for a predetermined amount of time, which leads to the monopolization of certain markets. Due to this exclusivity, patent holders are able to retain their high pricing in the absence of generic competition. Therefore, even after the patent term expires, patients could not have access to less expensive generic versions of necessary pharmaceuticals, extending the time of high pricing.
c. **Delayed Market Entry of Generic Medicines:** Data exclusivity clauses and other regulatory obstacles may cause a delay in the release of generic medications into the market. For a set amount of time, data exclusivity gives cutting-edge pharmaceutical businesses the only access to the data produced by clinical trials. The lack of data during this time prevents generic producers from using it to get marketing approval, which delays the release of less expensive generic equivalents.
d. **Limited Availability in poorer Countries:** Certain technology and drugs may not be readily available in poorer nations due to strong intellectual property protection. Pharmaceutical corporations could overlook areas with lower purchasing power in favor of those where they can fetch higher prices. This restriction on availability may deny citizens in underdeveloped nations access to technology and treatments that might save lives.
e. **Barriers to Research and Development for Neglected diseases:** Because of their poor economic potential, diseases that predominantly afflict communities in low-resource settings-known as neglected diseases-may not get enough funding for research and development (R&D). Robust intellectual property protection may serve as a deterrent for pharmaceutical companies seeking to engage in

research and development of neglected diseases, hence aggravating the scarcity of medicines for these ailments.

f. **Difficulties with Healthcare Budgets and Systems:** Strong intellectual property rights can lead to high medicine prices, which can put a pressure on healthcare systems and budgets, especially in nations where healthcare is publicly supported. Governments may find it difficult to pay for expensive patented medications, which might force them to choose between offering other healthcare services and necessary treatments.
g. **Legal Expenses and Litigation:** For generic producers, pursuing legal challenges to patents may be expensive and time-consuming. Access to reasonably priced medications may be further restricted if generic businesses are discouraged from joining the market by the possibility of lawsuits from patent holders.
h. **Effect on Access to Diagnostic Tools and Medical Devices:** In addition to medicines, diagnostic tools and medical devices are also covered by intellectual property protection. Robust defence of these breakthroughs may result in exorbitant expenses and restricted availability of vital diagnostic tools and technology.

CONCLUSION

With the advent of globalisation and the advancement of technologies, a need was felt to ensure the protection of these intellectual properties, which led to the framing of the TRIPS Agreement. The concept of Compulsory Licenses is although not explicitly mentioned under the TRIPS Agreement; however, Article 31 permits the Governments to determine the grounds wherein it has the right to allow the manufacturing and import of generic goods without the patent holder's consent. The protection of IPR of the inventors are crucial to protect their rights and interests. However, at the same time, the protection of public health also holds a significant position worldwide. The protection of human lives is a primary responsibility of the States and to ensure this various legal provisions such as Compulsory Licensing have been introduced and adopted by the States. At the same time, these initiatives comes with its own lacunaes and problems which has been discussed in this paper. Addressing these issues especially within the legal frameworks, as well as ensuring proper implementation of these provisions is very essential.

The waiver of these TRIPS provisions was proposed so as to promote open sharing of essential health innovations for everyone, especially crucial health technologies, materials and goods during the COVID-19 pandemic in the countries that could not procure these goods due to trade barriers.

The world witnessed the Covid-19 pandemic and it made the nations around the world realize the importance of preservation and protection of public health. During the pandemic, countries such as South Africa and India filed petitions to the WTO and called for a waiver or suspension on the granting and enforcement of any patents and any other IP related COVID-19 drugs, vaccines and diagnosis for the duration of the pandemic. Companies such as Moderna came forward and declared to openly share its patents during the pandemic. However, even during this crucial period, the WTO Member States failed to reach a consensus to waive off the IP rights for vaccines and treatments (Spence, E. A. 2022).

The purpose of "compulsory licensing" is to strike a balance between "promoting access to existing pharmaceuticals and encouraging research and development of new drugs." The Covid-19 pandemic which affected the world at large was not only a national emergency, but also a global concern. In such scenarios, it becomes the need of the hour to waive of the Agreement so as to save human lives and handle the pandemic more efficiently. Although there are provisions mentioned wherein the free flow of goods and production of generic products can be done during emergencies, however, it often supports a few pharmaceutical companies and the process is quite time taking. In an emergency situation, quick measures are required to be undertaken; the temporary waiver of the TRIPS is the only way out.

In summary, robust protection of intellectual property rights can erect severe obstacles to access to advances in healthcare, even while these rights are crucial for stimulating innovation. In order to overcome these obstacles, it is important to strike a careful balance between encouraging innovation and guaranteeing that everyone, regardless of financial situation, has access to necessary therapies. It is crucial for policymakers, business partners, and civil society organizations to strike a balance when putting policies in place to lessen the negative effects of intellectual property restrictions on healthcare access.

FUTURE RESEARCH DIRECTIONS

In this section, we'll delve into potential future directions for research and policy development concerning compulsory licensing under the TRIPS agreement in the context of India's public health priorities.

1. **Impact Assessment and Case Studies:** Conducting comprehensive impact assessments and case studies can provide valuable insights into the effectiveness of compulsory licensing mechanisms in India. Future research could focus on analyzing the economic, public health, and legal implications of specific com-

pulsory licensing cases, identifying key success factors, challenges, and lessons learned.

2. **Strengthening Legal Frameworks:** As India continues to refine its legal framework for compulsory licensing, future directions may involve exploring ways to streamline procedures, enhance transparency, and ensure consistency in decision-making. This could include clarifying the criteria for granting compulsory licenses, improving mechanisms for patent examination and dispute resolution, and aligning domestic legislation with evolving international norms.
3. **Promoting Access to Essential Medicines:** Given India's pivotal role as a provider of affordable generic medicines, future directions could focus on strategies to further enhance access to essential medicines through compulsory licensing. This could involve identifying priority therapeutic areas, engaging with patent holders to negotiate voluntary licensing agreements, and fostering partnerships with domestic and international stakeholders to expand production and distribution capacities.
4. **Addressing Emerging Public Health Challenges:** With the emergence of new health threats such as antimicrobial resistance, neglected tropical diseases, and pandemic preparedness, future directions may involve exploring the potential role of compulsory licensing in addressing these challenges. This could include facilitating access to patented technologies for diagnostics, vaccines, and treatments, as well as promoting collaborative research and innovation to develop new health solutions.
5. **Advancing Global Health Diplomacy:** India's experience with compulsory licensing can inform broader debates on intellectual property rights, access to medicines, and public health governance at the global level. Future directions may involve engaging in constructive dialogue and advocacy efforts within international forum such as the WTO, World Health Organization (WHO), and World Intellectual Property Organization (WIPO) to promote policy coherence, equity, and solidarity in addressing global health challenges.
6. **Capacity Building and Knowledge Sharing:** To effectively leverage compulsory licensing as a tool for public health, future directions could focus on strengthening institutional capacities, fostering interdisciplinary collaboration, and promoting knowledge sharing among policymakers, healthcare professionals, researchers, and civil society organizations. This could involve developing training programs, conducting policy workshops, and establishing networks for exchanging best practices and expertise.

By pursuing these future directions, India can continue to harness the potential of compulsory licensing under the TRIPS agreement to safeguard public health, promote equitable access to medicines, and contribute to global efforts towards achieving health for all.

REFRENCES

Athreye, S. S., Piscitello, L., & Shadlen, K. C. (2020). Twenty-five years since TRIPS: Patent policy and international business. *Journal of International Business Policy*, 3(4), 315–328. 10.1057/s42214-020-00079-1

Basheer, S., & Kochupillai, M. (2005). The 'compulsory licence'regime in India: past, present and future. *Present and Future*.

Bonadio, E., & Baldini, A. (2020). COVID-19, patents and the never-ending tension between proprietary rights and the protection of public health. *European Journal of Risk Regulation*, 11(2), 390–395. 10.1017/err.2020.24

Bunting, G. A. (1995). GATT and the Evolution of the Global Trade System: A Historical Perspective. *John's J. Legal Comment.*, 11, 505.

Chaudhuri, S. B. (2005). *The WTO and India's Pharmaceuticals Industry: Patent Protection*. TRIPS, and Developing Countries.

Desai, M. (2016). Compulsory licensing: Procedural requirements under the TRIPS agreement. *Pharmaceuticals, policy and law, 18*, 31-44.

Duffy, M., Scarles, C., Edensor, T., Waitt, G., & Franklin, A. (2021). Twenty years on: Reflections on the journeys travelled and future directions for tourist studies. *Tourist Studies*, 21(1), 3–8. 10.1177/1468797621997636

Erfani, P., Binagwaho, A., Jalloh, M. J., Yunus, M., Farmer, P., & Kerry, V. (2021). Intellectual property waiver for covid-19 vaccines will advance global health equity. *bmj, 374.*

Flynn, M. B., & Silva, E. O. (2021). Framing access to medicines during COVID-19: A qualitative content analysis of Gilead's Remdesivir. *Global Public Health: An International Journal for Research, Policy and Practice*, 16(8-9), 1499–1511. 10.1080/17441692.2020.187149833460356

Herget, G. (2006). WTO approves TRIPS amendment on importing under compulsory licensing. *HIV/AIDS Policy & Law Review*, 11(1), 23–24.16805011

Jumde, A., & Kumar, N. (2020). *Access to Medicines in the Light of Patent Law Regime in India*. Intellectual Property Rights and the Protection of Traditional Knowledge. 10.4018/978-1-7998-1835-9.ch002

Kamiike, A., & Sato, T. (2011, August). The TRIPs agreement and pharmaceutical industry: The Indian experience. In *Proceedings of conference on Comparative Aspects on Culture and Religion: India, Russia, China,* (*Vol. 31*, p. 2011). SRC.

Kamin-Friedman, S., & Peled Raz, M. (2021). Lessons from Israel's COVID-19 green pass program. *Israel Journal of Health Policy Research*, 10(1), 1–6. 10.1186/s13584-021-00496-434715931

Kumutha, N., Amutha, N., & Venkatesh, G. S. (2022). Compulsory licensing of patents. *Pharmaceutical Patent Analyst*, 11(6), 225–231. 10.4155/ppa-2022-003936802922

Lamping, M., Batista, P. H., Correa, J. I., Hilty, R. M., Kim, D., Slowinski, P. R., & Steinhart, M. (2023). Revisiting the Framework for Compulsory Licensing of Patents in the European Union. SSRN *Electronic Journal*. 10.2139/ssrn.4381959

Long, C. (2021). China Amends The Patent Law: A Stronger Protection Is On The Way. *les Nouvelles-Journal of the Licensing Executives Society, 56*(1).

Malhotra, P. (2010). TRIPS and the Indian Patents Regime. In *Impact of TRIPS in India: An Access to Medicines Perspective* (pp. 80-110). London: Palgrave Macmillan UK.

McGill, A. M. (2009). Compulsory licensing of patented pharmaceuticals: Why a WTO administrative body should determine what constitutes a public health crisis under the Doha Declaration. *Wake Forest Intell. Prop. LJ*, 10, 69.

Menell, P. S., Lemley, M. A., & Merges, R. P. (2016). *Intellectual Property in the New Technological Age: 2019*. Social Science Research Network.

Mucke, H. A. (2020). Patent highlights February-March 2020. *Pharmaceutical Patent Analyst*, 9(4), 129–136. 10.4155/ppa-2020-001032815491

Nomani, M., Alhalboosi, A. K., & Rauf, M. (2020). Legal & Intellectual Property Dimension of Health & Access to Medicines in India. *Indian Journal of Forensic Medicine Toxicology*.

Peter, K. Y. (2024). The COVID-19 TRIPS Waiver and the WTO Ministerial Decision. In *Intellectual Property Rights in Times of Crisis* (pp. 1-25). Edward Elgar Publishing.

Raju, K. D. (2016). The first compulsory licencing case in India under the TRIPS agreement: An analysis of Bayer versus Natco Pharma Ltd. *Journal of Development Policy and Practice*, 1(1), 71–88. 10.1177/2455133315612321

Ramanujam, P., & Goyal, Y. (2014). One view of compulsory licensing: Comparative perspectives from India and Canada. *Marq. Intell. Prop. L. Rev.*, 18, 369.

Rathod, S. K. (2017). Compulsory licences on pharmaceutical patents in India: A short article. *Journal of Generic Medicines*, 13(3), 108–113. 10.1177/1741134317691804

Rutschman, A. S. (2022). Ministerial Decision on the Trips Agreement (WTO). *International Legal Materials*, 62(2), 289–294. 10.1017/ilm.2022.47

Rutschman, A. S. (2023). Ministerial Decision on the Trips Agreement (WTO). *International Legal Materials*, 62(2), 289–294. 10.1017/ilm.2022.47

Sood, M. (2013). Nato Pharma Ltd. v. Bayer Corporation and the Compulsory Licensing Regime in India. *Nujs L. Rev., 6*, 99.

Spence, E. A. (2022). Existing Patent Laws Promote Competition and Lower Drug Prices, but Is This Appropriate for COVID-19 MRNA Vaccines? *Cal. WL Rev.*, 59, 183.

Thambisetty, S., McMahon, A., McDonagh, L., Kang, H. Y., & Dutfield, G. (2022). The COVID-19 TRIPS Waiver Process in Critical Review: An Appraisal of the WTO DG Text (IP/C/W/688) and Recommendations for Minimum Modifications. SSRN *Electronic Journal*. 10.2139/ssrn.4124497

Trebilcock, M. J., & Howse, R. (2005). *The regulation of international trade*.

Unni, V. (2019). India's TRIPS-Compliant Patent Decade – The Tumultuous Journey in Search of a Pragmatic Equilibrium. *IIC - International Review of Intellectual Property and Competition Law, 50*, 161-195.

Unni, V. (2019). India's TRIPS-Compliant Patent Decade – The Tumultuous Journey in Search of a Pragmatic Equilibrium. *IIC - International Review of Intellectual Property and Competition Law, 50*, 161-195.

Yurchyshyn, O., & Voitko, S. (2023). Development Of Innovative Activities In The 21st Century In Section Of Patent Activity And R&D Expenditures. *Intellect XXI*.

Zagashvili, V. S. (2023). Contradictions and Conflicts in the Multilateral Trading System. *Mirovaia Ekonomika i Mezhdunarodnye Otnosheniia*, 67(9), 5–14. 10.20542/0131-2227-2023-67-9-5-14

Compilation of References

. Ansari, A. I., & Singh, A. (2024). Growth and Opportunity of Medical Tourism in the Indian Healthcare Sector: A Critical Review. *Impact of AI and Robotics on the Medical Tourism Industry*, 290-301.

. Chen, C. P., & Zhang, C. Y. (2014). Data-intensive applications, challenges, techniques and technologies: A survey on Big Data. *Information sciences, 275*, 314-347. Mayer-Schönberger, V., & Cukier, K. (2013). *Big data: A revolution that will transform how we live, work, and think.* Houghton Mifflin Harcourt.

. Daniel, S., & Stephen, M. (2024). *Transforming Healthcare Delivery: The Role of AI in Telehealth Services.*

. Dratler J. Licensing of intellectual property. Law Journal Press; 2023 Dec 28.

. Drescher, T. D. (1992). The transformation and evolution of trademarks: From signals to symbols to myth. *The Trademark Reporter, 301.*

. Elias, B. (1992). Do scents signify source? An argument against trademark protection for fragrances. *Trademark Reporter, 82.*

. Ellwood, L. A. (1956). The Industrial Property Convention and the "Telle Quelle" clause. *Trademark Reporter, 46.*

. Gerke S, Minssen T & Cohen G (2020). Ethical and legal challenges of artificial intelligence-driven healthcare. *Artificial Intelligence in Healthcare*. Academic Press. .10.1016/B978-0-12-818438-7.00012-5

. Jimma, B. L. (March 2003). Artifical Intelligence in the Health Care: A Bibliometic Analysis. *Telematics and Informatics Reports, 4.*

. Ladas, S. P. (1948). Trademark and foreign trade. *Trademark Reporter, 38.*

. Landes, W. M., & Posner, R. A. (1986). The economics of trademark law. *Trademark Reporter, 78.*

. Liu, H., & Lang, B. (2019). Machine learning and deep learning methods for intrusion detection systems: A survey. *Applied Sciences, 9*(20), 4396.

. Luo, J., Wu, M., Gopukumar, D., & Zhao, Y. (2016). Big data application in biomedical research and health care: a literature review. *Biomedical informatics insights, 8*, BII-S31559.

. Marjani, M., Nasaruddin, F., Gani, A., Karim, A., Hashem, I. A. T., Siddiqa, A., & Yaqoob, I. (2017). Big IoT data analytics: architecture, opportunities, and open research challenges. *ieee access, 5*, 5247-5261.

. Reddy, B. M. (2023). Amalgamation of Internet of Things and Machine Learning for Smart Healthcare Applications–A Review. *Int. J Comp. Eng. Sci. Res, 5*, 08-36.

. Singh, B., & Kaunert, C. (2024). Future of Digital Marketing: Hyper-Personalized Customer Dynamic Experience with AI-Based Predictive Models. *Revolutionizing the AI-Digital Landscape: A Guide to Sustainable Emerging Technologies for Marketing Professionals*, 189.

.Kaledio, P., Doris, L., & Olaoye, F. (2024). *Optimizing Hospital Workflows with AI and Robotics.*

't Hoen, E. (2002). Number 1 Article 6 4-1-2002 From Seattle to Doha. *Chicago Journal of International Law Chicago Journal of International Law*, *3*(1), 27-29. https://chicagounbound.uchicago.edu/cgi/viewcontent.cgi?article=1171&context=cjil

Aaker, D. (2004). *Brand portfolio strategy* (1st ed.). Simon & Schuster.

Abbott, F. M. (2020). The TRIPs agreement article 73 security exceptions and the COVID-19 pandemic. *Research Paper, 116*, 20-16.

Abbott, F. M. (2011). *The Doha Declaration on the TRIPS Agreement and Public Health and the Contradictory Trend in Bilateral and Regional Free Trade Agreements.* SSRN. https://papers.ssrn.com/sol3/papers.cfm?abstract_id=1977300

Abbott, F. M., & Reichman, J. H. (2020). Facilitating access to Cross-border supplies of patented pharmaceuticals: The case of the COVID-19 pandemic. *Journal of International Economic Law*, 23(3), 535–561. 10.1093/jiel/jgaa022

Abebe, E., Seid, A., Gedefaw, G., Haile, Z. T., & Ice, G. (2019). Association between antenatal care follow-up and institutional delivery service utilization: Analysis of 2016 Ethiopia demographic and health survey. *BMC Public Health*, 19(1), 1472. 10.1186/s12889-019-7854-231699062

Abigail Swamidoss, S. K., Alghamdi, B., Hickman, R. L., Knighton, S., Pekarek, M., & Drummond, C. K. (2021, April). Medication Management System Design for Isolated Patient Care. In *Frontiers in Biomedical Devices* (*Vol. 84812*, p. V001T06A001). American Society of Mechanical Engineers. 10.1115/DMD2021-1036

Abomhara, M., & Køien, G. (2015). Cyber Security and the Internet of Things: Vulnerabilities, Threats, Intruders and Attacks. *Journal of Cybersecurity*, 65–88.

Abou Naja Intellectual Property. (2024). *7 Reasons Why Trademarks are Important for Startups*. Abounaja.com. https://abounaja.com/blogs/7-reasons-why-trademarks -are-important#:~:text=Trademarks%20also%20provide%20legal%20protection

Acar, A. Z., & Acar, P. (2012). The Effects of Organizational Culture and Innovativeness on Business Performance in Healthcare Industry. *Procedia: Social and Behavioral Sciences*, 58, 683–692. 10.1016/j.sbspro.2012.09.1046

Agaku, I. T., Adisa, A. O., Ayo-Yusuf, O. A., & Connolly, G. N. (2014). Concern about security and privacy, and perceived control over collection and use of health information are related to withholding of health information from healthcare providers. *Journal of the American Medical Informatics Association : JAMIA*, 21(2), 374–378. 10.1136/amiajnl-2013-00207923975624

Agaton, C. B., & Guila, P. M. C. (2024). Success Factors and Challenges: Implications of Real Options Valuation of Constructed Wetlands as Nature-Based Solutions for Wastewater Treatment. *Resources*, 13(1), 11. 10.3390/resources1301001138187013

Aghabiglou, A., Chu, C. S., Dabbech, A., & Wiaux, Y. (2024). The R2D2 deep neural network series paradigm for fast precision imaging in radio astronomy. *arXiv preprint arXiv:2403.05452*.

Agreement on the Trade Related Aspects of Intellectual Property Rights, 1994, Art. 27.

Ahmed, S. F., Islam, N., Tasannum, N., Mehjabin, A., Momtahin, A., Chowdhury, A. A., Almomani, F., & Mofijur, M. (2024). Microplastic removal and management strategies for wastewater treatment plants. *Chemosphere*, 347, 140648. 10.1016/j.chemosphere.2023.14064837952815

Ahmed, S. T., & Kadhem, S. M. (2021). Using Machine Learning via Deep Learning Algorithms to Diagnose the Lung Disease Based on Chest Imaging: A Survey. *International Journal of Interactive Mobile Technologies*, 15(16).

Ahmed, Y. A. E., Yue, B., Gu, Z., & Yang, J. (2023). An overview: Big data analysis by deep learning and image processing. *International Journal of Quantum Information*, 21(7), 2340009. 10.1142/S0219749923400099

Ahuja, V. K. (2010). Non-traditional trade marks: New dimension of trade marks law. *European Intellectual Property Review*, 32.

Ahuja, V. K. (2013). *Law relating to intellectual property rights* (2nd ed.). Lexis Nexis Butterworths.

Aiken, L. H., Sermeus, W., den Heede, K. V., Sloane, D. M., Busse, R., McKee, M., Bruyneel, L., Rafferty, A. M., Griffiths, P., Moreno-Casbas, M. T., Tishelman, C., Scott, A., Brzostek, T., Kinnunen, J., Schwendimann, R., Heinen, M., Zikos, D., Sjetne, I. S., Smith, H. L., & Kutney-Lee, A. (2012). Patient safety, satisfaction, and quality of hospital care: Cross sectional surveys of nurses and patients in 12 countries in Europe and the United States. *BMJ (Clinical Research Ed.)*, 344(mar20 2), e1717. 10.1136/bmj.e171722434089

AIPPI. (2014). *Report Q181*. AIPPI.

Aivalli, P. K., Elias, M. A., Pati, M. K., Bhanuprakash, S., Munegowda, C., Shroff, Z. C., & Srinivas, P. N. (2018). Perceptions of the quality of generic medicines: Implications for trust in public services within the local health system in Tumkur, India. *BMJ Global Health*, 2(Suppl 3), e000644. 10.1136/bmjgh-2017-00064429531844

Akhavan, P., Azizi, N., Akhtari, S., Haass, O., Jan, T., & Sajeev, S. (2023). Understanding critical success factors for implementing medical tourism in a multi-case analysis. *Knowledge Management & E-Learning*, 15(1), 43.

Al Kuwaiti, A., Nazer, K., Al-Reedy, A., Al-Shehri, S., Al-Muhanna, A., Subbarayalu, A. V., Al Muhanna, D., & Al-Muhanna, F. A. (2023). A Review of the Role of Artificial Intelligence in Healthcare. *Journal of Personalized Medicine*, 13(6), 951. 10.3390/jpm1306095137373940

AlAhmad, Y., Haggeer, D., Alsayed, A., Haik, M., AbuAfifeh, L., Aljaber, M., Mohamed, A., Balideh, M., Almutawa, N., & Mahmoud, M. (2021). The effect of telemedicine on patients' compliance in family medicine follow-ups in Qatar. *Avicenna (Doha)*. 10.5339/avi.2022.3

Al-Dahidi, S., Alrbai, M., Al-Ghussain, L., Alahmer, A., & Hayajneh, H. S. (2024). Data-driven analysis and prediction of wastewater treatment plant performance: Insights and forecasting for sustainable operations. *Bioresource Technology*, 391, 129937. 10.1016/j.biortech.2023.129937

Alenoghena, C. O., Onumanyi, A. J., Ohize, H. O., Adejo, A. O., Oligbi, M., Ali, S. I., & Okoh, S. A. (2022). eHealth: A survey of architectures, developments in mHealth, security concerns, and solutions. *International Journal of Environmental Research and Public Health*, 19(20), 13071. 10.3390/ijerph19201307136293656

Alessandrini, E., Gonakova, M., Batchelor, H., Gizurarson, S., Iurian, S., Klein, S., Schaufelberger, D., Turner, R., Walsh, J., & Tuleu, C. (2023). Colour of Medicines and Children's Acceptability? A Systematic Literature Review of Children's Perceptions about Colours of Oral Dosage Forms. *Pharmaceutics*, 15(7), 1992. 10.3390/pharmaceutics15071992 37514178

Alharam, A. K., & Elmedany, W. (2017). The Effects of Cyber-Security on Healthcare Industry. *2017 9th IEEE-GCC Conference and Exhibition (GCCCE)*, (pp. 1–9). IEEE. 10.1109/IEEEGCC.2017.8448206

Al-Jaroodi, J., Mohamed, N., & Abukhousa, E. (2020). Health 4.0: On the way to realizing the healthcare of the future. *IEEE Access : Practical Innovations, Open Solutions*, 8, 211189–211210. 10.1109/ACCESS.2020.303885834976565

Al-Jarrah, O. Y., Yoo, P. D., Muhaidat, S., Karagiannidis, G. K., & Taha, K. (2015). Efficient machine learning for big data: A review. *Big Data Research*, 2(3), 87–93. 10.1016/j.bdr.2015.04.001

Alowais, S. A., Alghamdi, S. S., Alsuhebany, N., Alqahtani, T., Alshaya, A. I., Almohareb, S. N., Aldairem, A., Alrashed, M., Bin Saleh, K., Badreldin, H. A., Al Yami, M. S., Al Harbi, S., & Albekairy, A. M. (2023). Revolutionizing healthcare: The role of artificial intelligence in clinical practice. *BMC Medical Education*, 23(1), 689. 10.1186/s12909-023-04698-z37740191

Alpay, L. L., Henkemans, O. B., Otten, W., Rövekamp, T. A., & Dumay, A. C. (2010). E-health applications and services for patient empowerment: Directions for best practices in The Netherlands. *Telemedicine Journal and e-Health*, 16(7), 787–791. 10.1089/tmj.2009.015620815745

Al-Shorbaji, N., & Al-Shorbaji, N. (2021). Improving healthcare access through digital health: the use of information and communication technologies. *Healthcare Access, 10.*

Alsubai, S., Dutta, A. K., Alkhayyat, A. H., Jaber, M. M., Abbas, A. H., & Kumar, A. (2023). Hybrid deep learning with improved Salp swarm optimization based multi-class grape disease classification model. *Computers & Electrical Engineering*, 108, 108733. 10.1016/j.compeleceng.2023.108733

Amjad, A., Kordel, P., & Fernandes, G. (2023). A review on innovation in healthcare sector (telehealth) through artificial intelligence. *Sustainability (Basel)*, 15(8), 6655. 10.3390/su15086655

Anand, E., Singh, J., & Unisa, S. (2015). Menstrual hygiene practices and its association with reproductive tract infections and abnormal vaginal discharge among women in India. *Sexual & Reproductive Healthcare : Official Journal of the Swedish Association of Midwives*, 6(4), 249–254. 10.1016/j.srhc.2015.06.00126614609

Anastasiadou, M. N., Isaia, P., Kolios, P., & Charalambous, C. (2023). Transitioning towards fit-for-purpose Public Health Surveillance Systems. arXiv preprint arXiv:2305.16821.

Anbesu, E. W., & Asgedom, D. K. (2023). Menstrual hygiene practice and associated factors among adolescent girls in sub-Saharan Africa: A systematic review and meta-analysis. *BMC Public Health*, 23(1), 33. 10.1186/s12889-022-14942-836604734

Angst, C. M., Block, E. S., D'Arcy, J., & Kelley, K. (2017). When Do IT Security Investments Matter? Accounting for the Influence of Institutional Factors in the Context of Healthcare Data Breaches. *Management Information Systems Quarterly*, 41(3), 893–916. 10.25300/MISQ/2017/41.3.10

Aniebue, U., Aniebue, P., & Nwankwo, T. (2010). The impact of pre-menarcheal training on menstrual practices and hygiene of Nigerian school girls. *The Pan African Medical Journal*, 2(1), 1–9. 10.4314/pamj.v2i1.5170821532905

Annoni, A., Nativi, S., Çöltekin, A., Desha, C., Eremchenko, E., Gevaert, C. M., Giuliani, G., Chen, M., Perez-Mora, L., Strobl, J., & Tumampos, S. (2023). Digital earth: Yesterday, today, and tomorrow. *International Journal of Digital Earth*, 16(1), 1022–1072. 10.1080/17538947.2023.2187467

Anshari, M., Almunawar, M. N., Younis, M. Z., & Kisa, A. (2021). Modeling users' empowerment in e-health systems. *Sustainability (Basel)*, 13(23), 12993. 10.3390/su132312993

Anwar, M. M., El-Haggar, R. S., & Zaghary, W. A. (2015). Salmeterol Xinafoate. *Profiles of Drug Substances, Excipients, and Related Methodology*, 40, 321–369. 10.1016/bs.podrm.2015.02.00226051688

Argaw, S. T., Troncoso-Pastoriza, J. R., Lacey, D., Florin, M.-V., Calcavecchia, F., Anderson, D., Burleson, W., Vogel, J.-M., O'Leary, C., Eshaya-Chauvin, B., & Flahault, A. (2020). Cybersecurity of Hospitals: Discussing the challenges and working towards mitigating the risks. *BMC Medical Informatics and Decision Making*, 20(1), 146. 10.1186/s12911-020-01161-732620167

Ariffin, N. A., Yunus, A. M., & Kadir, I. K. (2021). The role of big data in the healthcare industry. *Journal of Islamic*, 6(36), 235–245.

Arokiasamy P. & Pradhan J. (2014). Maternal health care in India: access and demand determinants. Prim Health Care Maternal Survival steering group. Maternal Mortality: Who, When, Where, and Why? *Maternal Survival. Lancet Mater Surv Series.*

Arti & Mittal J.K. (2020). Indian *Journal of Public Health Research & Development*, *2*(11). _https://doi.org/10.37506/ijphrd.v11i1

Arun, A. (2023). MedSync-App and Device to Promote Medication Adherence. [JIEEE]. *Journal of Informatics Electrical and Electronics Engineering*, 4(2), 1–8. 10.54060/jieee.2023.103

Aslam, F. (2023). The impact of artificial intelligence on chatbot technology: A study on the current advancements and leading innovations. *European Journal of Technology*, 7(3), 62–72. 10.47672/ejt.1561

AstraZeneca v. DRL Civ No.15-988 SLR. p.13-14.

Athreye, S. S., Piscitello, L., & Shadlen, K. C. (2020). Twenty-five years since TRIPS: Patent policy and international business. *Journal of International Business Policy*, 3(4), 315–328. 10.1057/s42214-020-00079-1

Attaran, A. (2001). Do Patents for Antiretroviral Drugs Constrain Access to AIDS Treatment in Africa? *Journal of the American Medical Association*, 286(15), 1886. 10.1001/jama.286.15.188611597292

Avci, O., Abdeljaber, O., Kiranyaz, S., Hussein, M., Gabbouj, M., & Inman, D. J. (2021). A review of vibration-based damage detection in civil structures: From traditional methods to Machine Learning and Deep Learning applications. *Mechanical Systems and Signal Processing*, 147, 107077. 10.1016/j.ymssp.2020.107077

Azaria, A., Ekblaw, A., Vieira, T., & Lippman, A. (2016). MedRec: Using Blockchain for Medical Data Access and Permission Management. *2016 2nd International Conference on Open and Big Data (OBD)*, (pp. 25–30). IEEE. 10.1109/OBD.2016.11

Babatunde, S. O., Odejide, O. A., Edunjobi, T. E., & Ogundipe, D. O. (2024). The role of AI in marketing personalization: A theoretical exploration of consumer engagement strategies. *International Journal of Management & Entrepreneurship Research*, 6(3), 936–949. 10.51594/ijmer.v6i3.964

Babbar, K., Martin, J., Ruiz, J., Parray, A. A., & Sommer, M. (2022). Menstrual health is a public health and human rights issue. *The Lancet. Public Health*, 7(1), e10–e11. 10.1016/S2468-2667(21)00212-734717798

Bahri, S., Zoghlami, N., Abed, M., & Tavares, J. M. R. (2018). Big data for healthcare: A survey. *IEEE Access : Practical Innovations, Open Solutions*, 7, 7397–7408. 10.1109/ACCESS.2018.2889180

Baisley, K., Changalucha, J., Weiss, H. A., Mugeye, K., Everett, D., Hambleton, I., Hay, P., Ross, D., Tanton, C., Chirwa, T., Hayes, R., & Watson-Jones, D. (2009). Bacterial vaginosis in female facility workers in north-western Tanzania: Prevalence and risk factors. *Sexually Transmitted Infections*, 85(5), 370–375. 10.1136/sti.2008.03554319473997

Balhasan, A., Dhillon, P., & Mohanty Sanjay, K. (2020). Inequalities in the utilization of maternal health care in the pre- and post-National Health Mission periods in India. *Journal of Biosocial Science*, 52(2), 198–216. 10.1017/S002193201900038531232249

Ballard-Reisch, D. S. (1990). A model of participative decision making for Physician-Patient interaction. *Health Communication*, 2(2), 91–104. 10.1207/s15327027hc0202_3

Banerjee, D. (2023). *Ethical Dilemmas and Legal Questions Involved in Use of AI in Surgeries: Discrepancies in Indian Medical Jurisprudence*.

Bangash, H., & Kullo, I. J. (2020, December 29). Implementation Science to Increase Adoption of Genomic Medicine: An Urgent Need. *Journal of Personalized Medicine*, 11(1), 19. 10.3390/jpm1101001933383675

Bansal, G., Zahedi, F., & Gefen, D. (2010). The impact of personal dispositions on information sensitivity, privacy concern and trust in disclosing health information online. *Decision Support Systems*, 49(2), 138–150. 10.1016/j.dss.2010.01.010

Bao, Y., Tang, Z., Li, H., & Zhang, Y. (2019). Computer vision and deep learning–based data anomaly detection method for structural health monitoring. *Structural Health Monitoring*, 18(2), 401–421. 10.1177/1475921718757405

Baran, Z., & Karaca, Ş. (2023). Next-Generation Technologies in Health Tourism. In *Global perspectives on the opportunities and future directions of health tourism* (pp. 138–164). IGI Global. 10.4018/978-1-6684-6692-6.ch006

Barbosa, I., Roberta, C., Silva, W. B. M., Cerqueira, G. S. G., Novo, N. F., Almeida, F. A., & Novo, J. L. V. G. (2015). Maternal and fetal outcome in women with hypertensive disorders of pregnancy: The impact of prenatal care. *Therapeutic Advances in Cardiovascular Disease*, 9(4), 140–175. 10.1177/175394471559762226220808

Barve, Y., & Saini, J. (2021). Healthcare misinformation detection and fact-checking: A novel approach. *International Journal of Advanced Computer Science and Applications*, 12(10), 407–414. 10.14569/IJACSA.2021.0121032

Basheer, S., & Kochupillai, M. (2005). The 'compulsory licence'regime in India: past, present and future. *Present and Future.*

Bastiaan, R. (2020, August 01). Bloem, M., E.RayDorsey, M., & MichaelS.Okun, M. (2020). The Coronavirus Disease 2019 Crisis as Catalyst for Telemedicine for Chronic Neurological Disorders. *JAMA Neurology*, 77(8), 927. 10.1001/jamaneurol.2020.1452

Bataineh, A. A., Reyes, V., Olukanni, T., Khalaf, M., Vibho, A., & Pedyuk, R. (2023). Advanced misinformation detection: A Bi-LSTM model optimized by genetic algorithms. *Electronics (Basel)*, 12(15), 3250. 10.3390/electronics12153250

Baumgart, D. C. (2005). Personal digital assistants in health care: Experienced clinicians in the palm of your hand? *Lancet*, 366(9492), 1210–1222. 10.1016/S0140-6736(05)67484-316198770

Bautista, J., Zhang, Y., & Gwizdka, J. (2021). Healthcare professionals' acts of correcting health misinformation on social media. *International Journal of Medical Informatics*, 148, 104375. 10.1016/j.ijmedinf.2021.10437533461008

Behura, A., Sahu, S., & Kabat, M. R. (2021). Advancement of Machine Learning and Cloud Computing in the Field of Smart Health Care. *Machine Learning Approach for Cloud Data Analytics in IoT*, 273-306.

Belayneh, Z., & Mekuriaw, B. (2019). Knowledge and menstrual hygiene practice among adolescent school girls in southern Ethiopia: A cross-sectional study. *BMC Public Health*, 19(1), 1–8. 10.1186/s12889-019-7973-931783741

Bender, D., & Sartipi, K. (2013). HL7 FHIR: An agile and RESTful approach to healthcare information exchange. In *Proceedings of the 26th IEEE International Symposium on Computer-Based Medical Systems* (pp. 326-331). IEEE. 10.1109/CBMS.2013.6627810

Bentley, L., & Davis, J., (Eds.). (2008). *Trademarks and brands: An interdisciplinary critique* (2nd ed.). Cambridge University Press. 10.1017/CBO9780511495212

Bently, L., Sherman, B., Gangjee, D., & Johnson, P. (2022). *Intellectual property law*. Oxford university press. 10.1093/he/9780198869917.001.0001

Bereskin, D. R. (1993). A comparison of the trademark provisions of NAFTA and TRIPS. *Trademark Reporter, 1.*

Bereskin, D. R., & Sawchuk, A. (2003). Crocker revisited: The protection of trademarks of foreign nationals in the United States. *Trademark Reporter, 93*.

Berg, M. (2001). Implementing information systems in health care organizations: Myths and challenges. *International Journal of Medical Informatics*, 64(2), 143–156. 10.1016/S1386-5056(01)00200-311734382

Bhattacharjee, B., Pal, P., Purkait, R., Chakraborty, P., & Choubey, G. (2023). Patient satisfaction survey for the telemedicine services during the second wave of the COVID-19 pandemic in the Homoeopathic Research Institutes of West Bengal. *Homoeopathic Links, 36*, 006-011. 10.1055/s-0043-1761429

Bhattacharya, S., & Saha, C. N. (2011). Intellectual property rights: An overview and implications in pharmaceutical industry. *Journal of Advanced Pharmaceutical Technology & Research, 2*(2), 88. 10.4103/2231-4040.82952

Bhattacharyya, D., Stephen Neal Joshua, E., & Thirupathi Rao, N. (2023). Medical Image Analysis of Lung Cancer CT Scans Using Deep Learning with Swarm Optimization Techniques. *Machine Intelligence, Big Data Analytics, and IoT in Image Processing: Practical Applications*, 23-50.

Bhatt, P. (2022, March 15). AI adoption in the hiring process – important criteria and extent of AI adoption. *Foresight*, 25(1), 144–163. 10.1108/FS-07-2021-0144

Binder, J., Ursu, O., Bologa, C., Jiang, S., Maphis, N., Dadras, S., Chisholm, D., Weick, J., Myers, O., Kumar, P., Yang, J. J., Bhaskar, K., & Oprea, T. I. (2022). Machine learning prediction and tau-based screening identifies potential Alzheimer's disease genes relevant to immunity. *Communications Biology*, 5(1), 125. 10.1038/s42003-022-03068-735149761

Bognar, C. L. F. B., Bychkovsky, B. L., & Lopes, G. de L.Jr. (2016). Compulsory Licenses for Cancer Drugs: Does Circumventing Patent Rights Improve Access to Oncology Medications? *Journal of Global Oncology*, 2(5), 292–301. 10.1200/JGO.2016.00536328717715

Bohan, D., & Dumbrell, A. (Eds.). (2023). *Advances in Ecological Research: Roadmaps Part B*. Elsevier.

Bonadio, E., & Baldini, A. (2020). COVID-19, patents and the never-ending tension between proprietary rights and the protection of public health. *European Journal of Risk Regulation*, 11(2), 390–395. 10.1017/err.2020.24

Borg, S. A., Bukenya, J. N., Kibira, S. P., Nakamya, P., Makumbi, F. E., Exum, N. G., Schwab, K. J., & Hennegan, J. (2023). The association between menstrual hygiene, workplace sanitation practices and self-reported urogenital symptoms in a cross-sectional survey of women working in Mukono District, Uganda. *PLoS One*, 18(7), e0288942. 10.1371/journal.pone.028894237471386

Braithwaite, J., & Drahos, P. (2004). *Global business regulation*. Cambridge University Press.

Bravo, G. (2001–2002). From Paris Convention to TRIPS: A brief history. *Journal of Contemporary Legal Issues, 12*.

Bravo, G. (2001). From Paris Convention to TRIPS: A Brief History. *Journal of Contemporary Legal Issues*, 12, 445.

Brennan, H. (2015). The cost of confusion: The paradox of trademarked pharmaceuticals. *SSRN*, 22(1), 14. 10.2139/ssrn.2690889

Brock, D. W. (1991). The ideal of shared decision making between physicians and patients. *Kennedy Institute of Ethics Journal*, 1(1), 28–47. 10.1353/ken.0.008410113819

Brown, G. (1948). Advertising and the public interest: The legal protection of trade symbols. *The Yale Law Journal*, 57(7), 57. 10.2307/793310

Bulgurcu, B., Cavusoglu, H., & Benbasat, I. (2010). Information Security Policy Compliance: An Empirical Study of Rationality-Based Beliefs and Information Security Awareness. *Management Information Systems Quarterly*, 34(3), 523–548. 10.2307/25750690

Bunting, G. A. (1995). GATT and the Evolution of the Global Trade System: A Historical Perspective. *John's J. Legal Comment.*, 11, 505.

Cabello, J. C., Karimipour, H., Jahromi, A. N., Dehghantanha, A., & Parizi, R. M. (2020). Big-data and cyber-physical systems in healthcare: Challenges and opportunities. *Handbook of Big Data Privacy*, 255-283.

Calboli, I. (2019). Beyond Patents: The Problems of Non-Traditional Trademark Protection for Medicines and Health Technologies. *IIC - International Review of Intellectual Property and Competition Law, 51*. 10.1007/s40319-019-00893-y

Cameron, H., & Hajhashem, M. (2015). *THE INTERSECTION OF INTELLECTUAL PROPERTY RIGHTS AND INNOVATION POLICY MAKING -A LITERATURE REVIEW*. WIPO. https://www.wipo.int/edocs/pubdocs/en/wipo_report_ip_inn.pdf

Carr, S. (2020). 'AI gone mental': Engagement and ethics in data-driven technology for mental health. *Journal of Mental Health (Abingdon, England)*, 29(2), 125–130. 10.1080/09638237.2020.171401132000544

Carter, S. (1990). The trouble with trademark. *The Yale Law Journal*, •••, 99.

Chandra-Mouli, V., & Patel, S. V. (2017). Mapping the knowledge and understanding of menarche, menstrual hygiene and menstrual health among adolescent girls in low- and middle-income countries. *Reproductive Health*, 14(1), 1–16. 10.1186/s12978-017-0293-628249610

Chandrasekharan, S., & Cook-Deegan, R. (2009). Gene patents and personalized medicine - what lies ahead? *Genome Medicine*, 1(9), 92. 10.1186/gm9219804612

Chandwani, A., Shrivastava, K., Sadashiv, S., Saha, I., & Mishra, P. (2023, April). Virtual Assistant for Appointment Booking. In *2023 IEEE 8th International Conference for Convergence in Technology (I2CT)* (pp. 1-5). IEEE. 10.1109/I2CT57861.2023.10126199

Chang, H.-J. (2001). Intellectual Property Rights and Economic Development: Historical lessons and emerging issues. *Journal of Human Development*, 2(2), 287–309. 10.1080/14649880120067293

Chan, M., Woon, I., & Kankanhalli, A. (2005). Perceptions of Information Security in the Workplace: Linking Information Security Climate to Compliant Behavior. *Journal of Information Privacy and Security*, 1(3), 18–41. 10.1080/15536548.2005.10855772

Chattu, V. K., Singh, B., Kaur, J., & Jakovljevic, M. (2021). COVID-19 vaccine, TRIPS, and global health diplomacy: India's role at the WTO platform. *BioMed Research International*, 2021, 2021. 10.1155/2021/665807034485525

Chaudhry, B., Wang, J., Wu, S., Maglione, M., Mojica, W., Roth, E., Morton, S. C., & Shekelle, P. G. (2006). Systematic Review: Impact of Health Information Technology on Quality, Efficiency, and Costs of Medical Care. *Annals of Internal Medicine*, 144(10), 742–752. 10.7326/0003-4819-144-10-200605160-0012516702590

Chaudhuri, S. B. (2005). *The WTO and India's Pharmaceuticals Industry: Patent Protection*. TRIPS, and Developing Countries.

Chauhan, P., Bali, A., & Kaur, S. (2024). Breaking Barriers for Accessible Health Programs: The Role of Telemedicine in a Global Healthcare Transformation. In *Transformative Approaches to Patient Literacy and Healthcare Innovation* (pp. 283-307). IGI Global.

Che, M., Yao, K., Che, C., Cao, Z., & Kong, F. (2021). Knowledge-graph-based drug repositioning against COVID-19 by graph convolutional network with attention mechanism. *Future Internet*, 13(1), 13. 10.3390/fi13010013

Chen, L., Wu, T., Wang, Z., Lin, X., & Cai, Y. (2023). A novel hybrid BPNN model based on adaptive evolutionary Artificial Bee Colony Algorithm for water quality index prediction. *Ecological Indicators*, 146, 109882. 10.1016/j.ecolind.2023.109882

Chen, M., Mao, S., Zhang, Y., & Leung, V. C. (2014). *Big data: related technologies, challenges and future prospects* (Vol. 100). Springer. 10.1007/978-3-319-06245-7

Chenthara, S., Ahmed, K., Wang, H., & Whittaker, F. (2019). Security and Privacy-Preserving Challenges of e-Health Solutions in Cloud Computing. *IEEE Access : Practical Innovations, Open Solutions*, 7, 74361–74382. 10.1109/ACCESS.2019.2919982

Chen, Y., & Esmaeilzadeh, P. (2024). Generative AI in medical practice: In-depth exploration of privacy and security challenges. *Journal of Medical Internet Research*, 26, e53008. 10.2196/5300838457208

Chidede, T. (2022). The role of intellectual property rights' protection in advancing development in South Africa. *Law, Democracy & Development, 26*(1).

Chintala, S. (2023). AI-Driven Personalised Treatment Plans: The Future of Precision Medicine. *Machine Intelligence Research*, 17(02), 9718–9728.

Chomutare, T., Fernandez-Luque, L., Årsand, E., & Hartvigsen, G. (2011). Features of Mobile Diabetes Applications: Review of the Literature and Analysis of Current Applications Compared Against Evidence-Based Guidelines. *Journal of Medical Internet Research*, 13(3), e65. 10.2196/jmir.187421979293

Chouhan, N. (2020, April 30). *Introduction to Pharmaceutical Trademarks*. Sagacious IP. https://sagaciousresearch.com/blog/introduction-pharmaceutical-trademarks/

Chow, D. (2012). Lessons from Pfizer's Disputes Over its Viagra Trademark in China. *Maryland Journal of International Law, 27*(1), 82. https://digitalcommons.law.umaryland.edu/mjil/vol27/iss1/9

Chung, G. S., Lawrence, R. E., Curlin, F. A., Arora, V., & Meltzer, D. O. (2011). Predictors of hospitalised patients' preferences for physician-directed medical decision-making. *Journal of Medical Ethics*, 38(2), 77–82. 10.1136/jme.2010.04061821697296

Claessen, V., Schmidt, A., & Heck, T. (2017). *Virtual Assistants*. Humboldt-Universität zu Berlin.

Classen, C., Howes, D., & Synnott, A. (1994). *Aroma: The cultural history of smell* (1st ed.). Routledge.

Cohen, I. G., Amarasingham, R., Shah, A., Xie, B., & Lo, B. (2020). The legal and ethical concerns that arise from using complex predictive analytics in health care. *Health Affairs*, 33(7), 1139–1147. 10.1377/hlthaff.2014.004825006139

Comito, C., Falcone, D., & Forestiero, A. (2020, December). Current trends and practices in smart health monitoring and clinical decision support. In *2020 IEEE International Conference on Bioinformatics and Biomedicine (BIBM)* (pp. 2577-2584). IEEE. 10.1109/BIBM49941.2020.9313449

Cornish, W., & Llewelyn, D. (2007). *Intellectual property: Patents, copyright, trade marks and allied rights* (6th ed.). Sweet & Maxwell.

Cornish, W., & Llewelyn, D. (2010). *Intellectual property: Patents, copyright, trademarks and allied rights* (7th ed.). Sweet & Maxwell Limited.

Cornish, W., Llewelyn, D., & Aplin, T. (2010). *Intellectual property, patents, copyrights, trademarks and allied rights* (7th ed.). Sweet & Maxwell.

Correa, C. M. (2006). Implications of bilateral free trade agreements on access to medicines. *Bulletin of the World Health Organization*, *84*(5), 399–404. https://www.ncbi.nlm.nih.gov/pmc/articles/PMC2627342/10.2471/BLT.05.023432

Correa, C. M., & Yusuf, A. A. (Eds.). (2008). *Intellectual property and international trade: The TRIPS Agreement* (1st ed.). Kluwer Law International.

Cousins, T., Pentecost, M., Alvergne, A., Chandler, C., Chigudu, S., Herrick, C., Kelly, A., Leonelli, S., Lezaun, J., Lorimer, J., Reubi, D., & Sekalala, S. (2021). The changing climates of global health. *BMJ Global Health*, 6(3), e005442. 10.1136/bmjgh-2021-00544233758015

Cui, L., Seo, H., Tabar, M., Ma, F., Wang, S., & Lee, D. (2020). DETERRENT: Knowledge guided graph attention network for detecting healthcare misinformation. In *Proceedings of the 26th ACM SIGKDD International Conference on Knowledge Discovery & Data Mining*. ACM. 10.1145/3394486.3403092

Cui, Z., Yuan, Z., Wu, Y., Sun, X., & Yu, K. (2023). Intelligent Recommendation for Departments Based on Medical Knowledge Graph. *IEEE Access : Practical Innovations, Open Solutions*, 11, 25372–25385. 10.1109/ACCESS.2023.3254303

Cutter, B. (1990). The rational basics of trademark protection; Control of quality and dilution - estranged bedfellows? *Journal Marshall Law Review, 24.*

D. I. (2004). Smell, sound, colour and shape trade marks: An unhappy flirtation. *Journal of Business Laws, 12.*

D'Alfonso, S. (2020). AI in mental health. *Current Opinion in Psychology*, 36, 112–117. 10.1016/j.copsyc.2020.04.00532604065

Dagher, G. G., Mohler, J., Milojkovic, M., & Marella, P. B. (2018). Ancile: Privacy-preserving framework for access control and interoperability of electronic health records using blockchain technology. *Sustainable Cities and Society*, 39, 283–297. 10.1016/j.scs.2018.02.014

Dalkıran, G. B. (2023). Health Tourism Components and Intermediary Institutions as Supplier Businesses in the Context of Health 4.0. In *Health 4.0 and Medical Supply Chain* (pp. 147–162). Springer Nature Singapore. 10.1007/978-981-99-1818-8_12

Danzon, P. M., & Towse, A. (2003). Differential Pricing for Pharmaceuticals: Reconciling Access, R&D and Patents. *International Journal of Health Care Finance and Economics*, 3(3), 183–205. https://www.jstor.org/stable/3528839. 10.1023/A:102538481957514625999

Dar, H., & Kashyap, K. (2023). Smart healthcare system (SHS): Medical tourism delivering, consumption, and elevating tool in the ages of smart technologies. *Tourism Planning & Development*, 20(3), 397–415. 10.1080/21568316.2022.2109206

Das, S. B. (2014). *Understanding the regional comprehensive economic partnership and the trans- pacific partnership: An ASEAN perspective*. Brookings. https://www.brookings.edu/wp-content/uploads/2014/01/11-asia-pacific-economic-integration-presentation-basu-das.pdf

Dasgupta, A., & Sarkar, M. (2008). Menstrual hygiene: How hygienic is the adolescent girl? *Indian Journal of Community Medicine*, 33(2), 77–80. 10.4103/0970-0218.4087219967028

Dash, S., Shakyawar, S. K., Sharma, M., & Kaushik, S. (2019). Big data in healthcare: Management, analysis and future prospects. *Journal of Big Data*, 6(1), 1–25. 10.1186/s40537-019-0217-0

Das, P., Baker, K. K., Dutta, A., Swain, T., Sahoo, S., Das, B. S., Panda, B., Nayak, A., Bara, M., Bilung, B., Mishra, P. R., Panigrahi, P., Cairncross, S., & Torondel, B. (2015). Menstrual hygiene practices, WASH access and the risk of urogenital infection in women from Odisha, India. *PLoS One*, 10(6), 1–16. 10.1371/journal.pone.013077726125184

Date, P., Pimprale, V., & Mandke, S. (2023, December 26). Explorative study on potential of machine learning and artificial intelligence for improved healthcare diagnosis and treatment. *Journal of Autonomous Intelligence*, 7(3). Advance online publication. 10.32629/jai.v7i3.1084

Davis, J. (2008). *Intellectual Property Law* (3rd ed.). Oxford University Press.

Davis, J. (2010). Between a sign and a brand: Mapping the boundaries of a registered trademark in European Union trademark law. In Bentley, L., (Eds.), *Trademarks and Brands* (pp. 65–81).

Davis, R. E., Sevdalis, N., & Vincent, C. A. (2012). Patient involvement in patient safety: The health-care professional's perspective. *Journal of Patient Safety*, 8(4), 182–188. 10.1097/PTS.0b013e318267c4aa23007240

De Fauw, J., Ledsam, J. R., Romera-Paredes, B., Nikolov, S., Tomasev, N., Blackwell, S., Askham, H., Glorot, X., O'Donoghue, B., Visentin, D., van den Driessche, G., Lakshminarayanan, B., Meyer, C., Mackinder, F., Bouton, S., Ayoub, K., Chopra, R., King, D., Karthikesalingam, A., & Ronneberger, O. (2018). Clinically applicable deep learning for diagnosis and referral in retinal disease. *Nature Medicine*, 24(9), 1342–1350. 10.1038/s41591-018-0107-630104768

De Giovanni, P. (2023). Sustainability of the Metaverse: A transition to Industry 5.0. *Sustainability (Basel)*, 15(7), 6079. 10.3390/su15076079

De Penning & De Penning. (2024, March 4). *Decoding Consumer Perception: How Trademarks Shape Your Choices*. De Penning & de Penning. https://depenning.com/blog/trademarks-on-consumer-perception/

Department of Economic and Social Affairs. (2022). *Population Division, World Population Prospects 2022, Online Edition*. UN. https://population. un.org/wpp/)

Derval, D. (2023). *Frontiers in Product Innovation Strategy: Predicting Market Outcomes and Creating Winning Products for a People and Planet-friendly Future*.

Desai, M. (2016). Compulsory licensing: Procedural requirements under the TRIPS agreement. *Pharmaceuticals, policy and law, 18*, 31-44.

Devika, G., & Karegowda, A. G. (2021). Deep Learning in IoT: Introduction, Applications, and Perspective in the Big Data Era. In *Deep Learning Applications and Intelligent Decision Making in Engineering* (pp. 1-54). IGI Global.

Dharmale, G., Shirsath, P., Shinde, A., Sawant, V., & Chougule, A. (2023, February). REMICARE—Medicine Intake Tracker and Healthcare Assistant. In *Proceedings of 3rd International Conference on Recent Trends in Machine Learning, IoT, Smart Cities and Applications: ICMISC 2022* (pp. 273-283). Singapore: Springer Nature Singapore.

Diependaele, L., Cockbain, J., & Sterckx, S. (2016). Raising the Barriers to Access to Medicines in the Developing World - The Relentless Push for Data Exclusivity. *Developing World Bioethics*, 17(1), 11–21. 10.1111/dewb.1210526818105

Dingler, T., Kwasnicka, D., Wei, J., Gong, E., & Oldenburg, B. (2021). The use and promise of conversational agents in digital health. *Yearbook of Medical Informatics*, 30(01), 191–199. 10.1055/s-0041-172651034479391

Dinwoodie, G. B. (1999). The death of ontology: A teleological approach to trademark law. *Iowa Law Review*, 84.

Dinwoodie, G. B., & Dreyfuss, R. C. (2009–2010). Designing a global intellectual property system responsive to change: The WTO, WIPO and beyond. *Houston Law Review*, 46.

Dobrauz-Saldapenna, G., & Huras, N. (Eds.). (2023). *Circular Economy: New solutions for a better tomorrow*. Stämpfli Verlag.

Doherty, P. (2023). *Smart Cities: Reimagining the Urban Experience*. Quality Press.

Drahos, P. (2004). Securing the Future of Intellectual Property: Intellectual Property Owners and Their Nodally Coordinated Enforcement Pyramid Recommended Citation. *Case Western Reserve Journal of International Law*, *36*(1), 55–61. https://scholarlycommons.law.case.edu/cgi/viewcontent.cgi?article=1385&context=jil.

Drahos, P. (2005). Bits and Bips. *The Journal of World Intellectual Property*, 4(6), 791–808. 10.1111/j.1747-1796.2001.tb00138.x

Drawnbaugh, K. (2001). *Brands in the balance: Meeting the challenges to commercial identity* (1st ed.). Reuters.

Drexl, J., Hilty, R., Desaunettes-Barbero, L., Globocnik, J., Otero, B. G., Hoffmann, J., & Kim, D. (2021). *Artificial intelligence and intellectual property law-Position statement of the max planck institute for innovation and competition of 9 april 2021 on the current debate*. Max Planck Institute for Innovation & Competition.

Duffy, M., Scarles, C., Edensor, T., Waitt, G., & Franklin, A. (2021). Twenty years on: Reflections on the journeys travelled and future directions for tourist studies. *Tourist Studies*, 21(1), 3–8. 10.1177/1468797621997636

Duggan, M., & Goyal, A. (2012). Pharmaceutical patents and prices: a preliminary empirical assessment using data from India. *Policy Research Working Paper Series*. https://ideas.repec.org/p/wbk/wbrwps/6063.html

Dutfield, G. (2005). Sharing the Benefits of Biodiversity. *The Journal of World Intellectual Property*, 5(6), 899–931. 10.1111/j.1747-1796.2002.tb00186.x

Dutfield, G., & Suthersanes, U. (2008). *Global intellectual property law* (1st ed.). Edward Elgar Publishing Ltd.

Ehrenfeld, J. (2017). WannaCry, cybersecurity and health information technology: A time to act. *Journal of Medical Systems*, 41(1), 1. 10.1007/s10916-017-0752-128540616

Elbadawi, M., Gaisford, S., & Basit, A. W. (2021). Advanced machine-learning techniques in drug discovery. *Drug Discovery Today*, 26(3), 769–777. 10.1016/j.drudis.2020.12.00333290820

Elhaddad, M., & Hamam, S. (2024). AI-Driven Clinical Decision Support Systems: An Ongoing Pursuit of Potential. *Cureus*, 16(4). 10.7759/cureus.5772838711724

Epstein, M. E. (2008). *Intellectual property*. Wolters Kluwer Law & Business.

Erfani, P., Binagwaho, A., Jalloh, M. J., Yunus, M., Farmer, P., & Kerry, V. (2021). Intellectual property waiver for covid-19 vaccines will advance global health equity. *bmj, 374*.

Eriksson, R. O., & Regoczi, B. (2023). *Diving into venture creation: An exploratory study of how external enabler combinations facilitate sustainable venture creation in the marine sector.*

Esposito, M., Halkias, D., Tse, T., & Harkiolakis, T. (2023). Environmental and Climate Impacts of the Metaverse. *Available atSSRN* 4616695. 10.2139/ssrn.4616695

Esteva, A., Robicquet, A., Ramsundar, B., Kuleshov, V., DePristo, M., Chou, K., Cui, C., Corrado, G., Thrun, S., & Dean, J. (2019). A guide to deep learning in healthcare. *Nature Medicine*, 25(1), 24–29. 10.1038/s41591-018-0316-z30617335

European Union. (2022). *Intellectual Property and the Pharma & Healthcare Sectors in India*. EU. https://www.cde.ual.es/wp-content/uploads/2022/06/EA0722284ENN.en-1.pdf

F.-K., & Reimer, A. (1955). Preparatory study for the establishment of a uniform international trademark definition. *Trademark Reporter, 5*.

Faaique, M. (2024). Overview of Big Data Analytics in Modern Astronomy. *International Journal of Mathematics, Statistics, and Computer Science*, 2, 96–113. 10.59543/ijmscs.v2i.8561

Fakhri, M., Hamzehgardeshi, Z., Hajikhani Golchin, N. A., & Komili, A. (2012). Promoting menstrual health among persian adolescent girls from low socioeconomic backgrounds: A quasi-experimental study. *BMC Public Health*, 12(1), 2–6. 10.1186/1471-2458-12-19322420743

Farhud, D. D., & Zokaei, S. (2021). Ethical issues of artificial intelligence in medicine and healthcare. *Iranian Journal of Public Health*, 50(11), i–v. 10.18502/ijph.v50i11.760035223619

Fekadu, A., Yitayal, M., & Alemayehu, G. (2019). Frequent Antenatal Care Visits Increase Institutional Delivery at Dabat Health and Demographic Surveillance System Site, Northwest Ethiopia. *J Pregn*.

Fernández-Alemán, J. L., Señor, I. C., Lozoya, P. Á. O., & Toval, A. (2013). Security and privacy in electronic health records: A systematic literature review. *Journal of Biomedical Informatics*, 46(3), 541–562. 10.1016/j.jbi.2012.12.00323305810

Filippo Amato, A. L.-M. (2013). Artificial neural networks in medical diagnosis. *Journal of Applied Biomedicine*, 11(2), 47–58. 10.2478/v10136-012-0031-x

Flynn, M. B., & Silva, E. O. (2021). Framing access to medicines during COVID-19: A qualitative content analysis of Gilead's Remdesivir. *Global Public Health: An International Journal for Research, Policy and Practice*, 16(8-9), 1499–1511. 10.1080/17441692.2020.187149833460356

Frank, E., & Olaoye, G. (2024). *Privacy and data protection in AI-enabled healthcare systems*. Research Gate. https://www.researchgate.net/publication/378287462_Privacy_and_data_protection_in_AI-enabled_healthcare_systems

Free, C., Phillips, G., Galli, L., Watson, L., Felix, L., Edwards, P., Patel, V., & Haines, A. (2013). The effectiveness of mobile-health technology-based health behaviour change or disease management interventions for health care consumers: A systematic review. *PLoS Medicine*, 10(1), e1001362. 10.1371/journal.pmed.100136223349621

Friedman, R. H., Stollerman, J. E., Mahoney, D. M., & Rozenblyum, L. (1997). The virtual visit: Using telecommunications technology to take care of patients. *Journal of the American Medical Informatics Association : JAMIA*, 4(6), 413–425. 10.1136/jamia.1997.00404139391929

Fritch, D. (2006). SHOULD "THE PURPLE PILL" BY ANY OTHER DRUG COMPANY STILL BE AS PURPLE? THE CHANGING FACE OF TRADE DRESS PROTECTION FOR PHARMACEUTICAL MANUFACTURERS. *IDEA - the Intellectual Property Law Review, 47*(2). https://ipmall.law.unh.edu/sites/default/files/hosted_resources/IDEA/idea-vol47-no2-fritch.pdf

Fritch, D. M. (2006-2007). Should the purple pill by any other drug company still be as purple? The changing face of trade dress protection for pharmaceutical manufacturers. *IDEA*, 47, 171–188.

Gajarawala, S. N., & Pelkowski, J. N. (2021). Telehealth benefits and barriers. *The Journal for Nurse Practitioners*, 17(2), 218–221. 10.1016/j.nurpra.2020.09.01333106751

Gajić, T., Minasyan, L. A., Petrović, M. D., Bakhtin, V. A., Kaneeva, A. V., & Wiegel, N. L. (2023). Travelers'(in) Resilience to environmental risks emphasized in the media and their redirecting to medical destinations: Enhancing sustainability. *Sustainability (Basel)*, 15(21), 15297. 10.3390/su152115297

Gallagher, T. A. (2015). Non-traditional trademarks: Taste/flavour. *Trademark Reporter, 105*.

Gallagher, T. A. (2015). Non traditional trademarks: Taste/Flavour. *Trademark Reporter*, 105, 806.

Ganapathy, K. (2021). Artificial intelligence and healthcare regulatory and legal concerns. *Telehealth and Medicine Today*, 6(2). 10.30953/tmt.v6.252

Garagancea, L. (2021). Access to Medicines: The Interplay between Parallel Imports, Compulsory Licensing, and Voluntary Licensing. *EPLR*, 5(1), 37–56. 10.21552/eplr/2021/1/6

Garg, R., Goyal, S., & Gupta, S. (2012). India moves towards menstrual hygiene: Subsidized sanitary napkins for rural adolescent girls - Issues and challenges. *Maternal and Child Health Journal*, 16(4), 767–774. 10.1007/s10995-011-0798-521505773

Garg, S., & Laskar, A. R. (2012). Community Based Monitoring; Key to success of National Health Programs, Department of community Medicine, MAMC, New Delhi, India. *Indian Journal of Community Medicine*, 35(2), 214–226.20922094

Gazzotti, R., Faron, C., Gandon, F., Lacroix-Hugues, V., & Darmon, D. (2022). Extending electronic medical records vector models with knowledge graphs to improve hospitalization prediction. *Journal of Biomedical Semantics*, 13(1), 1–20. 10.1186/s13326-022-00261-935193692

George. (2015, December 22). AstraZeneca v. Dr Reddy's - Colour as a pharmaceutical trade dress. *SPICY IP BLOG*. https://spicyip.com/2015/12/astrazeneca-v-dr-reddys-colour-as-a-pharmaceutical-trade-dress.html

Gerke, S., Minssen, T., & Cohen, G. (2020). *"Ethical and legal challenges of artificial intelligence-driven healthcare." Artificial intelligence in healthcare*. Academic Press.

Gervais, D. (2002). The Internationalization of Intellectual Property: New Challenges The Internationalization of Intellectual Property: New Challenges from the Very Old and the Very New from the Very Old and the Very New. *Fordham Intellectual Property, Media and Entertainment Law Fordham Intellectual Property, Media and Entertainment Law Journal Journal*, *12*(4). https://ir.lawnet.fordham.edu/cgi/viewcontent.cgi?article=1232&context=iplj

Ghayvat, H., Awais, M., Pandya, S., Ren, H., Akbarzadeh, S., Chandra Mukhopadhyay, S., Chen, C., Gope, P., Chouhan, A., & Chen, W. (2019). Smart aging system: Uncovering the hidden wellness parameter for well-being monitoring and anomaly detection. *Sensors (Basel)*, 19(4), 766. 10.3390/s1904076630781852

Ghosh. A. & Ghosh, R. (2020) Maternal health care in India: A reflection of 10 years of National Health Mission on the Indian maternal health scenario. *Sexual Reproductive health care, 25*, 1-8.

Giachos, I., Papakitsos, E. C., Savvidis, P., & Laskaris, N. (2023). Inquiring natural language processing capabilities on robotic systems through virtual assistants: A systemic approach. *Journal of Computer Science Research*, 5(2), 28–36. 10.30564/jcsr.v5i2.5537

Gilson, J., & LaLonde, A. G. (2005). Cinnamon buns, marching ducks and cherry-scented racecar exhaust: Protecting nontraditional trademarks. *Trademark Review, 95*(4).

Glaxo Wellcome UK Ltd & Anor v. Sandoz Ltd & Ors [2019] EWHC 2545 (Ch) (04 October 2019).

Gogia, S., & Sachdev, H. S. (2010). Home Visits by Community Health Workers to Prevent Neonatal Deaths in Developing Countries: A Systematic Review. *Bulletin of the World Health Organization*, 88(9), 658–666. 10.2471/BLT.09.06936920865070

Gomulkiewicz, R., Nguyen, X. T., & Conway, D. M. (2023). *Licensing intellectual property: law and application*. Aspen Publishing.

Gonzale, M. (2014). So let the paint be spread, we're painting the soles red. *Wake Forest Journal of Business and Intellectual Property Law, 52.*

Gore, C., Morin, S., Røttingen, J.-A., & Kieny, M. P. (2023). Negotiating public-health intellectual property licensing agreements to increase access to health technologies: An insider's story. *B. Journal of Global Health*, 8(9), e012964. 10.1136/bmjgh-2023-01296437669799

Goswami, A., Reddaiah, V. P., Kapoor, S. K., Singh, B., Dwivedi, S. N., & Kumar, G. (2005). *Tobacco and alcohol use in rural elderly Indian population*. Ind Joul of Psy. 10.4103/0019-5545.43050

Grabowski, H. (2002). Patents, Innovation and Access to New Pharmaceuticals. *Journal of International Economic Law*, 5(4), 849–860. https://ideas.repec.org/a/oup/jieclw/v5y2002i4p849-860.html. 10.1093/jiel/5.4.849

Graham, S., Depp, C., Lee, E. E., Nebeker, C., Tu, X., Kim, H. C., & Jeste, D. V. (2019). Artificial Intelligence for Mental Health and Mental Illnesses: An Overview. *Current Psychiatry Reports*, 21(11), 116. 10.1007/s11920-019-1094-031701320

Grassini, S., & Ratcliffe, E. (2024). The Virtual Wild: Exploring the Intersection of Virtual Reality and Natural Environments. *Managing Protected Areas*, 327.

Greene, J. A., & Kesselheim, A. S. (2011). Why do the same drugs look different? Pills, trade dress and public health. *The New England Journal of Medicine*, 365(1), 83–89. 10.1056/NEJMhle110172221732842

Greene, S. M., Tuzzio, L., & Cherkin, D. (2012). A framework for making patient-centered care front and center. *The Permanente Journal*, 16(3), 49–53. 10.7812/TPP/12-02523012599

Griffin, A. C., Xing, Z., Mikles, S. P., Bailey, S., Khairat, S., Arguello, J., Wang, Y., & Chung, A. E. (2021). Information needs and perceptions of chatbots for hypertension medication self-management: A mixed methods study. *JAMIA Open*, 4(2), ooab021. 10.1093/jamiaopen/ooab02133898936

Grimes, C. W., & Battersby, G. J. (1979). The protection of merchandising properties. *Trademark Reporter, 69.*

Grosse Ruse -Khan. H. (2011). *A Trade Agreement Creating Barriers to International Trade?: ACTA Border Measures and Goods in Transit*. Digital Commons. https://digitalcommons.wcl.american.edu/cgi/viewcontent.cgi?article=1711&context=auilr [Accessed 17 Nov. 2022].

Guan, J. (2019). Artificial intelligence in healthcare and medicine: Promises, ethical challenges and governance. *Chinese Medical Sciences Journal*, 34(2), 76–83.31315747

Guellec, D. (2007). Patents as an Incentive to Innovate. In D. Guellec & B. van P. Potterie (Eds.), *The Economics of the European Patent System: IP Policy for Innovation and Competition*. Oxford University Press.

Guoguang Rong, A. M. (2020). Artificial Intelligence in Healthcare: Review and Prediction Case Studies. *Engineering (Beijing)*, 6(3), 291–301. 10.1016/j.eng.2019.08.015

Guo, Y., Ren, X., Chen, Y. X., & Wang, T. J. (2019). Artificial intelligence meets Chinese medicine. *Chinese Journal of Integrative Medicine*, 25(9), 648–653. 10.1007/s11655-019-3169-531650485

Gupta, N., Pal, P., Bhargava, M., & Daga, M. (1992). Health of Women and Children in Rajasthan. *Economic and Political Weekly*, 27(42), 2323–2330.

Gupta, R., Srivastava, D., Sahu, M., Tiwari, S., Ambasta, R. K., & Kumar, P. (2021). Artificial intelligence to deep learning: Machine intelligence approach for drug discovery. *Molecular Diversity*, 25(3), 1315–1360. 10.1007/s11030-021-10217-333844136

Gupta, S. K. (2012). Impact of Janani Suraksha Yojana on Institutional Delivery Rate and Maternal Morbidity and Mortality: An Observational Study in India. *Journal of Health, Population and Nutrition*, 30(4), 464–471.23304913

Gurgula, O. (2020). Strategic patenting by pharmaceutical companies–should competition law intervene? *IIC; International Review of Industrial Property and Copyright Law*, 51(9), 1062–1085. 10.1007/s40319-020-00985-033132411

Gurung, P., Rajbanshi, R., Bastien, S., & Luitel, B. C. (2023). Menstrual Hygiene Management: A Case Study Through Participatory Action Research in Rural Nepal. In *Implementing Transformative Education With Participatory Action Research* (pp. 14-29). IGI Global. 10.4018/979-8-3693-0607-9.ch002

Halabi, S. F. (2021). Trademarks, Trade Dress, and the Patient Costs of Pharmaceutical Branding. *New York University Journal of Intellectual Property & Entertainment Law, 11*(2). https://jipel.law.nyu.edu/wp-content/uploads/2022/03/JIPEL-Halabi-Fall-2021.pdf

Haleem, A., Javaid, M., Singh, R. P., & Suman, R. (2021). Telemedicine for healthcare: Capabilities, features, barriers, and applications. *Sensors International*, 2, 100117. 10.1016/j.sintl.2021.10011734806053

Hanafi, I., & Lubis, A. F. (2023). Protection of Privacy and Intellectual Property Rights in Digital Data Management in Indonesia. *The Easta Journal Law and Human Rights*, 2(01), 33–40. 10.58812/eslhr.v2i01.151

Hao, F., & Zheng, K. (2022). Online disease identification and diagnosis and treatment based on machine learning technology. *Journal of Healthcare Engineering*, 2022, 2022. 10.1155/2022/673624935449857

Haskard-Zolnierek, K., Snyder, M., Hernandez, R., & Thompson, T. L. (2021). *Patient-Provider communication and health outcomes*. Routledge eBooks. 10.4324/9781003043379-18

Hassija, V., Chamola, V., Mahapatra, A., Singal, A., Goel, D., Huang, K., Scardapane, S., Spinelli, I., Mahmud, M., & Hussain, A. (2024). Interpreting Black-Box Models: A Review on Explainable Artificial Intelligence. *Cognitive Computation*, 16(1), 45–74. 10.1007/s12559-023-10179-8

Hemachandran, K., & Rodriguez, R. V. (Eds.). (2023). *The Business of the Metaverse: How to Maintain the Human Element Within this New Business Reality*. CRC Press.

Hennegan, J., Shannon, A. K., Rubli, J., Schwab, K. J., & Melendez-Torres, G. J. (2019). Women's and girls' experiences of menstruation in low-and middle-income countries: A systematic review and qualitative metasynthesis. In *PLoS Medicine, 16*(5). 10.1371/journal.pmed.1002803

Hennegan, J., Winkler, I. T., Bobel, C., Keiser, D., Hampton, J., Larsson, G., Chandra-Mouli, V., Plesons, M., & Mahon, T. (2021). Menstrual health: A definition for policy, practice, and research. *Sexual and Reproductive Health Matters*, 29(1), 31–38. 10.1080/26410397.2021.191161833910492

Herget, G. (2006). WTO approves TRIPS amendment on importing under compulsory licensing. *HIV/AIDS Policy & Law Review*, 11(1), 23–24.16805011

High-Level Panel on Access to Health Technologies. (2016). *Report of the UNITED NATIONS SECRETARY-GENERAL'S HIGH-LEVEL PANEL ON ACCESS TO MEDICINES Promoting innovation and access to health technologies.* https://static1.squarespace.com/static/562094dee4b0d00c1a3ef761/t/57d9c6ebf5e231b2f02cd3d4/1473890031320/UNSG+HLP+Report+FINAL+12+Sept+2016.pdf

Hilbert, M. (2016). Big data for development: A review of promises and challenges. *Development Policy Review*, 34(1), 135–174. 10.1111/dpr.12142

Hoffmann-La Roche' & Co. A.G. v. DDSA Pharmaceuticals Ltd., [1972] RPC 1, 20.

Hogan, M. C., Foreman, K. J., Naghavi, M., Ahn, S. Y., Wang, M., Makela, S. M., Lopez, A. D., Lozano, R., & Murray, C. J. L. (2010). Maternal mortality for 181 countries, 1980–2008: A systematic analysis of progress towards Millennium Development Goal 5. *Lancet*, 375(3), 1609–1623. 10.1016/S0140-6736(10)60518-120382417

Holst, A. S., Jacques-Aviñó, C., Berenguera, A., Pinzón-Sanabria, D., Valls-Llobet, C., Munrós-Feliu, J., Martínez-Bueno, C., López-Jiménez, T., Vicente-Hernández, M., & Medina-Perucha, L. (2022). Experiences of menstrual inequity and menstrual health among women and people who menstruate in the Barcelona area (Spain): A qualitative study. *Reproductive Health*, 19(1), 1–16. 10.1186/s12978-022-01354-535183195

Holzinger, A., Saranti, A., Hauschild, A. C., Beinecke, J., Heider, D., Roettger, R., & Pfeifer, B. (2023, August). Human-in-the-Loop Integration with Domain-Knowledge Graphs for Explainable Federated Deep Learning. In *International Cross-Domain Conference for Machine Learning and Knowledge Extraction* (pp. 45-64). Cham: Springer Nature Switzerland. 10.1007/978-3-031-40837-3_4

Hong, R., & Ruiz-Beltran, M. (2007). Impact of prenatal care on infant survival in Bangladesh. *Maternal and Child Health Journal*, 11(1), 199–206. 10.1007/s10995-006-0147-217136460

Househ, M. (2013). The use of social media in healthcare: Organizational, clinical, and patient perspectives. *Studies in Health Technology and Informatics*, 183, 244–248. 10.3233/978-1-61499-203-5-24423388291

Houtan, B., Hafid, A. S., & Makrakis, D. (2020). A Survey on Blockchain-Based Self-Sovereign Patient Identity in Healthcare. *IEEE Access : Practical Innovations, Open Solutions*, 8, 90478–90494. 10.1109/ACCESS.2020.2994090

Hu, G., Han, X., Zhou, H., & Liu, Y. (2019). Public perception on healthcare services: Evidence from social media platforms in China. *International Journal of Environmental Research and Public Health*, 16(7), 1273. 10.3390/ijerph1607127330974729

Huiying Liang, B. Y. (2019). Evaluation and accurate diagnoses of pediatric diseases using artificial intelligence. *Nature Medicine*, 25(3), 433–438. 10.1038/s41591-018-0335-930742121

Hu, Q., Hart, P., & Cooke, D. (2007). The role of external and internal influences on information systems security – a neo-institutional perspective. *The Journal of Strategic Information Systems*, 16(2), 153–172. 10.1016/j.jsis.2007.05.004

Hysong, S. J., Best, R. G., & Pugh, J. A. (2006). Audit and feedback and clinical practice guideline adherence: Making feedback actionable. *Implementation Science : IS*, 1(1), 9. 10.1186/1748-5908-1-916722539

IIPS and Macro International. (2007). *National Family Health Survey (NFHS 3), 2005–06; India* (Vol. I). IIPS.

Indian Council of Medical Research (ICMR), Ethical Guidelines for Application of Artificial Intelligence in Biomedical Research and Healthcare. (2023). Retrieved January 12, 2024, from https://main.icmr.nic.in/sites/default/files/upload_documents/Ethical_Guidelines_AI_Healthcare_2023.pdf

International Institute for Population Sciences. (2020). National Family Health Survey(NFHS-5) India 2019-21. *Ministry of Health and Family Welfare National*, 361, 2.

Inwood Labs Inc. v. Ives Labs Inc., 456 U.S. 844 (1982).

Ishida, S., Matsui, T., Haga, C., Hori, K., Hashimoto, S., & Saito, O. (2023). Twitter Mining for Detecting Interest Trends on Biodiversity: Messages from Seven Language Communities. *Sustainability (Basel)*, 15(17), 12893. 10.3390/su151712893

J, J. (2023a, June 30). Rapid transformation. artificial intelligence in indian healthcare: a promising future with challenges. *The Hindu*. https://www.thehindubusinessline.com/news/science/artificial-intelligence-in-indian-healthcare-a-promising-future-with challenges/article67015361.ece#:~:text=AI%20expenditure%20in%20India%20is,to%20%24102.7%20Billion%20by%202028.

Jain, L. (2023). *Artificial Intelligence and Machine Learning for Healthcare.*

Janett, R. S., & Yeracaris, P. P. (2020). Electronic Medical Records in the American Health System: Challenges and lessons learned. *Ciencia & Saude Coletiva*, 25(4), 1293–1304. 10.1590/1413-81232020254.28922019322674 32

Janwaar, A., & Singh, A. (2021, October). On the Design of Therapy Tracker: A Cross-platform Medication Management Application with Augmented Reality and Machine Learning. In *Proceedings of the Future Technologies Conference (FTC) 2021, (Vol. 358*, p. 29). Springer Nature.

Jesse, M. W. (2019). *Analysis of voice assistants in eHealth* [Doctoral dissertation, Master Thesis, Universität Klagenfurt].

Jeyaraman, M., Balaji, S., Jeyaraman, N., & Yadav, S. (2023). Unraveling the ethical enigma: Artificial intelligence in healthcare. *Cureus*, 15(8). 10.7759/cureus.4326237692617

Jeyaraman, M., Ramasubramanian, S., Kumar, S., Jeyaraman, N., Selvaraj, P., Nallakumarasamy, A., Bondili, S., & Yadav, S. (2023). Multifaceted role of social media in healthcare: Opportunities, challenges, and the need for quality control. *Cureus*, 15. 10.7759/cureus.3911137332420

Jiang, F., Jiang, Y., Zhi, H., Dong, Y., Li, H., Ma, S., Wang, Y., Dong, Q., Shen, H., & Wang, Y. (2017). Artificial intelligence in healthcare: Past, present and future. *Stroke and Vascular Neurology*, 2(4), 230–243. 10.1136/svn-2017-00010129507784

Jian, W.-S., Wen, H.-C., Scholl, J., Shabbir, S. A., Lee, P., Hsu, C.-Y., & Li, Y.-C. (2011). The Taiwanese method for providing patients data from multiple hospital EHR systems. *Journal of Biomedical Informatics*, 44(2), 326–332. 10.1016/j.jbi.2010.11.00421118726

Jinlei, L., Wenchao, D., Nuo, C., Wenjing, L., Peirong, Q., Hui, Z., & Jie, W. (2022, July). Knowledge Graph of Artificial Intelligence in Medicine: A Scientometric Analysis. In *2022 7th IEEE International Conference on Data Science in Cyberspace (DSC)* (pp. 142-153). IEEE. 10.1109/DSC55868.2022.00026

Jin, S., Zeng, X., Xia, F., Huang, W., & Liu, X. (2021). Application of deep learning methods in biological networks. *Briefings in Bioinformatics*, 22(2), 1902–1917. 10.1093/bib/bbaa04332363401

Jordan, M. I., & Mitchell, T. M. (2015). Machine learning: Trends, perspectives, and prospects. *Science*, 349(6245), 255–260. 10.1126/science.aaa841526185243

Jorstad, K. T. (2020). Intersection of artificial intelligence and medicine: Tort liability in the technological age. *Journal of Medical Artificial Intelligence*, 3, 3. 10.21037/jmai-20-57

Jumde, A., & Kumar, N. (2020). *Access to Medicines in the Light of Patent Law Regime in India*. Intellectual Property Rights and the Protection of Traditional Knowledge. 10.4018/978-1-7998-1835-9.ch002

Jung, Y., & Kwon, S. (2015). The Effects of Intellectual Property Rights on Access to Medicines and Catastrophic Expenditure. *International Journal of Health Services*, 45(3), 507–529. 10.1177/002073141558456026077858

Kachalia, A. (2010). Liability claims and costs before and after implementation of a medical error disclosure program. *Annals of Internal Medicine*, 153(4), 213. 10.7326/0003-4819-153-4-201008170-0000220713789

Kadam, R. A. (2017). Informed consent process: A step further towards making it meaningful! *Perspectives in Clinical Research*, 8(3), 107–112. 10.4103/picr.PICR_147_1628828304

Kaddoura, S., & Grati, R. (2021). Blockchain for Healthcare and Medical Systems. In *Enabling Blockchain Technology for Secure Networking and Communications* (pp. 249–270). IGI Global. 10.4018/978-1-7998-5839-3.ch011

Kadhim, K. T., Alsahlany, A. M., Wadi, S. M., & Kadhum, H. T. (2020). An Overview of Patient's Health Status Monitoring System Based on Internet of Things (IoT). *Wireless Personal Communications*, 114(3), 2235–2262. 10.1007/s11277-020-07474-0

Kahn, S., & Sheshadri, V. (2008). Medical Record Privacy and Security in a Digital Environment. *IT Professional*, 10(2), 46–52. 10.1109/MITP.2008.34

Kamath, R., Ghosh, D., Lena, A., & Chandrasekaran, V. (2013). A study on knowledge and practices regarding menstrual hygiene among rural and urban adolescent girls in Udupi Taluk, Manipal, India. *Global journal of medicine and public health, 2*(4), 1-9.

Kamiike, A., & Sato, T. (2011, August). The TRIPs agreement and pharmaceutical industry: The Indian experience. In *Proceedings of conference on Comparative Aspects on Culture and Religion: India, Russia, China,* (*Vol. 31*, p. 2011). SRC.

Kamin-Friedman, S., & Peled Raz, M. (2021). Lessons from Israel's COVID-19 green pass program. *Israel Journal of Health Policy Research*, 10(1), 1–6. 10.1186/s13584-021-00496-434715931

Kansal, S., Singh, S., & Kumar, A. (2016). Menstrual hygiene practices in context of schooling: A community study among rural adolescent girls in Varanasi. *Indian Journal of Community Medicine*, 41(1), 39–44. 10.4103/0970-0218.17096426917872

Karattuthodi, M. S., Krishnan, G., Aiswarya, A. V., Sarath Chandran, C., Nair, S. S., Thorakkatil, S. A., & Arain, S. (2023). A systematic review on pharmacist-led pharmaceutical care optimization through virtual platforms. *Journal of Pharmaceutical Health Services Research*, 14(1), 2–13. 10.1093/jphsr/rmac054

Kashyap, H., Ahmed, H. A., Hoque, N., Roy, S., & Bhattacharyya, D. K. (2015). Big data analytics in bioinformatics: A machine learning perspective. *arXiv preprint arXiv:1506.05101.*

Kashyap, H., Ahmed, H. A., Hoque, N., Roy, S., & Bhattacharyya, D. K. (2016). Big data analytics in bioinformatics: Architectures, techniques, tools and issues. *Network Modeling and Analysis in Health Informatics and Bioinformatics*, 5(1), 1–28. 10.1007/s13721-016-0135-4

Kaur, R., Kaur, K., & Kaur, R. (2018). Menstrual hygiene, management, and waste disposal: Practices and challenges faced by girls/women of developing countries. *Journal of Environmental and Public Health*, 2018, 2018. 10.1155/2018/173096429675047

Kaushal, S., & Mishra, D. (2024). *Strategic implications of AI in contemporary business and society*. 2024 2nd International Conference on Disruptive Technologies (ICDT), Greater Noida, India. 10.1109/ICDT61202.2024.10489027

Kaushal, S., Nyoni, A. M., Sharma, A., & Saidi, J. A. K. (2023). Drawbacks of technology as an antecedent for knowledge sharing: Focus on curbing misinformation. *2023 9th International Conference on Advanced Computing and Communication Systems (ICACCS)*. IEEE. 10.1109/ICACCS57279.2023.10112895

Keesara, S., Jonas, A., & Schulman, K. (2020). Covid-19 and health care's digital revolution. *The New England Journal of Medicine*, 382(23), e82. 10.1056/NEJMp200583532240581

Keikhosrokiani, P. (Ed.). (2022). *Big data analytics for healthcare: datasets, techniques, life cycles, management, and applications*. Academic Press.

Kerly. (2007). *Law of trademarks and trade names* (South Asian ed.). Sweet and Maxwell.

Kesselheim, A. S. (2012). Variations in pill appearance of antiepileptic drugs and the risk of nonadherence. *Archives of Internal Medicine*, 173(3), 1.23277164

Kesselheim, A. S., Bykov, K., Avorn, J., Tong, A., Doherty, M., & Choudhry, N. K. (2014). Burden of changes in pill appearance for patients receiving generic cardiovascular medications after myocardial infarction. *Annals of Internal Medicine*, 161(2), 96. 10.7326/M13-238125023248

Khachigian, L. M. (2020). Pharmaceutical patents: Reconciling the human right to health with the incentive to invent. *Drug Discovery Today*, 25(7), 1135–1141. 10.1016/j.drudis.2020.04.00932325020

Khan, A., Pin, K., Aziz, A., Han, J. W., & Nam, Y. (2023). Optical coherence tomography image classification using hybrid deep learning and ant colony optimization. *Sensors (Basel)*, 23(15), 6706. 10.3390/s2315670637571490

Khan, F. A., Ali, A., Abbas, H., & Haldar, N. A. H. (2014). A Cloud-based Healthcare Framework for Security and Patients' Data Privacy Using Wireless Body Area Networks. *Procedia Computer Science*, 34, 511–517. 10.1016/j.procs.2014.07.058

Khanna, N. N., Maindarkar, M. A., Viswanathan, V., Fernandes, J. F. E., Paul, S., Bhagawati, M., Ahluwalia, P., Ruzsa, Z., Sharma, A., Kolluri, R., Singh, I. M., Laird, J. R., Fatemi, M., Alizad, A., Saba, L., Agarwal, V., Sharma, A., Teji, J. S., Al-Maini, M., & Suri, J. S. (2022). Economics of Artificial Intelligence in Healthcare: Diagnosis vs. Treatment. *Healthcare (Basel)*, 10(12), 2493. 10.3390/healthcare1012249336554017

Khan, P., Kader, M. F., Islam, S. R., Rahman, A. B., Kamal, M. S., Toha, M. U., & Kwak, K. S. (2021). Machine learning and deep learning approaches for brain disease diagnosis: Principles and recent advances. *IEEE Access : Practical Innovations, Open Solutions*, 9, 37622–37655. 10.1109/ACCESS.2021.3062484

Khansa, L., Cook, D. F., James, T., & Bruyaka, O. (2012). Impact of HIPAA provisions on the stock market value of healthcare institutions, and information security and other information technology firms. *Computers & Security*, 31(6), 750–770. 10.1016/j.cose.2012.06.007

Khatoon, R., Ansari, S., Asghar, S. A., Sachan, B., Zaidi, Z. H., & Ahmad, S. (2023). Knowledge, attitude, and practices of adolescent school girls regarding menstrual hygiene in Lucknow district. *Asian Journal of Medical Sciences*, 14(2), 90–95. 10.3126/ajms.v14i2.49421

Khatri, M. R. (2023). Integration of natural language processing, self-service platforms, predictive maintenance, and prescriptive analytics for cost reduction, personalization, and real-time insights customer service and operational efficiency. *International Journal of Information and Cybersecurity*, 7(9), 1–30.

Khizar, H. M. U., Younas, A., Kumar, S., Akbar, A., & Poulova, P. (2023). The progression of sustainable development goals in tourism: A systematic literature review of past achievements and future promises. *Journal of Innovation & Knowledge*, 8(4), 100442. 10.1016/j.jik.2023.100442

Khurana, V. (2024). Accelerating Pace of Scientific Discovery and Innovation through Big Data Enabled Artificial Intelligence and Deep Learning. *Emerging Trends in Machine Intelligence and Big Data*, 16(1), 38–53.

Kianzad, B., & Wested, J. (2021). 'No-One Is Safe until Everyone Is Safe'-Patent Waiver, Compulsory Licensing and COVID-19. *EPLR*, 5(2), 71–91. 10.21552/eplr/2021/2/4

Kierkegaard, P. (2012). Medical data breaches: Notification delayed is notification denied. *Computer Law & Security Report*, 28(2), 163–183. 10.1016/j.clsr.2012.01.003

Kimani, K., Oduol, V., & Langat, K. (2019). Cyber security challenges for IoT-based smart grid networks. *International Journal of Critical Infrastructure Protection*, 25, 36–49. 10.1016/j.ijcip.2019.01.001

Kitada, M., Johannesen, E., Ojwala, R. A., Buckingham, S., Sun, Z., Rodríguez-Chaves, M., & Schofield, C. (2023). Barriers to the Collection of Gender-Disaggregated Data in Ocean Science. *Human Factors in Management and Leadership*, 71

Kitchin, D., & Llewelyn, D., (Eds.). (2005). *Kerly's law of trademarks and tradenames* (44th ed.). Sweet & Maxwell.

Kitchin, R. (2013). Big data and human geography: Opportunities, challenges and risks. *Dialogues in Human Geography*, 3(3), 262–267. 10.1177/2043820613513388

Kizza, P. (2023). *Implementation of Telemedicine to Reduce No-show Rates.*

Kjaerland, M. (2006). A taxonomy and comparison of computer security incidents from the commercial and government sectors. *Computers & Security*, 25(7), 522–538. 10.1016/j.cose.2006.08.004

Kong, W., You, Z., Lyu, S., & Lv, X. (2024). Multi-dimensional stereo face reconstruction for psychological assistant diagnosis in medical meta-universe. *Information Sciences*, 654, 119831. 10.1016/j.ins.2023.119831

Kopplin, C. S. (2023). Sports fashion and sustainability: A perfect match? *International Journal of Sports Marketing & Sponsorship*, 24(5), 891–912. 10.1108/IJSMS-04-2023-0078

Kou, Z., Shang, L., Zhang, Y., & Wang, D. (2022). Hc-covid: A hierarchical crowdsource knowledge graph approach to explainable covid-19 misinformation detection. *Proceedings of the ACM on Human-Computer Interaction, 6*(GROUP), (pp. 1-25). ACM. 10.1145/3492855

Kouicem, D. E., Bouabdallah, A., & Lakhlef, H. (2018). Internet of things security: A top-down survey. *Computer Networks*, 141, 199–221. 10.1016/j.comnet.2018.03.012

Kovács, B., Darida, M., & Simon, J. (2021). Drugs Becoming Generics—The Impact of Genericization on the Market Performance of Antihypertensive Active Pharmaceutical Ingredients. *International Journal of Environmental Research and Public Health*, 18(18), 9429. 10.3390/ijerph1818942934574353

Kraemer-Mbula, E., Tang, P., & Rush, H. (2013). The cybercrime ecosystem: Online innovation in the shadows? *Technological Forecasting and Social Change*, 80(3), 541–555. 10.1016/j.techfore.2012.07.002

Krikorian, G., & Torreele, E. (2021). We cannot win the access to medicines struggle using the same thinking that causes the chronic access crisis. *Health and Human Rights*, 23(1), 119.34194206

Krishnamoorthy, G. D., Balasubramanian, K., Govindaraj, S., Ayyavu, P. G., & Geetha, D. A. D. (2023, June). Energy management system using binary particle swarm optimization technique. In *AIP Conference Proceedings* (*Vol. 2766*, No. 1). AIP Publishing. 10.1063/5.0139459

Krishnan, S., & Twigg, J. (2016). Menstrual hygiene: A "silent" need during disaster recovery. *Waterlines*, 35(3), 265–276. 10.3362/1756-3488.2016.020

Kruse, C. S., Krowski, N., Rodriguez, B., Tran, L., Vela, J., & Brooks, M. (2017). Telehealth and patient satisfaction: A systematic review and narrative analysis. *BMJ Open*, 7(8), e016242. 10.1136/bmjopen-2017-01624228775188

Kuhnt, J., & Vollmer, S. (2017). Antenatal care services and its implications for vital and health outcomes of children: Evidence from 193 surveys in 69 low-income and middle income countries. *BMJ Open*, 7(11), e017122. 10.1136/bmjopen-2017-01712229146636

Kulyk, O. (2014). Personalized virtual coaching for lifestyle support: Principles for design and evaluation. *International Journal on Advances in Life Sciences*, 6(3-4), 300–309.

Kulynych, J., & Korn, D. (2003). The New HIPAA (Health Insurance Portability and Accountability Act of 1996) Medical Privacy Rule: Help or Hindrance for Clinical Research? *Circulation*, 108(8), 912–914. 10.1161/01.CIR.0000080642.35380.5012939240

Kumar, A., Khan, S. F., Sodhi, R. S., Khan, I. R., Kumar, S., & Tamrakar, A. K. (2022, February). Deep learning Based Patient-Friendly Clinical Expert Recommendation Framework. In *2022 2nd International Conference on Innovative Practices in Technology and Management (ICIPTM)* (*Vol. 2*, pp. 736-741). IEEE. 10.1109/ICIPTM54933.2022.9754157

Kumar, R., Gupta, S. K., Wang, H. C., Kumari, C. S., & Korlam, S. S. V. P. (2023). From Efficiency to Sustainability: Exploring the Potential of 6G for a Greener Future. *Sustainability (Basel)*, 15(23), 16387. 10.3390/su152316387

Kumutha, N., Amutha, N., & Venkatesh, G. S. (2022). Compulsory licensing of patents. *Pharmaceutical Patent Analyst*, 11(6), 225–231. 10.4155/ppa-2022-003936802922

Kuranga, C., Muwani, T. S., & Ranganai, N. (2023). A multi-population particle swarm optimization-based time series predictive technique. *Expert Systems with Applications*, 233, 120935. 10.1016/j.eswa.2023.120935

Kvedar, J., Coye, M. J., & Everett, W. (2014). Connected health: A review of technologies and strategies to improve patient care with telemedicine and telehealth. *Health Affairs (Project Hope)*, 33(2), 194–199. 10.1377/hlthaff.2013.099224493760

Kwon, J., & Johnson, M. (2014). Proactive versus reactive security investments in the healthcare sector. *Management Information Systems Quarterly*, 38(2), 451–471. 10.25300/MISQ/2014/38.2.06

Kwon, J., & Johnson, M. E. (2013). Security practices and regulatory compliance in the healthcare industry. *Journal of the American Medical Informatics Association : JAMIA*, 20(1), 44–51. 10.1136/amiajnl-2012-00090622955497

Lamping, M., Batista, P. H., Correa, J. I., Hilty, R. M., Kim, D., Slowinski, P. R., & Steinhart, M. (2023). Revisiting the Framework for Compulsory Licensing of Patents in the European Union. SSRN *Electronic Journal*. 10.2139/ssrn.4381959

Lavigne, M., Mussa, F., Creatore, M. I., Hoffman, S. J., & Buckeridge, D. L. (2019). A population health perspective on artificial intelligence. *Healthcare Management Forum*, 32(4), 173–177. 10.1177/084047041984842831106580

Lee, D. (2018). Strategies for technology-driven service encounters for patient experience satisfaction in hospitals. *International Journal Technological Forecasting and Social Change*, 118-127.

Lee, N., Nystén-Haarala, S., & Huhtilainen, L. (2010). *Interfacing Intellectual property rights and Open innovation*. WIPO. https://www.wipo.int/edocs/mdocs/mdocs/en/wipo_ipr_ge_11/wipo_ipr_ge_11_topic6.pdf

Lee, D. (2019). Effects of Key Value Co-creation Elements in the Healthcare System: Focusing on Technology Applications. *Service Business*, 13(2), 389–417. 10.1007/s11628-018-00388-9

Lee, J. A., Hilty, R., & Liu, K. C. (Eds.). (2021 Feb 25). *Artificial intelligence and intellectual property*. Oxford University Press. 10.1093/oso/9780198870944.001.0001

Lee, S. (2018). *Living Innovation: From Value Creation to the Greater Good*. Emerald Publishing Limited. 10.1108/9781787567139

Lei, Z., Sun, Y., Nanehkaran, Y. A., Yang, S., Islam, M. S., Lei, H., & Zhang, D. (2020). A novel data-driven robust framework based on machine learning and knowledge graph for disease classification. *Future Generation Computer Systems*, 102, 534–548. 10.1016/j.future.2019.08.030

Lemley, M. A., & Volokh, E. (1998). Freedom of speech and injunctions in intellectual property cases. *Duke Law Journal*, 48.

Leung, P. H., Chui, K. T., Lo, K., & de Pablos, P. O. (2021). A support vector machine–based voice disorders detection using human voice signal. In *Artificial Intelligence and Big Data Analytics for Smart Healthcare* (pp. 197–208). Academic Press. 10.1016/B978-0-12-822060-3.00014-0

Lindstrom, M. (2005). *Brand sense: Build powerful brands through touch, taste, smell, sight and sound* (1st ed.). Free Press.

Li, P., Williams, R., Gilbert, S., & Anderson, S. (2023). Regulating AI/ML-enabled medical devices in the UK. *Proceedings of the First International Symposium on Trustworthy Autonomous Systems*. ACM. 10.1145/3597512.3599704

Li, W., Chai, Y., Khan, F., Jan, S. R. U., Verma, S., Menon, V. G., & Li, X. (2021). A comprehensive survey on machine learning-based big data analytics for IoT-enabled smart healthcare system. *Mobile Networks and Applications*, 26(1), 234–252. 10.1007/s11036-020-01700-6

Li, Z. Q., Fu, Z. X., Li, W. J., Fan, H., Li, S. N., Wang, X. M., & Zhou, P. (2023). Prediction of Diabetic Macular Edema Using Knowledge Graph. *Diagnostics (Basel)*, 13(11), 1858. 10.3390/diagnostics1311185837296709

Long, C. (2021). China Amends The Patent Law: A Stronger Protection Is On The Way. *les Nouvelles-Journal of the Licensing Executives Society, 56*(1).

Long, J., Chen, Z., He, W., Wu, T., & Ren, J. (2020). An integrated framework of deep learning and knowledge graph for prediction of stock price trend: An application in Chinese stock exchange market. *Applied Soft Computing*, 91, 106205. 10.1016/j.asoc.2020.106205

Lopert, R., & Gleeson, D. (2013). The High Price of 'Free' Trade: U.S. Trade Agreements and Access to Medicines. *The Journal of Law, Medicine & Ethics*, 41(1), 199–223. 10.1111/jlme.1201423581666

Lown, B. A., Rosen, J., & Marttila, J. (2011). An agenda for improving compassionate care: A survey shows about half of patients say such care is missing. *Health Affairs*, 30(9), 1772–1778. 10.1377/hlthaff.2011.053921900669

Lukose, L. P. (2013). Consumer protection vis-a-vis trademark law. *Journal on Consumer Law and Practice*, 1(1).

Luna, R., Rhine, E., Myhra, M., Sullivan, R., & Kruse, C. S. (2016). Cyber threats to health information systems: A systematic review. *Technology and Health Care*, 24(1), 1–9. 10.3233/THC-15110226578272

Lv, H., Shi, L., Berkenpas, J. W., Dao, F. Y., Zulfiqar, H., Ding, H., Zhang, Y., Yang, L., & Cao, R. (2021). Application of artificial intelligence and machine learning for COVID-19 drug discovery and vaccine design. *Briefings in Bioinformatics*, 22(6), bbab320. 10.1093/bib/bbab32034410360

Lynn, L. A. (2019). Artificial intelligence systems for complex decision-making in acute Care Medicine: A Review. *Patient Safety in Surgery*, 13(1), 6. 10.1186/s13037-019-0188-230733829

MacIntyre, C. R., Chen, X., Kunasekaran, M., Quigley, A., Lim, S., Stone, H., Paik, H. Y., Yao, L., Heslop, D., Wei, W., Sarmiento, I., & Gurdasani, D. (2023, March). Artificial intelligence in public health: The potential of epidemic early warning systems. *The Journal of International Medical Research*, 51(3), 030006052311593. 10.1177/03000605231159335 36967669

MacLean, F. (2021). Knowledge graphs and their applications in drug discovery. *Expert Opinion on Drug Discovery*, 16(9), 1057–1069. 10.1080/17460441.2021.1910673 33843398

MacQueen, H., Waelde, C., & Laurie, G. (2008). *Contemporary intellectual property, law and policy* (1st ed.). Oxford University Press.

Maher, C., Singh, B., Wylde, A., & Chastin, S. (2024). Virtual health assistants: A grand challenge in health communications and behavior change. *Frontiers in Digital Health*, 6, 1418695. 10.3389/fdgth.2024.1418695 38827384

Majeed, J., Sharma, P., Ajmera, P., & Dalal, K. (2022). Menstrual hygiene practices and associated factors among Indian adolescent girls: A meta-analysis. *Reproductive Health*, 19(1), 148. 10.1186/s12978-022-01453-3 35739585

Malachi, A., Anders, E., & Asamoah, B. O. (2017). Effectiveness of antenatal care services in reducing neonatal mortality in Kenya: Analysis of national survey data. *Global Health Action*. 10.1080/16549716.2017.1272223 28621201

Malhotra, P. (2010). TRIPS and the Indian Patents Regime. In *Impact of TRIPS in India: An Access to Medicines Perspective* (pp. 80-110). London: Palgrave Macmillan UK.

Malik, S., & Tyagi, A. K. (Eds.). (2022). *Intelligent Interactive Multimedia Systems for E-Healthcare Applications*. CRC Press. 10.1201/9781003282112

Malik, V. S., Behmani, S., Singh, V., Behmani, R. K., Kumar, S., & Kumar, K. (2023). The effects of a menstrual distress coping education program for adolescents and young adult females. In *Perspectives on coping strategies for menstrual and premenstrual distress* (pp. 156–174). IGI Global. 10.4018/978-1-6684-5088-8.ch009

Mamanazarov, S. (2023). Intellectual Property Theories as Applied to Big Data. *International Journal of Law and Policy.*, 1(7). 10.59022/ijlp.164

Maniatis, S. M. (1998). *The communicative aspects of trade marks: a legal, functional and economic analysis* [Thesis]. https://core.ac.uk/download/pdf/30695616.pdf

Maniatis, S. (2006). *Trade marks in Europe: A practical jurisprudence* (1st ed.). Sweet & Maxwell.

Mann, K. D., Good, N. M., Fatehi, F., Khanna, S., Campbell, V., Conway, R., Sullivan, C., Staib, A., Joyce, C., & Cook, D. (2021). Predicting patient deterioration: A review of tools in the digital hospital setting. *Journal of Medical Internet Research*, 23(9), e28209. 10.2196/2820934591017

Manyika, J., Chui, M., Brown, B., Bughin, J., Dobbs, R., Roxburgh, C., & Hung Byers, A. (2011). *Big data: The next frontier for innovation, competition, and productivity*.

Marecos, J., Shattock, E., Bartlett, O., Goiana-da-Silva, F., Maheswaran, H., Ashrafian, H., & Darzi, A. (2023). Health misinformation and freedom of expression: Considerations for policymakers. *Health Economics, Policy, and Law*, 18(2), 1–14. 10.1017/S174413312200026336718749

Marsoof, A. (2012). TRIPS compatibility of Sri Lankan trademark law. *The Journal of World Intellectual Property*, 15(1), 15. 10.1111/j.1747-1796.2011.00430.x

Martin, G., Martin, P., Hankin, C., Darzi, A., & Kinross, J. (2017). Cybersecurity and healthcare: How safe are we? *BMJ (Clinical Research Ed.)*, 358, j3179. 10.1136/bmj.j317928684400

Mäses, S., Randmann, L., Maennel, O., & Lorenz, B. (2018). Stenmap: Framework for Evaluating Cybersecurity-Related Skills Based on Computer Simulations. In Zaphiris, P., & Ioannou, A. (Eds.), *Learning and Collaboration Technologies. Learning and Teaching* (pp. 492–504). Springer International Publishing. 10.1007/978-3-319-91152-6_38

Matebese, F., Mosai, A. K., Tutu, H., & Tshentu, Z. R. (2024). Mining wastewater treatment technologies and resource recovery techniques: A review. *Heliyon*, 10(3), e24730. 10.1016/j.heliyon.2024.e2473038317979

Matthews, D. (2002). *Globalising intellectual property rights: the TRIPs Agreement*. Routledge.

Mazhar, T., Talpur, D. B., Shloul, T. A., Ghadi, Y. Y., Haq, I., Ullah, I., Ouahada, K., & Hamam, H. (2023). Analysis of IoT Security Challenges and Its Solutions Using Artificial Intelligence. *Brain Sciences*, 13(4), 683. 10.3390/brainsci1304068337190648

McCarthy, J. T. (1998). *McCarthy on trademarks and unfair competition* (3rd ed.). Legal Solutions, Thomas Reuters.

McDowell, D. (2006). The polymerase chain reaction patents: Going, going, still going. *Journal of the Royal Society of Medicine*, 99(2), 62–64. 10.1258/jrsm.99.2.6216449778

McGill, A. M. (2009). Compulsory licensing of patented pharmaceuticals: Why a WTO administrative body should determine what constitutes a public health crisis under the Doha Declaration. *Wake Forest Intell. Prop. LJ*, 10, 69.

McGowan, P. T. (2012). Self-management education and support in chronic disease management. *Primary Care*, 39(2), 307–325. 10.1016/j.pop.2012.03.00522608868

Mead, N., & Bower, P. (2000). Patient-centredness: A conceptual framework and review of the empirical literature. *Social Science & Medicine*, 51(7), 1087–1110. 10.1016/S0277-9536(00)00098-811005395

Menell, P. S., Lemley, M. A., & Merges, R. P. (2016). *Intellectual Property in the New Technological Age: 2019*. Social Science Research Network.

Mensah, G. B. (2023). *Artificial Intelligence and Ethics: A Comprehensive Review of Bias Mitigation*. Transparency, and Accountability in AI Systems.

Merchant, R. M., & Lurie, N. (2020). Social media and emergency preparedness in response to novel coronavirus. *Journal of the American Medical Association*, 323(20), 2011–2012. 10.1001/jama.2020.446932202611

Mesko, B. (2016). Artificial Intelligence Will Redesign Healthcare. *Brain*.

Meskó, B., & Görög, M. (2020). A short guide for medical professionals in the era of artificial intelligence. *NPJ Digital Medicine*, 3(1), 126. 10.1038/s41746-020-00333-z33043150

Miller, E. (2003). *Introduction A Progress Report on TRIPS and Access to Medicines Médecins Sans Frontières Briefing for the 5th WTO Ministerial Conference, Cancún 2003 See back cover for recommendations*. https://www.msfaccess.org/sites/default/files/MSF_assets/Access/Docs/ACCESS_report_DohaDerailed_ENG_2003.pdf

Miller, D. D., & Brown, E. W. (2018). Artificial intelligence in medical practice: The question to the answer? *The American Journal of Medicine*, 131(2), 129–133. 10.1016/j.amjmed.2017.10.03529126825

Miller, F. G., Colloca, L., & Kaptchuk, T. J. (2009). The Placebo Effect: Illness and Interpersonal Healing. *Perspectives in Biology and Medicine*, 52(4), 518–539. 10.1353/pbm.0.011519855122

Ministry of social Justice & Empowerment. (2023). *Critical Insights Into Elderly Care In India*. Press information Bureau government of India. https://pib.gov.in/pressReleasePage.aspx?PRID=1961168)

Minnaar, A., & Herbig, F. J. (2021). Cyberattacks and the Cybercrime Threat of Ransomware to Hospitals and Healthcare Services During the COVID-19 Pandemic. *Acta Criminologica : African Journal of Criminology & Victimology*, 34(3), 155–185. 10.10520/ejc-crim_v34_n3_a10

Min, X. Z., Zhang, Z. F., Lu, X. M., Chen, J. C., Ma, W. L., Liu, L. Y., & Kallenborn, R. (2024). Occurrence and fate of pharmaceuticals and personal care products in a wastewater treatment plant with Bacillus bio-reactor treatment. *The Science of the Total Environment*, 924, 171589. 10.1016/j.scitotenv.2024.17158938461988

Mittal, S. (2017). *Effects of TRIPSPlus Provisions in International Trade Agreements Upon Access to Medicines in Developing Countries.* 10.2139/ssrn.2975649

Modarress-Fathi, B., Ansari, A., & Ansari, A. (2023). Examining Sustainability Alignment of Supplier Selection Criteria during Industrial Revolutions. *Sustainability (Basel)*, 15(22), 15930. 10.3390/su152215930

Mohammad Amini, M., Jesus, M., Fanaei Sheikholeslami, D., Alves, P., Hassanzadeh Benam, A., & Hariri, F. (2023). Artificial Intelligence Ethics and Challenges in Healthcare Applications: A Comprehensive Review in the Context of the European GDPR Mandate. *Machine Learning and Knowledge Extraction*, 5(3), 1023–1035. 10.3390/make5030053

Mohammadi, M., Al-Fuqaha, A., Sorour, S., & Guizani, M. (2018). Deep learning for IoT big data and streaming analytics: A survey. *IEEE Communications Surveys and Tutorials*, 20(4), 2923–2960. 10.1109/COMST.2018.2844341

Mohanty, S. K. (2012). Multiple Deprivations and Maternal Care in India. *International Perspectives on Sexual and Reproductive Health*, 38(1), 6–14. 10.1363/380061222481144

Moher, D., Liberati, A., Tetzlaff, J., & Altman, D. G. (2009). Preferred reporting items for systematic reviews and meta-analyses: The PRISMA statement. *BMJ (Clinical Research Ed.)*, 339(7716), 332–336. 10.1136/bmj.b253519622551

Mo, L., Zhang, L., Sun, X., & Zhou, Z. (2024). Unlock Happy Interactions: Voice Assistants Enable Autonomy and Timeliness. *Journal of Theoretical and Applied Electronic Commerce Research*, 19(2), 1013–1033. 10.3390/jtaer19020053

Molavi, H., Mirzaei, K., Jafarpour, E., Mohammadi, A., Salimi, M. S., Rezakazemi, M., Nadagouda, M. M., & Aminabhavi, T. M. (2024). Wastewater treatment using nanodiamond and related materials. *Journal of Environmental Management*, 349, 119349. 10.1016/j.jenvman.2023.119349

Monteiro, A. C. B., França, R. P., Arthur, R., & Iano, Y. (2021). An overview of medical Internet of Things, artificial intelligence, and cloud computing employed in health care from a modern panorama. *The Fusion of Internet of Things, Artificial Intelligence, and Cloud Computing in Health Care*, 3-23.

Morrison, A. M., & Buhalis, D. (Eds.). (2023). *Routledge Handbook of Trends and Issues in Global Tourism Supply and Demand*. Taylor & Francis. 10.4324/9781003260790

Mucke, H. A. (2020). Patent highlights February-March 2020. *Pharmaceutical Patent Analyst*, 9(4), 129–136. 10.4155/ppa-2020-001032815491

Muralidharan, A., Patil, H., & Patnaik, S. (2015). Unpacking the policy landscape for menstrual hygiene management: Implications for school WASH programmes in India. *Waterlines*, 34(1), 79–91. 10.3362/1756-3488.2015.008

Murdoch, B. (2021). Privacy and artificial intelligence: Challenges for protecting health information in a new era. *BMC Medical Ethics*, 22(1), 122. 10.1186/s12910-021-00687-334525993

Muthu, B., Sivaparthipan, C. B., Manogaran, G., Sundarasekar, R., Kadry, S., Shanthini, A., & Dasel, A. (2020). IOT based wearable sensor for diseases prediction and symptom analysis in healthcare sector. *Peer-to-Peer Networking and Applications*, 13(6), 2123–2134. 10.1007/s12083-019-00823-2

Muthuppalaniappan, M., & Stevenson, K. (2021). Healthcare cyber-attacks and the COVID-19 pandemic: An urgent threat to global health. *International Journal for Quality in Health Care : Journal of the International Society for Quality in Health Care*, 33(1), mzaa117. 10.1093/intqhc/mzaa11733351134

Muzeeb Ur Rehman, A. P. (2021). Review on Artificial Intelligence in Healthcare. *Innovations*, •••, 66.

Nahavandi, D., Alizadehsani, R., Khosravi, A., & Acharya, U. R. (2022). Application of artificial intelligence in wearable devices: Opportunities and challenges. *Computer Methods and Programs in Biomedicine*, 213, 106541. 10.1016/j.cmpb.2021.10654134837860

Naik, N., Hameed, B. M. Z., Shetty, D. K., Swain, D., Shah, M., Paul, R., Aggarwal, K., Ibrahim, S., Patil, V., Smriti, K., Shetty, S., Rai, B. P., Chlosta, P., & Somani, B. K. (2022). Legal and ethical consideration in artificial intelligence in healthcare: Who takes responsibility? *Frontiers in Surgery*, 9, 266. 10.3389/fsurg.2022.86232235360424

Nair, N. S., Darak, S., Parsekar, S. S., Parchure, R., Darak, T., Nelson, H., Vijayamma, R., & Menon, S. (2017). *Effectiveness of Behaviour Change Communication interventions in improving the delivery of health messages for ante-natal care in limited literacy settings: An evidence summary*. London: EPPI-Centre, Social Science Research Unit, UCL Institute of Education, University College London.

Nair, M. K. C., Chacko, D. S., Ranjith Darwin, M., Padma, K., George, B., & Ps, R. (2012). Menstrual disorders and menstrual hygiene practices in higher secondary school girls. *Indian Journal of Pediatrics*, 79(S1), 74–78. 10.1007/s12098-011-0431-z21625846

Nair, P., Aghoram, R., Thomas, B., Bharadwaj, B., & Chinnakali, P. (2021). Video teleconsultation services for persons with epilepsy during COVID-19 pandemic: An exploratory study from public tertiary care hospital in Southern India on feasibility, satisfaction, and effectiveness. *Epilepsy & Behavior*, 117, 107863. 10.1016/j.yebeh.2021.10786333677363

Napoleon, E. A. (2020). Patent Eligibility: Exploring the Intersection Between Patent Law and Biomedical Data. *Pitt. J. Tech. L. & Pol'y*, 21, 117.

Narayana Samy, G., Ahmad, R., & Ismail, Z. (2010). Security threats categories in healthcare information systems. *Health Informatics Journal*, 16(3), 201–209. 10.1177/14604582103774682O889850

Neely, S., Eldredge, C., & Sanders, R. (2021). Health information seeking behaviors on social media during the COVID-19 pandemic among American social networking site users: Survey study. *Journal of Medical Internet Research*, 23(6), e29802. 10.2196/2980234043526

Nimje, P. (2022, May 10). *The Need for Trademark in Pharmaceutical Industry*. Sagacious IP. https://sagaciousresearch.com/blog/the-need-for-trademark-in-pharmaceutical-industry/

Nizam, V., & Aslekar, A. (2021). Challenges of applying AI in healthcare in India. *Journal of Pharmaceutical Research International*, 203–209. 10.9734/jpri/2021/v33i36B31969

Nomani, M. Z. M., & Alaa, K. K. (2020). Alhalboosi, and Mohammad Rauf. "Legal & intellectual property dimension of health & access to medicines in India.". *Indian Journal of Forensic Medicine Toxicology*, 14(1), 118–122.

Nomani, M., Alhalboosi, A. K., & Rauf, M. (2020). Legal & Intellectual Property Dimension of Health & Access to Medicines in India. *Indian Journal of Forensic Medicine Toxicology*.

Norwich Pharmacal co: v. Sterling Drug, Inc., 271 F.2d 569 (1959)

O'Reilly, V. (2004). The Community Trademark System: A brief introduction and overview. *Marquette Intellectual Property Law Journal, 8.*

Obiuto, N. C., Ugwuanyi, E. D., Ninduwezuor-Ehiobu, N., Ani, E. C., & Olu-lawal, K. A. (2024). Advancing wastewater treatment technologies: The role of chemical engineering simulations in environmental sustainability. *World Journal of Advanced Research and Reviews, 21*(3), 019-031.

OECD. (2004). *Patents And Innovation: Trends And Policy Challenges Organisation For Economic Co-Operation And Development.* OECD. https://www.oecd.org/science/inno/24508541.pdf

Office of the Controller General of Patents, Designs and Trade Marks (India). (2007-2008). *Annual report.*

Office of the United States Trade Representative. (2005). *Australia-United States Free Trade Agreement.* USTR. ustr.gov.in. https://ustr.gov/sites/default/files/uploads/agreements/fta/australia/asset_upload_file469_5141.pdf

Olawunmi, B., & Babatunde, F. (2022). *Impact of mass media messaging on compliance with COVID-19 safety protocols among residents of Osogbo.* Caleb International Journal of Development Studies. 10.26772/cijds-2022-05-01-015

Olshannikova, E., Ometov, A., Koucheryavy, Y., & Olsson, T. (2015). Visualizing Big Data with augmented and virtual reality: Challenges and research agenda. *Journal of Big Data*, 2(1), 1–27. 10.1186/s40537-015-0031-2

Padmaja, M., Shitharth, S., Prasuna, K., Chaturvedi, A., Kshirsagar, P. R., & Vani, A. (2022). Grow of artificial intelligence to challenge security in IoT application. *Wireless Personal Communications*, 127(3), 1829–1845. 10.1007/s11277-021-08725-4

Paik, H.-Y., Xu, X., Bandara, H. M. N. D., Lee, S. U., & Lo, S. K. (2019). Analysis of Data Management in Blockchain-Based Systems: From Architecture to Governance. *IEEE Access : Practical Innovations, Open Solutions*, 7, 186091–186107. 10.1109/ACCESS.2019.2961404

Panch, T. S. P., Szolovits, P., & Atun, R. (2018). Artifcial intelligence, machine learning and Health System. *Journal of Global Health*, 8(2), 020303. 10.7189/jogh.08.02030330405904

Panesar, A. (2019). *Machine learning and AI for healthcare*. Apress. 10.1007/978-1-4842-3799-1

Pan, X., Lin, X., Cao, D., Zeng, X., Yu, P. S., He, L., Nussinov, R., & Cheng, F. (2022). Deep learning for drug repurposing: Methods, databases, and applications. *Wiley Interdisciplinary Reviews. Computational Molecular Science*, 12(4), e1597. 10.1002/wcms.1597

Paris Convention for the Protection of Industrial Property, 1883.

Park, J., Sandhu, R., Gupta, M., & Bhatt, S. (2021). Activity control design principles: Next-generation access control for smart and collaborative systems. *IEEE Access : Practical Innovations, Open Solutions*, 9, 151004–151022. 10.1109/ACCESS.2021.3126201

Pauwelyn, J. (2010). The dog that barked but didn't bite: 15 years of intellectual property disputes at the WTO. *Journal of International Dispute Settlement*, 1.

Pécoul, B. (1999). Access to Essential Drugs in Poor CountriesA Lost Battle? *Journal of the American Medical Association*, 281(4), 361. 10.1001/jama.281.4.3619929090

Pednekar, S., Some, S., Rivankar, K., & Thakore, R. (2022). Enabling factors for sustainable menstrual hygiene management practices: A rapid review. *Discover Sustainability*, 3(1), 28. 10.1007/s43621-022-00097-4

Peng, W., Yuan, S., & Holtz, B. (2016). Exploring the challenges and opportunities of health mobile apps for individuals with type 2 diabetes living in rural communities. *Telemedicine Journal and e-Health. Telemedicine Journal and e-Health*, 22(9), 733–738. 10.1089/tmj.2015.018026982017

Periyasamy, A. P., & Periyasami, S. (2023). Critical Review on Sustainability in Denim: A Step toward Sustainable Production and Consumption of Denim. *ACS Omega*, 8(5), 4472–4490. 10.1021/acsomega.2c0637436777581

Pesapane, F., Bracchi, D., Mulligan, J., Linnikov, A., Maslennikov, O., Lanzavecchia, M., Tantrige, P., Stasolla, A., Biondetti, P., Giuggioli, P., Cassano, E., & Carrafiello, G. (2021). Legal and regulatory framework for AI solutions in healthcare in EU, US, China, and Russia: New scenarios after a pandemic. *Radiation*, 1(4), 17–28. 10.3390/radiation1040022

Pesapane, F., Codari, M., & Sardanelli, F. (2018). *Artificial Intelligence in Medical Imaging: Threat or Opportunity? Radiologists again at tEuprohe Forefront of Innovation in Medicine*. European Radiology Exprimental.

Peter, K. Y. (2024). The COVID-19 TRIPS Waiver and the WTO Ministerial Decision. In *Intellectual Property Rights in Times of Crisis* (pp. 1-25). Edward Elgar Publishing.

Pfizer Products Inc. v. B.L. and Company, [Case citation]. Indian Kanoon. (2002). https://indiankanoon.org/doc/145093/

Pfizer. (n.d.). EUIPO Registration No: 001909472.

Pilkington, M. (2016). Blockchain technology: Principles and applications. In Olleros, F. X., & Zhegu, M. (Eds.), *Research Handbook on Digital Transformations*. Edward Elgar Publishing. 10.4337/9781784717766.00019

Pires de Carvalho, N. (2006). *The TRIPS regime of trademarks and designs* (5th ed.). Kluwer Law International.

Pley, C., van Der Heijden, M. R., & Tulinius, C. (2020). A health professional's guide to the intersection of public health with intellectual property rights in trade and investment: The case of tobacco plain packaging. *Journal of Public Health Policy*, 41(1), 52–62. 10.1057/s41271-019-00195-031685934

Poduval, S., Ahmed, S., Marston, L., Hamilton, F., & Murray, E. (2018). Crossing the digital divide in online self-management support: Analysis of usage data from HeLP-Diabetes. *JMIR Diabetes*, 3(4), e10925. 10.2196/1092530522988

Poonsuph, R. (2022). The design blueprint for a large-scale telehealth platform. *International Journal of Telemedicine and Applications*, 2022, 2022. 10.1155/2022/848650835035477

Poornima, A. S., & Subramanian, S. (2024, May). Fostering Global Wellness: Harnessing Social Media to Enhance Cross-Cultural Trust to propel Medical Tourism Ensuring Economic Growth. In *European Conference on Social Media* (Vol. 11, No. 1, pp. 216-224). 10.34190/ecsm.11.1.2408

Powell, R. E., Henstenburg, J. M., Cooper, G., Hollander, J. E., & Rising, K. L. (2017). Patient perceptions of telehealth primary care video visits. *Annals of Family Medicine*, 15(3), 225–229. 10.1370/afm.209528483887

Pradhan, T., Nimkar, P., & Jhajharia, K. (2024). Machine Learning and Deep Learning for Big Data Analysis. In *Big Data Analytics Techniques for Market Intelligence* (pp. 209–240). IGI Global. 10.4018/979-8-3693-0413-6.ch008

Prakash, S., Balaji, J. N., Joshi, A., & Surapaneni, K. M. (2022). Ethical Conundrums in the application of artificial intelligence (AI) in healthcare—A scoping review of reviews. *Journal of Personalized Medicine*, 12(11), 1914. 10.3390/jpm1211191436422090

Pramanik, P. K. D., Pal, S., & Mukhopadhyay, M. (2022). Healthcare big data: A comprehensive overview. *Research anthology on big data analytics, architectures, and applications*, 119-147.

Praniskas, J. (1968). Trade name creation: Processes and patterns. *Journal of Economics*, 101.

Preum, S. M., Munir, S., Ma, M., Yasar, M. S., Stone, D. J., Williams, R., & Stankovic, J. A. (2021). A review of cognitive assistants for healthcare: Trends, prospects, and future directions. *ACM Computing Surveys*, 53(6), 1–37. 10.1145/3419368

Putz, B., Menges, F., & Pernul, G. (2019). A secure and auditable logging infrastructure based on a permissioned blockchain. *Computers & Security*, 87, 101602. 10.1016/j.cose.2019.101602

Qadir, A. M. A., & Fatah, A. O. (2023). Platformization and the metaverse: Opportunities and challenges for urban sustainability and economic development. *EAI Endorsed Transactions on Energy Web, 10*(1).

Qadri, Y. A., Nauman, A., Zikria, Y. B., Vasilakos, A. V., & Kim, S. W. (2020). The future of healthcare internet of things: A survey of emerging technologies. *IEEE Communications Surveys and Tutorials*, 22(2), 1121–1167. 10.1109/COMST.2020.2973314

Quesada-Caballero, M., Carmona-García, A., Chami-Peña, S., Caballero-Mateos, A., Fernández-Martín, O., Fuente, G., & Romero-Béjar, J. (2023). Telemedicine in elderly hypertensive and patients with chronic diseases during the COVID-19 pandemic: A systematic review and meta-analysis. *Journal of Clinical Medicine*, 12(19), 6160. 10.3390/jcm1219616037834803

Qureshi, R., Irfan, M., Ali, H., Khan, A., Nittala, A. S., Ali, S., & Alam, T. (2023). Artificial Intelligence and Biosensors in Healthcare and its Clinical Relevance: A Review. *IEEE Access : Practical Innovations, Open Solutions*, 11, 61600–61620. 10.1109/ACCESS.2023.3285596

R120/2001-2, Eli Lilly & Company, Appeal Relating to Community Trade mark application no: 1452853. (2004).

Ragavan, S., & Vanni, A. (Eds.). (2021). *Intellectual property law and access to medicines: TRIPS agreement, health, and pharmaceuticals*. Taylor & Francis. 10.4324/9781003176602

Ragavi, V. S., Santha Sheela, A. C., & Narayanan Kannaiyan, G. (2021). Impact of Artificial Intelligence in the field of Health. *Journal of Physics: Conference Series*, 1831(1), 012006. 10.1088/1742-6596/1831/1/012006

Rahimieh, A., & Nosrati, M. (2024). A Review on Biochemistry, Microbiology and Thermodynamic Aspects of Propionate: The Key Intermediate in the Anaerobic Digestion and Wastewater Treatment. *Desalination and Water Treatment*, 317, 100191. 10.1016/j.dwt.2024.100191

Raju, K. D. (2016). The first compulsory licencing case in India under the TRIPS agreement: An analysis of Bayer versus Natco Pharma Ltd. *Journal of Development Policy and Practice*, 1(1), 71–88. 10.1177/2455133315612321

Ramalingam, R., & Chinnaiyan, V. (2023). A comparative analysis of chronic obstructive pulmonary disease using machine learning, and deep learning. *Iranian Journal of Electrical and Computer Engineering*, 13(1), 389. 10.11591/ijece.v13i1.pp389-399

Ramanujam, P., & Goyal, Y. (2014). One view of compulsory licensing: Comparative perspectives from India and Canada. *Marq. Intell. Prop. L. Rev.*, 18, 369.

Ramsey, L. P. (2010). Free speech and international obligations to protect trademarks. *The Yale Journal of International Law*, 35.

Ram, U., Pradhan, M. R., Patel, S., & Ram, F. (2020). Factors associated with disposable menstrual absorbent use among young women in India. *International Perspectives on Sexual and Reproductive Health*, 46, 223–234. 10.1363/46e032033108760

Rana, M., & Bhushan, M. (2023). Machine learning and deep learning approach for medical image analysis: Diagnosis to detection. *Multimedia Tools and Applications*, 82(17), 26731–26769. 10.1007/s11042-022-14305-w36588765

Rapacke, A. (2018, September 18). *The Role Trademarks Play in Medical Device Technologies - The Rapacke Law Group*. Arapackelaw.com. https://arapackelaw.com/trademarks/role-trademarks-medical-devices/

Rathert, C., Mittler, J. N., Banerjee, S., & McDaniel, J. (2017). Patient-centered communication in the era of electronic health records: What does the evidence say? *Patient Education and Counseling*, 100(1), 50–64. 10.1016/j.pec.2016.07.03127477917

Rathod, S. K. (2017). Compulsory licences on pharmaceutical patents in India: A short article. *Journal of Generic Medicines*, 13(3), 108–113. 10.1177/1741134317691804

Ratna, H. (2019). The importance of effective communication in healthcare practice. *HPHR Journal*, 23(23). 10.54111/0001/W4

Rauf, M., & Tamang, R. (2023). Access to Medicines and Intellectual Property Law: Balancing Innovation and Public Health. *Interdisciplinary Studies in Society, Law, and Politics*, 2(3), 37–43. 10.61838/kman.isslp.2.3.5

Raval, H. Y., Parikh, S. M., & Patel, H. R. (2022). Self-maintained health surveillance artificial intelligence assistant. In *Handbook of Research on Lifestyle Sustainability and Management Solutions Using AI, Big Data Analytics, and Visualization* (pp. 168-184). IGI Global. 10.4018/978-1-7998-8786-7.ch010

Rees, A. M. (1993). Communication in the physician-patient relationship. *Bulletin of the Medical Library Association*, 81(1), 1–10.8428183

Ricketson, S. (2015). *The Paris Convention for the Protection of Industrial Property: A commentary* (1st ed.). Oxford University Press.

Robinson, C. L., D'Souza, R. S., Yazdi, C., Diejomaoh, E. M., Schatman, M. E., Emerick, T., & Orhurhu, V. (2024). Reviewing the Potential Role of Artificial Intelligence in Delivering Personalized and Interactive Pain Medicine Education for Chronic Pain Patients. *Journal of Pain Research*, 17, 923–929. 10.2147/JPR.S43945238464902

Rode, S. J. (2018). Effect of Complete Antenatal Care on Birth Weight of Children in India: Evidence from National Family Health Survey (NFHS) Data. *Journal of Women's Health Care*, 7(1), 412. 10.4172/2167-0420.1000412

Rodrigues, J. F.Jr, Florea, L., de Oliveira, M. C., Diamond, D., & Oliveira, O. N.Jr. (2021). Big data and machine learning for materials science. *Discover Materials*, 1(1), 1–27. 10.1007/s43939-021-00012-033899049

Rosenbaum, L. (2020). Facing Covid-19 in Italy - Ethics, logistics, and therapeutics on the epidemic's front line. *The New England Journal of Medicine*, 382(20), 1873–1875. 10.1056/NEJMp200549232187459

Ross Whitney Corp v. SKF, 207 F.2d 190 (9th Cir. 1953).

Rossouw, L., & Ross, H. (2021). Understanding period poverty: Socio-economic inequalities in menstrual hygiene management in eight low-and middle-income countries. *International Journal of Environmental Research and Public Health*, 18(5), 1–15. 10.3390/ijerph1805257133806590

Rubeis, G. (2022). iHealth: The ethics of artificial intelligence and big data in mental healthcare. *Internet Interventions : the Application of Information Technology in Mental and Behavioural Health*, 28, 100518. 10.1016/j.invent.2022.10051835257003

Rudin, C. (2019). Stop explaining black box machine learning models for high stakes decisions and use interpretable models instead. *Nature Machine Intelligence*, 1(5), 206–215. 10.1038/s42256-019-0048-x35603010

Rupe, E. R., Rodean, J., Hurley, E. A., Miller, M. K., Boncoeur, M. D., & Masonbrink, A. R. (2022). Menstrual health among adolescents and young adults in rural Haiti. *Reproductive Health*, 19(1), 1–10. 10.1186/s12978-022-01533-436539795

Rutschman, A. S. (2022). Ministerial Decision on the Trips Agreement (WTO). *International Legal Materials*, 62(2), 289–294. 10.1017/ilm.2022.47

Ryals, C. A., Pierce, K. L., & Baker, J. W. (2011). INR Goal Attainment and Oral Anticoagulation Knowledge of Patients Enrolled in an Anticoagulation Clinic in a Veterans Affairs Medical Center. *Journal of Managed Care Pharmacy : JMCP*, 17(2), 133–142. 10.18553/jmcp.2011.17.2.13321348546

Saadat, M. N., & Shuaib, M. (2020). Advancements in deep learning theory and applications: Perspective in 2020 and beyond. *Advances and Applications in Deep Learning, 3*.

Sabrina, H. Z., & Chen, L. C. (2013). The Bangladesh Paradox: Exceptional Health Achievement despite Economic Poverty. *Lancet*, 382(9906), 1734–1745. 10.1016/S0140-6736(13)62148-024268002

Safavi, S., & Shukur, Z. (2014). Conceptual Privacy Framework for Health Information on Wearable Device. *PLoS One*, 9(12), e114306. 10.1371/journal.pone.011430625478915

Saggurti, N., Atmavilas, Y., Porwal, A., Schooley, J., Das, R., Kande, N., Irani, L., & Hay, K. (2018). Effect of health intervention integration within women's self-help groups on collectivization and healthy practices around reproductive, maternal neonatal and child health in rural India. *PLoS One*, 13(8), 2010–2020. 10.1371/journal.pone.020256230138397

Sahar, S. N., & Dar, H. (2024). Artificial Intelligence-Enhanced Global Healthcare: The Future of Medical Tourism. In *Impact of AI and Robotics on the Medical Tourism Industry* (pp. 194-216). IGI Global.

Salazar, S. (1998). *INTELLECTUAL PROPERTY AND THE RIGHT TO HEALTH*. WIPO. https://www.wipo.int/edocs/mdocs/tk/en/wipo_unhchr_ip_pnl_98/wipo_unhchr_ip_pnl_98_3.pdf

Sanchez-Segura, M. I., Dugarte-Peña, G. L., Medina-Dominguez, F., Amescua Seco, A., & Menchen Viso, R. (2023). Digital transformation in organizational health and safety to mitigate Burnout Syndrome. *Frontiers in Public Health*, 11, 1080620. 10.3389/fpubh.2023.108062037026125

Sanjaya, K. (2020). Competition Law and IPRs: Friends or Foes? *International Journal of Law Management & Humanities*, 3(6). 10.1732/IJLMH.25187

Sardar, T. H., Khatun, A., Sengupta, S., Alam, Y., & Ara, T. (2024). Machine Learning in the Healthcare Sector and the Biomedical Big Data: Techniques, Applications, and Challenges. *Big Data Computing*, 336-352.

Sarkar, G., & Shukla, S. K. (2024). Reconceptualizing online offenses: A framework for distinguishing cybercrime, cyberattacks, and cyberterrorism in the Indian legal context. *Journal of Economic Criminology*, 4, 100063. 10.1016/j.jeconc.2024.100063

Sarker, M. (2023). Assessing the Integration of AI Technologies in Enhancing Patient Care Delivery in US Hospitals. *Journal of Knowledge Learning and Science Technology, 2*(2), 338-351.

Sarpatwari, A., & Kesselheim, A. S. (2016). The Case for Reforming Drug Naming: Should Brand Name Trademark Protections Expire upon Generic Entry? *PLoS Medicine*, 13(2), e1001955. 10.1371/journal.pmed.100195526859662

Scarborough, B. M., & Smith, C. B. (2018). Optimal pain management for patients with cancer in the modern era. *CA: a Cancer Journal for Clinicians*, 68(3), 182–196. 10.3322/caac.2145329603142

Scaria, A. G., & Mammen, K. S. (2018). Non-Traditional Trademarks in the Pharmaceutical Sector. In Calboli, I., & Senftleben, M. (Eds.), *The Protection of Non-Traditional Trademarks: Critical Perspectives* (pp. 271–286). Oxford University Press. 10.1093/oso/9780198826576.003.0015

Scarpato, N., Pieroni, A., Di Nunzio, L., & Fallucchi, F. (2017). E-health-IoT universe: A review. *management, 21*(44), 46.

Schairer, C. E., Rubanovich, C. K., & Bloss, C. S. (2018). How could commercial terms of use and privacy policies undermine informed consent in the age of mobile health? *AMA Journal of Ethics*, 20(9), E864–E872. 10.1001/amajethics.2018.86430242818

Schechter, F. (1927). The rational basis of trademark protection. *Harvard Law Review*, •••, 40.

Secinaro, S., Calandra, D., Secinaro, A., Muthurangu, V., & Biancone, P. (2021). The role of artificial intelligence in healthcare: A structured literature review. *BMC Medical Informatics and Decision Making*, 21(1), 125. 10.1186/s12911-021-01488-933836752

Seh, A. H., Zarour, M., Alenezi, M., Sarkar, A. K., Agrawal, A., Kumar, R., & Ahmad Khan, R. (2020). Healthcare Data Breaches: Insights and Implications. *Health Care*, 8(2), 133. 10.3390/healthcare802013332414183

Sejdic, E., & Falk, T. H. (Eds.). (2018). *Signal processing and machine learning for biomedical big data*. CRC press. 10.1201/9781351061223

Sekalala, S., Forman, L., Hodgson, T., Mulumba, M., Namyalo-Ganafa, H., & Meier, B. M. (2021). Decolonising human rights: How intellectual property laws result in unequal access to the COVID-19 vaccine. *BMJ Global Health*, 6(7), e006169. 10.1136/bmjgh-2021-00616934253631

Seligsohn, E. (1973). Recent developments in the law of trademarks and unfair competition in Israel. *Trademark Reporter, 63*.

Sellin, J. A. (2015). Does One Size Fit All? Patents, the Right to Health and Access to Medicines. *Netherlands International Law Review*, 62(3), 445–473. 10.1007/s40802-015-0047-5

Sell, S. K. (2003). *Private power, public law: the globalization of intellectual property rights*. Cambridge University Press. 10.1017/CBO9780511491665

Sell, S. K. (2007). TRIPS-Plus Free Trade Agreements and Access to Medicines. *The Liverpool Law Review*, 28(1), 41–75. 10.1007/s10991-007-9011-8

Senarath, A., & Arachchilage, N. A. G. (2019). A data minimization model for embedding privacy into software systems. *Computers & Security*, 87, 101605. 10.1016/j.cose.2019.101605

Senbekov, M., Saliev, T., Bukeyeva, Z., Almabayeva, A., Zhanaliyeva, M., Aitenova, N., Toishibekov, Y., & Fakhradiyev, I. (2020). The recent progress and applications of digital technologies in healthcare: A review. *International Journal ofTelemedicine and Applications*, 2020, 2020. 10.1155/2020/883020033343657

Sengan, S., Kamalam, G. K., Vellingiri, J., Gopal, J., Velayutham, P., & Subramaniyaswamy, V. (2020). Medical information retrieval systems for e-Health care records using fuzzy based machine learning model. *Microprocessors and Microsystems*, 103344.

Seong No Yoon, D. L. (2019). Artificial Intelligence and Robots in Healthcare: What are the Success Factors for Technology-based Service Encounters? *International Journal of Healthcare Management*, 12(3), 218–225. 10.1080/20479700.2018.1498220

Sezgin, E., Militello, L. K., Huang, Y., & Lin, S. (2020). A scoping review of patient-facing, behavioral health interventions with voice assistant technology targeting self-management and healthy lifestyle behaviors. *Translational Behavioral Medicine*, 10(3), 606–628. 10.1093/tbm/ibz14132766865

Shabankareh, M., Nazarian, A., Golestaneh, M. H., & Dalouchi, F. (2023). Health tourism and government supports. *International Journal of Emerging Markets.*

Shah, F., Li, J., Shah, Y., & Shah, F. (2017, November). Broad big data domain via medical big data. In *2017 4th International Conference on Systems and Informatics (ICSAI)* (pp. 732-737). IEEE.

Shahabuddin, A. S. M., De Brouwere, V., & Adhikari, R. (2017). *Determinants of institutional delivery among young married women in Nepal: Evidence from the Nepal Demographic and Health Survey*. BMJ. bmj.com/content/bmjopen/7/4/e012446.full.pdfhttps://doi.org/10.1136/bmjopen-2016-012446

Shahid, Z. (2021). *Distributed Machine Learning for Anomalous Human Activity Recognition using IoT Systems.*

Shah, S. P., Nair, R., Shah, P. P., Modi, D. K., Desai, S. A., & Desai, L. (2013). Improving quality of life with new menstrual hygiene practices among adolescent tribal girls in rural Gujarat, India. *Reproductive Health Matters*, 21(41), 205–213. 10.1016/S0968-8080(13)41691-923684203

Shah, S. W., & Kanhere, S. S. (2019). Recent trends in user authentication–a survey. *IEEE Access : Practical Innovations, Open Solutions*, 7, 112505–112519. 10.1109/ACCESS.2019.2932400

Sharifi, A., Allam, Z., Bibri, S. E., & Khavarian-Garmsir, A. R. (2024). Smart cities and sustainable development goals (SDGs): A systematic literature review of co-benefits and trade-offs. *Cities (London, England)*, 146, 104659. 10.1016/j.cities.2023.104659

Sharma, A. K., & Dube, D. (2021). The relevance of criminal law in intellectual property law research. *Handbook of intellectual property research: Lenses, methods, and perspectives.* Oxford University Press. 10.1093/oso/9780198826743.001

Sharma, A., McCall-Hosenfeld, J. S., & Cuffee, Y. (2022). Systematic review of menstrual health and hygiene in Nepal employing a social ecological model. *Reproductive Health*, 19(1), 1–21. 10.1186/s12978-022-01456-035773696

Sharma, A., & Singh, B. (2022). Measuring Impact of E-commerce on Small Scale Business: A Systematic Review. *Journal of Corporate Governance and International Business Law*, 5(1).

Sharma, S., & Thakkalapelli, D. (2023). Corporate patenting AI and ML in healthcare: Regulatory and ethical considerations. *International Journal of New Media Studies: International Peer Reviewed Scholarly Indexed Journal*, 10(1), 232–235.

Sharmila Nirojini, P., Kanaga, K., Devika, S., & Pradeep, P. (2024). Exploring the impact of artificial intelligence on patient care: A comprehensive review of healthcare advancements. *Sch Acad J Pharm*, 13(2), 67–81. 10.36347/sajp.2024.v13i02.003

Shenoy, A., & Appel, J. M. (2017). Safeguarding Confidentiality in Electronic Health Records. *Cambridge Quarterly of Healthcare Ethics*, 26(2), 337–341. 10.1017/S0963180116000931 28361730

Shire v. Barr, 329 F.3d 348.

Shrank, W. H. (2009). Patients' perceptions of generic medicines. Health Affairs, 28 • Shapiro, A. K., & Shapiro, E. (1999). The placebo: Is it much ado about nothing? In Harrington, A. (Ed.), *The placebo effect* (pp. 12–30).

Shrestha, R., & Nam, S. Y. (2019). Regional Blockchain for Vehicular Networks to Prevent 51% Attacks. *IEEE Access : Practical Innovations, Open Solutions*, 7, 95033–95045. 10.1109/ACCESS.2019.2928753

Siegler, M. (2021). Clinical medical ethics and the historical background of shared decision making. In *Oxford University Press eBooks* (pp. 27–36). 10.1093/med/9780197598573.003.0003

Simões-Marques, M., Água, P., Frias, A., & Correia, A. (2023). Metaverse and Digital Twins: Contributions, Opportunities and Challenges to a Sustainable Use of the Ocean. *Human Factors and Systems Interaction, 84*(84).

Singh, B. (2023). Blockchain Technology in Renovating Healthcare: Legal and Future Perspectives. In *Revolutionizing Healthcare Through Artificial Intelligence and Internet of Things Applications* (pp. 177-186). IGI Global.

Singh, B. (2024). Evolutionary Global Neuroscience for Cognition and Brain Health: Strengthening Innovation in Brain Science. In *Biomedical Research Developments for Improved Healthcare* (pp. 246-272). IGI Global.

Singh, B., & Kaunert, C. (2024). Harnessing Sustainable Agriculture Through Climate-Smart Technologies: Artificial Intelligence for Climate Preservation and Futuristic Trends. In *Exploring Ethical Dimensions of Environmental Sustainability and Use of AI* (pp. 214-239). IGI Global.

Singh, B., & Kaunert, C. (2024). Salvaging Responsible Consumption and Production of Food in the Hospitality Industry: Harnessing Machine Learning and Deep Learning for Zero Food Waste. In *Sustainable Disposal Methods of Food Wastes in Hospitality Operations* (pp. 176-192). IGI Global.

Singh, A., Chakrabarty, M., Singh, S., Chandra, R., Chowdhury, S., & Singh, A. (2022). Menstrual hygiene practices among adolescent women in rural India: A cross-sectional study. *BMC Public Health*, 22(1), 1–18. 10.1186/s12889-022-14622-736401238

Singh, A., Pallikadavath, S., Ram, F., & Alagarajan, M. (2014). Do antenatal care interventions improve neonatal survival in India? *Health Policy and Planning*, 29(7), 842–848. 10.1093/heapol/czt06624038077

Singhal, A., Neveditsin, N., Tanveer, H., & Mago, V. (2024). Toward Fairness, Accountability, Transparency, and Ethics in AI for Social Media and Health Care: Scoping Review. *JMIR Medical Informatics*, 12, e50048. 10.2196/5004838568737

Singh, B. (2019). Profiling Public Healthcare: A Comparative Analysis Based on the Multidimensional Healthcare Management and Legal Approach. *Indian Journal of Health and Medical Law*, 2(2), 1–5.

Singh, B. (2020). GLOBAL SCIENCE AND JURISPRUDENTIAL APPROACH CONCERNING HEALTHCARE AND ILLNESS. *Indian Journal of Health and Medical Law*, 3(1), 7–13.

Singh, B. (2022). COVID-19 Pandemic and Public Healthcare: Endless Downward Spiral or Solution via Rapid Legal and Health Services Implementation with Patient Monitoring Program. *Justice and Law Bulletin*, 1(1), 1–7.

Singh, B. (2022). Relevance of Agriculture-Nutrition Linkage for Human Healthcare: A Conceptual Legal Framework of Implication and Pathways. *Justice and Law Bulletin*, 1(1), 44–49.

Singh, B. (2022). Understanding Legal Frameworks Concerning Transgender Healthcare in the Age of Dynamism. *ELECTRONIC JOURNAL OF SOCIAL AND STRATEGIC STUDIES*, 3(1), 56–65. 10.47362/EJSSS.2022.3104

Singh, B. (2023). Blockchain Technology in Renovating Healthcare: Legal and Future Perspectives. In Kaushik, K., Dahiya, S., Aggarwal, S., & Dwivedi, A. (Eds.), *Revolutionizing Healthcare Through Artificial Intelligence and Internet of Things Applications* (pp. 177–186). IGI Global. 10.4018/978-1-6684-5422-0.ch012

Singh, B. (2023). Unleashing Alternative Dispute Resolution (ADR) in Resolving Complex Legal-Technical Issues Arising in Cyberspace Lensing E-Commerce and Intellectual Property: Proliferation of E-Commerce Digital Economy. *Revista Brasileira de Alternative Dispute Resolution-Brazilian Journal of Alternative Dispute Resolution-RBADR*, 5(10), 81–105. 10.52028/rbadr.v5i10.ART04.Ind

Singh, B. (2024). Evolutionary Global Neuroscience for Cognition and Brain Health: Strengthening Innovation in Brain Science. In Prabhakar, P. (Ed.), *Biomedical Research Developments for Improved Healthcare* (pp. 246–272). IGI Global. 10.4018/979-8-3693-1922-2.ch012

Singh, B. (2024). Lensing Legal Dynamics for Examining Responsibility and Deliberation of Generative AI-Tethered Technological Privacy Concerns: Infringements and Use of Personal Data by Nefarious Actors. In Ara, A., & Ara, A. (Eds.), *Exploring the Ethical Implications of Generative AI* (pp. 146–167). IGI Global. 10.4018/979-8-3693-1565-1.ch009

Singh, B. (2024). Social Cognition of Incarcerated Women and Children: Addressing Exposure to Infectious Diseases and Legal Outcomes. In Reddy, K. (Ed.), *Principles and Clinical Interventions in Social Cognition* (pp. 236–251). IGI Global. 10.4018/979-8-3693-1265-0.ch014

Singh, B., Dutta, P. K., & Kaunert, C. (2024). Replenish Artificial Intelligence in Renewable Energy for Sustainable Development: Lensing SDG 7 Affordable and Clean Energy and SDG 13 Climate Actions With Legal-Financial Advisory. In Derbali, A. (Ed.), *Social and Ethical Implications of AI in Finance for Sustainability* (pp. 198–227). IGI Global. 10.4018/979-8-3693-2881-1.ch009

Singh, B., Jain, V., Kaunert, C., Dutta, P. K., & Singh, G. (2024). Privacy Matters: Espousing Blockchain and Artificial Intelligence (AI) for Consumer Data Protection on E-Commerce Platforms in Ethical Marketing. In Saluja, S., Nayyar, V., Rojhe, K., & Sharma, S. (Eds.), *Ethical Marketing Through Data Governance Standards and Effective Technology* (pp. 167–184). IGI Global. 10.4018/979-8-3693-2215-4.ch015

Singh, B., & Kaunert, C. (2024). Aroma of Highly Smart Internet of Medical Things (IoMT) and Lightweight EdgeTrust Expansion Medical Care Facilities for Electronic Healthcare Systems: Fortified-Chain Architecture for Remote Patient Monitoring and Privacy Protection Beyond Imagination. In Hassan, A., Bhattacharya, P., Tikadar, S., Dutta, P., & Sagayam, M. (Eds.), *Lightweight Digital Trust Architectures in the Internet of Medical Things (IoMT)* (pp. 196–212). IGI Global. 10.4018/979-8-3693-2109-6.ch011

Singh, B., & Kaunert, C. (2024). Augmented Reality and Virtual Reality Modules for Mindfulness: Boosting Emotional Intelligence and Mental Wellness. In Hiran, K., Doshi, R., & Patel, M. (Eds.), *Applications of Virtual and Augmented Reality for Health and Wellbeing* (pp. 111–128). IGI Global. 10.4018/979-8-3693-1123-3.ch007

Singh, B., & Kaunert, C. (2024). Computational Thinking for Innovative Solutions and Problem-Solving Techniques: Transforming Conventional Education to Futuristic Interdisciplinary Higher Education. In Fonkam, M., & Vajjhala, N. (Eds.), *Revolutionizing Curricula Through Computational Thinking, Logic, and Problem Solving* (pp. 60–82). IGI Global. 10.4018/979-8-3693-1974-1.ch004

Singh, B., & Kaunert, C. (2024). Harnessing Sustainable Agriculture Through Climate-Smart Technologies: Artificial Intelligence for Climate Preservation and Futuristic Trends. In Kannan, H., Rodriguez, R., Paprika, Z., & Ade-Ibijola, A. (Eds.), *Exploring Ethical Dimensions of Environmental Sustainability and Use of AI* (pp. 214–239). IGI Global. 10.4018/979-8-3693-0892-9.ch011

Singh, B., & Kaunert, C. (2024). Revealing Green Finance Mobilization: Harnessing FinTech and Blockchain Innovations to Surmount Barriers and Foster New Investment Avenues. In Jafar, S., Rodriguez, R., Kannan, H., Akhtar, S., & Plugmann, P. (Eds.), *Harnessing Blockchain-Digital Twin Fusion for Sustainable Investments* (pp. 265–286). IGI Global. 10.4018/979-8-3693-1878-2.ch011

Singh, B., & Kaunert, C. (2024). Salvaging Responsible Consumption and Production of Food in the Hospitality Industry: Harnessing Machine Learning and Deep Learning for Zero Food Waste. In Singh, A., Tyagi, P., & Garg, A. (Eds.), *Sustainable Disposal Methods of Food Wastes in Hospitality Operations* (pp. 176–192). IGI Global. 10.4018/979-8-3693-2181-2.ch012

Singh, B., & Kaunert, C. (2024). Wind and Solar Energy as Renewable Energy for Sustainable Global Future: Projecting Future Multi-Sector Sustainable Policies and Innovation. In Ara, A., & Thakore, R. (Eds.), *Promoting Multi-Sector Sustainability With Policy and Innovation* (pp. 210–245). IGI Global. 10.4018/979-8-3693-2113-3.ch009

Singh, B., & Kaunert, C. Reinventing Artificial Intelligence and Blockchain for Preserving Medical Data. In *Ethical Artificial Intelligence in Power Electronics* (pp. 77–91). CRC Press. 10.1201/9781032648323-6

Singh, B., Kaunert, C., & Vig, K. (2024). Reinventing Influence of Artificial Intelligence (AI) on Digital Consumer Lensing Transforming Consumer Recommendation Model: Exploring Stimulus Artificial Intelligence on Consumer Shopping Decisions. In Musiolik, T., Rodriguez, R., & Kannan, H. (Eds.), *AI Impacts in Digital Consumer Behavior* (pp. 141–169). IGI Global. 10.4018/979-8-3693-1918-5.ch006

Singh, B., Vig, K., Dutta, P. K., & Kaunert, C. (2024). Unraveling Agile Transformation for Customer Satisfaction in Changing Market Conditions: Roadmap for Industry Embracing Change in Project Management. In Misra, S., Jadeja, R., & Mittal, M. (Eds.), *Practical Approaches to Agile Project Management* (pp. 305–321). IGI Global. 10.4018/979-8-3693-3318-1.ch017

SK&F v. Premo Pharm. Labs., Inc., 625 F.2d 1055 (3rd Cir. 1980).

Skapetze, L., Zha, C., Yin, X., von Brueck, D., & Önkü, E. (2023). Promoting Pro-Environmental Behavior based on the Psychology of Perception. *Briefe zur Interdisziplinarität*, (31).

Skapetze, L., Zhao, C., Yin, X., von Brueck, D., & Önkü, E. (2023). 6 Promoting pro-environmental behaviour based on the. *Balanced Sustainability In A Changing World, 10*, 111.

Skapetze, L., Zhao, C., Yin, X., von Brueck, D., & Önkü, E. (2024). Promoting pro-environmental behaviour based on the psychology of perception—Can the metaverse be a potential solution? In *Balanced Sustainability in a Changing World* (pp. 111-136).

Smith, S. R. (2008). Introduction to Intellectual Property, Trade and Access to Medicines. In: *Our Health, Our Right: The Roles And Experiences Of PLHIV Networks in Securing Access to Generic ARV Medicines in Asia.* Asia Pacific Network of People Living with HIV/AIDS. https://rest.neptune-prod.its.unimelb.edu.au/server/api/core/bitstreams/cbf59c92-a665-5808-817b-e7d878d3dfc5/content

Soldrzano, R. (1952). Registrations of foreign trade-marks in Mexico. *Trademark Review, 42*.

Sood, M. (2013). Nato Pharma Ltd. v. Bayer Corporation and the Compulsory Licensing Regime in India. *Nujs L. Rev., 6*, 99.

Soofastaei, A. (Ed.). (2024). *Advanced Virtual Assistants-A Window to the Virtual Future*. BoD–Books on Demand.

Spence, E. A. (2022). Existing Patent Laws Promote Competition and Lower Drug Prices, but Is This Appropriate for COVID-19 MRNA Vaccines? *Cal. WL Rev.*, 59, 183.

Srivastav, S. (2023, June 19). AI in healthcare: the regulations conundrum. *Financial Express*. https://www.financialexpress.com/healthcare/healthtech/ai-in-healthcare-the-regulations-conundrum/3131045/

Stalla-Bourdillon, S., & Knight, A. (2016). Anonymous data v. personal data-false debate: An EU perspective on anonymization, pseudonymization and personal data. *Wis. Int'l LJ*, 34, 284.

Standing, K., & Parker, S. L. (2018). Girls' and Women's Rights to Menstrual Health in Nepal. In *Handbook of research on women's issues and rights in the developing world* (pp. 156-168). IGI Global.

Stanton, D. (2016, January 6). AstraZeneca's purple Reign? Dr Reddy's relaunches Nexium generic in blue. *IN-PHARMA TECHNOLOGIST BLOG*.http://www.in-pharmatechnologist.com/Processing/AZ-retains-purple-reign-Dr-Reddy-s-relaunches-Nexium-generic-in-blue

Stellios, I., Kotzanikolaou, P., Psarakis, M., Alcaraz, C., & Lopez, J. (2018). A Survey of IoT-Enabled Cyberattacks: Assessing Attack Paths to Critical Infrastructures and Services. *IEEE Communications Surveys and Tutorials*, 20(4), 3453–3495. 10.1109/COMST.2018.2855563

Stephens, Z. D., Lee, S. Y., Faghri, F., Campbell, R. H., Zhai, C., Efron, M. J., & Robinson, G. E. (2015). Big data: Astronomical or genomical? *PLoS Biology*, 13(7), e1002195. 10.1371/journal.pbio.100219526151137

Stim, R. (2024). *Patent, copyright & trademark: an intellectual property desk reference*. Nolo.

Street, R. L.Jr, Makoul, G., Arora, N. K., & Epstein, R. M. (2009). How does communication heal? Pathways linking clinician–patient communication to health outcomes. *Patient Education and Counseling*, 74(3), 295–301. 10.1016/j.pec.2008.11.01519150199

Sujatha, R., Chatterjee, J. M., Jhanjhi, N. Z., & Brohi, S. N. (2021). Performance of deep learning vs machine learning in plant leaf disease detection. *Microprocessors and Microsystems*, 80, 103615. 10.1016/j.micpro.2020.103615

Sukeshini, S., P., Ved, M., Chintalapti, J., & Pal, S. N. (2021). Big data analytics and machine learning technologies for HPC applications. In *Evolving Technologies for Computing, Communication and Smart World:Proceedings of ETCCS 2020* (pp. 411-424). Springer Singapore.

Sunyaev, A., Dehling, T., Taylor, P. L., & Mandl, K. D. (2014). Availability and quality of mobile health app privacy policies. *Journal of the American Medical Informatics Association : JAMIA*, 22(e1), e28–e33. 10.1136/amiajnl-2013-00260525147247

Suratiningsih, D. (2023). Strategy for Establishing the World Mangrove Center as a Climate Change Mitigation Effort. *Journal of Namibian Studies: History Politics Culture*, 34, 2474–2494.

Swann, J. B. (1986). The design of restaurant interiors – A new approach to aesthetic functionality. *Trademark Reporter, 76.*

Szalewski, J. (1998). The international protection of trademarks after the TRIPS Agreement. *Duke Journal of Comparative & International Law, 9.*

Tarzian, M., Ndrio, M., & Fakoya, A. O. (2023). An Introduction and Brief Overview of Psychoanalysis. *Cureus*, 15(9), e45171. 10.7759/cureus.4517137842377

Tavakoli, M. (2023). *Hybrid human-AI driven open personalized education.*

Telehealth: A Path to Virtual Integrated Care | AHA. (n.d.-b). American Hospital Association. https://www.aha.org/center/emerging-issues/market-insights/telehealth/path-virtual-integrated-care

Telehealth: Technology meets health care. (2022, June 18). Mayo Clinic. https://www.mayoclinic.org/healthy-lifestyle/consumer-health/in-depth/telehealth/art-20044878

Tembo, M., Renju, J., Weiss, H. A., Dauya, E., Gweshe, N., Ndlovu, P., Nzombe, P., Chikwari, C. D., Mavodza, C. V., Mackworth-Young, C. R. S., & Ferrand, A., R., & Francis, S. C. (. (2022). Integration of a menstrual health intervention in a community-based sexual and reproductive health service for young people in Zimbabwe: A qualitative acceptability study. *BMC Health Services Research*, 22(1), 1–12. 10.1186/s12913-022-07818-535354445

Tenni, B., Moir, H. V., Townsend, B., Kilic, B., Farrell, A. M., Keegel, T., & Gleeson, D. (2022). What is the impact of intellectual property rules on access to medicines? A systematic review. *Globalization and Health*, 18(1), 40. 10.1186/s12992-022-00826-435428250

Teremetskyi, V., Duliba, Y., Drozdova, O., Zhukovska, L., Sivash, O., & Dziuba, I. (2021). Access to Justice and Legal Aid for Vulnerable Groups: New Challenges Caused by the Covid-19 Pandemic. *J. Legal Ethical & Regul. Isses*, 24, 1.

Terhune, C. (2015, February 5). Anthem hack exposes data on 80 million; experts warn of identity theft - Los Angeles Times. *Los Angeles Times*. https://www.latimes.com/business/la-fi-anthem-hacked-20150204-story.html

Teutsch, C. (2003). Patient–doctor communication. *The Medical Clinics of North America*, 87(5), 1115–1145. 10.1016/S0025-7125(03)00066-X14621334

Thakre, S. B., Thakre, S. S., Reddy, M., Rathi, N., Pathak, K., & Ughade, S. (2011). Menstrual hygiene: Knowledge and practice among adolescent school girls of Saoner, Nagpur district. *Journal of Clinical and Diagnostic Research : JCDR*, 5(5), 1027–1033.

Thambisetty, S., McMahon, A., McDonagh, L., Kang, H. Y., & Dutfield, G. (2022). The COVID-19 TRIPS Waiver Process in Critical Review: An Appraisal of the WTO DG Text (IP/C/W/688) and Recommendations for Minimum Modifications. SSRN *Electronic Journal*. 10.2139/ssrn.4124497

Thapa, C., & Camtepe, S. (2021). Precision health data: Requirements, challenges and existing techniques for data security and privacy. *Computers in Biology and Medicine*, 129, 104130. 10.1016/j.compbiomed.2020.10413033271399

The Hindu. (2023). India must attune its policies to ensure the elderly live a life of dignity. *The Hindu.*

Tiwari, S. K., Kaur, J., Singla, P., & Hrisheekesha, P. N. (2022, September). A Comprehensive Review of Big Data Analysis Techniques in Health-Care. In *International Conference on Emergent Converging Technologies and Biomedical Systems* (pp. 401-420). Singapore: Springer Nature Singapore.

Tonelli, C., & Morandi, A. (2023). *The impact of 3D technology on sustainability in fashion luxury product design: evidences from an exploratory analysis.*

Tong, Y., Liao, X., He, Y., Cui, X., Wishart, M., Zhao, F., & Chen, G. (2024). Mitigating greenhouse gas emissions from municipal wastewater treatment in China. *Environmental Science and Ecotechnology*, 20, 100341. 10.1016/j.ese.2023.10034138094258

Topol, E. (2020). High-performance medicine: The convergence of human and artificial intelligence. *Nature Medicine*, 25(1), 44–56. 10.1038/s41591-018-0300-730617339

Torondel, B., Sinha, S., Mohanty, J. R., Swain, T., Sahoo, P., Panda, B., Nayak, A., Bara, M., Bilung, B., Cumming, O., Panigrahi, P., & Das, P. (2018). Association between unhygienic menstrual management practices and prevalence. *BMC Infectious Diseases*, 18(1), 473. https://bmcinfectdis.biomedcentral.com/articles/10.1186/s12879-018-3384-2. 10.1186/s12879-018-3384-230241498

Torremans, P. (2008). *Holyoak & Torremans, Intellectual Property Law* (5th ed.). Oxford University Press.

Townsend, B., Gleeson, D., & Lopert, R. (2016). The Regional Comprehensive Economic Partnership, Intellectual Property Protection, and Access to Medicines. *Asia-Pacific Journal of Public Health*, 28(8), 682–693. 10.1177/1010539516676 33827920239

Trebilcock, M. J., & Howse, R. (2005). *The regulation of international trade.*

Trinh, H., Shamekhi, A., Kimani, E., & Bickmore, T. W. (2018, November). Predicting user engagement in longitudinal interventions with virtual agents. In *Proceedings of the 18th International Conference on Intelligent Virtual Agents* (pp. 9-16). ACM. 10.1145/3267851.3267909

Trujillo, J. C., Carrillo, B., & Iglesias, W. J. (2014). Relationship between professional antenatal care and facility delivery: An assessment of Colombia. *Health Policy and Planning*, 29(4), 443–449. 10.1093/heapol/czt03323735737

Tyagi, A. K. (Ed.). (2023). *Privacy Preservation and Secured Data Storage in Cloud Computing*. IGI Global.

Tzanou, M. (2023). *Health Data Privacy Under the GDPR*. TAYLOR FRANCIS Limited.

U.N. Secretary-General's High-Level Panel on Access to Medicines. (2016). *Promoting innovation and access to health technologies.* Annex by Professor Ruth Okediji. High-Level Panel.

U.S. Department of Health and Human Services. (2022, October 19). *Summary of the HIPAA Security Rule.* HHS.gov. https://www.hhs.gov/hipaa/for-professionals/security/laws-regulations/index.html

UNICEF. (2019). Guidance on menstrual health and hygiene. *New York: UNICEF.*

United Nations Children's Fund. (2008) *The State Of The World's Children Maternal And Newborn Health*. UNICEF. https://www.unicef.org/sowc09/docs/SOWC09-FullReport-EN.pdf

United States -Morocco Free Trade Agreement. (2004). TCC. https://tcc.export.gov/static/final_text_Morocco_FTA.pdf

Unni, V. (2019). India's TRIPS-Compliant Patent Decade – The Tumultuous Journey in Search of a Pragmatic Equilibrium. *IIC - International Review of Intellectual Property and Competition Law, 50*, 161-195.

Upadhyay, N. K., & Rathee, M. 2020, June. Impact of Artificial Intelligence on Intellectual Property Rights. In *Proceedings of International Young Scholars Workshop* (Vol. 9). 10.47344/iysw.v9i0.192

Upashe, S. P., Tekelab, T., & Mekonnen, J. (2015). Assessment of knowledge and practice of menstrual hygiene among high school girls in Western Ethiopia. *BMC Women's Health*, 15(1), 1–8. 10.1186/s12905-015-0245-726466992

Urias, E., & Ramani, S. V. (2020). Access to medicines after TRIPS: Is compulsory licensing an effective mechanism to lower drug prices? A review of the existing evidence. *Journal of International Business Policy*, 3(4), 367–384. Advance online publication. 10.1057/s42214-020-00068-4

ustr.gov. (2016). *TPP Full Text.* United States Trade Representative. https://ustr.gov/trade-agreements/free-trade-agreements/trans-pacific-partnership/tpp-full-text

Valero, M., Clemente, J., Li, F., & Song, W. (2021). Health and sleep nursing assistant for real-time, contactless, and non-invasive monitoring. *Pervasive and Mobile Computing*, 75, 101422. 10.1016/j.pmcj.2021.101422

Van Deursen Hazelhoff Roelfze, N. (2014). *HI-Risk: A socio-technical method for the identification and monitoring of healthcare information security risks in the information society.* Naiper Repository. https://napier-repository.worktribe.com/output/181044

Van Eijk, A. M., Sivakami, M., Thakkar, M. B., Bauman, A., Laserson, K. F., Coates, S., & Phillips-Howard, P. A. (2016). Menstrual hygiene management among adolescent girls in India: A Systematic review and meta-analysis. *BMJ Open*, 6(3), e010290. Advance online publication. 10.1136/bmjopen-2015-01029026936906

Vats, S. (2022). 35% senior citizens in India suffer abuse by sons, 21% by daughters-in-law, finds survey. *The Print.* (https://theprint.in/india/35-senior-citizens-in-india-suffer-abuse-by-sons-21-by-daughters-in-law-finds-survey/997283/)

Vaver, D. (2005). Recent trends in European trademark law: Of shapes, senses and sensation. *The Trademark Reporter, 95.*

Velásquez, G., & Velásquez, G. (2022). *Medicines and intellectual property: 10 years of the WHO global strategy*. Springer International Publishing.

Venkat, A., Asher, S. L., Wolf, L., Geiderman, J. M., Marco, C. A., McGreevy, J., Derse, A. R., Otten, E. J., Jesus, J. E., Kreitzer, N. P., Escalante, M., & Levine, A. C. (2015). Ethical issues in the response to Ebola virus disease in United States Emergency Departments: A position paper of the American College of Emergency Physicians, the Emergency Nurses Association, and the Society for Academic Emergency Medicine. *Academic Emergency Medicine*, 22(5), 605–615. 10.1111/acem.1264225903144

Ventola, C. L. (2014). Social media and health care professionals: Benefits, risks, and best practices. *P&T*, 39(7), 491–520.25083128

Verma, A., Sharma, A., Singh, A., Malviya, R., & Fuloria, S. (2023). Digital Assistant in the Pharmaceutical Field for Advancing Healthcare Systems. In *Pharmaceutical industry 4.0: Future, Challenges & Application* (pp. 213-254). River Publishers. 10.1201/9781003442493-8

Verma, P., Singh, K. K., & Singh, A. (2017). Pregnancy risk during menstrual cycle: Misconceptions among urban men in India. *Reproductive Health*, 14(1), 1–8. 10.1186/s12978-017-0332-328606153

Viceconti, M., Hunter, P., & Hose, R. (2015). Big data, big knowledge: Big data for personalized healthcare. *IEEE Journal of Biomedical and Health Informatics*, 19(4), 1209–1215. 10.1109/JBHI.2015.240688326218867

Vilchez, G. C. (2018). *Legal and Policy Implications of the Trans-Pacific Partnership Agreement: Focus on Intellectual Property*. PidsWebs. pidswebs.pids.gov.phhttps://pidswebs.pids.gov.ph/CDN/PUBLICATIONS/pidspjd2016-2_intellectual_property.pdf [Accessed 16 Nov. 2022].

Vorisek, C., Stellmach, C., Mayer, P., Klopfenstein, S., Bures, D., Diehl, A., Henningsen, M., Ritter, K., & Thun, S. (2023). Artificial intelligence bias in health care: Web-based survey. *Journal of Medical Internet Research*, 25, e41089. 10.2196/4108937347528

Wager, K. A., Lee, F. W., & Glaser, J. P. (2021). *Health care information systems: a practical approach for health care management*. John Wiley & Sons.

Wang, M. H., Xing, L., Pan, Y., Gu, F., Fang, J., Yu, X., Pang, C. P., Chong, K. K.-L., Cheung, C. Y.-L., Liao, X., Fang, X., Yang, J., Zhou, R., Zhou, X., Wang, F., & Liu, W. (2024). AI-based Advanced approaches and dry eye disease detection based on multi-source evidence: Cases, applications, issues, and future directions. *Big Data Mining and Analytics*, 7(2), 445–484. 10.26599/BDMA.2023.9020024

Wang, S., Lin, M., Ghosal, T., Ding, Y., & Peng, Y. (2022). Knowledge Graph Applications in Medical Imaging Analysis: A Scoping Review. *Health Data Science*, 2022, 9841548. 10.34133/2022/984154835800847

Wang, S., Xu, F., Li, Y., Wang, J., Zhang, K., Liu, Y., Wu, M., & Zheng, J. (2021). KG4SL: Knowledge graph neural network for synthetic lethality prediction in human cancers. *Bioinformatics (Oxford, England)*, 37(Supplement_1), i418–i425. 10.1093/bioinformatics/btab27134252965

Wang, Y., Kung, L., & Byrd, T. A. (2018). Big data analytics: Understanding its capabilities and potential benefits for healthcare organizations. *Technological Forecasting and Social Change*, 126, 3–13. 10.1016/j.techfore.2015.12.019

West, J. K. (2008). Competition, Patents and Innovation. In SSRN *Electronic Journal*. 10.2139/ssrn.1081332

WHO-UNICEF. (2012). *Consultation on Draft Long List of Goal, Target and Indicator Options for Future Global Monitoring of Water, Sanitation and Hygiene*. World Health Organization. https://www.wssinfo.org/fileadmin/user_upload/resources/Consultation_JMP_post2015_August2012.pdf

Wiedermann, C. J., Mahlknecht, A., Piccoliori, G., & Engl, A. (2023). Redesigning Primary Care: The Emergence of Artificial-Intelligence-Driven Symptom Diagnostic Tools. *Journal of Personalized Medicine*, 13(9), 1379. 10.3390/jpm1309137937763147

William R Warner & Co. v. Eli lilly & Co., 265 US 526 (1924).

Williams, H. L. (2017). How Do Patents Affect Research Investments? *Annual Review of Economics*, 9(1), 441–469. 10.1146/annurev-economics-110216-10095929104716

Will, J. F. (2011). A brief historical and theoretical perspective on patient autonomy and medical decision making. *Chest*, 139(3), 669–673. 10.1378/chest.10-253221362653

Wilner, A. S., Luce, H., Ouellet, E., Williams, O., & Costa, N. (2021). From public health to cyber hygiene: Cybersecurity and Canada's healthcare sector. *International Journal (Toronto, Ont.)*, 76(4), 522–543. 10.1177/00207020211067946

Win, K. T., Susilo, W., & Mu, Y. (2006). Personal Health Record Systems and Their Security Protection. *Journal of Medical Systems*, 30(4), 309–315. 10.1007/s10916-006-9019-y16978011

Winker, M. A., Flanagin, A., Chi-Lum, B., White, J., Andrews, K., Kennett, R. L., DeAngelis, C. D., & Musacchio, R. A. (2000). Guidelines for Medical and Health Information Sites on the Internet: Principles Governing AMA Web Sites. *Journal of the American Medical Association*, 283(12), 1600. 10.1001/jama.283.12.160010735398

World Health Organisation, World Trade Organisation and World Intellectual Property Organisation. (2020). *Intersections between public health, intellectual property and trade Promoting Access to Medical Technologies and Innovation*. WHO. https://www.wto.org/english/res_e/booksp_e/who-wipo-wto_2020_e.pdf

World Health Organization (WHO). (n.d.). (rep.). *Ethics and Governance of Artificial Intelligence for Health*. WHO. https://www.ncdirindia.org/Downloads/WHO_AI_Ethics.pdf

World Health Organization, World Intellectual Property Organization and World Trade Organization. (2013). *Promoting Access to Medical Technologies and Innovation Intersections between public health, intellectual property and trade*. WHO. https://www.wto.org/english/res_e/booksp_e/pamtiwhowipowtoweb13_e.pdf

World Health Organization. (2002). *Implications of the Doha Declaration on the TRIPS agreement and public health*. WHO.

World Health Organization. (2015). *Trends in estimates of maternal mortality ratio 1990–2015*. WHO.

World Intellectual Property Organization. (2019a). *Patents*. WIPO. https://www.wipo.int/patents/en/

World Intellectual Property Organization. (2019b). *Trademarks*. WIPO. https://www.wipo.int/trademarks/en/

World Trade Organization. (2019). *WTO | intellectual property - overview of TRIPS Agreement*. WTO. https://www.wto.org/english/tratop_e/trips_e/intel2_e.htm

Wouters, J., Goddeeris, I., Natens, B., & Ciortuz, F. (2014). Some Critical Issues in the EU-India Free Trade Agreement Negotiations. *European Law Journal*, 20(6), 848–869. 10.1111/eulj.12109

Wright, D. W. M., & Zascerinska, S. (2023). Becoming immortal: Future wellness and medical tourism markets. *Journal of Tourism Futures*, 9(2), 168–195. 10.1108/JTF-05-2021-0119

Wu, X., Duan, J., Pan, Y., & Li, M. (2023). Medical knowledge graph: Data sources, construction, reasoning, and applications. *Big Data Mining and Analytics*, 6(2), 201–217. 10.26599/BDMA.2022.9020021

Wu, X., Zhu, X., Wu, G. Q., & Ding, W. (2013). Data mining with big data. *IEEE Transactions on Knowledge and Data Engineering*, 26(1), 97–107.

Xia, F., Sun, K., Yu, S., Aziz, A., Wan, L., Pan, S., & Liu, H. (2021). Graph learning: A survey. *IEEE Transactions on Artificial Intelligence*, 2(2), 109–127. 10.1109/TAI.2021.3076021

Xiong, W., Hoang, T., & Wang, W. Y. (2017). Deeppath: A reinforcement learning method for knowledge graph reasoning. *arXiv preprint arXiv:1707.06690*. 10.18653/v1/D17-1060

Xu, A., Johari, S. A., Khademolomoom, A. H., Khabaz, M. T., Umurzoqovich, R. S., Hosseini, S., & Semiromi, D. T. (2023). Investigation of management of international education considering sustainable medical tourism and entrepreneurship. *Heliyon*, 9(1), e12691. 10.1016/j.heliyon.2022.e1269136685466

Yaacoub, J. P. A., Noura, H. N., Salman, O., & Chehab, A. (2022). Robotics cyber security: Vulnerabilities, attacks, countermeasures, and recommendations. *International Journal of Information Security*, 21(1), 115–158. 10.1007/s10207-021-00545-833776611

Yamabhai, I., & Smith, R. D. (2012). A review of the health and economic implications of patent protection, with a specific focus on Thailand. *Health Research Policy and Systems*, 10(1), 24. 10.1186/1478-4505-10-2422849392

Yaraghi, N., & Gopal, R. D. (2018). The Role of HIPAA Omnibus Rules in Reducing the Frequency of Medical Data Breaches: Insights From an Empirical Study. *The Milbank Quarterly*, 96(1), 144–166. 10.1111/1468-0009.1231429504206

Yen, P. H., & Leasure, A. R. (2019). Use and effectiveness of the Teach-Back method in patient education and health outcomes. *Federal Practitioner*, 36(6), 284–289.31258322

Ye, Q., Xu, R., Li, D., Kang, Y., Deng, Y., Zhu, F., Chen, J., He, S., Hsieh, C.-Y., & Hou, T. (2023). Integrating multi-modal deep learning on knowledge graph for the discovery of synergistic drug combinations against infectious diseases. *Cell Reports. Physical Science*, 4(8), 101520. 10.1016/j.xcrp.2023.101520

Youn, S., Geismar, H. N., & Pinedo, M. (2022). Planning and scheduling in healthcare for better care coordination: Current understanding, trending topics, and future opportunities. *Production and Operations Management*, 31(12), 4407–4423. 10.1111/poms.13867

Yu, P. K. (2022). Intellectual property paradoxes in pandemic times. *GRUR International*, 71(4), 293–294. 10.1093/grurint/ikac014

Yurchyshyn, O., & Voitko, S. (2023). Development Of Innovative Activities In The 21st Century In Section Of Patent Activity And R&D Expenditures. *Intellect XXI*.

Zagashvili, V. S. (2023). Contradictions and Conflicts in the Multilateral Trading System. *Mirovaia Ekonomika i Mezhdunarodnye Otnosheniia*, 67(9), 5–14. 10.20542/0131-2227-2023-67-9-5-14

Zang, S., Zhang, X., Xing, Y., Chen, J., Lin, L., & Hou, Z. (2022). Applications of social media and digital technologies in COVID-19 vaccination: Scoping review. *Journal of Medical Internet Research*, 25, e40057. 10.2196/4005736649235

Zargar, S. T., Joshi, J., & Tipper, D. (2013). A Survey of Defense Mechanisms Against Distributed Denial of Service (DDoS) Flooding Attacks. *IEEE Communications Surveys and Tutorials*, 15(4), 2046–2069. 10.1109/SURV.2013.031413.00127

Zawish, M., Dharejo, F. A., Khowaja, S. A., Raza, S., Davy, S., Dev, K., & Bellavista, P. (2024). AI and 6G into the metaverse: Fundamentals, challenges and future research trends. *IEEE Open Journal of the Communications Society*, 5, 730–778. 10.1109/OJCOMS.2024.3349465

Zelnick, A. (1977). Shake the lemon tree: Use and Paris Union Treaty. *Trademark Reporter, 67.*

Zeng, D., Cao, Z., & Neill, D. B. (2021). Artificial intelligence–enabled public health surveillance—From local detection to global epidemic monitoring and control. *Artificial Intelligence in Medicine*, 437–453. 10.1016/B978-0-12-821259-2.00022-3

Zhan, J., Xu, S., Zhu, Y., Han, Y., Li, L., Liu, J., & Guo, X. (2024). Potential pathogenic microorganisms in rural wastewater treatment process: Succession characteristics, concentration variation, source exploration, and risk assessment. *Water Research*, 254, 121359. 10.1016/j.watres.2024.12135938428237

Zhou, B., Yang, G., Shi, Z., & Ma, S. (2022). Natural language processing for smart healthcare. *IEEE Reviews in Biomedical Engineering*.36170385

Zhou, L., Pan, S., Wang, J., & Vasilakos, A. V. (2017). Machine learning on big data: Opportunities and challenges. *Neurocomputing*, 237, 350–361. 10.1016/j.neucom.2017.01.026

Zhou, S. K., Greenspan, H., Davatzikos, C., Duncan, J. S., Van Ginneken, B., Madabhushi, A., Prince, J. L., Rueckert, D., & Summers, R. M. (2021). A review of deep learning in medical imaging: Imaging traits, technology trends, case studies with progress highlights, and future promises. *Proceedings of the IEEE*, 109(5), 820–838. 10.1109/JPROC.2021.305439037786449

Zhou, S., Zhang, R., Chen, D., & Zhu, X. (2021). A novel framework for bringing smart big data to proactive decision making in healthcare. *Health Informatics Journal*, 27(2), 14604582211024698. 10.1177/1460458221102469834159834

Zhu, D., Xie, L., Chen, B., Tan, J., Deng, R., Zheng, Y., & Andrew, W. H. (2023). Knowledge graph and deep learning based pest detection and identification system for fruit quality. *Internet of Things : Engineering Cyber Physical Human Systems*, 21, 100649. 10.1016/j.iot.2022.100649

Zhu, Y., Che, C., Jin, B., Zhang, N., Su, C., & Wang, F. (2020). Knowledge-driven drug repurposing using a comprehensive drug knowledge graph. *Health Informatics Journal*, 26(4), 2737–2750. 10.1177/146045822093710132674665

About the Contributors

Komal Vig is working as the Dean of Sharda School of Law, Sharda University, Greater Noida. She is LL.D. in Criminal Law and MBA (HR). Prof. (Dr.) Komal Vig has served in the field of academics in different capacities for more than 20 years. She has published more than 95 research papers in International and National Journals (including 11 Scopus), 20+ book chapters, 30+ conference paper publications. She supervised 6 scholars who have successfully completed PhD under her guidance and many others are pursuing. She has presented more than 65 research papers in national and international seminars/conferences. Her area of interest is Criminal law, Family law, and laws related to Women's rights. Prof. (Dr.) Komal Vig is a member of the inspection committees of various governing and accrediting bodies. Prof. (Dr.) Komal Vig has chaired numerous sessions in international and national conferences/ seminars. She is active member of Board of Studies of various universities, received Life membership of the Indian law Institute (Deemed University) New Delhi, "Women Empowerment Award- 2023" from Council of Research and Sustainable Development, India.

Christian Kaunert is Professor of International Security at Dublin City University, Ireland. He is also Professor of Policing and Security, as well as Director of the International Centre for Policing and Security at the University of South Wales. In addition, he is Jean Monnet Chair, Director of the Jean Monnet Centre of Excellence and Director of the Jean Monnet Network on EU Counter-Terrorism (www.eucter.net). Previously, he served as Academic Director and Professor at the Institute for European Studies, Vrije Universiteit Brussel, a Professor of International Politics, Head of Discipline in Politics, and the Director of the European Institute for Security and Justice, a Jean Monnet Centre for Excellence, at the University of Dundee. Prof Kaunert has researched and taught in many international universities, such as University of Shandong, Jinan, China, IBEI Barcelona, Spain, Diplomatic Academy Yerevan, Armenia – United Nations Development Mission, University of Cairo, Egypt, Collegio Carlo Alberto, Turin, Italy, Ecole nationale d'administration Paris, European Institute of Public Administration Maastricht, Netherlands, European Studies Institute (ESI) at Moscow, University of Porto, Portugal, etc. He was previously Senior Lecturer at the University of Dundee, Marie Curie Senior Research Fellow at the European University Institute Florence, and Senior Lecturer in EU Politics & International Relations, University of Salford. Christian has been invited expert for the European Institute for Public Administration (EIPA), the Counter-Terrorism Committee of the European Parliament, the European Union Institute for Security Studies (an agency of the EU), the United Nations Development Programme (UNDP) and the North Atlantic Treaty Organisation (NATO). Over his career, he has been awarded seven prestigious Marie Curie Fellowships, four Jean Monnet Chairs, and, finally, three Jean Monnet Centre of Excellence, as well as one Jean Monnet Network of Excellence 'EUCTER'. Additionally, he was awarded a large Horizon 2020 research grant on Terrorist Radicalisation processes – Mindb4Act. He is currently Editor of the Journal of Contemporary European Studies, was also previously an elected member of the national (UK) Executive Committee of the University Association for Contemporary European Studies (UACES) and co-founded and co-led the special interest section on the Area of Freedom, Security and Justice of the European Union Studies Association (EUSA).

Bhupinder Singh working as Professor in Sharda School of Law, Sharda University Greater Noida, India. Also, Honorary Professor in University of South Wales UK and Santo Tomas University Tunja, Colombia. He has 3 books, 133 paper publications, 167 paper presentations in international/national conferences and seminars, participated in more than 43 workshops/FDP's/QIP's, 25 courses from international universities of repute, organized more than 63 events with international and national academicians and industry people's, editor-in-chief and co-editor in journals, developed new courses. He has given talks at international universities, resource person in international conferences such as in Nanyang Technological University Singapore, Tashkent State University of Law Uzbekistan; KIMEP University Kazakhstan, All'ah meh Tabatabi University Iran, the Iranian Association of International Criminal law, Iran and Hague Center for International Law and Investment, The Netherlands, Northumbria University Newcastle UK, Taylor's University Malaysia, AFM Krakow University Poland, European Institute for Research and Development Georgia, Business and Technology University Georgia, Texas A & M University US name a few. His leadership, teaching, research and industry experience is of 16 years and 5 Months. His research interests are health law, criminal law, research methodology and emerging multidisciplinary areas as Blockchain Technology, IoT, Machine Learning, Artificial Intelligence, Genome-editing, Photovoltaic PV Glass, SDG's and many more.

***

Saurabh Chandra is currently working as an Associate Professor with the School of Law, Bennett University, Greater Noida, India. He has completed graduation in Law (B.A.LL.B.) from Aligarh Muslim University (AMU). He has completed Post Graduation in Law (LL.M. Business Laws) from the National Law School of India University (NLSIU) Bangalore. He has completed a Doctorate in Law (Ph.D.) From National Law University, Delhi. He has completed Master of Business Administration (MBA) with specialisation in Human Resource Management (HR). He has completed Master's degree in Journalism and Mass Communication. He has teaching experience of 15 years. He has various publications to his credit. His areas of expertise include Business and Corporate Laws and he has various publications to his credit. He has rich experience in Academic Administration and has handled various posts in Academic Administration.

Souvik Dhar is currently working as Assistant Professor at Department of Law, Brainware University. He has successfully passed both the UGC-NET and WB-SET examinations. He has completed his Ph.D. in Law from Amity University Noida. He has a diverse academic experience. Furthermore, he worked as a Research Investigator at the Centre for Child Rights, WB NUJS, contributing to a UNICEF project focusing on the 'Evaluation of the POCSO Act, 2012 in West Bengal'. His educational qualifications include a B.A. LL.B. from the Department of Law, University of Calcutta, and an LL.M. in Business Laws from Amity Law School, Amity University, Kolkata. Mr. Dhar has also practiced as an Advocate handling cases in consumer rights, banking, civil, and criminal law. He has actively participated, delivered special lectures as resource person, and presented papers at numerous national and international conferences, seminars, symposiums, and workshops. Additionally, he has organized several seminars and conferences as a faculty convenor. His scholarly contributions comprise numerous articles in reputable journals (including UGC-Care listed journals) and edited books covering diverse legal issues. He is the author and co-author of several books on various legal subjects. He has a total of over 30 publications which includes 15 books. With over 6 years of litigation experience and more than 5 years of academic experience, his area of interest includes Health Law, Criminal Law, Corporate Law, and Human Rights Law.

Kittisak Jermsittiparsert is a Research Fellow at Shinawatra University, Thailand, an Adjunct Professor at Sekolah Tinggi Ilmu Administrasi Abdul Haris, and an Adjunct Research Professor at Universitas Muhammadiyah Sinjai, Universitas Muhammadiyah Makassar & Universitas Muhammadiyah Sidenreng Rappang, Indonesia. Previously, he was a Full-Professor of Public Administration at Huanghe Business School, Henan University of Economics and Law, China, a Professor at Faculty of Education, University of City Island, Cyprus, a Lecturer at Faculty of Political Science, Rangsit University & College of Innovative Business and Accountancy, Dhurakij Pundit University, a Researcher at Chulalongkorn University Social Research Institute, Thailand, and an Adjunct Researcher at Ton Duc Thang University & Duy Tan University, Vietnam. He holds a Ph.D. (Social Sciences) from Kasetsart University, Thailand. His areas of expertise are Political Science, Public and Private Management, International Political Economy, and Social Research. He is named in the world's top 2% of scientists list by Stanford University, USA since 2020. Up to now, he has published more than 450 Scopus/WoS indexed documents.

Pooja Kansra is Head of the Department at Mittal School of Business, Lovely Professional University, Punjab, India. Her areas of interest include econometrics methods, microeconomics, macroeconomics, managerial economics, quantitative techniques, and economics of health and education. She holds a Master's in Economics from Guru Nanak Dev University, Amritsar, and a Doctorate degree from Punjab Technical University, Jalandhar. She is a member of the Indian Economic Association. Her research interests include health economics, insurance, and service operation management. She is an avid researcher and has presented papers in various national and international conferences. She has to her credit various research papers published in refereed national and international journals of repute.

Amiya Abdul Khadar is a Ph.D. scholar at Mittal School of Business, Lovely Professional University, Jalandhar. Her area of interest includes health economics, consumer behaviour, and development economics. She has to her credit research papers published in refereed national and international journals of repute. She has also presented several research papers at institutes with national repute.

Suparna Kundu is pursuing Ph.D (Law) from Amity Law School, Amity University, Kolkata, India . She has completed Master in Laws from Symbiosis Law School Noida, Symbiosis International (Deemed University). She has completed Bachelor in Law from KIIT School of Law - KSOL | KIIT Deemed to be University.

Sahil Lal is a Research Scholar at School of Law, Sharda University. He pursued his graduation from National Law University, Lucknow and completed his Master's in Law from Gujarat National Law University, Gandhinagar. Sahil has completed a certificate course on 'AI & Law' from Lund University, Sweden and on 'Cyber Law' from Indian Law Institute, New Delhi. Sahil Lal is a qualified UGC-NET & JRF candidate. He has a 10+ year Industry Experience and is an active member of Family Dispute Resolution Clinic, Mediation Center, Greater Noida. Sahil has attended 20+ International & National Conferences along with Paper Presentation and has also participated in more than 5+ Faculty Development Programme. Mr. Sahil has more than 20+ publications in various esteemed Journals & Books. Mr. Sahil has a keen interest in area of Artificial Intelligence, Machine Learning, Robotics, Block-Chain Technology and Intellectual Property Rights.

Kaushik Lodh is the CEO of Health USA, Los Angeles, California. He is also the Chairperson of the Maharashtra State Committee for disabled Children's Education Rights in Mumbai India.

Raniyal Niyada is currently an Assistant Professor of Law at B.M.S. College of Law and is also pursuing her PhD from the National Law School of India University, Bengaluru. She completed her LL.M. in IPR from Cochin University of Science and Technology, Kerala with a first-rank position and has qualified UGC-NET in Law. She has been the Editor-in-Chief of LJRF Voice, an online website that publishes legal content. She has also co-founded an NGO, Legal Collective for Students' Rights, which was instrumental in the Kerala High Court's declaration of the Internet as a fundamental right.

P.R.L. Rajavenkatesan is a Professor at VIT School of Law. He is an expert in the area of IPRs and Environmental Laws. At present, he is guiding four PhD candidates in VIT School of Law and one candidate has already been awarded PhD under his guidance. He is an external member of Doctoral Committee in other Institutions. He authored 12 books and published around 87 research papers. He has also received six research awards from VIT University. He is also active at the international level with paper presentations in conferences organised in the USA, Japan and Nepal.

Karun Sanjaya is an Assistant Professor at Symbiosis Law School, Nagpur and a Research Scholar at VIT School of Law, Vellore Institute of Technology, Chennai, India. He specializes in the area of Intellectual Property Laws. He is a recipient of many awards including the prestigious Justice V.R. Krishna Iyer Memorial Merit Awards in the year 2019 and 2022. He has published over fifty research items and is a keen researcher in diverse areas of law including Intellectual Property Laws.

Utsa Sarkar has a strong academic background and specialization in Criminal and Security Law. She holds an LL.M. from The West Bengal National University of Juridical Sciences, Kolkata (2020-21), and a B.A.LLB (Hons) from the National University of Study and Research in Law, Ranchi (2015-20). Having cleared the UGC-NET Examination in 2022, she has nearly 2 years of academic experience, having previously served at Presidency University, Bengaluru. Ms. Sarkar's research interests encompass criminal law, international criminal law, cyber security, constitutional law, and human rights. She has delivered lectures on substantive and procedural criminal laws, human rights, company law, and Code of Civil Procedure. Her contributions to legal scholarship include publications in reputable journals such as UGC Care and Scopus, along with several book chapters in edited volumes.

Anurag Singh is an Associate Professor of Law in Meerut College, Meerut. He also done post graduation in Maths and also passed company secretary exams. He joined Meerut college in 2001 as a Lecturer.

Index

A

Access 1, 2, 3, 4, 5, 7, 8, 12, 13, 14, 15, 16, 19, 20, 22, 26, 27, 33, 34, 35, 37, 41, 43, 53, 55, 61, 62, 66, 67, 68, 69, 70, 71, 73, 92, 93, 95, 96, 106, 107, 108, 110, 117, 118, 122, 123, 124, 125, 126, 127, 128, 129, 130, 131, 132, 133, 134, 135, 136, 137, 139, 140, 141, 149, 150, 151, 153, 154, 158, 159, 161, 162, 163, 165, 166, 167, 168, 169, 170, 171, 173, 175, 177, 178, 181, 185, 188, 189, 192, 193, 199, 201, 202, 207, 208, 210, 211, 212, 221, 237, 239, 242, 243, 246, 257, 265, 267, 273, 285, 286, 287, 290, 291, 292, 293, 294, 295, 296, 297, 300, 301, 302, 303, 304, 306, 307, 308, 312, 315, 323, 325, 326, 327, 328, 329, 330, 331, 332, 334, 335, 336, 338, 339, 340, 341, 342, 343, 344

Access to Medicine 165, 166, 168, 290, 292, 294, 306, 307, 312, 315, 328

Access to Medicines 117, 118, 124, 125, 126, 128, 129, 131, 132, 134, 139, 140, 141, 171, 173, 290, 291, 292, 294, 296, 301, 302, 303, 304, 308, 323, 327, 330, 335, 341, 342, 343, 344

Aging 24, 142, 143, 144

ANC 272, 273, 274, 275, 276, 280, 281, 282, 284, 285, 286

Application 25, 26, 28, 33, 37, 39, 41, 43, 61, 62, 65, 85, 87, 88, 92, 96, 97, 100, 101, 103, 112, 114, 121, 139, 191, 192, 218, 225, 232, 296, 301, 310, 311, 317, 326, 337

Artificial 6, 22, 23, 24, 26, 27, 28, 30, 31, 37, 38, 40, 42, 43, 46, 47, 50, 51, 74, 77, 78, 79, 81, 82, 83, 84, 85, 86, 87, 92, 93, 95, 96, 97, 98, 100, 101, 102, 103, 105, 107, 108, 109, 112, 114, 115, 116, 124, 139, 140, 141, 182, 187, 191, 192, 193, 194, 195, 197, 198, 201, 207, 217, 218, 224, 245, 311, 321, 322, 323

Artificial Intelligence 6, 22, 23, 24, 26, 27, 30, 31, 37, 38, 40, 42, 43, 46, 47, 50, 51, 77, 78, 79, 81, 82, 83, 84, 85, 86, 87, 92, 93, 95, 96, 97, 98, 100, 101, 102, 103, 105, 107, 108, 109, 112, 114, 115, 116, 124, 139, 140, 141, 182, 187, 191, 192, 193, 194, 195, 197, 198, 201, 207, 217, 218, 224, 245, 321, 322, 323

B

Biomedical 22, 24, 28, 57, 58, 64, 77, 87, 95, 112, 114, 140, 191, 193, 194, 195, 196, 229, 244, 321

C

care 1, 2, 3, 4, 5, 6, 9, 10, 11, 15, 16, 17, 18, 19, 21, 22, 23, 24, 25, 27, 28, 29, 30, 33, 34, 35, 37, 38, 39, 40, 41, 42, 43, 46, 47, 48, 49, 50, 51, 70, 76, 79, 83, 85, 88, 92, 101, 102, 103, 104, 106, 107, 108, 110, 111, 112, 113, 115, 131, 138, 142, 143, 148, 150, 151, 152, 153, 154, 155, 156, 157, 158, 159, 160, 161, 168, 169, 171, 176, 177, 179, 180, 181, 182, 184, 185, 186, 187, 188, 189, 191, 192, 194, 195, 198, 199, 200, 201, 204, 206, 207, 208, 209, 210, 211, 215, 216, 217, 218, 221, 224, 230, 231, 232, 236, 240, 241, 242, 243, 245, 246, 271, 272, 273, 274, 276, 282, 284, 285, 286, 287, 288, 289, 308, 322, 338

Clinical Decision Support 16, 23, 105, 201, 217

Clinical Practice 22, 82, 83, 89, 105, 204, 243

Compulsory license 132, 133, 134, 299, 325, 329, 330, 331, 332

Compulsory Licensing 118, 124, 126, 130, 132, 133, 134, 135, 139, 140, 173, 325, 326, 329, 330, 331, 332, 333,

334, 335, 336, 337, 339, 340, 341, 342, 343, 344, 345
Cyber security 28, 114, 225, 226, 229, 230, 231, 232, 236, 244
Cybersecurity 13, 25, 36, 43, 46, 48, 102, 114, 220, 221, 222, 223, 229, 230, 231, 232, 236, 241, 242, 245, 247
Cyber Terrorism 220, 222, 225, 226

D

Data Privacy 27, 38, 104, 109, 110, 112, 113, 190, 197, 198, 199, 200, 201, 202, 203, 211, 215, 216, 224, 244
Developed Nations 112
Developing Nations 92, 129, 138, 177, 178, 290, 292, 294, 301, 332
Diagnosis 3, 20, 35, 38, 41, 46, 83, 85, 91, 92, 93, 94, 96, 97, 101, 102, 103, 107, 114, 115, 175, 177, 191, 208, 216, 340

E

elderly 49, 87, 142, 143, 145, 146, 148, 149, 150, 151, 152, 153, 154, 155, 156, 157, 158, 159, 160, 314
Ethical considerations 20, 29, 39, 61, 66, 110, 111, 112, 123, 124, 141, 185, 188, 203, 207
Ethical Frameworks 65, 198, 207, 208, 215
Ethical Issues 35, 37, 42, 51, 54, 55, 60, 61, 63, 66, 88, 93, 108, 166, 187, 197, 198, 200, 201, 217
European Union 12, 41, 120, 162, 171, 295, 307, 318, 326, 344

F

Free Competition 126
Free Trade Agreements 290, 294, 295, 296, 297, 300, 301, 302, 304

G

Generic Drug 118, 125, 126, 127, 136, 299, 312, 315
Global Governance 43, 53, 55, 62, 64, 65, 331

H

Healthcare 1, 2, 3, 4, 5, 6, 7, 8, 9, 10, 11, 12, 13, 14, 15, 16, 17, 18, 20, 21, 22, 23, 24, 25, 26, 27, 28, 29, 30, 31, 32, 33, 34, 35, 36, 37, 38, 39, 40, 41, 42, 43, 44, 45, 46, 47, 48, 49, 51, 55, 57, 70, 71, 72, 73, 77, 79, 81, 82, 83, 84, 85, 86, 87, 88, 89, 90, 92, 94, 96, 97, 98, 101, 102, 103, 104, 105, 106, 107, 108, 109, 110, 111, 112, 113, 114, 115, 116, 123, 125, 126, 127, 130, 131, 132, 133, 134, 135, 136, 137, 138, 139, 141, 143, 147, 148, 149, 152, 156, 158, 159, 161, 162, 163, 164, 166, 167, 168, 169, 171, 175, 176, 177, 178, 180, 181, 182, 184, 185, 186, 187, 188, 189, 190, 191, 192, 193, 194, 196, 197, 198, 199, 200, 201, 202, 203, 204, 205, 206, 207, 209, 210, 211, 212, 213, 214, 215, 216, 217, 218, 220, 221, 222, 223, 224, 225, 229, 231, 232, 236, 237, 238, 239, 240, 241, 242, 243, 244, 245, 246, 247, 258, 264, 265, 266, 271, 272, 273, 274, 275, 286, 290, 291, 307, 308, 313, 321, 322, 330, 335, 336, 337, 338, 339, 340, 341
Health Care 23, 28, 33, 37, 38, 39, 42, 43, 46, 47, 50, 51, 101, 102, 115, 138, 143, 152, 153, 154, 155, 156, 161, 168, 169, 171, 177, 181, 184, 185, 189, 191, 192, 194, 198, 201, 207, 208, 209, 210, 211, 215, 217, 218, 224, 230, 231, 232, 236, 243, 245, 246, 271, 273, 274, 282, 286, 287, 288
Healthcare Communication 29, 30, 31, 33, 35, 40, 41, 42, 43, 44
Healthcare disparities 2, 20, 88, 135
Healthcare Regulations 12
Healthcare Services 1, 2, 5, 9, 13, 15, 16, 31, 36, 38, 43, 47, 70, 71, 94, 108, 127, 130, 131, 136, 137, 138, 147, 148, 156, 159, 166, 169, 178, 181, 185, 188, 221, 241, 245, 264, 273,

274, 291, 339
Health Gateways 174

I

India 1, 29, 41, 42, 47, 48, 49, 52, 81, 100, 108, 113, 117, 118, 124, 125, 127, 131, 132, 133, 135, 137, 138, 139, 140, 142, 145, 146, 147, 148, 149, 150, 151, 152, 155, 157, 158, 159, 160, 161, 170, 171, 174, 176, 180, 181, 186, 197, 198, 200, 201, 214, 215, 220, 224, 228, 234, 248, 249, 250, 253, 256, 257, 259, 264, 266, 267, 268, 269, 270, 271, 272, 273, 274, 275, 276, 277, 282, 283, 284, 285, 286, 287, 288, 289, 290, 291, 294, 295, 296, 297, 302, 305, 306, 309, 310, 312, 320, 325, 326, 327, 328, 333, 334, 335, 336, 340, 341, 342, 343, 344, 345
Information Security 28, 41, 113, 199, 222, 223, 240, 243, 244, 246
Informed Consent 29, 35, 36, 50, 61, 64, 88, 110, 197, 198, 199, 200, 203, 204, 205, 208, 209, 213, 214, 215, 216, 218
Innovation 3, 21, 22, 23, 43, 44, 74, 75, 77, 78, 102, 108, 113, 115, 116, 118, 119, 120, 121, 122, 123, 124, 125, 126, 127, 128, 129, 130, 131, 135, 136, 137, 138, 139, 140, 161, 162, 163, 166, 167, 168, 169, 170, 171, 172, 173, 175, 177, 188, 191, 192, 194, 211, 214, 221, 241, 244, 290, 292, 293, 303, 304, 321, 322, 323, 330, 331, 336, 337, 340, 341
Intellectual Property 117, 118, 119, 120, 121, 122, 123, 124, 125, 126, 127, 128, 129, 130, 131, 132, 133, 134, 135, 136, 137, 138, 139, 140, 141, 161, 162, 163, 166, 167, 168, 169, 170, 171, 172, 173, 194, 290, 291, 292, 293, 294, 295, 296, 297, 300, 302, 303, 304, 307, 308, 317, 318, 319, 320, 323, 325, 326, 327, 328, 329, 330, 331, 332, 333, 335, 338, 339, 340, 341, 343, 344, 345
Intellectual Property Protection 130, 138, 163, 290, 291, 292, 293, 294, 304, 330, 335, 338, 339
Intellectual Property Rights 118, 119, 120, 121, 122, 123, 124, 125, 126, 127, 128, 129, 130, 131, 133, 134, 135, 136, 137, 138, 139, 140, 141, 162, 163, 166, 167, 170, 172, 290, 291, 292, 302, 303, 304, 307, 308, 317, 325, 327, 331, 338, 339, 340, 341, 343, 344
Intelligence 1, 6, 22, 23, 24, 26, 27, 28, 30, 31, 37, 38, 40, 42, 43, 46, 47, 50, 51, 77, 78, 79, 81, 82, 83, 84, 85, 86, 87, 92, 93, 95, 96, 97, 98, 100, 101, 102, 103, 105, 107, 108, 109, 112, 114, 115, 116, 124, 139, 140, 141, 168, 182, 187, 190, 191, 192, 193, 194, 195, 197, 198, 201, 207, 217, 218, 224, 245, 321, 322, 323

L

legislation 72, 82, 89, 124, 151, 201, 211, 335, 336, 341

M

Machine Learning 24, 25, 29, 33, 34, 39, 41, 78, 82, 84, 87, 88, 92, 95, 96, 97, 98, 102, 103, 104, 105, 114, 116, 189, 191, 192, 193, 194, 195, 196, 204, 207, 218, 231, 232, 322
Medical and Healthcare 222
Medical devices 48, 135, 137, 163, 164, 224, 230, 231, 232, 339
Medical Industry 91
Medical Tourism 174, 175, 176, 177, 178, 179, 180, 181, 182, 183, 184, 185, 186, 187, 188, 189, 190, 192, 193, 196
Medication 1, 3, 4, 5, 6, 7, 9, 10, 11, 14, 16, 19, 20, 22, 23, 24, 25, 32, 35, 83, 125, 134, 138, 164, 166, 182, 294, 309, 314, 315, 331, 332, 336
Medicines 1, 57, 90, 117, 118, 123, 124, 125, 126, 127, 128, 129, 130, 131, 132, 133, 134, 135, 136, 138, 139, 140, 141, 167, 168, 170, 171, 173,

221, 290, 291, 292, 293, 294, 296, 298, 301, 302, 303, 304, 308, 314, 321, 323, 325, 327, 330, 331, 335, 338, 339, 341, 342, 343, 344
Menstrual Health 248, 249, 250, 251, 252, 254, 256, 258, 259, 264, 265, 266, 267, 269, 270
Menstrual Hygiene Management 250, 256, 257, 267, 268, 269, 270
Menstrual Products 248, 249, 250, 251, 252, 253, 255, 256, 264, 265
Menstrual Stigma 248, 250
Mental Healthcare 197, 198, 199, 200, 201, 202, 203, 204, 205, 206, 211, 212, 213, 214, 215, 218
Misinformation Management 29, 39
Mortality 70, 271, 272, 273, 274, 275, 286, 287, 288, 289, 314

N

National Rural Health Mission 273
Non-traditional Trademarks 161, 164, 165, 169, 173, 306, 307, 308, 312, 316, 319

P

Patent 118, 120, 121, 124, 125, 126, 127, 128, 129, 132, 133, 140, 141, 162, 163, 166, 167, 168, 170, 171, 173, 291, 292, 293, 294, 295, 296, 297, 298, 299, 300, 301, 307, 308, 313, 326, 327, 328, 330, 331, 332, 333, 335, 336, 337, 338, 339, 341, 343, 344, 345
Patents 117, 118, 120, 121, 122, 123, 124, 125, 126, 127, 128, 129, 131, 136, 140, 161, 162, 163, 166, 167, 168, 169, 170, 171, 172, 173, 291, 293, 294, 297, 299, 302, 303, 307, 308, 310, 317, 318, 320, 326, 327, 330, 331, 333, 335, 336, 338, 339, 340, 343, 344
Patient Autonomy 51, 111, 197, 199, 204, 206, 209, 215, 216
Patient-Provider Communication 7, 47
Pharmaceutical industry 28, 117, 125, 132, 135, 170, 172, 296, 308, 309, 316, 326, 327, 331, 343
pharmaceutical products 129, 291, 298, 306, 307, 316, 326
Pharmaceuticals 76, 125, 131, 132, 135, 137, 139, 140, 162, 163, 164, 165, 166, 171, 291, 294, 295, 300, 303, 306, 307, 312, 317, 319, 326, 330, 332, 338, 340, 343, 344
Policy reforms 161
population 18, 30, 40, 76, 83, 88, 89, 93, 102, 105, 106, 107, 115, 133, 135, 136, 137, 142, 143, 144, 145, 146, 147, 148, 149, 150, 151, 152, 158, 159, 160, 165, 176, 182, 184, 187, 259, 265, 268, 273, 274, 286, 287, 292, 315, 336
Public health 22, 26, 31, 32, 39, 47, 63, 82, 102, 115, 116, 118, 126, 127, 129, 130, 131, 132, 133, 135, 136, 137, 138, 140, 156, 160, 161, 162, 165, 166, 167, 172, 173, 176, 187, 217, 221, 247, 252, 253, 258, 266, 267, 268, 269, 273, 287, 293, 294, 302, 304, 307, 314, 315, 316, 319, 325, 330, 331, 332, 335, 336, 337, 339, 340, 341, 342, 343, 344

R

Ransomware 36, 220, 222, 237, 241, 245
Reproductive Justice 53, 54, 55, 60, 61, 67, 68, 69, 70, 71, 72, 73
right to health 140, 172, 173, 252, 301

S

Sanitation 148, 248, 250, 253, 255, 257, 264, 266, 270, 275
social 29, 30, 31, 32, 33, 35, 39, 40, 41, 42, 43, 45, 47, 48, 51, 52, 53, 54, 55, 57, 60, 61, 62, 65, 66, 68, 69, 70, 71, 72, 73, 77, 93, 98, 105, 106, 107, 115, 123, 124, 126, 135, 137, 142, 143, 144, 146, 148, 149, 150, 151, 152, 153, 154, 155, 156, 157, 158, 159, 160, 175, 177, 184, 185, 188, 193, 194, 201, 218, 226, 242, 244, 249, 250, 252, 256, 258, 259, 265, 269,

288, 291, 312, 321, 322, 344
Social Media 29, 30, 31, 32, 33, 35, 39, 40, 41, 42, 43, 45, 47, 48, 51, 93, 106, 193, 218
States 12, 35, 41, 51, 81, 120, 128, 142, 146, 149, 154, 179, 180, 214, 228, 229, 234, 240, 242, 253, 274, 276, 277, 278, 282, 285, 286, 290, 291, 292, 293, 294, 295, 296, 297, 298, 299, 300, 301, 303, 304, 310, 317, 326, 330, 336, 339, 340
Sustainability 22, 26, 74, 75, 76, 77, 78, 79, 174, 175, 176, 177, 178, 182, 184, 185, 187, 190, 195, 269, 322, 323
Sustainable development 75, 77, 138, 144, 185, 229, 250, 272, 276, 285, 322
Symptom Assessment 4

T

Technology 2, 11, 23, 24, 27, 30, 35, 36, 38, 41, 42, 43, 44, 46, 47, 50, 53, 54, 55, 57, 58, 59, 60, 61, 62, 63, 64, 65, 67, 69, 71, 72, 73, 74, 77, 78, 79, 82, 83, 84, 87, 90, 93, 94, 96, 98, 101, 102, 103, 108, 109, 111, 112, 113, 115, 116, 119, 121, 128, 129, 130, 131, 138, 147, 148, 161, 166, 168, 170, 175, 177, 178, 181, 194, 196, 198, 199, 203, 205, 206, 209, 211, 217, 218, 220, 221, 222, 229, 231, 236, 238, 239, 241, 243, 244, 245, 246, 292, 294, 308, 312, 321, 322, 328, 329, 336, 338, 339
Trademarks 117, 120, 122, 125, 128, 129, 131, 161, 162, 163, 164, 165, 166, 167, 168, 169, 170, 171, 172, 173, 306, 307, 308, 311, 312, 316, 317, 318, 319, 320, 321, 323
Transgenic Technology 59
TRIPS 118, 128, 129, 130, 139, 140, 169, 173, 290, 291, 292, 293, 294, 295, 296, 297, 298, 299, 300, 301, 302, 303, 304, 307, 317, 318, 320, 323, 325, 326, 327, 328, 329, 330, 331, 332, 333, 334, 335, 339, 340, 342, 343, 344, 345
TRIPS-plus 291, 293, 294, 295, 297, 301, 304

U

Unconventional Trademarks 164, 306, 307, 308, 312
United States 12, 35, 41, 51, 81, 120, 180, 228, 229, 234, 240, 242, 290, 291, 293, 294, 295, 296, 297, 298, 299, 300, 301, 303, 304, 310, 317
United States of America 41, 81, 228

W

wellbeing 78, 142, 148, 200, 322
Women's health 52, 61, 264, 265, 270, 288

www.ingramcontent.com/pod-product-compliance
Lightning Source LLC
LaVergne TN
LVHW080345011026
849161LV00009B/2198